GCC 7.0 Manual 2/2

A catalogue record for this book is available from the Hong Kong Public Libraries.

Published in Hong Kong by Samurai Media Limited.

Email: info@samuraimedia.org

ISBN 978-988-8406-92-0

Short Contents

Table of Contents

7   Extensions to the C++ Language 727

8   GNU Objective-C Features................. 741

6 Extensions to the C Language Family

GNU C provides several language features not found in ISO standard C. (The '-pedantic' option directs GCC to print a warning message if any of these features is used.) To test for the availability of these features in conditional compilation, check for a predefined macro __GNUC__, which is always defined under GCC.

These extensions are available in C and Objective-C. Most of them are also available in C++. See Chapter 7 [Extensions to the C++ Language], page 727, for extensions that apply *only* to C++.

Some features that are in ISO C99 but not C90 or C++ are also, as extensions, accepted by GCC in C90 mode and in C++.

6.1 Statements and Declarations in Expressions

A compound statement enclosed in parentheses may appear as an expression in GNU C. This allows you to use loops, switches, and local variables within an expression.

Recall that a compound statement is a sequence of statements surrounded by braces; in this construct, parentheses go around the braces. For example:

```
({ int y = foo (); int z;
   if (y > 0) z = y;
   else z = - y;
   z; })
```

is a valid (though slightly more complex than necessary) expression for the absolute value of foo ().

The last thing in the compound statement should be an expression followed by a semicolon; the value of this subexpression serves as the value of the entire construct. (If you use some other kind of statement last within the braces, the construct has type void, and thus effectively no value.)

This feature is especially useful in making macro definitions "safe" (so that they evaluate each operand exactly once). For example, the "maximum" function is commonly defined as a macro in standard C as follows:

```
#define max(a,b) ((a) > (b) ? (a) : (b))
```

But this definition computes either *a* or *b* twice, with bad results if the operand has side effects. In GNU C, if you know the type of the operands (here taken as int), you can define the macro safely as follows:

```
#define maxint(a,b) \
   ({int _a = (a), _b = (b); _a > _b ? _a : _b; })
```

Embedded statements are not allowed in constant expressions, such as the value of an enumeration constant, the width of a bit-field, or the initial value of a static variable.

If you don't know the type of the operand, you can still do this, but you must use typeof or __auto_type (see Section 6.6 [Typeof], page 410).

In G++, the result value of a statement expression undergoes array and function pointer decay, and is returned by value to the enclosing expression. For instance, if A is a class, then

```
        A a;

        ({a;}).Foo ()
```

constructs a temporary `A` object to hold the result of the statement expression, and that is used to invoke `Foo`. Therefore the `this` pointer observed by `Foo` is not the address of `a`.

In a statement expression, any temporaries created within a statement are destroyed at that statement's end. This makes statement expressions inside macros slightly different from function calls. In the latter case temporaries introduced during argument evaluation are destroyed at the end of the statement that includes the function call. In the statement expression case they are destroyed during the statement expression. For instance,

```
#define macro(a)  ({__typeof__(a) b = (a); b + 3; })
template<typename T> T function(T a) { T b = a; return b + 3; }

void foo ()
{
  macro (X ());
  function (X ());
}
```

has different places where temporaries are destroyed. For the `macro` case, the temporary `X` is destroyed just after the initialization of `b`. In the `function` case that temporary is destroyed when the function returns.

These considerations mean that it is probably a bad idea to use statement expressions of this form in header files that are designed to work with C++. (Note that some versions of the GNU C Library contained header files using statement expressions that lead to precisely this bug.)

Jumping into a statement expression with `goto` or using a `switch` statement outside the statement expression with a `case` or `default` label inside the statement expression is not permitted. Jumping into a statement expression with a computed `goto` (see Section 6.3 [Labels as Values], page 405) has undefined behavior. Jumping out of a statement expression is permitted, but if the statement expression is part of a larger expression then it is unspecified which other subexpressions of that expression have been evaluated except where the language definition requires certain subexpressions to be evaluated before or after the statement expression. In any case, as with a function call, the evaluation of a statement expression is not interleaved with the evaluation of other parts of the containing expression. For example,

```
    foo (), (({ bar1 (); goto a; 0; }) + bar2 ()), baz();
```

calls `foo` and `bar1` and does not call `baz` but may or may not call `bar2`. If `bar2` is called, it is called after `foo` and before `bar1`.

6.2 Locally Declared Labels

GCC allows you to declare *local labels* in any nested block scope. A local label is just like an ordinary label, but you can only reference it (with a `goto` statement, or by taking its address) within the block in which it is declared.

A local label declaration looks like this:

```
    __label__ label;
```

or

```
__label__ label1, label2, /* ... */;
```

Local label declarations must come at the beginning of the block, before any ordinary declarations or statements.

The label declaration defines the label *name*, but does not define the label itself. You must do this in the usual way, with **label:**, within the statements of the statement expression.

The local label feature is useful for complex macros. If a macro contains nested loops, a `goto` can be useful for breaking out of them. However, an ordinary label whose scope is the whole function cannot be used: if the macro can be expanded several times in one function, the label is multiply defined in that function. A local label avoids this problem. For example:

```
#define SEARCH(value, array, target)             \
do {                                             \
  __label__ found;                               \
  typeof (target) _SEARCH_target = (target);     \
  typeof (*(array)) *_SEARCH_array = (array);    \
  int i, j;                                      \
  int value;                                     \
  for (i = 0; i < max; i++)                      \
    for (j = 0; j < max; j++)                    \
      if (_SEARCH_array[i][j] == _SEARCH_target) \
        { (value) = i; goto found; }             \
  (value) = -1;                                  \
 found:;                                         \
} while (0)
```

This could also be written using a statement expression:

```
#define SEARCH(array, target)                    \
({                                               \
  __label__ found;                               \
  typeof (target) _SEARCH_target = (target);     \
  typeof (*(array)) *_SEARCH_array = (array);    \
  int i, j;                                      \
  int value;                                     \
  for (i = 0; i < max; i++)                      \
    for (j = 0; j < max; j++)                    \
      if (_SEARCH_array[i][j] == _SEARCH_target) \
        { value = i; goto found; }               \
  value = -1;                                    \
 found:                                          \
  value;                                         \
})
```

Local label declarations also make the labels they declare visible to nested functions, if there are any. See Section 6.4 [Nested Functions], page 406, for details.

6.3 Labels as Values

You can get the address of a label defined in the current function (or a containing function) with the unary operator '&&'. The value has type **void** *. This value is a constant and can be used wherever a constant of that type is valid. For example:

```
void *ptr;
/* ... */
ptr = &&foo;
```

To use these values, you need to be able to jump to one. This is done with the computed goto statement[1], `goto *exp;`. For example,

```
goto *ptr;
```

Any expression of type `void *` is allowed.

One way of using these constants is in initializing a static array that serves as a jump table:

```
static void *array[] = { &&foo, &&bar, &&hack };
```

Then you can select a label with indexing, like this:

```
goto *array[i];
```

Note that this does not check whether the subscript is in bounds—array indexing in C never does that.

Such an array of label values serves a purpose much like that of the `switch` statement. The `switch` statement is cleaner, so use that rather than an array unless the problem does not fit a `switch` statement very well.

Another use of label values is in an interpreter for threaded code. The labels within the interpreter function can be stored in the threaded code for super-fast dispatching.

You may not use this mechanism to jump to code in a different function. If you do that, totally unpredictable things happen. The best way to avoid this is to store the label address only in automatic variables and never pass it as an argument.

An alternate way to write the above example is

```
static const int array[] = { &&foo - &&foo, &&bar - &&foo,
                             &&hack - &&foo };
goto *(&&foo + array[i]);
```

This is more friendly to code living in shared libraries, as it reduces the number of dynamic relocations that are needed, and by consequence, allows the data to be read-only. This alternative with label differences is not supported for the AVR target, please use the first approach for AVR programs.

The `&&foo` expressions for the same label might have different values if the containing function is inlined or cloned. If a program relies on them being always the same, `__attribute__((__noinline__,__noclone__))` should be used to prevent inlining and cloning. If `&&foo` is used in a static variable initializer, inlining and cloning is forbidden.

6.4 Nested Functions

A *nested function* is a function defined inside another function. Nested functions are supported as an extension in GNU C, but are not supported by GNU C++.

The nested function's name is local to the block where it is defined. For example, here we define a nested function named `square`, and call it twice:

```
foo (double a, double b)
{
  double square (double z) { return z * z; }

  return square (a) + square (b);
}
```

---

[1] The analogous feature in Fortran is called an assigned goto, but that name seems inappropriate in C, where one can do more than simply store label addresses in label variables.

The nested function can access all the variables of the containing function that are visible at the point of its definition. This is called *lexical scoping*. For example, here we show a nested function which uses an inherited variable named `offset`:

```
bar (int *array, int offset, int size)
{
  int access (int *array, int index)
    { return array[index + offset]; }
  int i;
  /* ... */
  for (i = 0; i < size; i++)
    /* ... */ access (array, i) /* ... */
}
```

Nested function definitions are permitted within functions in the places where variable definitions are allowed; that is, in any block, mixed with the other declarations and statements in the block.

It is possible to call the nested function from outside the scope of its name by storing its address or passing the address to another function:

```
hack (int *array, int size)
{
  void store (int index, int value)
    { array[index] = value; }

  intermediate (store, size);
}
```

Here, the function `intermediate` receives the address of `store` as an argument. If `intermediate` calls `store`, the arguments given to `store` are used to store into `array`. But this technique works only so long as the containing function (`hack`, in this example) does not exit.

If you try to call the nested function through its address after the containing function exits, all hell breaks loose. If you try to call it after a containing scope level exits, and if it refers to some of the variables that are no longer in scope, you may be lucky, but it's not wise to take the risk. If, however, the nested function does not refer to anything that has gone out of scope, you should be safe.

GCC implements taking the address of a nested function using a technique called *trampolines*. This technique was described in *Lexical Closures for C++* (Thomas M. Breuel, USENIX C++ Conference Proceedings, October 17-21, 1988).

A nested function can jump to a label inherited from a containing function, provided the label is explicitly declared in the containing function (see Section 6.2 [Local Labels], page 404). Such a jump returns instantly to the containing function, exiting the nested function that did the `goto` and any intermediate functions as well. Here is an example:

```
      bar (int *array, int offset, int size)
      {
        __label__ failure;
        int access (int *array, int index)
          {
            if (index > size)
              goto failure;
            return array[index + offset];
          }
        int i;
        /* ... */
        for (i = 0; i < size; i++)
          /* ... */ access (array, i) /* ... */
        /* ... */
        return 0;

      /* Control comes here from access
         if it detects an error.  */
      failure:
        return -1;
      }
```

A nested function always has no linkage. Declaring one with **extern** or **static** is erroneous. If you need to declare the nested function before its definition, use **auto** (which is otherwise meaningless for function declarations).

```
      bar (int *array, int offset, int size)
      {
        __label__ failure;
        auto int access (int *, int);
        /* ... */
        int access (int *array, int index)
          {
            if (index > size)
              goto failure;
            return array[index + offset];
          }
        /* ... */
      }
```

6.5 Constructing Function Calls

Using the built-in functions described below, you can record the arguments a function received, and call another function with the same arguments, without knowing the number or types of the arguments.

You can also record the return value of that function call, and later return that value, without knowing what data type the function tried to return (as long as your caller expects that data type).

However, these built-in functions may interact badly with some sophisticated features or other extensions of the language. It is, therefore, not recommended to use them outside very simple functions acting as mere forwarders for their arguments.

void * __builtin_apply_args ()   [Built-in Function]
> This built-in function returns a pointer to data describing how to perform a call with the same arguments as are passed to the current function.

The function saves the arg pointer register, structure value address, and all registers that might be used to pass arguments to a function into a block of memory allocated on the stack. Then it returns the address of that block.

void * __builtin_apply (*void* (*`function`)(), *void*   [Built-in Function]
      `arguments`, *size_t* `size`)

This built-in function invokes *function* with a copy of the parameters described by *arguments* and *size*.

The value of *arguments* should be the value returned by __builtin_apply_args. The argument *size* specifies the size of the stack argument data, in bytes.

This function returns a pointer to data describing how to return whatever value is returned by *function*. The data is saved in a block of memory allocated on the stack.

It is not always simple to compute the proper value for *size*. The value is used by __builtin_apply to compute the amount of data that should be pushed on the stack and copied from the incoming argument area.

void __builtin_return (*void* *`result`*)   [Built-in Function]

This built-in function returns the value described by *result* from the containing function. You should specify, for *result*, a value returned by __builtin_apply.

__builtin_va_arg_pack ()   [Built-in Function]

This built-in function represents all anonymous arguments of an inline function. It can be used only in inline functions that are always inlined, never compiled as a separate function, such as those using __attribute__ ((__always_inline__)) or __attribute__ ((__gnu_inline__)) extern inline functions. It must be only passed as last argument to some other function with variable arguments. This is useful for writing small wrapper inlines for variable argument functions, when using preprocessor macros is undesirable. For example:

```
extern int myprintf (FILE *f, const char *format, ...);
extern inline __attribute__ ((__gnu_inline__)) int
myprintf (FILE *f, const char *format, ...)
{
  int r = fprintf (f, "myprintf: ");
  if (r < 0)
    return r;
  int s = fprintf (f, format, __builtin_va_arg_pack ());
  if (s < 0)
    return s;
  return r + s;
}
```

size_t __builtin_va_arg_pack_len ()   [Built-in Function]

This built-in function returns the number of anonymous arguments of an inline function. It can be used only in inline functions that are always inlined, never compiled as a separate function, such as those using __attribute__ ((__always_inline__)) or __attribute__ ((__gnu_inline__)) extern inline functions. For example following does link- or run-time checking of open arguments for optimized code:

```
#ifdef __OPTIMIZE__
extern inline __attribute__((__gnu_inline__)) int
myopen (const char *path, int oflag, ...)
```

```
        {
          if (__builtin_va_arg_pack_len () > 1)
            warn_open_too_many_arguments ();

          if (__builtin_constant_p (oflag))
            {
              if ((oflag & O_CREAT) != 0 && __builtin_va_arg_pack_len () < 1)
                {
                  warn_open_missing_mode ();
                  return __open_2 (path, oflag);
                }
              return open (path, oflag, __builtin_va_arg_pack ());
            }

          if (__builtin_va_arg_pack_len () < 1)
            return __open_2 (path, oflag);

          return open (path, oflag, __builtin_va_arg_pack ());
        }
        #endif
```

6.6 Referring to a Type with typeof

Another way to refer to the type of an expression is with typeof. The syntax of using of this keyword looks like sizeof, but the construct acts semantically like a type name defined with typedef.

There are two ways of writing the argument to typeof: with an expression or with a type. Here is an example with an expression:

```
        typeof (x[0](1))
```

This assumes that x is an array of pointers to functions; the type described is that of the values of the functions.

Here is an example with a typename as the argument:

```
        typeof (int *)
```

Here the type described is that of pointers to int.

If you are writing a header file that must work when included in ISO C programs, write __typeof__ instead of typeof. See Section 6.46 [Alternate Keywords], page 549.

A typeof construct can be used anywhere a typedef name can be used. For example, you can use it in a declaration, in a cast, or inside of sizeof or typeof.

The operand of typeof is evaluated for its side effects if and only if it is an expression of variably modified type or the name of such a type.

typeof is often useful in conjunction with statement expressions (see Section 6.1 [Statement Exprs], page 403). Here is how the two together can be used to define a safe "maximum" macro which operates on any arithmetic type and evaluates each of its arguments exactly once:

```
        #define max(a,b) \
          ({ typeof (a) _a = (a); \
             typeof (b) _b = (b); \
           _a > _b ? _a : _b; })
```

The reason for using names that start with underscores for the local variables is to avoid conflicts with variable names that occur within the expressions that are substituted for a and **b**. Eventually we hope to design a new form of declaration syntax that allows you to declare variables whose scopes start only after their initializers; this will be a more reliable way to prevent such conflicts.

Some more examples of the use of `typeof`:

- This declares y with the type of what x points to.

```
typeof (*x) y;
```

- This declares y as an array of such values.

```
typeof (*x) y[4];
```

- This declares y as an array of pointers to characters:

```
typeof (typeof (char *)[4]) y;
```

It is equivalent to the following traditional C declaration:

```
char *y[4];
```

To see the meaning of the declaration using `typeof`, and why it might be a useful way to write, rewrite it with these macros:

```
#define pointer(T)  typeof(T *)
#define array(T, N) typeof(T [N])
```

Now the declaration can be rewritten this way:

```
array (pointer (char), 4) y;
```

Thus, `array (pointer (char), 4)` is the type of arrays of 4 pointers to `char`.

In GNU C, but not GNU C++, you may also declare the type of a variable as `__auto_type`. In that case, the declaration must declare only one variable, whose declarator must just be an identifier, the declaration must be initialized, and the type of the variable is determined by the initializer; the name of the variable is not in scope until after the initializer. (In C++, you should use C++11 `auto` for this purpose.) Using `__auto_type`, the "maximum" macro above could be written as:

```
#define max(a,b) \
  ({ __auto_type _a = (a); \
      __auto_type _b = (b); \
    _a > _b ? _a : _b; })
```

Using `__auto_type` instead of `typeof` has two advantages:

- Each argument to the macro appears only once in the expansion of the macro. This prevents the size of the macro expansion growing exponentially when calls to such macros are nested inside arguments of such macros.

- If the argument to the macro has variably modified type, it is evaluated only once when using `__auto_type`, but twice if `typeof` is used.

6.7 Conditionals with Omitted Operands

The middle operand in a conditional expression may be omitted. Then if the first operand is nonzero, its value is the value of the conditional expression.

Therefore, the expression

```
x ? : y
```

has the value of x if that is nonzero; otherwise, the value of y.

This example is perfectly equivalent to

```
    x ? x : y
```

In this simple case, the ability to omit the middle operand is not especially useful. When it becomes useful is when the first operand does, or may (if it is a macro argument), contain a side effect. Then repeating the operand in the middle would perform the side effect twice. Omitting the middle operand uses the value already computed without the undesirable effects of recomputing it.

6.8 128-bit Integers

As an extension the integer scalar type `__int128` is supported for targets which have an integer mode wide enough to hold 128 bits. Simply write `__int128` for a signed 128-bit integer, or `unsigned __int128` for an unsigned 128-bit integer. There is no support in GCC for expressing an integer constant of type `__int128` for targets with `long long` integer less than 128 bits wide.

6.9 Double-Word Integers

ISO C99 supports data types for integers that are at least 64 bits wide, and as an extension GCC supports them in C90 mode and in C++. Simply write `long long int` for a signed integer, or `unsigned long long int` for an unsigned integer. To make an integer constant of type `long long int`, add the suffix 'LL' to the integer. To make an integer constant of type `unsigned long long int`, add the suffix 'ULL' to the integer.

You can use these types in arithmetic like any other integer types. Addition, subtraction, and bitwise boolean operations on these types are open-coded on all types of machines. Multiplication is open-coded if the machine supports a fullword-to-doubleword widening multiply instruction. Division and shifts are open-coded only on machines that provide special support. The operations that are not open-coded use special library routines that come with GCC.

There may be pitfalls when you use `long long` types for function arguments without function prototypes. If a function expects type `int` for its argument, and you pass a value of type `long long int`, confusion results because the caller and the subroutine disagree about the number of bytes for the argument. Likewise, if the function expects `long long int` and you pass `int`. The best way to avoid such problems is to use prototypes.

6.10 Complex Numbers

ISO C99 supports complex floating data types, and as an extension GCC supports them in C90 mode and in C++. GCC also supports complex integer data types which are not part of ISO C99. You can declare complex types using the keyword `_Complex`. As an extension, the older GNU keyword `__complex__` is also supported.

For example, '`_Complex double x;`' declares x as a variable whose real part and imaginary part are both of type `double`. '`_Complex short int y;`' declares y to have real and imaginary parts of type `short int`; this is not likely to be useful, but it shows that the set of complex types is complete.

To write a constant with a complex data type, use the suffix 'i' or 'j' (either one; they are equivalent). For example, `2.5fi` has type `_Complex float` and `3i` has type `_Complex int`. Such a constant always has a pure imaginary value, but you can form any complex value you like by adding one to a real constant. This is a GNU extension; if you have an ISO C99 conforming C library (such as the GNU C Library), and want to construct complex constants of floating type, you should include `<complex.h>` and use the macros `I` or `_Complex_I` instead.

To extract the real part of a complex-valued expression *exp*, write `__real__` *exp*. Likewise, use `__imag__` to extract the imaginary part. This is a GNU extension; for values of floating type, you should use the ISO C99 functions `crealf`, `creal`, `creall`, `cimagf`, `cimag` and `cimagl`, declared in `<complex.h>` and also provided as built-in functions by GCC.

The operator '`~`' performs complex conjugation when used on a value with a complex type. This is a GNU extension; for values of floating type, you should use the ISO C99 functions `conjf`, `conj` and `conjl`, declared in `<complex.h>` and also provided as built-in functions by GCC.

GCC can allocate complex automatic variables in a noncontiguous fashion; it's even possible for the real part to be in a register while the imaginary part is on the stack (or vice versa). Only the DWARF debug info format can represent this, so use of DWARF is recommended. If you are using the stabs debug info format, GCC describes a noncontiguous complex variable as if it were two separate variables of noncomplex type. If the variable's actual name is `foo`, the two fictitious variables are named `foo$real` and `foo$imag`. You can examine and set these two fictitious variables with your debugger.

6.11 Additional Floating Types

ISO/IEC TS 18661-3:2015 defines C support for additional floating types `_Float`*n* and `_Float`*n*`x`, and GCC supports these type names; the set of types supported depends on the target architecture. These types are not supported when compiling C++. Constants with these types use suffixes `f`*n* or `F`*n* and `f`*n*`x` or `F`*n*`x`. These type names can be used together with `_Complex` to declare complex types.

As an extension, GNU C and GNU C++ support additional floating types, `__float80` and `__float128` to support 80-bit (`XFmode`) and 128-bit (`TFmode`) floating types; these are aliases for the type names `_Float64x` and `_Float128`. Support for additional types includes the arithmetic operators: add, subtract, multiply, divide; unary arithmetic operators; relational operators; equality operators; and conversions to and from integer and other floating types. Use a suffix 'w' or 'W' in a literal constant of type `__float80` or type `__ibm128`. Use a suffix 'q' or 'Q' for `_float128`.

On the i386, x86_64, IA-64, and HP-UX targets, you can declare complex types using the corresponding internal complex type, `XCmode` for `__float80` type and `TCmode` for `__float128` type:

```
typedef _Complex float __attribute__((mode(TC))) _Complex128;
typedef _Complex float __attribute__((mode(XC))) _Complex80;
```

In order to use `_Float128`, `__float128` and `__ibm128` on PowerPC Linux systems, you must use the '-mfloat128'. It is expected in future versions of GCC that `_Float128` and `__float128` will be enabled automatically. In addition, there are currently problems in using the complex `__float128` type. When these problems are fixed, you would use the following syntax to declare `_Complex128` to be a complex `__float128` type:

On the PowerPC Linux VSX targets, you can declare complex types using the corresponding internal complex type, KCmode for __float128 type and ICmode for __ibm128 type:

```
typedef _Complex float __attribute__((mode(KC))) _Complex_float128;
typedef _Complex float __attribute__((mode(IC))) _Complex_ibm128;
```

Not all targets support additional floating-point types. __float80 and __float128 types are supported on x86 and IA-64 targets. The __float128 type is supported on hppa HP-UX. The __float128 type is supported on PowerPC 64-bit Linux systems by default if the vector scalar instruction set (VSX) is enabled. The _Float128 type is supported on all systems where __float128 is supported or where long double has the IEEE binary128 format. The _Float64x type is supported on all systems where __float128 is supported. The _Float32 type is supported on all systems supporting IEEE binary32; the _Float64 and Float32x types are supported on all systems supporting IEEE binary64. GCC does not currently support _Float16 or _Float128x on any systems.

On the PowerPC, __ibm128 provides access to the IBM extended double format, and it is intended to be used by the library functions that handle conversions if/when long double is changed to be IEEE 128-bit floating point.

6.12 Half-Precision Floating Point

On ARM targets, GCC supports half-precision (16-bit) floating point via the __fp16 type. You must enable this type explicitly with the '-mfp16-format' command-line option in order to use it.

ARM supports two incompatible representations for half-precision floating-point values. You must choose one of the representations and use it consistently in your program.

Specifying '-mfp16-format=ieee' selects the IEEE 754-2008 format. This format can represent normalized values in the range of 2^{-14} to 65504. There are 11 bits of significand precision, approximately 3 decimal digits.

Specifying '-mfp16-format=alternative' selects the ARM alternative format. This representation is similar to the IEEE format, but does not support infinities or NaNs. Instead, the range of exponents is extended, so that this format can represent normalized values in the range of 2^{-14} to 131008.

The __fp16 type is a storage format only. For purposes of arithmetic and other operations, __fp16 values in C or C++ expressions are automatically promoted to float. In addition, you cannot declare a function with a return value or parameters of type __fp16.

Note that conversions from double to __fp16 involve an intermediate conversion to float. Because of rounding, this can sometimes produce a different result than a direct conversion.

ARM provides hardware support for conversions between __fp16 and float values as an extension to VFP and NEON (Advanced SIMD). GCC generates code using these hardware instructions if you compile with options to select an FPU that provides them; for example, '-mfpu=neon-fp16 -mfloat-abi=softfp', in addition to the '-mfp16-format' option to select a half-precision format.

Language-level support for the __fp16 data type is independent of whether GCC generates code using hardware floating-point instructions. In cases where hardware support is not specified, GCC implements conversions between `__fp16` and `float` values as library calls.

6.13 Decimal Floating Types

As an extension, GNU C supports decimal floating types as defined in the N1312 draft of ISO/IEC WDTR24732. Support for decimal floating types in GCC will evolve as the draft technical report changes. Calling conventions for any target might also change. Not all targets support decimal floating types.

The decimal floating types are `_Decimal32`, `_Decimal64`, and `_Decimal128`. They use a radix of ten, unlike the floating types `float`, `double`, and `long double` whose radix is not specified by the C standard but is usually two.

Support for decimal floating types includes the arithmetic operators add, subtract, multiply, divide; unary arithmetic operators; relational operators; equality operators; and conversions to and from integer and other floating types. Use a suffix 'df' or 'DF' in a literal constant of type `_Decimal32`, 'dd' or 'DD' for `_Decimal64`, and 'dl' or 'DL' for `_Decimal128`.

GCC support of decimal float as specified by the draft technical report is incomplete:

- When the value of a decimal floating type cannot be represented in the integer type to which it is being converted, the result is undefined rather than the result value specified by the draft technical report.

- GCC does not provide the C library functionality associated with 'math.h', 'fenv.h', 'stdio.h', 'stdlib.h', and 'wchar.h', which must come from a separate C library implementation. Because of this the GNU C compiler does not define macro `__STDC_DEC_FP__` to indicate that the implementation conforms to the technical report.

Types `_Decimal32`, `_Decimal64`, and `_Decimal128` are supported by the DWARF debug information format.

6.14 Hex Floats

ISO C99 supports floating-point numbers written not only in the usual decimal notation, such as `1.55e1`, but also numbers such as `0x1.fp3` written in hexadecimal format. As a GNU extension, GCC supports this in C90 mode (except in some cases when strictly conforming) and in C++. In that format the '0x' hex introducer and the 'p' or 'P' exponent field are mandatory. The exponent is a decimal number that indicates the power of 2 by which the significant part is multiplied. Thus '0x1.f' is $1\frac{15}{16}$, 'p3' multiplies it by 8, and the value of `0x1.fp3` is the same as `1.55e1`.

Unlike for floating-point numbers in the decimal notation the exponent is always required in the hexadecimal notation. Otherwise the compiler would not be able to resolve the ambiguity of, e.g., `0x1.f`. This could mean `1.0f` or `1.9375` since 'f' is also the extension for floating-point constants of type `float`.

6.15 Fixed-Point Types

As an extension, GNU C supports fixed-point types as defined in the N1169 draft of ISO/IEC DTR 18037. Support for fixed-point types in GCC will evolve as the draft technical report changes. Calling conventions for any target might also change. Not all targets support fixed-point types.

The fixed-point types are short _Fract, _Fract, long _Fract, long long _Fract, unsigned short _Fract, unsigned _Fract, unsigned long _Fract, unsigned long long _Fract, _Sat short _Fract, _Sat _Fract, _Sat long _Fract, _Sat long long _Fract, _Sat unsigned short _Fract, _Sat unsigned _Fract, _Sat unsigned long _Fract, _Sat unsigned long long _Fract, short _Accum, _Accum, long _Accum, long long _Accum, unsigned short _Accum, unsigned _Accum, unsigned long _Accum, unsigned long long _Accum, _Sat short _Accum, _Sat _Accum, _Sat long _Accum, _Sat long long _Accum, _Sat unsigned short _Accum, _Sat unsigned _Accum, _Sat unsigned long _Accum, _Sat unsigned long long _Accum.

Fixed-point data values contain fractional and optional integral parts. The format of fixed-point data varies and depends on the target machine.

Support for fixed-point types includes:

- prefix and postfix increment and decrement operators (++, --)
- unary arithmetic operators (+, -, !)
- binary arithmetic operators (+, -, *, /)
- binary shift operators (<<, >>)
- relational operators (<, <=, >=, >)
- equality operators (==, !=)
- assignment operators (+=, -=, *=, /=, <<=, >>=)
- conversions to and from integer, floating-point, or fixed-point types

Use a suffix in a fixed-point literal constant:

- 'hr' or 'HR' for short _Fract and _Sat short _Fract
- 'r' or 'R' for _Fract and _Sat _Fract
- 'lr' or 'LR' for long _Fract and _Sat long _Fract
- 'llr' or 'LLR' for long long _Fract and _Sat long long _Fract
- 'uhr' or 'UHR' for unsigned short _Fract and _Sat unsigned short _Fract
- 'ur' or 'UR' for unsigned _Fract and _Sat unsigned _Fract
- 'ulr' or 'ULR' for unsigned long _Fract and _Sat unsigned long _Fract
- 'ullr' or 'ULLR' for unsigned long long _Fract and _Sat unsigned long long _Fract
- 'hk' or 'HK' for short _Accum and _Sat short _Accum
- 'k' or 'K' for _Accum and _Sat _Accum
- 'lk' or 'LK' for long _Accum and _Sat long _Accum
- 'llk' or 'LLK' for long long _Accum and _Sat long long _Accum
- 'uhk' or 'UHK' for unsigned short _Accum and _Sat unsigned short _Accum
- 'uk' or 'UK' for unsigned _Accum and _Sat unsigned _Accum
- 'ulk' or 'ULK' for unsigned long _Accum and _Sat unsigned long _Accum
- 'ullk' or 'ULLK' for unsigned long long _Accum and _Sat unsigned long long _Accum

GCC support of fixed-point types as specified by the draft technical report is incomplete:

- Pragmas to control overflow and rounding behaviors are not implemented.

Fixed-point types are supported by the DWARF debug information format.

6.16 Named Address Spaces

As an extension, GNU C supports named address spaces as defined in the N1275 draft of ISO/IEC DTR 18037. Support for named address spaces in GCC will evolve as the draft technical report changes. Calling conventions for any target might also change. At present, only the AVR, SPU, M32C, RL78, and x86 targets support address spaces other than the generic address space.

Address space identifiers may be used exactly like any other C type qualifier (e.g., `const` or `volatile`). See the N1275 document for more details.

6.16.1 AVR Named Address Spaces

On the AVR target, there are several address spaces that can be used in order to put read-only data into the flash memory and access that data by means of the special instructions `LPM` or `ELPM` needed to read from flash.

Per default, any data including read-only data is located in RAM (the generic address space) so that non-generic address spaces are needed to locate read-only data in flash memory *and* to generate the right instructions to access this data without using (inline) assembler code.

`__flash`   The `__flash` qualifier locates data in the `.progmem.data` section. Data is read using the `LPM` instruction. Pointers to this address space are 16 bits wide.

`__flash1`
`__flash2`
`__flash3`
`__flash4`
`__flash5`   These are 16-bit address spaces locating data in section `.progmemN.data` where *N* refers to address space `__flashN`. The compiler sets the `RAMPZ` segment register appropriately before reading data by means of the `ELPM` instruction.

`__memx`   This is a 24-bit address space that linearizes flash and RAM: If the high bit of the address is set, data is read from RAM using the lower two bytes as RAM address. If the high bit of the address is clear, data is read from flash with `RAMPZ` set according to the high byte of the address. See Section 6.60.10 [`__builtin_avr_flash_segment`], page 593.

Objects in this address space are located in `.progmemx.data`.

Example
```
char my_read (const __flash char ** p)
{
    /* p is a pointer to RAM that points to a pointer to flash.
       The first indirection of p reads that flash pointer
       from RAM and the second indirection reads a char from this
       flash address.  */

    return **p;
}

/* Locate array[] in flash memory */
const __flash int array[] = { 3, 5, 7, 11, 13, 17, 19 };
```

```
int i = 1;

int main (void)
{
    /* Return 17 by reading from flash memory */
    return array[array[i]];
}
```

For each named address space supported by avr-gcc there is an equally named but uppercase built-in macro defined. The purpose is to facilitate testing if respective address space support is available or not:

```
#ifdef __FLASH
const __flash int var = 1;

int read_var (void)
{
    return var;
}
#else
#include <avr/pgmspace.h> /* From AVR-LibC */

const int var PROGMEM = 1;

int read_var (void)
{
    return (int) pgm_read_word (&var);
}
#endif /* __FLASH */
```

Notice that attribute Section 6.32.2 [progmem], page 475 locates data in flash but accesses to these data read from generic address space, i.e. from RAM, so that you need special accessors like `pgm_read_byte` from AVR-LibC together with attribute `progmem`.

Limitations and caveats

- Reading across the 64 KiB section boundary of the `__flash` or `__flash`N address spaces shows undefined behavior. The only address space that supports reading across the 64 KiB flash segment boundaries is `__memx`.

- If you use one of the `__flash`N address spaces you must arrange your linker script to locate the `.progmem`N`.data` sections according to your needs.

- Any data or pointers to the non-generic address spaces must be qualified as `const`, i.e. as read-only data. This still applies if the data in one of these address spaces like software version number or calibration lookup table are intended to be changed after load time by, say, a boot loader. In this case the right qualification is `const volatile` so that the compiler must not optimize away known values or insert them as immediates into operands of instructions.

- The following code initializes a variable `pfoo` located in static storage with a 24-bit address:

```
extern const __memx char foo;
const __memx void *pfoo = &foo;
```

Such code requires at least binutils 2.23, see PR13503.

- On the reduced Tiny devices like ATtiny40, no address spaces are supported. Data can be put into and read from flash memory by means of attribute `progmem`, see Section 6.32.2 [AVR Variable Attributes], page 475.

6.16.2 M32C Named Address Spaces

On the M32C target, with the R8C and M16C CPU variants, variables qualified with `__far` are accessed using 32-bit addresses in order to access memory beyond the first 64 Ki bytes. If `__far` is used with the M32CM or M32C CPU variants, it has no effect.

6.16.3 RL78 Named Address Spaces

On the RL78 target, variables qualified with `__far` are accessed with 32-bit pointers (20-bit addresses) rather than the default 16-bit addresses. Non-far variables are assumed to appear in the topmost 64 KiB of the address space.

6.16.4 SPU Named Address Spaces

On the SPU target variables may be declared as belonging to another address space by qualifying the type with the `__ea` address space identifier:

```
extern int __ea i;
```

The compiler generates special code to access the variable `i`. It may use runtime library support, or generate special machine instructions to access that address space.

6.16.5 x86 Named Address Spaces

On the x86 target, variables may be declared as being relative to the `%fs` or `%gs` segments.

`__seg_fs`
`__seg_gs`   The object is accessed with the respective segment override prefix.

The respective segment base must be set via some method specific to the operating system. Rather than require an expensive system call to retrieve the segment base, these address spaces are not considered to be subspaces of the generic (flat) address space. This means that explicit casts are required to convert pointers between these address spaces and the generic address space. In practice the application should cast to `uintptr_t` and apply the segment base offset that it installed previously.

The preprocessor symbols `__SEG_FS` and `__SEG_GS` are defined when these address spaces are supported.

6.17 Arrays of Length Zero

Zero-length arrays are allowed in GNU C. They are very useful as the last element of a structure that is really a header for a variable-length object:

```
struct line {
  int length;
  char contents[0];
};

struct line *thisline = (struct line *)
  malloc (sizeof (struct line) + this_length);
thisline->length = this_length;
```

In ISO C90, you would have to give `contents` a length of 1, which means either you waste space or complicate the argument to `malloc`.

In ISO C99, you would use a *flexible array member*, which is slightly different in syntax and semantics:

- Flexible array members are written as `contents[]` without the 0.

- Flexible array members have incomplete type, and so the `sizeof` operator may not be applied. As a quirk of the original implementation of zero-length arrays, `sizeof` evaluates to zero.

- Flexible array members may only appear as the last member of a `struct` that is otherwise non-empty.

- A structure containing a flexible array member, or a union containing such a structure (possibly recursively), may not be a member of a structure or an element of an array. (However, these uses are permitted by GCC as extensions.)

Non-empty initialization of zero-length arrays is treated like any case where there are more initializer elements than the array holds, in that a suitable warning about "excess elements in array" is given, and the excess elements (all of them, in this case) are ignored.

GCC allows static initialization of flexible array members. This is equivalent to defining a new structure containing the original structure followed by an array of sufficient size to contain the data. E.g. in the following, `f1` is constructed as if it were declared like `f2`.

```
struct f1 {
  int x; int y[];
} f1 = { 1, { 2, 3, 4 } };

struct f2 {
  struct f1 f1; int data[3];
} f2 = { { 1 }, { 2, 3, 4 } };
```

The convenience of this extension is that `f1` has the desired type, eliminating the need to consistently refer to `f2.f1`.

This has symmetry with normal static arrays, in that an array of unknown size is also written with `[]`.

Of course, this extension only makes sense if the extra data comes at the end of a top-level object, as otherwise we would be overwriting data at subsequent offsets. To avoid undue complication and confusion with initialization of deeply nested arrays, we simply disallow any non-empty initialization except when the structure is the top-level object. For example:

```
struct foo { int x; int y[]; };
struct bar { struct foo z; };

struct foo a = { 1, { 2, 3, 4 } };        // Valid.
struct bar b = { { 1, { 2, 3, 4 } } };    // Invalid.
struct bar c = { { 1, { } } };            // Valid.
struct foo d[1] = { { 1, { 2, 3, 4 } } }; // Invalid.
```

6.18 Structures with No Members

GCC permits a C structure to have no members:

```
struct empty {
};
```

The structure has size zero. In C++, empty structures are part of the language. G++ treats empty structures as if they had a single member of type `char`.

6.19 Arrays of Variable Length

Variable-length automatic arrays are allowed in ISO C99, and as an extension GCC accepts them in C90 mode and in C++. These arrays are declared like any other automatic arrays, but with a length that is not a constant expression. The storage is allocated at the point of declaration and deallocated when the block scope containing the declaration exits. For example:

```
FILE *
concat_fopen (char *s1, char *s2, char *mode)
{
  char str[strlen (s1) + strlen (s2) + 1];
  strcpy (str, s1);
  strcat (str, s2);
  return fopen (str, mode);
}
```

Jumping or breaking out of the scope of the array name deallocates the storage. Jumping into the scope is not allowed; you get an error message for it.

As an extension, GCC accepts variable-length arrays as a member of a structure or a union. For example:

```
void
foo (int n)
{
  struct S { int x[n]; };
}
```

You can use the function **alloca** to get an effect much like variable-length arrays. The function **alloca** is available in many other C implementations (but not in all). On the other hand, variable-length arrays are more elegant.

There are other differences between these two methods. Space allocated with **alloca** exists until the containing *function* returns. The space for a variable-length array is deallocated as soon as the array name's scope ends, unless you also use **alloca** in this scope.

You can also use variable-length arrays as arguments to functions:

```
struct entry
tester (int len, char data[len][len])
{
  /* ... */
}
```

The length of an array is computed once when the storage is allocated and is remembered for the scope of the array in case you access it with **sizeof**.

If you want to pass the array first and the length afterward, you can use a forward declaration in the parameter list—another GNU extension.

```
struct entry
tester (int len; char data[len][len], int len)
{
  /* ... */
}
```

The 'int len' before the semicolon is a *parameter forward declaration*, and it serves the purpose of making the name **len** known when the declaration of **data** is parsed.

You can write any number of such parameter forward declarations in the parameter list. They can be separated by commas or semicolons, but the last one must end with a semicolon, which is followed by the "real" parameter declarations. Each forward declaration must match a "real" declaration in parameter name and data type. ISO C99 does not support parameter forward declarations.

6.20 Macros with a Variable Number of Arguments.

In the ISO C standard of 1999, a macro can be declared to accept a variable number of arguments much as a function can. The syntax for defining the macro is similar to that of a function. Here is an example:

```
#define debug(format, ...) fprintf (stderr, format, __VA_ARGS__)
```

Here '...' is a *variable argument*. In the invocation of such a macro, it represents the zero or more tokens until the closing parenthesis that ends the invocation, including any commas. This set of tokens replaces the identifier __VA_ARGS__ in the macro body wherever it appears. See the CPP manual for more information.

GCC has long supported variadic macros, and used a different syntax that allowed you to give a name to the variable arguments just like any other argument. Here is an example:

```
#define debug(format, args...) fprintf (stderr, format, args)
```

This is in all ways equivalent to the ISO C example above, but arguably more readable and descriptive.

GNU CPP has two further variadic macro extensions, and permits them to be used with either of the above forms of macro definition.

In standard C, you are not allowed to leave the variable argument out entirely; but you are allowed to pass an empty argument. For example, this invocation is invalid in ISO C, because there is no comma after the string:

```
debug ("A message")
```

GNU CPP permits you to completely omit the variable arguments in this way. In the above examples, the compiler would complain, though since the expansion of the macro still has the extra comma after the format string.

To help solve this problem, CPP behaves specially for variable arguments used with the token paste operator, '##'. If instead you write

```
#define debug(format, ...) fprintf (stderr, format, ## __VA_ARGS__)
```

and if the variable arguments are omitted or empty, the '##' operator causes the preprocessor to remove the comma before it. If you do provide some variable arguments in your macro invocation, GNU CPP does not complain about the paste operation and instead places the variable arguments after the comma. Just like any other pasted macro argument, these arguments are not macro expanded.

6.21 Slightly Looser Rules for Escaped Newlines

The preprocessor treatment of escaped newlines is more relaxed than that specified by the C90 standard, which requires the newline to immediately follow a backslash. GCC's implementation allows whitespace in the form of spaces, horizontal and vertical tabs, and form feeds between the backslash and the subsequent newline. The preprocessor issues a warning, but treats it as a valid escaped newline and combines the two lines to form a single logical line. This works within comments and tokens, as well as between tokens. Comments are *not* treated as whitespace for the purposes of this relaxation, since they have not yet been replaced with spaces.

6.22 Non-Lvalue Arrays May Have Subscripts

In ISO C99, arrays that are not lvalues still decay to pointers, and may be subscripted, although they may not be modified or used after the next sequence point and the unary '&' operator may not be applied to them. As an extension, GNU C allows such arrays to be subscripted in C90 mode, though otherwise they do not decay to pointers outside C99 mode. For example, this is valid in GNU C though not valid in C90:

```
struct foo {int a[4];};

struct foo f();

bar (int index)
{
  return f().a[index];
}
```

6.23 Arithmetic on `void`- and Function-Pointers

In GNU C, addition and subtraction operations are supported on pointers to `void` and on pointers to functions. This is done by treating the size of a `void` or of a function as 1.

A consequence of this is that `sizeof` is also allowed on `void` and on function types, and returns 1.

The option '`-Wpointer-arith`' requests a warning if these extensions are used.

6.24 Pointers to Arrays with Qualifiers Work as Expected

In GNU C, pointers to arrays with qualifiers work similar to pointers to other qualified types. For example, a value of type `int (*)[5]` can be used to initialize a variable of type `const int (*)[5]`. These types are incompatible in ISO C because the `const` qualifier is formally attached to the element type of the array and not the array itself.

```
extern void
transpose (int N, int M, double out[M][N], const double in[N][M]);
double x[3][2];
double y[2][3];
...
transpose(3, 2, y, x);
```

6.25 Non-Constant Initializers

As in standard C++ and ISO C99, the elements of an aggregate initializer for an automatic variable are not required to be constant expressions in GNU C. Here is an example of an initializer with run-time varying elements:

```
foo (float f, float g)
{
  float beat_freqs[2] = { f-g, f+g };
  /* ... */
}
```

6.26 Compound Literals

A compound literal looks like a cast of a brace-enclosed aggregate initializer list. Its value is an object of the type specified in the cast, containing the elements specified in the initializer.

Unlike the result of a cast, a compound literal is an lvalue. ISO C99 and later support compound literals. As an extension, GCC supports compound literals also in C90 mode and in C++, although as explained below, the C++ semantics are somewhat different.

Usually, the specified type of a compound literal is a structure. Assume that `struct foo` and `structure` are declared as shown:

```
struct foo {int a; char b[2];} structure;
```

Here is an example of constructing a `struct foo` with a compound literal:

```
structure = ((struct foo) {x + y, 'a', 0});
```

This is equivalent to writing the following:

```
{
  struct foo temp = {x + y, 'a', 0};
  structure = temp;
}
```

You can also construct an array, though this is dangerous in C++, as explained below. If all the elements of the compound literal are (made up of) simple constant expressions suitable for use in initializers of objects of static storage duration, then the compound literal can be coerced to a pointer to its first element and used in such an initializer, as shown here:

```
char **foo = (char *[]) { "x", "y", "z" };
```

Compound literals for scalar types and union types are also allowed. In the following example the variable `i` is initialized to the value 2, the result of incrementing the unnamed object created by the compound literal.

```
int i = ++(int) { 1 };
```

As a GNU extension, GCC allows initialization of objects with static storage duration by compound literals (which is not possible in ISO C99 because the initializer is not a constant). It is handled as if the object were initialized only with the brace-enclosed list if the types of the compound literal and the object match. The elements of the compound literal must be constant. If the object being initialized has array type of unknown size, the size is determined by the size of the compound literal.

```
static struct foo x = (struct foo) {1, 'a', 'b'};
static int y[] = (int []) {1, 2, 3};
static int z[] = (int [3]) {1};
```

The above lines are equivalent to the following:

```
static struct foo x = {1, 'a', 'b'};
static int y[] = {1, 2, 3};
static int z[] = {1, 0, 0};
```

In C, a compound literal designates an unnamed object with static or automatic storage duration. In C++, a compound literal designates a temporary object that only lives until the end of its full-expression. As a result, well-defined C code that takes the address of a subobject of a compound literal can be undefined in C++, so G++ rejects the conversion of a temporary array to a pointer. For instance, if the array compound literal example above appeared inside a function, any subsequent use of `foo` in C++ would have undefined behavior because the lifetime of the array ends after the declaration of `foo`.

As an optimization, G++ sometimes gives array compound literals longer lifetimes: when the array either appears outside a function or has a `const`-qualified type. If `foo` and its initializer had elements of type `char *const` rather than `char *`, or if `foo` were a global variable, the array would have static storage duration. But it is probably safest just to avoid the use of array compound literals in C++ code.

6.27 Designated Initializers

Standard C90 requires the elements of an initializer to appear in a fixed order, the same as the order of the elements in the array or structure being initialized.

In ISO C99 you can give the elements in any order, specifying the array indices or structure field names they apply to, and GNU C allows this as an extension in C90 mode as well. This extension is not implemented in GNU C++.

To specify an array index, write '[*index*] =' before the element value. For example,

```
int a[6] = { [4] = 29, [2] = 15 };
```

is equivalent to

```
int a[6] = { 0, 0, 15, 0, 29, 0 };
```

The index values must be constant expressions, even if the array being initialized is automatic.

An alternative syntax for this that has been obsolete since GCC 2.5 but GCC still accepts is to write '[*index*]' before the element value, with no '='.

To initialize a range of elements to the same value, write '[*first* ... *last*] = *value*'. This is a GNU extension. For example,

```
int widths[] = { [0 ... 9] = 1, [10 ... 99] = 2, [100] = 3 };
```

If the value in it has side-effects, the side-effects happen only once, not for each initialized field by the range initializer.

Note that the length of the array is the highest value specified plus one.

In a structure initializer, specify the name of a field to initialize with '.*fieldname* =' before the element value. For example, given the following structure,

```
struct point { int x, y; };
```

the following initialization

```
struct point p = { .y = yvalue, .x = xvalue };
```

is equivalent to

```
struct point p = { xvalue, yvalue };
```

Another syntax that has the same meaning, obsolete since GCC 2.5, is '*fieldname*:', as shown here:

```
struct point p = { y: yvalue, x: xvalue };
```

Omitted field members are implicitly initialized the same as objects that have static storage duration.

The '[*index*]' or '.*fieldname*' is known as a *designator*. You can also use a designator (or the obsolete colon syntax) when initializing a union, to specify which element of the union should be used. For example,

```
union foo { int i; double d; };
```

```
union foo f = { .d = 4 };
```

converts 4 to a **double** to store it in the union using the second element. By contrast, casting 4 to type **union foo** stores it into the union as the integer i, since it is an integer. (See Section 6.29 [Cast to Union], page 426.)

You can combine this technique of naming elements with ordinary C initialization of successive elements. Each initializer element that does not have a designator applies to the next consecutive element of the array or structure. For example,

```
int a[6] = { [1] = v1, v2, [4] = v4 };
```

is equivalent to

```
int a[6] = { 0, v1, v2, 0, v4, 0 };
```

Labeling the elements of an array initializer is especially useful when the indices are characters or belong to an `enum` type. For example:

```
int whitespace[256]
    = { [' '] = 1, ['\t'] = 1, ['\h'] = 1,
        ['\f'] = 1, ['\n'] = 1, ['\r'] = 1 };
```

You can also write a series of '.*fieldname*' and '[*index*]' designators before an '=' to specify a nested subobject to initialize; the list is taken relative to the subobject corresponding to the closest surrounding brace pair. For example, with the '`struct point`' declaration above:

```
struct point ptarray[10] = { [2].y = yv2, [2].x = xv2, [0].x = xv0 };
```

If the same field is initialized multiple times, it has the value from the last initialization. If any such overridden initialization has side-effect, it is unspecified whether the side-effect happens or not. Currently, GCC discards them and issues a warning.

6.28 Case Ranges

You can specify a range of consecutive values in a single `case` label, like this:

```
case low ... high:
```

This has the same effect as the proper number of individual `case` labels, one for each integer value from *low* to *high*, inclusive.

This feature is especially useful for ranges of ASCII character codes:

```
case 'A' ... 'Z':
```

Be careful: Write spaces around the ..., for otherwise it may be parsed wrong when you use it with integer values. For example, write this:

```
case 1 ... 5:
```

rather than this:

```
case 1...5:
```

6.29 Cast to a Union Type

A cast to union type looks similar to other casts, except that the type specified is a union type. You can specify the type either with the `union` keyword or with a `typedef` name that refers to a union. A cast to a union actually creates a compound literal and yields an lvalue, not an rvalue like true casts do. (See Section 6.26 [Compound Literals], page 423.)

The types that may be cast to the union type are those of the members of the union. Thus, given the following union and variables:

```
union foo { int i; double d; };
int x;
double y;
```

both `x` and `y` can be cast to type `union foo`.

Using the cast as the right-hand side of an assignment to a variable of union type is equivalent to storing in a member of the union:

```
union foo u;
/* ... */
u = (union foo) x  ≡  u.i = x
u = (union foo) y  ≡  u.d = y
```

You can also use the union cast as a function argument:

```
void hack (union foo);
/* ... */
hack ((union foo) x);
```

6.30 Mixed Declarations and Code

ISO C99 and ISO C++ allow declarations and code to be freely mixed within compound statements. As an extension, GNU C also allows this in C90 mode. For example, you could do:

```
int i;
/* ... */
i++;
int j = i + 2;
```

Each identifier is visible from where it is declared until the end of the enclosing block.

6.31 Declaring Attributes of Functions

In GNU C, you can use function attributes to declare certain things about functions called in your program which help the compiler optimize calls and check your code more carefully. For example, you can use attributes to declare that a function never returns (**noreturn**), returns a value depending only on its arguments (**pure**), or has **printf**-style arguments (**format**).

You can also use attributes to control memory placement, code generation options or call/return conventions within the function being annotated. Many of these attributes are target-specific. For example, many targets support attributes for defining interrupt handler functions, which typically must follow special register usage and return conventions.

Function attributes are introduced by the **__attribute__** keyword on a declaration, followed by an attribute specification inside double parentheses. You can specify multiple attributes in a declaration by separating them by commas within the double parentheses or by immediately following an attribute declaration with another attribute declaration. See Section 6.37 [Attribute Syntax], page 490, for the exact rules on attribute syntax and placement.

GCC also supports attributes on variable declarations (see Section 6.32 [Variable Attributes], page 471), labels (see Section 6.34 [Label Attributes], page 488), enumerators (see Section 6.35 [Enumerator Attributes], page 489), statements (see Section 6.36 [Statement Attributes], page 490), and types (see Section 6.33 [Type Attributes], page 482).

There is some overlap between the purposes of attributes and pragmas (see Section 6.62 [Pragmas Accepted by GCC], page 715). It has been found convenient to use **__attribute__** to achieve a natural attachment of attributes to their corresponding declarations, whereas **#pragma** is of use for compatibility with other compilers or constructs that do not naturally form part of the grammar.

In addition to the attributes documented here, GCC plugins may provide their own attributes.

6.31.1 Common Function Attributes

The following attributes are supported on most targets.

alias ("*target*")

> The **alias** attribute causes the declaration to be emitted as an alias for another symbol, which must be specified. For instance,
>
> ```
> void __f () { /* Do something. */; }
> void f () __attribute__ ((weak, alias ("__f")));
> ```
>
> defines 'f' to be a weak alias for '__f'. In C++, the mangled name for the target must be used. It is an error if '__f' is not defined in the same translation unit.
>
> This attribute requires assembler and object file support, and may not be available on all targets.

aligned (*alignment*)

> This attribute specifies a minimum alignment for the function, measured in bytes.
>
> You cannot use this attribute to decrease the alignment of a function, only to increase it. However, when you explicitly specify a function alignment this overrides the effect of the '-falign-functions' (see Section 3.10 [Optimize Options], page 102) option for this function.
>
> Note that the effectiveness of **aligned** attributes may be limited by inherent limitations in your linker. On many systems, the linker is only able to arrange for functions to be aligned up to a certain maximum alignment. (For some linkers, the maximum supported alignment may be very very small.) See your linker documentation for further information.
>
> The **aligned** attribute can also be used for variables and fields (see Section 6.32 [Variable Attributes], page 471.)

alloc_align

> The **alloc_align** attribute is used to tell the compiler that the function return value points to memory, where the returned pointer minimum alignment is given by one of the functions parameters. GCC uses this information to improve pointer alignment analysis.
>
> The function parameter denoting the allocated alignment is specified by one integer argument, whose number is the argument of the attribute. Argument numbering starts at one.
>
> For instance,
>
> ```
> void* my_memalign(size_t, size_t) __attribute__((alloc_align(1)))
> ```
>
> declares that **my_memalign** returns memory with minimum alignment given by parameter 1.

alloc_size

> The **alloc_size** attribute is used to tell the compiler that the function return value points to memory, where the size is given by one or two of the func-

tions parameters. GCC uses this information to improve the correctness of `__builtin_object_size`.

The function parameter(s) denoting the allocated size are specified by one or two integer arguments supplied to the attribute. The allocated size is either the value of the single function argument specified or the product of the two function arguments specified. Argument numbering starts at one.

For instance,

```
void* my_calloc(size_t, size_t) __attribute__((alloc_size(1,2)))
void* my_realloc(void*, size_t) __attribute__((alloc_size(2)))
```

declares that `my_calloc` returns memory of the size given by the product of parameter 1 and 2 and that `my_realloc` returns memory of the size given by parameter 2.

`always_inline`

Generally, functions are not inlined unless optimization is specified. For functions declared inline, this attribute inlines the function independent of any restrictions that otherwise apply to inlining. Failure to inline such a function is diagnosed as an error. Note that if such a function is called indirectly the compiler may or may not inline it depending on optimization level and a failure to inline an indirect call may or may not be diagnosed.

`artificial`

This attribute is useful for small inline wrappers that if possible should appear during debugging as a unit. Depending on the debug info format it either means marking the function as artificial or using the caller location for all instructions within the inlined body.

`assume_aligned`

The `assume_aligned` attribute is used to tell the compiler that the function return value points to memory, where the returned pointer minimum alignment is given by the first argument. If the attribute has two arguments, the second argument is misalignment offset.

For instance

```
void* my_alloc1(size_t) __attribute__((assume_aligned(16)))
void* my_alloc2(size_t) __attribute__((assume_aligned(32, 8)))
```

declares that `my_alloc1` returns 16-byte aligned pointer and that `my_alloc2` returns a pointer whose value modulo 32 is equal to 8.

`bnd_instrument`

The `bnd_instrument` attribute on functions is used to inform the compiler that the function should be instrumented when compiled with the '-fchkp-instrument-marked-only' option.

`bnd_legacy`

The `bnd_legacy` attribute on functions is used to inform the compiler that the function should not be instrumented when compiled with the '-fcheck-pointer-bounds' option.

`cold`   The `cold` attribute on functions is used to inform the compiler that the function is unlikely to be executed. The function is optimized for size rather than speed and on many targets it is placed into a special subsection of the text section so all cold functions appear close together, improving code locality of non-cold parts of program. The paths leading to calls of cold functions within code are marked as unlikely by the branch prediction mechanism. It is thus useful to mark functions used to handle unlikely conditions, such as **perror**, as cold to improve optimization of hot functions that do call marked functions in rare occasions.

When profile feedback is available, via '-fprofile-use', cold functions are automatically detected and this attribute is ignored.

const   Many functions do not examine any values except their arguments, and have no effects except the return value. Basically this is just slightly more strict class than the **pure** attribute below, since function is not allowed to read global memory.

         Note that a function that has pointer arguments and examines the data pointed to must *not* be declared **const**. Likewise, a function that calls a non-**const** function usually must not be **const**. It does not make sense for a **const** function to return **void**.

constructor
destructor
constructor (*priority*)
destructor (*priority*)

         The **constructor** attribute causes the function to be called automatically before execution enters **main ()**. Similarly, the **destructor** attribute causes the function to be called automatically after **main ()** completes or **exit ()** is called. Functions with these attributes are useful for initializing data that is used implicitly during the execution of the program.

         You may provide an optional integer priority to control the order in which constructor and destructor functions are run. A constructor with a smaller priority number runs before a constructor with a larger priority number; the opposite relationship holds for destructors. So, if you have a constructor that allocates a resource and a destructor that deallocates the same resource, both functions typically have the same priority. The priorities for constructor and destructor functions are the same as those specified for namespace-scope C++ objects (see Section 7.7 [C++ Attributes], page 733).

deprecated
deprecated (*msg*)

         The **deprecated** attribute results in a warning if the function is used anywhere in the source file. This is useful when identifying functions that are expected to be removed in a future version of a program. The warning also includes the location of the declaration of the deprecated function, to enable users to easily find further information about why the function is deprecated, or what they should do instead. Note that the warnings only occurs for uses:

```
int old_fn () __attribute__ ((deprecated));
int old_fn ();
int (*fn_ptr)() = old_fn;
```

results in a warning on line 3 but not line 2. The optional *msg* argument, which must be a string, is printed in the warning if present.

The `deprecated` attribute can also be used for variables and types (see Section 6.32 [Variable Attributes], page 471, see Section 6.33 [Type Attributes], page 482.)

`error ("message")`
`warning ("message")`

        If the `error` or `warning` attribute is used on a function declaration and a call to such a function is not eliminated through dead code elimination or other optimizations, an error or warning (respectively) that includes *message* is diagnosed. This is useful for compile-time checking, especially together with `__builtin_constant_p` and inline functions where checking the inline function arguments is not possible through `extern char [(condition) ? 1 : -1];` tricks.

        While it is possible to leave the function undefined and thus invoke a link failure (to define the function with a message in `.gnu.warning*` section), when using these attributes the problem is diagnosed earlier and with exact location of the call even in presence of inline functions or when not emitting debugging information.

`externally_visible`

        This attribute, attached to a global variable or function, nullifies the effect of the '`-fwhole-program`' command-line option, so the object remains visible outside the current compilation unit.

        If '`-fwhole-program`' is used together with '`-flto`' and `gold` is used as the linker plugin, `externally_visible` attributes are automatically added to functions (not variable yet due to a current `gold` issue) that are accessed outside of LTO objects according to resolution file produced by `gold`. For other linkers that cannot generate resolution file, explicit `externally_visible` attributes are still necessary.

`flatten`   Generally, inlining into a function is limited. For a function marked with this attribute, every call inside this function is inlined, if possible. Whether the function itself is considered for inlining depends on its size and the current inlining parameters.

`format (archetype, string-index, first-to-check)`

        The `format` attribute specifies that a function takes `printf`, `scanf`, `strftime` or `strfmon` style arguments that should be type-checked against a format string. For example, the declaration:

```
extern int
my_printf (void *my_object, const char *my_format, ...)
      __attribute__ ((format (printf, 2, 3)));
```

causes the compiler to check the arguments in calls to `my_printf` for consistency with the `printf` style format string argument `my_format`.

        The parameter *archetype* determines how the format string is interpreted, and should be `printf`, `scanf`, `strftime`, `gnu_printf`, `gnu_scanf`, `gnu_strftime` or `strfmon`. (You can also use `__printf__`, `__scanf__`, `__strftime__` or `__strfmon__`.) On MinGW targets, `ms_printf`, `ms_scanf`, and `ms_strftime` are also present. *archetype* values such as `printf` refer to the formats accepted by the system's C runtime library, while values prefixed with '`gnu_`' always refer to the formats accepted by the GNU C Library. On Microsoft Windows targets, values prefixed with '`ms_`' refer to the formats accepted by the '`msvcrt.dll`' library. The parameter *string-index* specifies which argument is the format string argument (starting from 1), while *first-to-check* is the number of the first argument to check against the format string. For functions where the arguments are not available to be checked (such as `vprintf`), specify the third parameter as zero. In this case the compiler only checks the format string for consistency. For `strftime` formats, the third parameter is required to be zero. Since non-static C++ methods have an implicit `this` argument, the arguments of such methods should be counted from two, not one, when giving values for *string-index* and *first-to-check*.

In the example above, the format string (`my_format`) is the second argument of the function `my_print`, and the arguments to check start with the third argument, so the correct parameters for the format attribute are 2 and 3.

The `format` attribute allows you to identify your own functions that take format strings as arguments, so that GCC can check the calls to these functions for errors. The compiler always (unless '`-ffreestanding`' or '`-fno-builtin`' is used) checks formats for the standard library functions `printf`, `fprintf`, `sprintf`, `scanf`, `fscanf`, `sscanf`, `strftime`, `vprintf`, `vfprintf` and `vsprintf` whenever such warnings are requested (using '`-Wformat`'), so there is no need to modify the header file '`stdio.h`'. In C99 mode, the functions `snprintf`, `vsnprintf`, `vscanf`, `vfscanf` and `vsscanf` are also checked. Except in strictly conforming C standard modes, the X/Open function `strfmon` is also checked as are `printf_unlocked` and `fprintf_unlocked`. See Section 3.4 [Options Controlling C Dialect], page 33.

For Objective-C dialects, `NSString` (or `__NSString__`) is recognized in the same context. Declarations including these format attributes are parsed for correct syntax, however the result of checking of such format strings is not yet defined, and is not carried out by this version of the compiler.

The target may also provide additional types of format checks. See Section 6.61 [Format Checks Specific to Particular Target Machines], page 715.

`format_arg (`*string-index*`)`

The `format_arg` attribute specifies that a function takes a format string for a `printf`, `scanf`, `strftime` or `strfmon` style function and modifies it (for example, to translate it into another language), so the result can be passed to a `printf`, `scanf`, `strftime` or `strfmon` style function (with the remaining arguments to the format function the same as they would have been for the unmodified string). For example, the declaration:

```
extern char *
my_dgettext (char *my_domain, const char *my_format)
        __attribute__ ((format_arg (2)));
```

causes the compiler to check the arguments in calls to a `printf`, `scanf`, `strftime` or `strfmon` type function, whose format string argument is a call to the `my_dgettext` function, for consistency with the format string argument `my_format`. If the `format_arg` attribute had not been specified, all the compiler could tell in such calls to format functions would be that the format string argument is not constant; this would generate a warning when '`-Wformat-nonliteral`' is used, but the calls could not be checked without the attribute.

The parameter *string-index* specifies which argument is the format string argument (starting from one). Since non-static C++ methods have an implicit `this` argument, the arguments of such methods should be counted from two.

The `format_arg` attribute allows you to identify your own functions that modify format strings, so that GCC can check the calls to `printf`, `scanf`, `strftime` or `strfmon` type function whose operands are a call to one of your own function. The compiler always treats `gettext`, `dgettext`, and `dcgettext` in this manner except when strict ISO C support is requested by '`-ansi`' or an appropriate '`-std`' option, or '`-ffreestanding`' or '`-fno-builtin`' is used. See Section 3.4 [Options Controlling C Dialect], page 33.

For Objective-C dialects, the `format-arg` attribute may refer to an `NSString` reference for compatibility with the `format` attribute above.

The target may also allow additional types in `format-arg` attributes. See Section 6.61 [Format Checks Specific to Particular Target Machines], page 715.

`gnu_inline`

This attribute should be used with a function that is also declared with the `inline` keyword. It directs GCC to treat the function as if it were defined in gnu90 mode even when compiling in C99 or gnu99 mode.

If the function is declared `extern`, then this definition of the function is used only for inlining. In no case is the function compiled as a standalone function, not even if you take its address explicitly. Such an address becomes an external reference, as if you had only declared the function, and had not defined it. This has almost the effect of a macro. The way to use this is to put a function definition in a header file with this attribute, and put another copy of the function, without `extern`, in a library file. The definition in the header file causes most calls to the function to be inlined. If any uses of the function remain, they refer to the single copy in the library. Note that the two definitions of the functions need not be precisely the same, although if they do not have the same effect your program may behave oddly.

In C, if the function is neither `extern` nor `static`, then the function is compiled as a standalone function, as well as being inlined where possible.

This is how GCC traditionally handled functions declared `inline`. Since ISO C99 specifies a different semantics for `inline`, this function attribute is provided as a transition measure and as a useful feature in its own right. This attribute is available in GCC 4.1.3 and later. It is available if either of the preprocessor macros `__GNUC_GNU_INLINE__` or `__GNUC_STDC_INLINE__` are defined. See Section 6.43 [An Inline Function is As Fast As a Macro], page 495.

In C++, this attribute does not depend on `extern` in any way, but it still requires the `inline` keyword to enable its special behavior.

hot   The hot attribute on a function is used to inform the compiler that the func-
                tion is a hot spot of the compiled program. The function is optimized more
                aggressively and on many targets it is placed into a special subsection of the
                text section so all hot functions appear close together, improving locality.

                When profile feedback is available, via '-fprofile-use', hot functions are au-
                tomatically detected and this attribute is ignored.

ifunc ("*resolver*")
                The ifunc attribute is used to mark a function as an indirect function using the
                STT_GNU_IFUNC symbol type extension to the ELF standard. This allows
                the resolution of the symbol value to be determined dynamically at load time,
                and an optimized version of the routine can be selected for the particular pro-
                cessor or other system characteristics determined then. To use this attribute,
                first define the implementation functions available, and a resolver function that
                returns a pointer to the selected implementation function. The implementation
                functions' declarations must match the API of the function being implemented,
                the resolver's declaration is be a function returning pointer to void function
                returning void:

```
void *my_memcpy (void *dst, const void *src, size_t len)
{
  ...
}

static void (*resolve_memcpy (void)) (void)
{
  return my_memcpy; // we'll just always select this routine
}
```

                The exported header file declaring the function the user calls would contain:

```
extern void *memcpy (void *, const void *, size_t);
```

                allowing the user to call this as a regular function, unaware of the implementa-
                tion. Finally, the indirect function needs to be defined in the same translation
                unit as the resolver function:

```
void *memcpy (void *, const void *, size_t)
     __attribute__ ((ifunc ("resolve_memcpy")));
```

                Indirect functions cannot be weak. Binutils version 2.20.1 or higher and GNU
                C Library version 2.11.1 are required to use this feature.

interrupt
interrupt_handler
                Many GCC back ends support attributes to indicate that a function is an in-
                terrupt handler, which tells the compiler to generate function entry and exit
                sequences that differ from those from regular functions. The exact syntax and
                behavior are target-specific; refer to the following subsections for details.

leaf   Calls to external functions with this attribute must return to the current com-
                pilation unit only by return or by exception handling. In particular, a leaf
                function is not allowed to invoke callback functions passed to it from the cur-
                rent compilation unit, directly call functions exported by the unit, or longjmp
                into the unit. Leaf functions might still call functions from other compilation

units and thus they are not necessarily leaf in the sense that they contain no function calls at all.

The attribute is intended for library functions to improve dataflow analysis. The compiler takes the hint that any data not escaping the current compilation unit cannot be used or modified by the leaf function. For example, the `sin` function is a leaf function, but `qsort` is not.

Note that leaf functions might indirectly run a signal handler defined in the current compilation unit that uses static variables. Similarly, when lazy symbol resolution is in effect, leaf functions might invoke indirect functions whose resolver function or implementation function is defined in the current compilation unit and uses static variables. There is no standard-compliant way to write such a signal handler, resolver function, or implementation function, and the best that you can do is to remove the `leaf` attribute or mark all such static variables `volatile`. Lastly, for ELF-based systems that support symbol interposition, care should be taken that functions defined in the current compilation unit do not unexpectedly interpose other symbols based on the defined standards mode and defined feature test macros; otherwise an inadvertent callback would be added.

The attribute has no effect on functions defined within the current compilation unit. This is to allow easy merging of multiple compilation units into one, for example, by using the link-time optimization. For this reason the attribute is not allowed on types to annotate indirect calls.

`malloc`   This tells the compiler that a function is `malloc`-like, i.e., that the pointer P returned by the function cannot alias any other pointer valid when the function returns, and moreover no pointers to valid objects occur in any storage addressed by P.

Using this attribute can improve optimization. Functions like `malloc` and `calloc` have this property because they return a pointer to uninitialized or zeroed-out storage. However, functions like `realloc` do not have this property, as they can return a pointer to storage containing pointers.

`no_icf`   This function attribute prevents a functions from being merged with another semantically equivalent function.

`no_instrument_function`

If '`-finstrument-functions`' is given, profiling function calls are generated at entry and exit of most user-compiled functions. Functions with this attribute are not so instrumented.

`no_profile_instrument_function`

The `no_profile_instrument_function` attribute on functions is used to inform the compiler that it should not process any profile feedback based optimization code instrumentation.

`no_reorder`

Do not reorder functions or variables marked `no_reorder` against each other or top level assembler statements the executable. The actual order in the program will depend on the linker command line. Static variables marked like this are also not removed. This has a similar effect as the '-fno-toplevel-reorder' option, but only applies to the marked symbols.

`no_sanitize_address`
`no_address_safety_analysis`

The `no_sanitize_address` attribute on functions is used to inform the compiler that it should not instrument memory accesses in the function when compiling with the '-fsanitize=address' option. The `no_address_safety_analysis` is a deprecated alias of the `no_sanitize_address` attribute, new code should use `no_sanitize_address`.

`no_sanitize_thread`

The `no_sanitize_thread` attribute on functions is used to inform the compiler that it should not instrument memory accesses in the function when compiling with the '-fsanitize=thread' option.

`no_sanitize_undefined`

The `no_sanitize_undefined` attribute on functions is used to inform the compiler that it should not check for undefined behavior in the function when compiling with the '-fsanitize=undefined' option.

`no_split_stack`

If '-fsplit-stack' is given, functions have a small prologue which decides whether to split the stack. Functions with the `no_split_stack` attribute do not have that prologue, and thus may run with only a small amount of stack space available.

`no_stack_limit`

This attribute locally overrides the '-fstack-limit-register' and '-fstack-limit-symbol' command-line options; it has the effect of disabling stack limit checking in the function it applies to.

`noclone`   This function attribute prevents a function from being considered for cloning—a mechanism that produces specialized copies of functions and which is (currently) performed by interprocedural constant propagation.

`noinline`   This function attribute prevents a function from being considered for inlining. If the function does not have side-effects, there are optimizations other than inlining that cause function calls to be optimized away, although the function call is live. To keep such calls from being optimized away, put

```
asm ("");
```

(see Section 6.45.2 [Extended Asm], page 500) in the called function, to serve as a special side-effect.

`nonnull (arg-index, ...)`

The `nonnull` attribute specifies that some function parameters should be non-null pointers. For instance, the declaration:

```
extern void *
my_memcpy (void *dest, const void *src, size_t len)
        __attribute__((nonnull (1, 2)));
```

causes the compiler to check that, in calls to `my_memcpy`, arguments *dest* and *src* are non-null. If the compiler determines that a null pointer is passed in an argument slot marked as non-null, and the '-Wnonnull' option is enabled, a warning is issued. The compiler may also choose to make optimizations based on the knowledge that certain function arguments will never be null.

If no argument index list is given to the `nonnull` attribute, all pointer arguments are marked as non-null. To illustrate, the following declaration is equivalent to the previous example:

```
extern void *
my_memcpy (void *dest, const void *src, size_t len)
          __attribute__((nonnull));
```

noplt
The `noplt` attribute is the counterpart to option '-fno-plt'. Calls to functions marked with this attribute in position-independent code do not use the PLT.

```
/* Externally defined function foo.  */
int foo () __attribute__ ((noplt));

int
main (/* ... */)
{
  /* ... */
  foo ();
  /* ... */
}
```

The `noplt` attribute on function `foo` tells the compiler to assume that the function `foo` is externally defined and that the call to `foo` must avoid the PLT in position-independent code.

In position-dependent code, a few targets also convert calls to functions that are marked to not use the PLT to use the GOT instead.

noreturn
A few standard library functions, such as `abort` and `exit`, cannot return. GCC knows this automatically. Some programs define their own functions that never return. You can declare them `noreturn` to tell the compiler this fact. For example,

```
void fatal () __attribute__ ((noreturn));

void
fatal (/* ... */)
{
  /* ... */ /* Print error message. */ /* ... */
  exit (1);
}
```

The `noreturn` keyword tells the compiler to assume that `fatal` cannot return. It can then optimize without regard to what would happen if `fatal` ever did return. This makes slightly better code. More importantly, it helps avoid spurious warnings of uninitialized variables.

The `noreturn` keyword does not affect the exceptional path when that applies: a `noreturn`-marked function may still return to the caller by throwing an exception or calling `longjmp`.

Do not assume that registers saved by the calling function are restored before calling the `noreturn` function.

It does not make sense for a `noreturn` function to have a return type other than `void`.

nothrow   The `nothrow` attribute is used to inform the compiler that a function cannot
               throw an exception. For example, most functions in the standard C library can
               be guaranteed not to throw an exception with the notable exceptions of `qsort`
               and `bsearch` that take function pointer arguments.

optimize   The `optimize` attribute is used to specify that a function is to be compiled with
               different optimization options than specified on the command line. Arguments
               can either be numbers or strings. Numbers are assumed to be an optimization
               level. Strings that begin with `O` are assumed to be an optimization option,
               while other options are assumed to be used with a `-f` prefix. You can also
               use the '`#pragma GCC optimize`' pragma to set the optimization options that
               affect more than one function. See Section 6.62.15 [Function Specific Option
               Pragmas], page 721, for details about the '`#pragma GCC optimize`' pragma.

               This attribute should be used for debugging purposes only. It is not suitable in
               production code.

pure   Many functions have no effects except the return value and their return value
               depends only on the parameters and/or global variables. Such a function can
               be subject to common subexpression elimination and loop optimization just as
               an arithmetic operator would be. These functions should be declared with the
               attribute `pure`. For example,

                       int square (int) __attribute__ ((pure));

               says that the hypothetical function `square` is safe to call fewer times than the
               program says.

               Some common examples of pure functions are `strlen` or `memcmp`. Interest-
               ing non-pure functions are functions with infinite loops or those depending on
               volatile memory or other system resource, that may change between two con-
               secutive calls (such as `feof` in a multithreading environment).

returns_nonnull
               The `returns_nonnull` attribute specifies that the function return value should
               be a non-null pointer. For instance, the declaration:

                       extern void *
                       mymalloc (size_t len) __attribute__((returns_nonnull));

               lets the compiler optimize callers based on the knowledge that the return value
               will never be null.

returns_twice
               The `returns_twice` attribute tells the compiler that a function may return
               more than one time. The compiler ensures that all registers are dead before
               calling such a function and emits a warning about the variables that may be
               clobbered after the second return from the function. Examples of such functions
               are `setjmp` and `vfork`. The `longjmp`-like counterpart of such function, if any,
               might need to be marked with the `noreturn` attribute.

section ("*section-name*")
               Normally, the compiler places the code it generates in the `text` section. Some-
               times, however, you need additional sections, or you need certain particular
               functions to appear in special sections. The `section` attribute specifies that a
               function lives in a particular section. For example, the declaration:

```
extern void foobar (void) __attribute__ ((section ("bar")));
```

puts the function `foobar` in the `bar` section.

Some file formats do not support arbitrary sections so the `section` attribute is not available on all platforms. If you need to map the entire contents of a module to a particular section, consider using the facilities of the linker instead.

`sentinel`   This function attribute ensures that a parameter in a function call is an explicit `NULL`. The attribute is only valid on variadic functions. By default, the sentinel is located at position zero, the last parameter of the function call. If an optional integer position argument P is supplied to the attribute, the sentinel must be located at position P counting backwards from the end of the argument list.

```
__attribute__ ((sentinel))
is equivalent to
__attribute__ ((sentinel(0)))
```

The attribute is automatically set with a position of 0 for the built-in functions `execl` and `execlp`. The built-in function `execle` has the attribute set with a position of 1.

A valid `NULL` in this context is defined as zero with any pointer type. If your system defines the `NULL` macro with an integer type then you need to add an explicit cast. GCC replaces `stddef.h` with a copy that redefines NULL appropriately.

The warnings for missing or incorrect sentinels are enabled with '`-Wformat`'.

`simd`
`simd("mask")`

This attribute enables creation of one or more function versions that can process multiple arguments using SIMD instructions from a single invocation. Specifying this attribute allows compiler to assume that such versions are available at link time (provided in the same or another translation unit). Generated versions are target-dependent and described in the corresponding Vector ABI document. For x86_64 target this document can be found here.

The optional argument *mask* may have the value `notinbranch` or `inbranch`, and instructs the compiler to generate non-masked or masked clones correspondingly. By default, all clones are generated.

The attribute should not be used together with Cilk Plus `vector` attribute on the same function.

If the attribute is specified and `#pragma omp declare simd` is present on a declaration and the '`-fopenmp`' or '`-fopenmp-simd`' switch is specified, then the attribute is ignored.

`stack_protect`

This attribute adds stack protection code to the function if flags '`-fstack-protector`', '`-fstack-protector-strong`' or '`-fstack-protector-explicit`' are set.

`target (options)`

Multiple target back ends implement the `target` attribute to specify that a function is to be compiled with different target options than specified on the command line. This can be used for instance to have functions compiled with a different ISA (instruction set architecture) than the default. You can also use the '#pragma GCC target' pragma to set more than one function to be compiled with specific target options. See Section 6.62.15 [Function Specific Option Pragmas], page 721, for details about the '#pragma GCC target' pragma.

For instance, on an x86, you could declare one function with the target("sse4.1,arch=core2") attribute and another with target("sse4a,arch=amdfam10"). This is equivalent to compiling the first function with '-msse4.1' and '-march=core2' options, and the second function with '-msse4a' and '-march=amdfam10' options. It is up to you to make sure that a function is only invoked on a machine that supports the particular ISA it is compiled for (for example by using cpuid on x86 to determine what feature bits and architecture family are used).

```
int core2_func (void) __attribute__ ((__target__ ("arch=core2")));
int sse3_func (void) __attribute__ ((__target__ ("sse3")));
```

You can either use multiple strings separated by commas to specify multiple options, or separate the options with a comma (',') within a single string.

The options supported are specific to each target; refer to Section 6.31.32 [x86 Function Attributes], page 466, Section 6.31.23 [PowerPC Function Attributes], page 459, Section 6.31.4 [ARM Function Attributes], page 445, and Section 6.31.21 [Nios II Function Attributes], page 459, for details.

target_clones (*options*)

> The target_clones attribute is used to specify that a function be cloned into multiple versions compiled with different target options than specified on the command line. The supported options and restrictions are the same as for target attribute.
>
> For instance, on an x86, you could compile a function with target_clones("sse4.1,avx"). GCC creates two function clones, one compiled with '-msse4.1' and another with '-mavx'. It also creates a resolver function (see the ifunc attribute above) that dynamically selects a clone suitable for current architecture.

unused   This attribute, attached to a function, means that the function is meant to be possibly unused. GCC does not produce a warning for this function.

used   This attribute, attached to a function, means that code must be emitted for the function even if it appears that the function is not referenced. This is useful, for example, when the function is referenced only in inline assembly.

> When applied to a member function of a C++ class template, the attribute also means that the function is instantiated if the class itself is instantiated.

visibility ("*visibility_type*")

> This attribute affects the linkage of the declaration to which it is attached. It can be applied to variables (see Section 6.32.1 [Common Variable Attributes], page 472) and types (see Section 6.33.1 [Common Type Attributes], page 482) as well as functions.
>
> There are four supported *visibility_type* values: default, hidden, protected or internal visibility.

```
void __attribute__ ((visibility ("protected")))
f () { /* Do something. */; }
int i __attribute__ ((visibility ("hidden")));
```

The possible values of *visibility_type* correspond to the visibility settings in the ELF gABI.

default   Default visibility is the normal case for the object file format. This value is available for the visibility attribute to override other options that may change the assumed visibility of entities.

On ELF, default visibility means that the declaration is visible to other modules and, in shared libraries, means that the declared entity may be overridden.

On Darwin, default visibility means that the declaration is visible to other modules.

Default visibility corresponds to "external linkage" in the language.

hidden   Hidden visibility indicates that the entity declared has a new form of linkage, which we call "hidden linkage". Two declarations of an object with hidden linkage refer to the same object if they are in the same shared object.

internal   Internal visibility is like hidden visibility, but with additional processor specific semantics. Unless otherwise specified by the psABI, GCC defines internal visibility to mean that a function is *never* called from another module. Compare this with hidden functions which, while they cannot be referenced directly by other modules, can be referenced indirectly via function pointers. By indicating that a function cannot be called from outside the module, GCC may for instance omit the load of a PIC register since it is known that the calling function loaded the correct value.

protected

Protected visibility is like default visibility except that it indicates that references within the defining module bind to the definition in that module. That is, the declared entity cannot be overridden by another module.

All visibilities are supported on many, but not all, ELF targets (supported when the assembler supports the '.visibility' pseudo-op). Default visibility is supported everywhere. Hidden visibility is supported on Darwin targets.

The visibility attribute should be applied only to declarations that would otherwise have external linkage. The attribute should be applied consistently, so that the same entity should not be declared with different settings of the attribute.

In C++, the visibility attribute applies to types as well as functions and objects, because in C++ types have linkage. A class must not have greater visibility than its non-static data member types and bases, and class members default to the visibility of their class. Also, a declaration without explicit visibility is limited to the visibility of its type.

In C++, you can mark member functions and static member variables of a class with the visibility attribute. This is useful if you know a particular method or static member variable should only be used from one shared object; then you can mark it hidden while the rest of the class has default visibility. Care must be taken to avoid breaking the One Definition Rule; for example, it is usually not useful to mark an inline method as hidden without marking the whole class as hidden.

A C++ namespace declaration can also have the visibility attribute.

```
namespace nspace1 __attribute__ ((visibility ("protected")))
{ /* Do something. */; }
```

This attribute applies only to the particular namespace body, not to other definitions of the same namespace; it is equivalent to using '#pragma GCC visibility' before and after the namespace definition (see Section 6.62.13 [Visibility Pragmas], page 721).

In C++, if a template argument has limited visibility, this restriction is implicitly propagated to the template instantiation. Otherwise, template instantiations and specializations default to the visibility of their template.

If both the template and enclosing class have explicit visibility, the visibility from the template is used.

warn_unused_result

The `warn_unused_result` attribute causes a warning to be emitted if a caller of the function with this attribute does not use its return value. This is useful for functions where not checking the result is either a security problem or always a bug, such as `realloc`.

```
int fn () __attribute__ ((warn_unused_result));
int foo ()
{
  if (fn () < 0) return -1;
  fn ();
  return 0;
}
```

results in warning on line 5.

weak

The `weak` attribute causes the declaration to be emitted as a weak symbol rather than a global. This is primarily useful in defining library functions that can be overridden in user code, though it can also be used with non-function declarations. Weak symbols are supported for ELF targets, and also for a.out targets when using the GNU assembler and linker.

weakref
weakref ("target")

The `weakref` attribute marks a declaration as a weak reference. Without arguments, it should be accompanied by an `alias` attribute naming the target symbol. Optionally, the target may be given as an argument to `weakref` itself. In either case, `weakref` implicitly marks the declaration as `weak`. Without a target, given as an argument to `weakref` or to `alias`, `weakref` is equivalent to weak.

```
static int x() __attribute__ ((weakref ("y")));
```

```
/* is equivalent to... */
static int x() __attribute__ ((weak, weakref, alias ("y")));
/* and to... */
static int x() __attribute__ ((weakref));
static int x() __attribute__ ((alias ("y")));
```

A weak reference is an alias that does not by itself require a definition to be given for the target symbol. If the target symbol is only referenced through weak references, then it becomes a **weak** undefined symbol. If it is directly referenced, however, then such strong references prevail, and a definition is required for the symbol, not necessarily in the same translation unit.

The effect is equivalent to moving all references to the alias to a separate translation unit, renaming the alias to the aliased symbol, declaring it as weak, compiling the two separate translation units and performing a reloadable link on them.

At present, a declaration to which **weakref** is attached can only be **static**.

6.31.2 AArch64 Function Attributes

The following target-specific function attributes are available for the AArch64 target. For the most part, these options mirror the behavior of similar command-line options (see Section 3.18.1 [AArch64 Options], page 217), but on a per-function basis.

general-regs-only
: Indicates that no floating-point or Advanced SIMD registers should be used when generating code for this function. If the function explicitly uses floating-point code, then the compiler gives an error. This is the same behavior as that of the command-line option '-mgeneral-regs-only'.

fix-cortex-a53-835769
: Indicates that the workaround for the Cortex-A53 erratum 835769 should be applied to this function. To explicitly disable the workaround for this function specify the negated form: no-fix-cortex-a53-835769. This corresponds to the behavior of the command line options '-mfix-cortex-a53-835769' and '-mno-fix-cortex-a53-835769'.

cmodel=
: Indicates that code should be generated for a particular code model for this function. The behavior and permissible arguments are the same as for the command line option '-mcmodel='.

strict-align
: Indicates that the compiler should not assume that unaligned memory references are handled by the system. The behavior is the same as for the command-line option '-mstrict-align'.

omit-leaf-frame-pointer
: Indicates that the frame pointer should be omitted for a leaf function call. To keep the frame pointer, the inverse attribute no-omit-leaf-frame-pointer can be specified. These attributes have the same behavior as the command-line options '-momit-leaf-frame-pointer' and '-mno-omit-leaf-frame-pointer'.

`tls-dialect=`

Specifies the TLS dialect to use for this function. The behavior and permissible arguments are the same as for the command-line option '`-mtls-dialect=`'.

`arch=`   Specifies the architecture version and architectural extensions to use for this function. The behavior and permissible arguments are the same as for the '`-march=`' command-line option.

`tune=`   Specifies the core for which to tune the performance of this function. The behavior and permissible arguments are the same as for the '`-mtune=`' command-line option.

`cpu=`   Specifies the core for which to tune the performance of this function and also whose architectural features to use. The behavior and valid arguments are the same as for the '`-mcpu=`' command-line option.

The above target attributes can be specified as follows:

```
__attribute__((target("attr-string")))
int
f (int a)
{
  return a + 5;
}
```

where *attr-string* is one of the attribute strings specified above.

Additionally, the architectural extension string may be specified on its own. This can be used to turn on and off particular architectural extensions without having to specify a particular architecture version or core. Example:

```
__attribute__((target("+crc+nocrypto")))
int
foo (int a)
{
  return a + 5;
}
```

In this example `target("+crc+nocrypto")` enables the `crc` extension and disables the `crypto` extension for the function `foo` without modifying an existing '`-march=`' or '`-mcpu`' option.

Multiple target function attributes can be specified by separating them with a comma. For example:

```
__attribute__((target("arch=armv8-a+crc+crypto,tune=cortex-a53")))
int
foo (int a)
{
  return a + 5;
}
```

is valid and compiles function `foo` for ARMv8-A with `crc` and `crypto` extensions and tunes it for `cortex-a53`.

6.31.2.1 Inlining rules

Specifying target attributes on individual functions or performing link-time optimization across translation units compiled with different target options can affect function inlining rules:

In particular, a caller function can inline a callee function only if the architectural features available to the callee are a subset of the features available to the caller. For example: A function `foo` compiled with '-march=armv8-a+crc', or tagged with the equivalent `arch=armv8-a+crc` attribute, can inline a function `bar` compiled with '-march=armv8-a+nocrc' because the all the architectural features that function `bar` requires are available to function `foo`. Conversely, function `bar` cannot inline function `foo`.

Additionally inlining a function compiled with '-mstrict-align' into a function compiled without -mstrict-align is not allowed. However, inlining a function compiled without '-mstrict-align' into a function compiled with '-mstrict-align' is allowed.

Note that CPU tuning options and attributes such as the '-mcpu=', '-mtune=' do not inhibit inlining unless the CPU specified by the '-mcpu=' option or the `cpu=` attribute conflicts with the architectural feature rules specified above.

6.31.3 ARC Function Attributes

These function attributes are supported by the ARC back end:

`interrupt`

> Use this attribute to indicate that the specified function is an interrupt handler. The compiler generates function entry and exit sequences suitable for use in an interrupt handler when this attribute is present.
>
> On the ARC, you must specify the kind of interrupt to be handled in a parameter to the interrupt attribute like this:
>
> ```
> void f () __attribute__ ((interrupt ("ilink1")));
> ```
>
> Permissible values for this parameter are: `ilink1` and `ilink2`.

`long_call`
`medium_call`
`short_call`

> These attributes specify how a particular function is called. These attributes override the '-mlong-calls' and '-mmedium-calls' (see Section 3.18.3 [ARC Options], page 223) command-line switches and `#pragma long_calls` settings.
>
> For ARC, a function marked with the `long_call` attribute is always called using register-indirect jump-and-link instructions, thereby enabling the called function to be placed anywhere within the 32-bit address space. A function marked with the `medium_call` attribute will always be close enough to be called with an unconditional branch-and-link instruction, which has a 25-bit offset from the call site. A function marked with the `short_call` attribute will always be close enough to be called with a conditional branch-and-link instruction, which has a 21-bit offset from the call site.

6.31.4 ARM Function Attributes

These function attributes are supported for ARM targets:

`interrupt`

> Use this attribute to indicate that the specified function is an interrupt handler. The compiler generates function entry and exit sequences suitable for use in an interrupt handler when this attribute is present.

You can specify the kind of interrupt to be handled by adding an optional parameter to the interrupt attribute like this:

```
void f () __attribute__ ((interrupt ("IRQ")));
```

Permissible values for this parameter are: `IRQ`, `FIQ`, `SWI`, `ABORT` and `UNDEF`.

On ARMv7-M the interrupt type is ignored, and the attribute means the function may be called with a word-aligned stack pointer.

`isr`   Use this attribute on ARM to write Interrupt Service Routines. This is an alias to the `interrupt` attribute above.

`long_call`
`short_call`

These attributes specify how a particular function is called. These attributes override the '-mlong-calls' (see Section 3.18.4 [ARM Options], page 231) command-line switch and #pragma `long_calls` settings. For ARM, the `long_call` attribute indicates that the function might be far away from the call site and require a different (more expensive) calling sequence. The `short_call` attribute always places the offset to the function from the call site into the 'BL' instruction directly.

`naked`   This attribute allows the compiler to construct the requisite function declaration, while allowing the body of the function to be assembly code. The specified function will not have prologue/epilogue sequences generated by the compiler. Only basic `asm` statements can safely be included in naked functions (see Section 6.45.1 [Basic Asm], page 498). While using extended `asm` or a mixture of basic `asm` and C code may appear to work, they cannot be depended upon to work reliably and are not supported.

`pcs`

The `pcs` attribute can be used to control the calling convention used for a function on ARM. The attribute takes an argument that specifies the calling convention to use.

When compiling using the AAPCS ABI (or a variant of it) then valid values for the argument are `"aapcs"` and `"aapcs-vfp"`. In order to use a variant other than `"aapcs"` then the compiler must be permitted to use the appropriate co-processor registers (i.e., the VFP registers must be available in order to use `"aapcs-vfp"`). For example,

```
/* Argument passed in r0, and result returned in r0+r1.  */
double f2d (float) __attribute__((pcs("aapcs")));
```

Variadic functions always use the `"aapcs"` calling convention and the compiler rejects attempts to specify an alternative.

`target (options)`

As discussed in Section 6.31.1 [Common Function Attributes], page 428, this attribute allows specification of target-specific compilation options.

On ARM, the following options are allowed:

'thumb'   Force code generation in the Thumb (T16/T32) ISA, depending on the architecture level.

'arm'   Force code generation in the ARM (A32) ISA.

                   Functions from different modes can be inlined in the caller's mode.

'fpu='   Specifies the fpu for which to tune the performance of this function. The behavior and permissible arguments are the same as for the '-mfpu=' command-line option.

6.31.5 AVR Function Attributes

These function attributes are supported by the AVR back end:

interrupt
                   Use this attribute to indicate that the specified function is an interrupt handler. The compiler generates function entry and exit sequences suitable for use in an interrupt handler when this attribute is present.

                   On the AVR, the hardware globally disables interrupts when an interrupt is executed. The first instruction of an interrupt handler declared with this attribute is a SEI instruction to re-enable interrupts. See also the signal function attribute that does not insert a SEI instruction. If both signal and interrupt are specified for the same function, signal is silently ignored.

naked   This attribute allows the compiler to construct the requisite function declaration, while allowing the body of the function to be assembly code. The specified function will not have prologue/epilogue sequences generated by the compiler. Only basic asm statements can safely be included in naked functions (see Section 6.45.1 [Basic Asm], page 498). While using extended asm or a mixture of basic asm and C code may appear to work, they cannot be depended upon to work reliably and are not supported.

OS_main
OS_task   On AVR, functions with the OS_main or OS_task attribute do not save/restore any call-saved register in their prologue/epilogue.

                   The OS_main attribute can be used when there *is guarantee* that interrupts are disabled at the time when the function is entered. This saves resources when the stack pointer has to be changed to set up a frame for local variables.

                   The OS_task attribute can be used when there is *no guarantee* that interrupts are disabled at that time when the function is entered like for, e.g. task functions in a multi-threading operating system. In that case, changing the stack pointer register is guarded by save/clear/restore of the global interrupt enable flag.

                   The differences to the naked function attribute are:

                   • naked functions do not have a return instruction whereas OS_main and OS_task functions have a RET or RETI return instruction.

                   • naked functions do not set up a frame for local variables or a frame pointer whereas OS_main and OS_task do this as needed.

signal   Use this attribute on the AVR to indicate that the specified function is an interrupt handler. The compiler generates function entry and exit sequences suitable for use in an interrupt handler when this attribute is present.

                   See also the interrupt function attribute.

The AVR hardware globally disables interrupts when an interrupt is executed. Interrupt handler functions defined with the **signal** attribute do not re-enable interrupts. It is save to enable interrupts in a **signal** handler. This "save" only applies to the code generated by the compiler and not to the IRQ layout of the application which is responsibility of the application.

If both **signal** and **interrupt** are specified for the same function, **signal** is silently ignored.

6.31.6 Blackfin Function Attributes

These function attributes are supported by the Blackfin back end:

exception_handler
> Use this attribute on the Blackfin to indicate that the specified function is an exception handler. The compiler generates function entry and exit sequences suitable for use in an exception handler when this attribute is present.

interrupt_handler
> Use this attribute to indicate that the specified function is an interrupt handler. The compiler generates function entry and exit sequences suitable for use in an interrupt handler when this attribute is present.

kspisusp
> When used together with **interrupt_handler**, **exception_handler** or **nmi_handler**, code is generated to load the stack pointer from the USP register in the function prologue.

l1_text
> This attribute specifies a function to be placed into L1 Instruction SRAM. The function is put into a specific section named **.l1.text**. With '**-mfdpic**', function calls with a such function as the callee or caller uses inlined PLT.

l2
> This attribute specifies a function to be placed into L2 SRAM. The function is put into a specific section named **.l2.text**. With '**-mfdpic**', callers of such functions use an inlined PLT.

longcall
shortcall
> The **longcall** attribute indicates that the function might be far away from the call site and require a different (more expensive) calling sequence. The **shortcall** attribute indicates that the function is always close enough for the shorter calling sequence to be used. These attributes override the '**-mlongcall**' switch.

nesting
> Use this attribute together with **interrupt_handler**, **exception_handler** or **nmi_handler** to indicate that the function entry code should enable nested interrupts or exceptions.

nmi_handler
> Use this attribute on the Blackfin to indicate that the specified function is an NMI handler. The compiler generates function entry and exit sequences suitable for use in an NMI handler when this attribute is present.

saveall
> Use this attribute to indicate that all registers except the stack pointer should be saved in the prologue regardless of whether they are used or not.

6.31.7 CR16 Function Attributes

These function attributes are supported by the CR16 back end:

`interrupt`

> Use this attribute to indicate that the specified function is an interrupt handler. The compiler generates function entry and exit sequences suitable for use in an interrupt handler when this attribute is present.

6.31.8 Epiphany Function Attributes

These function attributes are supported by the Epiphany back end:

`disinterrupt`

> This attribute causes the compiler to emit instructions to disable interrupts for the duration of the given function.

`forwarder_section`

> This attribute modifies the behavior of an interrupt handler. The interrupt handler may be in external memory which cannot be reached by a branch instruction, so generate a local memory trampoline to transfer control. The single parameter identifies the section where the trampoline is placed.

`interrupt`

> Use this attribute to indicate that the specified function is an interrupt handler. The compiler generates function entry and exit sequences suitable for use in an interrupt handler when this attribute is present. It may also generate a special section with code to initialize the interrupt vector table.
>
> On Epiphany targets one or more optional parameters can be added like this:
>
> ```
> void __attribute__ ((interrupt ("dma0, dma1"))) universal_dma_handler ();
> ```
>
> Permissible values for these parameters are: `reset`, `software_exception`, `page_miss`, `timer0`, `timer1`, `message`, `dma0`, `dma1`, `wand` and `swi`. Multiple parameters indicate that multiple entries in the interrupt vector table should be initialized for this function, i.e. for each parameter *name*, a jump to the function is emitted in the section ivt_entry_*name*. The parameter(s) may be omitted entirely, in which case no interrupt vector table entry is provided.
>
> Note that interrupts are enabled inside the function unless the `disinterrupt` attribute is also specified.
>
> The following examples are all valid uses of these attributes on Epiphany targets:
>
> ```
> void __attribute__ ((interrupt)) universal_handler ();
> void __attribute__ ((interrupt ("dma1"))) dma1_handler ();
> void __attribute__ ((interrupt ("dma0, dma1")))
>   universal_dma_handler ();
> void __attribute__ ((interrupt ("timer0"), disinterrupt))
>   fast_timer_handler ();
> void __attribute__ ((interrupt ("dma0, dma1"),
>                      forwarder_section ("tramp")))
>   external_dma_handler ();
> ```

```
long_call
short_call
```
These attributes specify how a particular function is called. These attributes override the '-mlong-calls' (see Section 3.18.2 [Adapteva Epiphany Options], page 221) command-line switch and #pragma long_calls settings.

6.31.9 H8/300 Function Attributes

These function attributes are available for H8/300 targets:

function_vector

Use this attribute on the H8/300, H8/300H, and H8S to indicate that the specified function should be called through the function vector. Calling a function through the function vector reduces code size; however, the function vector has a limited size (maximum 128 entries on the H8/300 and 64 entries on the H8/300H and H8S) and shares space with the interrupt vector.

interrupt_handler

Use this attribute on the H8/300, H8/300H, and H8S to indicate that the specified function is an interrupt handler. The compiler generates function entry and exit sequences suitable for use in an interrupt handler when this attribute is present.

saveall   Use this attribute on the H8/300, H8/300H, and H8S to indicate that all registers except the stack pointer should be saved in the prologue regardless of whether they are used or not.

6.31.10 IA-64 Function Attributes

These function attributes are supported on IA-64 targets:

syscall_linkage

This attribute is used to modify the IA-64 calling convention by marking all input registers as live at all function exits. This makes it possible to restart a system call after an interrupt without having to save/restore the input registers. This also prevents kernel data from leaking into application code.

version_id

This IA-64 HP-UX attribute, attached to a global variable or function, renames a symbol to contain a version string, thus allowing for function level versioning. HP-UX system header files may use function level versioning for some system calls.

```
extern int foo () __attribute__((version_id ("20040821")));
```

Calls to foo are mapped to calls to foo{20040821}.

6.31.11 M32C Function Attributes

These function attributes are supported by the M32C back end:

bank_switch

When added to an interrupt handler with the M32C port, causes the prologue and epilogue to use bank switching to preserve the registers rather than saving them on the stack.

`fast_interrupt`

Use this attribute on the M32C port to indicate that the specified function is a fast interrupt handler. This is just like the `interrupt` attribute, except that `freit` is used to return instead of `reit`.

`function_vector`

On M16C/M32C targets, the `function_vector` attribute declares a special page subroutine call function. Use of this attribute reduces the code size by 2 bytes for each call generated to the subroutine. The argument to the attribute is the vector number entry from the special page vector table which contains the 16 low-order bits of the subroutine's entry address. Each vector table has special page number (18 to 255) that is used in `jsrs` instructions. Jump addresses of the routines are generated by adding 0x0F0000 (in case of M16C targets) or 0xFF0000 (in case of M32C targets), to the 2-byte addresses set in the vector table. Therefore you need to ensure that all the special page vector routines should get mapped within the address range 0x0F0000 to 0x0FFFFF (for M16C) and 0xFF0000 to 0xFFFFFF (for M32C).

In the following example 2 bytes are saved for each call to function `foo`.

```
void foo (void) __attribute__((function_vector(0x18)));
void foo (void)
{
}

void bar (void)
{
    foo();
}
```

If functions are defined in one file and are called in another file, then be sure to write this declaration in both files.

This attribute is ignored for R8C target.

`interrupt`

Use this attribute to indicate that the specified function is an interrupt handler. The compiler generates function entry and exit sequences suitable for use in an interrupt handler when this attribute is present.

6.31.12 M32R/D Function Attributes

These function attributes are supported by the M32R/D back end:

`interrupt`

Use this attribute to indicate that the specified function is an interrupt handler. The compiler generates function entry and exit sequences suitable for use in an interrupt handler when this attribute is present.

`model (model-name)`

On the M32R/D, use this attribute to set the addressability of an object, and of the code generated for a function. The identifier *model-name* is one of `small`, `medium`, or `large`, representing each of the code models.

Small model objects live in the lower 16MB of memory (so that their addresses can be loaded with the `ld24` instruction), and are callable with the `bl` instruction.

Medium model objects may live anywhere in the 32-bit address space (the compiler generates `seth/add3` instructions to load their addresses), and are callable with the `bl` instruction.

Large model objects may live anywhere in the 32-bit address space (the compiler generates `seth/add3` instructions to load their addresses), and may not be reachable with the `bl` instruction (the compiler generates the much slower `seth/add3/jl` instruction sequence).

6.31.13 m68k Function Attributes

These function attributes are supported by the m68k back end:

`interrupt`
`interrupt_handler`

Use this attribute to indicate that the specified function is an interrupt handler. The compiler generates function entry and exit sequences suitable for use in an interrupt handler when this attribute is present. Either name may be used.

`interrupt_thread`

Use this attribute on fido, a subarchitecture of the m68k, to indicate that the specified function is an interrupt handler that is designed to run as a thread. The compiler omits generate prologue/epilogue sequences and replaces the return instruction with a `sleep` instruction. This attribute is available only on fido.

6.31.14 MCORE Function Attributes

These function attributes are supported by the MCORE back end:

`naked`   This attribute allows the compiler to construct the requisite function declaration, while allowing the body of the function to be assembly code. The specified function will not have prologue/epilogue sequences generated by the compiler. Only basic `asm` statements can safely be included in naked functions (see Section 6.45.1 [Basic Asm], page 498). While using extended `asm` or a mixture of basic `asm` and C code may appear to work, they cannot be depended upon to work reliably and are not supported.

6.31.15 MeP Function Attributes

These function attributes are supported by the MeP back end:

`disinterrupt`

On MeP targets, this attribute causes the compiler to emit instructions to disable interrupts for the duration of the given function.

`interrupt`

Use this attribute to indicate that the specified function is an interrupt handler. The compiler generates function entry and exit sequences suitable for use in an interrupt handler when this attribute is present.

near   This attribute causes the compiler to assume the called function is close enough to use the normal calling convention, overriding the '-mtf' command-line option.

far   On MeP targets this causes the compiler to use a calling convention that assumes the called function is too far away for the built-in addressing modes.

vliw   The vliw attribute tells the compiler to emit instructions in VLIW mode instead of core mode. Note that this attribute is not allowed unless a VLIW coprocessor has been configured and enabled through command-line options.

6.31.16 MicroBlaze Function Attributes

These function attributes are supported on MicroBlaze targets:

save_volatiles

Use this attribute to indicate that the function is an interrupt handler. All volatile registers (in addition to non-volatile registers) are saved in the function prologue. If the function is a leaf function, only volatiles used by the function are saved. A normal function return is generated instead of a return from interrupt.

break_handler

Use this attribute to indicate that the specified function is a break handler. The compiler generates function entry and exit sequences suitable for use in an break handler when this attribute is present. The return from break_handler is done through the rtbd instead of rtsd.

```
void f () __attribute__ ((break_handler));
```

interrupt_handler
fast_interrupt

These attributes indicate that the specified function is an interrupt handler. Use the fast_interrupt attribute to indicate handlers used in low-latency interrupt mode, and interrupt_handler for interrupts that do not use low-latency handlers. In both cases, GCC emits appropriate prologue code and generates a return from the handler using rtid instead of rtsd.

6.31.17 Microsoft Windows Function Attributes

The following attributes are available on Microsoft Windows and Symbian OS targets.

dllexport

On Microsoft Windows targets and Symbian OS targets the dllexport attribute causes the compiler to provide a global pointer to a pointer in a DLL, so that it can be referenced with the dllimport attribute. On Microsoft Windows targets, the pointer name is formed by combining _imp__ and the function or variable name.

You can use __declspec(dllexport) as a synonym for __attribute__ ((dllexport)) for compatibility with other compilers.

On systems that support the visibility attribute, this attribute also implies "default" visibility. It is an error to explicitly specify any other visibility.

GCC's default behavior is to emit all inline functions with the `dllexport` attribute. Since this can cause object file-size bloat, you can use '`-fno-keep-inline-dllexport`', which tells GCC to ignore the attribute for inlined functions unless the '`-fkeep-inline-functions`' flag is used instead.

The attribute is ignored for undefined symbols.

When applied to C++ classes, the attribute marks defined non-inlined member functions and static data members as exports. Static consts initialized in-class are not marked unless they are also defined out-of-class.

For Microsoft Windows targets there are alternative methods for including the symbol in the DLL's export table such as using a '`.def`' file with an `EXPORTS` section or, with GNU ld, using the '`--export-all`' linker flag.

`dllimport`

On Microsoft Windows and Symbian OS targets, the `dllimport` attribute causes the compiler to reference a function or variable via a global pointer to a pointer that is set up by the DLL exporting the symbol. The attribute implies `extern`. On Microsoft Windows targets, the pointer name is formed by combining `_imp__` and the function or variable name.

You can use `__declspec(dllimport)` as a synonym for `__attribute__` `((dllimport))` for compatibility with other compilers.

On systems that support the `visibility` attribute, this attribute also implies "default" visibility. It is an error to explicitly specify any other visibility.

Currently, the attribute is ignored for inlined functions. If the attribute is applied to a symbol *definition*, an error is reported. If a symbol previously declared `dllimport` is later defined, the attribute is ignored in subsequent references, and a warning is emitted. The attribute is also overridden by a subsequent declaration as `dllexport`.

When applied to C++ classes, the attribute marks non-inlined member functions and static data members as imports. However, the attribute is ignored for virtual methods to allow creation of vtables using thunks.

On the SH Symbian OS target the `dllimport` attribute also has another affect— it can cause the vtable and run-time type information for a class to be exported. This happens when the class has a dllimported constructor or a non-inline, non-pure virtual function and, for either of those two conditions, the class also has an inline constructor or destructor and has a key function that is defined in the current translation unit.

For Microsoft Windows targets the use of the `dllimport` attribute on functions is not necessary, but provides a small performance benefit by eliminating a thunk in the DLL. The use of the `dllimport` attribute on imported variables can be avoided by passing the '`--enable-auto-import`' switch to the GNU linker. As with functions, using the attribute for a variable eliminates a thunk in the DLL.

One drawback to using this attribute is that a pointer to a *variable* marked as `dllimport` cannot be used as a constant address. However, a pointer to a *function* with the `dllimport` attribute can be used as a constant initializer;

in this case, the address of a stub function in the import lib is referenced. On Microsoft Windows targets, the attribute can be disabled for functions by setting the '-mnop-fun-dllimport' flag.

6.31.18 MIPS Function Attributes

These function attributes are supported by the MIPS back end:

interrupt

> Use this attribute to indicate that the specified function is an interrupt handler. The compiler generates function entry and exit sequences suitable for use in an interrupt handler when this attribute is present. An optional argument is supported for the interrupt attribute which allows the interrupt mode to be described. By default GCC assumes the external interrupt controller (EIC) mode is in use, this can be explicitly set using eic. When interrupts are non-masked then the requested Interrupt Priority Level (IPL) is copied to the current IPL which has the effect of only enabling higher priority interrupts. To use vectored interrupt mode use the argument vector=[sw0|sw1|hw0|hw1|hw2|hw3|hw4|hw5], this will change the behavior of the non-masked interrupt support and GCC will arrange to mask all interrupts from sw0 up to and including the specified interrupt vector.

> You can use the following attributes to modify the behavior of an interrupt handler:

use_shadow_register_set

> Assume that the handler uses a shadow register set, instead of the main general-purpose registers. An optional argument intstack is supported to indicate that the shadow register set contains a valid stack pointer.

keep_interrupts_masked

> Keep interrupts masked for the whole function. Without this attribute, GCC tries to reenable interrupts for as much of the function as it can.

use_debug_exception_return

> Return using the deret instruction. Interrupt handlers that don't have this attribute return using eret instead.

> You can use any combination of these attributes, as shown below:

```
void __attribute__ ((interrupt)) v0 ();
void __attribute__ ((interrupt, use_shadow_register_set)) v1 ();
void __attribute__ ((interrupt, keep_interrupts_masked)) v2 ();
void __attribute__ ((interrupt, use_debug_exception_return)) v3 ();
void __attribute__ ((interrupt, use_shadow_register_set,
                     keep_interrupts_masked)) v4 ();
void __attribute__ ((interrupt, use_shadow_register_set,
                     use_debug_exception_return)) v5 ();
void __attribute__ ((interrupt, keep_interrupts_masked,
                     use_debug_exception_return)) v6 ();
void __attribute__ ((interrupt, use_shadow_register_set,
                     keep_interrupts_masked,
                     use_debug_exception_return)) v7 ();
```

```
void __attribute__ ((interrupt("eic"))) v8 ();
void __attribute__ ((interrupt("vector=hw3"))) v9 ();
```

long_call
near
far   These attributes specify how a particular function is called on MIPS. The
                 attributes override the '-mlong-calls' (see Section 3.18.26 [MIPS Options],
                 page 283) command-line switch. The long_call and far attributes are syn-
                 onyms, and cause the compiler to always call the function by first loading its
                 address into a register, and then using the contents of that register. The near
                 attribute has the opposite effect; it specifies that non-PIC calls should be made
                 using the more efficient jal instruction.

mips16
nomips16
                 On MIPS targets, you can use the mips16 and nomips16 function attributes to
                 locally select or turn off MIPS16 code generation. A function with the mips16
                 attribute is emitted as MIPS16 code, while MIPS16 code generation is dis-
                 abled for functions with the nomips16 attribute. These attributes override the
                 '-mips16' and '-mno-mips16' options on the command line (see Section 3.18.26
                 [MIPS Options], page 283).

                 When compiling files containing mixed MIPS16 and non-MIPS16 code, the pre-
                 processor symbol __mips16 reflects the setting on the command line, not that
                 within individual functions. Mixed MIPS16 and non-MIPS16 code may inter-
                 act badly with some GCC extensions such as __builtin_apply (see Section 6.5
                 [Constructing Calls], page 408).

micromips, MIPS
nomicromips, MIPS
                 On MIPS targets, you can use the micromips and nomicromips function at-
                 tributes to locally select or turn off microMIPS code generation. A function with
                 the micromips attribute is emitted as microMIPS code, while microMIPS code
                 generation is disabled for functions with the nomicromips attribute. These
                 attributes override the '-mmicromips' and '-mno-micromips' options on the
                 command line (see Section 3.18.26 [MIPS Options], page 283).

                 When compiling files containing mixed microMIPS and non-microMIPS code,
                 the preprocessor symbol __mips_micromips reflects the setting on the com-
                 mand line, not that within individual functions. Mixed microMIPS and non-
                 microMIPS code may interact badly with some GCC extensions such as __
                 builtin_apply (see Section 6.5 [Constructing Calls], page 408).

nocompression
                 On MIPS targets, you can use the nocompression function attribute to locally
                 turn off MIPS16 and microMIPS code generation. This attribute overrides the
                 '-mips16' and '-mmicromips' options on the command line (see Section 3.18.26
                 [MIPS Options], page 283).

6.31.19 MSP430 Function Attributes

These function attributes are supported by the MSP430 back end:

`critical`   Critical functions disable interrupts upon entry and restore the previous interrupt state upon exit. Critical functions cannot also have the **naked** or **reentrant** attributes. They can have the **interrupt** attribute.

`interrupt`
Use this attribute to indicate that the specified function is an interrupt handler. The compiler generates function entry and exit sequences suitable for use in an interrupt handler when this attribute is present.

You can provide an argument to the interrupt attribute which specifies a name or number. If the argument is a number it indicates the slot in the interrupt vector table (0 - 31) to which this handler should be assigned. If the argument is a name it is treated as a symbolic name for the vector slot. These names should match up with appropriate entries in the linker script. By default the names **watchdog** for vector 26, **nmi** for vector 30 and **reset** for vector 31 are recognized.

`naked`   This attribute allows the compiler to construct the requisite function declaration, while allowing the body of the function to be assembly code. The specified function will not have prologue/epilogue sequences generated by the compiler. Only basic **asm** statements can safely be included in naked functions (see Section 6.45.1 [Basic Asm], page 498). While using extended **asm** or a mixture of basic **asm** and C code may appear to work, they cannot be depended upon to work reliably and are not supported.

`reentrant`
Reentrant functions disable interrupts upon entry and enable them upon exit. Reentrant functions cannot also have the **naked** or **critical** attributes. They can have the **interrupt** attribute.

`wakeup`   This attribute only applies to interrupt functions. It is silently ignored if applied to a non-interrupt function. A wakeup interrupt function will rouse the processor from any low-power state that it might be in when the function exits.

`lower`
`upper`
`either`   On the MSP430 target these attributes can be used to specify whether the function or variable should be placed into low memory, high memory, or the placement should be left to the linker to decide. The attributes are only significant if compiling for the MSP430X architecture.

The attributes work in conjunction with a linker script that has been augmented to specify where to place sections with a `.lower` and a `.upper` prefix. So, for example, as well as placing the `.data` section, the script also specifies the placement of a `.lower.data` and a `.upper.data` section. The intention is that **lower** sections are placed into a small but easier to access memory region and the upper sections are placed into a larger, but slower to access, region.

The **either** attribute is special. It tells the linker to place the object into the corresponding **lower** section if there is room for it. If there is insufficient room then the object is placed into the corresponding **upper** section instead. Note that the placement algorithm is not very sophisticated. It does not attempt to find an optimal packing of the `lower` sections. It just makes one pass over the objects and does the best that it can. Using the '`-ffunction-sections`' and '`-fdata-sections`' command-line options can help the packing, however, since they produce smaller, easier to pack regions.

6.31.20 NDS32 Function Attributes

These function attributes are supported by the NDS32 back end:

`exception`

Use this attribute on the NDS32 target to indicate that the specified function is an exception handler. The compiler will generate corresponding sections for use in an exception handler.

`interrupt`

On NDS32 target, this attribute indicates that the specified function is an interrupt handler. The compiler generates corresponding sections for use in an interrupt handler. You can use the following attributes to modify the behavior:

`nested`   This interrupt service routine is interruptible.

`not_nested`
This interrupt service routine is not interruptible.

`nested_ready`
This interrupt service routine is interruptible after `PSW.GIE` (global interrupt enable) is set. This allows interrupt service routine to finish some short critical code before enabling interrupts.

`save_all`   The system will help save all registers into stack before entering interrupt handler.

`partial_save`
The system will help save caller registers into stack before entering interrupt handler.

`naked`   This attribute allows the compiler to construct the requisite function declaration, while allowing the body of the function to be assembly code. The specified function will not have prologue/epilogue sequences generated by the compiler. Only basic `asm` statements can safely be included in naked functions (see Section 6.45.1 [Basic Asm], page 498). While using extended `asm` or a mixture of basic `asm` and C code may appear to work, they cannot be depended upon to work reliably and are not supported.

`reset`   Use this attribute on the NDS32 target to indicate that the specified function is a reset handler. The compiler will generate corresponding sections for use in a reset handler. You can use the following attributes to provide extra exception handling:

`nmi`   Provide a user-defined function to handle NMI exception.

`warm`   Provide a user-defined function to handle warm reset exception.

6.31.21 Nios II Function Attributes

These function attributes are supported by the Nios II back end:

`target (options)`

>   As discussed in Section 6.31.1 [Common Function Attributes], page 428, this attribute allows specification of target-specific compilation options.

>   When compiling for Nios II, the following options are allowed:

>   `'custom-insn=N'`
>   `'no-custom-insn'`

>>   Each `'custom-insn=N'` attribute locally enables use of a custom instruction with encoding N when generating code that uses *insn*. Similarly, `'no-custom-insn'` locally inhibits use of the custom instruction *insn*. These target attributes correspond to the `'-mcustom-insn=N'` and `'-mno-custom-insn'` command-line options, and support the same set of *insn* keywords. See Section 3.18.32 [Nios II Options], page 302, for more information.

>   `'custom-fpu-cfg=name'`

>>   This attribute corresponds to the `'-mcustom-fpu-cfg=name'` command-line option, to select a predefined set of custom instructions named *name*. See Section 3.18.32 [Nios II Options], page 302, for more information.

6.31.22 Nvidia PTX Function Attributes

These function attributes are supported by the Nvidia PTX back end:

`kernel`   This attribute indicates that the corresponding function should be compiled as a kernel function, which can be invoked from the host via the CUDA RT library. By default functions are only callable only from other PTX functions.

>   Kernel functions must have `void` return type.

6.31.23 PowerPC Function Attributes

These function attributes are supported by the PowerPC back end:

`longcall`
`shortcall`

>   The `longcall` attribute indicates that the function might be far away from the call site and require a different (more expensive) calling sequence. The `shortcall` attribute indicates that the function is always close enough for the shorter calling sequence to be used. These attributes override both the `'-mlongcall'` switch and the `#pragma longcall` setting.

>   See Section 3.18.38 [RS/6000 and PowerPC Options], page 311, for more information on whether long calls are necessary.

`target (options)`

>   As discussed in Section 6.31.1 [Common Function Attributes], page 428, this attribute allows specification of target-specific compilation options.

>   On the PowerPC, the following options are allowed:

'altivec'
'no-altivec'
> Generate code that uses (does not use) AltiVec instructions. In 32-bit code, you cannot enable AltiVec instructions unless '-mabi=altivec' is used on the command line.

'cmpb'
'no-cmpb' Generate code that uses (does not use) the compare bytes instruction implemented on the POWER6 processor and other processors that support the PowerPC V2.05 architecture.

'dlmzb'
'no-dlmzb'
> Generate code that uses (does not use) the string-search 'dlmzb' instruction on the IBM 405, 440, 464 and 476 processors. This instruction is generated by default when targeting those processors.

'fprnd'
'no-fprnd'
> Generate code that uses (does not use) the FP round to integer instructions implemented on the POWER5+ processor and other processors that support the PowerPC V2.03 architecture.

'hard-dfp'
'no-hard-dfp'
> Generate code that uses (does not use) the decimal floating-point instructions implemented on some POWER processors.

'isel'
'no-isel' Generate code that uses (does not use) ISEL instruction.

'mfcrf'
'no-mfcrf'
> Generate code that uses (does not use) the move from condition register field instruction implemented on the POWER4 processor and other processors that support the PowerPC V2.01 architecture.

'mfpgpr'
'no-mfpgpr'
> Generate code that uses (does not use) the FP move to/from general purpose register instructions implemented on the POWER6X processor and other processors that support the extended PowerPC V2.05 architecture.

'mulhw'
'no-mulhw'
> Generate code that uses (does not use) the half-word multiply and multiply-accumulate instructions on the IBM 405, 440, 464 and 476 processors. These instructions are generated by default when targeting those processors.

'multiple'
'no-multiple'
> Generate code that uses (does not use) the load multiple word instructions and the store multiple word instructions.

'update'
'no-update'
> Generate code that uses (does not use) the load or store instructions that update the base register to the address of the calculated memory location.

'popcntb'
'no-popcntb'
> Generate code that uses (does not use) the popcount and double-precision FP reciprocal estimate instruction implemented on the POWER5 processor and other processors that support the PowerPC V2.02 architecture.

'popcntd'
'no-popcntd'
> Generate code that uses (does not use) the popcount instruction implemented on the POWER7 processor and other processors that support the PowerPC V2.06 architecture.

'powerpc-gfxopt'
'no-powerpc-gfxopt'
> Generate code that uses (does not use) the optional PowerPC architecture instructions in the Graphics group, including floating-point select.

'powerpc-gpopt'
'no-powerpc-gpopt'
> Generate code that uses (does not use) the optional PowerPC architecture instructions in the General Purpose group, including floating-point square root.

'recip-precision'
'no-recip-precision'
> Assume (do not assume) that the reciprocal estimate instructions provide higher-precision estimates than is mandated by the PowerPC ABI.

'string'
'no-string'
> Generate code that uses (does not use) the load string instructions and the store string word instructions to save multiple registers and do small block moves.

'vsx'
'no-vsx'   Generate code that uses (does not use) vector/scalar (VSX) instructions, and also enable the use of built-in functions that allow

more direct access to the VSX instruction set. In 32-bit code, you cannot enable VSX or AltiVec instructions unless '-mabi=altivec' is used on the command line.

'friz'
'no-friz'   Generate (do not generate) the friz instruction when the '-funsafe-math-optimizations' option is used to optimize rounding a floating-point value to 64-bit integer and back to floating point. The friz instruction does not return the same value if the floating-point number is too large to fit in an integer.

'avoid-indexed-addresses'
'no-avoid-indexed-addresses'
              Generate code that tries to avoid (not avoid) the use of indexed load or store instructions.

'paired'
'no-paired'
              Generate code that uses (does not use) the generation of PAIRED simd instructions.

'longcall'
'no-longcall'
              Generate code that assumes (does not assume) that all calls are far away so that a longer more expensive calling sequence is required.

'cpu=*CPU*'   Specify the architecture to generate code for when compiling the function. If you select the target("cpu=power7") attribute when generating 32-bit code, VSX and AltiVec instructions are not generated unless you use the '-mabi=altivec' option on the command line.

'tune=*TUNE*'
              Specify the architecture to tune for when compiling the function. If you do not specify the target("tune=*TUNE*") attribute and you do specify the target("cpu=*CPU*") attribute, compilation tunes for the *CPU* architecture, and not the default tuning specified on the command line.

On the PowerPC, the inliner does not inline a function that has different target options than the caller, unless the callee has a subset of the target options of the caller.

6.31.24 RL78 Function Attributes

These function attributes are supported by the RL78 back end:

interrupt
brk_interrupt
              These attributes indicate that the specified function is an interrupt handler. The compiler generates function entry and exit sequences suitable for use in an interrupt handler when this attribute is present.

Use `brk_interrupt` instead of `interrupt` for handlers intended to be used with the `BRK` opcode (i.e. those that must end with `RETB` instead of `RETI`).

naked   This attribute allows the compiler to construct the requisite function declaration, while allowing the body of the function to be assembly code. The specified function will not have prologue/epilogue sequences generated by the compiler. Only basic **asm** statements can safely be included in naked functions (see Section 6.45.1 [Basic Asm], page 498). While using extended **asm** or a mixture of basic **asm** and C code may appear to work, they cannot be depended upon to work reliably and are not supported.

6.31.25 RX Function Attributes

These function attributes are supported by the RX back end:

fast_interrupt

Use this attribute on the RX port to indicate that the specified function is a fast interrupt handler. This is just like the **interrupt** attribute, except that **freit** is used to return instead of **reit**.

interrupt

Use this attribute to indicate that the specified function is an interrupt handler. The compiler generates function entry and exit sequences suitable for use in an interrupt handler when this attribute is present.

On RX targets, you may specify one or more vector numbers as arguments to the attribute, as well as naming an alternate table name. Parameters are handled sequentially, so one handler can be assigned to multiple entries in multiple tables. One may also pass the magic string `"$default"` which causes the function to be used for any unfilled slots in the current table.

This example shows a simple assignment of a function to one vector in the default table (note that preprocessor macros may be used for chip-specific symbolic vector names):

```
void __attribute__ ((interrupt (5))) txd1_handler ();
```

This example assigns a function to two slots in the default table (using preprocessor macros defined elsewhere) and makes it the default for the `dct` table:

```
void __attribute__ ((interrupt (RXD1_VECT,RXD2_VECT,"dct","$default")))
txd1_handler ();
```

naked   This attribute allows the compiler to construct the requisite function declaration, while allowing the body of the function to be assembly code. The specified function will not have prologue/epilogue sequences generated by the compiler. Only basic **asm** statements can safely be included in naked functions (see Section 6.45.1 [Basic Asm], page 498). While using extended **asm** or a mixture of basic **asm** and C code may appear to work, they cannot be depended upon to work reliably and are not supported.

vector   This RX attribute is similar to the **interrupt** attribute, including its parameters, but does not make the function an interrupt-handler type function (i.e. it retains the normal C function calling ABI). See the **interrupt** attribute for a description of its arguments.

6.31.26 S/390 Function Attributes

These function attributes are supported on the S/390:

`hotpatch (`*`halfwords-before-function-label,halfwords-after-function-label`*`)`

> On S/390 System z targets, you can use this function attribute to make GCC generate a "hot-patching" function prologue. If the '`-mhotpatch=`' command-line option is used at the same time, the `hotpatch` attribute takes precedence. The first of the two arguments specifies the number of halfwords to be added before the function label. A second argument can be used to specify the number of halfwords to be added after the function label. For both arguments the maximum allowed value is 1000000.
>
> If both arguments are zero, hotpatching is disabled.

`target (`*`options`*`)`

> As discussed in Section 6.31.1 [Common Function Attributes], page 428, this attribute allows specification of target-specific compilation options.
>
> On S/390, the following options are supported:
>
> '`arch=`'
>
> '`tune=`'
>
> '`stack-guard=`'
> '`stack-size=`'
> '`branch-cost=`'
> '`warn-framesize=`'
> '`backchain`'
> '`no-backchain`'
> '`hard-dfp`'
> '`no-hard-dfp`'
> '`hard-float`'
> '`soft-float`'
> '`htm`'
> '`no-htm`'
>
> '`vx`'
> '`no-vx`'
>
> '`packed-stack`'
> '`no-packed-stack`'
> '`small-exec`'
> '`no-small-exec`'
> '`mvcle`'
> '`no-mvcle`'
> '`warn-dynamicstack`'
> '`no-warn-dynamicstack`'
>
> The options work exactly like the S/390 specific command line options (without the prefix '`-m`') except that they do not change any feature macros. For example,
>
> > `target("no-vx")`
>
> does not undefine the `__VEC__` macro.

6.31.27 SH Function Attributes

These function attributes are supported on the SH family of processors:

`function_vector`

On SH2A targets, this attribute declares a function to be called using the TBR relative addressing mode. The argument to this attribute is the entry number of the same function in a vector table containing all the TBR relative addressable functions. For correct operation the TBR must be setup accordingly to point to the start of the vector table before any functions with this attribute are invoked. Usually a good place to do the initialization is the startup routine. The TBR relative vector table can have at max 256 function entries. The jumps to these functions are generated using a SH2A specific, non delayed branch instruction JSR/N @(disp8,TBR). You must use GAS and GLD from GNU binutils version 2.7 or later for this attribute to work correctly.

In an application, for a function being called once, this attribute saves at least 8 bytes of code; and if other successive calls are being made to the same function, it saves 2 bytes of code per each of these calls.

`interrupt_handler`

Use this attribute to indicate that the specified function is an interrupt handler. The compiler generates function entry and exit sequences suitable for use in an interrupt handler when this attribute is present.

`nosave_low_regs`

Use this attribute on SH targets to indicate that an `interrupt_handler` function should not save and restore registers R0..R7. This can be used on SH3* and SH4* targets that have a second R0..R7 register bank for non-reentrant interrupt handlers.

`renesas` On SH targets this attribute specifies that the function or struct follows the Renesas ABI.

`resbank` On the SH2A target, this attribute enables the high-speed register saving and restoration using a register bank for `interrupt_handler` routines. Saving to the bank is performed automatically after the CPU accepts an interrupt that uses a register bank.

The nineteen 32-bit registers comprising general register R0 to R14, control register GBR, and system registers MACH, MACL, and PR and the vector table address offset are saved into a register bank. Register banks are stacked in first-in last-out (FILO) sequence. Restoration from the bank is executed by issuing a RESBANK instruction.

`sp_switch`

Use this attribute on the SH to indicate an `interrupt_handler` function should switch to an alternate stack. It expects a string argument that names a global variable holding the address of the alternate stack.

```
void *alt_stack;
void f () __attribute__ ((interrupt_handler,
                          sp_switch ("alt_stack")));
```

`trap_exit`

> Use this attribute on the SH for an `interrupt_handler` to return using `trapa` instead of `rte`. This attribute expects an integer argument specifying the trap number to be used.

`trapa_handler`

> On SH targets this function attribute is similar to `interrupt_handler` but it does not save and restore all registers.

6.31.28 SPU Function Attributes

These function attributes are supported by the SPU back end:

`naked`   This attribute allows the compiler to construct the requisite function declaration, while allowing the body of the function to be assembly code. The specified function will not have prologue/epilogue sequences generated by the compiler. Only basic `asm` statements can safely be included in naked functions (see Section 6.45.1 [Basic Asm], page 498). While using extended `asm` or a mixture of basic `asm` and C code may appear to work, they cannot be depended upon to work reliably and are not supported.

6.31.29 Symbian OS Function Attributes

See Section 6.31.17 [Microsoft Windows Function Attributes], page 453, for discussion of the `dllexport` and `dllimport` attributes.

6.31.30 V850 Function Attributes

The V850 back end supports these function attributes:

`interrupt`
`interrupt_handler`

> Use these attributes to indicate that the specified function is an interrupt handler. The compiler generates function entry and exit sequences suitable for use in an interrupt handler when either attribute is present.

6.31.31 Visium Function Attributes

These function attributes are supported by the Visium back end:

`interrupt`

> Use this attribute to indicate that the specified function is an interrupt handler. The compiler generates function entry and exit sequences suitable for use in an interrupt handler when this attribute is present.

6.31.32 x86 Function Attributes

These function attributes are supported by the x86 back end:

`cdecl`   On the x86-32 targets, the `cdecl` attribute causes the compiler to assume that the calling function pops off the stack space used to pass arguments. This is useful to override the effects of the '`-mrtd`' switch.

`fastcall`   On x86-32 targets, the `fastcall` attribute causes the compiler to pass the first argument (if of integral type) in the register ECX and the second argument (if of integral type) in the register EDX. Subsequent and other typed arguments are passed on the stack. The called function pops the arguments off the stack. If the number of arguments is variable all arguments are pushed on the stack.

thiscall   On x86-32 targets, the `thiscall` attribute causes the compiler to pass the first argument (if of integral type) in the register ECX. Subsequent and other typed arguments are passed on the stack. The called function pops the arguments off the stack. If the number of arguments is variable all arguments are pushed on the stack. The `thiscall` attribute is intended for C++ non-static member functions. As a GCC extension, this calling convention can be used for C functions and for static member methods.

ms_abi
sysv_abi

On 32-bit and 64-bit x86 targets, you can use an ABI attribute to indicate which calling convention should be used for a function. The `ms_abi` attribute tells the compiler to use the Microsoft ABI, while the `sysv_abi` attribute tells the compiler to use the ABI used on GNU/Linux and other systems. The default is to use the Microsoft ABI when targeting Windows. On all other systems, the default is the x86/AMD ABI.

Note, the `ms_abi` attribute for Microsoft Windows 64-bit targets currently requires the '`-maccumulate-outgoing-args`' option.

callee_pop_aggregate_return (*number*)

On x86-32 targets, you can use this attribute to control how aggregates are returned in memory. If the caller is responsible for popping the hidden pointer together with the rest of the arguments, specify *number* equal to zero. If callee is responsible for popping the hidden pointer, specify *number* equal to one.

The default x86-32 ABI assumes that the callee pops the stack for hidden pointer. However, on x86-32 Microsoft Windows targets, the compiler assumes that the caller pops the stack for hidden pointer.

ms_hook_prologue

On 32-bit and 64-bit x86 targets, you can use this function attribute to make GCC generate the "hot-patching" function prologue used in Win32 API functions in Microsoft Windows XP Service Pack 2 and newer.

regparm (*number*)

On x86-32 targets, the `regparm` attribute causes the compiler to pass arguments number one to *number* if they are of integral type in registers EAX, EDX, and ECX instead of on the stack. Functions that take a variable number of arguments continue to be passed all of their arguments on the stack.

Beware that on some ELF systems this attribute is unsuitable for global functions in shared libraries with lazy binding (which is the default). Lazy binding sends the first call via resolving code in the loader, which might assume EAX, EDX and ECX can be clobbered, as per the standard calling conventions. Solaris 8 is affected by this. Systems with the GNU C Library version 2.1 or higher and FreeBSD are believed to be safe since the loaders there save EAX,

EDX and ECX. (Lazy binding can be disabled with the linker or the loader if desired, to avoid the problem.)

sseregparm

On x86-32 targets with SSE support, the `sseregparm` attribute causes the compiler to pass up to 3 floating-point arguments in SSE registers instead of on the stack. Functions that take a variable number of arguments continue to pass all of their floating-point arguments on the stack.

force_align_arg_pointer

On x86 targets, the `force_align_arg_pointer` attribute may be applied to individual function definitions, generating an alternate prologue and epilogue that realigns the run-time stack if necessary. This supports mixing legacy codes that run with a 4-byte aligned stack with modern codes that keep a 16-byte stack for SSE compatibility.

stdcall

On x86-32 targets, the `stdcall` attribute causes the compiler to assume that the called function pops off the stack space used to pass arguments, unless it takes a variable number of arguments.

no_caller_saved_registers

Use this attribute to indicate that the specified function has no caller-saved registers. That is, all registers are callee-saved. For example, this attribute can be used for a function called from an interrupt handler. The compiler generates proper function entry and exit sequences to save and restore any modified registers, except for the EFLAGS register. Since GCC doesn't preserve MPX, SSE, MMX nor x87 states, the GCC option '`-mgeneral-regs-only`' should be used to compile functions with `no_caller_saved_registers` attribute.

interrupt

Use this attribute to indicate that the specified function is an interrupt handler or an exception handler (depending on parameters passed to the function, explained further). The compiler generates function entry and exit sequences suitable for use in an interrupt handler when this attribute is present. The `IRET` instruction, instead of the `RET` instruction, is used to return from interrupt handlers. All registers, except for the EFLAGS register which is restored by the `IRET` instruction, are preserved by the compiler. Since GCC doesn't preserve MPX, SSE, MMX nor x87 states, the GCC option '`-mgeneral-regs-only`' should be used to compile interrupt and exception handlers.

Any interruptible-without-stack-switch code must be compiled with '`-mno-red-zone`' since interrupt handlers can and will, because of the hardware design, touch the red zone.

An interrupt handler must be declared with a mandatory pointer argument:

```
struct interrupt_frame;

__attribute__ ((interrupt))
void
f (struct interrupt_frame *frame)
{
}
```

and you must define `struct interrupt_frame` as described in the processor's manual.

Exception handlers differ from interrupt handlers because the system pushes an error code on the stack. An exception handler declaration is similar to that for an interrupt handler, but with a different mandatory function signature. The compiler arranges to pop the error code off the stack before the `IRET` instruction.

```
#ifdef __x86_64__
typedef unsigned long long int uword_t;
#else
typedef unsigned int uword_t;
#endif

struct interrupt_frame;

__attribute__ ((interrupt))
void
f (struct interrupt_frame *frame, uword_t error_code)
{
    ...
}
```

Exception handlers should only be used for exceptions that push an error code; you should use an interrupt handler in other cases. The system will crash if the wrong kind of handler is used.

`target (options)`

As discussed in Section 6.31.1 [Common Function Attributes], page 428, this attribute allows specification of target-specific compilation options.

On the x86, the following options are allowed:

'abm'
'no-abm'   Enable/disable the generation of the advanced bit instructions.

'aes'
'no-aes'   Enable/disable the generation of the AES instructions.

'default'   See Section 7.8 [Function Multiversioning], page 734, where it is used to specify the default function version.

'mmx'
'no-mmx'   Enable/disable the generation of the MMX instructions.

'pclmul'
'no-pclmul'
            Enable/disable the generation of the PCLMUL instructions.

'popcnt'
'no-popcnt'
            Enable/disable the generation of the POPCNT instruction.

'sse'
'no-sse'   Enable/disable the generation of the SSE instructions.

'sse2'
'no-sse2'   Enable/disable the generation of the SSE2 instructions.

'sse3'
'no-sse3'   Enable/disable the generation of the SSE3 instructions.

'sse4'
'no-sse4'   Enable/disable the generation of the SSE4 instructions (both
             SSE4.1 and SSE4.2).

'sse4.1'
'no-sse4.1'
             Enable/disable the generation of the sse4.1 instructions.

'sse4.2'
'no-sse4.2'
             Enable/disable the generation of the sse4.2 instructions.

'sse4a'
'no-sse4a'
             Enable/disable the generation of the SSE4A instructions.

'fma4'
'no-fma4'   Enable/disable the generation of the FMA4 instructions.

'xop'
'no-xop'   Enable/disable the generation of the XOP instructions.

'lwp'
'no-lwp'   Enable/disable the generation of the LWP instructions.

'ssse3'
'no-ssse3'
             Enable/disable the generation of the SSSE3 instructions.

'cld'
'no-cld'   Enable/disable the generation of the CLD before string moves.

'fancy-math-387'
'no-fancy-math-387'
             Enable/disable the generation of the sin, cos, and sqrt instruc-
             tions on the 387 floating-point unit.

'ieee-fp'
'no-ieee-fp'
             Enable/disable the generation of floating point that depends on
             IEEE arithmetic.

'inline-all-stringops'
'no-inline-all-stringops'
             Enable/disable inlining of string operations.

'inline-stringops-dynamically'
'no-inline-stringops-dynamically'
             Enable/disable the generation of the inline code to do small string
             operations and calling the library routines for large operations.

'align-stringops'
'no-align-stringops'

> Do/do not align destination of inlined string operations.

'recip'
'no-recip'

> Enable/disable the generation of RCPSS, RCPPS, RSQRTSS and RSQRTPS instructions followed an additional Newton-Raphson step instead of doing a floating-point division.

'arch=*ARCH*'

> Specify the architecture to generate code for in compiling the function.

'tune=*TUNE*'

> Specify the architecture to tune for in compiling the function.

'fpmath=*FPMATH*'

> Specify which floating-point unit to use. You must specify the `target("fpmath=sse,387")` option as `target("fpmath=sse+387")` because the comma would separate different options.

On the x86, the inliner does not inline a function that has different target options than the caller, unless the callee has a subset of the target options of the caller. For example a function declared with `target("sse3")` can inline a function with `target("sse2")`, since `-msse3` implies `-msse2`.

6.31.33 Xstormy16 Function Attributes

These function attributes are supported by the Xstormy16 back end:

`interrupt`

> Use this attribute to indicate that the specified function is an interrupt handler. The compiler generates function entry and exit sequences suitable for use in an interrupt handler when this attribute is present.

6.32 Specifying Attributes of Variables

The keyword `__attribute__` allows you to specify special attributes of variables or structure fields. This keyword is followed by an attribute specification inside double parentheses. Some attributes are currently defined generically for variables. Other attributes are defined for variables on particular target systems. Other attributes are available for functions (see Section 6.31 [Function Attributes], page 427), labels (see Section 6.34 [Label Attributes], page 488), enumerators (see Section 6.35 [Enumerator Attributes], page 489), statements (see Section 6.36 [Statement Attributes], page 490), and for types (see Section 6.33 [Type Attributes], page 482). Other front ends might define more attributes (see Chapter 7 [Extensions to the C++ Language], page 727).

See Section 6.37 [Attribute Syntax], page 490, for details of the exact syntax for using attributes.

6.32.1 Common Variable Attributes

The following attributes are supported on most targets.

aligned (*alignment*)

    This attribute specifies a minimum alignment for the variable or structure field, measured in bytes. For example, the declaration:

```
int x __attribute__ ((aligned (16))) = 0;
```

    causes the compiler to allocate the global variable x on a 16-byte boundary. On a 68040, this could be used in conjunction with an asm expression to access the move16 instruction which requires 16-byte aligned operands.

    You can also specify the alignment of structure fields. For example, to create a double-word aligned int pair, you could write:

```
struct foo { int x[2] __attribute__ ((aligned (8))); };
```

    This is an alternative to creating a union with a double member, which forces the union to be double-word aligned.

    As in the preceding examples, you can explicitly specify the alignment (in bytes) that you wish the compiler to use for a given variable or structure field. Alternatively, you can leave out the alignment factor and just ask the compiler to align a variable or field to the default alignment for the target architecture you are compiling for. The default alignment is sufficient for all scalar types, but may not be enough for all vector types on a target that supports vector operations. The default alignment is fixed for a particular target ABI.

    GCC also provides a target specific macro __BIGGEST_ALIGNMENT__, which is the largest alignment ever used for any data type on the target machine you are compiling for. For example, you could write:

```
short array[3] __attribute__ ((aligned (__BIGGEST_ALIGNMENT__)));
```

    The compiler automatically sets the alignment for the declared variable or field to __BIGGEST_ALIGNMENT__. Doing this can often make copy operations more efficient, because the compiler can use whatever instructions copy the biggest chunks of memory when performing copies to or from the variables or fields that you have aligned this way. Note that the value of __BIGGEST_ALIGNMENT__ may change depending on command-line options.

    When used on a struct, or struct member, the aligned attribute can only increase the alignment; in order to decrease it, the packed attribute must be specified as well. When used as part of a typedef, the aligned attribute can both increase and decrease alignment, and specifying the packed attribute generates a warning.

    Note that the effectiveness of aligned attributes may be limited by inherent limitations in your linker. On many systems, the linker is only able to arrange for variables to be aligned up to a certain maximum alignment. (For some linkers, the maximum supported alignment may be very very small.) If your linker is only able to align variables up to a maximum of 8-byte alignment, then specifying aligned(16) in an __attribute__ still only provides you with 8-byte alignment. See your linker documentation for further information.

    The aligned attribute can also be used for functions (see Section 6.31.1 [Common Function Attributes], page 428.)

cleanup (*cleanup_function*)

> The **cleanup** attribute runs a function when the variable goes out of scope. This attribute can only be applied to auto function scope variables; it may not be applied to parameters or variables with static storage duration. The function must take one parameter, a pointer to a type compatible with the variable. The return value of the function (if any) is ignored.
>
> If '**-fexceptions**' is enabled, then *cleanup_function* is run during the stack unwinding that happens during the processing of the exception. Note that the **cleanup** attribute does not allow the exception to be caught, only to perform an action. It is undefined what happens if *cleanup_function* does not return normally.

common

nocommon The **common** attribute requests GCC to place a variable in "common" storage. The **nocommon** attribute requests the opposite—to allocate space for it directly.

> These attributes override the default chosen by the '**-fno-common**' and '**-fcommon**' flags respectively.

deprecated
deprecated (*msg*)

> The **deprecated** attribute results in a warning if the variable is used anywhere in the source file. This is useful when identifying variables that are expected to be removed in a future version of a program. The warning also includes the location of the declaration of the deprecated variable, to enable users to easily find further information about why the variable is deprecated, or what they should do instead. Note that the warning only occurs for uses:
>
> ```
> extern int old_var __attribute__ ((deprecated));
> extern int old_var;
> int new_fn () { return old_var; }
> ```
>
> results in a warning on line 3 but not line 2. The optional *msg* argument, which must be a string, is printed in the warning if present.
>
> The **deprecated** attribute can also be used for functions and types (see Section 6.31.1 [Common Function Attributes], page 428, see Section 6.33.1 [Common Type Attributes], page 482).

mode (*mode*)

> This attribute specifies the data type for the declaration—whichever type corresponds to the mode *mode*. This in effect lets you request an integer or floating-point type according to its width.
>
> You may also specify a mode of **byte** or **__byte__** to indicate the mode corresponding to a one-byte integer, **word** or **__word__** for the mode of a one-word integer, and **pointer** or **__pointer__** for the mode used to represent pointers.

packed   The **packed** attribute specifies that a variable or structure field should have the smallest possible alignment—one byte for a variable, and one bit for a field, unless you specify a larger value with the **aligned** attribute.

> Here is a structure in which the field **x** is packed, so that it immediately follows **a**:

```
struct foo
{
  char a;
  int x[2] __attribute__ ((packed));
};
```

Note: The 4.1, 4.2 and 4.3 series of GCC ignore the `packed` attribute on bit-fields of type `char`. This has been fixed in GCC 4.4 but the change can lead to differences in the structure layout. See the documentation of '-Wpacked-bitfield-compat' for more information.

section ("*section-name*")

Normally, the compiler places the objects it generates in sections like `data` and `bss`. Sometimes, however, you need additional sections, or you need certain particular variables to appear in special sections, for example to map to special hardware. The `section` attribute specifies that a variable (or function) lives in a particular section. For example, this small program uses several specific section names:

```
struct duart a __attribute__ ((section ("DUART_A"))) = { 0 };
struct duart b __attribute__ ((section ("DUART_B"))) = { 0 };
char stack[10000] __attribute__ ((section ("STACK"))) = { 0 };
int init_data __attribute__ ((section ("INITDATA")));

main()
{
  /* Initialize stack pointer */
  init_sp (stack + sizeof (stack));

  /* Initialize initialized data */
  memcpy (&init_data, &data, &edata - &data);

  /* Turn on the serial ports */
  init_duart (&a);
  init_duart (&b);
}
```

Use the `section` attribute with *global* variables and not *local* variables, as shown in the example.

You may use the `section` attribute with initialized or uninitialized global variables but the linker requires each object be defined once, with the exception that uninitialized variables tentatively go in the `common` (or `bss`) section and can be multiply "defined". Using the `section` attribute changes what section the variable goes into and may cause the linker to issue an error if an uninitialized variable has multiple definitions. You can force a variable to be initialized with the '-fno-common' flag or the `nocommon` attribute.

Some file formats do not support arbitrary sections so the `section` attribute is not available on all platforms. If you need to map the entire contents of a module to a particular section, consider using the facilities of the linker instead.

tls_model ("*tls_model*")

The `tls_model` attribute sets thread-local storage model (see Section 6.64 [Thread-Local], page 723) of a particular `__thread` variable, overriding '-ftls-model=' command-line switch on a per-variable basis. The *tls_model* argument should be one of `global-dynamic`, `local-dynamic`, `initial-exec` or `local-exec`.

Not all targets support this attribute.

`unused`   This attribute, attached to a variable, means that the variable is meant to be possibly unused. GCC does not produce a warning for this variable.

`used`   This attribute, attached to a variable with static storage, means that the variable must be emitted even if it appears that the variable is not referenced.

When applied to a static data member of a C++ class template, the attribute also means that the member is instantiated if the class itself is instantiated.

`vector_size (bytes)`

This attribute specifies the vector size for the variable, measured in bytes. For example, the declaration:

```
int foo __attribute__ ((vector_size (16)));
```

causes the compiler to set the mode for `foo`, to be 16 bytes, divided into `int` sized units. Assuming a 32-bit int (a vector of 4 units of 4 bytes), the corresponding mode of `foo` is V4SI.

This attribute is only applicable to integral and float scalars, although arrays, pointers, and function return values are allowed in conjunction with this construct.

Aggregates with this attribute are invalid, even if they are of the same size as a corresponding scalar. For example, the declaration:

```
struct S { int a; };
struct S  __attribute__ ((vector_size (16))) foo;
```

is invalid even if the size of the structure is the same as the size of the `int`.

`visibility ("visibility_type")`

This attribute affects the linkage of the declaration to which it is attached. The `visibility` attribute is described in Section 6.31.1 [Common Function Attributes], page 428.

`weak`   The `weak` attribute is described in Section 6.31.1 [Common Function Attributes], page 428.

6.32.2 AVR Variable Attributes

`progmem`   The `progmem` attribute is used on the AVR to place read-only data in the non-volatile program memory (flash). The `progmem` attribute accomplishes this by putting respective variables into a section whose name starts with `.progmem`.

This attribute works similar to the `section` attribute but adds additional checking.

- Ordinary AVR cores with 32 general purpose registers:

  `progmem` affects the location of the data but not how this data is accessed. In order to read data located with the `progmem` attribute (inline) assembler must be used.

  ```
  /* Use custom macros from AVR-LibC */
  #include <avr/pgmspace.h>
  ```

```
/* Locate var in flash memory */
const int var[2] PROGMEM = { 1, 2 };

int read_var (int i)
{
    /* Access var[] by accessor macro from avr/pgmspace.h */
    return (int) pgm_read_word (& var[i]);
}
```

AVR is a Harvard architecture processor and data and read-only data normally resides in the data memory (RAM).

See also the [AVR Named Address Spaces], page 417 section for an alternate way to locate and access data in flash memory.

- Reduced AVR Tiny cores like ATtiny40:

  The compiler adds 0x4000 to the addresses of objects and declarations in **progmem** and locates the objects in flash memory, namely in section `.progmem.data`. The offset is needed because the flash memory is visible in the RAM address space starting at address 0x4000.

  Data in **progmem** can be accessed by means of ordinary C code, no special functions or macros are needed.

  ```
  /* var is located in flash memory */
  extern const int var[2] __attribute__((progmem));

  int read_var (int i)
  {
      return var[i];
  }
  ```

  Please notice that on these devices, there is no need for **progmem** at all. Just use an appropriate linker description file like outlined below.

  ```
  .text :
  { ...
  } > text
  /* Leave .rodata in flash and add an offset of 0x4000 to all
     addresses so that respective objects can be accessed by LD
     instructions and open coded C/C++.  This means there is no
     need for progmem in the source and no overhead by read-only
     data in RAM.  */
  .rodata ADDR(.text) + SIZEOF (.text) + 0x4000 :
  {
    *(.rodata)
    *(.rodata*)
    *(.gnu.linkonce.r*)
  } AT> text
  /* No more need to put .rodata into .data:
     Removed all .rodata entries from .data.  */
  .data :
  { ...
  ```

io

io (*addr*) Variables with the `io` attribute are used to address memory-mapped peripherals in the io address range. If an address is specified, the variable is assigned that address, and the value is interpreted as an address in the data address space. Example:

```
volatile int porta __attribute__((io (0x22)));
```

The address specified in the address in the data address range.

Otherwise, the variable it is not assigned an address, but the compiler will still use in/out instructions where applicable, assuming some other module assigns an address in the io address range. Example:

```
extern volatile int porta __attribute__((io));
```

io_low
io_low (*addr*)

> This is like the io attribute, but additionally it informs the compiler that the object lies in the lower half of the I/O area, allowing the use of cbi, sbi, sbic and sbis instructions.

address
address (*addr*)

> Variables with the address attribute are used to address memory-mapped peripherals that may lie outside the io address range.
>
> ```
> volatile int porta __attribute__((address (0x600)));
> ```

absdata   Variables in static storage and with the absdata attribute can be accessed by the LDS and STS instructions which take absolute addresses.

- This attribute is only supported for the reduced AVR Tiny core like ATtiny40.

- You must make sure that respective data is located in the address range 0x40...0xbf accessible by LDS and STS. One way to achieve this as an appropriate linker description file.

- If the location does not fit the address range of LDS and STS, there is currently (Binutils 2.26) just an unspecific warning like

    ```
    module.c:(.text+0x1c): warning: internal error: out
    of range error
    ```

See also the '-mabsdata' Section 3.18.5 [AVR Options], page 238.

6.32.3 Blackfin Variable Attributes

Three attributes are currently defined for the Blackfin.

l1_data
l1_data_A
l1_data_B

> Use these attributes on the Blackfin to place the variable into L1 Data SRAM. Variables with l1_data attribute are put into the specific section named .l1.data. Those with l1_data_A attribute are put into the specific section named .l1.data.A. Those with l1_data_B attribute are put into the specific section named .l1.data.B.

l2   Use this attribute on the Blackfin to place the variable into L2 SRAM. Variables with l2 attribute are put into the specific section named .l2.data.

6.32.4 H8/300 Variable Attributes

These variable attributes are available for H8/300 targets:

eightbit_data

Use this attribute on the H8/300, H8/300H, and H8S to indicate that the specified variable should be placed into the eight-bit data section. The compiler generates more efficient code for certain operations on data in the eight-bit data area. Note the eight-bit data area is limited to 256 bytes of data.

You must use GAS and GLD from GNU binutils version 2.7 or later for this attribute to work correctly.

tiny_data

Use this attribute on the H8/300H and H8S to indicate that the specified variable should be placed into the tiny data section. The compiler generates more efficient code for loads and stores on data in the tiny data section. Note the tiny data area is limited to slightly under 32KB of data.

6.32.5 IA-64 Variable Attributes

The IA-64 back end supports the following variable attribute:

model (model-name)

On IA-64, use this attribute to set the addressability of an object. At present, the only supported identifier for model-name is small, indicating addressability via "small" (22-bit) addresses (so that their addresses can be loaded with the addl instruction). Caveat: such addressing is by definition not position independent and hence this attribute must not be used for objects defined by shared libraries.

6.32.6 M32R/D Variable Attributes

One attribute is currently defined for the M32R/D.

model (model-name)

Use this attribute on the M32R/D to set the addressability of an object. The identifier model-name is one of small, medium, or large, representing each of the code models.

Small model objects live in the lower 16MB of memory (so that their addresses can be loaded with the ld24 instruction).

Medium and large model objects may live anywhere in the 32-bit address space (the compiler generates seth/add3 instructions to load their addresses).

6.32.7 MeP Variable Attributes

The MeP target has a number of addressing modes and busses. The near space spans the standard memory space's first 16 megabytes (24 bits). The far space spans the entire 32-bit memory space. The based space is a 128-byte region in the memory space that is addressed relative to the $tp register. The tiny space is a 65536-byte region relative to the $gp register. In addition to these memory regions, the MeP target has a separate 16-bit control bus which is specified with cb attributes.

based   Any variable with the `based` attribute is assigned to the `.based` section, and is accessed with relative to the `$tp` register.

tiny   Likewise, the `tiny` attribute assigned variables to the `.tiny` section, relative to the `$gp` register.

near   Variables with the `near` attribute are assumed to have addresses that fit in a 24-bit addressing mode. This is the default for large variables (`-mtiny=4` is the default) but this attribute can override `-mtiny=` for small variables, or override `-ml`.

far   Variables with the `far` attribute are addressed using a full 32-bit address. Since this covers the entire memory space, this allows modules to make no assumptions about where variables might be stored.

io
io (*addr*)   Variables with the `io` attribute are used to address memory-mapped peripherals. If an address is specified, the variable is assigned that address, else it is not assigned an address (it is assumed some other module assigns an address). Example:

```
int timer_count __attribute__((io(0x123)));
```

cb
cb (*addr*)   Variables with the `cb` attribute are used to access the control bus, using special instructions. `addr` indicates the control bus address. Example:

```
int cpu_clock __attribute__((cb(0x123)));
```

6.32.8 Microsoft Windows Variable Attributes

You can use these attributes on Microsoft Windows targets. Section 6.32.15 [x86 Variable Attributes], page 481 for additional Windows compatibility attributes available on all x86 targets.

dllimport
dllexport

> The `dllimport` and `dllexport` attributes are described in Section 6.31.17 [Microsoft Windows Function Attributes], page 453.

selectany

> The `selectany` attribute causes an initialized global variable to have link-once semantics. When multiple definitions of the variable are encountered by the linker, the first is selected and the remainder are discarded. Following usage by the Microsoft compiler, the linker is told *not* to warn about size or content differences of the multiple definitions.
>
> Although the primary usage of this attribute is for POD types, the attribute can also be applied to global C++ objects that are initialized by a constructor. In this case, the static initialization and destruction code for the object is emitted in each translation defining the object, but the calls to the constructor and destructor are protected by a link-once guard variable.
>
> The `selectany` attribute is only available on Microsoft Windows targets. You can use `__declspec (selectany)` as a synonym for `__attribute__ ((selectany))` for compatibility with other compilers.

shared   On Microsoft Windows, in addition to putting variable definitions in a named
              section, the section can also be shared among all running copies of an executable
              or DLL. For example, this small program defines shared data by putting it in
              a named section shared and marking the section shareable:

```
int foo __attribute__((section ("shared"), shared)) = 0;

int
main()
{
  /* Read and write foo.  All running
     copies see the same value.  */
  return 0;
}
```

              You may only use the shared attribute along with section attribute with a
              fully-initialized global definition because of the way linkers work. See section
              attribute for more information.

              The shared attribute is only available on Microsoft Windows.

6.32.9 MSP430 Variable Attributes

noinit   Any data with the noinit attribute will not be initialised by the C runtime
              startup code, or the program loader. Not initialising data in this way can reduce
              program startup times.

persistent
              Any variable with the persistent attribute will not be initialised by the C
              runtime startup code. Instead its value will be set once, when the application
              is loaded, and then never initialised again, even if the processor is reset or the
              program restarts. Persistent data is intended to be placed into FLASH RAM,
              where its value will be retained across resets. The linker script being used to
              create the application should ensure that persistent data is correctly placed.

lower
upper
either   These attributes are the same as the MSP430 function attributes of the same
              name (see Section 6.31.19 [MSP430 Function Attributes], page 456). These
              attributes can be applied to both functions and variables.

6.32.10 Nvidia PTX Variable Attributes

These variable attributes are supported by the Nvidia PTX back end:

shared   Use this attribute to place a variable in the .shared memory space. This
              memory space is private to each cooperative thread array; only threads within
              one thread block refer to the same instance of the variable. The runtime does
              not initialize variables in this memory space.

6.32.11 PowerPC Variable Attributes

Three attributes currently are defined for PowerPC configurations: altivec, ms_struct
and gcc_struct.

For full documentation of the struct attributes please see the documentation in Section 6.32.15 [x86 Variable Attributes], page 481.

For documentation of `altivec` attribute please see the documentation in Section 6.33.4 [PowerPC Type Attributes], page 488.

6.32.12 RL78 Variable Attributes

The RL78 back end supports the `saddr` variable attribute. This specifies placement of the corresponding variable in the SADDR area, which can be accessed more efficiently than the default memory region.

6.32.13 SPU Variable Attributes

The SPU supports the `spu_vector` attribute for variables. For documentation of this attribute please see the documentation in Section 6.33.5 [SPU Type Attributes], page 488.

6.32.14 V850 Variable Attributes

These variable attributes are supported by the V850 back end:

sda   Use this attribute to explicitly place a variable in the small data area, which can hold up to 64 kilobytes.

tda   Use this attribute to explicitly place a variable in the tiny data area, which can hold up to 256 bytes in total.

zda   Use this attribute to explicitly place a variable in the first 32 kilobytes of memory.

6.32.15 x86 Variable Attributes

Two attributes are currently defined for x86 configurations: `ms_struct` and `gcc_struct`.

ms_struct
gcc_struct
            If `packed` is used on a structure, or if bit-fields are used, it may be that the Microsoft ABI lays out the structure differently than the way GCC normally does. Particularly when moving packed data between functions compiled with GCC and the native Microsoft compiler (either via function call or as data in a file), it may be necessary to access either format.

            The `ms_struct` and `gcc_struct` attributes correspond to the '-mms-bitfields' and '-mno-ms-bitfields' command-line options, respectively; see Section 3.18.54 [x86 Options], page 355, for details of how structure layout is affected. See Section 6.33.6 [x86 Type Attributes], page 488, for information about the corresponding attributes on types.

6.32.16 Xstormy16 Variable Attributes

One attribute is currently defined for xstormy16 configurations: `below100`.

below100
            If a variable has the `below100` attribute (`BELOW100` is allowed also), GCC places the variable in the first 0x100 bytes of memory and use special opcodes to access

it. Such variables are placed in either the `.bss_below100` section or the `.data_below100` section.

6.33 Specifying Attributes of Types

The keyword `__attribute__` allows you to specify special attributes of types. Some type attributes apply only to `struct` and `union` types, while others can apply to any type defined via a `typedef` declaration. Other attributes are defined for functions (see Section 6.31 [Function Attributes], page 427), labels (see Section 6.34 [Label Attributes], page 488), enumerators (see Section 6.35 [Enumerator Attributes], page 489), statements (see Section 6.36 [Statement Attributes], page 490), and for variables (see Section 6.32 [Variable Attributes], page 471).

The `__attribute__` keyword is followed by an attribute specification inside double parentheses.

You may specify type attributes in an enum, struct or union type declaration or definition by placing them immediately after the `struct`, `union` or `enum` keyword. A less preferred syntax is to place them just past the closing curly brace of the definition.

You can also include type attributes in a `typedef` declaration. See Section 6.37 [Attribute Syntax], page 490, for details of the exact syntax for using attributes.

6.33.1 Common Type Attributes

The following type attributes are supported on most targets.

`aligned (alignment)`

> This attribute specifies a minimum alignment (in bytes) for variables of the specified type. For example, the declarations:
>
> ```
> struct S { short f[3]; } __attribute__ ((aligned (8)));
> typedef int more_aligned_int __attribute__ ((aligned (8)));
> ```
>
> force the compiler to ensure (as far as it can) that each variable whose type is `struct S` or `more_aligned_int` is allocated and aligned *at least* on a 8-byte boundary. On a SPARC, having all variables of type `struct S` aligned to 8-byte boundaries allows the compiler to use the `ldd` and `std` (doubleword load and store) instructions when copying one variable of type `struct S` to another, thus improving run-time efficiency.
>
> Note that the alignment of any given `struct` or `union` type is required by the ISO C standard to be at least a perfect multiple of the lowest common multiple of the alignments of all of the members of the `struct` or `union` in question. This means that you *can* effectively adjust the alignment of a `struct` or `union` type by attaching an `aligned` attribute to any one of the members of such a type, but the notation illustrated in the example above is a more obvious, intuitive, and readable way to request the compiler to adjust the alignment of an entire `struct` or `union` type.
>
> As in the preceding example, you can explicitly specify the alignment (in bytes) that you wish the compiler to use for a given `struct` or `union` type. Alternatively, you can leave out the alignment factor and just ask the compiler to align a type to the maximum useful alignment for the target machine you are compiling for. For example, you could write:

```
struct S { short f[3]; } __attribute__ ((aligned));
```

Whenever you leave out the alignment factor in an **aligned** attribute specification, the compiler automatically sets the alignment for the type to the largest alignment that is ever used for any data type on the target machine you are compiling for. Doing this can often make copy operations more efficient, because the compiler can use whatever instructions copy the biggest chunks of memory when performing copies to or from the variables that have types that you have aligned this way.

In the example above, if the size of each **short** is 2 bytes, then the size of the entire **struct S** type is 6 bytes. The smallest power of two that is greater than or equal to that is 8, so the compiler sets the alignment for the entire **struct S** type to 8 bytes.

Note that although you can ask the compiler to select a time-efficient alignment for a given type and then declare only individual stand-alone objects of that type, the compiler's ability to select a time-efficient alignment is primarily useful only when you plan to create arrays of variables having the relevant (efficiently aligned) type. If you declare or use arrays of variables of an efficiently-aligned type, then it is likely that your program also does pointer arithmetic (or subscripting, which amounts to the same thing) on pointers to the relevant type, and the code that the compiler generates for these pointer arithmetic operations is often more efficient for efficiently-aligned types than for other types.

Note that the effectiveness of **aligned** attributes may be limited by inherent limitations in your linker. On many systems, the linker is only able to arrange for variables to be aligned up to a certain maximum alignment. (For some linkers, the maximum supported alignment may be very very small.) If your linker is only able to align variables up to a maximum of 8-byte alignment, then specifying **aligned(16)** in an **__attribute__** still only provides you with 8-byte alignment. See your linker documentation for further information.

The **aligned** attribute can only increase alignment. Alignment can be decreased by specifying the **packed** attribute. See below.

bnd_variable_size

When applied to a structure field, this attribute tells Pointer Bounds Checker that the size of this field should not be computed using static type information. It may be used to mark variably-sized static array fields placed at the end of a structure.

```
struct S
{
  int size;
  char data[1];
}
S *p = (S *)malloc (sizeof(S) + 100);
p->data[10] = 0; //Bounds violation
```

By using an attribute for the field we may avoid unwanted bound violation checks:

```
struct S
{
  int size;
```

```
      char data[1] __attribute__((bnd_variable_size));
    }
    S *p = (S *)malloc (sizeof(S) + 100);
    p->data[10] = 0; //OK
```

`deprecated`

`deprecated (`*msg*`)`

>The `deprecated` attribute results in a warning if the type is used anywhere in the source file. This is useful when identifying types that are expected to be removed in a future version of a program. If possible, the warning also includes the location of the declaration of the deprecated type, to enable users to easily find further information about why the type is deprecated, or what they should do instead. Note that the warnings only occur for uses and then only if the type is being applied to an identifier that itself is not being declared as deprecated.

>```
>typedef int T1 __attribute__ ((deprecated));
>T1 x;
>typedef T1 T2;
>T2 y;
>typedef T1 T3 __attribute__ ((deprecated));
>T3 z __attribute__ ((deprecated));
>```

>results in a warning on line 2 and 3 but not lines 4, 5, or 6. No warning is issued for line 4 because T2 is not explicitly deprecated. Line 5 has no warning because T3 is explicitly deprecated. Similarly for line 6. The optional *msg* argument, which must be a string, is printed in the warning if present.

>The `deprecated` attribute can also be used for functions and variables (see Section 6.31 [Function Attributes], page 427, see Section 6.32 [Variable Attributes], page 471.)

`designated_init`

>This attribute may only be applied to structure types. It indicates that any initialization of an object of this type must use designated initializers rather than positional initializers. The intent of this attribute is to allow the programmer to indicate that a structure's layout may change, and that therefore relying on positional initialization will result in future breakage.

>GCC emits warnings based on this attribute by default; use '`-Wno-designated-init`' to suppress them.

`may_alias`

>Accesses through pointers to types with this attribute are not subject to type-based alias analysis, but are instead assumed to be able to alias any other type of objects. In the context of section 6.5 paragraph 7 of the C99 standard, an lvalue expression dereferencing such a pointer is treated like having a character type. See '`-fstrict-aliasing`' for more information on aliasing issues. This extension exists to support some vector APIs, in which pointers to one vector type are permitted to alias pointers to a different vector type.

>Note that an object of a type with this attribute does not have any special semantics.

>Example of use:

>```
>typedef short __attribute__((__may_alias__)) short_a;
>```

```
                  int
                  main (void)
                  {
                    int a = 0x12345678;
                    short_a *b = (short_a *) &a;

                    b[1] = 0;

                    if (a == 0x12345678)
                      abort();

                    exit(0);
                  }
```

If you replaced `short_a` with `short` in the variable declaration, the above program would abort when compiled with '`-fstrict-aliasing`', which is on by default at '`-O2`' or above.

packed   This attribute, attached to `struct` or `union` type definition, specifies that each member (other than zero-width bit-fields) of the structure or union is placed to minimize the memory required. When attached to an `enum` definition, it indicates that the smallest integral type should be used.

Specifying the `packed` attribute for `struct` and `union` types is equivalent to specifying the `packed` attribute on each of the structure or union members. Specifying the '`-fshort-enums`' flag on the command line is equivalent to specifying the `packed` attribute on all `enum` definitions.

In the following example `struct my_packed_struct`'s members are packed closely together, but the internal layout of its `s` member is not packed—to do that, `struct my_unpacked_struct` needs to be packed too.

```
          struct my_unpacked_struct
           {
              char c;
              int i;
           };

          struct __attribute__ ((__packed__)) my_packed_struct
           {
              char c;
              int  i;
              struct my_unpacked_struct s;
           };
```

You may only specify the `packed` attribute attribute on the definition of an `enum`, `struct` or `union`, not on a `typedef` that does not also define the enumerated type, structure or union.

scalar_storage_order ("*endianness*")

When attached to a `union` or a `struct`, this attribute sets the storage order, aka endianness, of the scalar fields of the type, as well as the array fields whose component is scalar. The supported endiannesses are `big-endian` and `little-endian`. The attribute has no effects on fields which are themselves a `union`, a `struct` or an array whose component is a `union` or a `struct`, and it is possible for these fields to have a different scalar storage order than the enclosing type.

This attribute is supported only for targets that use a uniform default scalar storage order (fortunately, most of them), i.e. targets that store the scalars either all in big-endian or all in little-endian.

Additional restrictions are enforced for types with the reverse scalar storage order with regard to the scalar storage order of the target:

- Taking the address of a scalar field of a `union` or a `struct` with reverse scalar storage order is not permitted and yields an error.

- Taking the address of an array field, whose component is scalar, of a `union` or a `struct` with reverse scalar storage order is permitted but yields a warning, unless '`-Wno-scalar-storage-order`' is specified.

- Taking the address of a `union` or a `struct` with reverse scalar storage order is permitted.

These restrictions exist because the storage order attribute is lost when the address of a scalar or the address of an array with scalar component is taken, so storing indirectly through this address generally does not work. The second case is nevertheless allowed to be able to perform a block copy from or to the array.

Moreover, the use of type punning or aliasing to toggle the storage order is not supported; that is to say, a given scalar object cannot be accessed through distinct types that assign a different storage order to it.

`transparent_union`

This attribute, attached to a `union` type definition, indicates that any function parameter having that union type causes calls to that function to be treated in a special way.

First, the argument corresponding to a transparent union type can be of any type in the union; no cast is required. Also, if the union contains a pointer type, the corresponding argument can be a null pointer constant or a void pointer expression; and if the union contains a void pointer type, the corresponding argument can be any pointer expression. If the union member type is a pointer, qualifiers like `const` on the referenced type must be respected, just as with normal pointer conversions.

Second, the argument is passed to the function using the calling conventions of the first member of the transparent union, not the calling conventions of the union itself. All members of the union must have the same machine representation; this is necessary for this argument passing to work properly.

Transparent unions are designed for library functions that have multiple interfaces for compatibility reasons. For example, suppose the `wait` function must accept either a value of type `int *` to comply with POSIX, or a value of type `union wait *` to comply with the 4.1BSD interface. If `wait`'s parameter were `void *`, `wait` would accept both kinds of arguments, but it would also accept any other pointer type and this would make argument type checking less useful. Instead, `<sys/wait.h>` might define the interface as follows:

```
typedef union __attribute__ ((__transparent_union__))
  {
    int *__ip;
```

```
         union wait *__up;
       } wait_status_ptr_t;

       pid_t wait (wait_status_ptr_t);
```

This interface allows either `int *` or `union wait *` arguments to be passed, using the `int *` calling convention. The program can call `wait` with arguments of either type:

```
int w1 () { int w; return wait (&w); }
int w2 () { union wait w; return wait (&w); }
```

With this interface, `wait`'s implementation might look like this:

```
pid_t wait (wait_status_ptr_t p)
{
  return waitpid (-1, p.__ip, 0);
}
```

`unused`   When attached to a type (including a `union` or a `struct`), this attribute means that variables of that type are meant to appear possibly unused. GCC does not produce a warning for any variables of that type, even if the variable appears to do nothing. This is often the case with lock or thread classes, which are usually defined and then not referenced, but contain constructors and destructors that have nontrivial bookkeeping functions.

`visibility`

In C++, attribute visibility (see Section 6.31 [Function Attributes], page 427) can also be applied to class, struct, union and enum types. Unlike other type attributes, the attribute must appear between the initial keyword and the name of the type; it cannot appear after the body of the type.

Note that the type visibility is applied to vague linkage entities associated with the class (vtable, typeinfo node, etc.). In particular, if a class is thrown as an exception in one shared object and caught in another, the class must have default visibility. Otherwise the two shared objects are unable to use the same typeinfo node and exception handling will break.

To specify multiple attributes, separate them by commas within the double parentheses: for example, '`__attribute__ ((aligned (16), packed))`'.

6.33.2 ARM Type Attributes

On those ARM targets that support `dllimport` (such as Symbian OS), you can use the `notshared` attribute to indicate that the virtual table and other similar data for a class should not be exported from a DLL. For example:

```
class __declspec(notshared) C {
public:
  __declspec(dllimport) C();
  virtual void f();
}

__declspec(dllexport)
C::C() {}
```

In this code, `C::C` is exported from the current DLL, but the virtual table for `C` is not exported. (You can use `__attribute__` instead of `__declspec` if you prefer, but most Symbian OS code uses `__declspec`.)

6.33.3 MeP Type Attributes

Many of the MeP variable attributes may be applied to types as well. Specifically, the `based`, `tiny`, `near`, and `far` attributes may be applied to either. The `io` and `cb` attributes may not be applied to types.

6.33.4 PowerPC Type Attributes

Three attributes currently are defined for PowerPC configurations: `altivec`, `ms_struct` and `gcc_struct`.

For full documentation of the `ms_struct` and `gcc_struct` attributes please see the documentation in Section 6.33.6 [x86 Type Attributes], page 488.

The `altivec` attribute allows one to declare AltiVec vector data types supported by the AltiVec Programming Interface Manual. The attribute requires an argument to specify one of three vector types: `vector__`, `pixel__` (always followed by unsigned short), and `bool__` (always followed by unsigned).

```
__attribute__((altivec(vector__)))
__attribute__((altivec(pixel__))) unsigned short
__attribute__((altivec(bool__))) unsigned
```

These attributes mainly are intended to support the `__vector`, `__pixel`, and `__bool` AltiVec keywords.

6.33.5 SPU Type Attributes

The SPU supports the `spu_vector` attribute for types. This attribute allows one to declare vector data types supported by the Sony/Toshiba/IBM SPU Language Extensions Specification. It is intended to support the `__vector` keyword.

6.33.6 x86 Type Attributes

Two attributes are currently defined for x86 configurations: `ms_struct` and `gcc_struct`.

`ms_struct`
`gcc_struct`

>   If `packed` is used on a structure, or if bit-fields are used it may be that the Microsoft ABI packs them differently than GCC normally packs them. Particularly when moving packed data between functions compiled with GCC and the native Microsoft compiler (either via function call or as data in a file), it may be necessary to access either format.
>
>   The `ms_struct` and `gcc_struct` attributes correspond to the '-mms-bitfields' and '-mno-ms-bitfields' command-line options, respectively; see Section 3.18.54 [x86 Options], page 355, for details of how structure layout is affected. See Section 6.32.15 [x86 Variable Attributes], page 481, for information about the corresponding attributes on variables.

6.34 Label Attributes

GCC allows attributes to be set on C labels. See Section 6.37 [Attribute Syntax], page 490, for details of the exact syntax for using attributes. Other attributes are available for functions (see Section 6.31 [Function Attributes], page 427), variables (see Section 6.32 [Variable Attributes], page 471), enumerators (see Section 6.35 [Enumerator Attributes], page 489), statements (see Section 6.36 [Statement Attributes], page 490), and for types (see Section 6.33 [Type Attributes], page 482).

This example uses the `cold` label attribute to indicate the `ErrorHandling` branch is unlikely to be taken and that the `ErrorHandling` label is unused:

```
asm goto ("some asm" : : : : NoError);

/* This branch (the fall-through from the asm) is less commonly used */
ErrorHandling:
    __attribute__((cold, unused)); /* Semi-colon is required here */
    printf("error\n");
    return 0;

NoError:
    printf("no error\n");
    return 1;
```

unused   This feature is intended for program-generated code that may contain unused labels, but which is compiled with '-Wall'. It is not normally appropriate to use in it human-written code, though it could be useful in cases where the code that jumps to the label is contained within an `#ifdef` conditional.

hot   The `hot` attribute on a label is used to inform the compiler that the path following the label is more likely than paths that are not so annotated. This attribute is used in cases where `__builtin_expect` cannot be used, for instance with computed goto or `asm goto`.

cold   The `cold` attribute on labels is used to inform the compiler that the path following the label is unlikely to be executed. This attribute is used in cases where `__builtin_expect` cannot be used, for instance with computed goto or `asm goto`.

6.35 Enumerator Attributes

GCC allows attributes to be set on enumerators. See Section 6.37 [Attribute Syntax], page 490, for details of the exact syntax for using attributes. Other attributes are available for functions (see Section 6.31 [Function Attributes], page 427), variables (see Section 6.32 [Variable Attributes], page 471), labels (see Section 6.34 [Label Attributes], page 488), statements (see Section 6.36 [Statement Attributes], page 490), and for types (see Section 6.33 [Type Attributes], page 482).

This example uses the `deprecated` enumerator attribute to indicate the `oldval` enumerator is deprecated:

```
enum E {
  oldval __attribute__((deprecated)),
  newval
};

int
fn (void)
{
  return oldval;
}
```

deprecated

> The deprecated attribute results in a warning if the enumerator is used anywhere in the source file. This is useful when identifying enumerators that are expected to be removed in a future version of a program. The warning also includes the location of the declaration of the deprecated enumerator, to enable users to easily find further information about why the enumerator is deprecated, or what they should do instead. Note that the warnings only occurs for uses.

6.36 Statement Attributes

GCC allows attributes to be set on null statements. See Section 6.37 [Attribute Syntax], page 490, for details of the exact syntax for using attributes. Other attributes are available for functions (see Section 6.31 [Function Attributes], page 427), variables (see Section 6.32 [Variable Attributes], page 471), labels (see Section 6.34 [Label Attributes], page 488), enumerators (see Section 6.35 [Enumerator Attributes], page 489), and for types (see Section 6.33 [Type Attributes], page 482).

This example uses the fallthrough statement attribute to indicate that the '-Wimplicit-fallthrough' warning should not be emitted:

```
switch (cond)
  {
  case 1:
    bar (1);
    __attribute__((fallthrough));
  case 2:
    ...
  }
```

fallthrough

> The fallthrough attribute with a null statement serves as a fallthrough statement. It hints to the compiler that a statement that falls through to another case label, or user-defined label in a switch statement is intentional and thus the '-Wimplicit-fallthrough' warning must not trigger. The fallthrough attribute may appear at most once in each attribute list, and may not be mixed with other attributes. It can only be used in a switch statement (the compiler will issue an error otherwise), after a preceding statement and before a logically succeeding case label, or user-defined label.

6.37 Attribute Syntax

This section describes the syntax with which __attribute__ may be used, and the constructs to which attribute specifiers bind, for the C language. Some details may vary for C++ and Objective-C. Because of infelicities in the grammar for attributes, some forms described here may not be successfully parsed in all cases.

There are some problems with the semantics of attributes in C++. For example, there are no manglings for attributes, although they may affect code generation, so problems may arise when attributed types are used in conjunction with templates or overloading. Similarly, typeid does not distinguish between types with different attributes. Support for attributes in C++ may be restricted in future to attributes on declarations only, but not on nested declarators.

See Section 6.31 [Function Attributes], page 427, for details of the semantics of attributes applying to functions. See Section 6.32 [Variable Attributes], page 471, for details of the semantics of attributes applying to variables. See Section 6.33 [Type Attributes], page 482, for details of the semantics of attributes applying to structure, union and enumerated types. See Section 6.34 [Label Attributes], page 488, for details of the semantics of attributes applying to labels. See Section 6.35 [Enumerator Attributes], page 489, for details of the semantics of attributes applying to enumerators. See Section 6.36 [Statement Attributes], page 490, for details of the semantics of attributes applying to statements.

An *attribute specifier* is of the form `__attribute__ ((attribute-list))`. An *attribute list* is a possibly empty comma-separated sequence of *attributes*, where each attribute is one of the following:

- Empty. Empty attributes are ignored.

- An attribute name (which may be an identifier such as `unused`, or a reserved word such as `const`).

- An attribute name followed by a parenthesized list of parameters for the attribute. These parameters take one of the following forms:

  - An identifier. For example, `mode` attributes use this form.

  - An identifier followed by a comma and a non-empty comma-separated list of expressions. For example, `format` attributes use this form.

  - A possibly empty comma-separated list of expressions. For example, `format_arg` attributes use this form with the list being a single integer constant expression, and `alias` attributes use this form with the list being a single string constant.

An *attribute specifier list* is a sequence of one or more attribute specifiers, not separated by any other tokens.

You may optionally specify attribute names with '`__`' preceding and following the name. This allows you to use them in header files without being concerned about a possible macro of the same name. For example, you may use the attribute name `__noreturn__` instead of `noreturn`.

Label Attributes

In GNU C, an attribute specifier list may appear after the colon following a label, other than a `case` or `default` label. GNU C++ only permits attributes on labels if the attribute specifier is immediately followed by a semicolon (i.e., the label applies to an empty statement). If the semicolon is missing, C++ label attributes are ambiguous, as it is permissible for a declaration, which could begin with an attribute list, to be labelled in C++. Declarations cannot be labelled in C90 or C99, so the ambiguity does not arise there.

Enumerator Attributes

In GNU C, an attribute specifier list may appear as part of an enumerator. The attribute goes after the enumeration constant, before `=`, if present. The optional attribute in the enumerator appertains to the enumeration constant. It is not possible to place the attribute after the constant expression, if present.

Statement Attributes

In GNU C, an attribute specifier list may appear as part of a null statement. The attribute goes before the semicolon.

Type Attributes

An attribute specifier list may appear as part of a `struct`, `union` or `enum` specifier. It may go either immediately after the `struct`, `union` or `enum` keyword, or after the closing brace. The former syntax is preferred. Where attribute specifiers follow the closing brace, they are considered to relate to the structure, union or enumerated type defined, not to any enclosing declaration the type specifier appears in, and the type defined is not complete until after the attribute specifiers.

All other attributes

Otherwise, an attribute specifier appears as part of a declaration, counting declarations of unnamed parameters and type names, and relates to that declaration (which may be nested in another declaration, for example in the case of a parameter declaration), or to a particular declarator within a declaration. Where an attribute specifier is applied to a parameter declared as a function or an array, it should apply to the function or array rather than the pointer to which the parameter is implicitly converted, but this is not yet correctly implemented.

Any list of specifiers and qualifiers at the start of a declaration may contain attribute specifiers, whether or not such a list may in that context contain storage class specifiers. (Some attributes, however, are essentially in the nature of storage class specifiers, and only make sense where storage class specifiers may be used; for example, `section`.) There is one necessary limitation to this syntax: the first old-style parameter declaration in a function definition cannot begin with an attribute specifier, because such an attribute applies to the function instead by syntax described below (which, however, is not yet implemented in this case). In some other cases, attribute specifiers are permitted by this grammar but not yet supported by the compiler. All attribute specifiers in this place relate to the declaration as a whole. In the obsolescent usage where a type of `int` is implied by the absence of type specifiers, such a list of specifiers and qualifiers may be an attribute specifier list with no other specifiers or qualifiers.

At present, the first parameter in a function prototype must have some type specifier that is not an attribute specifier; this resolves an ambiguity in the interpretation of `void f(int (__attribute__((foo)) x))`, but is subject to change. At present, if the parentheses of a function declarator contain only attributes then those attributes are ignored, rather than yielding an error or warning or implying a single parameter of type int, but this is subject to change.

An attribute specifier list may appear immediately before a declarator (other than the first) in a comma-separated list of declarators in a declaration of more than one identifier using a single list of specifiers and qualifiers. Such attribute specifiers apply only to the identifier before whose declarator they appear. For example, in

```
__attribute__((noreturn)) void d0 (void),
    __attribute__((format(printf, 1, 2))) d1 (const char *, ...),
    d2 (void);
```

the `noreturn` attribute applies to all the functions declared; the `format` attribute only applies to `d1`.

An attribute specifier list may appear immediately before the comma, `=` or semicolon terminating the declaration of an identifier other than a function definition. Such attribute specifiers apply to the declared object or function. Where an assembler name for an object or function is specified (see Section 6.45.4 [Asm Labels], page 546), the attribute must follow the `asm` specification.

An attribute specifier list may, in future, be permitted to appear after the declarator in a function definition (before any old-style parameter declarations or the function body).

Attribute specifiers may be mixed with type qualifiers appearing inside the `[]` of a parameter array declarator, in the C99 construct by which such qualifiers are applied to the pointer to which the array is implicitly converted. Such attribute specifiers apply to the pointer, not to the array, but at present this is not implemented and they are ignored.

An attribute specifier list may appear at the start of a nested declarator. At present, there are some limitations in this usage: the attributes correctly apply to the declarator, but for most individual attributes the semantics this implies are not implemented. When attribute specifiers follow the `*` of a pointer declarator, they may be mixed with any type qualifiers present. The following describes the formal semantics of this syntax. It makes the most sense if you are familiar with the formal specification of declarators in the ISO C standard.

Consider (as in C99 subclause 6.7.5 paragraph 4) a declaration `T D1`, where `T` contains declaration specifiers that specify a type *Type* (such as `int`) and `D1` is a declarator that contains an identifier *ident*. The type specified for *ident* for derived declarators whose type does not include an attribute specifier is as in the ISO C standard.

If `D1` has the form (*attribute-specifier-list* D), and the declaration `T D` specifies the type "*derived-declarator-type-list Type*" for *ident*, then `T D1` specifies the type "*derived-declarator-type-list attribute-specifier-list Type*" for *ident*.

If `D1` has the form `*` *type-qualifier-and-attribute-specifier-list* D, and the declaration `T D` specifies the type "*derived-declarator-type-list Type*" for *ident*, then `T D1` specifies the type "*derived-declarator-type-list type-qualifier-and-attribute-specifier-list* pointer to *Type*" for *ident*.

For example,

```
void (__attribute__((noreturn)) ****f) (void);
```

specifies the type "pointer to pointer to pointer to pointer to non-returning function returning `void`". As another example,

```
char *__attribute__((aligned(8))) *f;
```

specifies the type "pointer to 8-byte-aligned pointer to `char`". Note again that this does not work with most attributes; for example, the usage of '`aligned`' and '`noreturn`' attributes given above is not yet supported.

For compatibility with existing code written for compiler versions that did not implement attributes on nested declarators, some laxity is allowed in the placing of attributes. If an attribute that only applies to types is applied to a declaration, it is treated as applying to the type of that declaration. If an attribute that only applies to declarations is applied to the type of a declaration, it is treated as applying to that declaration; and, for compatibility with code placing the attributes immediately before the identifier declared, such an attribute applied to a function return type is treated as applying to the function type, and such an attribute applied to an array element type is treated as applying to the array type. If an attribute that only applies to function types is applied to a pointer-to-function type, it is treated as applying to the pointer target type; if such an attribute is applied to a function return type that is not a pointer-to-function type, it is treated as applying to the function type.

6.38 Prototypes and Old-Style Function Definitions

GNU C extends ISO C to allow a function prototype to override a later old-style non-prototype definition. Consider the following example:

```
/* Use prototypes unless the compiler is old-fashioned.  */
#ifdef __STDC__
#define P(x) x
#else
#define P(x) ()
#endif

/* Prototype function declaration.  */
int isroot P((uid_t));

/* Old-style function definition.  */
int
isroot (x)   /* ??? lossage here ??? */
     uid_t x;
{
  return x == 0;
}
```

Suppose the type `uid_t` happens to be `short`. ISO C does not allow this example, because subword arguments in old-style non-prototype definitions are promoted. Therefore in this example the function definition's argument is really an `int`, which does not match the prototype argument type of `short`.

This restriction of ISO C makes it hard to write code that is portable to traditional C compilers, because the programmer does not know whether the `uid_t` type is `short`, `int`, or `long`. Therefore, in cases like these GNU C allows a prototype to override a later old-style definition. More precisely, in GNU C, a function prototype argument type overrides the argument type specified by a later old-style definition if the former type is the same as the latter type before promotion. Thus in GNU C the above example is equivalent to the following:

```
int isroot (uid_t);

int
isroot (uid_t x)
{
  return x == 0;
}
```

GNU C++ does not support old-style function definitions, so this extension is irrelevant.

6.39 C++ Style Comments

In GNU C, you may use C++ style comments, which start with '//' and continue until the end of the line. Many other C implementations allow such comments, and they are included in the 1999 C standard. However, C++ style comments are not recognized if you specify an '-std' option specifying a version of ISO C before C99, or '-ansi' (equivalent to '-std=c90').

6.40 Dollar Signs in Identifier Names

In GNU C, you may normally use dollar signs in identifier names. This is because many traditional C implementations allow such identifiers. However, dollar signs in identifiers are not supported on a few target machines, typically because the target assembler does not allow them.

6.41 The Character ESC in Constants

You can use the sequence '\e' in a string or character constant to stand for the ASCII character ESC.

6.42 Inquiring on Alignment of Types or Variables

The keyword `__alignof__` allows you to inquire about how an object is aligned, or the minimum alignment usually required by a type. Its syntax is just like `sizeof`.

For example, if the target machine requires a `double` value to be aligned on an 8-byte boundary, then `__alignof__ (double)` is 8. This is true on many RISC machines. On more traditional machine designs, `__alignof__ (double)` is 4 or even 2.

Some machines never actually require alignment; they allow reference to any data type even at an odd address. For these machines, `__alignof__` reports the smallest alignment that GCC gives the data type, usually as mandated by the target ABI.

If the operand of `__alignof__` is an lvalue rather than a type, its value is the required alignment for its type, taking into account any minimum alignment specified with GCC's `__attribute__` extension (see Section 6.32 [Variable Attributes], page 471). For example, after this declaration:

```
struct foo { int x; char y; } foo1;
```

the value of `__alignof__ (foo1.y)` is 1, even though its actual alignment is probably 2 or 4, the same as `__alignof__ (int)`.

It is an error to ask for the alignment of an incomplete type.

6.43 An Inline Function is As Fast As a Macro

By declaring a function inline, you can direct GCC to make calls to that function faster. One way GCC can achieve this is to integrate that function's code into the code for its callers. This makes execution faster by eliminating the function-call overhead; in addition, if any of the actual argument values are constant, their known values may permit simplifications at compile time so that not all of the inline function's code needs to be included. The effect on code size is less predictable; object code may be larger or smaller with function inlining, depending on the particular case. You can also direct GCC to try to integrate all "simple enough" functions into their callers with the option '-finline-functions'.

GCC implements three different semantics of declaring a function inline. One is available with '-std=gnu89' or '-fgnu89-inline' or when gnu_inline attribute is present on all inline declarations, another when '-std=c99', '-std=c11', '-std=gnu99' or '-std=gnu11' (without '-fgnu89-inline'), and the third is used when compiling C++.

To declare a function inline, use the inline keyword in its declaration, like this:

```
static inline int
inc (int *a)
{
  return (*a)++;
}
```

If you are writing a header file to be included in ISO C90 programs, write __inline__ instead of inline. See Section 6.46 [Alternate Keywords], page 549.

The three types of inlining behave similarly in two important cases: when the inline keyword is used on a static function, like the example above, and when a function is first declared without using the inline keyword and then is defined with inline, like this:

```
extern int inc (int *a);
inline int
inc (int *a)
{
  return (*a)++;
}
```

In both of these common cases, the program behaves the same as if you had not used the inline keyword, except for its speed.

When a function is both inline and static, if all calls to the function are integrated into the caller, and the function's address is never used, then the function's own assembler code is never referenced. In this case, GCC does not actually output assembler code for the function, unless you specify the option '-fkeep-inline-functions'. If there is a nonintegrated call, then the function is compiled to assembler code as usual. The function must also be compiled as usual if the program refers to its address, because that can't be inlined.

Note that certain usages in a function definition can make it unsuitable for inline substitution. Among these usages are: variadic functions, use of alloca, use of computed goto (see Section 6.3 [Labels as Values], page 405), use of nonlocal goto, use of nested functions, use of setjmp, use of __builtin_longjmp and use of __builtin_return or __builtin_apply_args. Using '-Winline' warns when a function marked inline could not be substituted, and gives the reason for the failure.

As required by ISO C++, GCC considers member functions defined within the body of a class to be marked inline even if they are not explicitly declared with the inline keyword. You can override this with '-fno-default-inline'; see Section 3.5 [Options Controlling C++ Dialect], page 40.

GCC does not inline any functions when not optimizing unless you specify the 'always_inline' attribute for the function, like this:

```
/* Prototype.  */
inline void foo (const char) __attribute__((always_inline));
```

The remainder of this section is specific to GNU C90 inlining.

When an inline function is not `static`, then the compiler must assume that there may be calls from other source files; since a global symbol can be defined only once in any program, the function must not be defined in the other source files, so the calls therein cannot be integrated. Therefore, a non-`static` inline function is always compiled on its own in the usual fashion.

If you specify both `inline` and `extern` in the function definition, then the definition is used only for inlining. In no case is the function compiled on its own, not even if you refer to its address explicitly. Such an address becomes an external reference, as if you had only declared the function, and had not defined it.

This combination of `inline` and `extern` has almost the effect of a macro. The way to use it is to put a function definition in a header file with these keywords, and put another copy of the definition (lacking `inline` and `extern`) in a library file. The definition in the header file causes most calls to the function to be inlined. If any uses of the function remain, they refer to the single copy in the library.

6.44 When is a Volatile Object Accessed?

C has the concept of volatile objects. These are normally accessed by pointers and used for accessing hardware or inter-thread communication. The standard encourages compilers to refrain from optimizations concerning accesses to volatile objects, but leaves it implementation defined as to what constitutes a volatile access. The minimum requirement is that at a sequence point all previous accesses to volatile objects have stabilized and no subsequent accesses have occurred. Thus an implementation is free to reorder and combine volatile accesses that occur between sequence points, but cannot do so for accesses across a sequence point. The use of volatile does not allow you to violate the restriction on updating objects multiple times between two sequence points.

Accesses to non-volatile objects are not ordered with respect to volatile accesses. You cannot use a volatile object as a memory barrier to order a sequence of writes to non-volatile memory. For instance:

```
int *ptr = something;
volatile int vobj;
*ptr = something;
vobj = 1;
```

Unless *ptr and vobj can be aliased, it is not guaranteed that the write to *ptr occurs by the time the update of vobj happens. If you need this guarantee, you must use a stronger memory barrier such as:

```
int *ptr = something;
volatile int vobj;
*ptr = something;
asm volatile ("" : : : "memory");
vobj = 1;
```

A scalar volatile object is read when it is accessed in a void context:

```
volatile int *src = somevalue;
*src;
```

Such expressions are rvalues, and GCC implements this as a read of the volatile object being pointed to.

Assignments are also expressions and have an rvalue. However when assigning to a scalar volatile, the volatile object is not reread, regardless of whether the assignment expression's rvalue is used or not. If the assignment's rvalue is used, the value is that assigned to the volatile object. For instance, there is no read of *vobj* in all the following cases:

```
int obj;
volatile int vobj;
vobj = something;
obj = vobj = something;
obj ? vobj = onething : vobj = anotherthing;
obj = (something, vobj = anotherthing);
```

If you need to read the volatile object after an assignment has occurred, you must use a separate expression with an intervening sequence point.

As bit-fields are not individually addressable, volatile bit-fields may be implicitly read when written to, or when adjacent bit-fields are accessed. Bit-field operations may be optimized such that adjacent bit-fields are only partially accessed, if they straddle a storage unit boundary. For these reasons it is unwise to use volatile bit-fields to access hardware.

6.45 How to Use Inline Assembly Language in C Code

The **asm** keyword allows you to embed assembler instructions within C code. GCC provides two forms of inline **asm** statements. A *basic* **asm** statement is one with no operands (see Section 6.45.1 [Basic Asm], page 498), while an *extended* **asm** statement (see Section 6.45.2 [Extended Asm], page 500) includes one or more operands. The extended form is preferred for mixing C and assembly language within a function, but to include assembly language at top level you must use basic **asm**.

You can also use the **asm** keyword to override the assembler name for a C symbol, or to place a C variable in a specific register.

6.45.1 Basic Asm — Assembler Instructions Without Operands

A basic **asm** statement has the following syntax:

```
asm [ volatile ] ( AssemblerInstructions )
```

The **asm** keyword is a GNU extension. When writing code that can be compiled with '-ansi' and the various '-std' options, use __asm__ instead of asm (see Section 6.46 [Alternate Keywords], page 549).

Qualifiers

volatile   The optional **volatile** qualifier has no effect. All basic **asm** blocks are implicitly volatile.

Parameters

AssemblerInstructions

This is a literal string that specifies the assembler code. The string can contain any instructions recognized by the assembler, including directives. GCC does not parse the assembler instructions themselves and does not know what they mean or even whether they are valid assembler input.

You may place multiple assembler instructions together in a single **asm** string, separated by the characters normally used in assembly code for the system. A combination that works in most places is a newline to break the line, plus a tab character (written as '\n\t'). Some assemblers allow semicolons as a line separator. However, note that some assembler dialects use semicolons to start a comment.

Remarks

Using extended **asm** (see Section 6.45.2 [Extended Asm], page 500) typically produces smaller, safer, and more efficient code, and in most cases it is a better solution than basic **asm**. However, there are two situations where only basic **asm** can be used:

- Extended **asm** statements have to be inside a C function, so to write inline assembly language at file scope ("top-level"), outside of C functions, you must use basic **asm**. You can use this technique to emit assembler directives, define assembly language macros that can be invoked elsewhere in the file, or write entire functions in assembly language.

- Functions declared with the **naked** attribute also require basic **asm** (see Section 6.31 [Function Attributes], page 427).

Safely accessing C data and calling functions from basic **asm** is more complex than it may appear. To access C data, it is better to use extended **asm**.

Do not expect a sequence of **asm** statements to remain perfectly consecutive after compilation. If certain instructions need to remain consecutive in the output, put them in a single multi-instruction **asm** statement. Note that GCC's optimizers can move **asm** statements relative to other code, including across jumps.

asm statements may not perform jumps into other **asm** statements. GCC does not know about these jumps, and therefore cannot take account of them when deciding how to optimize. Jumps from **asm** to C labels are only supported in extended **asm**.

Under certain circumstances, GCC may duplicate (or remove duplicates of) your assembly code when optimizing. This can lead to unexpected duplicate symbol errors during compilation if your assembly code defines symbols or labels.

Warning: The C standards do not specify semantics for **asm**, making it a potential source of incompatibilities between compilers. These incompatibilities may not produce compiler warnings/errors.

GCC does not parse basic **asm**'s *AssemblerInstructions*, which means there is no way to communicate to the compiler what is happening inside them. GCC has no visibility of symbols in the **asm** and may discard them as unreferenced. It also does not know about side effects of the assembler code, such as modifications to memory or registers. Unlike some compilers, GCC assumes that no changes to general purpose registers occur. This assumption may change in a future release.

To avoid complications from future changes to the semantics and the compatibility issues between compilers, consider replacing basic **asm** with extended **asm**. See How to convert from basic asm to extended asm for information about how to perform this conversion.

The compiler copies the assembler instructions in a basic **asm** verbatim to the assembly language output file, without processing dialects or any of the '%' operators that are available with extended **asm**. This results in minor differences between basic **asm** strings and extended **asm** templates. For example, to refer to registers you might use '%eax' in basic **asm** and '%%eax' in extended **asm**.

On targets such as x86 that support multiple assembler dialects, all basic **asm** blocks use the assembler dialect specified by the '-masm' command-line option (see Section 3.18.54 [x86 Options], page 355). Basic **asm** provides no mechanism to provide different assembler strings for different dialects.

For basic **asm** with non-empty assembler string GCC assumes the assembler block does not change any general purpose registers, but it may read or write any globally accessible variable.

Here is an example of basic **asm** for i386:

```
/* Note that this code will not compile with -masm=intel */
#define DebugBreak() asm("int $3")
```

6.45.2 Extended Asm - Assembler Instructions with C Expression Operands

With extended **asm** you can read and write C variables from assembler and perform jumps from assembler code to C labels. Extended **asm** syntax uses colons (':') to delimit the operand parameters after the assembler template:

```
asm [volatile] ( AssemblerTemplate
                 : OutputOperands
                 [ : InputOperands
                 [ : Clobbers ] ])

asm [volatile] goto ( AssemblerTemplate
                      :
                      : InputOperands
                      : Clobbers
                      : GotoLabels)
```

The **asm** keyword is a GNU extension. When writing code that can be compiled with '-ansi' and the various '-std' options, use __asm__ instead of **asm** (see Section 6.46 [Alternate Keywords], page 549).

Qualifiers

volatile   The typical use of extended **asm** statements is to manipulate input values to produce output values. However, your **asm** statements may also produce side effects. If so, you may need to use the **volatile** qualifier to disable certain optimizations. See [Volatile], page 501.

goto   This qualifier informs the compiler that the **asm** statement may perform a jump to one of the labels listed in the *GotoLabels*. See [GotoLabels], page 511.

Parameters

AssemblerTemplate
            This is a literal string that is the template for the assembler code. It is a combination of fixed text and tokens that refer to the input, output, and goto parameters. See [AssemblerTemplate], page 503.

OutputOperands

> A comma-separated list of the C variables modified by the instructions in the *AssemblerTemplate*. An empty list is permitted. See [OutputOperands], page 505.

InputOperands

> A comma-separated list of C expressions read by the instructions in the *AssemblerTemplate*. An empty list is permitted. See [InputOperands], page 509.

Clobbers A comma-separated list of registers or other values changed by the *AssemblerTemplate*, beyond those listed as outputs. An empty list is permitted. See [Clobbers], page 510.

GotoLabels

> When you are using the `goto` form of `asm`, this section contains the list of all C labels to which the code in the *AssemblerTemplate* may jump. See [GotoLabels], page 511.
>
> `asm` statements may not perform jumps into other `asm` statements, only to the listed *GotoLabels*. GCC's optimizers do not know about other jumps; therefore they cannot take account of them when deciding how to optimize.

The total number of input + output + goto operands is limited to 30.

Remarks

The `asm` statement allows you to include assembly instructions directly within C code. This may help you to maximize performance in time-sensitive code or to access assembly instructions that are not readily available to C programs.

Note that extended `asm` statements must be inside a function. Only basic `asm` may be outside functions (see Section 6.45.1 [Basic Asm], page 498). Functions declared with the **naked** attribute also require basic `asm` (see Section 6.31 [Function Attributes], page 427).

While the uses of `asm` are many and varied, it may help to think of an `asm` statement as a series of low-level instructions that convert input parameters to output parameters. So a simple (if not particularly useful) example for i386 using `asm` might look like this:

```
int src = 1;
int dst;

asm ("mov %1, %0\n\t"
    "add $1, %0"
    : "=r" (dst)
    : "r" (src));

printf("%d\n", dst);
```

This code copies `src` to `dst` and add 1 to `dst`.

6.45.2.1 Volatile

GCC's optimizers sometimes discard `asm` statements if they determine there is no need for the output variables. Also, the optimizers may move code out of loops if they believe that the code will always return the same result (i.e. none of its input values change between calls). Using the `volatile` qualifier disables these optimizations. `asm` statements that have no output operands, including `asm goto` statements, are implicitly volatile.

This i386 code demonstrates a case that does not use (or require) the `volatile` qualifier. If it is performing assertion checking, this code uses `asm` to perform the validation. Otherwise, `dwRes` is unreferenced by any code. As a result, the optimizers can discard the `asm` statement, which in turn removes the need for the entire `DoCheck` routine. By omitting the `volatile` qualifier when it isn't needed you allow the optimizers to produce the most efficient code possible.

```
void DoCheck(uint32_t dwSomeValue)
{
    uint32_t dwRes;

    // Assumes dwSomeValue is not zero.
    asm ("bsfl %1,%0"
      : "=r" (dwRes)
      : "r" (dwSomeValue)
      : "cc");

    assert(dwRes > 3);
}
```

The next example shows a case where the optimizers can recognize that the input (`dwSomeValue`) never changes during the execution of the function and can therefore move the `asm` outside the loop to produce more efficient code. Again, using `volatile` disables this type of optimization.

```
void do_print(uint32_t dwSomeValue)
{
    uint32_t dwRes;

    for (uint32_t x=0; x < 5; x++)
    {
        // Assumes dwSomeValue is not zero.
        asm ("bsfl %1,%0"
          : "=r" (dwRes)
          : "r" (dwSomeValue)
          : "cc");

        printf("%u: %u %u\n", x, dwSomeValue, dwRes);
    }
}
```

The following example demonstrates a case where you need to use the `volatile` qualifier. It uses the x86 `rdtsc` instruction, which reads the computer's time-stamp counter. Without the `volatile` qualifier, the optimizers might assume that the `asm` block will always return the same value and therefore optimize away the second call.

```
uint64_t msr;
```

```
asm volatile ( "rdtsc\n\t"    // Returns the time in EDX:EAX.
        "shl $32, %%rdx\n\t"  // Shift the upper bits left.
        "or %%rdx, %0"        // 'Or' in the lower bits.
        : "=a" (msr)
        :
        : "rdx");

printf("msr: %llx\n", msr);

// Do other work...

// Reprint the timestamp
asm volatile ( "rdtsc\n\t"    // Returns the time in EDX:EAX.
        "shl $32, %%rdx\n\t"  // Shift the upper bits left.
        "or %%rdx, %0"        // 'Or' in the lower bits.
        : "=a" (msr)
        :
        : "rdx");

printf("msr: %llx\n", msr);
```

GCC's optimizers do not treat this code like the non-volatile code in the earlier examples. They do not move it out of loops or omit it on the assumption that the result from a previous call is still valid.

Note that the compiler can move even volatile **asm** instructions relative to other code, including across jump instructions. For example, on many targets there is a system register that controls the rounding mode of floating-point operations. Setting it with a volatile **asm**, as in the following PowerPC example, does not work reliably.

```
asm volatile("mtfsf 255, %0" : : "f" (fpenv));
sum = x + y;
```

The compiler may move the addition back before the volatile **asm**. To make it work as expected, add an artificial dependency to the **asm** by referencing a variable in the subsequent code, for example:

```
asm volatile ("mtfsf 255,%1" : "=X" (sum) : "f" (fpenv));
sum = x + y;
```

Under certain circumstances, GCC may duplicate (or remove duplicates of) your assembly code when optimizing. This can lead to unexpected duplicate symbol errors during compilation if your asm code defines symbols or labels. Using '%=' (see [AssemblerTemplate], page 503) may help resolve this problem.

6.45.2.2 Assembler Template

An assembler template is a literal string containing assembler instructions. The compiler replaces tokens in the template that refer to inputs, outputs, and goto labels, and then outputs the resulting string to the assembler. The string can contain any instructions recognized by the assembler, including directives. GCC does not parse the assembler instructions themselves and does not know what they mean or even whether they are valid assembler input. However, it does count the statements (see Section 6.45.6 [Size of an asm], page 549).

You may place multiple assembler instructions together in a single **asm** string, separated by the characters normally used in assembly code for the system. A combination that works in most places is a newline to break the line, plus a tab character to move to the instruction field (written as '\n\t'). Some assemblers allow semicolons as a line separator. However, note that some assembler dialects use semicolons to start a comment.

Do not expect a sequence of **asm** statements to remain perfectly consecutive after compilation, even when you are using the **volatile** qualifier. If certain instructions need to remain consecutive in the output, put them in a single multi-instruction asm statement.

Accessing data from C programs without using input/output operands (such as by using global symbols directly from the assembler template) may not work as expected. Similarly, calling functions directly from an assembler template requires a detailed understanding of the target assembler and ABI.

Since GCC does not parse the assembler template, it has no visibility of any symbols it references. This may result in GCC discarding those symbols as unreferenced unless they are also listed as input, output, or goto operands.

Special format strings

In addition to the tokens described by the input, output, and goto operands, these tokens have special meanings in the assembler template:

'%%'   Outputs a single '%' into the assembler code.

'%='   Outputs a number that is unique to each instance of the **asm** statement in the entire compilation. This option is useful when creating local labels and referring to them multiple times in a single template that generates multiple assembler instructions.

'%{'
'%|'
'%}'   Outputs '{', '|', and '}' characters (respectively) into the assembler code. When unescaped, these characters have special meaning to indicate multiple assembler dialects, as described below.

Multiple assembler dialects in asm templates

On targets such as x86, GCC supports multiple assembler dialects. The '-masm' option controls which dialect GCC uses as its default for inline assembler. The target-specific documentation for the '-masm' option contains the list of supported dialects, as well as the default dialect if the option is not specified. This information may be important to understand, since assembler code that works correctly when compiled using one dialect will likely fail if compiled using another. See Section 3.18.54 [x86 Options], page 355.

If your code needs to support multiple assembler dialects (for example, if you are writing public headers that need to support a variety of compilation options), use constructs of this form:

```
{ dialect0 | dialect1 | dialect2... }
```

This construct outputs `dialect0` when using dialect #0 to compile the code, `dialect1` for dialect #1, etc. If there are fewer alternatives within the braces than the number of dialects the compiler supports, the construct outputs nothing.

For example, if an x86 compiler supports two dialects ('att', 'intel'), an assembler template such as this:

```
"bt{l %[Offset],%[Base] | %[Base],%[Offset]}; jc %l2"
```

is equivalent to one of

```
"btl %[Offset],%[Base] ; jc %l2"    /* att dialect */
"bt %[Base],%[Offset]; jc %l2"      /* intel dialect */
```

Using that same compiler, this code:

```
"xchg{l}\t{%%}ebx, %1"
```

corresponds to either

```
"xchgl\t%%ebx, %1"                  /* att dialect */
"xchg\tebx, %1"                     /* intel dialect */
```

There is no support for nesting dialect alternatives.

6.45.2.3 Output Operands

An `asm` statement has zero or more output operands indicating the names of C variables modified by the assembler code.

In this i386 example, `old` (referred to in the template string as `%0`) and `*Base` (as `%1`) are outputs and `Offset` (`%2`) is an input:

```
bool old;

__asm__ ("btsl %2,%1\n\t" // Turn on zero-based bit #Offset in Base.
         "sbb %0,%0"       // Use the CF to calculate old.
   : "=r" (old), "+rm" (*Base)
   : "Ir" (Offset)
   : "cc");

return old;
```

Operands are separated by commas. Each operand has this format:

[[asmSymbolicName]] constraint (cvariablename)

asmSymbolicName

> Specifies a symbolic name for the operand. Reference the name in the assembler template by enclosing it in square brackets (i.e. '%[Value]'). The scope of the name is the `asm` statement that contains the definition. Any valid C variable name is acceptable, including names already defined in the surrounding code. No two operands within the same `asm` statement can use the same symbolic name.

> When not using an asmSymbolicName, use the (zero-based) position of the operand in the list of operands in the assembler template. For example if there are three output operands, use '%0' in the template to refer to the first, '%1' for the second, and '%2' for the third.

constraint   A string constant specifying constraints on the placement of the operand; See
                 Section 6.45.3 [Constraints], page 514, for details.

> Output constraints must begin with either '=' (a variable overwriting an exist-
> ing value) or '+' (when reading and writing). When using '=', do not assume
> the location contains the existing value on entry to the asm, except when the
> operand is tied to an input; see [Input Operands], page 509.

> After the prefix, there must be one or more additional constraints (see
> Section 6.45.3 [Constraints], page 514) that describe where the value resides.
> Common constraints include 'r' for register and 'm' for memory. When you list
> more than one possible location (for example, "=rm"), the compiler chooses
> the most efficient one based on the current context. If you list as many
> alternates as the asm statement allows, you permit the optimizers to produce
> the best possible code. If you must use a specific register, but your Machine
> Constraints do not provide sufficient control to select the specific register you
> want, local register variables may provide a solution (see Section 6.45.5.2
> [Local Register Variables], page 548).

cvariablename

> Specifies a C lvalue expression to hold the output, typically a variable name.
> The enclosing parentheses are a required part of the syntax.

When the compiler selects the registers to use to represent the output operands, it does
not use any of the clobbered registers (see [Clobbers], page 510).

Output operand expressions must be lvalues. The compiler cannot check whether the
operands have data types that are reasonable for the instruction being executed. For output
expressions that are not directly addressable (for example a bit-field), the constraint must
allow a register. In that case, GCC uses the register as the output of the asm, and then
stores that register into the output.

Operands using the '+' constraint modifier count as two operands (that is, both as input
and output) towards the total maximum of 30 operands per asm statement.

Use the '&' constraint modifier (see Section 6.45.3.3 [Modifiers], page 517) on all output
operands that must not overlap an input. Otherwise, GCC may allocate the output operand
in the same register as an unrelated input operand, on the assumption that the assembler
code consumes its inputs before producing outputs. This assumption may be false if the
assembler code actually consists of more than one instruction.

The same problem can occur if one output parameter (*a*) allows a register constraint and
another output parameter (*b*) allows a memory constraint. The code generated by GCC
to access the memory address in *b* can contain registers which *might* be shared by *a*, and
GCC considers those registers to be inputs to the asm. As above, GCC assumes that such
input registers are consumed before any outputs are written. This assumption may result
in incorrect behavior if the asm writes to *a* before using *b*. Combining the '&' modifier with
the register constraint on *a* ensures that modifying *a* does not affect the address referenced
by *b*. Otherwise, the location of *b* is undefined if *a* is modified before using *b*.

asm supports operand modifiers on operands (for example '%k2' instead of simply '%2').
Typically these qualifiers are hardware dependent. The list of supported modifiers for x86
is found at [x86Operandmodifiers], page 512.

If the C code that follows the `asm` makes no use of any of the output operands, use `volatile` for the `asm` statement to prevent the optimizers from discarding the `asm` statement as unneeded (see [Volatile], page 501).

This code makes no use of the optional *asmSymbolicName*. Therefore it references the first output operand as `%0` (were there a second, it would be `%1`, etc). The number of the first input operand is one greater than that of the last output operand. In this i386 example, that makes `Mask` referenced as `%1`:

```
uint32_t Mask = 1234;
uint32_t Index;

asm ("bsfl %1, %0"
    : "=r" (Index)
    : "r" (Mask)
    : "cc");
```

That code overwrites the variable `Index` ('='), placing the value in a register ('r'). Using the generic 'r' constraint instead of a constraint for a specific register allows the compiler to pick the register to use, which can result in more efficient code. This may not be possible if an assembler instruction requires a specific register.

The following i386 example uses the *asmSymbolicName* syntax. It produces the same result as the code above, but some may consider it more readable or more maintainable since reordering index numbers is not necessary when adding or removing operands. The names `aIndex` and `aMask` are only used in this example to emphasize which names get used where. It is acceptable to reuse the names `Index` and `Mask`.

```
uint32_t Mask = 1234;
uint32_t Index;

asm ("bsfl %[aMask], %[aIndex]"
    : [aIndex] "=r" (Index)
    : [aMask] "r" (Mask)
    : "cc");
```

Here are some more examples of output operands.

```
uint32_t c = 1;
uint32_t d;
uint32_t *e = &c;

asm ("mov %[e], %[d]"
    : [d] "=rm" (d)
    : [e] "rm" (*e));
```

Here, `d` may either be in a register or in memory. Since the compiler might already have the current value of the `uint32_t` location pointed to by `e` in a register, you can enable it to choose the best location for `d` by specifying both constraints.

6.45.2.4 Flag Output Operands

Some targets have a special register that holds the "flags" for the result of an operation or comparison. Normally, the contents of that register are either unmodifed by the asm, or the asm is considered to clobber the contents.

On some targets, a special form of output operand exists by which conditions in the flags register may be outputs of the asm. The set of conditions supported are target specific, but the general rule is that the output variable must be a scalar integer, and the value is boolean. When supported, the target defines the preprocessor symbol `__GCC_ASM_FLAG_OUTPUTS__`.

Because of the special nature of the flag output operands, the constraint may not include alternatives.

Most often, the target has only one flags register, and thus is an implied operand of many instructions. In this case, the operand should not be referenced within the assembler template via `%0` etc, as there's no corresponding text in the assembly language.

x86 family   The flag output constraints for the x86 family are of the form '`=@cccond`' where *cond* is one of the standard conditions defined in the ISA manual for `jcc` or `setcc`.

a	"above" or unsigned greater than
ae	"above or equal" or unsigned greater than or equal
b	"below" or unsigned less than
be	"below or equal" or unsigned less than or equal
c	carry flag set
e z	"equal" or zero flag set
g	signed greater than
ge	signed greater than or equal
l	signed less than
le	signed less than or equal
o	overflow flag set
p	parity flag set
s	sign flag set

```
na
nae
nb
nbe
nc
ne
ng
nge
nl
nle
no
np
ns
nz                    "not" flag, or inverted versions of those above
```

6.45.2.5 Input Operands

Input operands make values from C variables and expressions available to the assembly
code.

Operands are separated by commas. Each operand has this format:

> [[asmSymbolicName]] constraint (cexpression)

asmSymbolicName

> Specifies a symbolic name for the operand. Reference the name in the assembler
> template by enclosing it in square brackets (i.e. '%[Value]'). The scope of the
> name is the asm statement that contains the definition. Any valid C variable
> name is acceptable, including names already defined in the surrounding code.
> No two operands within the same asm statement can use the same symbolic
> name.

> When not using an asmSymbolicName, use the (zero-based) position of the
> operand in the list of operands in the assembler template. For example if there
> are two output operands and three inputs, use '%2' in the template to refer to
> the first input operand, '%3' for the second, and '%4' for the third.

constraint A string constant specifying constraints on the placement of the operand; See
> Section 6.45.3 [Constraints], page 514, for details.

> Input constraint strings may not begin with either '=' or '+'. When you list
> more than one possible location (for example, '"irm"'), the compiler chooses
> the most efficient one based on the current context. If you must use a specific
> register, but your Machine Constraints do not provide sufficient control to select
> the specific register you want, local register variables may provide a solution
> (see Section 6.45.5.2 [Local Register Variables], page 548).

> Input constraints can also be digits (for example, "0"). This indicates that
> the specified input must be in the same place as the output constraint at the
> (zero-based) index in the output constraint list. When using asmSymbolicName
> syntax for the output operands, you may use these names (enclosed in brackets
> '[]') instead of digits.

cexpression

> This is the C variable or expression being passed to the `asm` statement as input. The enclosing parentheses are a required part of the syntax.

When the compiler selects the registers to use to represent the input operands, it does not use any of the clobbered registers (see [Clobbers], page 510).

If there are no output operands but there are input operands, place two consecutive colons where the output operands would go:

```
__asm__ ("some instructions"
    : /* No outputs. */
    : "r" (Offset / 8));
```

Warning: Do *not* modify the contents of input-only operands (except for inputs tied to outputs). The compiler assumes that on exit from the `asm` statement these operands contain the same values as they had before executing the statement. It is *not* possible to use clobbers to inform the compiler that the values in these inputs are changing. One common work-around is to tie the changing input variable to an output variable that never gets used. Note, however, that if the code that follows the `asm` statement makes no use of any of the output operands, the GCC optimizers may discard the `asm` statement as unneeded (see [Volatile], page 501).

`asm` supports operand modifiers on operands (for example '%k2' instead of simply '%2'). Typically these qualifiers are hardware dependent. The list of supported modifiers for x86 is found at [x86Operandmodifiers], page 512.

In this example using the fictitious `combine` instruction, the constraint "0" for input operand 1 says that it must occupy the same location as output operand 0. Only input operands may use numbers in constraints, and they must each refer to an output operand. Only a number (or the symbolic assembler name) in the constraint can guarantee that one operand is in the same place as another. The mere fact that `foo` is the value of both operands is not enough to guarantee that they are in the same place in the generated assembler code.

```
asm ("combine %2, %0"
    : "=r" (foo)
    : "0" (foo), "g" (bar));
```

Here is an example using symbolic names.

```
asm ("cmoveq %1, %2, %[result]"
    : [result] "=r"(result)
    : "r" (test), "r" (new), "[result]" (old));
```

6.45.2.6 Clobbers

While the compiler is aware of changes to entries listed in the output operands, the inline `asm` code may modify more than just the outputs. For example, calculations may require additional registers, or the processor may overwrite a register as a side effect of a particular assembler instruction. In order to inform the compiler of these changes, list them in the clobber list. Clobber list items are either register names or the special clobbers (listed below). Each clobber list item is a string constant enclosed in double quotes and separated by commas.

Clobber descriptions may not in any way overlap with an input or output operand. For example, you may not have an operand describing a register class with one member when listing that register in the clobber list. Variables declared to live in specific registers (see Section 6.45.5 [Explicit Register Variables], page 546) and used as **asm** input or output operands must have no part mentioned in the clobber description. In particular, there is no way to specify that input operands get modified without also specifying them as output operands.

When the compiler selects which registers to use to represent input and output operands, it does not use any of the clobbered registers. As a result, clobbered registers are available for any use in the assembler code.

Here is a realistic example for the VAX showing the use of clobbered registers:

```
asm volatile ("movc3 %0, %1, %2"
                  : /* No outputs. */
                  : "g" (from), "g" (to), "g" (count)
                  : "r0", "r1", "r2", "r3", "r4", "r5");
```

Also, there are two special clobber arguments:

"cc"   The **"cc"** clobber indicates that the assembler code modifies the flags register. On some machines, GCC represents the condition codes as a specific hardware register; **"cc"** serves to name this register. On other machines, condition code handling is different, and specifying **"cc"** has no effect. But it is valid no matter what the target.

"memory" The **"memory"** clobber tells the compiler that the assembly code performs memory reads or writes to items other than those listed in the input and output operands (for example, accessing the memory pointed to by one of the input parameters). To ensure memory contains correct values, GCC may need to flush specific register values to memory before executing the **asm**. Further, the compiler does not assume that any values read from memory before an **asm** remain unchanged after that **asm**; it reloads them as needed. Using the **"memory"** clobber effectively forms a read/write memory barrier for the compiler.

Note that this clobber does not prevent the *processor* from doing speculative reads past the **asm** statement. To prevent that, you need processor-specific fence instructions.

Flushing registers to memory has performance implications and may be an issue for time-sensitive code. You can use a trick to avoid this if the size of the memory being accessed is known at compile time. For example, if accessing ten bytes of a string, use a memory input like:

`{"m"( ({ struct { char x[10]; } *p = (void *)ptr ; *p; }) )}`.

6.45.2.7 Goto Labels

asm goto allows assembly code to jump to one or more C labels. The *GotoLabels* section in an **asm goto** statement contains a comma-separated list of all C labels to which the assembler code may jump. GCC assumes that **asm** execution falls through to the next statement (if this is not the case, consider using the **__builtin_unreachable** intrinsic after the **asm** statement). Optimization of **asm goto** may be improved by using the **hot** and **cold** label attributes (see Section 6.34 [Label Attributes], page 488).

An **asm goto** statement cannot have outputs. This is due to an internal restriction of the compiler: control transfer instructions cannot have outputs. If the assembler code does modify anything, use the `"memory"` clobber to force the optimizers to flush all register values to memory and reload them if necessary after the **asm** statement.

Also note that an **asm goto** statement is always implicitly considered volatile.

To reference a label in the assembler template, prefix it with '%l' (lowercase 'L') followed by its (zero-based) position in *GotoLabels* plus the number of input operands. For example, if the **asm** has three inputs and references two labels, refer to the first label as '%l3' and the second as '%l4').

Alternately, you can reference labels using the actual C label name enclosed in brackets. For example, to reference a label named **carry**, you can use '%l[carry]'. The label must still be listed in the *GotoLabels* section when using this approach.

Here is an example of **asm goto** for i386:

```
asm goto (
    "btl %1, %0\n\t"
    "jc %l2"
    : /* No outputs. */
    : "r" (p1), "r" (p2)
    : "cc"
    : carry);

return 0;

carry:
return 1;
```

The following example shows an **asm goto** that uses a memory clobber.

```
int frob(int x)
{
  int y;
  asm goto ("frob %%r5, %1; jc %l[error]; mov (%2), %%r5"
            : /* No outputs. */
            : "r"(x), "r"(&y)
            : "r5", "memory"
            : error);
  return y;
error:
  return -1;
}
```

6.45.2.8 x86 Operand Modifiers

References to input, output, and goto operands in the assembler template of extended **asm** statements can use modifiers to affect the way the operands are formatted in the code output to the assembler. For example, the following code uses the 'h' and 'b' modifiers for x86:

```
uint16_t  num;
asm volatile ("xchg %h0, %b0" : "+a" (num) );
```

These modifiers generate this assembler code:

```
xchg %ah, %al
```

The rest of this discussion uses the following code for illustrative purposes.

```
int main()
{
    int iInt = 1;

top:

    asm volatile goto ("some assembler instructions here"
    : /* No outputs. */
    : "q" (iInt), "X" (sizeof(unsigned char) + 1)
    : /* No clobbers. */
    : top);
}
```

With no modifiers, this is what the output from the operands would be for the 'att' and 'intel' dialects of assembler:

Operand	masm=att	masm=intel
%0	%eax	eax
%1	$2	2
%2	$.L2	OFFSET FLAT:.L2

The table below shows the list of supported modifiers and their effects.

Modifier	Description	Operand	'masm=att'	'masm=intel'
z	Print the opcode suffix for the size of the current integer operand (one of b/w/l/q).	%z0	l	
b	Print the QImode name of the register.	%b0	%al	al
h	Print the QImode name for a "high" register.	%h0	%ah	ah
w	Print the HImode name of the register.	%w0	%ax	ax
k	Print the SImode name of the register.	%k0	%eax	eax
q	Print the DImode name of the register.	%q0	%rax	rax
l	Print the label name with no punctuation.	%l2	.L2	.L2
c	Require a constant operand and print the constant expression with no punctuation.	%c1	2	2

6.45.2.9 x86 Floating-Point asm Operands

On x86 targets, there are several rules on the usage of stack-like registers in the operands of an asm. These rules apply only to the operands that are stack-like registers:

1. Given a set of input registers that die in an asm, it is necessary to know which are implicitly popped by the asm, and which must be explicitly popped by GCC.

   An input register that is implicitly popped by the asm must be explicitly clobbered, unless it is constrained to match an output operand.

2. For any input register that is implicitly popped by an `asm`, it is necessary to know how to adjust the stack to compensate for the pop. If any non-popped input is closer to the top of the reg-stack than the implicitly popped register, it would not be possible to know what the stack looked like—it's not clear how the rest of the stack "slides up".

   All implicitly popped input registers must be closer to the top of the reg-stack than any input that is not implicitly popped.

   It is possible that if an input dies in an `asm`, the compiler might use the input register for an output reload. Consider this example:

   ```
   asm ("foo" : "=t" (a) : "f" (b));
   ```

   This code says that input `b` is not popped by the `asm`, and that the `asm` pushes a result onto the reg-stack, i.e., the stack is one deeper after the `asm` than it was before. But, it is possible that reload may think that it can use the same register for both the input and the output.

   To prevent this from happening, if any input operand uses the '`f`' constraint, all output register constraints must use the '`&`' early-clobber modifier.

   The example above is correctly written as:

   ```
   asm ("foo" : "=&t" (a) : "f" (b));
   ```

3. Some operands need to be in particular places on the stack. All output operands fall in this category—GCC has no other way to know which registers the outputs appear in unless you indicate this in the constraints.

   Output operands must specifically indicate which register an output appears in after an `asm`. '`=f`' is not allowed: the operand constraints must select a class with a single register.

4. Output operands may not be "inserted" between existing stack registers. Since no 387 opcode uses a read/write operand, all output operands are dead before the `asm`, and are pushed by the `asm`. It makes no sense to push anywhere but the top of the reg-stack.

   Output operands must start at the top of the reg-stack: output operands may not "skip" a register.

5. Some `asm` statements may need extra stack space for internal calculations. This can be guaranteed by clobbering stack registers unrelated to the inputs and outputs.

This `asm` takes one input, which is internally popped, and produces two outputs.

```
asm ("fsincos" : "=t" (cos), "=u" (sin) : "0" (inp));
```

This `asm` takes two inputs, which are popped by the `fyl2xp1` opcode, and replaces them with one output. The `st(1)` clobber is necessary for the compiler to know that `fyl2xp1` pops both inputs.

```
asm ("fyl2xp1" : "=t" (result) : "0" (x), "u" (y) : "st(1)");
```

6.45.3 Constraints for asm Operands

Here are specific details on what constraint letters you can use with `asm` operands. Constraints can say whether an operand may be in a register, and which kinds of register; whether the operand can be a memory reference, and which kinds of address; whether the operand may be an immediate constant, and which possible values it may have. Constraints can also require two operands to match. Side-effects aren't allowed in operands of inline `asm`, unless '`<`' or '`>`' constraints are used, because there is no guarantee that the side-effects will happen exactly once in an instruction that can update the addressing register.

6.45.3.1 Simple Constraints

The simplest kind of constraint is a string full of letters, each of which describes one kind of operand that is permitted. Here are the letters that are allowed:

whitespace

Whitespace characters are ignored and can be inserted at any position except the first. This enables each alternative for different operands to be visually aligned in the machine description even if they have different number of constraints and modifiers.

'm'   A memory operand is allowed, with any kind of address that the machine supports in general. Note that the letter used for the general memory constraint can be re-defined by a back end using the `TARGET_MEM_CONSTRAINT` macro.

'o'   A memory operand is allowed, but only if the address is *offsettable*. This means that adding a small integer (actually, the width in bytes of the operand, as determined by its machine mode) may be added to the address and the result is also a valid memory address.

For example, an address which is constant is offsettable; so is an address that is the sum of a register and a constant (as long as a slightly larger constant is also within the range of address-offsets supported by the machine); but an autoincrement or autodecrement address is not offsettable. More complicated indirect/indexed addresses may or may not be offsettable depending on the other addressing modes that the machine supports.

Note that in an output operand which can be matched by another operand, the constraint letter 'o' is valid only when accompanied by both '<' (if the target machine has predecrement addressing) and '>' (if the target machine has preincrement addressing).

'V'   A memory operand that is not offsettable. In other words, anything that would fit the 'm' constraint but not the 'o' constraint.

'<'   A memory operand with autodecrement addressing (either predecrement or postdecrement) is allowed. In inline **asm** this constraint is only allowed if the operand is used exactly once in an instruction that can handle the side-effects. Not using an operand with '<' in constraint string in the inline **asm** pattern at all or using it in multiple instructions isn't valid, because the side-effects wouldn't be performed or would be performed more than once. Furthermore, on some targets the operand with '<' in constraint string must be accompanied by special instruction suffixes like %U0 instruction suffix on PowerPC or %P0 on IA-64.

'>'   A memory operand with autoincrement addressing (either preincrement or postincrement) is allowed. In inline **asm** the same restrictions as for '<' apply.

'r'   A register operand is allowed provided that it is in a general register.

'i'   An immediate integer operand (one with constant value) is allowed. This includes symbolic constants whose values will be known only at assembly time or later.

'n'   An immediate integer operand with a known numeric value is allowed. Many systems cannot support assembly-time constants for operands less than a word wide. Constraints for these operands should use 'n' rather than 'i'.

'I', 'J', 'K', ... 'P'
                Other letters in the range 'I' through 'P' may be defined in a machine-dependent fashion to permit immediate integer operands with explicit integer values in specified ranges. For example, on the 68000, 'I' is defined to stand for the range of values 1 to 8. This is the range permitted as a shift count in the shift instructions.

'E'   An immediate floating operand (expression code `const_double`) is allowed, but only if the target floating point format is the same as that of the host machine (on which the compiler is running).

'F'   An immediate floating operand (expression code `const_double` or `const_vector`) is allowed.

'G', 'H'   'G' and 'H' may be defined in a machine-dependent fashion to permit immediate floating operands in particular ranges of values.

's'   An immediate integer operand whose value is not an explicit integer is allowed.

                This might appear strange; if an insn allows a constant operand with a value not known at compile time, it certainly must allow any known value. So why use 's' instead of 'i'? Sometimes it allows better code to be generated.

                For example, on the 68000 in a fullword instruction it is possible to use an immediate operand; but if the immediate value is between −128 and 127, better code results from loading the value into a register and using the register. This is because the load into the register can be done with a 'moveq' instruction. We arrange for this to happen by defining the letter 'K' to mean "any integer outside the range −128 to 127", and then specifying 'Ks' in the operand constraints.

'g'   Any register, memory or immediate integer operand is allowed, except for registers that are not general registers.

'X'   Any operand whatsoever is allowed.

'0', '1', '2', ... '9'
                An operand that matches the specified operand number is allowed. If a digit is used together with letters within the same alternative, the digit should come last.

                This number is allowed to be more than a single digit. If multiple digits are encountered consecutively, they are interpreted as a single decimal integer. There is scant chance for ambiguity, since to-date it has never been desirable that '10' be interpreted as matching either operand 1 *or* operand 0. Should this be desired, one can use multiple alternatives instead.

                This is called a *matching constraint* and what it really means is that the assembler has only a single operand that fills two roles which `asm` distinguishes. For example, an add instruction uses two input operands and an output operand, but on most CISC machines an add instruction really has only two operands, one of them an input-output operand:

```
addl #35,r12
```

Matching constraints are used in these circumstances. More precisely, the two operands that match must include one input-only operand and one output-only operand. Moreover, the digit must be a smaller number than the number of the operand that uses it in the constraint.

'p'   An operand that is a valid memory address is allowed. This is for "load address" and "push address" instructions.

'p' in the constraint must be accompanied by **address_operand** as the predicate in the **match_operand**. This predicate interprets the mode specified in the **match_operand** as the mode of the memory reference for which the address would be valid.

other-letters

Other letters can be defined in machine-dependent fashion to stand for particular classes of registers or other arbitrary operand types. 'd', 'a' and 'f' are defined on the 68000/68020 to stand for data, address and floating point registers.

6.45.3.2 Multiple Alternative Constraints

Sometimes a single instruction has multiple alternative sets of possible operands. For example, on the 68000, a logical-or instruction can combine register or an immediate value into memory, or it can combine any kind of operand into a register; but it cannot combine one memory location into another.

These constraints are represented as multiple alternatives. An alternative can be described by a series of letters for each operand. The overall constraint for an operand is made from the letters for this operand from the first alternative, a comma, the letters for this operand from the second alternative, a comma, and so on until the last alternative. All operands for a single instruction must have the same number of alternatives.

So the first alternative for the 68000's logical-or could be written as "+m" (output) : "ir" (input). The second could be "+r" (output): "irm" (input). However, the fact that two memory locations cannot be used in a single instruction prevents simply using "+rm" (output) : "irm" (input). Using multi-alternatives, this might be written as "+m,r" (output) : "ir,irm" (input). This describes all the available alternatives to the compiler, allowing it to choose the most efficient one for the current conditions.

There is no way within the template to determine which alternative was chosen. However you may be able to wrap your **asm** statements with builtins such as **__builtin_constant_p** to achieve the desired results.

6.45.3.3 Constraint Modifier Characters

Here are constraint modifier characters.

'='   Means that this operand is written to by this instruction: the previous value is discarded and replaced by new data.

'+'   Means that this operand is both read and written by the instruction.

When the compiler fixes up the operands to satisfy the constraints, it needs to know which operands are read by the instruction and which are written by it.

'=' identifies an operand which is only written; '+' identifies an operand that is both read and written; all other operands are assumed to only be read.

If you specify '=' or '+' in a constraint, you put it in the first character of the constraint string.

'&'   Means (in a particular alternative) that this operand is an *earlyclobber* operand, which is written before the instruction is finished using the input operands. Therefore, this operand may not lie in a register that is read by the instruction or as part of any memory address.

'&' applies only to the alternative in which it is written. In constraints with multiple alternatives, sometimes one alternative requires '&' while others do not. See, for example, the 'movdf' insn of the 68000.

A operand which is read by the instruction can be tied to an earlyclobber operand if its only use as an input occurs before the early result is written. Adding alternatives of this form often allows GCC to produce better code when only some of the read operands can be affected by the earlyclobber. See, for example, the 'mulsi3' insn of the ARM.

Furthermore, if the *earlyclobber* operand is also a read/write operand, then that operand is written only after it's used.

'&' does not obviate the need to write '=' or '+'. As *earlyclobber* operands are always written, a read-only *earlyclobber* operand is ill-formed and will be rejected by the compiler.

'%'   Declares the instruction to be commutative for this operand and the following operand. This means that the compiler may interchange the two operands if that is the cheapest way to make all operands fit the constraints. '%' applies to all alternatives and must appear as the first character in the constraint. Only read-only operands can use '%'.

GCC can only handle one commutative pair in an asm; if you use more, the compiler may fail. Note that you need not use the modifier if the two alternatives are strictly identical; this would only waste time in the reload pass.

6.45.3.4 Constraints for Particular Machines

Whenever possible, you should use the general-purpose constraint letters in asm arguments, since they will convey meaning more readily to people reading your code. Failing that, use the constraint letters that usually have very similar meanings across architectures. The most commonly used constraints are 'm' and 'r' (for memory and general-purpose registers respectively; see Section 6.45.3.1 [Simple Constraints], page 515), and 'I', usually the letter indicating the most common immediate-constant format.

Each architecture defines additional constraints. These constraints are used by the compiler itself for instruction generation, as well as for asm statements; therefore, some of the constraints are not particularly useful for asm. Here is a summary of some of the machine-dependent constraints available on some particular machines; it includes both constraints that are useful for asm and constraints that aren't. The compiler source file mentioned in the table heading for each architecture is the definitive reference for the meanings of that architecture's constraints.

AArch64 family—'`config/aarch64/constraints.md`'

k	The stack pointer register (`SP`)
w	Floating point or SIMD vector register
I	Integer constant that is valid as an immediate operand in an `ADD` instruction
J	Integer constant that is valid as an immediate operand in a `SUB` instruction (once negated)
K	Integer constant that can be used with a 32-bit logical instruction
L	Integer constant that can be used with a 64-bit logical instruction
M	Integer constant that is valid as an immediate operand in a 32-bit `MOV` pseudo instruction. The `MOV` may be assembled to one of several different machine instructions depending on the value
N	Integer constant that is valid as an immediate operand in a 64-bit `MOV` pseudo instruction
S	An absolute symbolic address or a label reference
Y	Floating point constant zero
Z	Integer constant zero
Ush	The high part (bits 12 and upwards) of the pc-relative address of a symbol within 4GB of the instruction
Q	A memory address which uses a single base register with no offset
Ump	A memory address suitable for a load/store pair instruction in SI, DI, SF and DF modes

ARC —'`config/arc/constraints.md`'

q	Registers usable in ARCompact 16-bit instructions: `r0-r3`, `r12-r15`. This constraint can only match when the '`-mq`' option is in effect.
e	Registers usable as base-regs of memory addresses in ARCompact 16-bit memory instructions: `r0-r3`, `r12-r15`, `sp`. This constraint can only match when the '`-mq`' option is in effect.
D	ARC FPX (dpfp) 64-bit registers. `D0`, `D1`.
I	A signed 12-bit integer constant.
Cal	constant for arithmetic/logical operations. This might be any constant that can be put into a long immediate by the assmbler or linker without involving a PIC relocation.
K	A 3-bit unsigned integer constant.
L	A 6-bit unsigned integer constant.
CnL	One's complement of a 6-bit unsigned integer constant.

CmL	Two's complement of a 6-bit unsigned integer constant.
M	A 5-bit unsigned integer constant.
O	A 7-bit unsigned integer constant.
P	A 8-bit unsigned integer constant.
H	Any const_double value.

ARM family—`config/arm/constraints.md`

h	In Thumb state, the core registers r8-r15.
k	The stack pointer register.
l	In Thumb State the core registers r0-r7. In ARM state this is an alias for the r constraint.
t	VFP floating-point registers s0-s31. Used for 32 bit values.
w	VFP floating-point registers d0-d31 and the appropriate subset d0-d15 based on command line options. Used for 64 bit values only. Not valid for Thumb1.
y	The iWMMX co-processor registers.
z	The iWMMX GR registers.
G	The floating-point constant 0.0
I	Integer that is valid as an immediate operand in a data processing instruction. That is, an integer in the range 0 to 255 rotated by a multiple of 2
J	Integer in the range −4095 to 4095
K	Integer that satisfies constraint 'I' when inverted (ones complement)
L	Integer that satisfies constraint 'I' when negated (twos complement)
M	Integer in the range 0 to 32
Q	A memory reference where the exact address is in a single register (''m'' is preferable for asm statements)
R	An item in the constant pool
S	A symbol in the text segment of the current file
Uv	A memory reference suitable for VFP load/store insns (reg+constant offset)
Uy	A memory reference suitable for iWMMXt load/store instructions.
Uq	A memory reference suitable for the ARMv4 ldrsb instruction.

AVR family—`config/avr/constraints.md`

l	Registers from r0 to r15

a	Registers from r16 to r23
d	Registers from r16 to r31
w	Registers from r24 to r31. These registers can be used in 'adiw' command
e	Pointer register (r26–r31)
b	Base pointer register (r28–r31)
q	Stack pointer register (SPH:SPL)
t	Temporary register r0
x	Register pair X (r27:r26)
y	Register pair Y (r29:r28)
z	Register pair Z (r31:r30)
I	Constant greater than -1, less than 64
J	Constant greater than -64, less than 1
K	Constant integer 2
L	Constant integer 0
M	Constant that fits in 8 bits
N	Constant integer -1
O	Constant integer 8, 16, or 24
P	Constant integer 1
G	A floating point constant 0.0
Q	A memory address based on Y or Z pointer with displacement.

Blackfin family—'`config/bfin/constraints.md`'

a	P register
d	D register
z	A call clobbered P register.
q*n*	A single register. If *n* is in the range 0 to 7, the corresponding D register. If it is A, then the register P0.
D	Even-numbered D register
W	Odd-numbered D register
e	Accumulator register.
A	Even-numbered accumulator register.
B	Odd-numbered accumulator register.
b	I register

v	B register
f	M register
c	Registers used for circular buffering, i.e. I, B, or L registers.
C	The CC register.
t	LT0 or LT1.
k	LC0 or LC1.
u	LB0 or LB1.
x	Any D, P, B, M, I or L register.
y	Additional registers typically used only in prologues and epilogues: RETS, RETN, RETI, RETX, RETE, ASTAT, SEQSTAT and USP.
w	Any register except accumulators or CC.
Ksh	Signed 16 bit integer (in the range −32768 to 32767)
Kuh	Unsigned 16 bit integer (in the range 0 to 65535)
Ks7	Signed 7 bit integer (in the range −64 to 63)
Ku7	Unsigned 7 bit integer (in the range 0 to 127)
Ku5	Unsigned 5 bit integer (in the range 0 to 31)
Ks4	Signed 4 bit integer (in the range −8 to 7)
Ks3	Signed 3 bit integer (in the range −3 to 4)
Ku3	Unsigned 3 bit integer (in the range 0 to 7)
P*n*	Constant *n*, where *n* is a single-digit constant in the range 0 to 4.
PA	An integer equal to one of the MACFLAG_XXX constants that is suitable for use with either accumulator.
PB	An integer equal to one of the MACFLAG_XXX constants that is suitable for use only with accumulator A1.
M1	Constant 255.
M2	Constant 65535.
J	An integer constant with exactly a single bit set.
L	An integer constant with all bits set except exactly one.
H	
Q	Any SYMBOL_REF.

CR16 Architecture—'config/cr16/cr16.h'

b	Registers from r0 to r14 (registers without stack pointer)
t	Register from r0 to r11 (all 16-bit registers)
p	Register from r12 to r15 (all 32-bit registers)

I	Signed constant that fits in 4 bits
J	Signed constant that fits in 5 bits
K	Signed constant that fits in 6 bits
L	Unsigned constant that fits in 4 bits
M	Signed constant that fits in 32 bits
N	Check for 64 bits wide constants for add/sub instructions
G	Floating point constant that is legal for store immediate

Epiphany—'`config/epiphany/constraints.md`'

U16	An unsigned 16-bit constant.
K	An unsigned 5-bit constant.
L	A signed 11-bit constant.
Cm1	A signed 11-bit constant added to −1. Can only match when the '-m1reg-*reg*' option is active.
Cl1	Left-shift of −1, i.e., a bit mask with a block of leading ones, the rest being a block of trailing zeroes. Can only match when the '-m1reg-*reg*' option is active.
Cr1	Right-shift of −1, i.e., a bit mask with a trailing block of ones, the rest being zeroes. Or to put it another way, one less than a power of two. Can only match when the '-m1reg-*reg*' option is active.
Cal	Constant for arithmetic/logical operations. This is like i, except that for position independent code, no symbols / expressions needing relocations are allowed.
Csy	Symbolic constant for call/jump instruction.
Rcs	The register class usable in short insns. This is a register class constraint, and can thus drive register allocation. This constraint won't match unless '-mprefer-short-insn-regs' is in effect.
Rsc	The the register class of registers that can be used to hold a sibcall call address. I.e., a caller-saved register.
Rct	Core control register class.
Rgs	The register group usable in short insns. This constraint does not use a register class, so that it only passively matches suitable registers, and doesn't drive register allocation.
Rra	Matches the return address if it can be replaced with the link register.
Rcc	Matches the integer condition code register.
Sra	Matches the return address if it is in a stack slot.
Cfm	Matches control register values to switch fp mode, which are encapsulated in `UNSPEC_FP_MODE`.

FRV—'config/frv/frv.h'

a	Register in the class ACC_REGS (acc0 to acc7).
b	Register in the class EVEN_ACC_REGS (acc0 to acc7).
c	Register in the class CC_REGS (fcc0 to fcc3 and icc0 to icc3).
d	Register in the class GPR_REGS (gr0 to gr63).
e	Register in the class EVEN_REGS (gr0 to gr63). Odd registers are excluded not in the class but through the use of a machine mode larger than 4 bytes.
f	Register in the class FPR_REGS (fr0 to fr63).
h	Register in the class FEVEN_REGS (fr0 to fr63). Odd registers are excluded not in the class but through the use of a machine mode larger than 4 bytes.
l	Register in the class LR_REG (the lr register).
q	Register in the class QUAD_REGS (gr2 to gr63). Register numbers not divisible by 4 are excluded not in the class but through the use of a machine mode larger than 8 bytes.
t	Register in the class ICC_REGS (icc0 to icc3).
u	Register in the class FCC_REGS (fcc0 to fcc3).
v	Register in the class ICR_REGS (cc4 to cc7).
w	Register in the class FCR_REGS (cc0 to cc3).
x	Register in the class QUAD_FPR_REGS (fr0 to fr63). Register numbers not divisible by 4 are excluded not in the class but through the use of a machine mode larger than 8 bytes.
z	Register in the class SPR_REGS (lcr and lr).
A	Register in the class QUAD_ACC_REGS (acc0 to acc7).
B	Register in the class ACCG_REGS (accg0 to accg7).
C	Register in the class CR_REGS (cc0 to cc7).
G	Floating point constant zero
I	6-bit signed integer constant
J	10-bit signed integer constant
L	16-bit signed integer constant
M	16-bit unsigned integer constant
N	12-bit signed integer constant that is negative—i.e. in the range of -2048 to -1
O	Constant zero

P	12-bit signed integer constant that is greater than zero—i.e. in the range of 1 to 2047.

FT32—'`config/ft32/constraints.md`'

A	An absolute address
B	An offset address
W	A register indirect memory operand
e	An offset address.
f	An offset address.
O	The constant zero or one
I	A 16-bit signed constant ($-32768 \ldots 32767$)
w	A bitfield mask suitable for bext or bins
x	An inverted bitfield mask suitable for bext or bins
L	A 16-bit unsigned constant, multiple of 4 ($0 \ldots 65532$)
S	A 20-bit signed constant ($-524288 \ldots 524287$)
b	A constant for a bitfield width ($1 \ldots 16$)
KA	A 10-bit signed constant ($-512 \ldots 511$)

Hewlett-Packard PA-RISC—'`config/pa/pa.h`'

a	General register 1
f	Floating point register
q	Shift amount register
x	Floating point register (deprecated)
y	Upper floating point register (32-bit), floating point register (64-bit)
Z	Any register
I	Signed 11-bit integer constant
J	Signed 14-bit integer constant
K	Integer constant that can be deposited with a **zdepi** instruction
L	Signed 5-bit integer constant
M	Integer constant 0
N	Integer constant that can be loaded with a **ldil** instruction
O	Integer constant whose value plus one is a power of 2
P	Integer constant that can be used for **and** operations in **depi** and **extru** instructions
S	Integer constant 31

U	Integer constant 63
G	Floating-point constant 0.0
A	A `lo_sum` data-linkage-table memory operand
Q	A memory operand that can be used as the destination operand of an integer store instruction
R	A scaled or unscaled indexed memory operand
T	A memory operand for floating-point loads and stores
W	A register indirect memory operand

Intel IA-64—'config/ia64/ia64.h'

a	General register `r0` to `r3` for `addl` instruction
b	Branch register
c	Predicate register ('c' as in "conditional")
d	Application register residing in M-unit
e	Application register residing in I-unit
f	Floating-point register
m	Memory operand. If used together with '<' or '>', the operand can have postincrement and postdecrement which require printing with '%Pn' on IA-64.
G	Floating-point constant 0.0 or 1.0
I	14-bit signed integer constant
J	22-bit signed integer constant
K	8-bit signed integer constant for logical instructions
L	8-bit adjusted signed integer constant for compare pseudo-ops
M	6-bit unsigned integer constant for shift counts
N	9-bit signed integer constant for load and store postincrements
O	The constant zero
P	0 or −1 for `dep` instruction
Q	Non-volatile memory for floating-point loads and stores
R	Integer constant in the range 1 to 4 for `shladd` instruction
S	Memory operand except postincrement and postdecrement. This is now roughly the same as 'm' when not used together with '<' or '>'.

M32C—'config/m32c/m32c.c'

Rsp	
Rfb	
Rsb	'$sp', '$fb', '$sb'.

Rcr	Any control register, when they're 16 bits wide (nothing if control registers are 24 bits wide)
Rcl	Any control register, when they're 24 bits wide.
R0w R1w R2w R3w	$r0, $r1, $r2, $r3.
R02	$r0 or $r2, or $r2r0 for 32 bit values.
R13	$r1 or $r3, or $r3r1 for 32 bit values.
Rdi	A register that can hold a 64 bit value.
Rhl	$r0 or $r1 (registers with addressable high/low bytes)
R23	$r2 or $r3
Raa	Address registers
Raw	Address registers when they're 16 bits wide.
Ral	Address registers when they're 24 bits wide.
Rqi	Registers that can hold QI values.
Rad	Registers that can be used with displacements ($a0, $a1, $sb).
Rsi	Registers that can hold 32 bit values.
Rhi	Registers that can hold 16 bit values.
Rhc	Registers chat can hold 16 bit values, including all control registers.
Rra	$r0 through R1, plus $a0 and $a1.
Rfl	The flags register.
Rmm	The memory-based pseudo-registers $mem0 through $mem15.
Rpi	Registers that can hold pointers (16 bit registers for r8c, m16c; 24 bit registers for m32cm, m32c).
Rpa	Matches multiple registers in a PARALLEL to form a larger register. Used to match function return values.
Is3	−8 . . . 7
IS1	−128 . . . 127
IS2	−32768 . . . 32767
IU2	0 . . . 65535
In4	−8 . . . −1 or 1 . . . 8
In5	−16 . . . −1 or 1 . . . 16
In6	−32 . . . −1 or 1 . . . 32
IM2	−65536 . . . −1

Ilb	An 8 bit value with exactly one bit set.
Ilw	A 16 bit value with exactly one bit set.
Sd	The common src/dest memory addressing modes.
Sa	Memory addressed using $a0 or $a1.
Si	Memory addressed with immediate addresses.
Ss	Memory addressed using the stack pointer ($sp).
Sf	Memory addressed using the frame base register ($fb).
Ss	Memory addressed using the small base register ($sb).
S1	$r1h

MicroBlaze—'config/microblaze/constraints.md'

d	A general register (r0 to r31).
z	A status register (rmsr, $fcc1 to $fcc7).

MIPS—'config/mips/constraints.md'

d	A general-purpose register. This is equivalent to r unless generating MIPS16 code, in which case the MIPS16 register set is used.
f	A floating-point register (if available).
h	Formerly the hi register. This constraint is no longer supported.
l	The lo register. Use this register to store values that are no bigger than a word.
x	The concatenated hi and lo registers. Use this register to store doubleword values.
c	A register suitable for use in an indirect jump. This will always be $25 for '-mabicalls'.
v	Register $3. Do not use this constraint in new code; it is retained only for compatibility with glibc.
y	Equivalent to r; retained for backwards compatibility.
z	A floating-point condition code register.
I	A signed 16-bit constant (for arithmetic instructions).
J	Integer zero.
K	An unsigned 16-bit constant (for logic instructions).
L	A signed 32-bit constant in which the lower 16 bits are zero. Such constants can be loaded using lui.
M	A constant that cannot be loaded using lui, addiu or ori.
N	A constant in the range -65535 to -1 (inclusive).
O	A signed 15-bit constant.

P	A constant in the range 1 to 65535 (inclusive).
G	Floating-point zero.
R	An address that can be used in a non-macro load or store.
ZC	A memory operand whose address is formed by a base register and offset that is suitable for use in instructions with the same addressing mode as `ll` and `sc`.
ZD	An address suitable for a `prefetch` instruction, or for any other instruction with the same addressing mode as `prefetch`.

Motorola 680x0—`config/m68k/constraints.md`

a	Address register
d	Data register
f	68881 floating-point register, if available
I	Integer in the range 1 to 8
J	16-bit signed number
K	Signed number whose magnitude is greater than 0x80
L	Integer in the range −8 to −1
M	Signed number whose magnitude is greater than 0x100
N	Range 24 to 31, rotatert:SI 8 to 1 expressed as rotate
O	16 (for rotate using swap)
P	Range 8 to 15, rotatert:HI 8 to 1 expressed as rotate
R	Numbers that mov3q can handle
G	Floating point constant that is not a 68881 constant
S	Operands that satisfy 'm' when -mpcrel is in effect
T	Operands that satisfy 's' when -mpcrel is not in effect
Q	Address register indirect addressing mode
U	Register offset addressing
W	const_call_operand
Cs	symbol_ref or const
Ci	const_int
CO	const_int 0
Cj	Range of signed numbers that don't fit in 16 bits
Cmvq	Integers valid for mvq
Capsw	Integers valid for a moveq followed by a swap
Cmvz	Integers valid for mvz

Cmvs	Integers valid for mvs
Ap	push_operand
Ac	Non-register operands allowed in clr

Moxie—'config/moxie/constraints.md'

A	An absolute address
B	An offset address
W	A register indirect memory operand
I	A constant in the range of 0 to 255.
N	A constant in the range of 0 to −255.

MSP430–'config/msp430/constraints.md'

R12	Register R12.
R13	Register R13.
K	Integer constant 1.
L	Integer constant -1^20..1^19.
M	Integer constant 1-4.
Ya	Memory references which do not require an extended MOVX instruction.
Yl	Memory reference, labels only.
Ys	Memory reference, stack only.

NDS32—'config/nds32/constraints.md'

w	LOW register class $r0 to $r7 constraint for V3/V3M ISA.
l	LOW register class $r0 to $r7.
d	MIDDLE register class $r0 to $r11, $r16 to $r19.
h	HIGH register class $r12 to $r14, $r20 to $r31.
t	Temporary assist register $ta (i.e. $r15).
k	Stack register $sp.
Iu03	Unsigned immediate 3-bit value.
In03	Negative immediate 3-bit value in the range of −7–0.
Iu04	Unsigned immediate 4-bit value.
Is05	Signed immediate 5-bit value.
Iu05	Unsigned immediate 5-bit value.
In05	Negative immediate 5-bit value in the range of −31–0.
Ip05	Unsigned immediate 5-bit value for movpi45 instruction with range 16–47.

Iu06   Unsigned immediate 6-bit value constraint for addri36.sp instruction.

Iu08   Unsigned immediate 8-bit value.

Iu09   Unsigned immediate 9-bit value.

Is10   Signed immediate 10-bit value.

Is11   Signed immediate 11-bit value.

Is15   Signed immediate 15-bit value.

Iu15   Unsigned immediate 15-bit value.

Ic15   A constant which is not in the range of imm15u but ok for bclr instruction.

Ie15   A constant which is not in the range of imm15u but ok for bset instruction.

It15   A constant which is not in the range of imm15u but ok for btgl instruction.

Ii15   A constant whose compliment value is in the range of imm15u and ok for bitci instruction.

Is16   Signed immediate 16-bit value.

Is17   Signed immediate 17-bit value.

Is19   Signed immediate 19-bit value.

Is20   Signed immediate 20-bit value.

Ihig   The immediate value that can be simply set high 20-bit.

Izeb   The immediate value 0xff.

Izeh   The immediate value 0xffff.

Ixls   The immediate value 0x01.

Ix11   The immediate value 0x7ff.

Ibms   The immediate value with power of 2.

Ifex   The immediate value with power of 2 minus 1.

U33   Memory constraint for 333 format.

U45   Memory constraint for 45 format.

U37   Memory constraint for 37 format.

Nios II family—'config/nios2/constraints.md'

I   Integer that is valid as an immediate operand in an instruction taking a signed 16-bit number. Range −32768 to 32767.

J   Integer that is valid as an immediate operand in an instruction taking an unsigned 16-bit number. Range 0 to 65535.

K | Integer that is valid as an immediate operand in an instruction taking only the upper 16-bits of a 32-bit number. Range 32-bit numbers with the lower 16-bits being 0.

L | Integer that is valid as an immediate operand for a shift instruction. Range 0 to 31.

M | Integer that is valid as an immediate operand for only the value 0. Can be used in conjunction with the format modifier z to use r0 instead of 0 in the assembly output.

N | Integer that is valid as an immediate operand for a custom instruction opcode. Range 0 to 255.

P | An immediate operand for R2 andchi/andci instructions.

S | Matches immediates which are addresses in the small data section and therefore can be added to **gp** as a 16-bit immediate to re-create their 32-bit value.

U | Matches constants suitable as an operand for the rdprs and cache instructions.

v | A memory operand suitable for Nios II R2 load/store exclusive instructions.

w | A memory operand suitable for load/store IO and cache instructions.

PDP-11—'config/pdp11/constraints.md'

a | Floating point registers AC0 through AC3. These can be loaded from/to memory with a single instruction.

d | Odd numbered general registers (R1, R3, R5). These are used for 16-bit multiply operations.

f | Any of the floating point registers (AC0 through AC5).

G | Floating point constant 0.

I | An integer constant that fits in 16 bits.

J | An integer constant whose low order 16 bits are zero.

K | An integer constant that does not meet the constraints for codes 'I' or 'J'.

L | The integer constant 1.

M | The integer constant −1.

N | The integer constant 0.

O | Integer constants −4 through −1 and 1 through 4; shifts by these amounts are handled as multiple single-bit shifts rather than a single variable-length shift.

Q   A memory reference which requires an additional word (address or offset) after the opcode.

R   A memory reference that is encoded within the opcode.

PowerPC and IBM RS6000—'config/rs6000/constraints.md'

b   Address base register

d   Floating point register (containing 64-bit value)

f   Floating point register (containing 32-bit value)

v   Altivec vector register

wa   Any VSX register if the -mvsx option was used or NO_REGS.

When using any of the register constraints (wa, wd, wf, wg, wh, wi, wj, wk, wl, wm, wo, wp, wq, ws, wt, wu, wv, ww, or wy) that take VSX registers, you must use %x<n> in the template so that the correct register is used. Otherwise the register number output in the assembly file will be incorrect if an Altivec register is an operand of a VSX instruction that expects VSX register numbering.

```
asm ("xvadddp %x0,%x1,%x2" : "=wa" (v1) : "wa" (v2), "wa" (v3));
```

is correct, but:

```
asm ("xvadddp %0,%1,%2" : "=wa" (v1) : "wa" (v2), "wa" (v3));
```

is not correct.

If an instruction only takes Altivec registers, you do not want to use %x<n>.

```
asm ("xsaddqp %0,%1,%2" : "=v" (v1) : "v" (v2), "v" (v3));
```

is correct because the **xsaddqp** instruction only takes Altivec registers, while:

```
asm ("xsaddqp %x0,%x1,%x2" : "=v" (v1) : "v" (v2), "v" (v3));
```

is incorrect.

wb   Altivec register if '-mcpu=power9' is used or NO_REGS.

wd   VSX vector register to hold vector double data or NO_REGS.

we   VSX register if the '-mcpu=power9' and '-m64' options were used or NO_REGS.

wf   VSX vector register to hold vector float data or NO_REGS.

wg   If '-mmfpgpr' was used, a floating point register or NO_REGS.

wh   Floating point register if direct moves are available, or NO_REGS.

wi   FP or VSX register to hold 64-bit integers for VSX insns or NO_REGS.

wj   FP or VSX register to hold 64-bit integers for direct moves or NO_REGS.

wk   FP or VSX register to hold 64-bit doubles for direct moves or NO_REGS.

wl	Floating point register if the LFIWAX instruction is enabled or NO_REGS.
wm	VSX register if direct move instructions are enabled, or NO_REGS.
wn	No register (NO_REGS).
wo	VSX register to use for ISA 3.0 vector instructions, or NO_REGS.
wp	VSX register to use for IEEE 128-bit floating point TFmode, or NO_REGS.
wq	VSX register to use for IEEE 128-bit floating point, or NO_REGS.
wr	General purpose register if 64-bit instructions are enabled or NO_REGS.
ws	VSX vector register to hold scalar double values or NO_REGS.
wt	VSX vector register to hold 128 bit integer or NO_REGS.
wu	Altivec register to use for float/32-bit int loads/stores or NO_REGS.
wv	Altivec register to use for double loads/stores or NO_REGS.
ww	FP or VSX register to perform float operations under '-mvsx' or NO_REGS.
wx	Floating point register if the STFIWX instruction is enabled or NO_REGS.
wy	FP or VSX register to perform ISA 2.07 float ops or NO_REGS.
wz	Floating point register if the LFIWZX instruction is enabled or NO_REGS.
wB	Signed 5-bit constant integer that can be loaded into an altivec register.
wD	Int constant that is the element number of the 64-bit scalar in a vector.
wE	Vector constant that can be loaded with the XXSPLTIB instruction.
wF	Memory operand suitable for power9 fusion load/stores.
wG	Memory operand suitable for TOC fusion memory references.
wH	Altivec register if '-mvsx-small-integer'.
wI	Floating point register if '-mvsx-small-integer'.
wJ	FP register if '-mvsx-small-integer' and '-mpower9-vector'.
wK	Altivec register if '-mvsx-small-integer' and '-mpower9-vector'.
wL	Int constant that is the element number that the MFVSRLD instruction. targets.

wM	Match vector constant with all 1's if the XXLORC instruction is available.
wO	A memory operand suitable for the ISA 3.0 vector d-form instructions.
wQ	A memory address that will work with the `lq` and `stq` instructions.
wS	Vector constant that can be loaded with XXSPLTIB & sign extension.
h	'MQ', 'CTR', or 'LINK' register
c	'CTR' register
l	'LINK' register
x	'CR' register (condition register) number 0
y	'CR' register (condition register)
z	'XER[CA]' carry bit (part of the XER register)
I	Signed 16-bit constant
J	Unsigned 16-bit constant shifted left 16 bits (use 'L' instead for SImode constants)
K	Unsigned 16-bit constant
L	Signed 16-bit constant shifted left 16 bits
M	Constant larger than 31
N	Exact power of 2
O	Zero
P	Constant whose negation is a signed 16-bit constant
G	Floating point constant that can be loaded into a register with one instruction per word
H	Integer/Floating point constant that can be loaded into a register using three instructions
m	Memory operand. Normally, m does not allow addresses that update the base register. If '<' or '>' constraint is also used, they are allowed and therefore on PowerPC targets in that case it is only safe to use 'm<>' in an asm statement if that asm statement accesses the operand exactly once. The asm statement must also use '%U<opno>' as a placeholder for the "update" flag in the corresponding load or store instruction. For example:

```
asm ("st%U0 %1,%0" : "=m<>" (mem) : "r" (val));
```

is correct but:

```
asm ("st %1,%0" : "=m<>" (mem) : "r" (val));
```

is not.

es	A "stable" memory operand; that is, one which does not include any automodification of the base register. This used to be useful when 'm' allowed automodification of the base register, but as those are now only allowed when '<' or '>' is used, 'es' is basically the same as 'm' without '<' and '>'.
Q	Memory operand that is an offset from a register (it is usually better to use 'm' or 'es' in **asm** statements)
Z	Memory operand that is an indexed or indirect from a register (it is usually better to use 'm' or 'es' in **asm** statements)
R	AIX TOC entry
a	Address operand that is an indexed or indirect from a register ('p' is preferable for **asm** statements)
U	System V Release 4 small data area reference
W	Vector constant that does not require memory
j	Vector constant that is all zeros.

RL78—'config/rl78/constraints.md'

Int3	An integer constant in the range 1 . . . 7.
Int8	An integer constant in the range 0 . . . 255.
J	An integer constant in the range -255 . . . 0
K	The integer constant 1.
L	The integer constant -1.
M	The integer constant 0.
N	The integer constant 2.
O	The integer constant -2.
P	An integer constant in the range 1 . . . 15.
Qbi	The built-in compare types–eq, ne, gtu, ltu, geu, and leu.
Qsc	The synthetic compare types–gt, lt, ge, and le.
Wab	A memory reference with an absolute address.
Wbc	A memory reference using BC as a base register, with an optional offset.
Wca	A memory reference using AX, BC, DE, or HL for the address, for calls.
Wcv	A memory reference using any 16-bit register pair for the address, for calls.
Wd2	A memory reference using DE as a base register, with an optional offset.

Wde	A memory reference using DE as a base register, without any offset.
Wfr	Any memory reference to an address in the far address space.
Wh1	A memory reference using HL as a base register, with an optional one-byte offset.
Whb	A memory reference using HL as a base register, with B or C as the index register.
Whl	A memory reference using HL as a base register, without any offset.
Ws1	A memory reference using SP as a base register, with an optional one-byte offset.
Y	Any memory reference to an address in the near address space.
A	The AX register.
B	The BC register.
D	The DE register.
R	A through L registers.
S	The SP register.
T	The HL register.
Z08W	The 16-bit R8 register.
Z10W	The 16-bit R10 register.
Zint	The registers reserved for interrupts (R24 to R31).
a	The A register.
b	The B register.
c	The C register.
d	The D register.
e	The E register.
h	The H register.
l	The L register.
v	The virtual registers.
w	The PSW register.
x	The X register.

RX—'config/rx/constraints.md'

Q	An address which does not involve register indirect addressing or pre/post increment/decrement addressing.
Symbol	A symbol reference.
Int08	A constant in the range −256 to 255, inclusive.

Sint08	A constant in the range −128 to 127, inclusive.	
Sint16	A constant in the range −32768 to 32767, inclusive.	
Sint24	A constant in the range −8388608 to 8388607, inclusive.	
Uint04	A constant in the range 0 to 15, inclusive.	

S/390 and zSeries—'config/s390/s390.h'

a	Address register (general purpose register except r0)
c	Condition code register
d	Data register (arbitrary general purpose register)
f	Floating-point register
I	Unsigned 8-bit constant (0–255)
J	Unsigned 12-bit constant (0–4095)
K	Signed 16-bit constant (−32768–32767)
L	Value appropriate as displacement.

    (0..4095)
            for short displacement

    (−524288..524287)
            for long displacement

M	Constant integer with a value of 0x7fffffff.
N	Multiple letter constraint followed by 4 parameter letters.

0..9:	number of the part counting from most to least significant
H,Q:	mode of the part
D,S,H:	mode of the containing operand
0,F:	value of the other parts (F—all bits set)

The constraint matches if the specified part of a constant has a value different from its other parts.

Q	Memory reference without index register and with short displacement.
R	Memory reference with index register and short displacement.
S	Memory reference without index register but with long displacement.
T	Memory reference with index register and long displacement.
U	Pointer with short displacement.
W	Pointer with long displacement.
Y	Shift count operand.

SPARC—'config/sparc/sparc.h'

f	Floating-point register on the SPARC-V8 architecture and lower floating-point register on the SPARC-V9 architecture.
e	Floating-point register. It is equivalent to 'f' on the SPARC-V8 architecture and contains both lower and upper floating-point registers on the SPARC-V9 architecture.
c	Floating-point condition code register.
d	Lower floating-point register. It is only valid on the SPARC-V9 architecture when the Visual Instruction Set is available.
b	Floating-point register. It is only valid on the SPARC-V9 architecture when the Visual Instruction Set is available.
h	64-bit global or out register for the SPARC-V8+ architecture.
C	The constant all-ones, for floating-point.
A	Signed 5-bit constant
D	A vector constant
I	Signed 13-bit constant
J	Zero
K	32-bit constant with the low 12 bits clear (a constant that can be loaded with the **sethi** instruction)
L	A constant in the range supported by **movcc** instructions (11-bit signed immediate)
M	A constant in the range supported by **movrcc** instructions (10-bit signed immediate)
N	Same as 'K', except that it verifies that bits that are not in the lower 32-bit range are all zero. Must be used instead of 'K' for modes wider than **SImode**
O	The constant 4096
G	Floating-point zero
H	Signed 13-bit constant, sign-extended to 32 or 64 bits
P	The constant -1
Q	Floating-point constant whose integral representation can be moved into an integer register using a single sethi instruction
R	Floating-point constant whose integral representation can be moved into an integer register using a single mov instruction
S	Floating-point constant whose integral representation can be moved into an integer register using a high/lo_sum instruction sequence
T	Memory address aligned to an 8-byte boundary

U	Even register
W	Memory address for 'e' constraint registers
w	Memory address with only a base register
Y	Vector zero

SPU—'config/spu/spu.h'

a	An immediate which can be loaded with the il/ila/ilh/ilhu instructions. const_int is treated as a 64 bit value.
c	An immediate for and/xor/or instructions. const_int is treated as a 64 bit value.
d	An immediate for the iohl instruction. const_int is treated as a 64 bit value.
f	An immediate which can be loaded with fsmbi.
A	An immediate which can be loaded with the il/ila/ilh/ilhu instructions. const_int is treated as a 32 bit value.
B	An immediate for most arithmetic instructions. const_int is treated as a 32 bit value.
C	An immediate for and/xor/or instructions. const_int is treated as a 32 bit value.
D	An immediate for the iohl instruction. const_int is treated as a 32 bit value.
I	A constant in the range [−64, 63] for shift/rotate instructions.
J	An unsigned 7-bit constant for conversion/nop/channel instructions.
K	A signed 10-bit constant for most arithmetic instructions.
M	A signed 16 bit immediate for stop.
N	An unsigned 16-bit constant for iohl and fsmbi.
O	An unsigned 7-bit constant whose 3 least significant bits are 0.
P	An unsigned 3-bit constant for 16-byte rotates and shifts
R	Call operand, reg, for indirect calls
S	Call operand, symbol, for relative calls.
T	Call operand, const_int, for absolute calls.
U	An immediate which can be loaded with the il/ila/ilh/ilhu instructions. const_int is sign extended to 128 bit.
W	An immediate for shift and rotate instructions. const_int is treated as a 32 bit value.
Y	An immediate for and/xor/or instructions. const_int is sign extended as a 128 bit.

Z	An immediate for the `iohl` instruction. const_int is sign extended to 128 bit.

TI C6X family— '`config/c6x/constraints.md`'

a	Register file A (A0–A31).
b	Register file B (B0–B31).
A	Predicate registers in register file A (A0–A2 on C64X and higher, A1 and A2 otherwise).
B	Predicate registers in register file B (B0–B2).
C	A call-used register in register file B (B0–B9, B16–B31).
Da	Register file A, excluding predicate registers (A3–A31, plus A0 if not C64X or higher).
Db	Register file B, excluding predicate registers (B3–B31).
Iu4	Integer constant in the range 0 ... 15.
Iu5	Integer constant in the range 0 ... 31.
In5	Integer constant in the range −31 ... 0.
Is5	Integer constant in the range −16 ... 15.
I5x	Integer constant that can be the operand of an ADDA or a SUBA insn.
IuB	Integer constant in the range 0 ... 65535.
IsB	Integer constant in the range −32768 ... 32767.
IsC	Integer constant in the range -2^{20} ... $2^{20} - 1$.
Jc	Integer constant that is a valid mask for the clr instruction.
Js	Integer constant that is a valid mask for the set instruction.
Q	Memory location with A base register.
R	Memory location with B base register.
Z	Register B14 (aka DP).

TILE-Gx— '`config/tilegx/constraints.md`'

R00	
R01	
R02	
R03	
R04	
R05	
R06	
R07	
R08	
R09	
R10	Each of these represents a register constraint for an individual register, from r0 to r10.

I   Signed 8-bit integer constant.

J   Signed 16-bit integer constant.

K   Unsigned 16-bit integer constant.

L   Integer constant that fits in one signed byte when incremented by one (−129 . . . 126).

m   Memory operand. If used together with '<' or '>', the operand can have postincrement which requires printing with '%In' and '%in' on TILE-Gx. For example:

```
asm ("st_add %I0,%1,%i0" : "=m<>" (*mem) : "r" (val));
```

M   A bit mask suitable for the BFINS instruction.

N   Integer constant that is a byte tiled out eight times.

O   The integer zero constant.

P   Integer constant that is a sign-extended byte tiled out as four shorts.

Q   Integer constant that fits in one signed byte when incremented (−129 . . . 126), but excluding -1.

S   Integer constant that has all 1 bits consecutive and starting at bit 0.

T   A 16-bit fragment of a got, tls, or pc-relative reference.

U   Memory operand except postincrement. This is roughly the same as 'm' when not used together with '<' or '>'.

W   An 8-element vector constant with identical elements.

Y   A 4-element vector constant with identical elements.

Z0   The integer constant 0xffffffff.

Z1   The integer constant 0xffffffff00000000.

TILEPro—'config/tilepro/constraints.md'

R00
R01
R02
R03
R04
R05
R06
R07
R08
R09
R10   Each of these represents a register constraint for an individual register, from r0 to r10.

I   Signed 8-bit integer constant.

J	Signed 16-bit integer constant.
K	Nonzero integer constant with low 16 bits zero.
L	Integer constant that fits in one signed byte when incremented by one (−129 ... 126).
m	Memory operand. If used together with '<' or '>', the operand can have postincrement which requires printing with '%In' and '%in' on TILEPro. For example:

```
asm ("swadd %I0,%1,%i0" : "=m<>" (mem) : "r" (val));
```

M	A bit mask suitable for the MM instruction.
N	Integer constant that is a byte tiled out four times.
O	The integer zero constant.
P	Integer constant that is a sign-extended byte tiled out as two shorts.
Q	Integer constant that fits in one signed byte when incremented (−129 ... 126), but excluding -1.
T	A symbolic operand, or a 16-bit fragment of a got, tls, or pc-relative reference.
U	Memory operand except postincrement. This is roughly the same as 'm' when not used together with '<' or '>'.
W	A 4-element vector constant with identical elements.
Y	A 2-element vector constant with identical elements.

Visium—'config/visium/constraints.md'

b	EAM register mdb
c	EAM register mdc
f	Floating point register
l	General register, but not r29, r30 and r31
t	Register r1
u	Register r2
v	Register r3
G	Floating-point constant 0.0
J	Integer constant in the range 0 .. 65535 (16-bit immediate)
K	Integer constant in the range 1 .. 31 (5-bit immediate)
L	Integer constant in the range −65535 .. −1 (16-bit negative immediate)
M	Integer constant −1
O	Integer constant 0

P	Integer constant 32

x86 family—'config/i386/constraints.md'

R	Legacy register—the eight integer registers available on all i386 processors (**a**, **b**, **c**, **d**, **si**, **di**, **bp**, **sp**).
q	Any register accessible as **rl**. In 32-bit mode, **a**, **b**, **c**, and **d**; in 64-bit mode, any integer register.
Q	Any register accessible as **rh**: **a**, **b**, **c**, and **d**.
a	The **a** register.
b	The **b** register.
c	The **c** register.
d	The **d** register.
S	The **si** register.
D	The **di** register.
A	The **a** and **d** registers. This class is used for instructions that return double word results in the **ax:dx** register pair. Single word values will be allocated either in **ax** or **dx**. For example on i386 the following implements **rdtsc**:

```
unsigned long long rdtsc (void)
{
  unsigned long long tick;
  __asm__ __volatile__("rdtsc":"=A"(tick));
  return tick;
}
```

This is not correct on x86-64 as it would allocate tick in either **ax** or **dx**. You have to use the following variant instead:

```
unsigned long long rdtsc (void)
{
  unsigned int tickl, tickh;
  __asm__ __volatile__("rdtsc":"=a"(tickl),"=d"(tickh));
  return ((unsigned long long)tickh << 32)|tickl;
}
```

f	Any 80387 floating-point (stack) register.
t	Top of 80387 floating-point stack (**%st(0)**).
u	Second from top of 80387 floating-point stack (**%st(1)**).
y	Any MMX register.
x	Any SSE register.
Yz	First SSE register (**%xmm0**).
I	Integer constant in the range 0 ... 31, for 32-bit shifts.
J	Integer constant in the range 0 ... 63, for 64-bit shifts.
K	Signed 8-bit integer constant.

L	0xFF or 0xFFFF, for andsi as a zero-extending move.
M	0, 1, 2, or 3 (shifts for the **lea** instruction).
N	Unsigned 8-bit integer constant (for **in** and **out** instructions).
G	Standard 80387 floating point constant.
C	SSE constant zero operand.
e	32-bit signed integer constant, or a symbolic reference known to fit that range (for immediate operands in sign-extending x86-64 instructions).
Z	32-bit unsigned integer constant, or a symbolic reference known to fit that range (for immediate operands in zero-extending x86-64 instructions).

Xstormy16—'`config/stormy16/stormy16.h`'

a	Register r0.
b	Register r1.
c	Register r2.
d	Register r8.
e	Registers r0 through r7.
t	Registers r0 and r1.
y	The carry register.
z	Registers r8 and r9.
I	A constant between 0 and 3 inclusive.
J	A constant that has exactly one bit set.
K	A constant that has exactly one bit clear.
L	A constant between 0 and 255 inclusive.
M	A constant between −255 and 0 inclusive.
N	A constant between −3 and 0 inclusive.
O	A constant between 1 and 4 inclusive.
P	A constant between −4 and −1 inclusive.
Q	A memory reference that is a stack push.
R	A memory reference that is a stack pop.
S	A memory reference that refers to a constant address of known value.
T	The register indicated by Rx (not implemented yet).
U	A constant that is not between 2 and 15 inclusive.

Z	The constant 0.

Xtensa—'config/xtensa/constraints.md'

a	General-purpose 32-bit register
b	One-bit boolean register
A	MAC16 40-bit accumulator register
I	Signed 12-bit integer constant, for use in MOVI instructions
J	Signed 8-bit integer constant, for use in ADDI instructions
K	Integer constant valid for BccI instructions
L	Unsigned constant valid for BccUI instructions

6.45.4 Controlling Names Used in Assembler Code

You can specify the name to be used in the assembler code for a C function or variable by writing the asm (or __asm__) keyword after the declarator. It is up to you to make sure that the assembler names you choose do not conflict with any other assembler symbols, or reference registers.

Assembler names for data:

This sample shows how to specify the assembler name for data:

```
int foo asm ("myfoo") = 2;
```

This specifies that the name to be used for the variable foo in the assembler code should be 'myfoo' rather than the usual '_foo'.

On systems where an underscore is normally prepended to the name of a C variable, this feature allows you to define names for the linker that do not start with an underscore.

GCC does not support using this feature with a non-static local variable since such variables do not have assembler names. If you are trying to put the variable in a particular register, see Section 6.45.5 [Explicit Register Variables], page 546.

Assembler names for functions:

To specify the assembler name for functions, write a declaration for the function before its definition and put asm there, like this:

```
int func (int x, int y) asm ("MYFUNC");

int func (int x, int y)
{
   /* ... */
```

This specifies that the name to be used for the function func in the assembler code should be MYFUNC.

6.45.5 Variables in Specified Registers

GNU C allows you to associate specific hardware registers with C variables. In almost all cases, allowing the compiler to assign registers produces the best code. However under certain unusual circumstances, more precise control over the variable storage is required.

Both global and local variables can be associated with a register. The consequences of performing this association are very different between the two, as explained in the sections below.

6.45.5.1 Defining Global Register Variables

You can define a global register variable and associate it with a specified register like this:

```
register int *foo asm ("r12");
```

Here `r12` is the name of the register that should be used. Note that this is the same syntax used for defining local register variables, but for a global variable the declaration appears outside a function. The **register** keyword is required, and cannot be combined with **static**. The register name must be a valid register name for the target platform.

Registers are a scarce resource on most systems and allowing the compiler to manage their usage usually results in the best code. However, under special circumstances it can make sense to reserve some globally. For example this may be useful in programs such as programming language interpreters that have a couple of global variables that are accessed very often.

After defining a global register variable, for the current compilation unit:

- The register is reserved entirely for this use, and will not be allocated for any other purpose.

- The register is not saved and restored by any functions.

- Stores into this register are never deleted even if they appear to be dead, but references may be deleted, moved or simplified.

Note that these points *only* apply to code that is compiled with the definition. The behavior of code that is merely linked in (for example code from libraries) is not affected.

If you want to recompile source files that do not actually use your global register variable so they do not use the specified register for any other purpose, you need not actually add the global register declaration to their source code. It suffices to specify the compiler option '**-ffixed-reg**' (see Section 3.16 [Code Gen Options], page 190) to reserve the register.

Declaring the variable

Global register variables can not have initial values, because an executable file has no means to supply initial contents for a register.

When selecting a register, choose one that is normally saved and restored by function calls on your machine. This ensures that code which is unaware of this reservation (such as library routines) will restore it before returning.

On machines with register windows, be sure to choose a global register that is not affected magically by the function call mechanism.

Using the variable

When calling routines that are not aware of the reservation, be cautious if those routines call back into code which uses them. As an example, if you call the system library version of **qsort**, it may clobber your registers during execution, but (if you have selected appropriate registers) it will restore them before returning. However it will *not* restore them before calling **qsort**'s comparison function. As a result, global values will not reliably be available to the comparison function unless the **qsort** function itself is rebuilt.

Similarly, it is not safe to access the global register variables from signal handlers or from more than one thread of control. Unless you recompile them specially for the task at hand, the system library routines may temporarily use the register for other things.

On most machines, **longjmp** restores to each global register variable the value it had at the time of the **setjmp**. On some machines, however, **longjmp** does not change the value of global register variables. To be portable, the function that called **setjmp** should make other arrangements to save the values of the global register variables, and to restore them in a **longjmp**. This way, the same thing happens regardless of what **longjmp** does.

Eventually there may be a way of asking the compiler to choose a register automatically, but first we need to figure out how it should choose and how to enable you to guide the choice. No solution is evident.

6.45.5.2 Specifying Registers for Local Variables

You can define a local register variable and associate it with a specified register like this:

```
register int *foo asm ("r12");
```

Here **r12** is the name of the register that should be used. Note that this is the same syntax used for defining global register variables, but for a local variable the declaration appears within a function. The **register** keyword is required, and cannot be combined with **static**. The register name must be a valid register name for the target platform.

As with global register variables, it is recommended that you choose a register that is normally saved and restored by function calls on your machine, so that calls to library routines will not clobber it.

The only supported use for this feature is to specify registers for input and output operands when calling Extended **asm** (see Section 6.45.2 [Extended Asm], page 500). This may be necessary if the constraints for a particular machine don't provide sufficient control to select the desired register. To force an operand into a register, create a local variable and specify the register name after the variable's declaration. Then use the local variable for the **asm** operand and specify any constraint letter that matches the register:

```
register int *p1 asm ("r0") = ...;
register int *p2 asm ("r1") = ...;
register int *result asm ("r0");
asm ("sysint" : "=r" (result) : "0" (p1), "r" (p2));
```

Warning: In the above example, be aware that a register (for example **r0**) can be call-clobbered by subsequent code, including function calls and library calls for arithmetic operators on other variables (for example the initialization of **p2**). In this case, use temporary variables for expressions between the register assignments:

```
int t1 = ...;
register int *p1 asm ("r0") = ...;
register int *p2 asm ("r1") = t1;
register int *result asm ("r0");
asm ("sysint" : "=r" (result) : "0" (p1), "r" (p2));
```

Defining a register variable does not reserve the register. Other than when invoking the Extended **asm**, the contents of the specified register are not guaranteed. For this reason, the following uses are explicitly *not* supported. If they appear to work, it is only happenstance, and may stop working as intended due to (seemingly) unrelated changes in surrounding code, or even minor changes in the optimization of a future version of gcc:

- Passing parameters to or from Basic `asm`
- Passing parameters to or from Extended `asm` without using input or output operands.
- Passing parameters to or from routines written in assembler (or other languages) using non-standard calling conventions.

Some developers use Local Register Variables in an attempt to improve gcc's allocation of registers, especially in large functions. In this case the register name is essentially a hint to the register allocator. While in some instances this can generate better code, improvements are subject to the whims of the allocator/optimizers. Since there are no guarantees that your improvements won't be lost, this usage of Local Register Variables is discouraged.

On the MIPS platform, there is related use for local register variables with slightly different characteristics (see Section "Defining coprocessor specifics for MIPS targets" in *GNU Compiler Collection (GCC) Internals*).

6.45.6 Size of an `asm`

Some targets require that GCC track the size of each instruction used in order to generate correct code. Because the final length of the code produced by an `asm` statement is only known by the assembler, GCC must make an estimate as to how big it will be. It does this by counting the number of instructions in the pattern of the `asm` and multiplying that by the length of the longest instruction supported by that processor. (When working out the number of instructions, it assumes that any occurrence of a newline or of whatever statement separator character is supported by the assembler – typically ';' — indicates the end of an instruction.)

Normally, GCC's estimate is adequate to ensure that correct code is generated, but it is possible to confuse the compiler if you use pseudo instructions or assembler macros that expand into multiple real instructions, or if you use assembler directives that expand to more space in the object file than is needed for a single instruction. If this happens then the assembler may produce a diagnostic saying that a label is unreachable.

6.46 Alternate Keywords

'-ansi' and the various '-std' options disable certain keywords. This causes trouble when you want to use GNU C extensions, or a general-purpose header file that should be usable by all programs, including ISO C programs. The keywords `asm`, `typeof` and `inline` are not available in programs compiled with '-ansi' or '-std' (although `inline` can be used in a program compiled with '-std=c99' or '-std=c11'). The ISO C99 keyword `restrict` is only available when '-std=gnu99' (which will eventually be the default) or '-std=c99' (or the equivalent '-std=iso9899:1999'), or an option for a later standard version, is used.

The way to solve these problems is to put '__' at the beginning and end of each problematical keyword. For example, use `__asm__` instead of `asm`, and `__inline__` instead of `inline`.

Other C compilers won't accept these alternative keywords; if you want to compile with another compiler, you can define the alternate keywords as macros to replace them with the customary keywords. It looks like this:

```
#ifndef __GNUC__
#define __asm__ asm
#endif
```

'-pedantic' and other options cause warnings for many GNU C extensions. You can prevent such warnings within one expression by writing __extension__ before the expression. __extension__ has no effect aside from this.

6.47 Incomplete enum Types

You can define an enum tag without specifying its possible values. This results in an incomplete type, much like what you get if you write struct foo without describing the elements. A later declaration that does specify the possible values completes the type.

You can't allocate variables or storage using the type while it is incomplete. However, you can work with pointers to that type.

This extension may not be very useful, but it makes the handling of enum more consistent with the way struct and union are handled.

This extension is not supported by GNU C++.

6.48 Function Names as Strings

GCC provides three magic constants that hold the name of the current function as a string. In C++11 and later modes, all three are treated as constant expressions and can be used in constexpr constexts. The first of these constants is __func__, which is part of the C99 standard:

The identifier __func__ is implicitly declared by the translator as if, immediately following the opening brace of each function definition, the declaration

```
static const char __func__[] = "function-name";
```

appeared, where function-name is the name of the lexically-enclosing function. This name is the unadorned name of the function. As an extension, at file (or, in C++, namespace scope), __func__ evaluates to the empty string.

__FUNCTION__ is another name for __func__, provided for backward compatibility with old versions of GCC.

In C, __PRETTY_FUNCTION__ is yet another name for __func__, except that at file (or, in C++, namespace scope), it evaluates to the string "top level". In addition, in C++, __PRETTY_FUNCTION__ contains the signature of the function as well as its bare name. For example, this program:

```
extern "C" int printf (const char *, ...);

class a {
 public:
  void sub (int i)
    {
      printf ("__FUNCTION__ = %s\n", __FUNCTION__);
      printf ("__PRETTY_FUNCTION__ = %s\n", __PRETTY_FUNCTION__);
    }
};

int
main (void)
```

```
{
  a ax;
  ax.sub (0);
  return 0;
}
```

gives this output:

```
__FUNCTION__ = sub
__PRETTY_FUNCTION__ = void a::sub(int)
```

These identifiers are variables, not preprocessor macros, and may not be used to initialize char arrays or be concatenated with string literals.

6.49 Getting the Return or Frame Address of a Function

These functions may be used to get information about the callers of a function.

void * __builtin_return_address (*unsigned int* **level**)   [Built-in Function]
> This function returns the return address of the current function, or of one of its callers. The *level* argument is number of frames to scan up the call stack. A value of 0 yields the return address of the current function, a value of 1 yields the return address of the caller of the current function, and so forth. When inlining the expected behavior is that the function returns the address of the function that is returned to. To work around this behavior use the noinline function attribute.
>
> The *level* argument must be a constant integer.
>
> On some machines it may be impossible to determine the return address of any function other than the current one; in such cases, or when the top of the stack has been reached, this function returns 0 or a random value. In addition, __builtin_frame_address may be used to determine if the top of the stack has been reached.
>
> Additional post-processing of the returned value may be needed, see __builtin_extract_return_addr.
>
> Calling this function with a nonzero argument can have unpredictable effects, including crashing the calling program. As a result, calls that are considered unsafe are diagnosed when the '-Wframe-address' option is in effect. Such calls should only be made in debugging situations.

void * __builtin_extract_return_addr (*void* *addr*)   [Built-in Function]
> The address as returned by __builtin_return_address may have to be fed through this function to get the actual encoded address. For example, on the 31-bit S/390 platform the highest bit has to be masked out, or on SPARC platforms an offset has to be added for the true next instruction to be executed.
>
> If no fixup is needed, this function simply passes through *addr*.

void * __builtin_frob_return_address (*void* *addr*)   [Built-in Function]
> This function does the reverse of __builtin_extract_return_addr.

void * __builtin_frame_address (*unsigned int* **level**)   [Built-in Function]
> This function is similar to __builtin_return_address, but it returns the address of the function frame rather than the return address of the function. Calling __builtin_frame_address with a value of 0 yields the frame address of the current function, a value of 1 yields the frame address of the caller of the current function, and so forth.

The frame is the area on the stack that holds local variables and saved registers. The frame address is normally the address of the first word pushed on to the stack by the function. However, the exact definition depends upon the processor and the calling convention. If the processor has a dedicated frame pointer register, and the function has a frame, then `__builtin_frame_address` returns the value of the frame pointer register.

On some machines it may be impossible to determine the frame address of any function other than the current one; in such cases, or when the top of the stack has been reached, this function returns 0 if the first frame pointer is properly initialized by the startup code.

Calling this function with a nonzero argument can have unpredictable effects, including crashing the calling program. As a result, calls that are considered unsafe are diagnosed when the '-Wframe-address' option is in effect. Such calls should only be made in debugging situations.

6.50 Using Vector Instructions through Built-in Functions

On some targets, the instruction set contains SIMD vector instructions which operate on multiple values contained in one large register at the same time. For example, on the x86 the MMX, 3DNow! and SSE extensions can be used this way.

The first step in using these extensions is to provide the necessary data types. This should be done using an appropriate `typedef`:

```
typedef int v4si __attribute__ ((vector_size (16)));
```

The `int` type specifies the base type, while the attribute specifies the vector size for the variable, measured in bytes. For example, the declaration above causes the compiler to set the mode for the `v4si` type to be 16 bytes wide and divided into `int` sized units. For a 32-bit `int` this means a vector of 4 units of 4 bytes, and the corresponding mode of `foo` is V4SI.

The `vector_size` attribute is only applicable to integral and float scalars, although arrays, pointers, and function return values are allowed in conjunction with this construct. Only sizes that are a power of two are currently allowed.

All the basic integer types can be used as base types, both as signed and as unsigned: `char`, `short`, `int`, `long`, `long long`. In addition, `float` and `double` can be used to build floating-point vector types.

Specifying a combination that is not valid for the current architecture causes GCC to synthesize the instructions using a narrower mode. For example, if you specify a variable of type `V4SI` and your architecture does not allow for this specific SIMD type, GCC produces code that uses 4 `SIs`.

The types defined in this manner can be used with a subset of normal C operations. Currently, GCC allows using the following operators on these types: `+`, `-`, `*`, `/`, unary minus, `^`, `|`, `&`, `~`, `%`.

The operations behave like C++ `valarrays`. Addition is defined as the addition of the corresponding elements of the operands. For example, in the code below, each of the 4 elements in a is added to the corresponding 4 elements in b and the resulting vector is stored in c.

```
typedef int v4si __attribute__ ((vector_size (16)));

v4si a, b, c;

c = a + b;
```

Subtraction, multiplication, division, and the logical operations operate in a similar manner. Likewise, the result of using the unary minus or complement operators on a vector type is a vector whose elements are the negative or complemented values of the corresponding elements in the operand.

It is possible to use shifting operators `<<`, `>>` on integer-type vectors. The operation is defined as following: `{a0, a1, ..., an} >> {b0, b1, ..., bn} == {a0 >> b0, a1 >> b1, ..., an >> bn}`. Vector operands must have the same number of elements.

For convenience, it is allowed to use a binary vector operation where one operand is a scalar. In that case the compiler transforms the scalar operand into a vector where each element is the scalar from the operation. The transformation happens only if the scalar could be safely converted to the vector-element type. Consider the following code.

```
typedef int v4si __attribute__ ((vector_size (16)));

v4si a, b, c;
long l;

a = b + 1;    /* a = b + {1,1,1,1}; */
a = 2 * b;    /* a = {2,2,2,2} * b; */

a = l + a;    /* Error, cannot convert long to int. */
```

Vectors can be subscripted as if the vector were an array with the same number of elements and base type. Out of bound accesses invoke undefined behavior at run time. Warnings for out of bound accesses for vector subscription can be enabled with '`-Warray-bounds`'.

Vector comparison is supported with standard comparison operators: `==`, `!=`, `<`, `<=`, `>`, `>=`. Comparison operands can be vector expressions of integer-type or real-type. Comparison between integer-type vectors and real-type vectors are not supported. The result of the comparison is a vector of the same width and number of elements as the comparison operands with a signed integral element type.

Vectors are compared element-wise producing 0 when comparison is false and -1 (constant of the appropriate type where all bits are set) otherwise. Consider the following example.

```
typedef int v4si __attribute__ ((vector_size (16)));

v4si a = {1,2,3,4};
v4si b = {3,2,1,4};
v4si c;

c = a >  b;    /* The result would be {0, 0,-1, 0} */
c = a == b;    /* The result would be {0,-1, 0,-1} */
```

In C++, the ternary operator `?:` is available. `a?b:c`, where b and c are vectors of the same type and a is an integer vector with the same number of elements of the same size as b and c, computes all three arguments and creates a vector `{a[0]?b[0]:c[0], a[1]?b[1]:c[1], ...}`. Note that unlike in OpenCL, a is thus interpreted as `a != 0` and not `a < 0`. As in the case of binary operations, this syntax is also accepted when one of b or c is a scalar that is then transformed into a vector. If both b and c are scalars and the type of `true?b:c` has the same size as the element type of a, then b and c are converted to a vector type whose elements have this type and with the same number of elements as a.

In C++, the logic operators !, &&, || are available for vectors. !v is equivalent to v == 0, a && b is equivalent to a!=0 & b!=0 and a || b is equivalent to a!=0 | b!=0. For mixed operations between a scalar s and a vector v, s && v is equivalent to s?v!=0:0 (the evaluation is short-circuit) and v && s is equivalent to v!=0 & (s?-1:0).

Vector shuffling is available using functions __builtin_shuffle (vec, mask) and __builtin_shuffle (vec0, vec1, mask). Both functions construct a permutation of elements from one or two vectors and return a vector of the same type as the input vector(s). The *mask* is an integral vector with the same width (W) and element count (N) as the output vector.

The elements of the input vectors are numbered in memory ordering of *vec0* beginning at 0 and *vec1* beginning at N. The elements of *mask* are considered modulo N in the single-operand case and modulo $2*N$ in the two-operand case.

Consider the following example,

```
typedef int v4si __attribute__ ((vector_size (16)));

v4si a = {1,2,3,4};
v4si b = {5,6,7,8};
v4si mask1 = {0,1,1,3};
v4si mask2 = {0,4,2,5};
v4si res;

res = __builtin_shuffle (a, mask1);      /* res is {1,2,2,4}  */
res = __builtin_shuffle (a, b, mask2);   /* res is {1,5,3,6}  */
```

Note that __builtin_shuffle is intentionally semantically compatible with the OpenCL shuffle and shuffle2 functions.

You can declare variables and use them in function calls and returns, as well as in assignments and some casts. You can specify a vector type as a return type for a function. Vector types can also be used as function arguments. It is possible to cast from one vector type to another, provided they are of the same size (in fact, you can also cast vectors to and from other datatypes of the same size).

You cannot operate between vectors of different lengths or different signedness without a cast.

6.51 Support for offsetof

GCC implements for both C and C++ a syntactic extension to implement the offsetof macro.

```
primary:
        "__builtin_offsetof" "(" typename "," offsetof_member_designator ")"

offsetof_member_designator:
          identifier
        | offsetof_member_designator "." identifier
        | offsetof_member_designator "[" expr "]"
```

This extension is sufficient such that

```
#define offsetof(type, member)  __builtin_offsetof (type, member)
```

is a suitable definition of the `offsetof` macro. In C++, *type* may be dependent. In either case, *member* may consist of a single identifier, or a sequence of member accesses and array references.

6.52 Legacy `__sync` Built-in Functions for Atomic Memory Access

The following built-in functions are intended to be compatible with those described in the *Intel Itanium Processor-specific Application Binary Interface*, section 7.4. As such, they depart from normal GCC practice by not using the '`__builtin_`' prefix and also by being overloaded so that they work on multiple types.

The definition given in the Intel documentation allows only for the use of the types `int`, `long`, `long long` or their unsigned counterparts. GCC allows any scalar type that is 1, 2, 4 or 8 bytes in size other than the C type `_Bool` or the C++ type `bool`. Operations on pointer arguments are performed as if the operands were of the `uintptr_t` type. That is, they are not scaled by the size of the type to which the pointer points.

These functions are implemented in terms of the '`__atomic`' builtins (see Section 6.53 [__atomic Builtins], page 557). They should not be used for new code which should use the '`__atomic`' builtins instead.

Not all operations are supported by all target processors. If a particular operation cannot be implemented on the target processor, a warning is generated and a call to an external function is generated. The external function carries the same name as the built-in version, with an additional suffix '`_n`' where *n* is the size of the data type.

In most cases, these built-in functions are considered a *full barrier*. That is, no memory operand is moved across the operation, either forward or backward. Further, instructions are issued as necessary to prevent the processor from speculating loads across the operation and from queuing stores after the operation.

All of the routines are described in the Intel documentation to take "an optional list of variables protected by the memory barrier". It's not clear what is meant by that; it could mean that *only* the listed variables are protected, or it could mean a list of additional variables to be protected. The list is ignored by GCC which treats it as empty. GCC interprets an empty list as meaning that all globally accessible variables should be protected.

type `__sync_fetch_and_add` (*type* `*ptr`, *type* `value`, ...)
type `__sync_fetch_and_sub` (*type* `*ptr`, *type* `value`, ...)
type `__sync_fetch_and_or` (*type* `*ptr`, *type* `value`, ...)
type `__sync_fetch_and_and` (*type* `*ptr`, *type* `value`, ...)
type `__sync_fetch_and_xor` (*type* `*ptr`, *type* `value`, ...)
type `__sync_fetch_and_nand` (*type* `*ptr`, *type* `value`, ...)

> These built-in functions perform the operation suggested by the name, and returns the value that had previously been in memory. That is, operations on integer operands have the following semantics. Operations on pointer arguments are performed as if the operands were of the `uintptr_t` type. That is, they are not scaled by the size of the type to which the pointer points.

```
{ tmp = *ptr; *ptr op= value; return tmp; }
{ tmp = *ptr; *ptr = ~(tmp & value); return tmp; }    // nand
```

The object pointed to by the first argument must be of integer or pointer type. It must not be a boolean type.

Note: GCC 4.4 and later implement `__sync_fetch_and_nand` as `*ptr = ~(tmp & value)` instead of `*ptr = ~tmp & value`.

`type __sync_add_and_fetch (type *ptr, type value, ...)`
`type __sync_sub_and_fetch (type *ptr, type value, ...)`
`type __sync_or_and_fetch (type *ptr, type value, ...)`
`type __sync_and_and_fetch (type *ptr, type value, ...)`
`type __sync_xor_and_fetch (type *ptr, type value, ...)`
`type __sync_nand_and_fetch (type *ptr, type value, ...)`

These built-in functions perform the operation suggested by the name, and return the new value. That is, operations on integer operands have the following semantics. Operations on pointer operands are performed as if the operand's type were `uintptr_t`.

```
{ *ptr op= value; return *ptr; }
{ *ptr = ~(*ptr & value); return *ptr; }   // nand
```

The same constraints on arguments apply as for the corresponding `__sync_op_and_fetch` built-in functions.

Note: GCC 4.4 and later implement `__sync_nand_and_fetch` as `*ptr = ~(*ptr & value)` instead of `*ptr = ~*ptr & value`.

`bool __sync_bool_compare_and_swap (type *ptr, type oldval, type newval, ...)`
`type __sync_val_compare_and_swap (type *ptr, type oldval, type newval, ...)`

These built-in functions perform an atomic compare and swap. That is, if the current value of *ptr* is *oldval*, then write *newval* into *ptr*.

The "bool" version returns true if the comparison is successful and *newval* is written. The "val" version returns the contents of *ptr* before the operation.

`__sync_synchronize (...)`

This built-in function issues a full memory barrier.

`type __sync_lock_test_and_set (type *ptr, type value, ...)`

This built-in function, as described by Intel, is not a traditional test-and-set operation, but rather an atomic exchange operation. It writes *value* into *ptr*, and returns the previous contents of *ptr*.

Many targets have only minimal support for such locks, and do not support a full exchange operation. In this case, a target may support reduced functionality here by which the *only* valid value to store is the immediate constant 1. The exact value actually stored in *ptr* is implementation defined.

This built-in function is not a full barrier, but rather an *acquire barrier*. This means that references after the operation cannot move to (or be speculated to) before the operation, but previous memory stores may not be globally visible yet, and previous memory loads may not yet be satisfied.

`void __sync_lock_release (type *ptr, ...)`

This built-in function releases the lock acquired by `__sync_lock_test_and_set`. Normally this means writing the constant 0 to *ptr*.

This built-in function is not a full barrier, but rather a *release barrier*. This means that all previous memory stores are globally visible, and all previous memory loads have been satisfied, but following memory reads are not prevented from being speculated to before the barrier.

6.53 Built-in Functions for Memory Model Aware Atomic Operations

The following built-in functions approximately match the requirements for the C++11 memory model. They are all identified by being prefixed with '`__atomic`' and most are overloaded so that they work with multiple types.

These functions are intended to replace the legacy '`__sync`' builtins. The main difference is that the memory order that is requested is a parameter to the functions. New code should always use the '`__atomic`' builtins rather than the '`__sync`' builtins.

Note that the '`__atomic`' builtins assume that programs will conform to the C++11 memory model. In particular, they assume that programs are free of data races. See the C++11 standard for detailed requirements.

The '`__atomic`' builtins can be used with any integral scalar or pointer type that is 1, 2, 4, or 8 bytes in length. 16-byte integral types are also allowed if '`__int128`' (see Section 6.8 [__int128], page 412) is supported by the architecture.

The four non-arithmetic functions (load, store, exchange, and compare_exchange) all have a generic version as well. This generic version works on any data type. It uses the lock-free built-in function if the specific data type size makes that possible; otherwise, an external call is left to be resolved at run time. This external call is the same format with the addition of a '`size_t`' parameter inserted as the first parameter indicating the size of the object being pointed to. All objects must be the same size.

There are 6 different memory orders that can be specified. These map to the C++11 memory orders with the same names, see the C++11 standard or the GCC wiki on atomic synchronization for detailed definitions. Individual targets may also support additional memory orders for use on specific architectures. Refer to the target documentation for details of these.

An atomic operation can both constrain code motion and be mapped to hardware instructions for synchronization between threads (e.g., a fence). To which extent this happens is controlled by the memory orders, which are listed here in approximately ascending order of strength. The description of each memory order is only meant to roughly illustrate the effects and is not a specification; see the C++11 memory model for precise semantics.

`__ATOMIC_RELAXED`

> Implies no inter-thread ordering constraints.

`__ATOMIC_CONSUME`

> This is currently implemented using the stronger `__ATOMIC_ACQUIRE` memory order because of a deficiency in C++11's semantics for `memory_order_consume`.

`__ATOMIC_ACQUIRE`

> Creates an inter-thread happens-before constraint from the release (or stronger) semantic store to this acquire load. Can prevent hoisting of code to before the operation.

`__ATOMIC_RELEASE`

>   Creates an inter-thread happens-before constraint to acquire (or stronger) semantic loads that read from this release store. Can prevent sinking of code to after the operation.

`__ATOMIC_ACQ_REL`

>   Combines the effects of both `__ATOMIC_ACQUIRE` and `__ATOMIC_RELEASE`.

`__ATOMIC_SEQ_CST`

>   Enforces total ordering with all other `__ATOMIC_SEQ_CST` operations.

Note that in the C++11 memory model, *fences* (e.g., '`__atomic_thread_fence`') take effect in combination with other atomic operations on specific memory locations (e.g., atomic loads); operations on specific memory locations do not necessarily affect other operations in the same way.

Target architectures are encouraged to provide their own patterns for each of the atomic built-in functions. If no target is provided, the original non-memory model set of '`__sync`' atomic built-in functions are used, along with any required synchronization fences surrounding it in order to achieve the proper behavior. Execution in this case is subject to the same restrictions as those built-in functions.

If there is no pattern or mechanism to provide a lock-free instruction sequence, a call is made to an external routine with the same parameters to be resolved at run time.

When implementing patterns for these built-in functions, the memory order parameter can be ignored as long as the pattern implements the most restrictive `__ATOMIC_SEQ_CST` memory order. Any of the other memory orders execute correctly with this memory order but they may not execute as efficiently as they could with a more appropriate implementation of the relaxed requirements.

Note that the C++11 standard allows for the memory order parameter to be determined at run time rather than at compile time. These built-in functions map any run-time value to `__ATOMIC_SEQ_CST` rather than invoke a runtime library call or inline a switch statement. This is standard compliant, safe, and the simplest approach for now.

The memory order parameter is a signed int, but only the lower 16 bits are reserved for the memory order. The remainder of the signed int is reserved for target use and should be 0. Use of the predefined atomic values ensures proper usage.

type `__atomic_load_n` (*type* *ptr, *int memorder*)   [Built-in Function]

>   This built-in function implements an atomic load operation. It returns the contents of *ptr.

>   The valid memory order variants are `__ATOMIC_RELAXED`, `__ATOMIC_SEQ_CST`, `__ATOMIC_ACQUIRE`, and `__ATOMIC_CONSUME`.

`void` `__atomic_load` (*type* *ptr, *type* *ret, *int memorder*)   [Built-in Function]

>   This is the generic version of an atomic load. It returns the contents of *ptr in *ret.

`void` `__atomic_store_n` (*type* *ptr, *type val*, *int memorder*)   [Built-in Function]

>   This built-in function implements an atomic store operation. It writes `val` into *ptr.

>   The valid memory order variants are `__ATOMIC_RELAXED`, `__ATOMIC_SEQ_CST`, and `__ATOMIC_RELEASE`.

void __atomic_store (*type* *ptr, *type* *val, *int memorder*)   [Built-in Function]
>   This is the generic version of an atomic store. It stores the value of *val into *ptr.

type __atomic_exchange_n (*type* *ptr, *type* val, int   [Built-in Function]
>   *memorder*)
>
>   This built-in function implements an atomic exchange operation. It writes *val* into
>   *ptr, and returns the previous contents of *ptr.
>
>   The valid memory order variants are __ATOMIC_RELAXED, __ATOMIC_SEQ_CST, __
>   ATOMIC_ACQUIRE, __ATOMIC_RELEASE, and __ATOMIC_ACQ_REL.

void __atomic_exchange (*type* *ptr, *type* *val, *type* *ret, int   [Built-in Function]
>   *memorder*)
>
>   This is the generic version of an atomic exchange. It stores the contents of *val into
>   *ptr. The original value of *ptr is copied into *ret.

bool __atomic_compare_exchange_n (*type* *ptr, *type*   [Built-in Function]
>   *expected, *type* desired, bool weak, int success_memorder, int
>   failure_memorder)
>
>   This built-in function implements an atomic compare and exchange operation. This
>   compares the contents of *ptr with the contents of *expected. If equal, the operation
>   is a *read-modify-write* operation that writes *desired* into *ptr. If they are not equal,
>   the operation is a *read* and the current contents of *ptr are written into *expected.
>   *weak* is true for weak compare_exchange, which may fail spuriously, and false for
>   the strong variation, which never fails spuriously. Many targets only offer the strong
>   variation and ignore the parameter. When in doubt, use the strong variation.
>
>   If *desired* is written into *ptr then true is returned and memory is affected according
>   to the memory order specified by *success_memorder*. There are no restrictions on
>   what memory order can be used here.
>
>   Otherwise, false is returned and memory is affected according to *failure_memorder*.
>   This memory order cannot be __ATOMIC_RELEASE nor __ATOMIC_ACQ_REL. It also
>   cannot be a stronger order than that specified by *success_memorder*.

bool __atomic_compare_exchange (*type* *ptr, *type*   [Built-in Function]
>   *expected, *type* *desired, bool weak, int success_memorder, int
>   failure_memorder)
>
>   This built-in function implements the generic version of __atomic_compare_
>   exchange. The function is virtually identical to __atomic_compare_exchange_n,
>   except the desired value is also a pointer.

type __atomic_add_fetch (*type* *ptr, *type* val, int memorder)   [Built-in Function]
type __atomic_sub_fetch (*type* *ptr, *type* val, int memorder)   [Built-in Function]
type __atomic_and_fetch (*type* *ptr, *type* val, int memorder)   [Built-in Function]
type __atomic_xor_fetch (*type* *ptr, *type* val, int memorder)   [Built-in Function]
type __atomic_or_fetch (*type* *ptr, *type* val, int memorder)   [Built-in Function]
type __atomic_nand_fetch (*type* *ptr, *type* val, int   [Built-in Function]
>   *memorder*)
>
>   These built-in functions perform the operation suggested by the name, and return
>   the result of the operation. Operations on pointer arguments are performed as if the

operands were of the `uintptr_t` type. That is, they are not scaled by the size of the type to which the pointer points.

> `{ *ptr op= val; return *ptr; }`

The object pointed to by the first argument must be of integer or pointer type. It must not be a boolean type. All memory orders are valid.

`type __atomic_fetch_add (type *ptr, type val, int memorder)`   [Built-in Function]
`type __atomic_fetch_sub (type *ptr, type val, int memorder)`   [Built-in Function]
`type __atomic_fetch_and (type *ptr, type val, int memorder)`   [Built-in Function]
`type __atomic_fetch_xor (type *ptr, type val, int memorder)`   [Built-in Function]
`type __atomic_fetch_or (type *ptr, type val, int memorder)`   [Built-in Function]
`type __atomic_fetch_nand (type *ptr, type val, int`   [Built-in Function]
      `memorder)`

These built-in functions perform the operation suggested by the name, and return the value that had previously been in `*ptr`. Operations on pointer arguments are performed as if the operands were of the `uintptr_t` type. That is, they are not scaled by the size of the type to which the pointer points.

> `{ tmp = *ptr; *ptr op= val; return tmp; }`

The same constraints on arguments apply as for the corresponding `__atomic_op_fetch` built-in functions. All memory orders are valid.

`bool __atomic_test_and_set (void *ptr, int memorder)`   [Built-in Function]
This built-in function performs an atomic test-and-set operation on the byte at `*ptr`. The byte is set to some implementation defined nonzero "set" value and the return value is `true` if and only if the previous contents were "set". It should be only used for operands of type `bool` or `char`. For other types only part of the value may be set.

All memory orders are valid.

`void __atomic_clear (bool *ptr, int memorder)`   [Built-in Function]
This built-in function performs an atomic clear operation on `*ptr`. After the operation, `*ptr` contains 0. It should be only used for operands of type `bool` or `char` and in conjunction with `__atomic_test_and_set`. For other types it may only clear partially. If the type is not `bool` prefer using `__atomic_store`.

The valid memory order variants are `__ATOMIC_RELAXED`, `__ATOMIC_SEQ_CST`, and `__ATOMIC_RELEASE`.

`void __atomic_thread_fence (int memorder)`   [Built-in Function]
This built-in function acts as a synchronization fence between threads based on the specified memory order.

All memory orders are valid.

`void __atomic_signal_fence (int memorder)`   [Built-in Function]
This built-in function acts as a synchronization fence between a thread and signal handlers based in the same thread.

All memory orders are valid.

`bool __atomic_always_lock_free` (*size_t size, void *ptr*)   [Built-in Function]
  This built-in function returns true if objects of *size* bytes always generate lock-free atomic instructions for the target architecture. *size* must resolve to a compile-time constant and the result also resolves to a compile-time constant.

  ptr is an optional pointer to the object that may be used to determine alignment. A value of 0 indicates typical alignment should be used. The compiler may also ignore this parameter.

```
if (__atomic_always_lock_free (sizeof (long long), 0))
```

`bool __atomic_is_lock_free` (*size_t size, void *ptr*)   [Built-in Function]
  This built-in function returns true if objects of *size* bytes always generate lock-free atomic instructions for the target architecture. If the built-in function is not known to be lock-free, a call is made to a runtime routine named `__atomic_is_lock_free`.

  ptr is an optional pointer to the object that may be used to determine alignment. A value of 0 indicates typical alignment should be used. The compiler may also ignore this parameter.

6.54 Built-in Functions to Perform Arithmetic with Overflow Checking

The following built-in functions allow performing simple arithmetic operations together with checking whether the operations overflowed.

`bool __builtin_add_overflow` (***type1** a,* ***type2** b,* ***type3***   [Built-in Function]
    ***res*)
`bool __builtin_sadd_overflow` (*int a, int b, int *res*)   [Built-in Function]
`bool __builtin_saddl_overflow` (*long int a, long int b, long*   [Built-in Function]
    *int *res*)
`bool __builtin_saddll_overflow` (*long long int a, long long*   [Built-in Function]
    *int b, long long int *res*)
`bool __builtin_uadd_overflow` (*unsigned int a, unsigned int*   [Built-in Function]
    *b, unsigned int *res*)
`bool __builtin_uaddl_overflow` (*unsigned long int a,*   [Built-in Function]
    *unsigned long int b, unsigned long int *res*)
`bool __builtin_uaddll_overflow` (*unsigned long long int a,*   [Built-in Function]
    *unsigned long long int b, unsigned long long int *res*)
  These built-in functions promote the first two operands into infinite precision signed type and perform addition on those promoted operands. The result is then cast to the type the third pointer argument points to and stored there. If the stored result is equal to the infinite precision result, the built-in functions return false, otherwise they return true. As the addition is performed in infinite signed precision, these built-in functions have fully defined behavior for all argument values.

  The first built-in function allows arbitrary integral types for operands and the result type must be pointer to some integral type other than enumerated or boolean type, the rest of the built-in functions have explicit integer types.

  The compiler will attempt to use hardware instructions to implement these built-in functions where possible, like conditional jump on overflow after addition, conditional jump on carry etc.

`bool __builtin_sub_overflow` (*type1* a, *type2* b, *type3*   [Built-in Function]
        **res*)

`bool __builtin_ssub_overflow` (*int a, int b, int *res*)   [Built-in Function]

`bool __builtin_ssubl_overflow` (*long int a, long int b, long*   [Built-in Function]
        *int *res*)

`bool __builtin_ssubll_overflow` (*long long int a, long long*   [Built-in Function]
        *int b, long long int *res*)

`bool __builtin_usub_overflow` (*unsigned int a, unsigned int*   [Built-in Function]
        *b, unsigned int *res*)

`bool __builtin_usubl_overflow` (*unsigned long int a,*   [Built-in Function]
        *unsigned long int b, unsigned long int *res*)

`bool __builtin_usubll_overflow` (*unsigned long long int a,*   [Built-in Function]
        *unsigned long long int b, unsigned long long int *res*)

> These built-in functions are similar to the add overflow checking built-in functions
> above, except they perform subtraction, subtract the second argument from the first
> one, instead of addition.

`bool __builtin_mul_overflow` (*type1* a, *type2* b, *type3*   [Built-in Function]
        **res*)

`bool __builtin_smul_overflow` (*int a, int b, int *res*)   [Built-in Function]

`bool __builtin_smull_overflow` (*long int a, long int b, long*   [Built-in Function]
        *int *res*)

`bool __builtin_smulll_overflow` (*long long int a, long long*   [Built-in Function]
        *int b, long long int *res*)

`bool __builtin_umul_overflow` (*unsigned int a, unsigned int*   [Built-in Function]
        *b, unsigned int *res*)

`bool __builtin_umull_overflow` (*unsigned long int a,*   [Built-in Function]
        *unsigned long int b, unsigned long int *res*)

`bool __builtin_umulll_overflow` (*unsigned long long int a,*   [Built-in Function]
        *unsigned long long int b, unsigned long long int *res*)

> These built-in functions are similar to the add overflow checking built-in functions
> above, except they perform multiplication, instead of addition.

The following built-in functions allow checking if simple arithmetic operation would overflow.

`bool __builtin_add_overflow_p` (*type1* a, *type2* b, *type3*   [Built-in Function]
        c)

`bool __builtin_sub_overflow_p` (*type1* a, *type2* b, *type3*   [Built-in Function]
        c)

`bool __builtin_mul_overflow_p` (*type1* a, *type2* b, *type3*   [Built-in Function]
        c)

> These built-in functions are similar to `__builtin_add_overflow`, `__builtin_sub_`
> `overflow`, or `__builtin_mul_overflow`, except that they don't store the result of
> the arithmetic operation anywhere and the last argument is not a pointer, but some
> expression with integral type other than enumerated or boolean type.

> The built-in functions promote the first two operands into infinite precision signed
> type and perform addition on those promoted operands. The result is then cast to

the type of the third argument. If the cast result is equal to the infinite precision result, the built-in functions return false, otherwise they return true. The value of the third argument is ignored, just the side-effects in the third argument are evaluated, and no integral argument promotions are performed on the last argument. If the third argument is a bit-field, the type used for the result cast has the precision and signedness of the given bit-field, rather than precision and signedness of the underlying type.

For example, the following macro can be used to portably check, at compile-time, whether or not adding two constant integers will overflow, and perform the addition only when it is known to be safe and not to trigger a '-Woverflow' warning.

```
#define INT_ADD_OVERFLOW_P(a, b) \
    __builtin_add_overflow_p (a, b, (__typeof__ ((a) + (b))) 0)

enum {
    A = INT_MAX, B = 3,
    C = INT_ADD_OVERFLOW_P (A, B) ? 0 : A + B,
    D = __builtin_add_overflow_p (1, SCHAR_MAX, (signed char) 0)
};
```

The compiler will attempt to use hardware instructions to implement these built-in functions where possible, like conditional jump on overflow after addition, conditional jump on carry etc.

6.55 x86-Specific Memory Model Extensions for Transactional Memory

The x86 architecture supports additional memory ordering flags to mark lock critical sections for hardware lock elision. These must be specified in addition to an existing memory order to atomic intrinsics.

__ATOMIC_HLE_ACQUIRE

> Start lock elision on a lock variable. Memory order must be __ATOMIC_ACQUIRE or stronger.

__ATOMIC_HLE_RELEASE

> End lock elision on a lock variable. Memory order must be __ATOMIC_RELEASE or stronger.

When a lock acquire fails, it is required for good performance to abort the transaction quickly. This can be done with a _mm_pause.

```
#include <immintrin.h> // For _mm_pause

int lockvar;

/* Acquire lock with lock elision */
while (__atomic_exchange_n(&lockvar, 1, __ATOMIC_ACQUIRE|__ATOMIC_HLE_ACQUIRE))
    _mm_pause(); /* Abort failed transaction */
...
/* Free lock with lock elision */
__atomic_store_n(&lockvar, 0, __ATOMIC_RELEASE|__ATOMIC_HLE_RELEASE);
```

6.56 Object Size Checking Built-in Functions

GCC implements a limited buffer overflow protection mechanism that can prevent some buffer overflow attacks by determining the sizes of objects into which data is about to be written and preventing the writes when the size isn't sufficient. The built-in functions described below yield the best results when used together and when optimization is enabled. For example, to detect object sizes across function boundaries or to follow pointer assignments through non-trivial control flow they rely on various optimization passes enabled with '-O2'. However, to a limited extent, they can be used without optimization as well.

size_t __builtin_object_size (*const void * ptr, int type*)   [Built-in Function]
> is a built-in construct that returns a constant number of bytes from *ptr* to the end of the object *ptr* pointer points to (if known at compile time). __builtin_object_size never evaluates its arguments for side-effects. If there are any side-effects in them, it returns (size_t) -1 for *type* 0 or 1 and (size_t) 0 for *type* 2 or 3. If there are multiple objects *ptr* can point to and all of them are known at compile time, the returned number is the maximum of remaining byte counts in those objects if *type* & 2 is 0 and minimum if nonzero. If it is not possible to determine which objects *ptr* points to at compile time, __builtin_object_size should return (size_t) -1 for *type* 0 or 1 and (size_t) 0 for *type* 2 or 3.
>
> *type* is an integer constant from 0 to 3. If the least significant bit is clear, objects are whole variables, if it is set, a closest surrounding subobject is considered the object a pointer points to. The second bit determines if maximum or minimum of remaining bytes is computed.

```
struct V { char buf1[10]; int b; char buf2[10]; } var;
char *p = &var.buf1[1], *q = &var.b;

/* Here the object p points to is var.  */
assert (__builtin_object_size (p, 0) == sizeof (var) - 1);
/* The subobject p points to is var.buf1.  */
assert (__builtin_object_size (p, 1) == sizeof (var.buf1) - 1);
/* The object q points to is var.  */
assert (__builtin_object_size (q, 0)
            == (char *) (&var + 1) - (char *) &var.b);
/* The subobject q points to is var.b.  */
assert (__builtin_object_size (q, 1) == sizeof (var.b));
```

There are built-in functions added for many common string operation functions, e.g., for memcpy __builtin___memcpy_chk built-in is provided. This built-in has an additional last argument, which is the number of bytes remaining in object the *dest* argument points to or (size_t) -1 if the size is not known.

The built-in functions are optimized into the normal string functions like memcpy if the last argument is (size_t) -1 or if it is known at compile time that the destination object will not be overflown. If the compiler can determine at compile time the object will be always overflown, it issues a warning.

The intended use can be e.g.

```
#undef memcpy
#define bos0(dest) __builtin_object_size (dest, 0)
#define memcpy(dest, src, n) \
  __builtin___memcpy_chk (dest, src, n, bos0 (dest))
```

```
char *volatile p;
char buf[10];
/* It is unknown what object p points to, so this is optimized
   into plain memcpy - no checking is possible.  */
memcpy (p, "abcde", n);
/* Destination is known and length too.  It is known at compile
   time there will be no overflow.  */
memcpy (&buf[5], "abcde", 5);
/* Destination is known, but the length is not known at compile time.
   This will result in __memcpy_chk call that can check for overflow
   at run time.  */
memcpy (&buf[5], "abcde", n);
/* Destination is known and it is known at compile time there will
   be overflow.  There will be a warning and __memcpy_chk call that
   will abort the program at run time.  */
memcpy (&buf[6], "abcde", 5);
```

Such built-in functions are provided for `memcpy`, `mempcpy`, `memmove`, `memset`, `strcpy`, `stpcpy`, `strncpy`, `strcat` and `strncat`.

There are also checking built-in functions for formatted output functions.

```
int __builtin___sprintf_chk (char *s, int flag, size_t os, const char *fmt, ...);
int __builtin___snprintf_chk (char *s, size_t maxlen, int flag, size_t os,
                              const char *fmt, ...);
int __builtin___vsprintf_chk (char *s, int flag, size_t os, const char *fmt,
                              va_list ap);
int __builtin___vsnprintf_chk (char *s, size_t maxlen, int flag, size_t os,
                               const char *fmt, va_list ap);
```

The added *flag* argument is passed unchanged to `__sprintf_chk` etc. functions and can contain implementation specific flags on what additional security measures the checking function might take, such as handling `%n` differently.

The *os* argument is the object size *s* points to, like in the other built-in functions. There is a small difference in the behavior though, if *os* is `(size_t) -1`, the built-in functions are optimized into the non-checking functions only if *flag* is 0, otherwise the checking function is called with *os* argument set to `(size_t) -1`.

In addition to this, there are checking built-in functions `__builtin___printf_chk`, `__builtin___vprintf_chk`, `__builtin___fprintf_chk` and `__builtin___vfprintf_chk`. These have just one additional argument, *flag*, right before format string *fmt*. If the compiler is able to optimize them to `fputc` etc. functions, it does, otherwise the checking function is called and the *flag* argument passed to it.

6.57 Pointer Bounds Checker Built-in Functions

GCC provides a set of built-in functions to control Pointer Bounds Checker instrumentation. Note that all Pointer Bounds Checker builtins can be used even if you compile with Pointer Bounds Checker off ('`-fno-check-pointer-bounds`'). The behavior may differ in such case as documented below.

void * __builtin___bnd_set_ptr_bounds (*const void *q*,   [Built-in Function]
         size_t size)

This built-in function returns a new pointer with the value of q, and associate it with the bounds [q, q+size-1]. With Pointer Bounds Checker off, the built-in function just returns the first argument.

```
extern void *__wrap_malloc (size_t n)
{
  void *p = (void *)__real_malloc (n);
  if (!p) return __builtin___bnd_null_ptr_bounds (p);
  return __builtin___bnd_set_ptr_bounds (p, n);
}
```

void * __builtin___bnd_narrow_ptr_bounds (*const void*   [Built-in Function]
         **p*, *const void *q*, *size_t size*)

This built-in function returns a new pointer with the value of p and associates it with the narrowed bounds formed by the intersection of bounds associated with q and the bounds [p, p + size - 1]. With Pointer Bounds Checker off, the built-in function just returns the first argument.

```
void init_objects (object *objs, size_t size)
{
  size_t i;
  /* Initialize objects one-by-one passing pointers with bounds of
     an object, not the full array of objects.  */
  for (i = 0; i < size; i++)
    init_object (__builtin___bnd_narrow_ptr_bounds (objs + i, objs,
                                                    sizeof(object)));
}
```

void * __builtin___bnd_copy_ptr_bounds (*const void *q*,   [Built-in Function]
         *const void *r*)

This built-in function returns a new pointer with the value of q, and associates it with the bounds already associated with pointer r. With Pointer Bounds Checker off, the built-in function just returns the first argument.

```
/* Here is a way to get pointer to object's field but
   still with the full object's bounds.  */
int *field_ptr = __builtin___bnd_copy_ptr_bounds (&objptr->int_field,
                                                  objptr);
```

void * __builtin___bnd_init_ptr_bounds (*const void *q*)   [Built-in Function]

This built-in function returns a new pointer with the value of q, and associates it with INIT (allowing full memory access) bounds. With Pointer Bounds Checker off, the built-in function just returns the first argument.

void * __builtin___bnd_null_ptr_bounds (*const void *q*)   [Built-in Function]

This built-in function returns a new pointer with the value of q, and associates it with NULL (allowing no memory access) bounds. With Pointer Bounds Checker off, the built-in function just returns the first argument.

void __builtin___bnd_store_ptr_bounds (*const void*   [Built-in Function]
         ***ptr_addr*, *const void *ptr_val*)

This built-in function stores the bounds associated with pointer *ptr_val* and location *ptr_addr* into Bounds Table. This can be useful to propagate bounds from legacy code without touching the associated pointer's memory when pointers are copied as integers. With Pointer Bounds Checker off, the built-in function call is ignored.

void __builtin___bnd_chk_ptr_lbounds (*const void *q*)   [Built-in Function]
This built-in function checks if the pointer *q* is within the lower bound of its associated bounds. With Pointer Bounds Checker off, the built-in function call is ignored.

```
extern void *__wrap_memset (void *dst, int c, size_t len)
{
  if (len > 0)
    {
      __builtin___bnd_chk_ptr_lbounds (dst);
      __builtin___bnd_chk_ptr_ubounds ((char *)dst + len - 1);
      __real_memset (dst, c, len);
    }
  return dst;
}
```

void __builtin___bnd_chk_ptr_ubounds (*const void *q*)   [Built-in Function]
This built-in function checks if the pointer *q* is within the upper bound of its associated bounds. With Pointer Bounds Checker off, the built-in function call is ignored.

void __builtin___bnd_chk_ptr_bounds (*const void *q, size_t*   [Built-in Function]
        size)
This built-in function checks if [*q*, *q* + *size* - 1] is within the lower and upper bounds associated with *q*. With Pointer Bounds Checker off, the built-in function call is ignored.

```
extern void *__wrap_memcpy (void *dst, const void *src, size_t n)
{
  if (n > 0)
    {
      __bnd_chk_ptr_bounds (dst, n);
      __bnd_chk_ptr_bounds (src, n);
      __real_memcpy (dst, src, n);
    }
  return dst;
}
```

const void * __builtin___bnd_get_ptr_lbound (*const*   [Built-in Function]
        *void *q*)
This built-in function returns the lower bound associated with the pointer *q*, as a pointer value. This is useful for debugging using printf. With Pointer Bounds Checker off, the built-in function returns 0.

```
void *lb = __builtin___bnd_get_ptr_lbound (q);
void *ub = __builtin___bnd_get_ptr_ubound (q);
printf ("q = %p  lb(q) = %p  ub(q) = %p", q, lb, ub);
```

const void * __builtin___bnd_get_ptr_ubound (*const*   [Built-in Function]
        *void *q*)
This built-in function returns the upper bound (which is a pointer) associated with the pointer *q*. With Pointer Bounds Checker off, the built-in function returns -1.

6.58 Cilk Plus C/C++ Language Extension Built-in Functions

GCC provides support for the following built-in reduction functions if Cilk Plus is enabled. Cilk Plus can be enabled using the '-fcilkplus' flag.

- __sec_implicit_index
- __sec_reduce
- __sec_reduce_add
- __sec_reduce_all_nonzero
- __sec_reduce_all_zero
- __sec_reduce_any_nonzero
- __sec_reduce_any_zero
- __sec_reduce_max
- __sec_reduce_min
- __sec_reduce_max_ind
- __sec_reduce_min_ind
- __sec_reduce_mul
- __sec_reduce_mutating

Further details and examples about these built-in functions are described in the Cilk Plus language manual which can be found at http://www.cilkplus.org.

6.59 Other Built-in Functions Provided by GCC

GCC provides a large number of built-in functions other than the ones mentioned above. Some of these are for internal use in the processing of exceptions or variable-length argument lists and are not documented here because they may change from time to time; we do not recommend general use of these functions.

The remaining functions are provided for optimization purposes.

With the exception of built-ins that have library equivalents such as the standard C library functions discussed below, or that expand to library calls, GCC built-in functions are always expanded inline and thus do not have corresponding entry points and their address cannot be obtained. Attempting to use them in an expression other than a function call results in a compile-time error.

GCC includes built-in versions of many of the functions in the standard C library. These functions come in two forms: one whose names start with the __builtin_ prefix, and the other without. Both forms have the same type (including prototype), the same address (when their address is taken), and the same meaning as the C library functions even if you specify the '-fno-builtin' option see Section 3.4 [C Dialect Options], page 33). Many of these functions are only optimized in certain cases; if they are not optimized in a particular case, a call to the library function is emitted.

Outside strict ISO C mode ('-ansi', '-std=c90', '-std=c99' or '-std=c11'), the functions _exit, alloca, bcmp, bzero, dcgettext, dgettext, dremf, dreml, drem, exp10f, exp10l, exp10, ffsll, ffsl, ffs, fprintf_unlocked, fputs_unlocked, gammaf, gammal, gamma, gammaf_r, gammal_r, gamma_r, gettext, index, isascii, j0f, j0l, j0, j1f, j1l, j1, jnf, jnl, jn, lgammaf_r, lgammal_r, lgamma_r, mempcpy, pow10f, pow10l, pow10, printf_unlocked, rindex, scalbf, scalbl, scalb, signbit, signbitf, signbitl, signbitd32, signbitd64, signbitd128, significandf, significandl, significand, sincosf, sincosl, sincos, stpcpy, stpncpy, strcasecmp, strdup, strfmon, strncasecmp, strndup, toascii, y0f, y0l, y0, y1f, y1l, y1, ynf, ynl and yn may be handled as built-in functions. All these functions have corresponding versions prefixed with __builtin_, which may be used even in strict C90 mode.

The ISO C99 functions _Exit, acoshf, acoshl, acosh, asinhf, asinhl, asinh, atanhf, atanhl, atanh, cabsf, cabsl, cabs, cacosf, cacoshf, cacoshl, cacosh, cacosl, cacos, cargf, cargl, carg, casinf, casinhf, casinhl, casinh, casinl, casin, catanf, catanhf, catanhl, catanh, catanl, catan, cbrtf, cbrtl, cbrt, ccosf, ccoshf, ccoshl, ccosh, ccosl, ccos, cexpf, cexpl, cexp, cimagf, cimagl, cimag, clogf, clogl, clog, conjf, conjl, conj, copysignf, copysignl, copysign, cpowf, cpowl, cpow, cprojf, cprojl, cproj, crealf, creall, creal, csinf, csinhf, csinhl, csinh, csinl, csin, csqrtf, csqrtl, csqrt, ctanf, ctanhf, ctanhl, ctanh, ctanl, ctan, erfcf, erfcl, erfc, erff, erfl, erf, exp2f, exp2l, exp2, expm1f, expm1l, expm1, fdimf, fdiml, fdim, fmaf, fmal, fmaxf, fmaxl, fmax, fma, fminf, fminl, fmin, hypotf, hypotl, hypot, ilogbf, ilogbl, ilogb, imaxabs, isblank, iswblank, lgammaf, lgammal, lgamma, llabs, llrintf, llrintl, llrint, llroundf, llroundl, llround, log1pf, log1pl, log1p, log2f, log2l, log2, logbf, logbl, logb, lrintf, lrintl, lrint, lroundf, lroundl, lround, nearbyintf, nearbyintl, nearbyint, nextafterf, nextafterl, nextafter, nexttowardf, nexttowardl, nexttoward, remainderf, remainderl, remainder, remquof, remquol, remquo, rintf, rintl, rint, roundf, roundl, round, scalblnf, scalblnl, scalbln, scalbnf, scalbnl, scalbn, snprintf, tgammaf, tgammal, tgamma, truncf, truncl, trunc, vfscanf, vscanf, vsnprintf and vsscanf are handled as built-in functions except in strict ISO C90 mode ('-ansi' or '-std=c90').

There are also built-in versions of the ISO C99 functions acosf, acosl, asinf, asinl, atan2f, atan2l, atanf, atanl, ceilf, ceill, cosf, coshf, coshl, cosl, expf, expl, fabsf, fabsl, floorf, floorl, fmodf, fmodl, frexpf, frexpl, ldexpf, ldexpl, log10f, log10l, logf, logl, modfl, modf, powf, powl, sinf, sinhf, sinhl, sinl, sqrtf, sqrtl, tanf, tanhf, tanhl and tanl that are recognized in any mode since ISO C90 reserves these names for the purpose to which ISO C99 puts them. All these functions have corresponding versions prefixed with __builtin_.

There are also built-in functions __builtin_fabsf*n*, __builtin_fabsf*n*x, __builtin_copysignf*n* and __builtin_copysignf*n*x, corresponding to the TS 18661-3 functions fabsf*n*, fabsf*n*x, copysignf*n* and copysignf*n*x, for supported types _Float*n* and _Float*n*x.

There are also GNU extension functions clog10, clog10f and clog10l which names are reserved by ISO C99 for future use. All these functions have versions prefixed with __builtin_.

The ISO C94 functions iswalnum, iswalpha, iswcntrl, iswdigit, iswgraph, iswlower, iswprint, iswpunct, iswspace, iswupper, iswxdigit, towlower and towupper are handled as built-in functions except in strict ISO C90 mode ('-ansi' or '-std=c90').

The ISO C90 functions abort, abs, acos, asin, atan2, atan, calloc, ceil, cosh, cos, exit, exp, fabs, floor, fmod, fprintf, fputs, frexp, fscanf, isalnum, isalpha, iscntrl, isdigit, isgraph, islower, isprint, ispunct, isspace, isupper, isxdigit, `tolower`, `toupper`, `labs`, `ldexp`, `log10`, `log`, `malloc`, `memchr`, `memcmp`, `memcpy`, `memset`, `modf`, `pow`, `printf`, `putchar`, `puts`, `scanf`, `sinh`, `sin`, `snprintf`, `sprintf`, `sqrt`, `sscanf`, `strcat`, `strchr`, `strcmp`, `strcpy`, `strcspn`, `strlen`, `strncat`, `strncmp`, `strncpy`, `strpbrk`, `strrchr`, `strspn`, `strstr`, `tanh`, `tan`, `vfprintf`, `vprintf` and `vsprintf` are all recognized as built-in functions unless '`-fno-builtin`' is specified (or '`-fno-builtin-`*function*' is specified for an individual function). All of these functions have corresponding versions prefixed with `__builtin_`.

GCC provides built-in versions of the ISO C99 floating-point comparison macros that avoid raising exceptions for unordered operands. They have the same names as the standard macros (`isgreater`, `isgreaterequal`, `isless`, `islessequal`, `islessgreater`, and `isunordered`) , with `__builtin_` prefixed. We intend for a library implementor to be able to simply `#define` each standard macro to its built-in equivalent. In the same fashion, GCC provides `fpclassify`, `isfinite`, `isinf_sign`, `isnormal` and `signbit` built-ins used with `__builtin_` prefixed. The `isinf` and `isnan` built-in functions appear both with and without the `__builtin_` prefix.

`void *__builtin_alloca (`*size_t size*`)`   [Built-in Function]
    The `__builtin_alloca` function must be called at block scope. The function allocates an object *size* bytes large on the stack of the calling function. The object is aligned on the default stack alignment boundary for the target determined by the `__BIGGEST_ALIGNMENT__` macro. The `__builtin_alloca` function returns a pointer to the first byte of the allocated object. The lifetime of the allocated object ends just before the calling function returns to its caller. This is so even when `__builtin_alloca` is called within a nested block.

    For example, the following function allocates eight objects of `n` bytes each on the stack, storing a pointer to each in consecutive elements of the array `a`. It then passes the array to function `g` which can safely use the storage pointed to by each of the array elements.

```
void f (unsigned n)
{
  void *a [8];
  for (int i = 0; i != 8; ++i)
    a [i] = __builtin_alloca (n);

  g (a, n);   // safe
}
```

    Since the `__builtin_alloca` function doesn't validate its argument it is the responsibility of its caller to make sure the argument doesn't cause it to exceed the stack size limit. The `__builtin_alloca` function is provided to make it possible to allocate on the stack arrays of bytes with an upper bound that may be computed at run time. Since C99 Variable Length Arrays offer similar functionality under a portable, more convenient, and safer interface they are recommended instead, in both C99 and C++ programs where GCC provides them as an extension. See Section 6.19 [Variable Length], page 421, for details.

`void *__builtin_alloca_with_align (`*size_t size*`, size_t`   [Built-in Function]
        alignment`)`
    The `__builtin_alloca_with_align` function must be called at block scope. The function allocates an object *size* bytes large on the stack of the calling function.

The allocated object is aligned on the boundary specified by the argument *alignment* whose unit is given in bits (not bytes). The *size* argument must be positive and not exceed the stack size limit. The *alignment* argument must be a constant integer expression that evaluates to a power of 2 greater than or equal to `CHAR_BIT` and less than some unspecified maximum. Invocations with other values are rejected with an error indicating the valid bounds. The function returns a pointer to the first byte of the allocated object. The lifetime of the allocated object ends at the end of the block in which the function was called. The allocated storage is released no later than just before the calling function returns to its caller, but may be released at the end of the block in which the function was called.

For example, in the following function the call to g is unsafe because when `overalign` is non-zero, the space allocated by `__builtin_alloca_with_align` may have been released at the end of the `if` statement in which it was called.

```
void f (unsigned n, bool overalign)
{
  void *p;
  if (overalign)
    p = __builtin_alloca_with_align (n, 64 /* bits */);
  else
    p = __builtin_alloc (n);

  g (p, n);   // unsafe
}
```

Since the `__builtin_alloca_with_align` function doesn't validate its *size* argument it is the responsibility of its caller to make sure the argument doesn't cause it to exceed the stack size limit. The `__builtin_alloca_with_align` function is provided to make it possible to allocate on the stack overaligned arrays of bytes with an upper bound that may be computed at run time. Since C99 Variable Length Arrays offer the same functionality under a portable, more convenient, and safer interface they are recommended instead, in both C99 and C++ programs where GCC provides them as an extension. See Section 6.19 [Variable Length], page 421, for details.

`int __builtin_types_compatible_p (`*type1*`, `*type2*`)`   [Built-in Function]
    You can use the built-in function `__builtin_types_compatible_p` to determine whether two types are the same.

    This built-in function returns 1 if the unqualified versions of the types *type1* and *type2* (which are types, not expressions) are compatible, 0 otherwise. The result of this built-in function can be used in integer constant expressions.

    This built-in function ignores top level qualifiers (e.g., `const`, `volatile`). For example, `int` is equivalent to `const int`.

    The type `int[]` and `int[5]` are compatible. On the other hand, `int` and `char *` are not compatible, even if the size of their types, on the particular architecture are the same. Also, the amount of pointer indirection is taken into account when determining similarity. Consequently, `short *` is not similar to `short **`. Furthermore, two types that are typedefed are considered compatible if their underlying types are compatible.

    An `enum` type is not considered to be compatible with another `enum` type even if both are compatible with the same integer type; this is what the C standard specifies. For example, `enum {foo, bar}` is not similar to `enum {hot, dog}`.

You typically use this function in code whose execution varies depending on the arguments' types. For example:

```
#define foo(x)                                                    \
  ({                                                              \
     typeof (x) tmp = (x);                                        \
     if (__builtin_types_compatible_p (typeof (x), long double)) \
       tmp = foo_long_double (tmp);                               \
     else if (__builtin_types_compatible_p (typeof (x), double)) \
       tmp = foo_double (tmp);                                    \
     else if (__builtin_types_compatible_p (typeof (x), float))  \
       tmp = foo_float (tmp);                                     \
     else                                                         \
       abort ();                                                  \
     tmp;                                                         \
  })
```

Note: This construct is only available for C.

type **__builtin_call_with_static_chain (***call_exp*,   [Built-in Function]
       *pointer_exp***)**

The *call_exp* expression must be a function call, and the *pointer_exp* expression must be a pointer. The *pointer_exp* is passed to the function call in the target's static chain location. The result of builtin is the result of the function call.

Note: This builtin is only available for C. This builtin can be used to call Go closures from C.

type **__builtin_choose_expr (***const_exp*, *exp1*, *exp2***)**   [Built-in Function]

You can use the built-in function **__builtin_choose_expr** to evaluate code depending on the value of a constant expression. This built-in function returns *exp1* if *const_exp*, which is an integer constant expression, is nonzero. Otherwise it returns *exp2*.

This built-in function is analogous to the '? :' operator in C, except that the expression returned has its type unaltered by promotion rules. Also, the built-in function does not evaluate the expression that is not chosen. For example, if *const_exp* evaluates to true, *exp2* is not evaluated even if it has side-effects.

This built-in function can return an lvalue if the chosen argument is an lvalue.

If *exp1* is returned, the return type is the same as *exp1*'s type. Similarly, if *exp2* is returned, its return type is the same as *exp2*.

Example:

```
#define foo(x)                                              \
  __builtin_choose_expr (                                   \
    __builtin_types_compatible_p (typeof (x), double),      \
    foo_double (x),                                         \
    __builtin_choose_expr (                                 \
      __builtin_types_compatible_p (typeof (x), float),     \
      foo_float (x),                                        \
      /* The void expression results in a compile-time error \
         when assigning the result to something.  */        \
      (void)0))
```

Note: This construct is only available for C. Furthermore, the unused expression (*exp1* or *exp2* depending on the value of *const_exp*) may still generate syntax errors. This may change in future revisions.

type **__builtin_complex** (*real*, *imag*)   [Built-in Function]

    The built-in function **__builtin_complex** is provided for use in implementing the ISO C11 macros `CMPLXF`, `CMPLX` and `CMPLXL`. *real* and *imag* must have the same type, a real binary floating-point type, and the result has the corresponding complex type with real and imaginary parts *real* and *imag*. Unlike '`real + I * imag`', this works even when infinities, NaNs and negative zeros are involved.

int **__builtin_constant_p** (*exp*)   [Built-in Function]

    You can use the built-in function **__builtin_constant_p** to determine if a value is known to be constant at compile time and hence that GCC can perform constant-folding on expressions involving that value. The argument of the function is the value to test. The function returns the integer 1 if the argument is known to be a compile-time constant and 0 if it is not known to be a compile-time constant. A return of 0 does not indicate that the value is *not* a constant, but merely that GCC cannot prove it is a constant with the specified value of the '`-O`' option.

    You typically use this function in an embedded application where memory is a critical resource. If you have some complex calculation, you may want it to be folded if it involves constants, but need to call a function if it does not. For example:

```
#define Scale_Value(X)      \
  (__builtin_constant_p (X) \
  ? ((X) * SCALE + OFFSET) : Scale (X))
```

    You may use this built-in function in either a macro or an inline function. However, if you use it in an inlined function and pass an argument of the function as the argument to the built-in, GCC never returns 1 when you call the inline function with a string constant or compound literal (see Section 6.26 [Compound Literals], page 423) and does not return 1 when you pass a constant numeric value to the inline function unless you specify the '`-O`' option.

    You may also use **__builtin_constant_p** in initializers for static data. For instance, you can write

```
static const int table[] = {
  __builtin_constant_p (EXPRESSION) ? (EXPRESSION) : -1,
  /* ... */
};
```

    This is an acceptable initializer even if *EXPRESSION* is not a constant expression, including the case where **__builtin_constant_p** returns 1 because *EXPRESSION* can be folded to a constant but *EXPRESSION* contains operands that are not otherwise permitted in a static initializer (for example, `0 && foo ()`). GCC must be more conservative about evaluating the built-in in this case, because it has no opportunity to perform optimization.

long **__builtin_expect** (*long exp*, *long c*)   [Built-in Function]

    You may use **__builtin_expect** to provide the compiler with branch prediction information. In general, you should prefer to use actual profile feedback for this ('`-fprofile-arcs`'), as programmers are notoriously bad at predicting how their programs actually perform. However, there are applications in which this data is hard to collect.

    The return value is the value of *exp*, which should be an integral expression. The semantics of the built-in are that it is expected that *exp* == *c*. For example:

```
if (__builtin_expect (x, 0))
  foo ();
```

indicates that we do not expect to call foo, since we expect x to be zero. Since you are limited to integral expressions for *exp*, you should use constructions such as

```
if (__builtin_expect (ptr != NULL, 1))
  foo (*ptr);
```

when testing pointer or floating-point values.

void __builtin_trap (*void*)   [Built-in Function]

This function causes the program to exit abnormally. GCC implements this function by using a target-dependent mechanism (such as intentionally executing an illegal instruction) or by calling abort. The mechanism used may vary from release to release so you should not rely on any particular implementation.

void __builtin_unreachable (*void*)   [Built-in Function]

If control flow reaches the point of the __builtin_unreachable, the program is undefined. It is useful in situations where the compiler cannot deduce the unreachability of the code.

One such case is immediately following an asm statement that either never terminates, or one that transfers control elsewhere and never returns. In this example, without the __builtin_unreachable, GCC issues a warning that control reaches the end of a non-void function. It also generates code to return after the asm.

```
int f (int c, int v)
{
  if (c)
    {
      return v;
    }
  else
    {
      asm("jmp error_handler");
      __builtin_unreachable ();
    }
}
```

Because the asm statement unconditionally transfers control out of the function, control never reaches the end of the function body. The __builtin_unreachable is in fact unreachable and communicates this fact to the compiler.

Another use for __builtin_unreachable is following a call a function that never returns but that is not declared __attribute__((noreturn)), as in this example:

```
void function_that_never_returns (void);

int g (int c)
{
  if (c)
    {
      return 1;
    }
  else
    {
      function_that_never_returns ();
      __builtin_unreachable ();
```

```
        }
      }
```

void * __builtin_assume_aligned (*const void *exp, size_t*   [Built-in Function]
    align, ...)

This function returns its first argument, and allows the compiler to assume that the returned pointer is at least *align* bytes aligned. This built-in can have either two or three arguments, if it has three, the third argument should have integer type, and if it is nonzero means misalignment offset. For example:

```
        void *x = __builtin_assume_aligned (arg, 16);
```

means that the compiler can assume x, set to **arg**, is at least 16-byte aligned, while:

```
        void *x = __builtin_assume_aligned (arg, 32, 8);
```

means that the compiler can assume for x, set to **arg**, that (**char ***) x − 8 is 32-byte aligned.

int __builtin_LINE ()   [Built-in Function]

This function is the equivalent of the preprocessor **__LINE__** macro and returns a constant integer expression that evaluates to the line number of the invocation of the built-in. When used as a C++ default argument for a function *F*, it returns the line number of the call to *F*.

const char * __builtin_FUNCTION ()   [Built-in Function]

This function is the equivalent of the **__FUNCTION__** symbol and returns an address constant pointing to the name of the function from which the built-in was invoked, or the empty string if the invocation is not at function scope. When used as a C++ default argument for a function *F*, it returns the name of *F*'s caller or the empty string if the call was not made at function scope.

const char * __builtin_FILE ()   [Built-in Function]

This function is the equivalent of the preprocessor **__FILE__** macro and returns an address constant pointing to the file name containing the invocation of the built-in, or the empty string if the invocation is not at function scope. When used as a C++ default argument for a function *F*, it returns the file name of the call to *F* or the empty string if the call was not made at function scope.

For example, in the following, each call to function **foo** will print a line similar to `"file.c:123: foo: message"` with the name of the file and the line number of the `printf` call, the name of the function **foo**, followed by the word **message**.

```
        const char*
        function (const char *func = __builtin_FUNCTION ())
        {
          return func;
        }

        void foo (void)
        {
          printf ("%s:%i: %s: message\n", file (), line (), function ());
        }
```

`void __builtin___clear_cache (char *begin, char *end)`   [Built-in Function]

> This function is used to flush the processor's instruction cache for the region of memory between *begin* inclusive and *end* exclusive. Some targets require that the instruction cache be flushed, after modifying memory containing code, in order to obtain deterministic behavior.
>
> If the target does not require instruction cache flushes, `__builtin___clear_cache` has no effect. Otherwise either instructions are emitted in-line to clear the instruction cache or a call to the `__clear_cache` function in libgcc is made.

`void __builtin_prefetch (const void *addr, ...)`   [Built-in Function]

> This function is used to minimize cache-miss latency by moving data into a cache before it is accessed. You can insert calls to `__builtin_prefetch` into code for which you know addresses of data in memory that is likely to be accessed soon. If the target supports them, data prefetch instructions are generated. If the prefetch is done early enough before the access then the data will be in the cache by the time it is accessed.
>
> The value of *addr* is the address of the memory to prefetch. There are two optional arguments, *rw* and *locality*. The value of *rw* is a compile-time constant one or zero; one means that the prefetch is preparing for a write to the memory address and zero, the default, means that the prefetch is preparing for a read. The value *locality* must be a compile-time constant integer between zero and three. A value of zero means that the data has no temporal locality, so it need not be left in the cache after the access. A value of three means that the data has a high degree of temporal locality and should be left in all levels of cache possible. Values of one and two mean, respectively, a low or moderate degree of temporal locality. The default is three.
>
> ```
>     for (i = 0; i < n; i++)
>       {
>         a[i] = a[i] + b[i];
>         __builtin_prefetch (&a[i+j], 1, 1);
>         __builtin_prefetch (&b[i+j], 0, 1);
>         /* ... */
>       }
> ```
>
> Data prefetch does not generate faults if *addr* is invalid, but the address expression itself must be valid. For example, a prefetch of `p->next` does not fault if `p->next` is not a valid address, but evaluation faults if `p` is not a valid address.
>
> If the target does not support data prefetch, the address expression is evaluated if it includes side effects but no other code is generated and GCC does not issue a warning.

`double __builtin_huge_val (void)`   [Built-in Function]

> Returns a positive infinity, if supported by the floating-point format, else `DBL_MAX`. This function is suitable for implementing the ISO C macro `HUGE_VAL`.

`float __builtin_huge_valf (void)`   [Built-in Function]

> Similar to `__builtin_huge_val`, except the return type is `float`.

`long double __builtin_huge_vall (void)`   [Built-in Function]

> Similar to `__builtin_huge_val`, except the return type is `long double`.

`_Floatn __builtin_huge_valfn (void)`   [Built-in Function]

> Similar to `__builtin_huge_val`, except the return type is `_Floatn`.

_Float*nx* __builtin_huge_valf*nx* (*void*)   [Built-in Function]
    Similar to __builtin_huge_val, except the return type is _Float*nx*.

int __builtin_fpclassify (*int, int, int, int, int, ...*)   [Built-in Function]
    This built-in implements the C99 fpclassify functionality. The first five int arguments
    should be the target library's notion of the possible FP classes and are used for return
    values. They must be constant values and they must appear in this order: FP_NAN,
    FP_INFINITE, FP_NORMAL, FP_SUBNORMAL and FP_ZERO. The ellipsis is for exactly one
    floating-point value to classify. GCC treats the last argument as type-generic, which
    means it does not do default promotion from float to double.

double __builtin_inf (*void*)   [Built-in Function]
    Similar to __builtin_huge_val, except a warning is generated if the target floating-
    point format does not support infinities.

_Decimal32 __builtin_infd32 (*void*)   [Built-in Function]
    Similar to __builtin_inf, except the return type is _Decimal32.

_Decimal64 __builtin_infd64 (*void*)   [Built-in Function]
    Similar to __builtin_inf, except the return type is _Decimal64.

_Decimal128 __builtin_infd128 (*void*)   [Built-in Function]
    Similar to __builtin_inf, except the return type is _Decimal128.

float __builtin_inff (*void*)   [Built-in Function]
    Similar to __builtin_inf, except the return type is float. This function is suitable
    for implementing the ISO C99 macro INFINITY.

long double __builtin_infl (*void*)   [Built-in Function]
    Similar to __builtin_inf, except the return type is long double.

_Float*n* __builtin_inff*n* (*void*)   [Built-in Function]
    Similar to __builtin_inf, except the return type is _Float*n*.

_Float*n* __builtin_inff*n*x (*void*)   [Built-in Function]
    Similar to __builtin_inf, except the return type is _Float*n*x.

int __builtin_isinf_sign (*...*)   [Built-in Function]
    Similar to isinf, except the return value is -1 for an argument of −Inf and 1 for
    an argument of +Inf. Note while the parameter list is an ellipsis, this function only
    accepts exactly one floating-point argument. GCC treats this parameter as type-
    generic, which means it does not do default promotion from float to double.

double __builtin_nan (*const char *str*)   [Built-in Function]
    This is an implementation of the ISO C99 function nan.

    Since ISO C99 defines this function in terms of strtod, which we do not implement,
    a description of the parsing is in order. The string is parsed as by strtol; that is, the
    base is recognized by leading '0' or '0x' prefixes. The number parsed is placed in the
    significand such that the least significant bit of the number is at the least significant
    bit of the significand. The number is truncated to fit the significand field provided.
    The significand is forced to be a quiet NaN.

This function, if given a string literal all of which would have been consumed by strtol, is evaluated early enough that it is considered a compile-time constant.

_Decimal32 __builtin_nand32 (*const char *str*)   [Built-in Function]
> Similar to __builtin_nan, except the return type is _Decimal32.

_Decimal64 __builtin_nand64 (*const char *str*)   [Built-in Function]
> Similar to __builtin_nan, except the return type is _Decimal64.

_Decimal128 __builtin_nand128 (*const char *str*)   [Built-in Function]
> Similar to __builtin_nan, except the return type is _Decimal128.

float __builtin_nanf (*const char *str*)   [Built-in Function]
> Similar to __builtin_nan, except the return type is float.

long double __builtin_nanl (*const char *str*)   [Built-in Function]
> Similar to __builtin_nan, except the return type is long double.

_Float*n* __builtin_nanf*n* (*const char *str*)   [Built-in Function]
> Similar to __builtin_nan, except the return type is _Float*n*.

_Float*nx* __builtin_nanf*nx* (*const char *str*)   [Built-in Function]
> Similar to __builtin_nan, except the return type is _Float*nx*.

double __builtin_nans (*const char *str*)   [Built-in Function]
> Similar to __builtin_nan, except the significand is forced to be a signaling NaN. The nans function is proposed by WG14 N965.

float __builtin_nansf (*const char *str*)   [Built-in Function]
> Similar to __builtin_nans, except the return type is float.

long double __builtin_nansl (*const char *str*)   [Built-in Function]
> Similar to __builtin_nans, except the return type is long double.

_Float*n* __builtin_nansf*n* (*const char *str*)   [Built-in Function]
> Similar to __builtin_nans, except the return type is _Float*n*.

_Float*nx* __builtin_nansf*nx* (*const char *str*)   [Built-in Function]
> Similar to __builtin_nans, except the return type is _Float*nx*.

int __builtin_ffs (*int x*)   [Built-in Function]
> Returns one plus the index of the least significant 1-bit of x, or if x is zero, returns zero.

int __builtin_clz (*unsigned int x*)   [Built-in Function]
> Returns the number of leading 0-bits in x, starting at the most significant bit position. If x is 0, the result is undefined.

int __builtin_ctz (*unsigned int x*)   [Built-in Function]
> Returns the number of trailing 0-bits in x, starting at the least significant bit position. If x is 0, the result is undefined.

int __builtin_clrsb (*int x*)   [Built-in Function]
> Returns the number of leading redundant sign bits in *x*, i.e. the number of bits
> following the most significant bit that are identical to it. There are no special cases
> for 0 or other values.

int __builtin_popcount (*unsigned int x*)   [Built-in Function]
> Returns the number of 1-bits in *x*.

int __builtin_parity (*unsigned int x*)   [Built-in Function]
> Returns the parity of *x*, i.e. the number of 1-bits in *x* modulo 2.

int __builtin_ffsl (*long*)   [Built-in Function]
> Similar to __builtin_ffs, except the argument type is long.

int __builtin_clzl (*unsigned long*)   [Built-in Function]
> Similar to __builtin_clz, except the argument type is unsigned long.

int __builtin_ctzl (*unsigned long*)   [Built-in Function]
> Similar to __builtin_ctz, except the argument type is unsigned long.

int __builtin_clrsbl (*long*)   [Built-in Function]
> Similar to __builtin_clrsb, except the argument type is long.

int __builtin_popcountl (*unsigned long*)   [Built-in Function]
> Similar to __builtin_popcount, except the argument type is unsigned long.

int __builtin_parityl (*unsigned long*)   [Built-in Function]
> Similar to __builtin_parity, except the argument type is unsigned long.

int __builtin_ffsll (*long long*)   [Built-in Function]
> Similar to __builtin_ffs, except the argument type is long long.

int __builtin_clzll (*unsigned long long*)   [Built-in Function]
> Similar to __builtin_clz, except the argument type is unsigned long long.

int __builtin_ctzll (*unsigned long long*)   [Built-in Function]
> Similar to __builtin_ctz, except the argument type is unsigned long long.

int __builtin_clrsbll (*long long*)   [Built-in Function]
> Similar to __builtin_clrsb, except the argument type is long long.

int __builtin_popcountll (*unsigned long long*)   [Built-in Function]
> Similar to __builtin_popcount, except the argument type is unsigned long long.

int __builtin_parityll (*unsigned long long*)   [Built-in Function]
> Similar to __builtin_parity, except the argument type is unsigned long long.

double __builtin_powi (*double, int*)   [Built-in Function]
> Returns the first argument raised to the power of the second. Unlike the pow function
> no guarantees about precision and rounding are made.

float __builtin_powif (*float, int*)   [Built-in Function]
> Similar to __builtin_powi, except the argument and return types are float.

`long double __builtin_powil` (*long double, int*)   [Built-in Function]
    Similar to `__builtin_powi`, except the argument and return types are `long double`.

`uint16_t __builtin_bswap16` (*uint16_t x*)   [Built-in Function]
    Returns *x* with the order of the bytes reversed; for example, `0xaabb` becomes `0xbbaa`.
    Byte here always means exactly 8 bits.

`uint32_t __builtin_bswap32` (*uint32_t x*)   [Built-in Function]
    Similar to `__builtin_bswap16`, except the argument and return types are 32 bit.

`uint64_t __builtin_bswap64` (*uint64_t x*)   [Built-in Function]
    Similar to `__builtin_bswap32`, except the argument and return types are 64 bit.

6.60 Built-in Functions Specific to Particular Target Machines

On some target machines, GCC supports many built-in functions specific to those machines. Generally these generate calls to specific machine instructions, but allow the compiler to schedule those calls.

6.60.1 AArch64 Built-in Functions

These built-in functions are available for the AArch64 family of processors.

```
unsigned int __builtin_aarch64_get_fpcr ()
void __builtin_aarch64_set_fpcr (unsigned int)
unsigned int __builtin_aarch64_get_fpsr ()
void __builtin_aarch64_set_fpsr (unsigned int)
```

6.60.2 Alpha Built-in Functions

These built-in functions are available for the Alpha family of processors, depending on the command-line switches used.

The following built-in functions are always available. They all generate the machine instruction that is part of the name.

```
long __builtin_alpha_implver (void)
long __builtin_alpha_rpcc (void)
long __builtin_alpha_amask (long)
long __builtin_alpha_cmpbge (long, long)
long __builtin_alpha_extbl (long, long)
long __builtin_alpha_extwl (long, long)
long __builtin_alpha_extll (long, long)
long __builtin_alpha_extql (long, long)
long __builtin_alpha_extwh (long, long)
long __builtin_alpha_extlh (long, long)
long __builtin_alpha_extqh (long, long)
long __builtin_alpha_insbl (long, long)
long __builtin_alpha_inswl (long, long)
long __builtin_alpha_insll (long, long)
long __builtin_alpha_insql (long, long)
long __builtin_alpha_inswh (long, long)
long __builtin_alpha_inslh (long, long)
long __builtin_alpha_insqh (long, long)
long __builtin_alpha_mskbl (long, long)
long __builtin_alpha_mskwl (long, long)
```

```
long __builtin_alpha_mskll (long, long)
long __builtin_alpha_mskql (long, long)
long __builtin_alpha_mskwh (long, long)
long __builtin_alpha_msklh (long, long)
long __builtin_alpha_mskqh (long, long)
long __builtin_alpha_umulh (long, long)
long __builtin_alpha_zap (long, long)
long __builtin_alpha_zapnot (long, long)
```

The following built-in functions are always with '-mmax' or '-mcpu=*cpu*' where *cpu* is pca56 or later. They all generate the machine instruction that is part of the name.

```
long __builtin_alpha_pklb (long)
long __builtin_alpha_pkwb (long)
long __builtin_alpha_unpkbl (long)
long __builtin_alpha_unpkbw (long)
long __builtin_alpha_minub8 (long, long)
long __builtin_alpha_minsb8 (long, long)
long __builtin_alpha_minuw4 (long, long)
long __builtin_alpha_minsw4 (long, long)
long __builtin_alpha_maxub8 (long, long)
long __builtin_alpha_maxsb8 (long, long)
long __builtin_alpha_maxuw4 (long, long)
long __builtin_alpha_maxsw4 (long, long)
long __builtin_alpha_perr (long, long)
```

The following built-in functions are always with '-mcix' or '-mcpu=*cpu*' where *cpu* is ev67 or later. They all generate the machine instruction that is part of the name.

```
long __builtin_alpha_cttz (long)
long __builtin_alpha_ctlz (long)
long __builtin_alpha_ctpop (long)
```

The following built-in functions are available on systems that use the OSF/1 PAL-code. Normally they invoke the rduniq and wruniq PAL calls, but when invoked with '-mtls-kernel', they invoke rdval and wrval.

```
void *__builtin_thread_pointer (void)
void __builtin_set_thread_pointer (void *)
```

6.60.3 Altera Nios II Built-in Functions

These built-in functions are available for the Altera Nios II family of processors.

The following built-in functions are always available. They all generate the machine instruction that is part of the name.

```
int __builtin_ldbio (volatile const void *)
int __builtin_ldbuio (volatile const void *)
int __builtin_ldhio (volatile const void *)
int __builtin_ldhuio (volatile const void *)
int __builtin_ldwio (volatile const void *)
void __builtin_stbio (volatile void *, int)
void __builtin_sthio (volatile void *, int)
void __builtin_stwio (volatile void *, int)
void __builtin_sync (void)
int __builtin_rdctl (int)
int __builtin_rdprs (int, int)
void __builtin_wrctl (int, int)
```

```
void __builtin_flushd (volatile void *)
void __builtin_flushda (volatile void *)
int __builtin_wrpie (int);
void __builtin_eni (int);
int __builtin_ldex (volatile const void *)
int __builtin_stex (volatile void *, int)
int __builtin_ldsex (volatile const void *)
int __builtin_stsex (volatile void *, int)
```

The following built-in functions are always available. They all generate a Nios II Custom Instruction. The name of the function represents the types that the function takes and returns. The letter before the **n** is the return type or void if absent. The **n** represents the first parameter to all the custom instructions, the custom instruction number. The two letters after the **n** represent the up to two parameters to the function.

The letters represent the following data types:

<no letter>
        `void` for return type and no parameter for parameter types.

i   `int` for return type and parameter type

f   `float` for return type and parameter type

p   `void *` for return type and parameter type

And the function names are:

```
void __builtin_custom_n (void)
void __builtin_custom_ni (int)
void __builtin_custom_nf (float)
void __builtin_custom_np (void *)
void __builtin_custom_nii (int, int)
void __builtin_custom_nif (int, float)
void __builtin_custom_nip (int, void *)
void __builtin_custom_nfi (float, int)
void __builtin_custom_nff (float, float)
void __builtin_custom_nfp (float, void *)
void __builtin_custom_npi (void *, int)
void __builtin_custom_npf (void *, float)
void __builtin_custom_npp (void *, void *)
int __builtin_custom_in (void)
int __builtin_custom_ini (int)
int __builtin_custom_inf (float)
int __builtin_custom_inp (void *)
int __builtin_custom_inii (int, int)
int __builtin_custom_inif (int, float)
int __builtin_custom_inip (int, void *)
int __builtin_custom_infi (float, int)
int __builtin_custom_inff (float, float)
int __builtin_custom_infp (float, void *)
int __builtin_custom_inpi (void *, int)
```

```
int __builtin_custom_inpf (void *, float)
int __builtin_custom_inpp (void *, void *)
float __builtin_custom_fn (void)
float __builtin_custom_fni (int)
float __builtin_custom_fnf (float)
float __builtin_custom_fnp (void *)
float __builtin_custom_fnii (int, int)
float __builtin_custom_fnif (int, float)
float __builtin_custom_fnip (int, void *)
float __builtin_custom_fnfi (float, int)
float __builtin_custom_fnff (float, float)
float __builtin_custom_fnfp (float, void *)
float __builtin_custom_fnpi (void *, int)
float __builtin_custom_fnpf (void *, float)
float __builtin_custom_fnpp (void *, void *)
void * __builtin_custom_pn (void)
void * __builtin_custom_pni (int)
void * __builtin_custom_pnf (float)
void * __builtin_custom_pnp (void *)
void * __builtin_custom_pnii (int, int)
void * __builtin_custom_pnif (int, float)
void * __builtin_custom_pnip (int, void *)
void * __builtin_custom_pnfi (float, int)
void * __builtin_custom_pnff (float, float)
void * __builtin_custom_pnfp (float, void *)
void * __builtin_custom_pnpi (void *, int)
void * __builtin_custom_pnpf (void *, float)
void * __builtin_custom_pnpp (void *, void *)
```

6.60.4 ARC Built-in Functions

The following built-in functions are provided for ARC targets. The built-ins generate the corresponding assembly instructions. In the examples given below, the generated code often requires an operand or result to be in a register. Where necessary further code will be generated to ensure this is true, but for brevity this is not described in each case.

Note: Using a built-in to generate an instruction not supported by a target may cause problems. At present the compiler is not guaranteed to detect such misuse, and as a result an internal compiler error may be generated.

int __builtin_arc_aligned (*void *val*, *int* alignval)   [Built-in Function]
    Return 1 if *val* is known to have the byte alignment given by *alignval*, otherwise return 0. Note that this is different from

```
__alignof__(*(char *)val) >= alignval
```

    because __alignof__ sees only the type of the dereference, whereas __builtin_arc_align uses alignment information from the pointer as well as from the pointed-to type. The information available will depend on optimization level.

`void __builtin_arc_brk` (*void*)   [Built-in Function]

> Generates
>
> > `brk`

`unsigned int __builtin_arc_core_read` (*unsigned int*   [Built-in Function]
> `regno`)
>
> The operand is the number of a register to be read. Generates:
>
> > `mov   dest, rregno`
>
> where the value in *dest* will be the result returned from the built-in.

`void __builtin_arc_core_write` (*unsigned int* **regno**,   [Built-in Function]
> *unsigned int* **val**)
>
> The first operand is the number of a register to be written, the second operand is a
> compile time constant to write into that register. Generates:
>
> > `mov   rregno, val`

`int __builtin_arc_divaw` (*int* **a**, *int* **b**)   [Built-in Function]
> Only available if either '-mcpu=ARC700' or '-meA' is set. Generates:
>
> > `divaw   dest, a, b`
>
> where the value in *dest* will be the result returned from the built-in.

`void __builtin_arc_flag` (*unsigned int* **a**)   [Built-in Function]

> Generates
>
> > `flag   a`

`unsigned int __builtin_arc_lr` (*unsigned int* **auxr**)   [Built-in Function]
> The operand, *auxv*, is the address of an auxiliary register and must be a compile time
> constant. Generates:
>
> > `lr   dest, [auxr]`
>
> Where the value in *dest* will be the result returned from the built-in.

`void __builtin_arc_mul64` (*int* **a**, *int* **b**)   [Built-in Function]
> Only available with '-mmul64'. Generates:
>
> > `mul64   a, b`

`void __builtin_arc_mulu64` (*unsigned int* **a**, *unsigned int* **b**)   [Built-in Function]
> Only available with '-mmul64'. Generates:
>
> > `mulu64   a, b`

`void __builtin_arc_nop` (*void*)   [Built-in Function]

> Generates:
>
> > `nop`

`int __builtin_arc_norm` (*int* **src**)   [Built-in Function]
> Only valid if the 'norm' instruction is available through the '-mnorm' option or by
> default with '-mcpu=ARC700'. Generates:
>
> > `norm   dest, src`
>
> Where the value in *dest* will be the result returned from the built-in.

short int __builtin_arc_normw (*short int* **src**)   [Built-in Function]
    Only valid if the 'normw' instruction is available through the '-mnorm' option or by
    default with '-mcpu=ARC700'. Generates:

        `normw  dest, src`

    Where the value in *dest* will be the result returned from the built-in.

void __builtin_arc_rtie (*void*)   [Built-in Function]
    Generates:

        `rtie`

void __builtin_arc_sleep (*int* **a**   [Built-in Function]
    Generates:

        `sleep  a`

void __builtin_arc_sr (*unsigned int* **auxr**, *unsigned int* **val**)   [Built-in Function]
    The first argument, *auxv*, is the address of an auxiliary register, the second argument,
    val, is a compile time constant to be written to the register. Generates:

        `sr  auxr, [val]`

int __builtin_arc_swap (*int* **src**)   [Built-in Function]
    Only valid with '-mswap'. Generates:

        `swap  dest, src`

    Where the value in *dest* will be the result returned from the built-in.

void __builtin_arc_swi (*void*)   [Built-in Function]
    Generates:

        `swi`

void __builtin_arc_sync (*void*)   [Built-in Function]
    Only available with '-mcpu=ARC700'. Generates:

        `sync`

void __builtin_arc_trap_s (*unsigned int* **c**)   [Built-in Function]
    Only available with '-mcpu=ARC700'. Generates:

        `trap_s  c`

void __builtin_arc_unimp_s (*void*)   [Built-in Function]
    Only available with '-mcpu=ARC700'. Generates:

        `unimp_s`

The instructions generated by the following builtins are not considered as candidates for
scheduling. They are not moved around by the compiler during scheduling, and thus can
be expected to appear where they are put in the C code:

```
__builtin_arc_brk()
__builtin_arc_core_read()
__builtin_arc_core_write()
__builtin_arc_flag()
```

```
__builtin_arc_lr()
__builtin_arc_sleep()
__builtin_arc_sr()
__builtin_arc_swi()
```

6.60.5 ARC SIMD Built-in Functions

SIMD builtins provided by the compiler can be used to generate the vector instructions. This section describes the available builtins and their usage in programs. With the '-msimd' option, the compiler provides 128-bit vector types, which can be specified using the vector_size attribute. The header file 'arc-simd.h' can be included to use the following predefined types:

```
typedef int __v4si  __attribute__((vector_size(16)));
typedef short __v8hi __attribute__((vector_size(16)));
```

These types can be used to define 128-bit variables. The built-in functions listed in the following section can be used on these variables to generate the vector operations.

For all builtins, __builtin_arc_*someinsn*, the header file 'arc-simd.h' also provides equivalent macros called _*someinsn* that can be used for programming ease and improved readability. The following macros for DMA control are also provided:

```
#define _setup_dma_in_channel_reg _vdiwr
#define _setup_dma_out_channel_reg _vdowr
```

The following is a complete list of all the SIMD built-ins provided for ARC, grouped by calling signature.

The following take two __v8hi arguments and return a __v8hi result:

```
__v8hi __builtin_arc_vaddaw (__v8hi, __v8hi)
__v8hi __builtin_arc_vaddw (__v8hi, __v8hi)
__v8hi __builtin_arc_vand (__v8hi, __v8hi)
__v8hi __builtin_arc_vandaw (__v8hi, __v8hi)
__v8hi __builtin_arc_vavb (__v8hi, __v8hi)
__v8hi __builtin_arc_vavrb (__v8hi, __v8hi)
__v8hi __builtin_arc_vbic (__v8hi, __v8hi)
__v8hi __builtin_arc_vbicaw (__v8hi, __v8hi)
__v8hi __builtin_arc_vdifaw (__v8hi, __v8hi)
__v8hi __builtin_arc_vdifw (__v8hi, __v8hi)
__v8hi __builtin_arc_veqw (__v8hi, __v8hi)
__v8hi __builtin_arc_vh264f (__v8hi, __v8hi)
__v8hi __builtin_arc_vh264ft (__v8hi, __v8hi)
__v8hi __builtin_arc_vh264fw (__v8hi, __v8hi)
__v8hi __builtin_arc_vlew (__v8hi, __v8hi)
__v8hi __builtin_arc_vltw (__v8hi, __v8hi)
__v8hi __builtin_arc_vmaxaw (__v8hi, __v8hi)
__v8hi __builtin_arc_vmaxw (__v8hi, __v8hi)
__v8hi __builtin_arc_vminaw (__v8hi, __v8hi)
__v8hi __builtin_arc_vminw (__v8hi, __v8hi)
__v8hi __builtin_arc_vmr1aw (__v8hi, __v8hi)
__v8hi __builtin_arc_vmr1w (__v8hi, __v8hi)
```

```
__v8hi __builtin_arc_vmr2aw (__v8hi, __v8hi)
__v8hi __builtin_arc_vmr2w (__v8hi, __v8hi)
__v8hi __builtin_arc_vmr3aw (__v8hi, __v8hi)
__v8hi __builtin_arc_vmr3w (__v8hi, __v8hi)
__v8hi __builtin_arc_vmr4aw (__v8hi, __v8hi)
__v8hi __builtin_arc_vmr4w (__v8hi, __v8hi)
__v8hi __builtin_arc_vmr5aw (__v8hi, __v8hi)
__v8hi __builtin_arc_vmr5w (__v8hi, __v8hi)
__v8hi __builtin_arc_vmr6aw (__v8hi, __v8hi)
__v8hi __builtin_arc_vmr6w (__v8hi, __v8hi)
__v8hi __builtin_arc_vmr7aw (__v8hi, __v8hi)
__v8hi __builtin_arc_vmr7w (__v8hi, __v8hi)
__v8hi __builtin_arc_vmrb (__v8hi, __v8hi)
__v8hi __builtin_arc_vmulaw (__v8hi, __v8hi)
__v8hi __builtin_arc_vmulfaw (__v8hi, __v8hi)
__v8hi __builtin_arc_vmulfw (__v8hi, __v8hi)
__v8hi __builtin_arc_vmulw (__v8hi, __v8hi)
__v8hi __builtin_arc_vnew (__v8hi, __v8hi)
__v8hi __builtin_arc_vor (__v8hi, __v8hi)
__v8hi __builtin_arc_vsubaw (__v8hi, __v8hi)
__v8hi __builtin_arc_vsubw (__v8hi, __v8hi)
__v8hi __builtin_arc_vsummw (__v8hi, __v8hi)
__v8hi __builtin_arc_vvc1f (__v8hi, __v8hi)
__v8hi __builtin_arc_vvc1ft (__v8hi, __v8hi)
__v8hi __builtin_arc_vxor (__v8hi, __v8hi)
__v8hi __builtin_arc_vxoraw (__v8hi, __v8hi)
```

The following take one `__v8hi` and one `int` argument and return a `__v8hi` result:

```
__v8hi __builtin_arc_vbaddw (__v8hi, int)
__v8hi __builtin_arc_vbmaxw (__v8hi, int)
__v8hi __builtin_arc_vbminw (__v8hi, int)
__v8hi __builtin_arc_vbmulaw (__v8hi, int)
__v8hi __builtin_arc_vbmulfw (__v8hi, int)
__v8hi __builtin_arc_vbmulw (__v8hi, int)
__v8hi __builtin_arc_vbrsubw (__v8hi, int)
__v8hi __builtin_arc_vbsubw (__v8hi, int)
```

The following take one `__v8hi` argument and one `int` argument which must be a 3-bit compile time constant indicating a register number I0-I7. They return a `__v8hi` result.

```
__v8hi __builtin_arc_vasrw (__v8hi, const int)
__v8hi __builtin_arc_vsr8 (__v8hi, const int)
__v8hi __builtin_arc_vsr8aw (__v8hi, const int)
```

The following take one `__v8hi` argument and one `int` argument which must be a 6-bit compile time constant. They return a `__v8hi` result.

```
__v8hi __builtin_arc_vasrpwbi (__v8hi, const int)
__v8hi __builtin_arc_vasrrpwbi (__v8hi, const int)
__v8hi __builtin_arc_vasrrwi (__v8hi, const int)
```

```
__v8hi __builtin_arc_vasrsrwi (__v8hi, const int)
__v8hi __builtin_arc_vasrwi (__v8hi, const int)
__v8hi __builtin_arc_vsr8awi (__v8hi, const int)
__v8hi __builtin_arc_vsr8i (__v8hi, const int)
```

The following take one `__v8hi` argument and one `int` argument which must be a 8-bit compile time constant. They return a `__v8hi` result.

```
__v8hi __builtin_arc_vd6tapf (__v8hi, const int)
__v8hi __builtin_arc_vmvaw (__v8hi, const int)
__v8hi __builtin_arc_vmvw (__v8hi, const int)
__v8hi __builtin_arc_vmvzw (__v8hi, const int)
```

The following take two `int` arguments, the second of which which must be a 8-bit compile time constant. They return a `__v8hi` result:

```
__v8hi __builtin_arc_vmovaw (int, const int)
__v8hi __builtin_arc_vmovw (int, const int)
__v8hi __builtin_arc_vmovzw (int, const int)
```

The following take a single `__v8hi` argument and return a `__v8hi` result:

```
__v8hi __builtin_arc_vabsaw (__v8hi)
__v8hi __builtin_arc_vabsw (__v8hi)
__v8hi __builtin_arc_vaddsuw (__v8hi)
__v8hi __builtin_arc_vexch1 (__v8hi)
__v8hi __builtin_arc_vexch2 (__v8hi)
__v8hi __builtin_arc_vexch4 (__v8hi)
__v8hi __builtin_arc_vsignw (__v8hi)
__v8hi __builtin_arc_vupbaw (__v8hi)
__v8hi __builtin_arc_vupbw (__v8hi)
__v8hi __builtin_arc_vupsbaw (__v8hi)
__v8hi __builtin_arc_vupsbw (__v8hi)
```

The following take two `int` arguments and return no result:

```
void __builtin_arc_vdirun (int, int)
void __builtin_arc_vdorun (int, int)
```

The following take two `int` arguments and return no result. The first argument must a 3-bit compile time constant indicating one of the DR0-DR7 DMA setup channels:

```
void __builtin_arc_vdiwr (const int, int)
void __builtin_arc_vdowr (const int, int)
```

The following take an `int` argument and return no result:

```
void __builtin_arc_vendrec (int)
void __builtin_arc_vrec (int)
void __builtin_arc_vrecrun (int)
void __builtin_arc_vrun (int)
```

The following take a `__v8hi` argument and two `int` arguments and return a `__v8hi` result. The second argument must be a 3-bit compile time constants, indicating one the registers I0-I7, and the third argument must be an 8-bit compile time constant.

Note: Although the equivalent hardware instructions do not take an SIMD register as an operand, these builtins overwrite the relevant bits of the `__v8hi` register provided as the first argument with the value loaded from the [Ib, u8] location in the SDM.

```
__v8hi __builtin_arc_vld32 (__v8hi, const int, const int)
__v8hi __builtin_arc_vld32wh (__v8hi, const int, const int)
__v8hi __builtin_arc_vld32wl (__v8hi, const int, const int)
__v8hi __builtin_arc_vld64 (__v8hi, const int, const int)
```

The following take two `int` arguments and return a `__v8hi` result. The first argument must be a 3-bit compile time constants, indicating one the registers I0-I7, and the second argument must be an 8-bit compile time constant.

```
__v8hi __builtin_arc_vld128 (const int, const int)
__v8hi __builtin_arc_vld64w (const int, const int)
```

The following take a `__v8hi` argument and two `int` arguments and return no result. The second argument must be a 3-bit compile time constants, indicating one the registers I0-I7, and the third argument must be an 8-bit compile time constant.

```
void __builtin_arc_vst128 (__v8hi, const int, const int)
void __builtin_arc_vst64 (__v8hi, const int, const int)
```

The following take a `__v8hi` argument and three `int` arguments and return no result. The second argument must be a 3-bit compile-time constant, identifying the 16-bit sub-register to be stored, the third argument must be a 3-bit compile time constants, indicating one the registers I0-I7, and the fourth argument must be an 8-bit compile time constant.

```
void __builtin_arc_vst16_n (__v8hi, const int, const int, const int)
void __builtin_arc_vst32_n (__v8hi, const int, const int, const int)
```

6.60.6 ARM iWMMXt Built-in Functions

These built-in functions are available for the ARM family of processors when the '-mcpu=iwmmxt' switch is used:

```
typedef int v2si __attribute__ ((vector_size (8)));
typedef short v4hi __attribute__ ((vector_size (8)));
typedef char v8qi __attribute__ ((vector_size (8)));

int __builtin_arm_getwcgr0 (void)
void __builtin_arm_setwcgr0 (int)
int __builtin_arm_getwcgr1 (void)
void __builtin_arm_setwcgr1 (int)
int __builtin_arm_getwcgr2 (void)
void __builtin_arm_setwcgr2 (int)
int __builtin_arm_getwcgr3 (void)
void __builtin_arm_setwcgr3 (int)
int __builtin_arm_textrmsb (v8qi, int)
int __builtin_arm_textrmsh (v4hi, int)
int __builtin_arm_textrmsw (v2si, int)
int __builtin_arm_textrmub (v8qi, int)
int __builtin_arm_textrmuh (v4hi, int)
int __builtin_arm_textrmuw (v2si, int)
v8qi __builtin_arm_tinsrb (v8qi, int, int)
v4hi __builtin_arm_tinsrh (v4hi, int, int)
v2si __builtin_arm_tinsrw (v2si, int, int)
long long __builtin_arm_tmia (long long, int, int)
long long __builtin_arm_tmiabb (long long, int, int)
```

```
long long __builtin_arm_tmiabt (long long, int, int)
long long __builtin_arm_tmiaph (long long, int, int)
long long __builtin_arm_tmiatb (long long, int, int)
long long __builtin_arm_tmiatt (long long, int, int)
int __builtin_arm_tmovmskb (v8qi)
int __builtin_arm_tmovmskh (v4hi)
int __builtin_arm_tmovmskw (v2si)
long long __builtin_arm_waccb (v8qi)
long long __builtin_arm_wacch (v4hi)
long long __builtin_arm_waccw (v2si)
v8qi __builtin_arm_waddb (v8qi, v8qi)
v8qi __builtin_arm_waddbss (v8qi, v8qi)
v8qi __builtin_arm_waddbus (v8qi, v8qi)
v4hi __builtin_arm_waddh (v4hi, v4hi)
v4hi __builtin_arm_waddhss (v4hi, v4hi)
v4hi __builtin_arm_waddhus (v4hi, v4hi)
v2si __builtin_arm_waddw (v2si, v2si)
v2si __builtin_arm_waddwss (v2si, v2si)
v2si __builtin_arm_waddwus (v2si, v2si)
v8qi __builtin_arm_walign (v8qi, v8qi, int)
long long __builtin_arm_wand(long long, long long)
long long __builtin_arm_wandn (long long, long long)
v8qi __builtin_arm_wavg2b (v8qi, v8qi)
v8qi __builtin_arm_wavg2br (v8qi, v8qi)
v4hi __builtin_arm_wavg2h (v4hi, v4hi)
v4hi __builtin_arm_wavg2hr (v4hi, v4hi)
v8qi __builtin_arm_wcmpeqb (v8qi, v8qi)
v4hi __builtin_arm_wcmpeqh (v4hi, v4hi)
v2si __builtin_arm_wcmpeqw (v2si, v2si)
v8qi __builtin_arm_wcmpgtsb (v8qi, v8qi)
v4hi __builtin_arm_wcmpgtsh (v4hi, v4hi)
v2si __builtin_arm_wcmpgtsw (v2si, v2si)
v8qi __builtin_arm_wcmpgtub (v8qi, v8qi)
v4hi __builtin_arm_wcmpgtuh (v4hi, v4hi)
v2si __builtin_arm_wcmpgtuw (v2si, v2si)
long long __builtin_arm_wmacs (long long, v4hi, v4hi)
long long __builtin_arm_wmacsz (v4hi, v4hi)
long long __builtin_arm_wmacu (long long, v4hi, v4hi)
long long __builtin_arm_wmacuz (v4hi, v4hi)
v4hi __builtin_arm_wmadds (v4hi, v4hi)
v4hi __builtin_arm_wmaddu (v4hi, v4hi)
v8qi __builtin_arm_wmaxsb (v8qi, v8qi)
v4hi __builtin_arm_wmaxsh (v4hi, v4hi)
v2si __builtin_arm_wmaxsw (v2si, v2si)
v8qi __builtin_arm_wmaxub (v8qi, v8qi)
v4hi __builtin_arm_wmaxuh (v4hi, v4hi)
v2si __builtin_arm_wmaxuw (v2si, v2si)
v8qi __builtin_arm_wminsb (v8qi, v8qi)
v4hi __builtin_arm_wminsh (v4hi, v4hi)
v2si __builtin_arm_wminsw (v2si, v2si)
v8qi __builtin_arm_wminub (v8qi, v8qi)
v4hi __builtin_arm_wminuh (v4hi, v4hi)
v2si __builtin_arm_wminuw (v2si, v2si)
v4hi __builtin_arm_wmulsm (v4hi, v4hi)
v4hi __builtin_arm_wmulul (v4hi, v4hi)
v4hi __builtin_arm_wmulum (v4hi, v4hi)
long long __builtin_arm_wor (long long, long long)
v2si __builtin_arm_wpackdss (long long, long long)
```

```
v2si __builtin_arm_wpackdus (long long, long long)
v8qi __builtin_arm_wpackhss (v4hi, v4hi)
v8qi __builtin_arm_wpackhus (v4hi, v4hi)
v4hi __builtin_arm_wpackwss (v2si, v2si)
v4hi __builtin_arm_wpackwus (v2si, v2si)
long long __builtin_arm_wrord (long long, long long)
long long __builtin_arm_wrordi (long long, int)
v4hi __builtin_arm_wrorh (v4hi, long long)
v4hi __builtin_arm_wrorhi (v4hi, int)
v2si __builtin_arm_wrorw (v2si, long long)
v2si __builtin_arm_wrorwi (v2si, int)
v2si __builtin_arm_wsadb (v2si, v8qi, v8qi)
v2si __builtin_arm_wsadbz (v8qi, v8qi)
v2si __builtin_arm_wsadh (v2si, v4hi, v4hi)
v2si __builtin_arm_wsadhz (v4hi, v4hi)
v4hi __builtin_arm_wshufh (v4hi, int)
long long __builtin_arm_wslld (long long, long long)
long long __builtin_arm_wslldi (long long, int)
v4hi __builtin_arm_wsllh (v4hi, long long)
v4hi __builtin_arm_wsllhi (v4hi, int)
v2si __builtin_arm_wsllw (v2si, long long)
v2si __builtin_arm_wsllwi (v2si, int)
long long __builtin_arm_wsrad (long long, long long)
long long __builtin_arm_wsradi (long long, int)
v4hi __builtin_arm_wsrah (v4hi, long long)
v4hi __builtin_arm_wsrahi (v4hi, int)
v2si __builtin_arm_wsraw (v2si, long long)
v2si __builtin_arm_wsrawi (v2si, int)
long long __builtin_arm_wsrld (long long, long long)
long long __builtin_arm_wsrldi (long long, int)
v4hi __builtin_arm_wsrlh (v4hi, long long)
v4hi __builtin_arm_wsrlhi (v4hi, int)
v2si __builtin_arm_wsrlw (v2si, long long)
v2si __builtin_arm_wsrlwi (v2si, int)
v8qi __builtin_arm_wsubb (v8qi, v8qi)
v8qi __builtin_arm_wsubbss (v8qi, v8qi)
v8qi __builtin_arm_wsubbus (v8qi, v8qi)
v4hi __builtin_arm_wsubh (v4hi, v4hi)
v4hi __builtin_arm_wsubhss (v4hi, v4hi)
v4hi __builtin_arm_wsubhus (v4hi, v4hi)
v2si __builtin_arm_wsubw (v2si, v2si)
v2si __builtin_arm_wsubwss (v2si, v2si)
v2si __builtin_arm_wsubwus (v2si, v2si)
v4hi __builtin_arm_wunpckehsb (v8qi)
v2si __builtin_arm_wunpckehsh (v4hi)
long long __builtin_arm_wunpckehsw (v2si)
v4hi __builtin_arm_wunpckehub (v8qi)
v2si __builtin_arm_wunpckehuh (v4hi)
long long __builtin_arm_wunpckehuw (v2si)
v4hi __builtin_arm_wunpckelsb (v8qi)
v2si __builtin_arm_wunpckelsh (v4hi)
long long __builtin_arm_wunpckelsw (v2si)
v4hi __builtin_arm_wunpckelub (v8qi)
v2si __builtin_arm_wunpckeluh (v4hi)
long long __builtin_arm_wunpckeluw (v2si)
v8qi __builtin_arm_wunpckihb (v8qi, v8qi)
v4hi __builtin_arm_wunpckihh (v4hi, v4hi)
v2si __builtin_arm_wunpckihw (v2si, v2si)
```

```
v8qi __builtin_arm_wunpckilb (v8qi, v8qi)
v4hi __builtin_arm_wunpckilh (v4hi, v4hi)
v2si __builtin_arm_wunpckilw (v2si, v2si)
long long __builtin_arm_wxor (long long, long long)
long long __builtin_arm_wzero ()
```

6.60.7 ARM C Language Extensions (ACLE)

GCC implements extensions for C as described in the ARM C Language Extensions (ACLE) specification, which can be found at http://infocenter.arm.com/help/topic/com.arm. doc.ihi0053c/IHI0053C_acle_2_0.pdf.

As a part of ACLE, GCC implements extensions for Advanced SIMD as described in the ARM C Language Extensions Specification. The complete list of Advanced SIMD intrinsics can be found at http://infocenter.arm.com/help/topic/com.arm.doc.ihi0073a/ IHI0073A_arm_neon_intrinsics_ref.pdf. The built-in intrinsics for the Advanced SIMD extension are available when NEON is enabled.

Currently, ARM and AArch64 back ends do not support ACLE 2.0 fully. Both back ends support CRC32 intrinsics from 'arm_acle.h'. The ARM back end's 16-bit floating-point Advanced SIMD intrinsics currently comply to ACLE v1.1. AArch64's back end does not have support for 16-bit floating point Advanced SIMD intrinsics yet.

See Section 3.18.4 [ARM Options], page 231 and Section 3.18.1 [AArch64 Options], page 217 for more information on the availability of extensions.

6.60.8 ARM Floating Point Status and Control Intrinsics

These built-in functions are available for the ARM family of processors with floating-point unit.

```
unsigned int __builtin_arm_get_fpscr ()
void __builtin_arm_set_fpscr (unsigned int)
```

6.60.9 ARM ARMv8-M Security Extensions

GCC implements the ARMv8-M Security Extensions as described in the ARMv8-M Security Extensions: Requiremenets on Development Tools Engineering Specification, which can be found at http://infocenter.arm.com/help/topic/com.arm.doc.ecm0359818/ ECM0359818_armv8m_security_extensions_reqs_on_dev_tools_1_0.pdf.

As part of the Security Extensions GCC implements two new function attributes: cmse_nonsecure_entry and cmse_nonsecure_call.

As part of the Security Extensions GCC implements the intrinsics below. FPTR is used here to mean any function pointer type.

```
cmse_address_info_t cmse_TT (void *)
cmse_address_info_t cmse_TT_fptr (FPTR)
cmse_address_info_t cmse_TTT (void *)
cmse_address_info_t cmse_TTT_fptr (FPTR)
cmse_address_info_t cmse_TTA (void *)
cmse_address_info_t cmse_TTA_fptr (FPTR)
cmse_address_info_t cmse_TTAT (void *)
cmse_address_info_t cmse_TTAT_fptr (FPTR)
void * cmse_check_address_range (void *, size_t, int)
typeof(p) cmse_nsfptr_create (FPTR p)
intptr_t cmse_is_nsfptr (FPTR)
int cmse_nonsecure_caller (void)
```

6.60.10 AVR Built-in Functions

For each built-in function for AVR, there is an equally named, uppercase built-in macro defined. That way users can easily query if or if not a specific built-in is implemented or not. For example, if `__builtin_avr_nop` is available the macro `__BUILTIN_AVR_NOP` is defined to 1 and undefined otherwise.

The following built-in functions map to the respective machine instruction, i.e. `nop`, `sei`, `cli`, `sleep`, `wdr`, `swap`, `fmul`, `fmuls` resp. `fmulsu`. The three `fmul*` built-ins are implemented as library call if no hardware multiplier is available.

```
void __builtin_avr_nop (void)
void __builtin_avr_sei (void)
void __builtin_avr_cli (void)
void __builtin_avr_sleep (void)
void __builtin_avr_wdr (void)
unsigned char __builtin_avr_swap (unsigned char)
unsigned int __builtin_avr_fmul (unsigned char, unsigned char)
int __builtin_avr_fmuls (char, char)
int __builtin_avr_fmulsu (char, unsigned char)
```

In order to delay execution for a specific number of cycles, GCC implements

```
void __builtin_avr_delay_cycles (unsigned long ticks)
```

`ticks` is the number of ticks to delay execution. Note that this built-in does not take into account the effect of interrupts that might increase delay time. `ticks` must be a compile-time integer constant; delays with a variable number of cycles are not supported.

```
char __builtin_avr_flash_segment (const __memx void*)
```

This built-in takes a byte address to the 24-bit [AVR Named Address Spaces], page 417 `__memx` and returns the number of the flash segment (the 64 KiB chunk) where the address points to. Counting starts at 0. If the address does not point to flash memory, return −1.

```
unsigned char __builtin_avr_insert_bits (unsigned long map, unsigned char bits, unsigned char val)
```

Insert bits from *bits* into *val* and return the resulting value. The nibbles of *map* determine how the insertion is performed: Let X be the n-th nibble of *map*

1. If X is `0xf`, then the n-th bit of *val* is returned unaltered.

2. If X is in the range 0...7, then the n-th result bit is set to the X-th bit of *bits*

3. If X is in the range 8...`0xe`, then the n-th result bit is undefined.

One typical use case for this built-in is adjusting input and output values to non-contiguous port layouts. Some examples:

```
// same as val, bits is unused
__builtin_avr_insert_bits (0xffffffff, bits, val)

// same as bits, val is unused
__builtin_avr_insert_bits (0x76543210, bits, val)

// same as rotating bits by 4
__builtin_avr_insert_bits (0x32107654, bits, 0)

// high nibble of result is the high nibble of val
// low nibble of result is the low nibble of bits
__builtin_avr_insert_bits (0xffff3210, bits, val)

// reverse the bit order of bits
__builtin_avr_insert_bits (0x01234567, bits, 0)

void __builtin_avr_nops (unsigned count)
```

Insert `count` NOP instructions. The number of instructions must be a compile-time integer constant.

6.60.11 Blackfin Built-in Functions

Currently, there are two Blackfin-specific built-in functions. These are used for generating `CSYNC` and `SSYNC` machine insns without using inline assembly; by using these built-in functions the compiler can automatically add workarounds for hardware errata involving these instructions. These functions are named as follows:

```
void __builtin_bfin_csync (void)
void __builtin_bfin_ssync (void)
```

6.60.12 FR-V Built-in Functions

GCC provides many FR-V-specific built-in functions. In general, these functions are intended to be compatible with those described by *FR-V Family, Softune C/C++ Compiler Manual (V6), Fujitsu Semiconductor*. The two exceptions are `__MDUNPACKH` and `__MBTOHE`, the GCC forms of which pass 128-bit values by pointer rather than by value.

Most of the functions are named after specific FR-V instructions. Such functions are said to be "directly mapped" and are summarized here in tabular form.

6.60.12.1 Argument Types

The arguments to the built-in functions can be divided into three groups: register numbers, compile-time constants and run-time values. In order to make this classification clear at a glance, the arguments and return values are given the following pseudo types:

Pseudo type	Real C type	Constant?	Description
uh	unsigned short	No	an unsigned halfword
uw1	unsigned int	No	an unsigned word
sw1	int	No	a signed word
uw2	unsigned long long	No	an unsigned doubleword
sw2	long long	No	a signed doubleword
const	int	Yes	an integer constant
acc	int	Yes	an ACC register number
iacc	int	Yes	an IACC register number

These pseudo types are not defined by GCC, they are simply a notational convenience used in this manual.

Arguments of type `uh`, `uw1`, `sw1`, `uw2` and `sw2` are evaluated at run time. They correspond to register operands in the underlying FR-V instructions.

`const` arguments represent immediate operands in the underlying FR-V instructions. They must be compile-time constants.

`acc` arguments are evaluated at compile time and specify the number of an accumulator register. For example, an `acc` argument of 2 selects the ACC2 register.

`iacc` arguments are similar to `acc` arguments but specify the number of an IACC register. See see Section 6.60.12.5 [Other Built-in Functions], page 597 for more details.

6.60.12.2 Directly-Mapped Integer Functions

The functions listed below map directly to FR-V I-type instructions.

Function prototype	Example usage	Assembly output
sw1 __ADDSS (sw1, sw1)	c = __ADDSS (a, b)	ADDSS a,b,c

Function prototype	Example usage	Assembly output
sw1 __SCAN (sw1, sw1)	c = __SCAN (a, b)	SCAN a,b,c
sw1 __SCUTSS (sw1)	b = __SCUTSS (a)	SCUTSS a,b
sw1 __SLASS (sw1, sw1)	c = __SLASS (a, b)	SLASS a,b,c
void __SMASS (sw1, sw1)	__SMASS (a, b)	SMASS a,b
void __SMSSS (sw1, sw1)	__SMSSS (a, b)	SMSSS a,b
void __SMU (sw1, sw1)	__SMU (a, b)	SMU a,b
sw2 __SMUL (sw1, sw1)	c = __SMUL (a, b)	SMUL a,b,c
sw1 __SUBSS (sw1, sw1)	c = __SUBSS (a, b)	SUBSS a,b,c
uw2 __UMUL (uw1, uw1)	c = __UMUL (a, b)	UMUL a,b,c

6.60.12.3 Directly-Mapped Media Functions

The functions listed below map directly to FR-V M-type instructions.

Function prototype	Example usage	Assembly output
uw1 __MABSHS (sw1)	b = __MABSHS (a)	MABSHS a,b
void __MADDACCS (acc, acc)	__MADDACCS (b, a)	MADDACCS a,b
sw1 __MADDHSS (sw1, sw1)	c = __MADDHSS (a, b)	MADDHSS a,b,c
uw1 __MADDHUS (uw1, uw1)	c = __MADDHUS (a, b)	MADDHUS a,b,c
uw1 __MAND (uw1, uw1)	c = __MAND (a, b)	MAND a,b,c
void __MASACCS (acc, acc)	__MASACCS (b, a)	MASACCS a,b
uw1 __MAVEH (uw1, uw1)	c = __MAVEH (a, b)	MAVEH a,b,c
uw2 __MBTOH (uw1)	b = __MBTOH (a)	MBTOH a,b
void __MBTOHE (uw1 *, uw1)	__MBTOHE (&b, a)	MBTOHE a,b
void __MCLRACC (acc)	__MCLRACC (a)	MCLRACC a
void __MCLRACCA (void)	__MCLRACCA ()	MCLRACCA
uw1 __Mcop1 (uw1, uw1)	c = __Mcop1 (a, b)	Mcop1 a,b,c
uw1 __Mcop2 (uw1, uw1)	c = __Mcop2 (a, b)	Mcop2 a,b,c
uw1 __MCPLHI (uw2, const)	c = __MCPLHI (a, b)	MCPLHI a,#b,c
uw1 __MCPLI (uw2, const)	c = __MCPLI (a, b)	MCPLI a,#b,c
void __MCPXIS (acc, sw1, sw1)	__MCPXIS (c, a, b)	MCPXIS a,b,c
void __MCPXIU (acc, uw1, uw1)	__MCPXIU (c, a, b)	MCPXIU a,b,c
void __MCPXRS (acc, sw1, sw1)	__MCPXRS (c, a, b)	MCPXRS a,b,c
void __MCPXRU (acc, uw1, uw1)	__MCPXRU (c, a, b)	MCPXRU a,b,c
uw1 __MCUT (acc, uw1)	c = __MCUT (a, b)	MCUT a,b,c
uw1 __MCUTSS (acc, sw1)	c = __MCUTSS (a, b)	MCUTSS a,b,c
void __MDADDACCS (acc, acc)	__MDADDACCS (b, a)	MDADDACCS a,b
void __MDASACCS (acc, acc)	__MDASACCS (b, a)	MDASACCS a,b
uw2 __MDCUTSSI (acc, const)	c = __MDCUTSSI (a, b)	MDCUTSSI a,#b,c
uw2 __MDPACKH (uw2, uw2)	c = __MDPACKH (a, b)	MDPACKH a,b,c
uw2 __MDROTLI (uw2, const)	c = __MDROTLI (a, b)	MDROTLI a,#b,c
void __MDSUBACCS (acc, acc)	__MDSUBACCS (b, a)	MDSUBACCS a,b
void __MDUNPACKH (uw1 *, uw2)	__MDUNPACKH (&b, a)	MDUNPACKH a,b
uw2 __MEXPDHD (uw1, const)	c = __MEXPDHD (a, b)	MEXPDHD a,#b,c
uw1 __MEXPDHW (uw1, const)	c = __MEXPDHW (a, b)	MEXPDHW a,#b,c
uw1 __MHDSETH (uw1, const)	c = __MHDSETH (a, b)	MHDSETH a,#b,c
sw1 __MHDSETS (const)	b = __MHDSETS (a)	MHDSETS #a,b
uw1 __MHSETHIH (uw1, const)	b = __MHSETHIH (b, a)	MHSETHIH #a,b

sw1 __MHSETHIS (sw1, const)	b = __MHSETHIS (b, a)	MHSETHIS #a,b
uw1 __MHSETLOH (uw1, const)	b = __MHSETLOH (b, a)	MHSETLOH #a,b
sw1 __MHSETLOS (sw1, const)	b = __MHSETLOS (b, a)	MHSETLOS #a,b
uw1 __MHTOB (uw2)	b = __MHTOB (a)	MHTOB a,b
void __MMACHS (acc, sw1, sw1)	__MMACHS (c, a, b)	MMACHS a,b,c
void __MMACHU (acc, uw1, uw1)	__MMACHU (c, a, b)	MMACHU a,b,c
void __MMRDHS (acc, sw1, sw1)	__MMRDHS (c, a, b)	MMRDHS a,b,c
void __MMRDHU (acc, uw1, uw1)	__MMRDHU (c, a, b)	MMRDHU a,b,c
void __MMULHS (acc, sw1, sw1)	__MMULHS (c, a, b)	MMULHS a,b,c
void __MMULHU (acc, uw1, uw1)	__MMULHU (c, a, b)	MMULHU a,b,c
void __MMULXHS (acc, sw1, sw1)	__MMULXHS (c, a, b)	MMULXHS a,b,c
void __MMULXHU (acc, uw1, uw1)	__MMULXHU (c, a, b)	MMULXHU a,b,c
uw1 __MNOT (uw1)	b = __MNOT (a)	MNOT a,b
uw1 __MOR (uw1, uw1)	c = __MOR (a, b)	MOR a,b,c
uw1 __MPACKH (uh, uh)	c = __MPACKH (a, b)	MPACKH a,b,c
sw2 __MQADDHSS (sw2, sw2)	c = __MQADDHSS (a, b)	MQADDHSS a,b,c
uw2 __MQADDHUS (uw2, uw2)	c = __MQADDHUS (a, b)	MQADDHUS a,b,c
void __MQCPXIS (acc, sw2, sw2)	__MQCPXIS (c, a, b)	MQCPXIS a,b,c
void __MQCPXIU (acc, uw2, uw2)	__MQCPXIU (c, a, b)	MQCPXIU a,b,c
void __MQCPXRS (acc, sw2, sw2)	__MQCPXRS (c, a, b)	MQCPXRS a,b,c
void __MQCPXRU (acc, uw2, uw2)	__MQCPXRU (c, a, b)	MQCPXRU a,b,c
sw2 __MQLCLRHS (sw2, sw2)	c = __MQLCLRHS (a, b)	MQLCLRHS a,b,c
sw2 __MQLMTHS (sw2, sw2)	c = __MQLMTHS (a, b)	MQLMTHS a,b,c
void __MQMACHS (acc, sw2, sw2)	__MQMACHS (c, a, b)	MQMACHS a,b,c
void __MQMACHU (acc, uw2, uw2)	__MQMACHU (c, a, b)	MQMACHU a,b,c
void __MQMACXHS (acc, sw2, sw2)	__MQMACXHS (c, a, b)	MQMACXHS a,b,c
void __MQMULHS (acc, sw2, sw2)	__MQMULHS (c, a, b)	MQMULHS a,b,c
void __MQMULHU (acc, uw2, uw2)	__MQMULHU (c, a, b)	MQMULHU a,b,c
void __MQMULXHS (acc, sw2, sw2)	__MQMULXHS (c, a, b)	MQMULXHS a,b,c
void __MQMULXHU (acc, uw2, uw2)	__MQMULXHU (c, a, b)	MQMULXHU a,b,c
sw2 __MQSATHS (sw2, sw2)	c = __MQSATHS (a, b)	MQSATHS a,b,c
uw2 __MQSLLHI (uw2, int)	c = __MQSLLHI (a, b)	MQSLLHI a,b,c
sw2 __MQSRAHI (sw2, int)	c = __MQSRAHI (a, b)	MQSRAHI a,b,c
sw2 __MQSUBHSS (sw2, sw2)	c = __MQSUBHSS (a, b)	MQSUBHSS a,b,c
uw2 __MQSUBHUS (uw2, uw2)	c = __MQSUBHUS (a, b)	MQSUBHUS a,b,c
void __MQXMACHS (acc, sw2, sw2)	__MQXMACHS (c, a, b)	MQXMACHS a,b,c
void __MQXMACXHS (acc, sw2, sw2)	__MQXMACXHS (c, a, b)	MQXMACXHS a,b,c
uw1 __MRDACC (acc)	b = __MRDACC (a)	MRDACC a,b
uw1 __MRDACCG (acc)	b = __MRDACCG (a)	MRDACCG a,b
uw1 __MROTLI (uw1, const)	c = __MROTLI (a, b)	MROTLI a,#b,c
uw1 __MROTRI (uw1, const)	c = __MROTRI (a, b)	MROTRI a,#b,c
sw1 __MSATHS (sw1, sw1)	c = __MSATHS (a, b)	MSATHS a,b,c
uw1 __MSATHU (uw1, uw1)	c = __MSATHU (a, b)	MSATHU a,b,c
uw1 __MSLLHI (uw1, const)	c = __MSLLHI (a, b)	MSLLHI a,#b,c
sw1 __MSRAHI (sw1, const)	c = __MSRAHI (a, b)	MSRAHI a,#b,c
uw1 __MSRLHI (uw1, const)	c = __MSRLHI (a, b)	MSRLHI a,#b,c
void __MSUBACCS (acc, acc)	__MSUBACCS (b, a)	MSUBACCS a,b

```
sw1 __MSUBHSS (sw1, sw1)        c = __MSUBHSS (a, b)      MSUBHSS a,b,c
uw1 __MSUBHUS (uw1, uw1)        c = __MSUBHUS (a, b)      MSUBHUS a,b,c
void __MTRAP (void)             __MTRAP ()                MTRAP
uw2 __MUNPACKH (uw1)            b = __MUNPACKH (a)        MUNPACKH a,b
uw1 __MWCUT (uw2, uw1)          c = __MWCUT (a, b)        MWCUT a,b,c
void __MWTACC (acc, uw1)        __MWTACC (b, a)           MWTACC a,b
void __MWTACCG (acc, uw1)       __MWTACCG (b, a)          MWTACCG a,b
uw1 __MXOR (uw1, uw1)           c = __MXOR (a, b)         MXOR a,b,c
```

6.60.12.4 Raw Read/Write Functions

This sections describes built-in functions related to read and write instructions to access memory. These functions generate `membar` instructions to flush the I/O load and stores where appropriate, as described in Fujitsu's manual described above.

```
unsigned char __builtin_read8 (void *data)
unsigned short __builtin_read16 (void *data)
unsigned long __builtin_read32 (void *data)
unsigned long long __builtin_read64 (void *data)
void __builtin_write8 (void *data, unsigned char datum)
void __builtin_write16 (void *data, unsigned short datum)
void __builtin_write32 (void *data, unsigned long datum)
void __builtin_write64 (void *data, unsigned long long datum)
```

6.60.12.5 Other Built-in Functions

This section describes built-in functions that are not named after a specific FR-V instruction.

`sw2 __IACCreadll (iacc reg)`

> Return the full 64-bit value of IACC0. The *reg* argument is reserved for future expansion and must be 0.

`sw1 __IACCreadl (iacc reg)`

> Return the value of IACC0H if *reg* is 0 and IACC0L if *reg* is 1. Other values of *reg* are rejected as invalid.

`void __IACCsetll (iacc reg, sw2 x)`

> Set the full 64-bit value of IACC0 to *x*. The *reg* argument is reserved for future expansion and must be 0.

`void __IACCsetl (iacc reg, sw1 x)`

> Set IACC0H to *x* if *reg* is 0 and IACC0L to *x* if *reg* is 1. Other values of *reg* are rejected as invalid.

`void __data_prefetch0 (const void *x)`

> Use the `dcpl` instruction to load the contents of address *x* into the data cache.

`void __data_prefetch (const void *x)`

> Use the `nldub` instruction to load the contents of address *x* into the data cache. The instruction is issued in slot I1.

6.60.13 MIPS DSP Built-in Functions

The MIPS DSP Application-Specific Extension (ASE) includes new instructions that are designed to improve the performance of DSP and media applications. It provides instructions that operate on packed 8-bit/16-bit integer data, Q7, Q15 and Q31 fractional data.

GCC supports MIPS DSP operations using both the generic vector extensions (see Section 6.50 [Vector Extensions], page 552) and a collection of MIPS-specific built-in functions. Both kinds of support are enabled by the '-mdsp' command-line option.

Revision 2 of the ASE was introduced in the second half of 2006. This revision adds extra instructions to the original ASE, but is otherwise backwards-compatible with it. You can select revision 2 using the command-line option '-mdspr2'; this option implies '-mdsp'.

The SCOUNT and POS bits of the DSP control register are global. The WRDSP, EXTPDP, EXTPDPV and MTHLIP instructions modify the SCOUNT and POS bits. During optimization, the compiler does not delete these instructions and it does not delete calls to functions containing these instructions.

At present, GCC only provides support for operations on 32-bit vectors. The vector type associated with 8-bit integer data is usually called v4i8, the vector type associated with Q7 is usually called v4q7, the vector type associated with 16-bit integer data is usually called v2i16, and the vector type associated with Q15 is usually called v2q15. They can be defined in C as follows:

```
typedef signed char v4i8 __attribute__ ((vector_size(4)));
typedef signed char v4q7 __attribute__ ((vector_size(4)));
typedef short v2i16 __attribute__ ((vector_size(4)));
typedef short v2q15 __attribute__ ((vector_size(4)));
```

v4i8, v4q7, v2i16 and v2q15 values are initialized in the same way as aggregates. For example:

```
v4i8 a = {1, 2, 3, 4};
v4i8 b;
b = (v4i8) {5, 6, 7, 8};

v2q15 c = {0x0fcb, 0x3a75};
v2q15 d;
d = (v2q15) {0.1234 * 0x1.0p15, 0.4567 * 0x1.0p15};
```

Note: The CPU's endianness determines the order in which values are packed. On little-endian targets, the first value is the least significant and the last value is the most significant. The opposite order applies to big-endian targets. For example, the code above sets the lowest byte of a to 1 on little-endian targets and 4 on big-endian targets.

Note: Q7, Q15 and Q31 values must be initialized with their integer representation. As shown in this example, the integer representation of a Q7 value can be obtained by multiplying the fractional value by 0x1.0p7. The equivalent for Q15 values is to multiply by 0x1.0p15. The equivalent for Q31 values is to multiply by 0x1.0p31.

The table below lists the v4i8 and v2q15 operations for which hardware support exists. a and b are v4i8 values, and c and d are v2q15 values.

C code	MIPS instruction
a + b	addu.qb
c + d	addq.ph
a - b	subu.qb

```
c - d                                          subq.ph
```

The table below lists the `v2i16` operation for which hardware support exists for the DSP ASE REV 2. `e` and `f` are `v2i16` values.

C code   MIPS instruction

```
e * f                                          mul.ph
```

It is easier to describe the DSP built-in functions if we first define the following types:

```
typedef int q31;
typedef int i32;
typedef unsigned int ui32;
typedef long long a64;
```

`q31` and `i32` are actually the same as `int`, but we use `q31` to indicate a Q31 fractional value and `i32` to indicate a 32-bit integer value. Similarly, `a64` is the same as `long long`, but we use `a64` to indicate values that are placed in one of the four DSP accumulators (`$ac0`, `$ac1`, `$ac2` or `$ac3`).

Also, some built-in functions prefer or require immediate numbers as parameters, because the corresponding DSP instructions accept both immediate numbers and register operands, or accept immediate numbers only. The immediate parameters are listed as follows.

```
imm0_3: 0 to 3.
imm0_7: 0 to 7.
imm0_15: 0 to 15.
imm0_31: 0 to 31.
imm0_63: 0 to 63.
imm0_255: 0 to 255.
imm_n32_31: -32 to 31.
imm_n512_511: -512 to 511.
```

The following built-in functions map directly to a particular MIPS DSP instruction. Please refer to the architecture specification for details on what each instruction does.

```
v2q15 __builtin_mips_addq_ph (v2q15, v2q15)
v2q15 __builtin_mips_addq_s_ph (v2q15, v2q15)
q31 __builtin_mips_addq_s_w (q31, q31)
v4i8 __builtin_mips_addu_qb (v4i8, v4i8)
v4i8 __builtin_mips_addu_s_qb (v4i8, v4i8)
v2q15 __builtin_mips_subq_ph (v2q15, v2q15)
v2q15 __builtin_mips_subq_s_ph (v2q15, v2q15)
q31 __builtin_mips_subq_s_w (q31, q31)
v4i8 __builtin_mips_subu_qb (v4i8, v4i8)
v4i8 __builtin_mips_subu_s_qb (v4i8, v4i8)
i32 __builtin_mips_addsc (i32, i32)
i32 __builtin_mips_addwc (i32, i32)
i32 __builtin_mips_modsub (i32, i32)
i32 __builtin_mips_raddu_w_qb (v4i8)
v2q15 __builtin_mips_absq_s_ph (v2q15)
q31 __builtin_mips_absq_s_w (q31)
v4i8 __builtin_mips_precrq_qb_ph (v2q15, v2q15)
v2q15 __builtin_mips_precrq_ph_w (q31, q31)
v2q15 __builtin_mips_precrq_rs_ph_w (q31, q31)
v4i8 __builtin_mips_precrqu_s_qb_ph (v2q15, v2q15)
q31 __builtin_mips_preceq_w_phl (v2q15)
q31 __builtin_mips_preceq_w_phr (v2q15)
v2q15 __builtin_mips_precequ_ph_qbl (v4i8)
v2q15 __builtin_mips_precequ_ph_qbr (v4i8)
v2q15 __builtin_mips_precequ_ph_qbla (v4i8)
v2q15 __builtin_mips_precequ_ph_qbra (v4i8)
```

```
v2q15 __builtin_mips_preceu_ph_qbl (v4i8)
v2q15 __builtin_mips_preceu_ph_qbr (v4i8)
v2q15 __builtin_mips_preceu_ph_qbla (v4i8)
v2q15 __builtin_mips_preceu_ph_qbra (v4i8)
v4i8 __builtin_mips_shll_qb (v4i8, imm0_7)
v4i8 __builtin_mips_shll_qb (v4i8, i32)
v2q15 __builtin_mips_shll_ph (v2q15, imm0_15)
v2q15 __builtin_mips_shll_ph (v2q15, i32)
v2q15 __builtin_mips_shll_s_ph (v2q15, imm0_15)
v2q15 __builtin_mips_shll_s_ph (v2q15, i32)
q31 __builtin_mips_shll_s_w (q31, imm0_31)
q31 __builtin_mips_shll_s_w (q31, i32)
v4i8 __builtin_mips_shrl_qb (v4i8, imm0_7)
v4i8 __builtin_mips_shrl_qb (v4i8, i32)
v2q15 __builtin_mips_shra_ph (v2q15, imm0_15)
v2q15 __builtin_mips_shra_ph (v2q15, i32)
v2q15 __builtin_mips_shra_r_ph (v2q15, imm0_15)
v2q15 __builtin_mips_shra_r_ph (v2q15, i32)
q31 __builtin_mips_shra_r_w (q31, imm0_31)
q31 __builtin_mips_shra_r_w (q31, i32)
v2q15 __builtin_mips_muleu_s_ph_qbl (v4i8, v2q15)
v2q15 __builtin_mips_muleu_s_ph_qbr (v4i8, v2q15)
v2q15 __builtin_mips_mulq_rs_ph (v2q15, v2q15)
q31 __builtin_mips_muleq_s_w_phl (v2q15, v2q15)
q31 __builtin_mips_muleq_s_w_phr (v2q15, v2q15)
a64 __builtin_mips_dpau_h_qbl (a64, v4i8, v4i8)
a64 __builtin_mips_dpau_h_qbr (a64, v4i8, v4i8)
a64 __builtin_mips_dpsu_h_qbl (a64, v4i8, v4i8)
a64 __builtin_mips_dpsu_h_qbr (a64, v4i8, v4i8)
a64 __builtin_mips_dpaq_s_w_ph (a64, v2q15, v2q15)
a64 __builtin_mips_dpaq_sa_l_w (a64, q31, q31)
a64 __builtin_mips_dpsq_s_w_ph (a64, v2q15, v2q15)
a64 __builtin_mips_dpsq_sa_l_w (a64, q31, q31)
a64 __builtin_mips_mulsaq_s_w_ph (a64, v2q15, v2q15)
a64 __builtin_mips_maq_s_w_phl (a64, v2q15, v2q15)
a64 __builtin_mips_maq_s_w_phr (a64, v2q15, v2q15)
a64 __builtin_mips_maq_sa_w_phl (a64, v2q15, v2q15)
a64 __builtin_mips_maq_sa_w_phr (a64, v2q15, v2q15)
i32 __builtin_mips_bitrev (i32)
i32 __builtin_mips_insv (i32, i32)
v4i8 __builtin_mips_repl_qb (imm0_255)
v4i8 __builtin_mips_repl_qb (i32)
v2q15 __builtin_mips_repl_ph (imm_n512_511)
v2q15 __builtin_mips_repl_ph (i32)
void __builtin_mips_cmpu_eq_qb (v4i8, v4i8)
void __builtin_mips_cmpu_lt_qb (v4i8, v4i8)
void __builtin_mips_cmpu_le_qb (v4i8, v4i8)
i32 __builtin_mips_cmpgu_eq_qb (v4i8, v4i8)
i32 __builtin_mips_cmpgu_lt_qb (v4i8, v4i8)
i32 __builtin_mips_cmpgu_le_qb (v4i8, v4i8)
void __builtin_mips_cmp_eq_ph (v2q15, v2q15)
void __builtin_mips_cmp_lt_ph (v2q15, v2q15)
void __builtin_mips_cmp_le_ph (v2q15, v2q15)
v4i8 __builtin_mips_pick_qb (v4i8, v4i8)
v2q15 __builtin_mips_pick_ph (v2q15, v2q15)
v2q15 __builtin_mips_packrl_ph (v2q15, v2q15)
i32 __builtin_mips_extr_w (a64, imm0_31)
i32 __builtin_mips_extr_w (a64, i32)
```

```
i32 __builtin_mips_extr_r_w (a64, imm0_31)
i32 __builtin_mips_extr_s_h (a64, i32)
i32 __builtin_mips_extr_rs_w (a64, imm0_31)
i32 __builtin_mips_extr_rs_w (a64, i32)
i32 __builtin_mips_extr_s_h (a64, imm0_31)
i32 __builtin_mips_extr_r_w (a64, i32)
i32 __builtin_mips_extp (a64, imm0_31)
i32 __builtin_mips_extp (a64, i32)
i32 __builtin_mips_extpdp (a64, imm0_31)
i32 __builtin_mips_extpdp (a64, i32)
a64 __builtin_mips_shilo (a64, imm_n32_31)
a64 __builtin_mips_shilo (a64, i32)
a64 __builtin_mips_mthlip (a64, i32)
void __builtin_mips_wrdsp (i32, imm0_63)
i32 __builtin_mips_rddsp (imm0_63)
i32 __builtin_mips_lbux (void *, i32)
i32 __builtin_mips_lhx (void *, i32)
i32 __builtin_mips_lwx (void *, i32)
a64 __builtin_mips_ldx (void *, i32) [MIPS64 only]
i32 __builtin_mips_bposge32 (void)
a64 __builtin_mips_madd (a64, i32, i32);
a64 __builtin_mips_maddu (a64, ui32, ui32);
a64 __builtin_mips_msub (a64, i32, i32);
a64 __builtin_mips_msubu (a64, ui32, ui32);
a64 __builtin_mips_mult (i32, i32);
a64 __builtin_mips_multu (ui32, ui32);
```

The following built-in functions map directly to a particular MIPS DSP REV 2 instruction. Please refer to the architecture specification for details on what each instruction does.

```
v4q7 __builtin_mips_absq_s_qb (v4q7);
v2i16 __builtin_mips_addu_ph (v2i16, v2i16);
v2i16 __builtin_mips_addu_s_ph (v2i16, v2i16);
v4i8 __builtin_mips_adduh_qb (v4i8, v4i8);
v4i8 __builtin_mips_adduh_r_qb (v4i8, v4i8);
i32 __builtin_mips_append (i32, i32, imm0_31);
i32 __builtin_mips_balign (i32, i32, imm0_3);
i32 __builtin_mips_cmpgdu_eq_qb (v4i8, v4i8);
i32 __builtin_mips_cmpgdu_lt_qb (v4i8, v4i8);
i32 __builtin_mips_cmpgdu_le_qb (v4i8, v4i8);
a64 __builtin_mips_dpa_w_ph (a64, v2i16, v2i16);
a64 __builtin_mips_dps_w_ph (a64, v2i16, v2i16);
v2i16 __builtin_mips_mul_ph (v2i16, v2i16);
v2i16 __builtin_mips_mul_s_ph (v2i16, v2i16);
q31 __builtin_mips_mulq_rs_w (q31, q31);
v2q15 __builtin_mips_mulq_s_ph (v2q15, v2q15);
q31 __builtin_mips_mulq_s_w (q31, q31);
a64 __builtin_mips_mulsa_w_ph (a64, v2i16, v2i16);
v4i8 __builtin_mips_precr_qb_ph (v2i16, v2i16);
v2i16 __builtin_mips_precr_sra_ph_w (i32, i32, imm0_31);
v2i16 __builtin_mips_precr_sra_r_ph_w (i32, i32, imm0_31);
i32 __builtin_mips_prepend (i32, i32, imm0_31);
v4i8 __builtin_mips_shra_qb (v4i8, imm0_7);
v4i8 __builtin_mips_shra_r_qb (v4i8, imm0_7);
v4i8 __builtin_mips_shra_qb (v4i8, i32);
v4i8 __builtin_mips_shra_r_qb (v4i8, i32);
v2i16 __builtin_mips_shrl_ph (v2i16, imm0_15);
v2i16 __builtin_mips_shrl_ph (v2i16, i32);
v2i16 __builtin_mips_subu_ph (v2i16, v2i16);
```

```
v2i16 __builtin_mips_subu_s_ph (v2i16, v2i16);
v4i8 __builtin_mips_subuh_qb (v4i8, v4i8);
v4i8 __builtin_mips_subuh_r_qb (v4i8, v4i8);
v2q15 __builtin_mips_addqh_ph (v2q15, v2q15);
v2q15 __builtin_mips_addqh_r_ph (v2q15, v2q15);
q31 __builtin_mips_addqh_w (q31, q31);
q31 __builtin_mips_addqh_r_w (q31, q31);
v2q15 __builtin_mips_subqh_ph (v2q15, v2q15);
v2q15 __builtin_mips_subqh_r_ph (v2q15, v2q15);
q31 __builtin_mips_subqh_w (q31, q31);
q31 __builtin_mips_subqh_r_w (q31, q31);
a64 __builtin_mips_dpax_w_ph (a64, v2i16, v2i16);
a64 __builtin_mips_dpsx_w_ph (a64, v2i16, v2i16);
a64 __builtin_mips_dpaqx_s_w_ph (a64, v2q15, v2q15);
a64 __builtin_mips_dpaqx_sa_w_ph (a64, v2q15, v2q15);
a64 __builtin_mips_dpsqx_s_w_ph (a64, v2q15, v2q15);
a64 __builtin_mips_dpsqx_sa_w_ph (a64, v2q15, v2q15);
```

6.60.14 MIPS Paired-Single Support

The MIPS64 architecture includes a number of instructions that operate on pairs of single-precision floating-point values. Each pair is packed into a 64-bit floating-point register, with one element being designated the "upper half" and the other being designated the "lower half".

GCC supports paired-single operations using both the generic vector extensions (see Section 6.50 [Vector Extensions], page 552) and a collection of MIPS-specific built-in functions. Both kinds of support are enabled by the '-mpaired-single' command-line option.

The vector type associated with paired-single values is usually called v2sf. It can be defined in C as follows:

```
typedef float v2sf __attribute__ ((vector_size (8)));
```

v2sf values are initialized in the same way as aggregates. For example:

```
v2sf a = {1.5, 9.1};
v2sf b;
float e, f;
b = (v2sf) {e, f};
```

Note: The CPU's endianness determines which value is stored in the upper half of a register and which value is stored in the lower half. On little-endian targets, the first value is the lower one and the second value is the upper one. The opposite order applies to big-endian targets. For example, the code above sets the lower half of a to 1.5 on little-endian targets and 9.1 on big-endian targets.

6.60.15 MIPS Loongson Built-in Functions

GCC provides intrinsics to access the SIMD instructions provided by the ST Microelectronics Loongson-2E and -2F processors. These intrinsics, available after inclusion of the loongson.h header file, operate on the following 64-bit vector types:

- uint8x8_t, a vector of eight unsigned 8-bit integers;
- uint16x4_t, a vector of four unsigned 16-bit integers;
- uint32x2_t, a vector of two unsigned 32-bit integers;
- int8x8_t, a vector of eight signed 8-bit integers;

- `int16x4_t`, a vector of four signed 16-bit integers;

- `int32x2_t`, a vector of two signed 32-bit integers.

The intrinsics provided are listed below; each is named after the machine instruction to which it corresponds, with suffixes added as appropriate to distinguish intrinsics that expand to the same machine instruction yet have different argument types. Refer to the architecture documentation for a description of the functionality of each instruction.

```
int16x4_t packsswh (int32x2_t s, int32x2_t t);
int8x8_t packsshb (int16x4_t s, int16x4_t t);
uint8x8_t packushb (uint16x4_t s, uint16x4_t t);
uint32x2_t paddw_u (uint32x2_t s, uint32x2_t t);
uint16x4_t paddh_u (uint16x4_t s, uint16x4_t t);
uint8x8_t paddb_u (uint8x8_t s, uint8x8_t t);
int32x2_t paddw_s (int32x2_t s, int32x2_t t);
int16x4_t paddh_s (int16x4_t s, int16x4_t t);
int8x8_t paddb_s (int8x8_t s, int8x8_t t);
uint64_t paddd_u (uint64_t s, uint64_t t);
int64_t paddd_s (int64_t s, int64_t t);
int16x4_t paddsh (int16x4_t s, int16x4_t t);
int8x8_t paddsb (int8x8_t s, int8x8_t t);
uint16x4_t paddush (uint16x4_t s, uint16x4_t t);
uint8x8_t paddusb (uint8x8_t s, uint8x8_t t);
uint64_t pandn_ud (uint64_t s, uint64_t t);
uint32x2_t pandn_uw (uint32x2_t s, uint32x2_t t);
uint16x4_t pandn_uh (uint16x4_t s, uint16x4_t t);
uint8x8_t pandn_ub (uint8x8_t s, uint8x8_t t);
int64_t pandn_sd (int64_t s, int64_t t);
int32x2_t pandn_sw (int32x2_t s, int32x2_t t);
int16x4_t pandn_sh (int16x4_t s, int16x4_t t);
int8x8_t pandn_sb (int8x8_t s, int8x8_t t);
uint16x4_t pavgh (uint16x4_t s, uint16x4_t t);
uint8x8_t pavgb (uint8x8_t s, uint8x8_t t);
uint32x2_t pcmpeqw_u (uint32x2_t s, uint32x2_t t);
uint16x4_t pcmpeqh_u (uint16x4_t s, uint16x4_t t);
uint8x8_t pcmpeqb_u (uint8x8_t s, uint8x8_t t);
int32x2_t pcmpeqw_s (int32x2_t s, int32x2_t t);
int16x4_t pcmpeqh_s (int16x4_t s, int16x4_t t);
int8x8_t pcmpeqb_s (int8x8_t s, int8x8_t t);
uint32x2_t pcmpgtw_u (uint32x2_t s, uint32x2_t t);
uint16x4_t pcmpgth_u (uint16x4_t s, uint16x4_t t);
uint8x8_t pcmpgtb_u (uint8x8_t s, uint8x8_t t);
int32x2_t pcmpgtw_s (int32x2_t s, int32x2_t t);
int16x4_t pcmpgth_s (int16x4_t s, int16x4_t t);
int8x8_t pcmpgtb_s (int8x8_t s, int8x8_t t);
uint16x4_t pextrh_u (uint16x4_t s, int field);
int16x4_t pextrh_s (int16x4_t s, int field);
uint16x4_t pinsrh_0_u (uint16x4_t s, uint16x4_t t);
uint16x4_t pinsrh_1_u (uint16x4_t s, uint16x4_t t);
uint16x4_t pinsrh_2_u (uint16x4_t s, uint16x4_t t);
uint16x4_t pinsrh_3_u (uint16x4_t s, uint16x4_t t);
int16x4_t pinsrh_0_s (int16x4_t s, int16x4_t t);
int16x4_t pinsrh_1_s (int16x4_t s, int16x4_t t);
int16x4_t pinsrh_2_s (int16x4_t s, int16x4_t t);
int16x4_t pinsrh_3_s (int16x4_t s, int16x4_t t);
int32x2_t pmaddhw (int16x4_t s, int16x4_t t);
int16x4_t pmaxsh (int16x4_t s, int16x4_t t);
uint8x8_t pmaxub (uint8x8_t s, uint8x8_t t);
```

```
int16x4_t pminsh (int16x4_t s, int16x4_t t);
uint8x8_t pminub (uint8x8_t s, uint8x8_t t);
uint8x8_t pmovmskb_u (uint8x8_t s);
int8x8_t pmovmskb_s (int8x8_t s);
uint16x4_t pmulhuh (uint16x4_t s, uint16x4_t t);
int16x4_t pmulhh (int16x4_t s, int16x4_t t);
int16x4_t pmullh (int16x4_t s, int16x4_t t);
int64_t pmuluw (uint32x2_t s, uint32x2_t t);
uint8x8_t pasubub (uint8x8_t s, uint8x8_t t);
uint16x4_t biadd (uint8x8_t s);
uint16x4_t psadbh (uint8x8_t s, uint8x8_t t);
uint16x4_t pshufh_u (uint16x4_t dest, uint16x4_t s, uint8_t order);
int16x4_t pshufh_s (int16x4_t dest, int16x4_t s, uint8_t order);
uint16x4_t psllh_u (uint16x4_t s, uint8_t amount);
int16x4_t psllh_s (int16x4_t s, uint8_t amount);
uint32x2_t psllw_u (uint32x2_t s, uint8_t amount);
int32x2_t psllw_s (int32x2_t s, uint8_t amount);
uint16x4_t psrlh_u (uint16x4_t s, uint8_t amount);
int16x4_t psrlh_s (int16x4_t s, uint8_t amount);
uint32x2_t psrlw_u (uint32x2_t s, uint8_t amount);
int32x2_t psrlw_s (int32x2_t s, uint8_t amount);
uint16x4_t psrah_u (uint16x4_t s, uint8_t amount);
int16x4_t psrah_s (int16x4_t s, uint8_t amount);
uint32x2_t psraw_u (uint32x2_t s, uint8_t amount);
int32x2_t psraw_s (int32x2_t s, uint8_t amount);
uint32x2_t psubw_u (uint32x2_t s, uint32x2_t t);
uint16x4_t psubh_u (uint16x4_t s, uint16x4_t t);
uint8x8_t psubb_u (uint8x8_t s, uint8x8_t t);
int32x2_t psubw_s (int32x2_t s, int32x2_t t);
int16x4_t psubh_s (int16x4_t s, int16x4_t t);
int8x8_t psubb_s (int8x8_t s, int8x8_t t);
uint64_t psubd_u (uint64_t s, uint64_t t);
int64_t psubd_s (int64_t s, int64_t t);
int16x4_t psubsh (int16x4_t s, int16x4_t t);
int8x8_t psubsb (int8x8_t s, int8x8_t t);
uint16x4_t psubush (uint16x4_t s, uint16x4_t t);
uint8x8_t psubusb (uint8x8_t s, uint8x8_t t);
uint32x2_t punpckhwd_u (uint32x2_t s, uint32x2_t t);
uint16x4_t punpckhhw_u (uint16x4_t s, uint16x4_t t);
uint8x8_t punpckhbh_u (uint8x8_t s, uint8x8_t t);
int32x2_t punpckhwd_s (int32x2_t s, int32x2_t t);
int16x4_t punpckhhw_s (int16x4_t s, int16x4_t t);
int8x8_t punpckhbh_s (int8x8_t s, int8x8_t t);
uint32x2_t punpcklwd_u (uint32x2_t s, uint32x2_t t);
uint16x4_t punpcklhw_u (uint16x4_t s, uint16x4_t t);
uint8x8_t punpcklbh_u (uint8x8_t s, uint8x8_t t);
int32x2_t punpcklwd_s (int32x2_t s, int32x2_t t);
int16x4_t punpcklhw_s (int16x4_t s, int16x4_t t);
int8x8_t punpcklbh_s (int8x8_t s, int8x8_t t);
```

6.60.15.1 Paired-Single Arithmetic

The table below lists the v2sf operations for which hardware support exists. a, b and c are v2sf values and x is an integral value.

C code	MIPS instruction
a + b	add.ps
a - b	sub.ps

```
-a                                   neg.ps
a * b                                mul.ps
a * b + c                            madd.ps
a * b - c                            msub.ps
-(a * b + c)                         nmadd.ps
-(a * b - c)                         nmsub.ps
x ? a : b                            movn.ps/movz.ps
```

Note that the multiply-accumulate instructions can be disabled using the command-line option -mno-fused-madd.

6.60.15.2 Paired-Single Built-in Functions

The following paired-single functions map directly to a particular MIPS instruction. Please refer to the architecture specification for details on what each instruction does.

v2sf __builtin_mips_pll_ps (v2sf, v2sf)
          Pair lower lower (pll.ps).

v2sf __builtin_mips_pul_ps (v2sf, v2sf)
          Pair upper lower (pul.ps).

v2sf __builtin_mips_plu_ps (v2sf, v2sf)
          Pair lower upper (plu.ps).

v2sf __builtin_mips_puu_ps (v2sf, v2sf)
          Pair upper upper (puu.ps).

v2sf __builtin_mips_cvt_ps_s (float, float)
          Convert pair to paired single (cvt.ps.s).

float __builtin_mips_cvt_s_pl (v2sf)
          Convert pair lower to single (cvt.s.pl).

float __builtin_mips_cvt_s_pu (v2sf)
          Convert pair upper to single (cvt.s.pu).

v2sf __builtin_mips_abs_ps (v2sf)
          Absolute value (abs.ps).

v2sf __builtin_mips_alnv_ps (v2sf, v2sf, int)
          Align variable (alnv.ps).

          Note: The value of the third parameter must be 0 or 4 modulo 8, otherwise the result is unpredictable. Please read the instruction description for details.

The following multi-instruction functions are also available. In each case, *cond* can be any of the 16 floating-point conditions: f, un, eq, ueq, olt, ult, ole, ule, sf, ngle, seq, ngl, lt, nge, le or ngt.

v2sf __builtin_mips_movt_c_*cond*_ps (v2sf *a*, v2sf *b*, v2sf *c*, v2sf *d*)
v2sf __builtin_mips_movf_c_*cond*_ps (v2sf *a*, v2sf *b*, v2sf *c*, v2sf *d*)
          Conditional move based on floating-point comparison (c.*cond*.ps, movt.ps/movf.ps).

          The movt functions return the value x computed by:

```
c.cond.ps cc,a,b
mov.ps x,c
movt.ps x,d,cc
```

The movf functions are similar but use `movf.ps` instead of `movt.ps`.

`int __builtin_mips_upper_c_`*cond*`_ps (v2sf a, v2sf b)`
`int __builtin_mips_lower_c_`*cond*`_ps (v2sf a, v2sf b)`

Comparison of two paired-single values (`c.`*cond*`.ps`, `bc1t/bc1f`).

These functions compare *a* and *b* using `c.`*cond*`.ps` and return either the upper or lower half of the result. For example:

```
v2sf a, b;
if (__builtin_mips_upper_c_eq_ps (a, b))
  upper_halves_are_equal ();
else
  upper_halves_are_unequal ();

if (__builtin_mips_lower_c_eq_ps (a, b))
  lower_halves_are_equal ();
else
  lower_halves_are_unequal ();
```

6.60.15.3 MIPS-3D Built-in Functions

The MIPS-3D Application-Specific Extension (ASE) includes additional paired-single instructions that are designed to improve the performance of 3D graphics operations. Support for these instructions is controlled by the '-mips3d' command-line option.

The functions listed below map directly to a particular MIPS-3D instruction. Please refer to the architecture specification for more details on what each instruction does.

`v2sf __builtin_mips_addr_ps (v2sf, v2sf)`

Reduction add (`addr.ps`).

`v2sf __builtin_mips_mulr_ps (v2sf, v2sf)`

Reduction multiply (`mulr.ps`).

`v2sf __builtin_mips_cvt_pw_ps (v2sf)`

Convert paired single to paired word (`cvt.pw.ps`).

`v2sf __builtin_mips_cvt_ps_pw (v2sf)`

Convert paired word to paired single (`cvt.ps.pw`).

`float __builtin_mips_recip1_s (float)`
`double __builtin_mips_recip1_d (double)`
`v2sf __builtin_mips_recip1_ps (v2sf)`

Reduced-precision reciprocal (sequence step 1) (`recip1.`*fmt*).

`float __builtin_mips_recip2_s (float, float)`
`double __builtin_mips_recip2_d (double, double)`
`v2sf __builtin_mips_recip2_ps (v2sf, v2sf)`

Reduced-precision reciprocal (sequence step 2) (`recip2.`*fmt*).

`float __builtin_mips_rsqrt1_s (float)`
`double __builtin_mips_rsqrt1_d (double)`
`v2sf __builtin_mips_rsqrt1_ps (v2sf)`

Reduced-precision reciprocal square root (sequence step 1) (`rsqrt1.`*fmt*).

```
float __builtin_mips_rsqrt2_s (float, float)
double __builtin_mips_rsqrt2_d (double, double)
v2sf __builtin_mips_rsqrt2_ps (v2sf, v2sf)
```
> Reduced-precision reciprocal square root (sequence step 2) (`rsqrt2.`*fmt*).

The following multi-instruction functions are also available. In each case, *cond* can be any of the 16 floating-point conditions: f, un, eq, ueq, olt, ult, ole, ule, sf, ngle, seq, ngl, lt, nge, le or ngt.

```
int __builtin_mips_cabs_cond_s (float a, float b)
int __builtin_mips_cabs_cond_d (double a, double b)
```
> Absolute comparison of two scalar values (`cabs.`*cond*`.`*fmt*, `bc1t`/`bc1f`).

> These functions compare *a* and *b* using `cabs.`*cond*`.s` or `cabs.`*cond*`.d` and return the result as a boolean value. For example:
> ```
> float a, b;
> if (__builtin_mips_cabs_eq_s (a, b))
>   true ();
> else
>   false ();
> ```

```
int __builtin_mips_upper_cabs_cond_ps (v2sf a, v2sf b)
int __builtin_mips_lower_cabs_cond_ps (v2sf a, v2sf b)
```
> Absolute comparison of two paired-single values (`cabs.`*cond*`.ps`, `bc1t`/`bc1f`).

> These functions compare *a* and *b* using `cabs.`*cond*`.ps` and return either the upper or lower half of the result. For example:
> ```
> v2sf a, b;
> if (__builtin_mips_upper_cabs_eq_ps (a, b))
>   upper_halves_are_equal ();
> else
>   upper_halves_are_unequal ();
>
> if (__builtin_mips_lower_cabs_eq_ps (a, b))
>   lower_halves_are_equal ();
> else
>   lower_halves_are_unequal ();
> ```

```
v2sf __builtin_mips_movt_cabs_cond_ps (v2sf a, v2sf b, v2sf c, v2sf d)
v2sf __builtin_mips_movf_cabs_cond_ps (v2sf a, v2sf b, v2sf c, v2sf d)
```
> Conditional move based on absolute comparison (`cabs.`*cond*`.ps`, `movt.ps`/`movf.ps`).

> The `movt` functions return the value *x* computed by:
> ```
> cabs.cond.ps cc,a,b
> mov.ps x,c
> movt.ps x,d,cc
> ```

> The `movf` functions are similar but use `movf.ps` instead of `movt.ps`.

```
int __builtin_mips_any_c_cond_ps (v2sf a, v2sf b)
int __builtin_mips_all_c_cond_ps (v2sf a, v2sf b)
int __builtin_mips_any_cabs_cond_ps (v2sf a, v2sf b)
int __builtin_mips_all_cabs_cond_ps (v2sf a, v2sf b)
```
> Comparison of two paired-single values (`c.`*cond*`.ps`/`cabs.`*cond*`.ps`, `bc1any2t`/`bc1any2f`).

These functions compare a and b using `c.cond.ps` or `cabs.cond.ps`. The `any` forms return true if either result is true and the `all` forms return true if both results are true. For example:

```
v2sf a, b;
if (__builtin_mips_any_c_eq_ps (a, b))
  one_is_true ();
else
  both_are_false ();

if (__builtin_mips_all_c_eq_ps (a, b))
  both_are_true ();
else
  one_is_false ();
```

int __builtin_mips_any_c_*cond*_4s (v2sf *a*, v2sf *b*, v2sf *c*, v2sf *d*)
int __builtin_mips_all_c_*cond*_4s (v2sf *a*, v2sf *b*, v2sf *c*, v2sf *d*)
int __builtin_mips_any_cabs_*cond*_4s (v2sf *a*, v2sf *b*, v2sf *c*, v2sf *d*)
int __builtin_mips_all_cabs_*cond*_4s (v2sf *a*, v2sf *b*, v2sf *c*, v2sf *d*)

Comparison of four paired-single values (`c.cond.ps`/`cabs.cond.ps`, `bc1any4t`/`bc1any4f`).

These functions use `c.cond.ps` or `cabs.cond.ps` to compare a with b and to compare c with d. The `any` forms return true if any of the four results are true and the `all` forms return true if all four results are true. For example:

```
v2sf a, b, c, d;
if (__builtin_mips_any_c_eq_4s (a, b, c, d))
  some_are_true ();
else
  all_are_false ();

if (__builtin_mips_all_c_eq_4s (a, b, c, d))
  all_are_true ();
else
  some_are_false ();
```

6.60.16 MIPS SIMD Architecture (MSA) Support

GCC provides intrinsics to access the SIMD instructions provided by the MSA MIPS SIMD Architecture. The interface is made available by including `<msa.h>` and using '`-mmsa -mhard-float -mfp64 -mnan=2008`'. For each `__builtin_msa_*`, there is a shortened name of the intrinsic, `__msa_*`.

MSA implements 128-bit wide vector registers, operating on 8-, 16-, 32- and 64-bit integer, 16- and 32-bit fixed-point, or 32- and 64-bit floating point data elements. The following vectors typedefs are included in `msa.h`:

- `v16i8`, a vector of sixteen signed 8-bit integers;
- `v16u8`, a vector of sixteen unsigned 8-bit integers;
- `v8i16`, a vector of eight signed 16-bit integers;
- `v8u16`, a vector of eight unsigned 16-bit integers;
- `v4i32`, a vector of four signed 32-bit integers;
- `v4u32`, a vector of four unsigned 32-bit integers;
- `v2i64`, a vector of two signed 64-bit integers;

- v2u64, a vector of two unsigned 64-bit integers;
- v4f32, a vector of four 32-bit floats;
- v2f64, a vector of two 64-bit doubles.

Intructions and corresponding built-ins may have additional restrictions and/or input/output values manipulated:

- imm0_1, an integer literal in range 0 to 1;
- imm0_3, an integer literal in range 0 to 3;
- imm0_7, an integer literal in range 0 to 7;
- imm0_15, an integer literal in range 0 to 15;
- imm0_31, an integer literal in range 0 to 31;
- imm0_63, an integer literal in range 0 to 63;
- imm0_255, an integer literal in range 0 to 255;
- imm_n16_15, an integer literal in range -16 to 15;
- imm_n512_511, an integer literal in range -512 to 511;
- imm_n1024_1022, an integer literal in range -512 to 511 left shifted by 1 bit, i.e., -1024, -1022, ..., 1020, 1022;
- imm_n2048_2044, an integer literal in range -512 to 511 left shifted by 2 bits, i.e., -2048, -2044, ..., 2040, 2044;
- imm_n4096_4088, an integer literal in range -512 to 511 left shifted by 3 bits, i.e., -4096, -4088, ..., 4080, 4088;
- imm1_4, an integer literal in range 1 to 4;
- i32, i64, u32, u64, f32, f64, defined as follows:

```
{
typedef int i32;
#if __LONG_MAX__ == __LONG_LONG_MAX__
typedef long i64;
#else
typedef long long i64;
#endif

typedef unsigned int u32;
#if __LONG_MAX__ == __LONG_LONG_MAX__
typedef unsigned long u64;
#else
typedef unsigned long long u64;
#endif

typedef double f64;
typedef float f32;
}
```

6.60.16.1 MIPS SIMD Architecture Built-in Functions

The intrinsics provided are listed below; each is named after the machine instruction.

```
v16i8 __builtin_msa_add_a_b (v16i8, v16i8);
v8i16 __builtin_msa_add_a_h (v8i16, v8i16);
v4i32 __builtin_msa_add_a_w (v4i32, v4i32);
v2i64 __builtin_msa_add_a_d (v2i64, v2i64);
```

```
v16i8 __builtin_msa_adds_a_b (v16i8, v16i8);
v8i16 __builtin_msa_adds_a_h (v8i16, v8i16);
v4i32 __builtin_msa_adds_a_w (v4i32, v4i32);
v2i64 __builtin_msa_adds_a_d (v2i64, v2i64);

v16i8 __builtin_msa_adds_s_b (v16i8, v16i8);
v8i16 __builtin_msa_adds_s_h (v8i16, v8i16);
v4i32 __builtin_msa_adds_s_w (v4i32, v4i32);
v2i64 __builtin_msa_adds_s_d (v2i64, v2i64);

v16u8 __builtin_msa_adds_u_b (v16u8, v16u8);
v8u16 __builtin_msa_adds_u_h (v8u16, v8u16);
v4u32 __builtin_msa_adds_u_w (v4u32, v4u32);
v2u64 __builtin_msa_adds_u_d (v2u64, v2u64);

v16i8 __builtin_msa_addv_b (v16i8, v16i8);
v8i16 __builtin_msa_addv_h (v8i16, v8i16);
v4i32 __builtin_msa_addv_w (v4i32, v4i32);
v2i64 __builtin_msa_addv_d (v2i64, v2i64);

v16i8 __builtin_msa_addvi_b (v16i8, imm0_31);
v8i16 __builtin_msa_addvi_h (v8i16, imm0_31);
v4i32 __builtin_msa_addvi_w (v4i32, imm0_31);
v2i64 __builtin_msa_addvi_d (v2i64, imm0_31);

v16u8 __builtin_msa_and_v (v16u8, v16u8);

v16u8 __builtin_msa_andi_b (v16u8, imm0_255);

v16i8 __builtin_msa_asub_s_b (v16i8, v16i8);
v8i16 __builtin_msa_asub_s_h (v8i16, v8i16);
v4i32 __builtin_msa_asub_s_w (v4i32, v4i32);
v2i64 __builtin_msa_asub_s_d (v2i64, v2i64);

v16u8 __builtin_msa_asub_u_b (v16u8, v16u8);
v8u16 __builtin_msa_asub_u_h (v8u16, v8u16);
v4u32 __builtin_msa_asub_u_w (v4u32, v4u32);
v2u64 __builtin_msa_asub_u_d (v2u64, v2u64);

v16i8 __builtin_msa_ave_s_b (v16i8, v16i8);
v8i16 __builtin_msa_ave_s_h (v8i16, v8i16);
v4i32 __builtin_msa_ave_s_w (v4i32, v4i32);
v2i64 __builtin_msa_ave_s_d (v2i64, v2i64);

v16u8 __builtin_msa_ave_u_b (v16u8, v16u8);
v8u16 __builtin_msa_ave_u_h (v8u16, v8u16);
v4u32 __builtin_msa_ave_u_w (v4u32, v4u32);
v2u64 __builtin_msa_ave_u_d (v2u64, v2u64);

v16i8 __builtin_msa_aver_s_b (v16i8, v16i8);
v8i16 __builtin_msa_aver_s_h (v8i16, v8i16);
v4i32 __builtin_msa_aver_s_w (v4i32, v4i32);
v2i64 __builtin_msa_aver_s_d (v2i64, v2i64);

v16u8 __builtin_msa_aver_u_b (v16u8, v16u8);
v8u16 __builtin_msa_aver_u_h (v8u16, v8u16);
v4u32 __builtin_msa_aver_u_w (v4u32, v4u32);
```

```
v2u64 __builtin_msa_aver_u_d (v2u64, v2u64);

v16u8 __builtin_msa_bclr_b (v16u8, v16u8);
v8u16 __builtin_msa_bclr_h (v8u16, v8u16);
v4u32 __builtin_msa_bclr_w (v4u32, v4u32);
v2u64 __builtin_msa_bclr_d (v2u64, v2u64);

v16u8 __builtin_msa_bclri_b (v16u8, imm0_7);
v8u16 __builtin_msa_bclri_h (v8u16, imm0_15);
v4u32 __builtin_msa_bclri_w (v4u32, imm0_31);
v2u64 __builtin_msa_bclri_d (v2u64, imm0_63);

v16u8 __builtin_msa_binsl_b (v16u8, v16u8, v16u8);
v8u16 __builtin_msa_binsl_h (v8u16, v8u16, v8u16);
v4u32 __builtin_msa_binsl_w (v4u32, v4u32, v4u32);
v2u64 __builtin_msa_binsl_d (v2u64, v2u64, v2u64);

v16u8 __builtin_msa_binsli_b (v16u8, v16u8, imm0_7);
v8u16 __builtin_msa_binsli_h (v8u16, v8u16, imm0_15);
v4u32 __builtin_msa_binsli_w (v4u32, v4u32, imm0_31);
v2u64 __builtin_msa_binsli_d (v2u64, v2u64, imm0_63);

v16u8 __builtin_msa_binsr_b (v16u8, v16u8, v16u8);
v8u16 __builtin_msa_binsr_h (v8u16, v8u16, v8u16);
v4u32 __builtin_msa_binsr_w (v4u32, v4u32, v4u32);
v2u64 __builtin_msa_binsr_d (v2u64, v2u64, v2u64);

v16u8 __builtin_msa_binsri_b (v16u8, v16u8, imm0_7);
v8u16 __builtin_msa_binsri_h (v8u16, v8u16, imm0_15);
v4u32 __builtin_msa_binsri_w (v4u32, v4u32, imm0_31);
v2u64 __builtin_msa_binsri_d (v2u64, v2u64, imm0_63);

v16u8 __builtin_msa_bmnz_v (v16u8, v16u8, v16u8);

v16u8 __builtin_msa_bmnzi_b (v16u8, v16u8, imm0_255);

v16u8 __builtin_msa_bmz_v (v16u8, v16u8, v16u8);

v16u8 __builtin_msa_bmzi_b (v16u8, v16u8, imm0_255);

v16u8 __builtin_msa_bneg_b (v16u8, v16u8);
v8u16 __builtin_msa_bneg_h (v8u16, v8u16);
v4u32 __builtin_msa_bneg_w (v4u32, v4u32);
v2u64 __builtin_msa_bneg_d (v2u64, v2u64);

v16u8 __builtin_msa_bnegi_b (v16u8, imm0_7);
v8u16 __builtin_msa_bnegi_h (v8u16, imm0_15);
v4u32 __builtin_msa_bnegi_w (v4u32, imm0_31);
v2u64 __builtin_msa_bnegi_d (v2u64, imm0_63);

i32 __builtin_msa_bnz_b (v16u8);
i32 __builtin_msa_bnz_h (v8u16);
i32 __builtin_msa_bnz_w (v4u32);
i32 __builtin_msa_bnz_d (v2u64);

i32 __builtin_msa_bnz_v (v16u8);

v16u8 __builtin_msa_bsel_v (v16u8, v16u8, v16u8);
```

```
v16u8 __builtin_msa_bseli_b (v16u8, v16u8, imm0_255);

v16u8 __builtin_msa_bset_b (v16u8, v16u8);
v8u16 __builtin_msa_bset_h (v8u16, v8u16);
v4u32 __builtin_msa_bset_w (v4u32, v4u32);
v2u64 __builtin_msa_bset_d (v2u64, v2u64);

v16u8 __builtin_msa_bseti_b (v16u8, imm0_7);
v8u16 __builtin_msa_bseti_h (v8u16, imm0_15);
v4u32 __builtin_msa_bseti_w (v4u32, imm0_31);
v2u64 __builtin_msa_bseti_d (v2u64, imm0_63);

i32 __builtin_msa_bz_b (v16u8);
i32 __builtin_msa_bz_h (v8u16);
i32 __builtin_msa_bz_w (v4u32);
i32 __builtin_msa_bz_d (v2u64);

i32 __builtin_msa_bz_v (v16u8);

v16i8 __builtin_msa_ceq_b (v16i8, v16i8);
v8i16 __builtin_msa_ceq_h (v8i16, v8i16);
v4i32 __builtin_msa_ceq_w (v4i32, v4i32);
v2i64 __builtin_msa_ceq_d (v2i64, v2i64);

v16i8 __builtin_msa_ceqi_b (v16i8, imm_n16_15);
v8i16 __builtin_msa_ceqi_h (v8i16, imm_n16_15);
v4i32 __builtin_msa_ceqi_w (v4i32, imm_n16_15);
v2i64 __builtin_msa_ceqi_d (v2i64, imm_n16_15);

i32 __builtin_msa_cfcmsa (imm0_31);

v16i8 __builtin_msa_cle_s_b (v16i8, v16i8);
v8i16 __builtin_msa_cle_s_h (v8i16, v8i16);
v4i32 __builtin_msa_cle_s_w (v4i32, v4i32);
v2i64 __builtin_msa_cle_s_d (v2i64, v2i64);

v16i8 __builtin_msa_cle_u_b (v16u8, v16u8);
v8i16 __builtin_msa_cle_u_h (v8u16, v8u16);
v4i32 __builtin_msa_cle_u_w (v4u32, v4u32);
v2i64 __builtin_msa_cle_u_d (v2u64, v2u64);

v16i8 __builtin_msa_clei_s_b (v16i8, imm_n16_15);
v8i16 __builtin_msa_clei_s_h (v8i16, imm_n16_15);
v4i32 __builtin_msa_clei_s_w (v4i32, imm_n16_15);
v2i64 __builtin_msa_clei_s_d (v2i64, imm_n16_15);

v16i8 __builtin_msa_clei_u_b (v16u8, imm0_31);
v8i16 __builtin_msa_clei_u_h (v8u16, imm0_31);
v4i32 __builtin_msa_clei_u_w (v4u32, imm0_31);
v2i64 __builtin_msa_clei_u_d (v2u64, imm0_31);

v16i8 __builtin_msa_clt_s_b (v16i8, v16i8);
v8i16 __builtin_msa_clt_s_h (v8i16, v8i16);
v4i32 __builtin_msa_clt_s_w (v4i32, v4i32);
v2i64 __builtin_msa_clt_s_d (v2i64, v2i64);

v16i8 __builtin_msa_clt_u_b (v16u8, v16u8);
```

```
v8i16 __builtin_msa_clt_u_h (v8u16, v8u16);
v4i32 __builtin_msa_clt_u_w (v4u32, v4u32);
v2i64 __builtin_msa_clt_u_d (v2u64, v2u64);

v16i8 __builtin_msa_clti_s_b (v16i8, imm_n16_15);
v8i16 __builtin_msa_clti_s_h (v8i16, imm_n16_15);
v4i32 __builtin_msa_clti_s_w (v4i32, imm_n16_15);
v2i64 __builtin_msa_clti_s_d (v2i64, imm_n16_15);

v16i8 __builtin_msa_clti_u_b (v16u8, imm0_31);
v8i16 __builtin_msa_clti_u_h (v8u16, imm0_31);
v4i32 __builtin_msa_clti_u_w (v4u32, imm0_31);
v2i64 __builtin_msa_clti_u_d (v2u64, imm0_31);

i32 __builtin_msa_copy_s_b (v16i8, imm0_15);
i32 __builtin_msa_copy_s_h (v8i16, imm0_7);
i32 __builtin_msa_copy_s_w (v4i32, imm0_3);
i64 __builtin_msa_copy_s_d (v2i64, imm0_1);

u32 __builtin_msa_copy_u_b (v16i8, imm0_15);
u32 __builtin_msa_copy_u_h (v8i16, imm0_7);
u32 __builtin_msa_copy_u_w (v4i32, imm0_3);
u64 __builtin_msa_copy_u_d (v2i64, imm0_1);

void __builtin_msa_ctcmsa (imm0_31, i32);

v16i8 __builtin_msa_div_s_b (v16i8, v16i8);
v8i16 __builtin_msa_div_s_h (v8i16, v8i16);
v4i32 __builtin_msa_div_s_w (v4i32, v4i32);
v2i64 __builtin_msa_div_s_d (v2i64, v2i64);

v16u8 __builtin_msa_div_u_b (v16u8, v16u8);
v8u16 __builtin_msa_div_u_h (v8u16, v8u16);
v4u32 __builtin_msa_div_u_w (v4u32, v4u32);
v2u64 __builtin_msa_div_u_d (v2u64, v2u64);

v8i16 __builtin_msa_dotp_s_h (v16i8, v16i8);
v4i32 __builtin_msa_dotp_s_w (v8i16, v8i16);
v2i64 __builtin_msa_dotp_s_d (v4i32, v4i32);

v8u16 __builtin_msa_dotp_u_h (v16u8, v16u8);
v4u32 __builtin_msa_dotp_u_w (v8u16, v8u16);
v2u64 __builtin_msa_dotp_u_d (v4u32, v4u32);

v8i16 __builtin_msa_dpadd_s_h (v8i16, v16i8, v16i8);
v4i32 __builtin_msa_dpadd_s_w (v4i32, v8i16, v8i16);
v2i64 __builtin_msa_dpadd_s_d (v2i64, v4i32, v4i32);

v8u16 __builtin_msa_dpadd_u_h (v8u16, v16u8, v16u8);
v4u32 __builtin_msa_dpadd_u_w (v4u32, v8u16, v8u16);
v2u64 __builtin_msa_dpadd_u_d (v2u64, v4u32, v4u32);

v8i16 __builtin_msa_dpsub_s_h (v8i16, v16i8, v16i8);
v4i32 __builtin_msa_dpsub_s_w (v4i32, v8i16, v8i16);
v2i64 __builtin_msa_dpsub_s_d (v2i64, v4i32, v4i32);

v8i16 __builtin_msa_dpsub_u_h (v8i16, v16u8, v16u8);
v4i32 __builtin_msa_dpsub_u_w (v4i32, v8u16, v8u16);
```

```
v2i64 __builtin_msa_dpsub_u_d (v2i64, v4u32, v4u32);

v4f32 __builtin_msa_fadd_w (v4f32, v4f32);
v2f64 __builtin_msa_fadd_d (v2f64, v2f64);

v4i32 __builtin_msa_fcaf_w (v4f32, v4f32);
v2i64 __builtin_msa_fcaf_d (v2f64, v2f64);

v4i32 __builtin_msa_fceq_w (v4f32, v4f32);
v2i64 __builtin_msa_fceq_d (v2f64, v2f64);

v4i32 __builtin_msa_fclass_w (v4f32);
v2i64 __builtin_msa_fclass_d (v2f64);

v4i32 __builtin_msa_fcle_w (v4f32, v4f32);
v2i64 __builtin_msa_fcle_d (v2f64, v2f64);

v4i32 __builtin_msa_fclt_w (v4f32, v4f32);
v2i64 __builtin_msa_fclt_d (v2f64, v2f64);

v4i32 __builtin_msa_fcne_w (v4f32, v4f32);
v2i64 __builtin_msa_fcne_d (v2f64, v2f64);

v4i32 __builtin_msa_fcor_w (v4f32, v4f32);
v2i64 __builtin_msa_fcor_d (v2f64, v2f64);

v4i32 __builtin_msa_fcueq_w (v4f32, v4f32);
v2i64 __builtin_msa_fcueq_d (v2f64, v2f64);

v4i32 __builtin_msa_fcule_w (v4f32, v4f32);
v2i64 __builtin_msa_fcule_d (v2f64, v2f64);

v4i32 __builtin_msa_fcult_w (v4f32, v4f32);
v2i64 __builtin_msa_fcult_d (v2f64, v2f64);

v4i32 __builtin_msa_fcun_w (v4f32, v4f32);
v2i64 __builtin_msa_fcun_d (v2f64, v2f64);

v4i32 __builtin_msa_fcune_w (v4f32, v4f32);
v2i64 __builtin_msa_fcune_d (v2f64, v2f64);

v4f32 __builtin_msa_fdiv_w (v4f32, v4f32);
v2f64 __builtin_msa_fdiv_d (v2f64, v2f64);

v8i16 __builtin_msa_fexdo_h (v4f32, v4f32);
v4f32 __builtin_msa_fexdo_w (v2f64, v2f64);

v4f32 __builtin_msa_fexp2_w (v4f32, v4i32);
v2f64 __builtin_msa_fexp2_d (v2f64, v2i64);

v4f32 __builtin_msa_fexupl_w (v8i16);
v2f64 __builtin_msa_fexupl_d (v4f32);

v4f32 __builtin_msa_fexupr_w (v8i16);
v2f64 __builtin_msa_fexupr_d (v4f32);

v4f32 __builtin_msa_ffint_s_w (v4i32);
v2f64 __builtin_msa_ffint_s_d (v2i64);
```

```
v4f32 __builtin_msa_ffint_u_w (v4u32);
v2f64 __builtin_msa_ffint_u_d (v2u64);

v4f32 __builtin_msa_ffql_w (v8i16);
v2f64 __builtin_msa_ffql_d (v4i32);

v4f32 __builtin_msa_ffqr_w (v8i16);
v2f64 __builtin_msa_ffqr_d (v4i32);

v16i8 __builtin_msa_fill_b (i32);
v8i16 __builtin_msa_fill_h (i32);
v4i32 __builtin_msa_fill_w (i32);
v2i64 __builtin_msa_fill_d (i64);

v4f32 __builtin_msa_flog2_w (v4f32);
v2f64 __builtin_msa_flog2_d (v2f64);

v4f32 __builtin_msa_fmadd_w (v4f32, v4f32, v4f32);
v2f64 __builtin_msa_fmadd_d (v2f64, v2f64, v2f64);

v4f32 __builtin_msa_fmax_w (v4f32, v4f32);
v2f64 __builtin_msa_fmax_d (v2f64, v2f64);

v4f32 __builtin_msa_fmax_a_w (v4f32, v4f32);
v2f64 __builtin_msa_fmax_a_d (v2f64, v2f64);

v4f32 __builtin_msa_fmin_w (v4f32, v4f32);
v2f64 __builtin_msa_fmin_d (v2f64, v2f64);

v4f32 __builtin_msa_fmin_a_w (v4f32, v4f32);
v2f64 __builtin_msa_fmin_a_d (v2f64, v2f64);

v4f32 __builtin_msa_fmsub_w (v4f32, v4f32, v4f32);
v2f64 __builtin_msa_fmsub_d (v2f64, v2f64, v2f64);

v4f32 __builtin_msa_fmul_w (v4f32, v4f32);
v2f64 __builtin_msa_fmul_d (v2f64, v2f64);

v4f32 __builtin_msa_frint_w (v4f32);
v2f64 __builtin_msa_frint_d (v2f64);

v4f32 __builtin_msa_frcp_w (v4f32);
v2f64 __builtin_msa_frcp_d (v2f64);

v4f32 __builtin_msa_frsqrt_w (v4f32);
v2f64 __builtin_msa_frsqrt_d (v2f64);

v4i32 __builtin_msa_fsaf_w (v4f32, v4f32);
v2i64 __builtin_msa_fsaf_d (v2f64, v2f64);

v4i32 __builtin_msa_fseq_w (v4f32, v4f32);
v2i64 __builtin_msa_fseq_d (v2f64, v2f64);

v4i32 __builtin_msa_fsle_w (v4f32, v4f32);
v2i64 __builtin_msa_fsle_d (v2f64, v2f64);

v4i32 __builtin_msa_fslt_w (v4f32, v4f32);
```

```
v2i64 __builtin_msa_fslt_d (v2f64, v2f64);

v4i32 __builtin_msa_fsne_w (v4f32, v4f32);
v2i64 __builtin_msa_fsne_d (v2f64, v2f64);

v4i32 __builtin_msa_fsor_w (v4f32, v4f32);
v2i64 __builtin_msa_fsor_d (v2f64, v2f64);

v4f32 __builtin_msa_fsqrt_w (v4f32);
v2f64 __builtin_msa_fsqrt_d (v2f64);

v4f32 __builtin_msa_fsub_w (v4f32, v4f32);
v2f64 __builtin_msa_fsub_d (v2f64, v2f64);

v4i32 __builtin_msa_fsueq_w (v4f32, v4f32);
v2i64 __builtin_msa_fsueq_d (v2f64, v2f64);

v4i32 __builtin_msa_fsule_w (v4f32, v4f32);
v2i64 __builtin_msa_fsule_d (v2f64, v2f64);

v4i32 __builtin_msa_fsult_w (v4f32, v4f32);
v2i64 __builtin_msa_fsult_d (v2f64, v2f64);

v4i32 __builtin_msa_fsun_w (v4f32, v4f32);
v2i64 __builtin_msa_fsun_d (v2f64, v2f64);

v4i32 __builtin_msa_fsune_w (v4f32, v4f32);
v2i64 __builtin_msa_fsune_d (v2f64, v2f64);

v4i32 __builtin_msa_ftint_s_w (v4f32);
v2i64 __builtin_msa_ftint_s_d (v2f64);

v4u32 __builtin_msa_ftint_u_w (v4f32);
v2u64 __builtin_msa_ftint_u_d (v2f64);

v8i16 __builtin_msa_ftq_h (v4f32, v4f32);
v4i32 __builtin_msa_ftq_w (v2f64, v2f64);

v4i32 __builtin_msa_ftrunc_s_w (v4f32);
v2i64 __builtin_msa_ftrunc_s_d (v2f64);

v4u32 __builtin_msa_ftrunc_u_w (v4f32);
v2u64 __builtin_msa_ftrunc_u_d (v2f64);

v8i16 __builtin_msa_hadd_s_h (v16i8, v16i8);
v4i32 __builtin_msa_hadd_s_w (v8i16, v8i16);
v2i64 __builtin_msa_hadd_s_d (v4i32, v4i32);

v8u16 __builtin_msa_hadd_u_h (v16u8, v16u8);
v4u32 __builtin_msa_hadd_u_w (v8u16, v8u16);
v2u64 __builtin_msa_hadd_u_d (v4u32, v4u32);

v8i16 __builtin_msa_hsub_s_h (v16i8, v16i8);
v4i32 __builtin_msa_hsub_s_w (v8i16, v8i16);
v2i64 __builtin_msa_hsub_s_d (v4i32, v4i32);

v8i16 __builtin_msa_hsub_u_h (v16u8, v16u8);
v4i32 __builtin_msa_hsub_u_w (v8u16, v8u16);
```

```
v2i64 __builtin_msa_hsub_u_d (v4u32, v4u32);

v16i8 __builtin_msa_ilvev_b (v16i8, v16i8);
v8i16 __builtin_msa_ilvev_h (v8i16, v8i16);
v4i32 __builtin_msa_ilvev_w (v4i32, v4i32);
v2i64 __builtin_msa_ilvev_d (v2i64, v2i64);

v16i8 __builtin_msa_ilvl_b (v16i8, v16i8);
v8i16 __builtin_msa_ilvl_h (v8i16, v8i16);
v4i32 __builtin_msa_ilvl_w (v4i32, v4i32);
v2i64 __builtin_msa_ilvl_d (v2i64, v2i64);

v16i8 __builtin_msa_ilvod_b (v16i8, v16i8);
v8i16 __builtin_msa_ilvod_h (v8i16, v8i16);
v4i32 __builtin_msa_ilvod_w (v4i32, v4i32);
v2i64 __builtin_msa_ilvod_d (v2i64, v2i64);

v16i8 __builtin_msa_ilvr_b (v16i8, v16i8);
v8i16 __builtin_msa_ilvr_h (v8i16, v8i16);
v4i32 __builtin_msa_ilvr_w (v4i32, v4i32);
v2i64 __builtin_msa_ilvr_d (v2i64, v2i64);

v16i8 __builtin_msa_insert_b (v16i8, imm0_15, i32);
v8i16 __builtin_msa_insert_h (v8i16, imm0_7, i32);
v4i32 __builtin_msa_insert_w (v4i32, imm0_3, i32);
v2i64 __builtin_msa_insert_d (v2i64, imm0_1, i64);

v16i8 __builtin_msa_insve_b (v16i8, imm0_15, v16i8);
v8i16 __builtin_msa_insve_h (v8i16, imm0_7, v8i16);
v4i32 __builtin_msa_insve_w (v4i32, imm0_3, v4i32);
v2i64 __builtin_msa_insve_d (v2i64, imm0_1, v2i64);

v16i8 __builtin_msa_ld_b (void *, imm_n512_511);
v8i16 __builtin_msa_ld_h (void *, imm_n1024_1022);
v4i32 __builtin_msa_ld_w (void *, imm_n2048_2044);
v2i64 __builtin_msa_ld_d (void *, imm_n4096_4088);

v16i8 __builtin_msa_ldi_b (imm_n512_511);
v8i16 __builtin_msa_ldi_h (imm_n512_511);
v4i32 __builtin_msa_ldi_w (imm_n512_511);
v2i64 __builtin_msa_ldi_d (imm_n512_511);

v8i16 __builtin_msa_madd_q_h (v8i16, v8i16, v8i16);
v4i32 __builtin_msa_madd_q_w (v4i32, v4i32, v4i32);

v8i16 __builtin_msa_maddr_q_h (v8i16, v8i16, v8i16);
v4i32 __builtin_msa_maddr_q_w (v4i32, v4i32, v4i32);

v16i8 __builtin_msa_maddv_b (v16i8, v16i8, v16i8);
v8i16 __builtin_msa_maddv_h (v8i16, v8i16, v8i16);
v4i32 __builtin_msa_maddv_w (v4i32, v4i32, v4i32);
v2i64 __builtin_msa_maddv_d (v2i64, v2i64, v2i64);

v16i8 __builtin_msa_max_a_b (v16i8, v16i8);
v8i16 __builtin_msa_max_a_h (v8i16, v8i16);
v4i32 __builtin_msa_max_a_w (v4i32, v4i32);
v2i64 __builtin_msa_max_a_d (v2i64, v2i64);
```

```
v16i8 __builtin_msa_max_s_b (v16i8, v16i8);
v8i16 __builtin_msa_max_s_h (v8i16, v8i16);
v4i32 __builtin_msa_max_s_w (v4i32, v4i32);
v2i64 __builtin_msa_max_s_d (v2i64, v2i64);

v16u8 __builtin_msa_max_u_b (v16u8, v16u8);
v8u16 __builtin_msa_max_u_h (v8u16, v8u16);
v4u32 __builtin_msa_max_u_w (v4u32, v4u32);
v2u64 __builtin_msa_max_u_d (v2u64, v2u64);

v16i8 __builtin_msa_maxi_s_b (v16i8, imm_n16_15);
v8i16 __builtin_msa_maxi_s_h (v8i16, imm_n16_15);
v4i32 __builtin_msa_maxi_s_w (v4i32, imm_n16_15);
v2i64 __builtin_msa_maxi_s_d (v2i64, imm_n16_15);

v16u8 __builtin_msa_maxi_u_b (v16u8, imm0_31);
v8u16 __builtin_msa_maxi_u_h (v8u16, imm0_31);
v4u32 __builtin_msa_maxi_u_w (v4u32, imm0_31);
v2u64 __builtin_msa_maxi_u_d (v2u64, imm0_31);

v16i8 __builtin_msa_min_a_b (v16i8, v16i8);
v8i16 __builtin_msa_min_a_h (v8i16, v8i16);
v4i32 __builtin_msa_min_a_w (v4i32, v4i32);
v2i64 __builtin_msa_min_a_d (v2i64, v2i64);

v16i8 __builtin_msa_min_s_b (v16i8, v16i8);
v8i16 __builtin_msa_min_s_h (v8i16, v8i16);
v4i32 __builtin_msa_min_s_w (v4i32, v4i32);
v2i64 __builtin_msa_min_s_d (v2i64, v2i64);

v16u8 __builtin_msa_min_u_b (v16u8, v16u8);
v8u16 __builtin_msa_min_u_h (v8u16, v8u16);
v4u32 __builtin_msa_min_u_w (v4u32, v4u32);
v2u64 __builtin_msa_min_u_d (v2u64, v2u64);

v16i8 __builtin_msa_mini_s_b (v16i8, imm_n16_15);
v8i16 __builtin_msa_mini_s_h (v8i16, imm_n16_15);
v4i32 __builtin_msa_mini_s_w (v4i32, imm_n16_15);
v2i64 __builtin_msa_mini_s_d (v2i64, imm_n16_15);

v16u8 __builtin_msa_mini_u_b (v16u8, imm0_31);
v8u16 __builtin_msa_mini_u_h (v8u16, imm0_31);
v4u32 __builtin_msa_mini_u_w (v4u32, imm0_31);
v2u64 __builtin_msa_mini_u_d (v2u64, imm0_31);

v16i8 __builtin_msa_mod_s_b (v16i8, v16i8);
v8i16 __builtin_msa_mod_s_h (v8i16, v8i16);
v4i32 __builtin_msa_mod_s_w (v4i32, v4i32);
v2i64 __builtin_msa_mod_s_d (v2i64, v2i64);

v16u8 __builtin_msa_mod_u_b (v16u8, v16u8);
v8u16 __builtin_msa_mod_u_h (v8u16, v8u16);
v4u32 __builtin_msa_mod_u_w (v4u32, v4u32);
v2u64 __builtin_msa_mod_u_d (v2u64, v2u64);

v16i8 __builtin_msa_move_v (v16i8);

v8i16 __builtin_msa_msub_q_h (v8i16, v8i16, v8i16);
```

```
v4i32 __builtin_msa_msub_q_w (v4i32, v4i32, v4i32);

v8i16 __builtin_msa_msubr_q_h (v8i16, v8i16, v8i16);
v4i32 __builtin_msa_msubr_q_w (v4i32, v4i32, v4i32);

v16i8 __builtin_msa_msubv_b (v16i8, v16i8, v16i8);
v8i16 __builtin_msa_msubv_h (v8i16, v8i16, v8i16);
v4i32 __builtin_msa_msubv_w (v4i32, v4i32, v4i32);
v2i64 __builtin_msa_msubv_d (v2i64, v2i64, v2i64);

v8i16 __builtin_msa_mul_q_h (v8i16, v8i16);
v4i32 __builtin_msa_mul_q_w (v4i32, v4i32);

v8i16 __builtin_msa_mulr_q_h (v8i16, v8i16);
v4i32 __builtin_msa_mulr_q_w (v4i32, v4i32);

v16i8 __builtin_msa_mulv_b (v16i8, v16i8);
v8i16 __builtin_msa_mulv_h (v8i16, v8i16);
v4i32 __builtin_msa_mulv_w (v4i32, v4i32);
v2i64 __builtin_msa_mulv_d (v2i64, v2i64);

v16i8 __builtin_msa_nloc_b (v16i8);
v8i16 __builtin_msa_nloc_h (v8i16);
v4i32 __builtin_msa_nloc_w (v4i32);
v2i64 __builtin_msa_nloc_d (v2i64);

v16i8 __builtin_msa_nlzc_b (v16i8);
v8i16 __builtin_msa_nlzc_h (v8i16);
v4i32 __builtin_msa_nlzc_w (v4i32);
v2i64 __builtin_msa_nlzc_d (v2i64);

v16u8 __builtin_msa_nor_v (v16u8, v16u8);

v16u8 __builtin_msa_nori_b (v16u8, imm0_255);

v16u8 __builtin_msa_or_v (v16u8, v16u8);

v16u8 __builtin_msa_ori_b (v16u8, imm0_255);

v16i8 __builtin_msa_pckev_b (v16i8, v16i8);
v8i16 __builtin_msa_pckev_h (v8i16, v8i16);
v4i32 __builtin_msa_pckev_w (v4i32, v4i32);
v2i64 __builtin_msa_pckev_d (v2i64, v2i64);

v16i8 __builtin_msa_pckod_b (v16i8, v16i8);
v8i16 __builtin_msa_pckod_h (v8i16, v8i16);
v4i32 __builtin_msa_pckod_w (v4i32, v4i32);
v2i64 __builtin_msa_pckod_d (v2i64, v2i64);

v16i8 __builtin_msa_pcnt_b (v16i8);
v8i16 __builtin_msa_pcnt_h (v8i16);
v4i32 __builtin_msa_pcnt_w (v4i32);
v2i64 __builtin_msa_pcnt_d (v2i64);

v16i8 __builtin_msa_sat_s_b (v16i8, imm0_7);
v8i16 __builtin_msa_sat_s_h (v8i16, imm0_15);
v4i32 __builtin_msa_sat_s_w (v4i32, imm0_31);
v2i64 __builtin_msa_sat_s_d (v2i64, imm0_63);
```

```
v16u8 __builtin_msa_sat_u_b (v16u8, imm0_7);
v8u16 __builtin_msa_sat_u_h (v8u16, imm0_15);
v4u32 __builtin_msa_sat_u_w (v4u32, imm0_31);
v2u64 __builtin_msa_sat_u_d (v2u64, imm0_63);

v16i8 __builtin_msa_shf_b (v16i8, imm0_255);
v8i16 __builtin_msa_shf_h (v8i16, imm0_255);
v4i32 __builtin_msa_shf_w (v4i32, imm0_255);

v16i8 __builtin_msa_sld_b (v16i8, v16i8, i32);
v8i16 __builtin_msa_sld_h (v8i16, v8i16, i32);
v4i32 __builtin_msa_sld_w (v4i32, v4i32, i32);
v2i64 __builtin_msa_sld_d (v2i64, v2i64, i32);

v16i8 __builtin_msa_sldi_b (v16i8, v16i8, imm0_15);
v8i16 __builtin_msa_sldi_h (v8i16, v8i16, imm0_7);
v4i32 __builtin_msa_sldi_w (v4i32, v4i32, imm0_3);
v2i64 __builtin_msa_sldi_d (v2i64, v2i64, imm0_1);

v16i8 __builtin_msa_sll_b (v16i8, v16i8);
v8i16 __builtin_msa_sll_h (v8i16, v8i16);
v4i32 __builtin_msa_sll_w (v4i32, v4i32);
v2i64 __builtin_msa_sll_d (v2i64, v2i64);

v16i8 __builtin_msa_slli_b (v16i8, imm0_7);
v8i16 __builtin_msa_slli_h (v8i16, imm0_15);
v4i32 __builtin_msa_slli_w (v4i32, imm0_31);
v2i64 __builtin_msa_slli_d (v2i64, imm0_63);

v16i8 __builtin_msa_splat_b (v16i8, i32);
v8i16 __builtin_msa_splat_h (v8i16, i32);
v4i32 __builtin_msa_splat_w (v4i32, i32);
v2i64 __builtin_msa_splat_d (v2i64, i32);

v16i8 __builtin_msa_splati_b (v16i8, imm0_15);
v8i16 __builtin_msa_splati_h (v8i16, imm0_7);
v4i32 __builtin_msa_splati_w (v4i32, imm0_3);
v2i64 __builtin_msa_splati_d (v2i64, imm0_1);

v16i8 __builtin_msa_sra_b (v16i8, v16i8);
v8i16 __builtin_msa_sra_h (v8i16, v8i16);
v4i32 __builtin_msa_sra_w (v4i32, v4i32);
v2i64 __builtin_msa_sra_d (v2i64, v2i64);

v16i8 __builtin_msa_srai_b (v16i8, imm0_7);
v8i16 __builtin_msa_srai_h (v8i16, imm0_15);
v4i32 __builtin_msa_srai_w (v4i32, imm0_31);
v2i64 __builtin_msa_srai_d (v2i64, imm0_63);

v16i8 __builtin_msa_srar_b (v16i8, v16i8);
v8i16 __builtin_msa_srar_h (v8i16, v8i16);
v4i32 __builtin_msa_srar_w (v4i32, v4i32);
v2i64 __builtin_msa_srar_d (v2i64, v2i64);

v16i8 __builtin_msa_srari_b (v16i8, imm0_7);
v8i16 __builtin_msa_srari_h (v8i16, imm0_15);
v4i32 __builtin_msa_srari_w (v4i32, imm0_31);
```

```
v2i64 __builtin_msa_srari_d (v2i64, imm0_63);

v16i8 __builtin_msa_srl_b (v16i8, v16i8);
v8i16 __builtin_msa_srl_h (v8i16, v8i16);
v4i32 __builtin_msa_srl_w (v4i32, v4i32);
v2i64 __builtin_msa_srl_d (v2i64, v2i64);

v16i8 __builtin_msa_srli_b (v16i8, imm0_7);
v8i16 __builtin_msa_srli_h (v8i16, imm0_15);
v4i32 __builtin_msa_srli_w (v4i32, imm0_31);
v2i64 __builtin_msa_srli_d (v2i64, imm0_63);

v16i8 __builtin_msa_srlr_b (v16i8, v16i8);
v8i16 __builtin_msa_srlr_h (v8i16, v8i16);
v4i32 __builtin_msa_srlr_w (v4i32, v4i32);
v2i64 __builtin_msa_srlr_d (v2i64, v2i64);

v16i8 __builtin_msa_srlri_b (v16i8, imm0_7);
v8i16 __builtin_msa_srlri_h (v8i16, imm0_15);
v4i32 __builtin_msa_srlri_w (v4i32, imm0_31);
v2i64 __builtin_msa_srlri_d (v2i64, imm0_63);

void __builtin_msa_st_b (v16i8, void *, imm_n512_511);
void __builtin_msa_st_h (v8i16, void *, imm_n1024_1022);
void __builtin_msa_st_w (v4i32, void *, imm_n2048_2044);
void __builtin_msa_st_d (v2i64, void *, imm_n4096_4088);

v16i8 __builtin_msa_subs_s_b (v16i8, v16i8);
v8i16 __builtin_msa_subs_s_h (v8i16, v8i16);
v4i32 __builtin_msa_subs_s_w (v4i32, v4i32);
v2i64 __builtin_msa_subs_s_d (v2i64, v2i64);

v16u8 __builtin_msa_subs_u_b (v16u8, v16u8);
v8u16 __builtin_msa_subs_u_h (v8u16, v8u16);
v4u32 __builtin_msa_subs_u_w (v4u32, v4u32);
v2u64 __builtin_msa_subs_u_d (v2u64, v2u64);

v16u8 __builtin_msa_subsus_u_b (v16u8, v16i8);
v8u16 __builtin_msa_subsus_u_h (v8u16, v8i16);
v4u32 __builtin_msa_subsus_u_w (v4u32, v4i32);
v2u64 __builtin_msa_subsus_u_d (v2u64, v2i64);

v16i8 __builtin_msa_subsuu_s_b (v16u8, v16u8);
v8i16 __builtin_msa_subsuu_s_h (v8u16, v8u16);
v4i32 __builtin_msa_subsuu_s_w (v4u32, v4u32);
v2i64 __builtin_msa_subsuu_s_d (v2u64, v2u64);

v16i8 __builtin_msa_subv_b (v16i8, v16i8);
v8i16 __builtin_msa_subv_h (v8i16, v8i16);
v4i32 __builtin_msa_subv_w (v4i32, v4i32);
v2i64 __builtin_msa_subv_d (v2i64, v2i64);

v16i8 __builtin_msa_subvi_b (v16i8, imm0_31);
v8i16 __builtin_msa_subvi_h (v8i16, imm0_31);
v4i32 __builtin_msa_subvi_w (v4i32, imm0_31);
v2i64 __builtin_msa_subvi_d (v2i64, imm0_31);

v16i8 __builtin_msa_vshf_b (v16i8, v16i8, v16i8);
```

```
v8i16 __builtin_msa_vshf_h (v8i16, v8i16, v8i16);
v4i32 __builtin_msa_vshf_w (v4i32, v4i32, v4i32);
v2i64 __builtin_msa_vshf_d (v2i64, v2i64, v2i64);

v16u8 __builtin_msa_xor_v (v16u8, v16u8);

v16u8 __builtin_msa_xori_b (v16u8, imm0_255);
```

6.60.17 Other MIPS Built-in Functions

GCC provides other MIPS-specific built-in functions:

`void __builtin_mips_cache (int op, const volatile void *addr)`

> Insert a 'cache' instruction with operands op and addr. GCC defines the preprocessor macro `___GCC_HAVE_BUILTIN_MIPS_CACHE` when this function is available.

`unsigned int __builtin_mips_get_fcsr (void)`
`void __builtin_mips_set_fcsr (unsigned int value)`

> Get and set the contents of the floating-point control and status register (FPU control register 31). These functions are only available in hard-float code but can be called in both MIPS16 and non-MIPS16 contexts.
>
> `__builtin_mips_set_fcsr` can be used to change any bit of the register except the condition codes, which GCC assumes are preserved.

6.60.18 MSP430 Built-in Functions

GCC provides a couple of special builtin functions to aid in the writing of interrupt handlers in C.

`__bic_SR_register_on_exit (int mask)`

> This clears the indicated bits in the saved copy of the status register currently residing on the stack. This only works inside interrupt handlers and the changes to the status register will only take affect once the handler returns.

`__bis_SR_register_on_exit (int mask)`

> This sets the indicated bits in the saved copy of the status register currently residing on the stack. This only works inside interrupt handlers and the changes to the status register will only take affect once the handler returns.

`__delay_cycles (long long cycles)`

> This inserts an instruction sequence that takes exactly cycles cycles (between 0 and about 17E9) to complete. The inserted sequence may use jumps, loops, or no-ops, and does not interfere with any other instructions. Note that cycles must be a compile-time constant integer - that is, you must pass a number, not a variable that may be optimized to a constant later. The number of cycles delayed by this builtin is exact.

6.60.19 NDS32 Built-in Functions

These built-in functions are available for the NDS32 target:

`void __builtin_nds32_isync (int *addr)`   [Built-in Function]

> Insert an ISYNC instruction into the instruction stream where addr is an instruction address for serialization.

`void __builtin_nds32_isb` (*void*)   [Built-in Function]
    Insert an ISB instruction into the instruction stream.

`int __builtin_nds32_mfsr` (*int* `sr`)   [Built-in Function]
    Return the content of a system register which is mapped by *sr*.

`int __builtin_nds32_mfusr` (*int* `usr`)   [Built-in Function]
    Return the content of a user space register which is mapped by *usr*.

`void __builtin_nds32_mtsr` (*int* `value`, *int* `sr`)   [Built-in Function]
    Move the *value* to a system register which is mapped by *sr*.

`void __builtin_nds32_mtusr` (*int* `value`, *int* `usr`)   [Built-in Function]
    Move the *value* to a user space register which is mapped by *usr*.

`void __builtin_nds32_setgie_en` (*void*)   [Built-in Function]
    Enable global interrupt.

`void __builtin_nds32_setgie_dis` (*void*)   [Built-in Function]
    Disable global interrupt.

6.60.20 picoChip Built-in Functions

GCC provides an interface to selected machine instructions from the picoChip instruction set.

`int __builtin_sbc (int value)`
    Sign bit count. Return the number of consecutive bits in *value* that have the same value as the sign bit. The result is the number of leading sign bits minus one, giving the number of redundant sign bits in *value*.

`int __builtin_byteswap (int value)`
    Byte swap. Return the result of swapping the upper and lower bytes of *value*.

`int __builtin_brev (int value)`
    Bit reversal. Return the result of reversing the bits in *value*. Bit 15 is swapped with bit 0, bit 14 is swapped with bit 1, and so on.

`int __builtin_adds (int x, int y)`
    Saturating addition. Return the result of adding *x* and *y*, storing the value 32767 if the result overflows.

`int __builtin_subs (int x, int y)`
    Saturating subtraction. Return the result of subtracting *y* from *x*, storing the value -32768 if the result overflows.

`void __builtin_halt (void)`
    Halt. The processor stops execution. This built-in is useful for implementing assertions.

6.60.21 PowerPC Built-in Functions

The following built-in functions are always available and can be used to check the PowerPC target platform type:

void __builtin_cpu_init (*void*)   [Built-in Function]

This function is a nop on the PowerPC platform and is included solely to maintain API compatibility with the x86 builtins.

int __builtin_cpu_is (*const char *cpuname*)   [Built-in Function]

This function returns a value of 1 if the run-time CPU is of type *cpuname* and returns 0 otherwise. The following CPU names can be detected:

'power9'   IBM POWER9 Server CPU.

'power8'   IBM POWER8 Server CPU.

'power7'   IBM POWER7 Server CPU.

'power6x'   IBM POWER6 Server CPU (RAW mode).

'power6'   IBM POWER6 Server CPU (Architected mode).

'power5+'   IBM POWER5+ Server CPU.

'power5'   IBM POWER5 Server CPU.

'ppc970'   IBM 970 Server CPU (ie, Apple G5).

'power4'   IBM POWER4 Server CPU.

'ppca2'   IBM A2 64-bit Embedded CPU.

'ppc476'   IBM PowerPC 476FP 32-bit Embedded CPU.

'ppc464'   IBM PowerPC 464 32-bit Embedded CPU.

'ppc440'   PowerPC 440 32-bit Embedded CPU.

'ppc405'   PowerPC 405 32-bit Embedded CPU.

'ppc-cell-be'
            IBM PowerPC Cell Broadband Engine Architecture CPU.

Here is an example:

```
if (__builtin_cpu_is ("power8"))
  {
    do_power8 (); // POWER8 specific implementation.
  }
else
  {
    do_generic (); // Generic implementation.
  }
```

int __builtin_cpu_supports (*const char *feature*)   [Built-in Function]

This function returns a value of 1 if the run-time CPU supports the HWCAP feature *feature* and returns 0 otherwise. The following features can be detected:

'4xxmac'   4xx CPU has a Multiply Accumulator.

`'altivec'`   CPU has a SIMD/Vector Unit.

`'arch_2_05'`
          CPU supports ISA 2.05 (eg, POWER6)

`'arch_2_06'`
          CPU supports ISA 2.06 (eg, POWER7)

`'arch_2_07'`
          CPU supports ISA 2.07 (eg, POWER8)

`'arch_3_00'`
          CPU supports ISA 3.0 (eg, POWER9)

`'archpmu'`   CPU supports the set of compatible performance monitoring events.

`'booke'`   CPU supports the Embedded ISA category.

`'cellbe'`   CPU has a CELL broadband engine.

`'dfp'`   CPU has a decimal floating point unit.

`'dscr'`   CPU supports the data stream control register.

`'ebb'`   CPU supports event base branching.

`'efpdouble'`
          CPU has a SPE double precision floating point unit.

`'efpsingle'`
          CPU has a SPE single precision floating point unit.

`'fpu'`   CPU has a floating point unit.

`'htm'`   CPU has hardware transaction memory instructions.

`'htm-nosc'`
          Kernel aborts hardware transactions when a syscall is made.

`'ic_snoop'`
          CPU supports icache snooping capabilities.

`'ieee128'`   CPU supports 128-bit IEEE binary floating point instructions.

`'isel'`   CPU supports the integer select instruction.

`'mmu'`   CPU has a memory management unit.

`'notb'`   CPU does not have a timebase (eg, 601 and 403gx).

`'pa6t'`   CPU supports the PA Semi 6T CORE ISA.

`'power4'`   CPU supports ISA 2.00 (eg, POWER4)

`'power5'`   CPU supports ISA 2.02 (eg, POWER5)

`'power5+'`   CPU supports ISA 2.03 (eg, POWER5+)

`'power6x'`   CPU supports ISA 2.05 (eg, POWER6) extended opcodes mffgpr and
          mftgpr.

'ppc32'   CPU supports 32-bit mode execution.

'ppc601'   CPU supports the old POWER ISA (eg, 601)

'ppc64'   CPU supports 64-bit mode execution.

'ppcle'   CPU supports a little-endian mode that uses address swizzling.

'smt'   CPU support simultaneous multi-threading.

'spe'   CPU has a signal processing extension unit.

'tar'   CPU supports the target address register.

'true_le'   CPU supports true little-endian mode.

'ucache'   CPU has unified I/D cache.

'vcrypto'   CPU supports the vector cryptography instructions.

'vsx'   CPU supports the vector-scalar extension.

Here is an example:

```
if (__builtin_cpu_supports ("fpu"))
  {
    asm("fadd %0,%1,%2" : "=d"(dst) : "d"(src1), "d"(src2));
  }
else
  {
    dst = __fadd (src1, src2); // Software FP addition function.
  }
```

These built-in functions are available for the PowerPC family of processors:

```
float __builtin_recipdivf (float, float);
float __builtin_rsqrtf (float);
double __builtin_recipdiv (double, double);
double __builtin_rsqrt (double);
uint64_t __builtin_ppc_get_timebase ();
unsigned long __builtin_ppc_mftb ();
double __builtin_unpack_longdouble (long double, int);
long double __builtin_pack_longdouble (double, double);
```

The `vec_rsqrt`, `__builtin_rsqrt`, and `__builtin_rsqrtf` functions generate multiple instructions to implement the reciprocal sqrt functionality using reciprocal sqrt estimate instructions.

The `__builtin_recipdiv`, and `__builtin_recipdivf` functions generate multiple instructions to implement division using the reciprocal estimate instructions.

The `__builtin_ppc_get_timebase` and `__builtin_ppc_mftb` functions generate instructions to read the Time Base Register. The `__builtin_ppc_get_timebase` function may generate multiple instructions and always returns the 64 bits of the Time Base Register. The `__builtin_ppc_mftb` function always generates one instruction and returns the Time Base Register value as an unsigned long, throwing away the most significant word on 32-bit environments.

Additional built-in functions are available for the 64-bit PowerPC family of processors, for efficient use of 128-bit floating point (`__float128`) values.

The following floating-point built-in functions are available with `-mfloat128` and Altivec support. All of them implement the function that is part of the name.

```
__float128 __builtin_fabsq (__float128)
__float128 __builtin_copysignq (__float128, __float128)
```

The following built-in functions are available with -mfloat128 and Altivec support.

`__float128 __builtin_infq (void)`
> Similar to __builtin_inf, except the return type is __float128.

`__float128 __builtin_huge_valq (void)`
> Similar to __builtin_huge_val, except the return type is __float128.

`__float128 __builtin_nanq (void)`
> Similar to __builtin_nan, except the return type is __float128.

`__float128 __builtin_nansq (void)`
> Similar to __builtin_nans, except the return type is __float128.

The following built-in functions are available for the PowerPC family of processors, starting with ISA 2.06 or later ('-mcpu=power7' or '-mpopcntd'):

```
long __builtin_bpermd (long, long);
int __builtin_divwe (int, int);
int __builtin_divweo (int, int);
unsigned int __builtin_divweu (unsigned int, unsigned int);
unsigned int __builtin_divweuo (unsigned int, unsigned int);
long __builtin_divde (long, long);
long __builtin_divdeo (long, long);
unsigned long __builtin_divdeu (unsigned long, unsigned long);
unsigned long __builtin_divdeuo (unsigned long, unsigned long);
unsigned int cdtbcd (unsigned int);
unsigned int cbcdtd (unsigned int);
unsigned int addg6s (unsigned int, unsigned int);
```

The __builtin_divde, __builtin_divdeo, __builtin_divdeu, __builtin_divdeou functions require a 64-bit environment support ISA 2.06 or later.

The following built-in functions are available for the PowerPC family of processors, starting with ISA 3.0 or later ('-mcpu=power9'):

```
long long __builtin_darn (void);
long long __builtin_darn_raw (void);
int __builtin_darn_32 (void);

int __builtin_dfp_dtstsfi_lt (unsigned int comparison, _Decimal64 value);
int __builtin_dfp_dtstsfi_lt (unsigned int comparison, _Decimal128 value);
int __builtin_dfp_dtstsfi_lt_dd (unsigned int comparison, _Decimal64 value);
int __builtin_dfp_dtstsfi_lt_td (unsigned int comparison, _Decimal128 value);

int __builtin_dfp_dtstsfi_gt (unsigned int comparison, _Decimal64 value);
int __builtin_dfp_dtstsfi_gt (unsigned int comparison, _Decimal128 value);
int __builtin_dfp_dtstsfi_gt_dd (unsigned int comparison, _Decimal64 value);
int __builtin_dfp_dtstsfi_gt_td (unsigned int comparison, _Decimal128 value);

int __builtin_dfp_dtstsfi_eq (unsigned int comparison, _Decimal64 value);
int __builtin_dfp_dtstsfi_eq (unsigned int comparison, _Decimal128 value);
int __builtin_dfp_dtstsfi_eq_dd (unsigned int comparison, _Decimal64 value);
int __builtin_dfp_dtstsfi_eq_td (unsigned int comparison, _Decimal128 value);

int __builtin_dfp_dtstsfi_ov (unsigned int comparison, _Decimal64 value);
int __builtin_dfp_dtstsfi_ov (unsigned int comparison, _Decimal128 value);
int __builtin_dfp_dtstsfi_ov_dd (unsigned int comparison, _Decimal64 value);
```

```
int __builtin_dfp_dtstsfi_ov_td (unsigned int comparison, _Decimal128 value);

unsigned int scalar_extract_exp (double source);
unsigned long long int scalar_extract_sig (double source);

double
scalar_insert_exp (unsigned long long int significand, unsigned long long int exponent);

int scalar_cmp_exp_gt (double arg1, double arg2);
int scalar_cmp_exp_lt (double arg1, double arg2);
int scalar_cmp_exp_eq (double arg1, double arg2);
int scalar_cmp_exp_unordered (double arg1, double arg2);

int scalar_test_data_class (float source, unsigned int condition);
int scalar_test_data_class (double source, unsigned int condition);

int scalar_test_neg (float source);
int scalar_test_neg (double source);
```

The `__builtin_darn` and `__builtin_darn_raw` functions require a 64-bit environment supporting ISA 3.0 or later. The `__builtin_darn` function provides a 64-bit conditioned random number. The `__builtin_darn_raw` function provides a 64-bit raw random number. The `__builtin_darn_32` function provides a 32-bit random number.

The `scalar_extract_sig` and `scalar_insert_exp` functions require a 64-bit environment supporting ISA 3.0 or later. The `scalar_extract_exp` and `vec_extract_sig` built-in functions return the significand and exponent respectively of their `source` arguments. The `scalar_insert_exp` built-in function returns a double-precision floating point value that is constructed by assembling the values of its `significand` and `exponent` arguments. The sign of the result is copied from the most significant bit of the `significand` argument. The significand and exponent components of the result are composed of the least significant 11 bits of the `significand` argument and the least significant 52 bits of the `exponent` argument.

The `scalar_cmp_exp_gt`, `scalar_cmp_exp_lt`, `scalar_cmp_exp_eq`, and `scalar_cmp_exp_unordered` built-in functions return a non-zero value if `arg1` is greater than, less than, equal to, or not comparable to `arg2` respectively. The arguments are not comparable if one or the other equals NaN (not a number).

The `scalar_test_data_class` built-in functions return a non-zero value if any of the condition tests enabled by the value of the `condition` variable are true. The `condition` argument must be an unsigned integer with value not exceeding 127. The `condition` argument is encoded as a bitmask with each bit enabling the testing of a different condition, as characterized by the following:

```
0x40    Test for NaN
0x20    Test for +Infinity
0x10    Test for -Infinity
0x08    Test for +Zero
0x04    Test for -Zero
0x02    Test for +Denormal
0x01    Test for -Denormal
```

If all of the enabled test conditions are false, the return value is 0.

The `scalar_test_neg` built-in functions return a non-zero value if their `source` argument holds a negative value.

The `__builtin_dfp_dtstsfi_lt` function returns a non-zero value if and only if the number of signficant digits of its `value` argument is less than its `comparison` argument. The `__builtin_dfp_dtstsfi_lt_dd` and `__builtin_dfp_dtstsfi_lt_td` functions behave similarly, but require that the type of the `value` argument be `__Decimal64` and `__Decimal128` respectively.

The `__builtin_dfp_dtstsfi_gt` function returns a non-zero value if and only if the number of signficant digits of its `value` argument is greater than its `comparison` argument. The `__builtin_dfp_dtstsfi_gt_dd` and `__builtin_dfp_dtstsfi_gt_td` functions behave similarly, but require that the type of the `value` argument be `__Decimal64` and `__Decimal128` respectively.

The `__builtin_dfp_dtstsfi_eq` function returns a non-zero value if and only if the number of signficant digits of its `value` argument equals its `comparison` argument. The `__builtin_dfp_dtstsfi_eq_dd` and `__builtin_dfp_dtstsfi_eq_td` functions behave similarly, but require that the type of the `value` argument be `__Decimal64` and `__Decimal128` respectively.

The `__builtin_dfp_dtstsfi_ov` function returns a non-zero value if and only if its `value` argument has an undefined number of significant digits, such as when `value` is an encoding of `NaN`. The `__builtin_dfp_dtstsfi_ov_dd` and `__builtin_dfp_dtstsfi_ov_td` functions behave similarly, but require that the type of the `value` argument be `__Decimal64` and `__Decimal128` respectively.

The following built-in functions are also available for the PowerPC family of processors, starting with ISA 3.0 or later ('`-mcpu=power9`'). These string functions are described separately in order to group the descriptions closer to the function prototypes:

```
int vec_all_nez (vector signed char, vector signed char);
int vec_all_nez (vector unsigned char, vector unsigned char);
int vec_all_nez (vector signed short, vector signed short);
int vec_all_nez (vector unsigned short, vector unsigned short);
int vec_all_nez (vector signed int, vector signed int);
int vec_all_nez (vector unsigned int, vector unsigned int);

int vec_any_eqz (vector signed char, vector signed char);
int vec_any_eqz (vector unsigned char, vector unsigned char);
int vec_any_eqz (vector signed short, vector signed short);
int vec_any_eqz (vector unsigned short, vector unsigned short);
int vec_any_eqz (vector signed int, vector signed int);
int vec_any_eqz (vector unsigned int, vector unsigned int);

vector bool char vec_cmpnez (vector signed char arg1, vector signed char arg2);
vector bool char vec_cmpnez (vector unsigned char arg1, vector unsigned char arg2);
vector bool short vec_cmpnez (vector signed short arg1, vector signed short arg2);
vector bool short vec_cmpnez (vector unsigned short arg1, vector unsigned short arg2);
vector bool int vec_cmpnez (vector signed int arg1, vector signed int arg2);
vector bool int vec_cmpnez (vector unsigned int, vector unsigned int);

signed int vec_cntlz_lsbb (vector signed char);
signed int vec_cntlz_lsbb (vector unsigned char);

signed int vec_cnttz_lsbb (vector signed char);
signed int vec_cnttz_lsbb (vector unsigned char);

vector signed char vec_xl_len (signed char *addr, size_t len);
vector unsigned char vec_xl_len (unsigned char *addr, size_t len);
```

```
vector signed int vec_xl_len (signed int *addr, size_t len);
vector unsigned int vec_xl_len (unsigned int *addr, size_t len);
vector signed __int128 vec_xl_len (signed __int128 *addr, size_t len);
vector unsigned __int128 vec_xl_len (unsigned __int128 *addr, size_t len);
vector signed long long vec_xl_len (signed long long *addr, size_t len);
vector unsigned long long vec_xl_len (unsigned long long *addr, size_t len);
vector signed short vec_xl_len (signed short *addr, size_t len);
vector unsigned short vec_xl_len (unsigned short *addr, size_t len);
vector double vec_xl_len (double *addr, size_t len);
vector float vec_xl_len (float *addr, size_t len);

void vec_xst_len (vector signed char data, signed char *addr, size_t len);
void vec_xst_len (vector unsigned char data, unsigned char *addr, size_t len);
void vec_xst_len (vector signed int data, signed int *addr, size_t len);
void vec_xst_len (vector unsigned int data, unsigned int *addr, size_t len);
void vec_xst_len (vector unsigned __int128 data, unsigned __int128 *addr, size_t len);
void vec_xst_len (vector signed long long data, signed long long *addr, size_t len);
void vec_xst_len (vector unsigned long long data, unsigned long long *addr, size_t len);
void vec_xst_len (vector signed short data, signed short *addr, size_t len);
void vec_xst_len (vector unsigned short data, unsigned short *addr, size_t len);
void vec_xst_len (vector signed __int128 data, signed __int128 *addr, size_t len);
void vec_xst_len (vector double data, double *addr, size_t len);
void vec_xst_len (vector float data, float *addr, size_t len);

signed char vec_xlx (unsigned int index, vector signed char data);
unsigned char vec_xlx (unsigned int index, vector unsigned char data);
signed short vec_xlx (unsigned int index, vector signed short data);
unsigned short vec_xlx (unsigned int index, vector unsigned short data);
signed int vec_xlx (unsigned int index, vector signed int data);
unsigned int vec_xlx (unsigned int index, vector unsigned int data);
float vec_xlx (unsigned int index, vector float data);

signed char vec_xrx (unsigned int index, vector signed char data);
unsigned char vec_xrx (unsigned int index, vector unsigned char data);
signed short vec_xrx (unsigned int index, vector signed short data);
unsigned short vec_xrx (unsigned int index, vector unsigned short data);
signed int vec_xrx (unsigned int index, vector signed int data);
unsigned int vec_xrx (unsigned int index, vector unsigned int data);
float vec_xrx (unsigned int index, vector float data);
```

The `vec_all_nez`, `vec_any_eqz`, and `vec_cmpnez` perform pairwise comparisons between the elements at the same positions within their two vector arguments. The `vec_all_nez` function returns a non-zero value if and only if all pairwise comparisons are not equal and no element of either vector argument contains a zero. The `vec_any_eqz` function returns a non-zero value if and only if at least one pairwise comparison is equal or if at least one element of either vector argument contains a zero. The `vec_cmpnez` function returns a vector of the same type as its two arguments, within which each element consists of all ones to denote that either the corresponding elements of the incoming arguments are not equal or that at least one of the corresponding elements contains zero. Otherwise, the element of the returned vector contains all zeros.

The `vec_cntlz_lsbb` function returns the count of the number of consecutive leading byte elements (starting from position 0 within the supplied vector argument) for which the least-significant bit equals zero. The `vec_cnttz_lsbb` function returns the count of the number of consecutive trailing byte elements (starting from position 15 and counting backwards within the supplied vector argument) for which the least-significant bit equals zero.

The `vec_xl_len` and `vec_xst_len` functions require a 64-bit environment supporting ISA 3.0 or later. The `vec_xl_len` function loads a variable length vector from memory. The `vec_xst_len` function stores a variable length vector to memory. With both the `vec_xl_len` and `vec_xst_len` functions, the `addr` argument represents the memory address to or from which data will be transferred, and the `len` argument represents the number of bytes to be transferred, as computed by the C expression `min((len & 0xff), 16)`. If this expression's value is not a multiple of the vector element's size, the behavior of this function is undefined. In the case that the underlying computer is configured to run in big-endian mode, the data transfer moves bytes 0 to (`len - 1`) of the corresponding vector. In little-endian mode, the data transfer moves bytes (`16 - len`) to `15` of the corresponding vector. For the load function, any bytes of the result vector that are not loaded from memory are set to zero. The value of the `addr` argument need not be aligned on a multiple of the vector's element size.

The `vec_xlx` and `vec_xrx` functions extract the single element selected by the `index` argument from the vector represented by the `data` argument. The `index` argument always specifies a byte offset, regardless of the size of the vector element. With `vec_xlx`, `index` is the offset of the first byte of the element to be extracted. With `vec_xrx`, `index` represents the last byte of the element to be extracted, measured from the right end of the vector. In other words, the last byte of the element to be extracted is found at position (`15 - index`). There is no requirement that `index` be a multiple of the vector element size. However, if the size of the vector element added to `index` is greater than 15, the content of the returned value is undefined.

The following built-in functions are available for the PowerPC family of processors when hardware decimal floating point ('`-mhard-dfp`') is available:

```
_Decimal64 __builtin_dxex (_Decimal64);
_Decimal128 __builtin_dxexq (_Decimal128);
_Decimal64 __builtin_ddedpd (int, _Decimal64);
_Decimal128 __builtin_ddedpdq (int, _Decimal128);
_Decimal64 __builtin_denbcd (int, _Decimal64);
_Decimal128 __builtin_denbcdq (int, _Decimal128);
_Decimal64 __builtin_diex (_Decimal64, _Decimal64);
_Decimal128 _builtin_diexq (_Decimal128, _Decimal128);
_Decimal64 __builtin_dscli (_Decimal64, int);
_Decimal128 __builtin_dscliq (_Decimal128, int);
_Decimal64 __builtin_dscri (_Decimal64, int);
_Decimal128 __builtin_dscriq (_Decimal128, int);
unsigned long long __builtin_unpack_dec128 (_Decimal128, int);
_Decimal128 __builtin_pack_dec128 (unsigned long long, unsigned long long);
```

The following built-in functions are available for the PowerPC family of processors when the Vector Scalar (vsx) instruction set is available:

```
unsigned long long __builtin_unpack_vector_int128 (vector __int128_t, int);
vector __int128_t __builtin_pack_vector_int128 (unsigned long long,
                                                unsigned long long);
```

6.60.22 PowerPC AltiVec Built-in Functions

GCC provides an interface for the PowerPC family of processors to access the AltiVec operations described in Motorola's AltiVec Programming Interface Manual. The interface is made available by including `<altivec.h>` and using '`-maltivec`' and '`-mabi=altivec`'. The interface supports the following vector types.

```
vector unsigned char
vector signed char
vector bool char

vector unsigned short
vector signed short
vector bool short
vector pixel

vector unsigned int
vector signed int
vector bool int
vector float
```

If '`-mvsx`' is used the following additional vector types are implemented.

```
vector unsigned long
vector signed long
vector double
```

The long types are only implemented for 64-bit code generation, and the long type is only used in the floating point/integer conversion instructions.

GCC's implementation of the high-level language interface available from C and C++ code differs from Motorola's documentation in several ways.

- A vector constant is a list of constant expressions within curly braces.

- A vector initializer requires no cast if the vector constant is of the same type as the variable it is initializing.

- If `signed` or `unsigned` is omitted, the signedness of the vector type is the default signedness of the base type. The default varies depending on the operating system, so a portable program should always specify the signedness.

- Compiling with '`-maltivec`' adds keywords `__vector`, `vector`, `__pixel`, `pixel`, `__bool` and `bool`. When compiling ISO C, the context-sensitive substitution of the keywords `vector`, `pixel` and `bool` is disabled. To use them, you must include `<altivec.h>` instead.

- GCC allows using a `typedef` name as the type specifier for a vector type.

- For C, overloaded functions are implemented with macros so the following does not work:

  ```
  vec_add ((vector signed int){1, 2, 3, 4}, foo);
  ```

  Since `vec_add` is a macro, the vector constant in the example is treated as four separate arguments. Wrap the entire argument in parentheses for this to work.

Note: Only the `<altivec.h>` interface is supported. Internally, GCC uses built-in functions to achieve the functionality in the aforementioned header file, but they are not supported and are subject to change without notice.

The following interfaces are supported for the generic and specific AltiVec operations and the AltiVec predicates. In cases where there is a direct mapping between generic and specific operations, only the generic names are shown here, although the specific operations can also be used.

Arguments that are documented as `const int` require literal integral values within the range required for that operation.

```
vector signed char vec_abs (vector signed char);
vector signed short vec_abs (vector signed short);
vector signed int vec_abs (vector signed int);
vector float vec_abs (vector float);

vector signed char vec_abss (vector signed char);
vector signed short vec_abss (vector signed short);
vector signed int vec_abss (vector signed int);

vector signed char vec_add (vector bool char, vector signed char);
vector signed char vec_add (vector signed char, vector bool char);
vector signed char vec_add (vector signed char, vector signed char);
vector unsigned char vec_add (vector bool char, vector unsigned char);
vector unsigned char vec_add (vector unsigned char, vector bool char);
vector unsigned char vec_add (vector unsigned char,
                              vector unsigned char);
vector signed short vec_add (vector bool short, vector signed short);
vector signed short vec_add (vector signed short, vector bool short);
vector signed short vec_add (vector signed short, vector signed short);
vector unsigned short vec_add (vector bool short,
                               vector unsigned short);
vector unsigned short vec_add (vector unsigned short,
                               vector bool short);
vector unsigned short vec_add (vector unsigned short,
                               vector unsigned short);
vector signed int vec_add (vector bool int, vector signed int);
vector signed int vec_add (vector signed int, vector bool int);
vector signed int vec_add (vector signed int, vector signed int);
vector unsigned int vec_add (vector bool int, vector unsigned int);
vector unsigned int vec_add (vector unsigned int, vector bool int);
vector unsigned int vec_add (vector unsigned int, vector unsigned int);
vector float vec_add (vector float, vector float);

vector float vec_vaddfp (vector float, vector float);

vector signed int vec_vadduwm (vector bool int, vector signed int);
vector signed int vec_vadduwm (vector signed int, vector bool int);
vector signed int vec_vadduwm (vector signed int, vector signed int);
vector unsigned int vec_vadduwm (vector bool int, vector unsigned int);
vector unsigned int vec_vadduwm (vector unsigned int, vector bool int);
vector unsigned int vec_vadduwm (vector unsigned int,
                                 vector unsigned int);

vector signed short vec_vadduhm (vector bool short,
                                 vector signed short);
vector signed short vec_vadduhm (vector signed short,
                                 vector bool short);
vector signed short vec_vadduhm (vector signed short,
                                 vector signed short);
vector unsigned short vec_vadduhm (vector bool short,
                                   vector unsigned short);
vector unsigned short vec_vadduhm (vector unsigned short,
                                   vector bool short);
vector unsigned short vec_vadduhm (vector unsigned short,
                                   vector unsigned short);
```

```
vector signed char vec_vaddubm (vector bool char, vector signed char);
vector signed char vec_vaddubm (vector signed char, vector bool char);
vector signed char vec_vaddubm (vector signed char, vector signed char);
vector unsigned char vec_vaddubm (vector bool char,
                                  vector unsigned char);
vector unsigned char vec_vaddubm (vector unsigned char,
                                  vector bool char);
vector unsigned char vec_vaddubm (vector unsigned char,
                                  vector unsigned char);

vector unsigned int vec_addc (vector unsigned int, vector unsigned int);

vector unsigned char vec_adds (vector bool char, vector unsigned char);
vector unsigned char vec_adds (vector unsigned char, vector bool char);
vector unsigned char vec_adds (vector unsigned char,
                               vector unsigned char);
vector signed char vec_adds (vector bool char, vector signed char);
vector signed char vec_adds (vector signed char, vector bool char);
vector signed char vec_adds (vector signed char, vector signed char);
vector unsigned short vec_adds (vector bool short,
                                vector unsigned short);
vector unsigned short vec_adds (vector unsigned short,
                                vector bool short);
vector unsigned short vec_adds (vector unsigned short,
                                vector unsigned short);
vector signed short vec_adds (vector bool short, vector signed short);
vector signed short vec_adds (vector signed short, vector bool short);
vector signed short vec_adds (vector signed short, vector signed short);
vector unsigned int vec_adds (vector bool int, vector unsigned int);
vector unsigned int vec_adds (vector unsigned int, vector bool int);
vector unsigned int vec_adds (vector unsigned int, vector unsigned int);
vector signed int vec_adds (vector bool int, vector signed int);
vector signed int vec_adds (vector signed int, vector bool int);
vector signed int vec_adds (vector signed int, vector signed int);

vector signed int vec_vaddsws (vector bool int, vector signed int);
vector signed int vec_vaddsws (vector signed int, vector bool int);
vector signed int vec_vaddsws (vector signed int, vector signed int);

vector unsigned int vec_vadduws (vector bool int, vector unsigned int);
vector unsigned int vec_vadduws (vector unsigned int, vector bool int);
vector unsigned int vec_vadduws (vector unsigned int,
                                 vector unsigned int);

vector signed short vec_vaddshs (vector bool short,
                                 vector signed short);
vector signed short vec_vaddshs (vector signed short,
                                 vector bool short);
vector signed short vec_vaddshs (vector signed short,
                                 vector signed short);

vector unsigned short vec_vadduhs (vector bool short,
                                   vector unsigned short);
vector unsigned short vec_vadduhs (vector unsigned short,
                                   vector bool short);
vector unsigned short vec_vadduhs (vector unsigned short,
                                   vector unsigned short);
```

```
vector signed char vec_vaddsbs (vector bool char, vector signed char);
vector signed char vec_vaddsbs (vector signed char, vector bool char);
vector signed char vec_vaddsbs (vector signed char, vector signed char);

vector unsigned char vec_vaddubs (vector bool char,
                                  vector unsigned char);
vector unsigned char vec_vaddubs (vector unsigned char,
                                  vector bool char);
vector unsigned char vec_vaddubs (vector unsigned char,
                                  vector unsigned char);

vector float vec_and (vector float, vector float);
vector float vec_and (vector float, vector bool int);
vector float vec_and (vector bool int, vector float);
vector bool int vec_and (vector bool int, vector bool int);
vector signed int vec_and (vector bool int, vector signed int);
vector signed int vec_and (vector signed int, vector bool int);
vector signed int vec_and (vector signed int, vector signed int);
vector unsigned int vec_and (vector bool int, vector unsigned int);
vector unsigned int vec_and (vector unsigned int, vector bool int);
vector unsigned int vec_and (vector unsigned int, vector unsigned int);
vector bool short vec_and (vector bool short, vector bool short);
vector signed short vec_and (vector bool short, vector signed short);
vector signed short vec_and (vector signed short, vector bool short);
vector signed short vec_and (vector signed short, vector signed short);
vector unsigned short vec_and (vector bool short,
                               vector unsigned short);
vector unsigned short vec_and (vector unsigned short,
                               vector bool short);
vector unsigned short vec_and (vector unsigned short,
                               vector unsigned short);
vector signed char vec_and (vector bool char, vector signed char);
vector bool char vec_and (vector bool char, vector bool char);
vector signed char vec_and (vector signed char, vector bool char);
vector signed char vec_and (vector signed char, vector signed char);
vector unsigned char vec_and (vector bool char, vector unsigned char);
vector unsigned char vec_and (vector unsigned char, vector bool char);
vector unsigned char vec_and (vector unsigned char,
                              vector unsigned char);

vector float vec_andc (vector float, vector float);
vector float vec_andc (vector float, vector bool int);
vector float vec_andc (vector bool int, vector float);
vector bool int vec_andc (vector bool int, vector bool int);
vector signed int vec_andc (vector bool int, vector signed int);
vector signed int vec_andc (vector signed int, vector bool int);
vector signed int vec_andc (vector signed int, vector signed int);
vector unsigned int vec_andc (vector bool int, vector unsigned int);
vector unsigned int vec_andc (vector unsigned int, vector bool int);
vector unsigned int vec_andc (vector unsigned int, vector unsigned int);
vector bool short vec_andc (vector bool short, vector bool short);
vector signed short vec_andc (vector bool short, vector signed short);
vector signed short vec_andc (vector signed short, vector bool short);
vector signed short vec_andc (vector signed short, vector signed short);
vector unsigned short vec_andc (vector bool short,
                                vector unsigned short);
vector unsigned short vec_andc (vector unsigned short,
                                vector bool short);
```

```
vector unsigned short vec_andc (vector unsigned short,
                                vector unsigned short);
vector signed char vec_andc (vector bool char, vector signed char);
vector bool char vec_andc (vector bool char, vector bool char);
vector signed char vec_andc (vector signed char, vector bool char);
vector signed char vec_andc (vector signed char, vector signed char);
vector unsigned char vec_andc (vector bool char, vector unsigned char);
vector unsigned char vec_andc (vector unsigned char, vector bool char);
vector unsigned char vec_andc (vector unsigned char,
                               vector unsigned char);

vector unsigned char vec_avg (vector unsigned char,
                              vector unsigned char);
vector signed char vec_avg (vector signed char, vector signed char);
vector unsigned short vec_avg (vector unsigned short,
                               vector unsigned short);
vector signed short vec_avg (vector signed short, vector signed short);
vector unsigned int vec_avg (vector unsigned int, vector unsigned int);
vector signed int vec_avg (vector signed int, vector signed int);

vector signed int vec_vavgsw (vector signed int, vector signed int);

vector unsigned int vec_vavguw (vector unsigned int,
                                vector unsigned int);

vector signed short vec_vavgsh (vector signed short,
                                vector signed short);

vector unsigned short vec_vavguh (vector unsigned short,
                                  vector unsigned short);

vector signed char vec_vavgsb (vector signed char, vector signed char);

vector unsigned char vec_vavgub (vector unsigned char,
                                 vector unsigned char);

vector float vec_copysign (vector float);

vector float vec_ceil (vector float);

vector signed int vec_cmpb (vector float, vector float);

vector bool char vec_cmpeq (vector bool char, vector bool char);
vector bool short vec_cmpeq (vector bool short, vector bool short);
vector bool int vec_cmpeq (vector bool int, vector bool int);
vector bool char vec_cmpeq (vector signed char, vector signed char);
vector bool char vec_cmpeq (vector unsigned char, vector unsigned char);
vector bool short vec_cmpeq (vector signed short, vector signed short);
vector bool short vec_cmpeq (vector unsigned short,
                             vector unsigned short);
vector bool int vec_cmpeq (vector signed int, vector signed int);
vector bool int vec_cmpeq (vector unsigned int, vector unsigned int);
vector bool int vec_cmpeq (vector float, vector float);

vector bool int vec_vcmpeqfp (vector float, vector float);

vector bool int vec_vcmpequw (vector signed int, vector signed int);
vector bool int vec_vcmpequw (vector unsigned int, vector unsigned int);
```

```
vector bool short vec_vcmpequh (vector signed short,
                               vector signed short);
vector bool short vec_vcmpequh (vector unsigned short,
                               vector unsigned short);

vector bool char vec_vcmpequb (vector signed char, vector signed char);
vector bool char vec_vcmpequb (vector unsigned char,
                               vector unsigned char);

vector bool int vec_cmpge (vector float, vector float);

vector bool char vec_cmpgt (vector unsigned char, vector unsigned char);
vector bool char vec_cmpgt (vector signed char, vector signed char);
vector bool short vec_cmpgt (vector unsigned short,
                             vector unsigned short);
vector bool short vec_cmpgt (vector signed short, vector signed short);
vector bool int vec_cmpgt (vector unsigned int, vector unsigned int);
vector bool int vec_cmpgt (vector signed int, vector signed int);
vector bool int vec_cmpgt (vector float, vector float);

vector bool int vec_vcmpgtfp (vector float, vector float);

vector bool int vec_vcmpgtsw (vector signed int, vector signed int);

vector bool int vec_vcmpgtuw (vector unsigned int, vector unsigned int);

vector bool short vec_vcmpgtsh (vector signed short,
                                vector signed short);

vector bool short vec_vcmpgtuh (vector unsigned short,
                                vector unsigned short);

vector bool char vec_vcmpgtsb (vector signed char, vector signed char);

vector bool char vec_vcmpgtub (vector unsigned char,
                               vector unsigned char);

vector bool int vec_cmple (vector float, vector float);

vector bool char vec_cmplt (vector unsigned char, vector unsigned char);
vector bool char vec_cmplt (vector signed char, vector signed char);
vector bool short vec_cmplt (vector unsigned short,
                             vector unsigned short);
vector bool short vec_cmplt (vector signed short, vector signed short);
vector bool int vec_cmplt (vector unsigned int, vector unsigned int);
vector bool int vec_cmplt (vector signed int, vector signed int);
vector bool int vec_cmplt (vector float, vector float);

vector float vec_cpsgn (vector float, vector float);

vector float vec_ctf (vector unsigned int, const int);
vector float vec_ctf (vector signed int, const int);
vector double vec_ctf (vector unsigned long, const int);
vector double vec_ctf (vector signed long, const int);

vector float vec_vcfsx (vector signed int, const int);
```

```
vector float vec_vcfux (vector unsigned int, const int);

vector signed int vec_cts (vector float, const int);
vector signed long vec_cts (vector double, const int);

vector unsigned int vec_ctu (vector float, const int);
vector unsigned long vec_ctu (vector double, const int);

void vec_dss (const int);

void vec_dssall (void);

void vec_dst (const vector unsigned char *, int, const int);
void vec_dst (const vector signed char *, int, const int);
void vec_dst (const vector bool char *, int, const int);
void vec_dst (const vector unsigned short *, int, const int);
void vec_dst (const vector signed short *, int, const int);
void vec_dst (const vector bool short *, int, const int);
void vec_dst (const vector pixel *, int, const int);
void vec_dst (const vector unsigned int *, int, const int);
void vec_dst (const vector signed int *, int, const int);
void vec_dst (const vector bool int *, int, const int);
void vec_dst (const vector float *, int, const int);
void vec_dst (const unsigned char *, int, const int);
void vec_dst (const signed char *, int, const int);
void vec_dst (const unsigned short *, int, const int);
void vec_dst (const short *, int, const int);
void vec_dst (const unsigned int *, int, const int);
void vec_dst (const int *, int, const int);
void vec_dst (const unsigned long *, int, const int);
void vec_dst (const long *, int, const int);
void vec_dst (const float *, int, const int);

void vec_dstst (const vector unsigned char *, int, const int);
void vec_dstst (const vector signed char *, int, const int);
void vec_dstst (const vector bool char *, int, const int);
void vec_dstst (const vector unsigned short *, int, const int);
void vec_dstst (const vector signed short *, int, const int);
void vec_dstst (const vector bool short *, int, const int);
void vec_dstst (const vector pixel *, int, const int);
void vec_dstst (const vector unsigned int *, int, const int);
void vec_dstst (const vector signed int *, int, const int);
void vec_dstst (const vector bool int *, int, const int);
void vec_dstst (const vector float *, int, const int);
void vec_dstst (const unsigned char *, int, const int);
void vec_dstst (const signed char *, int, const int);
void vec_dstst (const unsigned short *, int, const int);
void vec_dstst (const short *, int, const int);
void vec_dstst (const unsigned int *, int, const int);
void vec_dstst (const int *, int, const int);
void vec_dstst (const unsigned long *, int, const int);
void vec_dstst (const long *, int, const int);
void vec_dstst (const float *, int, const int);

void vec_dststt (const vector unsigned char *, int, const int);
void vec_dststt (const vector signed char *, int, const int);
void vec_dststt (const vector bool char *, int, const int);
void vec_dststt (const vector unsigned short *, int, const int);
```

```
void vec_dststt (const vector signed short *, int, const int);
void vec_dststt (const vector bool short *, int, const int);
void vec_dststt (const vector pixel *, int, const int);
void vec_dststt (const vector unsigned int *, int, const int);
void vec_dststt (const vector signed int *, int, const int);
void vec_dststt (const vector bool int *, int, const int);
void vec_dststt (const vector float *, int, const int);
void vec_dststt (const unsigned char *, int, const int);
void vec_dststt (const signed char *, int, const int);
void vec_dststt (const unsigned short *, int, const int);
void vec_dststt (const short *, int, const int);
void vec_dststt (const unsigned int *, int, const int);
void vec_dststt (const int *, int, const int);
void vec_dststt (const unsigned long *, int, const int);
void vec_dststt (const long *, int, const int);
void vec_dststt (const float *, int, const int);

void vec_dstt (const vector unsigned char *, int, const int);
void vec_dstt (const vector signed char *, int, const int);
void vec_dstt (const vector bool char *, int, const int);
void vec_dstt (const vector unsigned short *, int, const int);
void vec_dstt (const vector signed short *, int, const int);
void vec_dstt (const vector bool short *, int, const int);
void vec_dstt (const vector pixel *, int, const int);
void vec_dstt (const vector unsigned int *, int, const int);
void vec_dstt (const vector signed int *, int, const int);
void vec_dstt (const vector bool int *, int, const int);
void vec_dstt (const vector float *, int, const int);
void vec_dstt (const unsigned char *, int, const int);
void vec_dstt (const signed char *, int, const int);
void vec_dstt (const unsigned short *, int, const int);
void vec_dstt (const short *, int, const int);
void vec_dstt (const unsigned int *, int, const int);
void vec_dstt (const int *, int, const int);
void vec_dstt (const unsigned long *, int, const int);
void vec_dstt (const long *, int, const int);
void vec_dstt (const float *, int, const int);

vector float vec_expte (vector float);

vector float vec_floor (vector float);

vector float vec_ld (int, const vector float *);
vector float vec_ld (int, const float *);
vector bool int vec_ld (int, const vector bool int *);
vector signed int vec_ld (int, const vector signed int *);
vector signed int vec_ld (int, const int *);
vector signed int vec_ld (int, const long *);
vector unsigned int vec_ld (int, const vector unsigned int *);
vector unsigned int vec_ld (int, const unsigned int *);
vector unsigned int vec_ld (int, const unsigned long *);
vector bool short vec_ld (int, const vector bool short *);
vector pixel vec_ld (int, const vector pixel *);
vector signed short vec_ld (int, const vector signed short *);
vector signed short vec_ld (int, const short *);
vector unsigned short vec_ld (int, const vector unsigned short *);
vector unsigned short vec_ld (int, const unsigned short *);
vector bool char vec_ld (int, const vector bool char *);
```

```
vector signed char vec_ld (int, const vector signed char *);
vector signed char vec_ld (int, const signed char *);
vector unsigned char vec_ld (int, const vector unsigned char *);
vector unsigned char vec_ld (int, const unsigned char *);

vector signed char vec_lde (int, const signed char *);
vector unsigned char vec_lde (int, const unsigned char *);
vector signed short vec_lde (int, const short *);
vector unsigned short vec_lde (int, const unsigned short *);
vector float vec_lde (int, const float *);
vector signed int vec_lde (int, const int *);
vector unsigned int vec_lde (int, const unsigned int *);
vector signed int vec_lde (int, const long *);
vector unsigned int vec_lde (int, const unsigned long *);

vector float vec_lvewx (int, float *);
vector signed int vec_lvewx (int, int *);
vector unsigned int vec_lvewx (int, unsigned int *);
vector signed int vec_lvewx (int, long *);
vector unsigned int vec_lvewx (int, unsigned long *);

vector signed short vec_lvehx (int, short *);
vector unsigned short vec_lvehx (int, unsigned short *);

vector signed char vec_lvebx (int, char *);
vector unsigned char vec_lvebx (int, unsigned char *);

vector float vec_ldl (int, const vector float *);
vector float vec_ldl (int, const float *);
vector bool int vec_ldl (int, const vector bool int *);
vector signed int vec_ldl (int, const vector signed int *);
vector signed int vec_ldl (int, const int *);
vector signed int vec_ldl (int, const long *);
vector unsigned int vec_ldl (int, const vector unsigned int *);
vector unsigned int vec_ldl (int, const unsigned int *);
vector unsigned int vec_ldl (int, const unsigned long *);
vector bool short vec_ldl (int, const vector bool short *);
vector pixel vec_ldl (int, const vector pixel *);
vector signed short vec_ldl (int, const vector signed short *);
vector signed short vec_ldl (int, const short *);
vector unsigned short vec_ldl (int, const vector unsigned short *);
vector unsigned short vec_ldl (int, const unsigned short *);
vector bool char vec_ldl (int, const vector bool char *);
vector signed char vec_ldl (int, const vector signed char *);
vector signed char vec_ldl (int, const signed char *);
vector unsigned char vec_ldl (int, const vector unsigned char *);
vector unsigned char vec_ldl (int, const unsigned char *);

vector float vec_loge (vector float);

vector unsigned char vec_lvsl (int, const volatile unsigned char *);
vector unsigned char vec_lvsl (int, const volatile signed char *);
vector unsigned char vec_lvsl (int, const volatile unsigned short *);
vector unsigned char vec_lvsl (int, const volatile short *);
vector unsigned char vec_lvsl (int, const volatile unsigned int *);
vector unsigned char vec_lvsl (int, const volatile int *);
vector unsigned char vec_lvsl (int, const volatile unsigned long *);
vector unsigned char vec_lvsl (int, const volatile long *);
```

```
vector unsigned char vec_lvsl (int, const volatile float *);

vector unsigned char vec_lvsr (int, const volatile unsigned char *);
vector unsigned char vec_lvsr (int, const volatile signed char *);
vector unsigned char vec_lvsr (int, const volatile unsigned short *);
vector unsigned char vec_lvsr (int, const volatile short *);
vector unsigned char vec_lvsr (int, const volatile unsigned int *);
vector unsigned char vec_lvsr (int, const volatile int *);
vector unsigned char vec_lvsr (int, const volatile unsigned long *);
vector unsigned char vec_lvsr (int, const volatile long *);
vector unsigned char vec_lvsr (int, const volatile float *);

vector float vec_madd (vector float, vector float, vector float);

vector signed short vec_madds (vector signed short,
                               vector signed short,
                               vector signed short);

vector unsigned char vec_max (vector bool char, vector unsigned char);
vector unsigned char vec_max (vector unsigned char, vector bool char);
vector unsigned char vec_max (vector unsigned char,
                              vector unsigned char);
vector signed char vec_max (vector bool char, vector signed char);
vector signed char vec_max (vector signed char, vector bool char);
vector signed char vec_max (vector signed char, vector signed char);
vector unsigned short vec_max (vector bool short,
                               vector unsigned short);
vector unsigned short vec_max (vector unsigned short,
                               vector bool short);
vector unsigned short vec_max (vector unsigned short,
                               vector unsigned short);
vector signed short vec_max (vector bool short, vector signed short);
vector signed short vec_max (vector signed short, vector bool short);
vector signed short vec_max (vector signed short, vector signed short);
vector unsigned int vec_max (vector bool int, vector unsigned int);
vector unsigned int vec_max (vector unsigned int, vector bool int);
vector unsigned int vec_max (vector unsigned int, vector unsigned int);
vector signed int vec_max (vector bool int, vector signed int);
vector signed int vec_max (vector signed int, vector bool int);
vector signed int vec_max (vector signed int, vector signed int);
vector float vec_max (vector float, vector float);

vector float vec_vmaxfp (vector float, vector float);

vector signed int vec_vmaxsw (vector bool int, vector signed int);
vector signed int vec_vmaxsw (vector signed int, vector bool int);
vector signed int vec_vmaxsw (vector signed int, vector signed int);

vector unsigned int vec_vmaxuw (vector bool int, vector unsigned int);
vector unsigned int vec_vmaxuw (vector unsigned int, vector bool int);
vector unsigned int vec_vmaxuw (vector unsigned int,
                                vector unsigned int);

vector signed short vec_vmaxsh (vector bool short, vector signed short);
vector signed short vec_vmaxsh (vector signed short, vector bool short);
vector signed short vec_vmaxsh (vector signed short,
                                vector signed short);
```

```
vector unsigned short vec_vmaxuh (vector bool short,
                                  vector unsigned short);
vector unsigned short vec_vmaxuh (vector unsigned short,
                                  vector bool short);
vector unsigned short vec_vmaxuh (vector unsigned short,
                                  vector unsigned short);

vector signed char vec_vmaxsb (vector bool char, vector signed char);
vector signed char vec_vmaxsb (vector signed char, vector bool char);
vector signed char vec_vmaxsb (vector signed char, vector signed char);

vector unsigned char vec_vmaxub (vector bool char,
                                 vector unsigned char);
vector unsigned char vec_vmaxub (vector unsigned char,
                                 vector bool char);
vector unsigned char vec_vmaxub (vector unsigned char,
                                 vector unsigned char);

vector bool char vec_mergeh (vector bool char, vector bool char);
vector signed char vec_mergeh (vector signed char, vector signed char);
vector unsigned char vec_mergeh (vector unsigned char,
                                 vector unsigned char);
vector bool short vec_mergeh (vector bool short, vector bool short);
vector pixel vec_mergeh (vector pixel, vector pixel);
vector signed short vec_mergeh (vector signed short,
                                vector signed short);
vector unsigned short vec_mergeh (vector unsigned short,
                                  vector unsigned short);
vector float vec_mergeh (vector float, vector float);
vector bool int vec_mergeh (vector bool int, vector bool int);
vector signed int vec_mergeh (vector signed int, vector signed int);
vector unsigned int vec_mergeh (vector unsigned int,
                                vector unsigned int);

vector float vec_vmrghw (vector float, vector float);
vector bool int vec_vmrghw (vector bool int, vector bool int);
vector signed int vec_vmrghw (vector signed int, vector signed int);
vector unsigned int vec_vmrghw (vector unsigned int,
                                vector unsigned int);

vector bool short vec_vmrghh (vector bool short, vector bool short);
vector signed short vec_vmrghh (vector signed short,
                                vector signed short);
vector unsigned short vec_vmrghh (vector unsigned short,
                                  vector unsigned short);
vector pixel vec_vmrghh (vector pixel, vector pixel);

vector bool char vec_vmrghb (vector bool char, vector bool char);
vector signed char vec_vmrghb (vector signed char, vector signed char);
vector unsigned char vec_vmrghb (vector unsigned char,
                                 vector unsigned char);

vector bool char vec_mergel (vector bool char, vector bool char);
vector signed char vec_mergel (vector signed char, vector signed char);
vector unsigned char vec_mergel (vector unsigned char,
                                 vector unsigned char);
vector bool short vec_mergel (vector bool short, vector bool short);
vector pixel vec_mergel (vector pixel, vector pixel);
```

```
vector signed short vec_mergel (vector signed short,
                                vector signed short);
vector unsigned short vec_mergel (vector unsigned short,
                                  vector unsigned short);
vector float vec_mergel (vector float, vector float);
vector bool int vec_mergel (vector bool int, vector bool int);
vector signed int vec_mergel (vector signed int, vector signed int);
vector unsigned int vec_mergel (vector unsigned int,
                                vector unsigned int);

vector float vec_vmrglw (vector float, vector float);
vector signed int vec_vmrglw (vector signed int, vector signed int);
vector unsigned int vec_vmrglw (vector unsigned int,
                                vector unsigned int);
vector bool int vec_vmrglw (vector bool int, vector bool int);

vector bool short vec_vmrglh (vector bool short, vector bool short);
vector signed short vec_vmrglh (vector signed short,
                                vector signed short);
vector unsigned short vec_vmrglh (vector unsigned short,
                                  vector unsigned short);
vector pixel vec_vmrglh (vector pixel, vector pixel);

vector bool char vec_vmrglb (vector bool char, vector bool char);
vector signed char vec_vmrglb (vector signed char, vector signed char);
vector unsigned char vec_vmrglb (vector unsigned char,
                                 vector unsigned char);

vector unsigned short vec_mfvscr (void);

vector unsigned char vec_min (vector bool char, vector unsigned char);
vector unsigned char vec_min (vector unsigned char, vector bool char);
vector unsigned char vec_min (vector unsigned char,
                              vector unsigned char);
vector signed char vec_min (vector bool char, vector signed char);
vector signed char vec_min (vector signed char, vector bool char);
vector signed char vec_min (vector signed char, vector signed char);
vector unsigned short vec_min (vector bool short,
                               vector unsigned short);
vector unsigned short vec_min (vector unsigned short,
                               vector bool short);
vector unsigned short vec_min (vector unsigned short,
                               vector unsigned short);
vector signed short vec_min (vector bool short, vector signed short);
vector signed short vec_min (vector signed short, vector bool short);
vector signed short vec_min (vector signed short, vector signed short);
vector unsigned int vec_min (vector bool int, vector unsigned int);
vector unsigned int vec_min (vector unsigned int, vector bool int);
vector unsigned int vec_min (vector unsigned int, vector unsigned int);
vector signed int vec_min (vector bool int, vector signed int);
vector signed int vec_min (vector signed int, vector bool int);
vector signed int vec_min (vector signed int, vector signed int);
vector float vec_min (vector float, vector float);

vector float vec_vminfp (vector float, vector float);

vector signed int vec_vminsw (vector bool int, vector signed int);
vector signed int vec_vminsw (vector signed int, vector bool int);
```

```
vector signed int vec_vminsw (vector signed int, vector signed int);

vector unsigned int vec_vminuw (vector bool int, vector unsigned int);
vector unsigned int vec_vminuw (vector unsigned int, vector bool int);
vector unsigned int vec_vminuw (vector unsigned int,
                                vector unsigned int);

vector signed short vec_vminsh (vector bool short, vector signed short);
vector signed short vec_vminsh (vector signed short, vector bool short);
vector signed short vec_vminsh (vector signed short,
                                vector signed short);

vector unsigned short vec_vminuh (vector bool short,
                                  vector unsigned short);
vector unsigned short vec_vminuh (vector unsigned short,
                                  vector bool short);
vector unsigned short vec_vminuh (vector unsigned short,
                                  vector unsigned short);

vector signed char vec_vminsb (vector bool char, vector signed char);
vector signed char vec_vminsb (vector signed char, vector bool char);
vector signed char vec_vminsb (vector signed char, vector signed char);

vector unsigned char vec_vminub (vector bool char,
                                 vector unsigned char);
vector unsigned char vec_vminub (vector unsigned char,
                                 vector bool char);
vector unsigned char vec_vminub (vector unsigned char,
                                 vector unsigned char);

vector signed short vec_mladd (vector signed short,
                               vector signed short,
                               vector signed short);
vector signed short vec_mladd (vector signed short,
                               vector unsigned short,
                               vector unsigned short);
vector signed short vec_mladd (vector unsigned short,
                               vector signed short,
                               vector signed short);
vector unsigned short vec_mladd (vector unsigned short,
                                 vector unsigned short,
                                 vector unsigned short);

vector signed short vec_mradds (vector signed short,
                                vector signed short,
                                vector signed short);

vector unsigned int vec_msum (vector unsigned char,
                              vector unsigned char,
                              vector unsigned int);
vector signed int vec_msum (vector signed char,
                            vector unsigned char,
                            vector signed int);
vector unsigned int vec_msum (vector unsigned short,
                              vector unsigned short,
                              vector unsigned int);
vector signed int vec_msum (vector signed short,
                            vector signed short,
```

```
                            vector signed int);

vector signed int vec_vmsumshm (vector signed short,
                               vector signed short,
                               vector signed int);

vector unsigned int vec_vmsumuhm (vector unsigned short,
                                 vector unsigned short,
                                 vector unsigned int);

vector signed int vec_vmsummbm (vector signed char,
                               vector unsigned char,
                               vector signed int);

vector unsigned int vec_vmsumubm (vector unsigned char,
                                 vector unsigned char,
                                 vector unsigned int);

vector unsigned int vec_msums (vector unsigned short,
                              vector unsigned short,
                              vector unsigned int);
vector signed int vec_msums (vector signed short,
                            vector signed short,
                            vector signed int);

vector signed int vec_vmsumshs (vector signed short,
                               vector signed short,
                               vector signed int);

vector unsigned int vec_vmsumuhs (vector unsigned short,
                                 vector unsigned short,
                                 vector unsigned int);

void vec_mtvscr (vector signed int);
void vec_mtvscr (vector unsigned int);
void vec_mtvscr (vector bool int);
void vec_mtvscr (vector signed short);
void vec_mtvscr (vector unsigned short);
void vec_mtvscr (vector bool short);
void vec_mtvscr (vector pixel);
void vec_mtvscr (vector signed char);
void vec_mtvscr (vector unsigned char);
void vec_mtvscr (vector bool char);

vector unsigned short vec_mule (vector unsigned char,
                               vector unsigned char);
vector signed short vec_mule (vector signed char,
                             vector signed char);
vector unsigned int vec_mule (vector unsigned short,
                             vector unsigned short);
vector signed int vec_mule (vector signed short, vector signed short);

vector signed int vec_vmulesh (vector signed short,
                              vector signed short);

vector unsigned int vec_vmuleuh (vector unsigned short,
                                vector unsigned short);
```

```
vector signed short vec_vmulesb (vector signed char,
                                 vector signed char);

vector unsigned short vec_vmuleub (vector unsigned char,
                                   vector unsigned char);

vector unsigned short vec_mulo (vector unsigned char,
                                vector unsigned char);
vector signed short vec_mulo (vector signed char, vector signed char);
vector unsigned int vec_mulo (vector unsigned short,
                              vector unsigned short);
vector signed int vec_mulo (vector signed short, vector signed short);

vector signed int vec_vmulosh (vector signed short,
                               vector signed short);

vector unsigned int vec_vmulouh (vector unsigned short,
                                 vector unsigned short);

vector signed short vec_vmulosb (vector signed char,
                                 vector signed char);

vector unsigned short vec_vmuloub (vector unsigned char,
                                   vector unsigned char);

vector float vec_nmsub (vector float, vector float, vector float);

vector float vec_nor (vector float, vector float);
vector signed int vec_nor (vector signed int, vector signed int);
vector unsigned int vec_nor (vector unsigned int, vector unsigned int);
vector bool int vec_nor (vector bool int, vector bool int);
vector signed short vec_nor (vector signed short, vector signed short);
vector unsigned short vec_nor (vector unsigned short,
                               vector unsigned short);
vector bool short vec_nor (vector bool short, vector bool short);
vector signed char vec_nor (vector signed char, vector signed char);
vector unsigned char vec_nor (vector unsigned char,
                              vector unsigned char);
vector bool char vec_nor (vector bool char, vector bool char);

vector float vec_or (vector float, vector float);
vector float vec_or (vector float, vector bool int);
vector float vec_or (vector bool int, vector float);
vector bool int vec_or (vector bool int, vector bool int);
vector signed int vec_or (vector bool int, vector signed int);
vector signed int vec_or (vector signed int, vector bool int);
vector signed int vec_or (vector signed int, vector signed int);
vector unsigned int vec_or (vector bool int, vector unsigned int);
vector unsigned int vec_or (vector unsigned int, vector bool int);
vector unsigned int vec_or (vector unsigned int, vector unsigned int);
vector bool short vec_or (vector bool short, vector bool short);
vector signed short vec_or (vector bool short, vector signed short);
vector signed short vec_or (vector signed short, vector bool short);
vector signed short vec_or (vector signed short, vector signed short);
vector unsigned short vec_or (vector bool short, vector unsigned short);
vector unsigned short vec_or (vector unsigned short, vector bool short);
vector unsigned short vec_or (vector unsigned short,
                              vector unsigned short);
```

```
vector signed char vec_or (vector bool char, vector signed char);
vector bool char vec_or (vector bool char, vector bool char);
vector signed char vec_or (vector signed char, vector bool char);
vector signed char vec_or (vector signed char, vector signed char);
vector unsigned char vec_or (vector bool char, vector unsigned char);
vector unsigned char vec_or (vector unsigned char, vector bool char);
vector unsigned char vec_or (vector unsigned char,
                             vector unsigned char);

vector signed char vec_pack (vector signed short, vector signed short);
vector unsigned char vec_pack (vector unsigned short,
                               vector unsigned short);
vector bool char vec_pack (vector bool short, vector bool short);
vector signed short vec_pack (vector signed int, vector signed int);
vector unsigned short vec_pack (vector unsigned int,
                                vector unsigned int);
vector bool short vec_pack (vector bool int, vector bool int);

vector bool short vec_vpkuwum (vector bool int, vector bool int);
vector signed short vec_vpkuwum (vector signed int, vector signed int);
vector unsigned short vec_vpkuwum (vector unsigned int,
                                   vector unsigned int);

vector bool char vec_vpkuhum (vector bool short, vector bool short);
vector signed char vec_vpkuhum (vector signed short,
                                vector signed short);
vector unsigned char vec_vpkuhum (vector unsigned short,
                                  vector unsigned short);

vector pixel vec_packpx (vector unsigned int, vector unsigned int);

vector unsigned char vec_packs (vector unsigned short,
                                vector unsigned short);
vector signed char vec_packs (vector signed short, vector signed short);
vector unsigned short vec_packs (vector unsigned int,
                                 vector unsigned int);
vector signed short vec_packs (vector signed int, vector signed int);

vector signed short vec_vpkswss (vector signed int, vector signed int);

vector unsigned short vec_vpkuwus (vector unsigned int,
                                   vector unsigned int);

vector signed char vec_vpkshss (vector signed short,
                                vector signed short);

vector unsigned char vec_vpkuhus (vector unsigned short,
                                  vector unsigned short);

vector unsigned char vec_packsu (vector unsigned short,
                                 vector unsigned short);
vector unsigned char vec_packsu (vector signed short,
                                 vector signed short);
vector unsigned short vec_packsu (vector unsigned int,
                                  vector unsigned int);
vector unsigned short vec_packsu (vector signed int, vector signed int);

vector unsigned short vec_vpkswus (vector signed int,
```

```
                                       vector signed int);

       vector unsigned char vec_vpkshus (vector signed short,
                                         vector signed short);

       vector float vec_perm (vector float,
                              vector float,
                              vector unsigned char);
       vector signed int vec_perm (vector signed int,
                                   vector signed int,
                                   vector unsigned char);
       vector unsigned int vec_perm (vector unsigned int,
                                     vector unsigned int,
                                     vector unsigned char);
       vector bool int vec_perm (vector bool int,
                                 vector bool int,
                                 vector unsigned char);
       vector signed short vec_perm (vector signed short,
                                     vector signed short,
                                     vector unsigned char);
       vector unsigned short vec_perm (vector unsigned short,
                                       vector unsigned short,
                                       vector unsigned char);
       vector bool short vec_perm (vector bool short,
                                   vector bool short,
                                   vector unsigned char);
       vector pixel vec_perm (vector pixel,
                              vector pixel,
                              vector unsigned char);
       vector signed char vec_perm (vector signed char,
                                    vector signed char,
                                    vector unsigned char);
       vector unsigned char vec_perm (vector unsigned char,
                                      vector unsigned char,
                                      vector unsigned char);
       vector bool char vec_perm (vector bool char,
                                  vector bool char,
                                  vector unsigned char);

       vector float vec_re (vector float);

       vector signed char vec_rl (vector signed char,
                                  vector unsigned char);
       vector unsigned char vec_rl (vector unsigned char,
                                    vector unsigned char);
       vector signed short vec_rl (vector signed short, vector unsigned short);
       vector unsigned short vec_rl (vector unsigned short,
                                     vector unsigned short);
       vector signed int vec_rl (vector signed int, vector unsigned int);
       vector unsigned int vec_rl (vector unsigned int, vector unsigned int);

       vector signed int vec_vrlw (vector signed int, vector unsigned int);
       vector unsigned int vec_vrlw (vector unsigned int, vector unsigned int);

       vector signed short vec_vrlh (vector signed short,
                                     vector unsigned short);
       vector unsigned short vec_vrlh (vector unsigned short,
                                       vector unsigned short);
```

```
vector signed char vec_vrlb (vector signed char, vector unsigned char);
vector unsigned char vec_vrlb (vector unsigned char,
                               vector unsigned char);

vector float vec_round (vector float);

vector float vec_recip (vector float, vector float);

vector float vec_rsqrt (vector float);

vector float vec_rsqrte (vector float);

vector float vec_sel (vector float, vector float, vector bool int);
vector float vec_sel (vector float, vector float, vector unsigned int);
vector signed int vec_sel (vector signed int,
                           vector signed int,
                           vector bool int);
vector signed int vec_sel (vector signed int,
                           vector signed int,
                           vector unsigned int);
vector unsigned int vec_sel (vector unsigned int,
                             vector unsigned int,
                             vector bool int);
vector unsigned int vec_sel (vector unsigned int,
                             vector unsigned int,
                             vector unsigned int);
vector bool int vec_sel (vector bool int,
                         vector bool int,
                         vector bool int);
vector bool int vec_sel (vector bool int,
                         vector bool int,
                         vector unsigned int);
vector signed short vec_sel (vector signed short,
                             vector signed short,
                             vector bool short);
vector signed short vec_sel (vector signed short,
                             vector signed short,
                             vector unsigned short);
vector unsigned short vec_sel (vector unsigned short,
                               vector unsigned short,
                               vector bool short);
vector unsigned short vec_sel (vector unsigned short,
                               vector unsigned short,
                               vector unsigned short);
vector bool short vec_sel (vector bool short,
                           vector bool short,
                           vector bool short);
vector bool short vec_sel (vector bool short,
                           vector bool short,
                           vector unsigned short);
vector signed char vec_sel (vector signed char,
                            vector signed char,
                            vector bool char);
vector signed char vec_sel (vector signed char,
                            vector signed char,
                            vector unsigned char);
vector unsigned char vec_sel (vector unsigned char,
```

```
                          vector unsigned char,
                          vector bool char);
vector unsigned char vec_sel (vector unsigned char,
                          vector unsigned char,
                          vector unsigned char);
vector bool char vec_sel (vector bool char,
                    vector bool char,
                    vector bool char);
vector bool char vec_sel (vector bool char,
                    vector bool char,
                    vector unsigned char);

vector signed char vec_sl (vector signed char,
                      vector unsigned char);
vector unsigned char vec_sl (vector unsigned char,
                        vector unsigned char);
vector signed short vec_sl (vector signed short, vector unsigned short);
vector unsigned short vec_sl (vector unsigned short,
                          vector unsigned short);
vector signed int vec_sl (vector signed int, vector unsigned int);
vector unsigned int vec_sl (vector unsigned int, vector unsigned int);

vector signed int vec_vslw (vector signed int, vector unsigned int);
vector unsigned int vec_vslw (vector unsigned int, vector unsigned int);

vector signed short vec_vslh (vector signed short,
                          vector unsigned short);
vector unsigned short vec_vslh (vector unsigned short,
                            vector unsigned short);

vector signed char vec_vslb (vector signed char, vector unsigned char);
vector unsigned char vec_vslb (vector unsigned char,
                          vector unsigned char);

vector float vec_sld (vector float, vector float, const int);
vector signed int vec_sld (vector signed int,
                      vector signed int,
                      const int);
vector unsigned int vec_sld (vector unsigned int,
                        vector unsigned int,
                        const int);
vector bool int vec_sld (vector bool int,
                    vector bool int,
                    const int);
vector signed short vec_sld (vector signed short,
                        vector signed short,
                        const int);
vector unsigned short vec_sld (vector unsigned short,
                          vector unsigned short,
                          const int);
vector bool short vec_sld (vector bool short,
                      vector bool short,
                      const int);
vector pixel vec_sld (vector pixel,
                 vector pixel,
                 const int);
vector signed char vec_sld (vector signed char,
                       vector signed char,
```

```
                                         const int);
vector unsigned char vec_sld (vector unsigned char,
                              vector unsigned char,
                              const int);
vector bool char vec_sld (vector bool char,
                          vector bool char,
                          const int);

vector signed int vec_sll (vector signed int,
                           vector unsigned int);
vector signed int vec_sll (vector signed int,
                           vector unsigned short);
vector signed int vec_sll (vector signed int,
                           vector unsigned char);
vector unsigned int vec_sll (vector unsigned int,
                             vector unsigned int);
vector unsigned int vec_sll (vector unsigned int,
                             vector unsigned short);
vector unsigned int vec_sll (vector unsigned int,
                             vector unsigned char);
vector bool int vec_sll (vector bool int,
                         vector unsigned int);
vector bool int vec_sll (vector bool int,
                         vector unsigned short);
vector bool int vec_sll (vector bool int,
                         vector unsigned char);
vector signed short vec_sll (vector signed short,
                             vector unsigned int);
vector signed short vec_sll (vector signed short,
                             vector unsigned short);
vector signed short vec_sll (vector signed short,
                             vector unsigned char);
vector unsigned short vec_sll (vector unsigned short,
                               vector unsigned int);
vector unsigned short vec_sll (vector unsigned short,
                               vector unsigned short);
vector unsigned short vec_sll (vector unsigned short,
                               vector unsigned char);
vector bool short vec_sll (vector bool short, vector unsigned int);
vector bool short vec_sll (vector bool short, vector unsigned short);
vector bool short vec_sll (vector bool short, vector unsigned char);
vector pixel vec_sll (vector pixel, vector unsigned int);
vector pixel vec_sll (vector pixel, vector unsigned short);
vector pixel vec_sll (vector pixel, vector unsigned char);
vector signed char vec_sll (vector signed char, vector unsigned int);
vector signed char vec_sll (vector signed char, vector unsigned short);
vector signed char vec_sll (vector signed char, vector unsigned char);
vector unsigned char vec_sll (vector unsigned char,
                              vector unsigned int);
vector unsigned char vec_sll (vector unsigned char,
                              vector unsigned short);
vector unsigned char vec_sll (vector unsigned char,
                              vector unsigned char);
vector bool char vec_sll (vector bool char, vector unsigned int);
vector bool char vec_sll (vector bool char, vector unsigned short);
vector bool char vec_sll (vector bool char, vector unsigned char);

vector float vec_slo (vector float, vector signed char);
```

```
vector float vec_slo (vector float, vector unsigned char);
vector signed int vec_slo (vector signed int, vector signed char);
vector signed int vec_slo (vector signed int, vector unsigned char);
vector unsigned int vec_slo (vector unsigned int, vector signed char);
vector unsigned int vec_slo (vector unsigned int, vector unsigned char);
vector signed short vec_slo (vector signed short, vector signed char);
vector signed short vec_slo (vector signed short, vector unsigned char);
vector unsigned short vec_slo (vector unsigned short,
                               vector signed char);
vector unsigned short vec_slo (vector unsigned short,
                               vector unsigned char);
vector pixel vec_slo (vector pixel, vector signed char);
vector pixel vec_slo (vector pixel, vector unsigned char);
vector signed char vec_slo (vector signed char, vector signed char);
vector signed char vec_slo (vector signed char, vector unsigned char);
vector unsigned char vec_slo (vector unsigned char, vector signed char);
vector unsigned char vec_slo (vector unsigned char,
                              vector unsigned char);

vector signed char vec_splat (vector signed char, const int);
vector unsigned char vec_splat (vector unsigned char, const int);
vector bool char vec_splat (vector bool char, const int);
vector signed short vec_splat (vector signed short, const int);
vector unsigned short vec_splat (vector unsigned short, const int);
vector bool short vec_splat (vector bool short, const int);
vector pixel vec_splat (vector pixel, const int);
vector float vec_splat (vector float, const int);
vector signed int vec_splat (vector signed int, const int);
vector unsigned int vec_splat (vector unsigned int, const int);
vector bool int vec_splat (vector bool int, const int);
vector signed long vec_splat (vector signed long, const int);
vector unsigned long vec_splat (vector unsigned long, const int);

vector signed char vec_splats (signed char);
vector unsigned char vec_splats (unsigned char);
vector signed short vec_splats (signed short);
vector unsigned short vec_splats (unsigned short);
vector signed int vec_splats (signed int);
vector unsigned int vec_splats (unsigned int);
vector float vec_splats (float);

vector float vec_vspltw (vector float, const int);
vector signed int vec_vspltw (vector signed int, const int);
vector unsigned int vec_vspltw (vector unsigned int, const int);
vector bool int vec_vspltw (vector bool int, const int);

vector bool short vec_vsplth (vector bool short, const int);
vector signed short vec_vsplth (vector signed short, const int);
vector unsigned short vec_vsplth (vector unsigned short, const int);
vector pixel vec_vsplth (vector pixel, const int);

vector signed char vec_vspltb (vector signed char, const int);
vector unsigned char vec_vspltb (vector unsigned char, const int);
vector bool char vec_vspltb (vector bool char, const int);

vector signed char vec_splat_s8 (const int);

vector signed short vec_splat_s16 (const int);
```

```
vector signed int vec_splat_s32 (const int);

vector unsigned char vec_splat_u8 (const int);

vector unsigned short vec_splat_u16 (const int);

vector unsigned int vec_splat_u32 (const int);

vector signed char vec_sr (vector signed char, vector unsigned char);
vector unsigned char vec_sr (vector unsigned char,
                             vector unsigned char);
vector signed short vec_sr (vector signed short,
                            vector unsigned short);
vector unsigned short vec_sr (vector unsigned short,
                              vector unsigned short);
vector signed int vec_sr (vector signed int, vector unsigned int);
vector unsigned int vec_sr (vector unsigned int, vector unsigned int);

vector signed int vec_vsrw (vector signed int, vector unsigned int);
vector unsigned int vec_vsrw (vector unsigned int, vector unsigned int);

vector signed short vec_vsrh (vector signed short,
                              vector unsigned short);
vector unsigned short vec_vsrh (vector unsigned short,
                                vector unsigned short);

vector signed char vec_vsrb (vector signed char, vector unsigned char);
vector unsigned char vec_vsrb (vector unsigned char,
                               vector unsigned char);

vector signed char vec_sra (vector signed char, vector unsigned char);
vector unsigned char vec_sra (vector unsigned char,
                              vector unsigned char);
vector signed short vec_sra (vector signed short,
                             vector unsigned short);
vector unsigned short vec_sra (vector unsigned short,
                               vector unsigned short);
vector signed int vec_sra (vector signed int, vector unsigned int);
vector unsigned int vec_sra (vector unsigned int, vector unsigned int);

vector signed int vec_vsraw (vector signed int, vector unsigned int);
vector unsigned int vec_vsraw (vector unsigned int,
                               vector unsigned int);

vector signed short vec_vsrah (vector signed short,
                               vector unsigned short);
vector unsigned short vec_vsrah (vector unsigned short,
                                 vector unsigned short);

vector signed char vec_vsrab (vector signed char, vector unsigned char);
vector unsigned char vec_vsrab (vector unsigned char,
                                vector unsigned char);

vector signed int vec_srl (vector signed int, vector unsigned int);
vector signed int vec_srl (vector signed int, vector unsigned short);
vector signed int vec_srl (vector signed int, vector unsigned char);
vector unsigned int vec_srl (vector unsigned int, vector unsigned int);
```

```
vector unsigned int vec_srl (vector unsigned int,
                             vector unsigned short);
vector unsigned int vec_srl (vector unsigned int, vector unsigned char);
vector bool int vec_srl (vector bool int, vector unsigned int);
vector bool int vec_srl (vector bool int, vector unsigned short);
vector bool int vec_srl (vector bool int, vector unsigned char);
vector signed short vec_srl (vector signed short, vector unsigned int);
vector signed short vec_srl (vector signed short,
                             vector unsigned short);
vector signed short vec_srl (vector signed short, vector unsigned char);
vector unsigned short vec_srl (vector unsigned short,
                               vector unsigned int);
vector unsigned short vec_srl (vector unsigned short,
                               vector unsigned short);
vector unsigned short vec_srl (vector unsigned short,
                               vector unsigned char);
vector bool short vec_srl (vector bool short, vector unsigned int);
vector bool short vec_srl (vector bool short, vector unsigned short);
vector bool short vec_srl (vector bool short, vector unsigned char);
vector pixel vec_srl (vector pixel, vector unsigned int);
vector pixel vec_srl (vector pixel, vector unsigned short);
vector pixel vec_srl (vector pixel, vector unsigned char);
vector signed char vec_srl (vector signed char, vector unsigned int);
vector signed char vec_srl (vector signed char, vector unsigned short);
vector signed char vec_srl (vector signed char, vector unsigned char);
vector unsigned char vec_srl (vector unsigned char,
                              vector unsigned int);
vector unsigned char vec_srl (vector unsigned char,
                              vector unsigned short);
vector unsigned char vec_srl (vector unsigned char,
                              vector unsigned char);
vector bool char vec_srl (vector bool char, vector unsigned int);
vector bool char vec_srl (vector bool char, vector unsigned short);
vector bool char vec_srl (vector bool char, vector unsigned char);

vector float vec_sro (vector float, vector signed char);
vector float vec_sro (vector float, vector unsigned char);
vector signed int vec_sro (vector signed int, vector signed char);
vector signed int vec_sro (vector signed int, vector unsigned char);
vector unsigned int vec_sro (vector unsigned int, vector signed char);
vector unsigned int vec_sro (vector unsigned int, vector unsigned char);
vector signed short vec_sro (vector signed short, vector signed char);
vector signed short vec_sro (vector signed short, vector unsigned char);
vector unsigned short vec_sro (vector unsigned short,
                               vector signed char);
vector unsigned short vec_sro (vector unsigned short,
                               vector unsigned char);
vector pixel vec_sro (vector pixel, vector signed char);
vector pixel vec_sro (vector pixel, vector unsigned char);
vector signed char vec_sro (vector signed char, vector signed char);
vector signed char vec_sro (vector signed char, vector unsigned char);
vector unsigned char vec_sro (vector unsigned char, vector signed char);
vector unsigned char vec_sro (vector unsigned char,
                              vector unsigned char);

void vec_st (vector float, int, vector float *);
void vec_st (vector float, int, float *);
void vec_st (vector signed int, int, vector signed int *);
```

```
void vec_st (vector signed int, int, int *);
void vec_st (vector unsigned int, int, vector unsigned int *);
void vec_st (vector unsigned int, int, unsigned int *);
void vec_st (vector bool int, int, vector bool int *);
void vec_st (vector bool int, int, unsigned int *);
void vec_st (vector bool int, int, int *);
void vec_st (vector signed short, int, vector signed short *);
void vec_st (vector signed short, int, short *);
void vec_st (vector unsigned short, int, vector unsigned short *);
void vec_st (vector unsigned short, int, unsigned short *);
void vec_st (vector bool short, int, vector bool short *);
void vec_st (vector bool short, int, unsigned short *);
void vec_st (vector pixel, int, vector pixel *);
void vec_st (vector pixel, int, unsigned short *);
void vec_st (vector pixel, int, short *);
void vec_st (vector bool short, int, short *);
void vec_st (vector signed char, int, vector signed char *);
void vec_st (vector signed char, int, signed char *);
void vec_st (vector unsigned char, int, vector unsigned char *);
void vec_st (vector unsigned char, int, unsigned char *);
void vec_st (vector bool char, int, vector bool char *);
void vec_st (vector bool char, int, unsigned char *);
void vec_st (vector bool char, int, signed char *);

void vec_ste (vector signed char, int, signed char *);
void vec_ste (vector unsigned char, int, unsigned char *);
void vec_ste (vector bool char, int, signed char *);
void vec_ste (vector bool char, int, unsigned char *);
void vec_ste (vector signed short, int, short *);
void vec_ste (vector unsigned short, int, unsigned short *);
void vec_ste (vector bool short, int, short *);
void vec_ste (vector bool short, int, unsigned short *);
void vec_ste (vector pixel, int, short *);
void vec_ste (vector pixel, int, unsigned short *);
void vec_ste (vector float, int, float *);
void vec_ste (vector signed int, int, int *);
void vec_ste (vector unsigned int, int, unsigned int *);
void vec_ste (vector bool int, int, int *);
void vec_ste (vector bool int, int, unsigned int *);

void vec_stvewx (vector float, int, float *);
void vec_stvewx (vector signed int, int, int *);
void vec_stvewx (vector unsigned int, int, unsigned int *);
void vec_stvewx (vector bool int, int, int *);
void vec_stvewx (vector bool int, int, unsigned int *);

void vec_stvehx (vector signed short, int, short *);
void vec_stvehx (vector unsigned short, int, unsigned short *);
void vec_stvehx (vector bool short, int, short *);
void vec_stvehx (vector bool short, int, unsigned short *);
void vec_stvehx (vector pixel, int, short *);
void vec_stvehx (vector pixel, int, unsigned short *);

void vec_stvebx (vector signed char, int, signed char *);
void vec_stvebx (vector unsigned char, int, unsigned char *);
void vec_stvebx (vector bool char, int, signed char *);
void vec_stvebx (vector bool char, int, unsigned char *);
```

```
void vec_stl (vector float, int, vector float *);
void vec_stl (vector float, int, float *);
void vec_stl (vector signed int, int, vector signed int *);
void vec_stl (vector signed int, int, int *);
void vec_stl (vector unsigned int, int, vector unsigned int *);
void vec_stl (vector unsigned int, int, unsigned int *);
void vec_stl (vector bool int, int, vector bool int *);
void vec_stl (vector bool int, int, unsigned int *);
void vec_stl (vector bool int, int, int *);
void vec_stl (vector signed short, int, vector signed short *);
void vec_stl (vector signed short, int, short *);
void vec_stl (vector unsigned short, int, vector unsigned short *);
void vec_stl (vector unsigned short, int, unsigned short *);
void vec_stl (vector bool short, int, vector bool short *);
void vec_stl (vector bool short, int, unsigned short *);
void vec_stl (vector bool short, int, short *);
void vec_stl (vector pixel, int, vector pixel *);
void vec_stl (vector pixel, int, unsigned short *);
void vec_stl (vector pixel, int, short *);
void vec_stl (vector signed char, int, vector signed char *);
void vec_stl (vector signed char, int, signed char *);
void vec_stl (vector unsigned char, int, vector unsigned char *);
void vec_stl (vector unsigned char, int, unsigned char *);
void vec_stl (vector bool char, int, vector bool char *);
void vec_stl (vector bool char, int, unsigned char *);
void vec_stl (vector bool char, int, signed char *);

vector signed char vec_sub (vector bool char, vector signed char);
vector signed char vec_sub (vector signed char, vector bool char);
vector signed char vec_sub (vector signed char, vector signed char);
vector unsigned char vec_sub (vector bool char, vector unsigned char);
vector unsigned char vec_sub (vector unsigned char, vector bool char);
vector unsigned char vec_sub (vector unsigned char,
                              vector unsigned char);
vector signed short vec_sub (vector bool short, vector signed short);
vector signed short vec_sub (vector signed short, vector bool short);
vector signed short vec_sub (vector signed short, vector signed short);
vector unsigned short vec_sub (vector bool short,
                               vector unsigned short);
vector unsigned short vec_sub (vector unsigned short,
                               vector bool short);
vector unsigned short vec_sub (vector unsigned short,
                               vector unsigned short);
vector signed int vec_sub (vector bool int, vector signed int);
vector signed int vec_sub (vector signed int, vector bool int);
vector signed int vec_sub (vector signed int, vector signed int);
vector unsigned int vec_sub (vector bool int, vector unsigned int);
vector unsigned int vec_sub (vector unsigned int, vector bool int);
vector unsigned int vec_sub (vector unsigned int, vector unsigned int);
vector float vec_sub (vector float, vector float);

vector float vec_vsubfp (vector float, vector float);

vector signed int vec_vsubuwm (vector bool int, vector signed int);
vector signed int vec_vsubuwm (vector signed int, vector bool int);
vector signed int vec_vsubuwm (vector signed int, vector signed int);
vector unsigned int vec_vsubuwm (vector bool int, vector unsigned int);
vector unsigned int vec_vsubuwm (vector unsigned int, vector bool int);
```

```
vector unsigned int vec_vsubuwm (vector unsigned int,
                                 vector unsigned int);

vector signed short vec_vsubuhm (vector bool short,
                                 vector signed short);
vector signed short vec_vsubuhm (vector signed short,
                                 vector bool short);
vector signed short vec_vsubuhm (vector signed short,
                                 vector signed short);
vector unsigned short vec_vsubuhm (vector bool short,
                                   vector unsigned short);
vector unsigned short vec_vsubuhm (vector unsigned short,
                                   vector bool short);
vector unsigned short vec_vsubuhm (vector unsigned short,
                                   vector unsigned short);

vector signed char vec_vsububm (vector bool char, vector signed char);
vector signed char vec_vsububm (vector signed char, vector bool char);
vector signed char vec_vsububm (vector signed char, vector signed char);
vector unsigned char vec_vsububm (vector bool char,
                                  vector unsigned char);
vector unsigned char vec_vsububm (vector unsigned char,
                                  vector bool char);
vector unsigned char vec_vsububm (vector unsigned char,
                                  vector unsigned char);

vector unsigned int vec_subc (vector unsigned int, vector unsigned int);

vector unsigned char vec_subs (vector bool char, vector unsigned char);
vector unsigned char vec_subs (vector unsigned char, vector bool char);
vector unsigned char vec_subs (vector unsigned char,
                               vector unsigned char);
vector signed char vec_subs (vector bool char, vector signed char);
vector signed char vec_subs (vector signed char, vector bool char);
vector signed char vec_subs (vector signed char, vector signed char);
vector unsigned short vec_subs (vector bool short,
                                vector unsigned short);
vector unsigned short vec_subs (vector unsigned short,
                                vector bool short);
vector unsigned short vec_subs (vector unsigned short,
                                vector unsigned short);
vector signed short vec_subs (vector bool short, vector signed short);
vector signed short vec_subs (vector signed short, vector bool short);
vector signed short vec_subs (vector signed short, vector signed short);
vector unsigned int vec_subs (vector bool int, vector unsigned int);
vector unsigned int vec_subs (vector unsigned int, vector bool int);
vector unsigned int vec_subs (vector unsigned int, vector unsigned int);
vector signed int vec_subs (vector bool int, vector signed int);
vector signed int vec_subs (vector signed int, vector bool int);
vector signed int vec_subs (vector signed int, vector signed int);

vector signed int vec_vsubsws (vector bool int, vector signed int);
vector signed int vec_vsubsws (vector signed int, vector bool int);
vector signed int vec_vsubsws (vector signed int, vector signed int);

vector unsigned int vec_vsubuws (vector bool int, vector unsigned int);
vector unsigned int vec_vsubuws (vector unsigned int, vector bool int);
vector unsigned int vec_vsubuws (vector unsigned int,
```

```
                                        vector unsigned int);

vector signed short vec_vsubshs (vector bool short,
                                 vector signed short);
vector signed short vec_vsubshs (vector signed short,
                                 vector bool short);
vector signed short vec_vsubshs (vector signed short,
                                 vector signed short);

vector unsigned short vec_vsubuhs (vector bool short,
                                   vector unsigned short);
vector unsigned short vec_vsubuhs (vector unsigned short,
                                   vector bool short);
vector unsigned short vec_vsubuhs (vector unsigned short,
                                   vector unsigned short);

vector signed char vec_vsubsbs (vector bool char, vector signed char);
vector signed char vec_vsubsbs (vector signed char, vector bool char);
vector signed char vec_vsubsbs (vector signed char, vector signed char);

vector unsigned char vec_vsububs (vector bool char,
                                  vector unsigned char);
vector unsigned char vec_vsububs (vector unsigned char,
                                  vector bool char);
vector unsigned char vec_vsububs (vector unsigned char,
                                  vector unsigned char);

vector unsigned int vec_sum4s (vector unsigned char,
                               vector unsigned int);
vector signed int vec_sum4s (vector signed char, vector signed int);
vector signed int vec_sum4s (vector signed short, vector signed int);

vector signed int vec_vsum4shs (vector signed short, vector signed int);

vector signed int vec_vsum4sbs (vector signed char, vector signed int);

vector unsigned int vec_vsum4ubs (vector unsigned char,
                                  vector unsigned int);

vector signed int vec_sum2s (vector signed int, vector signed int);

vector signed int vec_sums (vector signed int, vector signed int);

vector float vec_trunc (vector float);

vector signed short vec_unpackh (vector signed char);
vector bool short vec_unpackh (vector bool char);
vector signed int vec_unpackh (vector signed short);
vector bool int vec_unpackh (vector bool short);
vector unsigned int vec_unpackh (vector pixel);

vector bool int vec_vupkhsh (vector bool short);
vector signed int vec_vupkhsh (vector signed short);

vector unsigned int vec_vupkhpx (vector pixel);

vector bool short vec_vupkhsb (vector bool char);
vector signed short vec_vupkhsb (vector signed char);
```

```
vector signed short vec_unpackl (vector signed char);
vector bool short vec_unpackl (vector bool char);
vector unsigned int vec_unpackl (vector pixel);
vector signed int vec_unpackl (vector signed short);
vector bool int vec_unpackl (vector bool short);

vector unsigned int vec_vupklpx (vector pixel);

vector bool int vec_vupklsh (vector bool short);
vector signed int vec_vupklsh (vector signed short);

vector bool short vec_vupklsb (vector bool char);
vector signed short vec_vupklsb (vector signed char);

vector float vec_xor (vector float, vector float);
vector float vec_xor (vector float, vector bool int);
vector float vec_xor (vector bool int, vector float);
vector bool int vec_xor (vector bool int, vector bool int);
vector signed int vec_xor (vector bool int, vector signed int);
vector signed int vec_xor (vector signed int, vector bool int);
vector signed int vec_xor (vector signed int, vector signed int);
vector unsigned int vec_xor (vector bool int, vector unsigned int);
vector unsigned int vec_xor (vector unsigned int, vector bool int);
vector unsigned int vec_xor (vector unsigned int, vector unsigned int);
vector bool short vec_xor (vector bool short, vector bool short);
vector signed short vec_xor (vector bool short, vector signed short);
vector signed short vec_xor (vector signed short, vector bool short);
vector signed short vec_xor (vector signed short, vector signed short);
vector unsigned short vec_xor (vector bool short,
                               vector unsigned short);
vector unsigned short vec_xor (vector unsigned short,
                               vector bool short);
vector unsigned short vec_xor (vector unsigned short,
                               vector unsigned short);
vector signed char vec_xor (vector bool char, vector signed char);
vector bool char vec_xor (vector bool char, vector bool char);
vector signed char vec_xor (vector signed char, vector bool char);
vector signed char vec_xor (vector signed char, vector signed char);
vector unsigned char vec_xor (vector bool char, vector unsigned char);
vector unsigned char vec_xor (vector unsigned char, vector bool char);
vector unsigned char vec_xor (vector unsigned char,
                              vector unsigned char);

int vec_all_eq (vector signed char, vector bool char);
int vec_all_eq (vector signed char, vector signed char);
int vec_all_eq (vector unsigned char, vector bool char);
int vec_all_eq (vector unsigned char, vector unsigned char);
int vec_all_eq (vector bool char, vector bool char);
int vec_all_eq (vector bool char, vector unsigned char);
int vec_all_eq (vector bool char, vector signed char);
int vec_all_eq (vector signed short, vector bool short);
int vec_all_eq (vector signed short, vector signed short);
int vec_all_eq (vector unsigned short, vector bool short);
int vec_all_eq (vector unsigned short, vector unsigned short);
int vec_all_eq (vector bool short, vector bool short);
int vec_all_eq (vector bool short, vector unsigned short);
int vec_all_eq (vector bool short, vector signed short);
```

```
int vec_all_eq (vector pixel, vector pixel);
int vec_all_eq (vector signed int, vector bool int);
int vec_all_eq (vector signed int, vector signed int);
int vec_all_eq (vector unsigned int, vector bool int);
int vec_all_eq (vector unsigned int, vector unsigned int);
int vec_all_eq (vector bool int, vector bool int);
int vec_all_eq (vector bool int, vector unsigned int);
int vec_all_eq (vector bool int, vector signed int);
int vec_all_eq (vector float, vector float);

int vec_all_ge (vector bool char, vector unsigned char);
int vec_all_ge (vector unsigned char, vector bool char);
int vec_all_ge (vector unsigned char, vector unsigned char);
int vec_all_ge (vector bool char, vector signed char);
int vec_all_ge (vector signed char, vector bool char);
int vec_all_ge (vector signed char, vector signed char);
int vec_all_ge (vector bool short, vector unsigned short);
int vec_all_ge (vector unsigned short, vector bool short);
int vec_all_ge (vector unsigned short, vector unsigned short);
int vec_all_ge (vector signed short, vector signed short);
int vec_all_ge (vector bool short, vector signed short);
int vec_all_ge (vector signed short, vector bool short);
int vec_all_ge (vector bool int, vector unsigned int);
int vec_all_ge (vector unsigned int, vector bool int);
int vec_all_ge (vector unsigned int, vector unsigned int);
int vec_all_ge (vector bool int, vector signed int);
int vec_all_ge (vector signed int, vector bool int);
int vec_all_ge (vector signed int, vector signed int);
int vec_all_ge (vector float, vector float);

int vec_all_gt (vector bool char, vector unsigned char);
int vec_all_gt (vector unsigned char, vector bool char);
int vec_all_gt (vector unsigned char, vector unsigned char);
int vec_all_gt (vector bool char, vector signed char);
int vec_all_gt (vector signed char, vector bool char);
int vec_all_gt (vector signed char, vector signed char);
int vec_all_gt (vector bool short, vector unsigned short);
int vec_all_gt (vector unsigned short, vector bool short);
int vec_all_gt (vector unsigned short, vector unsigned short);
int vec_all_gt (vector bool short, vector signed short);
int vec_all_gt (vector signed short, vector bool short);
int vec_all_gt (vector signed short, vector signed short);
int vec_all_gt (vector bool int, vector unsigned int);
int vec_all_gt (vector unsigned int, vector bool int);
int vec_all_gt (vector unsigned int, vector unsigned int);
int vec_all_gt (vector bool int, vector signed int);
int vec_all_gt (vector signed int, vector bool int);
int vec_all_gt (vector signed int, vector signed int);
int vec_all_gt (vector float, vector float);

int vec_all_in (vector float, vector float);

int vec_all_le (vector bool char, vector unsigned char);
int vec_all_le (vector unsigned char, vector bool char);
int vec_all_le (vector unsigned char, vector unsigned char);
int vec_all_le (vector bool char, vector signed char);
int vec_all_le (vector signed char, vector bool char);
int vec_all_le (vector signed char, vector signed char);
```

```
int vec_all_le (vector bool short, vector unsigned short);
int vec_all_le (vector unsigned short, vector bool short);
int vec_all_le (vector unsigned short, vector unsigned short);
int vec_all_le (vector bool short, vector signed short);
int vec_all_le (vector signed short, vector bool short);
int vec_all_le (vector signed short, vector signed short);
int vec_all_le (vector bool int, vector unsigned int);
int vec_all_le (vector unsigned int, vector bool int);
int vec_all_le (vector unsigned int, vector unsigned int);
int vec_all_le (vector bool int, vector signed int);
int vec_all_le (vector signed int, vector bool int);
int vec_all_le (vector signed int, vector signed int);
int vec_all_le (vector float, vector float);

int vec_all_lt (vector bool char, vector unsigned char);
int vec_all_lt (vector unsigned char, vector bool char);
int vec_all_lt (vector unsigned char, vector unsigned char);
int vec_all_lt (vector bool char, vector signed char);
int vec_all_lt (vector signed char, vector bool char);
int vec_all_lt (vector signed char, vector signed char);
int vec_all_lt (vector bool short, vector unsigned short);
int vec_all_lt (vector unsigned short, vector bool short);
int vec_all_lt (vector unsigned short, vector unsigned short);
int vec_all_lt (vector bool short, vector signed short);
int vec_all_lt (vector signed short, vector bool short);
int vec_all_lt (vector signed short, vector signed short);
int vec_all_lt (vector bool int, vector unsigned int);
int vec_all_lt (vector unsigned int, vector bool int);
int vec_all_lt (vector unsigned int, vector unsigned int);
int vec_all_lt (vector bool int, vector signed int);
int vec_all_lt (vector signed int, vector bool int);
int vec_all_lt (vector signed int, vector signed int);
int vec_all_lt (vector float, vector float);

int vec_all_nan (vector float);

int vec_all_ne (vector signed char, vector bool char);
int vec_all_ne (vector signed char, vector signed char);
int vec_all_ne (vector unsigned char, vector bool char);
int vec_all_ne (vector unsigned char, vector unsigned char);
int vec_all_ne (vector bool char, vector bool char);
int vec_all_ne (vector bool char, vector unsigned char);
int vec_all_ne (vector bool char, vector signed char);
int vec_all_ne (vector signed short, vector bool short);
int vec_all_ne (vector signed short, vector signed short);
int vec_all_ne (vector unsigned short, vector bool short);
int vec_all_ne (vector unsigned short, vector unsigned short);
int vec_all_ne (vector bool short, vector bool short);
int vec_all_ne (vector bool short, vector unsigned short);
int vec_all_ne (vector bool short, vector signed short);
int vec_all_ne (vector pixel, vector pixel);
int vec_all_ne (vector signed int, vector bool int);
int vec_all_ne (vector signed int, vector signed int);
int vec_all_ne (vector unsigned int, vector bool int);
int vec_all_ne (vector unsigned int, vector unsigned int);
int vec_all_ne (vector bool int, vector bool int);
int vec_all_ne (vector bool int, vector unsigned int);
int vec_all_ne (vector bool int, vector signed int);
```

```
int vec_all_ne (vector float, vector float);

int vec_all_nge (vector float, vector float);

int vec_all_ngt (vector float, vector float);

int vec_all_nle (vector float, vector float);

int vec_all_nlt (vector float, vector float);

int vec_all_numeric (vector float);

int vec_any_eq (vector signed char, vector bool char);
int vec_any_eq (vector signed char, vector signed char);
int vec_any_eq (vector unsigned char, vector bool char);
int vec_any_eq (vector unsigned char, vector unsigned char);
int vec_any_eq (vector bool char, vector bool char);
int vec_any_eq (vector bool char, vector unsigned char);
int vec_any_eq (vector bool char, vector signed char);
int vec_any_eq (vector signed short, vector bool short);
int vec_any_eq (vector signed short, vector signed short);
int vec_any_eq (vector unsigned short, vector bool short);
int vec_any_eq (vector unsigned short, vector unsigned short);
int vec_any_eq (vector bool short, vector bool short);
int vec_any_eq (vector bool short, vector unsigned short);
int vec_any_eq (vector bool short, vector signed short);
int vec_any_eq (vector pixel, vector pixel);
int vec_any_eq (vector signed int, vector bool int);
int vec_any_eq (vector signed int, vector signed int);
int vec_any_eq (vector unsigned int, vector bool int);
int vec_any_eq (vector unsigned int, vector unsigned int);
int vec_any_eq (vector bool int, vector bool int);
int vec_any_eq (vector bool int, vector unsigned int);
int vec_any_eq (vector bool int, vector signed int);
int vec_any_eq (vector float, vector float);

int vec_any_ge (vector signed char, vector bool char);
int vec_any_ge (vector unsigned char, vector bool char);
int vec_any_ge (vector unsigned char, vector unsigned char);
int vec_any_ge (vector signed char, vector signed char);
int vec_any_ge (vector bool char, vector unsigned char);
int vec_any_ge (vector bool char, vector signed char);
int vec_any_ge (vector unsigned short, vector bool short);
int vec_any_ge (vector unsigned short, vector unsigned short);
int vec_any_ge (vector signed short, vector signed short);
int vec_any_ge (vector signed short, vector bool short);
int vec_any_ge (vector bool short, vector unsigned short);
int vec_any_ge (vector bool short, vector signed short);
int vec_any_ge (vector signed int, vector bool int);
int vec_any_ge (vector unsigned int, vector bool int);
int vec_any_ge (vector unsigned int, vector unsigned int);
int vec_any_ge (vector signed int, vector signed int);
int vec_any_ge (vector bool int, vector unsigned int);
int vec_any_ge (vector bool int, vector signed int);
int vec_any_ge (vector float, vector float);

int vec_any_gt (vector bool char, vector unsigned char);
int vec_any_gt (vector unsigned char, vector bool char);
```

```
int vec_any_gt (vector unsigned char, vector unsigned char);
int vec_any_gt (vector bool char, vector signed char);
int vec_any_gt (vector signed char, vector bool char);
int vec_any_gt (vector signed char, vector signed char);
int vec_any_gt (vector bool short, vector unsigned short);
int vec_any_gt (vector unsigned short, vector bool short);
int vec_any_gt (vector unsigned short, vector unsigned short);
int vec_any_gt (vector bool short, vector signed short);
int vec_any_gt (vector signed short, vector bool short);
int vec_any_gt (vector signed short, vector signed short);
int vec_any_gt (vector bool int, vector unsigned int);
int vec_any_gt (vector unsigned int, vector bool int);
int vec_any_gt (vector unsigned int, vector unsigned int);
int vec_any_gt (vector bool int, vector signed int);
int vec_any_gt (vector signed int, vector bool int);
int vec_any_gt (vector signed int, vector signed int);
int vec_any_gt (vector float, vector float);

int vec_any_le (vector bool char, vector unsigned char);
int vec_any_le (vector unsigned char, vector bool char);
int vec_any_le (vector unsigned char, vector unsigned char);
int vec_any_le (vector bool char, vector signed char);
int vec_any_le (vector signed char, vector bool char);
int vec_any_le (vector signed char, vector signed char);
int vec_any_le (vector bool short, vector unsigned short);
int vec_any_le (vector unsigned short, vector bool short);
int vec_any_le (vector unsigned short, vector unsigned short);
int vec_any_le (vector bool short, vector signed short);
int vec_any_le (vector signed short, vector bool short);
int vec_any_le (vector signed short, vector signed short);
int vec_any_le (vector bool int, vector unsigned int);
int vec_any_le (vector unsigned int, vector bool int);
int vec_any_le (vector unsigned int, vector unsigned int);
int vec_any_le (vector bool int, vector signed int);
int vec_any_le (vector signed int, vector bool int);
int vec_any_le (vector signed int, vector signed int);
int vec_any_le (vector float, vector float);

int vec_any_lt (vector bool char, vector unsigned char);
int vec_any_lt (vector unsigned char, vector bool char);
int vec_any_lt (vector unsigned char, vector unsigned char);
int vec_any_lt (vector bool char, vector signed char);
int vec_any_lt (vector signed char, vector bool char);
int vec_any_lt (vector signed char, vector signed char);
int vec_any_lt (vector bool short, vector unsigned short);
int vec_any_lt (vector unsigned short, vector bool short);
int vec_any_lt (vector unsigned short, vector unsigned short);
int vec_any_lt (vector bool short, vector signed short);
int vec_any_lt (vector signed short, vector bool short);
int vec_any_lt (vector signed short, vector signed short);
int vec_any_lt (vector bool int, vector unsigned int);
int vec_any_lt (vector unsigned int, vector bool int);
int vec_any_lt (vector unsigned int, vector unsigned int);
int vec_any_lt (vector bool int, vector signed int);
int vec_any_lt (vector signed int, vector bool int);
int vec_any_lt (vector signed int, vector signed int);
int vec_any_lt (vector float, vector float);
```

```
int vec_any_nan (vector float);

int vec_any_ne (vector signed char, vector bool char);
int vec_any_ne (vector signed char, vector signed char);
int vec_any_ne (vector unsigned char, vector bool char);
int vec_any_ne (vector unsigned char, vector unsigned char);
int vec_any_ne (vector bool char, vector bool char);
int vec_any_ne (vector bool char, vector unsigned char);
int vec_any_ne (vector bool char, vector signed char);
int vec_any_ne (vector signed short, vector bool short);
int vec_any_ne (vector signed short, vector signed short);
int vec_any_ne (vector unsigned short, vector bool short);
int vec_any_ne (vector unsigned short, vector unsigned short);
int vec_any_ne (vector bool short, vector bool short);
int vec_any_ne (vector bool short, vector unsigned short);
int vec_any_ne (vector bool short, vector signed short);
int vec_any_ne (vector pixel, vector pixel);
int vec_any_ne (vector signed int, vector bool int);
int vec_any_ne (vector signed int, vector signed int);
int vec_any_ne (vector unsigned int, vector bool int);
int vec_any_ne (vector unsigned int, vector unsigned int);
int vec_any_ne (vector bool int, vector bool int);
int vec_any_ne (vector bool int, vector unsigned int);
int vec_any_ne (vector bool int, vector signed int);
int vec_any_ne (vector float, vector float);

int vec_any_nge (vector float, vector float);

int vec_any_ngt (vector float, vector float);

int vec_any_nle (vector float, vector float);

int vec_any_nlt (vector float, vector float);

int vec_any_numeric (vector float);

int vec_any_out (vector float, vector float);
```

If the vector/scalar (VSX) instruction set is available, the following additional functions
are available:

```
vector double vec_abs (vector double);
vector double vec_add (vector double, vector double);
vector double vec_and (vector double, vector double);
vector double vec_and (vector double, vector bool long);
vector double vec_and (vector bool long, vector double);
vector long vec_and (vector long, vector long);
vector long vec_and (vector long, vector bool long);
vector long vec_and (vector bool long, vector long);
vector unsigned long vec_and (vector unsigned long, vector unsigned long);
vector unsigned long vec_and (vector unsigned long, vector bool long);
vector unsigned long vec_and (vector bool long, vector unsigned long);
vector double vec_andc (vector double, vector double);
vector double vec_andc (vector double, vector bool long);
vector double vec_andc (vector bool long, vector double);
vector long vec_andc (vector long, vector long);
vector long vec_andc (vector long, vector bool long);
vector long vec_andc (vector bool long, vector long);
vector unsigned long vec_andc (vector unsigned long, vector unsigned long);
```

```
vector unsigned long vec_andc (vector unsigned long, vector bool long);
vector unsigned long vec_andc (vector bool long, vector unsigned long);
vector double vec_ceil (vector double);
vector bool long vec_cmpeq (vector double, vector double);
vector bool long vec_cmpge (vector double, vector double);
vector bool long vec_cmpgt (vector double, vector double);
vector bool long vec_cmple (vector double, vector double);
vector bool long vec_cmplt (vector double, vector double);
vector double vec_cpsgn (vector double, vector double);
vector float vec_div (vector float, vector float);
vector double vec_div (vector double, vector double);
vector long vec_div (vector long, vector long);
vector unsigned long vec_div (vector unsigned long, vector unsigned long);
vector double vec_floor (vector double);
vector double vec_ld (int, const vector double *);
vector double vec_ld (int, const double *);
vector double vec_ldl (int, const vector double *);
vector double vec_ldl (int, const double *);
vector unsigned char vec_lvsl (int, const volatile double *);
vector unsigned char vec_lvsr (int, const volatile double *);
vector double vec_madd (vector double, vector double, vector double);
vector double vec_max (vector double, vector double);
vector signed long vec_mergeh (vector signed long, vector signed long);
vector signed long vec_mergeh (vector signed long, vector bool long);
vector signed long vec_mergeh (vector bool long, vector signed long);
vector unsigned long vec_mergeh (vector unsigned long, vector unsigned long);
vector unsigned long vec_mergeh (vector unsigned long, vector bool long);
vector unsigned long vec_mergeh (vector bool long, vector unsigned long);
vector signed long vec_mergel (vector signed long, vector signed long);
vector signed long vec_mergel (vector signed long, vector bool long);
vector signed long vec_mergel (vector bool long, vector signed long);
vector unsigned long vec_mergel (vector unsigned long, vector unsigned long);
vector unsigned long vec_mergel (vector unsigned long, vector bool long);
vector unsigned long vec_mergel (vector bool long, vector unsigned long);
vector double vec_min (vector double, vector double);
vector float vec_msub (vector float, vector float, vector float);
vector double vec_msub (vector double, vector double, vector double);
vector float vec_mul (vector float, vector float);
vector double vec_mul (vector double, vector double);
vector long vec_mul (vector long, vector long);
vector unsigned long vec_mul (vector unsigned long, vector unsigned long);
vector float vec_nearbyint (vector float);
vector double vec_nearbyint (vector double);
vector float vec_nmadd (vector float, vector float, vector float);
vector double vec_nmadd (vector double, vector double, vector double);
vector double vec_nmsub (vector double, vector double, vector double);
vector double vec_nor (vector double, vector double);
vector long vec_nor (vector long, vector long);
vector long vec_nor (vector long, vector bool long);
vector long vec_nor (vector bool long, vector long);
vector unsigned long vec_nor (vector unsigned long, vector unsigned long);
vector unsigned long vec_nor (vector unsigned long, vector bool long);
vector unsigned long vec_nor (vector bool long, vector unsigned long);
vector double vec_or (vector double, vector double);
vector double vec_or (vector double, vector bool long);
vector double vec_or (vector bool long, vector double);
vector long vec_or (vector long, vector long);
vector long vec_or (vector long, vector bool long);
```

```
vector long vec_or (vector bool long, vector long);
vector unsigned long vec_or (vector unsigned long, vector unsigned long);
vector unsigned long vec_or (vector unsigned long, vector bool long);
vector unsigned long vec_or (vector bool long, vector unsigned long);
vector double vec_perm (vector double, vector double, vector unsigned char);
vector long vec_perm (vector long, vector long, vector unsigned char);
vector unsigned long vec_perm (vector unsigned long, vector unsigned long,
                               vector unsigned char);
vector double vec_rint (vector double);
vector double vec_recip (vector double, vector double);
vector double vec_rsqrt (vector double);
vector double vec_rsqrte (vector double);
vector double vec_sel (vector double, vector double, vector bool long);
vector double vec_sel (vector double, vector double, vector unsigned long);
vector long vec_sel (vector long, vector long, vector long);
vector long vec_sel (vector long, vector long, vector unsigned long);
vector long vec_sel (vector long, vector long, vector bool long);
vector unsigned long vec_sel (vector unsigned long, vector unsigned long,
                              vector long);
vector unsigned long vec_sel (vector unsigned long, vector unsigned long,
                              vector unsigned long);
vector unsigned long vec_sel (vector unsigned long, vector unsigned long,
                              vector bool long);
vector double vec_splats (double);
vector signed long vec_splats (signed long);
vector unsigned long vec_splats (unsigned long);
vector float vec_sqrt (vector float);
vector double vec_sqrt (vector double);
void vec_st (vector double, int, vector double *);
void vec_st (vector double, int, double *);
vector double vec_sub (vector double, vector double);
vector double vec_trunc (vector double);
vector double vec_xl (int, vector double *);
vector double vec_xl (int, double *);
vector long long vec_xl (int, vector long long *);
vector long long vec_xl (int, long long *);
vector unsigned long long vec_xl (int, vector unsigned long long *);
vector unsigned long long vec_xl (int, unsigned long long *);
vector float vec_xl (int, vector float *);
vector float vec_xl (int, float *);
vector int vec_xl (int, vector int *);
vector int vec_xl (int, int *);
vector unsigned int vec_xl (int, vector unsigned int *);
vector unsigned int vec_xl (int, unsigned int *);
vector double vec_xor (vector double, vector double);
vector double vec_xor (vector double, vector bool long);
vector double vec_xor (vector bool long, vector double);
vector long vec_xor (vector long, vector long);
vector long vec_xor (vector long, vector bool long);
vector long vec_xor (vector bool long, vector long);
vector unsigned long vec_xor (vector unsigned long, vector unsigned long);
vector unsigned long vec_xor (vector unsigned long, vector bool long);
vector unsigned long vec_xor (vector bool long, vector unsigned long);
void vec_xst (vector double, int, vector double *);
void vec_xst (vector double, int, double *);
void vec_xst (vector long long, int, vector long long *);
void vec_xst (vector long long, int, long long *);
void vec_xst (vector unsigned long long, int, vector unsigned long long *);
```

```
void vec_xst (vector unsigned long long, int, unsigned long long *);
void vec_xst (vector float, int, vector float *);
void vec_xst (vector float, int, float *);
void vec_xst (vector int, int, vector int *);
void vec_xst (vector int, int, int *);
void vec_xst (vector unsigned int, int, vector unsigned int *);
void vec_xst (vector unsigned int, int, unsigned int *);
int vec_all_eq (vector double, vector double);
int vec_all_ge (vector double, vector double);
int vec_all_gt (vector double, vector double);
int vec_all_le (vector double, vector double);
int vec_all_lt (vector double, vector double);
int vec_all_nan (vector double);
int vec_all_ne (vector double, vector double);
int vec_all_nge (vector double, vector double);
int vec_all_ngt (vector double, vector double);
int vec_all_nle (vector double, vector double);
int vec_all_nlt (vector double, vector double);
int vec_all_numeric (vector double);
int vec_any_eq (vector double, vector double);
int vec_any_ge (vector double, vector double);
int vec_any_gt (vector double, vector double);
int vec_any_le (vector double, vector double);
int vec_any_lt (vector double, vector double);
int vec_any_nan (vector double);
int vec_any_ne (vector double, vector double);
int vec_any_nge (vector double, vector double);
int vec_any_ngt (vector double, vector double);
int vec_any_nle (vector double, vector double);
int vec_any_nlt (vector double, vector double);
int vec_any_numeric (vector double);

vector double vec_vsx_ld (int, const vector double *);
vector double vec_vsx_ld (int, const double *);
vector float vec_vsx_ld (int, const vector float *);
vector float vec_vsx_ld (int, const float *);
vector bool int vec_vsx_ld (int, const vector bool int *);
vector signed int vec_vsx_ld (int, const vector signed int *);
vector signed int vec_vsx_ld (int, const int *);
vector signed int vec_vsx_ld (int, const long *);
vector unsigned int vec_vsx_ld (int, const vector unsigned int *);
vector unsigned int vec_vsx_ld (int, const unsigned int *);
vector unsigned int vec_vsx_ld (int, const unsigned long *);
vector bool short vec_vsx_ld (int, const vector bool short *);
vector pixel vec_vsx_ld (int, const vector pixel *);
vector signed short vec_vsx_ld (int, const vector signed short *);
vector signed short vec_vsx_ld (int, const short *);
vector unsigned short vec_vsx_ld (int, const vector unsigned short *);
vector unsigned short vec_vsx_ld (int, const unsigned short *);
vector bool char vec_vsx_ld (int, const vector bool char *);
vector signed char vec_vsx_ld (int, const vector signed char *);
vector signed char vec_vsx_ld (int, const signed char *);
vector unsigned char vec_vsx_ld (int, const vector unsigned char *);
vector unsigned char vec_vsx_ld (int, const unsigned char *);

void vec_vsx_st (vector double, int, vector double *);
void vec_vsx_st (vector double, int, double *);
void vec_vsx_st (vector float, int, vector float *);
```

```
void vec_vsx_st (vector float, int, float *);
void vec_vsx_st (vector signed int, int, vector signed int *);
void vec_vsx_st (vector signed int, int, int *);
void vec_vsx_st (vector unsigned int, int, vector unsigned int *);
void vec_vsx_st (vector unsigned int, int, unsigned int *);
void vec_vsx_st (vector bool int, int, vector bool int *);
void vec_vsx_st (vector bool int, int, unsigned int *);
void vec_vsx_st (vector bool int, int, int *);
void vec_vsx_st (vector signed short, int, vector signed short *);
void vec_vsx_st (vector signed short, int, short *);
void vec_vsx_st (vector unsigned short, int, vector unsigned short *);
void vec_vsx_st (vector unsigned short, int, unsigned short *);
void vec_vsx_st (vector bool short, int, vector bool short *);
void vec_vsx_st (vector bool short, int, unsigned short *);
void vec_vsx_st (vector pixel, int, vector pixel *);
void vec_vsx_st (vector pixel, int, unsigned short *);
void vec_vsx_st (vector pixel, int, short *);
void vec_vsx_st (vector bool short, int, short *);
void vec_vsx_st (vector signed char, int, vector signed char *);
void vec_vsx_st (vector signed char, int, signed char *);
void vec_vsx_st (vector unsigned char, int, vector unsigned char *);
void vec_vsx_st (vector unsigned char, int, unsigned char *);
void vec_vsx_st (vector bool char, int, vector bool char *);
void vec_vsx_st (vector bool char, int, unsigned char *);
void vec_vsx_st (vector bool char, int, signed char *);

vector double vec_xxpermdi (vector double, vector double, int);
vector float vec_xxpermdi (vector float, vector float, int);
vector long long vec_xxpermdi (vector long long, vector long long, int);
vector unsigned long long vec_xxpermdi (vector unsigned long long,
                                         vector unsigned long long, int);
vector int vec_xxpermdi (vector int, vector int, int);
vector unsigned int vec_xxpermdi (vector unsigned int,
                                   vector unsigned int, int);
vector short vec_xxpermdi (vector short, vector short, int);
vector unsigned short vec_xxpermdi (vector unsigned short,
                                     vector unsigned short, int);
vector signed char vec_xxpermdi (vector signed char, vector signed char, int);
vector unsigned char vec_xxpermdi (vector unsigned char,
                                    vector unsigned char, int);

vector double vec_xxsldi (vector double, vector double, int);
vector float vec_xxsldi (vector float, vector float, int);
vector long long vec_xxsldi (vector long long, vector long long, int);
vector unsigned long long vec_xxsldi (vector unsigned long long,
                                       vector unsigned long long, int);
vector int vec_xxsldi (vector int, vector int, int);
vector unsigned int vec_xxsldi (vector unsigned int, vector unsigned int, int);
vector short vec_xxsldi (vector short, vector short, int);
vector unsigned short vec_xxsldi (vector unsigned short,
                                   vector unsigned short, int);
vector signed char vec_xxsldi (vector signed char, vector signed char, int);
vector unsigned char vec_xxsldi (vector unsigned char,
                                  vector unsigned char, int);
```

Note that the 'vec_ld' and 'vec_st' built-in functions always generate the AltiVec 'LVX' and 'STVX' instructions even if the VSX instruction set is available. The 'vec_vsx_ld' and 'vec_vsx_st' built-in functions always generate the VSX 'LXVD2X', 'LXVW4X', 'STXVD2X', and 'STXVW4X' instructions.

If the ISA 2.07 additions to the vector/scalar (power8-vector) instruction set are available, the following additional functions are available for both 32-bit and 64-bit targets. For 64-bit targets, you can use *vector long* instead of *vector long long*, *vector bool long* instead of *vector bool long long*, and *vector unsigned long* instead of *vector unsigned long long*.

```
vector long long vec_abs (vector long long);

vector long long vec_add (vector long long, vector long long);
vector unsigned long long vec_add (vector unsigned long long,
                                   vector unsigned long long);

int vec_all_eq (vector long long, vector long long);
int vec_all_eq (vector unsigned long long, vector unsigned long long);
int vec_all_ge (vector long long, vector long long);
int vec_all_ge (vector unsigned long long, vector unsigned long long);
int vec_all_gt (vector long long, vector long long);
int vec_all_gt (vector unsigned long long, vector unsigned long long);
int vec_all_le (vector long long, vector long long);
int vec_all_le (vector unsigned long long, vector unsigned long long);
int vec_all_lt (vector long long, vector long long);
int vec_all_lt (vector unsigned long long, vector unsigned long long);
int vec_all_ne (vector long long, vector long long);
int vec_all_ne (vector unsigned long long, vector unsigned long long);

int vec_any_eq (vector long long, vector long long);
int vec_any_eq (vector unsigned long long, vector unsigned long long);
int vec_any_ge (vector long long, vector long long);
int vec_any_ge (vector unsigned long long, vector unsigned long long);
int vec_any_gt (vector long long, vector long long);
int vec_any_gt (vector unsigned long long, vector unsigned long long);
int vec_any_le (vector long long, vector long long);
int vec_any_le (vector unsigned long long, vector unsigned long long);
int vec_any_lt (vector long long, vector long long);
int vec_any_lt (vector unsigned long long, vector unsigned long long);
int vec_any_ne (vector long long, vector long long);
int vec_any_ne (vector unsigned long long, vector unsigned long long);

vector bool long long vec_cmpeq (vector bool long long, vector bool long long);

vector long long vec_eqv (vector long long, vector long long);
vector long long vec_eqv (vector bool long long, vector long long);
vector long long vec_eqv (vector long long, vector bool long long);
vector unsigned long long vec_eqv (vector unsigned long long,
                                   vector unsigned long long);
vector unsigned long long vec_eqv (vector bool long long,
                                   vector unsigned long long);
vector unsigned long long vec_eqv (vector unsigned long long,
                                   vector bool long long);
vector int vec_eqv (vector int, vector int);
vector int vec_eqv (vector bool int, vector int);
vector int vec_eqv (vector int, vector bool int);
vector unsigned int vec_eqv (vector unsigned int, vector unsigned int);
vector unsigned int vec_eqv (vector bool unsigned int,
                             vector unsigned int);
vector unsigned int vec_eqv (vector unsigned int,
                             vector bool unsigned int);
```

```
vector short vec_eqv (vector short, vector short);
vector short vec_eqv (vector bool short, vector short);
vector short vec_eqv (vector short, vector bool short);
vector unsigned short vec_eqv (vector unsigned short, vector unsigned short);
vector unsigned short vec_eqv (vector bool unsigned short,
                               vector unsigned short);
vector unsigned short vec_eqv (vector unsigned short,
                               vector bool unsigned short);
vector signed char vec_eqv (vector signed char, vector signed char);
vector signed char vec_eqv (vector bool signed char, vector signed char);
vector signed char vec_eqv (vector signed char, vector bool signed char);
vector unsigned char vec_eqv (vector unsigned char, vector unsigned char);
vector unsigned char vec_eqv (vector bool unsigned char, vector unsigned char);
vector unsigned char vec_eqv (vector unsigned char, vector bool unsigned char);

vector long long vec_max (vector long long, vector long long);
vector unsigned long long vec_max (vector unsigned long long,
                                   vector unsigned long long);

vector signed int vec_mergee (vector signed int, vector signed int);
vector unsigned int vec_mergee (vector unsigned int, vector unsigned int);
vector bool int vec_mergee (vector bool int, vector bool int);

vector signed int vec_mergeo (vector signed int, vector signed int);
vector unsigned int vec_mergeo (vector unsigned int, vector unsigned int);
vector bool int vec_mergeo (vector bool int, vector bool int);

vector long long vec_min (vector long long, vector long long);
vector unsigned long long vec_min (vector unsigned long long,
                                   vector unsigned long long);

vector long long vec_nand (vector long long, vector long long);
vector long long vec_nand (vector bool long long, vector long long);
vector long long vec_nand (vector long long, vector bool long long);
vector unsigned long long vec_nand (vector unsigned long long,
                                    vector unsigned long long);
vector unsigned long long vec_nand (vector bool long long,
                                    vector unsigned long long);
vector unsigned long long vec_nand (vector unsigned long long,
                                    vector bool long long);
vector int vec_nand (vector int, vector int);
vector int vec_nand (vector bool int, vector int);
vector int vec_nand (vector int, vector bool int);
vector unsigned int vec_nand (vector unsigned int, vector unsigned int);
vector unsigned int vec_nand (vector bool unsigned int,
                              vector unsigned int);
vector unsigned int vec_nand (vector unsigned int,
                              vector bool unsigned int);
vector short vec_nand (vector short, vector short);
vector short vec_nand (vector bool short, vector short);
vector short vec_nand (vector short, vector bool short);
vector unsigned short vec_nand (vector unsigned short, vector unsigned short);
vector unsigned short vec_nand (vector bool unsigned short,
                                vector unsigned short);
vector unsigned short vec_nand (vector unsigned short,
                                vector bool unsigned short);
vector signed char vec_nand (vector signed char, vector signed char);
vector signed char vec_nand (vector bool signed char, vector signed char);
```

```
vector signed char vec_nand (vector signed char, vector bool signed char);
vector unsigned char vec_nand (vector unsigned char, vector unsigned char);
vector unsigned char vec_nand (vector bool unsigned char, vector unsigned char);
vector unsigned char vec_nand (vector unsigned char, vector bool unsigned char);

vector long long vec_orc (vector long long, vector long long);
vector long long vec_orc (vector bool long long, vector long long);
vector long long vec_orc (vector long long, vector bool long long);
vector unsigned long long vec_orc (vector unsigned long long,
                                   vector unsigned long long);
vector unsigned long long vec_orc (vector bool long long,
                                   vector unsigned long long);
vector unsigned long long vec_orc (vector unsigned long long,
                                   vector bool long long);
vector int vec_orc (vector int, vector int);
vector int vec_orc (vector bool int, vector int);
vector int vec_orc (vector int, vector bool int);
vector unsigned int vec_orc (vector unsigned int, vector unsigned int);
vector unsigned int vec_orc (vector bool unsigned int,
                             vector unsigned int);
vector unsigned int vec_orc (vector unsigned int,
                             vector bool unsigned int);
vector short vec_orc (vector short, vector short);
vector short vec_orc (vector bool short, vector short);
vector short vec_orc (vector short, vector bool short);
vector unsigned short vec_orc (vector unsigned short, vector unsigned short);
vector unsigned short vec_orc (vector bool unsigned short,
                               vector unsigned short);
vector unsigned short vec_orc (vector unsigned short,
                               vector bool unsigned short);
vector signed char vec_orc (vector signed char, vector signed char);
vector signed char vec_orc (vector bool signed char, vector signed char);
vector signed char vec_orc (vector signed char, vector bool signed char);
vector unsigned char vec_orc (vector unsigned char, vector unsigned char);
vector unsigned char vec_orc (vector bool unsigned char, vector unsigned char);
vector unsigned char vec_orc (vector unsigned char, vector bool unsigned char);

vector int vec_pack (vector long long, vector long long);
vector unsigned int vec_pack (vector unsigned long long,
                              vector unsigned long long);
vector bool int vec_pack (vector bool long long, vector bool long long);

vector int vec_packs (vector long long, vector long long);
vector unsigned int vec_packs (vector unsigned long long,
                               vector unsigned long long);

vector unsigned int vec_packsu (vector long long, vector long long);
vector unsigned int vec_packsu (vector unsigned long long,
                                vector unsigned long long);

vector long long vec_rl (vector long long,
                         vector unsigned long long);
vector long long vec_rl (vector unsigned long long,
                         vector unsigned long long);

vector long long vec_sl (vector long long, vector unsigned long long);
vector long long vec_sl (vector unsigned long long,
                         vector unsigned long long);
```

```
vector long long vec_sr (vector long long, vector unsigned long long);
vector unsigned long long char vec_sr (vector unsigned long long,
                                       vector unsigned long long);

vector long long vec_sra (vector long long, vector unsigned long long);
vector unsigned long long vec_sra (vector unsigned long long,
                                   vector unsigned long long);

vector long long vec_sub (vector long long, vector long long);
vector unsigned long long vec_sub (vector unsigned long long,
                                   vector unsigned long long);

vector long long vec_unpackh (vector int);
vector unsigned long long vec_unpackh (vector unsigned int);

vector long long vec_unpackl (vector int);
vector unsigned long long vec_unpackl (vector unsigned int);

vector long long vec_vaddudm (vector long long, vector long long);
vector long long vec_vaddudm (vector bool long long, vector long long);
vector long long vec_vaddudm (vector long long, vector bool long long);
vector unsigned long long vec_vaddudm (vector unsigned long long,
                                       vector unsigned long long);
vector unsigned long long vec_vaddudm (vector bool unsigned long long,
                                       vector unsigned long long);
vector unsigned long long vec_vaddudm (vector unsigned long long,
                                       vector bool unsigned long long);

vector long long vec_vbpermq (vector signed char, vector signed char);
vector long long vec_vbpermq (vector unsigned char, vector unsigned char);

vector long long vec_cntlz (vector long long);
vector unsigned long long vec_cntlz (vector unsigned long long);
vector int vec_cntlz (vector int);
vector unsigned int vec_cntlz (vector int);
vector short vec_cntlz (vector short);
vector unsigned short vec_cntlz (vector unsigned short);
vector signed char vec_cntlz (vector signed char);
vector unsigned char vec_cntlz (vector unsigned char);

vector long long vec_vclz (vector long long);
vector unsigned long long vec_vclz (vector unsigned long long);
vector int vec_vclz (vector int);
vector unsigned int vec_vclz (vector int);
vector short vec_vclz (vector short);
vector unsigned short vec_vclz (vector unsigned short);
vector signed char vec_vclz (vector signed char);
vector unsigned char vec_vclz (vector unsigned char);

vector signed char vec_vclzb (vector signed char);
vector unsigned char vec_vclzb (vector unsigned char);

vector long long vec_vclzd (vector long long);
vector unsigned long long vec_vclzd (vector unsigned long long);

vector short vec_vclzh (vector short);
vector unsigned short vec_vclzh (vector unsigned short);
```

```
vector int vec_vclzw (vector int);
vector unsigned int vec_vclzw (vector int);

vector signed char vec_vgbbd (vector signed char);
vector unsigned char vec_vgbbd (vector unsigned char);

vector long long vec_vmaxsd (vector long long, vector long long);

vector unsigned long long vec_vmaxud (vector unsigned long long,
                                      unsigned vector long long);

vector long long vec_vminsd (vector long long, vector long long);

vector unsigned long long vec_vminud (vector long long,
                                      vector long long);

vector int vec_vpksdss (vector long long, vector long long);
vector unsigned int vec_vpksdss (vector long long, vector long long);

vector unsigned int vec_vpkudus (vector unsigned long long,
                                 vector unsigned long long);

vector int vec_vpkudum (vector long long, vector long long);
vector unsigned int vec_vpkudum (vector unsigned long long,
                                 vector unsigned long long);
vector bool int vec_vpkudum (vector bool long long, vector bool long long);

vector long long vec_vpopcnt (vector long long);
vector unsigned long long vec_vpopcnt (vector unsigned long long);
vector int vec_vpopcnt (vector int);
vector unsigned int vec_vpopcnt (vector int);
vector short vec_vpopcnt (vector short);
vector unsigned short vec_vpopcnt (vector unsigned short);
vector signed char vec_vpopcnt (vector signed char);
vector unsigned char vec_vpopcnt (vector unsigned char);

vector signed char vec_vpopcntb (vector signed char);
vector unsigned char vec_vpopcntb (vector unsigned char);

vector long long vec_vpopcntd (vector long long);
vector unsigned long long vec_vpopcntd (vector unsigned long long);

vector short vec_vpopcnth (vector short);
vector unsigned short vec_vpopcnth (vector unsigned short);

vector int vec_vpopcntw (vector int);
vector unsigned int vec_vpopcntw (vector int);

vector long long vec_vrld (vector long long, vector unsigned long long);
vector unsigned long long vec_vrld (vector unsigned long long,
                                    vector unsigned long long);

vector long long vec_vsld (vector long long, vector unsigned long long);
vector long long vec_vsld (vector unsigned long long,
                           vector unsigned long long);

vector long long vec_vsrad (vector long long, vector unsigned long long);
```

```
vector unsigned long long vec_vsrad (vector unsigned long long,
                                     vector unsigned long long);

vector long long vec_vsrd (vector long long, vector unsigned long long);
vector unsigned long long char vec_vsrd (vector unsigned long long,
                                         vector unsigned long long);

vector long long vec_vsubudm (vector long long, vector long long);
vector long long vec_vsubudm (vector bool long long, vector long long);
vector long long vec_vsubudm (vector long long, vector bool long long);
vector unsigned long long vec_vsubudm (vector unsigned long long,
                                       vector unsigned long long);
vector unsigned long long vec_vsubudm (vector bool long long,
                                       vector unsigned long long);
vector unsigned long long vec_vsubudm (vector unsigned long long,
                                       vector bool long long);

vector long long vec_vupkhsw (vector int);
vector unsigned long long vec_vupkhsw (vector unsigned int);

vector long long vec_vupklsw (vector int);
vector unsigned long long vec_vupklsw (vector int);
```

If the ISA 2.07 additions to the vector/scalar (power8-vector) instruction set are available, the following additional functions are available for 64-bit targets. New vector types (*vector __int128_t* and *vector __uint128_t*) are available to hold the *__int128_t* and *__uint128_t* types to use these builtins.

The normal vector extract, and set operations work on *vector __int128_t* and *vector __uint128_t* types, but the index value must be 0.

```
vector __int128_t vec_vaddcuq (vector __int128_t, vector __int128_t);
vector __uint128_t vec_vaddcuq (vector __uint128_t, vector __uint128_t);

vector __int128_t vec_vadduqm (vector __int128_t, vector __int128_t);
vector __uint128_t vec_vadduqm (vector __uint128_t, vector __uint128_t);

vector __int128_t vec_vaddecuq (vector __int128_t, vector __int128_t,
                                vector __int128_t);
vector __uint128_t vec_vaddecuq (vector __uint128_t, vector __uint128_t,
                                 vector __uint128_t);

vector __int128_t vec_vaddeuqm (vector __int128_t, vector __int128_t,
                                vector __int128_t);
vector __uint128_t vec_vaddeuqm (vector __uint128_t, vector __uint128_t,
                                 vector __uint128_t);

vector __int128_t vec_vsubecuq (vector __int128_t, vector __int128_t,
                                vector __int128_t);
vector __uint128_t vec_vsubecuq (vector __uint128_t, vector __uint128_t,
                                 vector __uint128_t);

vector __int128_t vec_vsubeuqm (vector __int128_t, vector __int128_t,
                                vector __int128_t);
vector __uint128_t vec_vsubeuqm (vector __uint128_t, vector __uint128_t,
                                 vector __uint128_t);

vector __int128_t vec_vsubcuq (vector __int128_t, vector __int128_t);
vector __uint128_t vec_vsubcuq (vector __uint128_t, vector __uint128_t);
```

```
__int128_t vec_vsubuqm (__int128_t, __int128_t);
__uint128_t vec_vsubuqm (__uint128_t, __uint128_t);

vector __int128_t __builtin_bcdadd (vector __int128_t, vector__int128_t);
int __builtin_bcdadd_lt (vector __int128_t, vector__int128_t);
int __builtin_bcdadd_eq (vector __int128_t, vector__int128_t);
int __builtin_bcdadd_gt (vector __int128_t, vector__int128_t);
int __builtin_bcdadd_ov (vector __int128_t, vector__int128_t);
vector __int128_t bcdsub (vector __int128_t, vector__int128_t);
int __builtin_bcdsub_lt (vector __int128_t, vector__int128_t);
int __builtin_bcdsub_eq (vector __int128_t, vector__int128_t);
int __builtin_bcdsub_gt (vector __int128_t, vector__int128_t);
int __builtin_bcdsub_ov (vector __int128_t, vector__int128_t);
```

If the ISA 3.0 instruction set additions ('-mcpu=power9') are available:

```
vector bool char vec_cmpne (vector bool char, vector bool char);
vector bool short vec_cmpne (vector bool short, vector bool short);
vector bool int vec_cmpne (vector bool int, vector bool int);
vector bool long long vec_cmpne (vector bool long long, vector bool long long);

vector long long vec_vctz (vector long long);
vector unsigned long long vec_vctz (vector unsigned long long);
vector int vec_vctz (vector int);
vector unsigned int vec_vctz (vector int);
vector short vec_vctz (vector short);
vector unsigned short vec_vctz (vector unsigned short);
vector signed char vec_vctz (vector signed char);
vector unsigned char vec_vctz (vector unsigned char);

vector signed char vec_vctzb (vector signed char);
vector unsigned char vec_vctzb (vector unsigned char);

vector long long vec_vctzd (vector long long);
vector unsigned long long vec_vctzd (vector unsigned long long);

vector short vec_vctzh (vector short);
vector unsigned short vec_vctzh (vector unsigned short);

vector int vec_vctzw (vector int);
vector unsigned int vec_vctzw (vector int);

vector int vec_vprtyb (vector int);
vector unsigned int vec_vprtyb (vector unsigned int);
vector long long vec_vprtyb (vector long long);
vector unsigned long long vec_vprtyb (vector unsigned long long);

vector int vec_vprtybw (vector int);
vector unsigned int vec_vprtybw (vector unsigned int);

vector long long vec_vprtybd (vector long long);
vector unsigned long long vec_vprtybd (vector unsigned long long);
```

On 64-bit targets, if the ISA 3.0 additions ('-mcpu=power9') are available:

```
vector long vec_vprtyb (vector long);
vector unsigned long vec_vprtyb (vector unsigned long);
vector __int128_t vec_vprtyb (vector __int128_t);
vector __uint128_t vec_vprtyb (vector __uint128_t);
```

```
vector long vec_vprtybd (vector long);
vector unsigned long vec_vprtybd (vector unsigned long);

vector __int128_t vec_vprtybq (vector __int128_t);
vector __uint128_t vec_vprtybd (vector __uint128_t);
```

The following built-in vector functions are available for the PowerPC family of processors, starting with ISA 3.0 or later ('-mcpu=power9'):

```
__vector unsigned char
vec_slv (__vector unsigned char src, __vector unsigned char shift_distance);
__vector unsigned char
vec_srv (__vector unsigned char src, __vector unsigned char shift_distance);
```

The vec_slv and vec_srv functions operate on all of the bytes of their src and shift_distance arguments in parallel. The behavior of the vec_slv is as if there existed a temporary array of 17 unsigned characters slv_array within which elements 0 through 15 are the same as the entries in the src array and element 16 equals 0. The result returned from the vec_slv function is a __vector of 16 unsigned characters within which element i is computed using the C expression 0xff & (*((unsigned short *)(slv_array + i)) << (0x07 & shift_distance[i])), with this resulting value coerced to the unsigned char type. The behavior of the vec_srv is as if there existed a temporary array of 17 unsigned characters srv_array within which element 0 equals zero and elements 1 through 16 equal the elements 0 through 15 of the src array. The result returned from the vec_srv function is a __vector of 16 unsigned characters within which element i is computed using the C expression 0xff & (*((unsigned short *)(srv_array + i)) >> (0x07 & shift_distance[i])), with this resulting value coerced to the unsigned char type.

The following built-in functions are available for the PowerPC family of processors, starting with ISA 3.0 or later ('-mcpu=power9'):

```
__vector unsigned char
vec_absd (__vector unsigned char arg1, __vector unsigned char arg2);
__vector unsigned short
vec_absd (__vector unsigned short arg1, __vector unsigned short arg2);
__vector unsigned int
vec_absd (__vector unsigned int arg1, __vector unsigned int arg2);

__vector unsigned char
vec_absdb (__vector unsigned char arg1, __vector unsigned char arg2);
__vector unsigned short
vec_absdh (__vector unsigned short arg1, __vector unsigned short arg2);
__vector unsigned int
vec_absdw (__vector unsigned int arg1, __vector unsigned int arg2);
```

The vec_absd, vec_absdb, vec_absdh, and vec_absdw built-in functions each computes the absolute differences of the pairs of vector elements supplied in its two vector arguments, placing the absolute differences into the corresponding elements of the vector result.

The following built-in functions are available for the PowerPC family of processors, starting with ISA 3.0 or later ('-mcpu=power9'):

```
__vector int
vec_extract_exp (__vector float source);
__vector long long int
vec_extract_exp (__vector double source);

__vector int
vec_extract_sig (__vector float source);
```

```
__vector long long int
vec_extract_sig (__vector double source);

__vector float
vec_insert_exp (__vector unsigned int significands,  __vector unsigned int exponents);
__vector double
vec_insert_exp (__vector unsigned long long int significands,
                __vector unsigned long long int exponents);

__vector int vec_test_data_class (__vector float source, unsigned int condition);
__vector long long int vec_test_data_class (__vector double source, unsigned int condition);
```

The `vec_extract_sig` and `vec_extract_exp` built-in functions return vectors repre-
senting the significands and exponents of their `source` arguments respectively. The `vec_insert_exp` built-in functions return a vector of single- or double-precision floating point
values constructed by assembling the values of their `significands` and `exponents` argu-
ments into the corresponding elements of the returned vector. The sign of each element
of the result is copied from the most significant bit of the corresponding entry within the
`significands` argument. The significand and exponent components of each element of the
result are composed of the least significant bits of the corresponding `significands` element
and the least significant bits of the corresponding `exponents` element.

The `vec_test_data_class` built-in function returns a vector representing the results
of testing the `source` vector for the condition selected by the `condition` argument. The
`condition` argument must be an unsigned integer with value not exceeding 127. The
`condition` argument is encoded as a bitmask with each bit enabling the testing of a different
condition, as characterized by the following:

```
0x40      Test for NaN
0x20      Test for +Infinity
0x10      Test for -Infinity
0x08      Test for +Zero
0x04      Test for -Zero
0x02      Test for +Denormal
0x01      Test for -Denormal
```

If any of the enabled test conditions is true, the corresponding entry in the result vector
is -1. Otherwise (all of the enabled test conditions are false), the corresponding entry of the
result vector is 0.

If the cryptographic instructions are enabled ('-mcrypto' or '-mcpu=power8'), the following builtins are enabled.

```
vector unsigned long long __builtin_crypto_vsbox (vector unsigned long long);

vector unsigned long long __builtin_crypto_vcipher (vector unsigned long long,
                                                    vector unsigned long long);

vector unsigned long long __builtin_crypto_vcipherlast
                               (vector unsigned long long,
                                vector unsigned long long);

vector unsigned long long __builtin_crypto_vncipher (vector unsigned long long,
                                                     vector unsigned long long);

vector unsigned long long __builtin_crypto_vncipherlast
                               (vector unsigned long long,
                                vector unsigned long long);
```

```
vector unsigned char __builtin_crypto_vpermxor (vector unsigned char,
                                                vector unsigned char,
                                                vector unsigned char);

vector unsigned short __builtin_crypto_vpermxor (vector unsigned short,
                                                 vector unsigned short,
                                                 vector unsigned short);

vector unsigned int __builtin_crypto_vpermxor (vector unsigned int,
                                               vector unsigned int,
                                               vector unsigned int);

vector unsigned long long __builtin_crypto_vpermxor (vector unsigned long long,
                                                     vector unsigned long long,
                                                     vector unsigned long long);

vector unsigned char __builtin_crypto_vpmsumb (vector unsigned char,
                                               vector unsigned char);

vector unsigned short __builtin_crypto_vpmsumb (vector unsigned short,
                                                vector unsigned short);

vector unsigned int __builtin_crypto_vpmsumb (vector unsigned int,
                                              vector unsigned int);

vector unsigned long long __builtin_crypto_vpmsumb (vector unsigned long long,
                                                    vector unsigned long long);

vector unsigned long long __builtin_crypto_vshasigmad
                              (vector unsigned long long, int, int);

vector unsigned int __builtin_crypto_vshasigmaw (vector unsigned int,
                                                 int, int);
```

The second argument to the _ _*builtin_ crypto_ vshasigmad* and _ _*builtin_ crypto_ vshasigmaw*■
builtin functions must be a constant integer that is 0 or 1. The third argument to these
builtin functions must be a constant integer in the range of 0 to 15.

If the ISA 3.0 instruction set additions are enabled ('-mcpu=power9'), the following additional functions are available for both 32-bit and 64-bit targets.

vector short vec_xl (int, vector short *); vector short vec_xl (int, short *); vector unsigned short vec_xl (int, vector unsigned short *); vector unsigned short vec_xl (int, unsigned short *); vector char vec_xl (int, vector char *); vector char vec_xl (int, char *); vector unsigned char vec_xl (int, vector unsigned char *); vector unsigned char vec_xl (int, unsigned char *);

void vec_xst (vector short, int, vector short *); void vec_xst (vector short, int, short *); void vec_xst (vector unsigned short, int, vector unsigned short *); void vec_xst (vector unsigned short, int, unsigned short *); void vec_xst (vector char, int, vector char *); void vec_xst (vector char, int, char *); void vec_xst (vector unsigned char, int, vector unsigned char *); void vec_xst (vector unsigned char, int, unsigned char *);

6.60.23 PowerPC Hardware Transactional Memory Built-in Functions

GCC provides two interfaces for accessing the Hardware Transactional Memory (HTM) instructions available on some of the PowerPC family of processors (eg, POWER8). The two interfaces come in a low level interface, consisting of built-in functions specific to PowerPC and a higher level interface consisting of inline functions that are common between PowerPC and S/390.

6.60.23.1 PowerPC HTM Low Level Built-in Functions

The following low level built-in functions are available with '-mhtm' or '-mcpu=CPU' where CPU is 'power8' or later. They all generate the machine instruction that is part of the name.

The HTM builtins (with the exception of `__builtin_tbegin`) return the full 4-bit condition register value set by their associated hardware instruction. The header file `htmintrin.h` defines some macros that can be used to decipher the return value. The `__builtin_tbegin` builtin returns a simple true or false value depending on whether a transaction was successfully started or not. The arguments of the builtins match exactly the type and order of the associated hardware instruction's operands, except for the `__builtin_tcheck` builtin, which does not take any input arguments. Refer to the ISA manual for a description of each instruction's operands.

```
unsigned int __builtin_tbegin (unsigned int)
unsigned int __builtin_tend (unsigned int)

unsigned int __builtin_tabort (unsigned int)
unsigned int __builtin_tabortdc (unsigned int, unsigned int, unsigned int)
unsigned int __builtin_tabortdci (unsigned int, unsigned int, int)
unsigned int __builtin_tabortwc (unsigned int, unsigned int, unsigned int)
unsigned int __builtin_tabortwci (unsigned int, unsigned int, int)

unsigned int __builtin_tcheck (void)
unsigned int __builtin_treclaim (unsigned int)
unsigned int __builtin_trechkpt (void)
unsigned int __builtin_tsr (unsigned int)
```

In addition to the above HTM built-ins, we have added built-ins for some common extended mnemonics of the HTM instructions:

```
unsigned int __builtin_tendall (void)
unsigned int __builtin_tresume (void)
unsigned int __builtin_tsuspend (void)
```

Note that the semantics of the above HTM builtins are required to mimic the locking semantics used for critical sections. Builtins that are used to create a new transaction or restart a suspended transaction must have lock acquisition like semantics while those builtins that end or suspend a transaction must have lock release like semantics. Specifically, this must mimic lock semantics as specified by C++11, for example: Lock acquisition is as-if an execution of __atomic_exchange_n(&globallock,1,__ATOMIC_ACQUIRE) that returns 0, and lock release is as-if an execution of __atomic_store(&globallock,0,__ATOMIC_RELEASE), with globallock being an implicit implementation-defined lock used for all transactions. The HTM instructions associated with with the builtins inherently provide the correct acquisition and release hardware barriers required. However, the compiler must also be prohibited from moving loads and stores across the builtins in a way that would violate their semantics. This has been accomplished by adding memory barriers to the associated HTM instructions (which is a conservative approach to provide acquire and release semantics). Earlier versions of the compiler did not treat the HTM instructions as memory barriers. A `__TM_FENCE__` macro has been added, which can be used to determine whether the current compiler treats HTM instructions as memory barriers or not. This allows the user to explicitly add memory barriers to their code when using an older version of the compiler.

The following set of built-in functions are available to gain access to the HTM specific special purpose registers.

```
unsigned long __builtin_get_texasr (void)
unsigned long __builtin_get_texasru (void)
unsigned long __builtin_get_tfhar (void)
unsigned long __builtin_get_tfiar (void)

void __builtin_set_texasr (unsigned long);
void __builtin_set_texasru (unsigned long);
void __builtin_set_tfhar (unsigned long);
void __builtin_set_tfiar (unsigned long);
```

Example usage of these low level built-in functions may look like:

```
#include <htmintrin.h>

int num_retries = 10;

while (1)
  {
    if (__builtin_tbegin (0))
      {
        /* Transaction State Initiated.  */
        if (is_locked (lock))
          __builtin_tabort (0);
        ... transaction code...
        __builtin_tend (0);
        break;
      }
    else
      {
        /* Transaction State Failed.  Use locks if the transaction
           failure is "persistent" or we've tried too many times.  */
        if (num_retries-- <= 0
            || _TEXASRU_FAILURE_PERSISTENT (__builtin_get_texasru ()))
          {
            acquire_lock (lock);
            ... non transactional fallback path...
            release_lock (lock);
            break;
          }
      }
  }
```

One final built-in function has been added that returns the value of the 2-bit Transaction State field of the Machine Status Register (MSR) as stored in CR0.

```
unsigned long __builtin_ttest (void)
```

This built-in can be used to determine the current transaction state using the following code example:

```
#include <htmintrin.h>

unsigned char tx_state = _HTM_STATE (__builtin_ttest ());

if (tx_state == _HTM_TRANSACTIONAL)
  {
    /* Code to use in transactional state.  */
  }
else if (tx_state == _HTM_NONTRANSACTIONAL)
  {
    /* Code to use in non-transactional state.  */
  }
else if (tx_state == _HTM_SUSPENDED)
  {
    /* Code to use in transaction suspended state.  */
  }
```

6.60.23.2 PowerPC HTM High Level Inline Functions

The following high level HTM interface is made available by including `<htmxlintrin.h>`
and using '-mhtm' or '-mcpu=CPU' where CPU is 'power8' or later. This interface is common
between PowerPC and S/390, allowing users to write one HTM source implementation that
can be compiled and executed on either system.

```
long __TM_simple_begin (void)
long __TM_begin (void* const TM_buff)
long __TM_end (void)
void __TM_abort (void)
void __TM_named_abort (unsigned char const code)
void __TM_resume (void)
void __TM_suspend (void)

long __TM_is_user_abort (void* const TM_buff)
long __TM_is_named_user_abort (void* const TM_buff, unsigned char *code)
long __TM_is_illegal (void* const TM_buff)
long __TM_is_footprint_exceeded (void* const TM_buff)
long __TM_nesting_depth (void* const TM_buff)
long __TM_is_nested_too_deep(void* const TM_buff)
long __TM_is_conflict(void* const TM_buff)
long __TM_is_failure_persistent(void* const TM_buff)
long __TM_failure_address(void* const TM_buff)
long long __TM_failure_code(void* const TM_buff)
```

Using these common set of HTM inline functions, we can create a more portable version
of the HTM example in the previous section that will work on either PowerPC or S/390:

```
#include <htmxlintrin.h>

int num_retries = 10;
TM_buff_type TM_buff;

while (1)
  {
    if (__TM_begin (TM_buff) == _HTM_TBEGIN_STARTED)
      {
        /* Transaction State Initiated.  */
        if (is_locked (lock))
          __TM_abort ();
        ... transaction code...
        __TM_end ();
```

```
        break;
      }
    else
      {
        /* Transaction State Failed.  Use locks if the transaction
           failure is "persistent" or we've tried too many times.  */
        if (num_retries-- <= 0
            || __TM_is_failure_persistent (TM_buff))
          {
            acquire_lock (lock);
            ... non transactional fallback path...
            release_lock (lock);
            break;
          }
      }
  }
```

6.60.24 RX Built-in Functions

GCC supports some of the RX instructions which cannot be expressed in the C programming language via the use of built-in functions. The following functions are supported:

void __builtin_rx_brk (*void*)   [Built-in Function]
> Generates the brk machine instruction.

void __builtin_rx_clrpsw (*int*)   [Built-in Function]
> Generates the clrpsw machine instruction to clear the specified bit in the processor status word.

void __builtin_rx_int (*int*)   [Built-in Function]
> Generates the int machine instruction to generate an interrupt with the specified value.

void __builtin_rx_machi (*int, int*)   [Built-in Function]
> Generates the machi machine instruction to add the result of multiplying the top 16 bits of the two arguments into the accumulator.

void __builtin_rx_maclo (*int, int*)   [Built-in Function]
> Generates the maclo machine instruction to add the result of multiplying the bottom 16 bits of the two arguments into the accumulator.

void __builtin_rx_mulhi (*int, int*)   [Built-in Function]
> Generates the mulhi machine instruction to place the result of multiplying the top 16 bits of the two arguments into the accumulator.

void __builtin_rx_mullo (*int, int*)   [Built-in Function]
> Generates the mullo machine instruction to place the result of multiplying the bottom 16 bits of the two arguments into the accumulator.

int __builtin_rx_mvfachi (*void*)   [Built-in Function]
> Generates the mvfachi machine instruction to read the top 32 bits of the accumulator.

int __builtin_rx_mvfacmi (*void*)   [Built-in Function]
> Generates the mvfacmi machine instruction to read the middle 32 bits of the accumulator.

`int __builtin_rx_mvfc` (*int*)   [Built-in Function]

> Generates the `mvfc` machine instruction which reads the control register specified in its argument and returns its value.

`void __builtin_rx_mvtachi` (*int*)   [Built-in Function]

> Generates the `mvtachi` machine instruction to set the top 32 bits of the accumulator.

`void __builtin_rx_mvtaclo` (*int*)   [Built-in Function]

> Generates the `mvtaclo` machine instruction to set the bottom 32 bits of the accumulator.

`void __builtin_rx_mvtc` (*int reg, int val*)   [Built-in Function]

> Generates the `mvtc` machine instruction which sets control register number `reg` to `val`.

`void __builtin_rx_mvtipl` (*int*)   [Built-in Function]

> Generates the `mvtipl` machine instruction set the interrupt priority level.

`void __builtin_rx_racw` (*int*)   [Built-in Function]

> Generates the `racw` machine instruction to round the accumulator according to the specified mode.

`int __builtin_rx_revw` (*int*)   [Built-in Function]

> Generates the `revw` machine instruction which swaps the bytes in the argument so that bits 0–7 now occupy bits 8–15 and vice versa, and also bits 16–23 occupy bits 24–31 and vice versa.

`void __builtin_rx_rmpa` (*void*)   [Built-in Function]

> Generates the `rmpa` machine instruction which initiates a repeated multiply and accumulate sequence.

`void __builtin_rx_round` (*float*)   [Built-in Function]

> Generates the `round` machine instruction which returns the floating-point argument rounded according to the current rounding mode set in the floating-point status word register.

`int __builtin_rx_sat` (*int*)   [Built-in Function]

> Generates the `sat` machine instruction which returns the saturated value of the argument.

`void __builtin_rx_setpsw` (*int*)   [Built-in Function]

> Generates the `setpsw` machine instruction to set the specified bit in the processor status word.

`void __builtin_rx_wait` (*void*)   [Built-in Function]

> Generates the `wait` machine instruction.

6.60.25 S/390 System z Built-in Functions

`int __builtin_tbegin` (*void**)   [Built-in Function]

Generates the `tbegin` machine instruction starting a non-constrained hardware transaction. If the parameter is non-NULL the memory area is used to store the transaction diagnostic buffer and will be passed as first operand to `tbegin`. This buffer can be defined using the `struct __htm_tdb` C struct defined in `htmintrin.h` and must reside on a double-word boundary. The second tbegin operand is set to `0xff0c`. This enables save/restore of all GPRs and disables aborts for FPR and AR manipulations inside the transaction body. The condition code set by the tbegin instruction is returned as integer value. The tbegin instruction by definition overwrites the content of all FPRs. The compiler will generate code which saves and restores the FPRs. For soft-float code it is recommended to used the `*_nofloat` variant. In order to prevent a TDB from being written it is required to pass a constant zero value as parameter. Passing a zero value through a variable is not sufficient. Although modifications of access registers inside the transaction will not trigger an transaction abort it is not supported to actually modify them. Access registers do not get saved when entering a transaction. They will have undefined state when reaching the abort code.

Macros for the possible return codes of tbegin are defined in the `htmintrin.h` header file:

`_HTM_TBEGIN_STARTED`

`tbegin` has been executed as part of normal processing. The transaction body is supposed to be executed.

`_HTM_TBEGIN_INDETERMINATE`

The transaction was aborted due to an indeterminate condition which might be persistent.

`_HTM_TBEGIN_TRANSIENT`

The transaction aborted due to a transient failure. The transaction should be re-executed in that case.

`_HTM_TBEGIN_PERSISTENT`

The transaction aborted due to a persistent failure. Re-execution under same circumstances will not be productive.

`_HTM_FIRST_USER_ABORT_CODE`   [Macro]

The `_HTM_FIRST_USER_ABORT_CODE` defined in `htmintrin.h` specifies the first abort code which can be used for `__builtin_tabort`. Values below this threshold are reserved for machine use.

`struct __htm_tdb`   [Data type]

The `struct __htm_tdb` defined in `htmintrin.h` describes the structure of the transaction diagnostic block as specified in the Principles of Operation manual chapter 5-91.

`int __builtin_tbegin_nofloat` (*void**)   [Built-in Function]

Same as `__builtin_tbegin` but without FPR saves and restores. Using this variant in code making use of FPRs will leave the FPRs in undefined state when entering the transaction abort handler code.

int __builtin_tbegin_retry (*void**, *int*)   [Built-in Function]
> In addition to __builtin_tbegin a loop for transient failures is generated. If tbegin returns a condition code of 2 the transaction will be retried as often as specified in the second argument. The perform processor assist instruction is used to tell the CPU about the number of fails so far.

int __builtin_tbegin_retry_nofloat (*void**, *int*)   [Built-in Function]
> Same as __builtin_tbegin_retry but without FPR saves and restores. Using this variant in code making use of FPRs will leave the FPRs in undefined state when entering the transaction abort handler code.

void __builtin_tbeginc (*void*)   [Built-in Function]
> Generates the tbeginc machine instruction starting a constrained hardware transaction. The second operand is set to 0xff08.

int __builtin_tend (*void*)   [Built-in Function]
> Generates the tend machine instruction finishing a transaction and making the changes visible to other threads. The condition code generated by tend is returned as integer value.

void __builtin_tabort (*int*)   [Built-in Function]
> Generates the tabort machine instruction with the specified abort code. Abort codes from 0 through 255 are reserved and will result in an error message.

void __builtin_tx_assist (*int*)   [Built-in Function]
> Generates the ppa rX,rY,1 machine instruction. Where the integer parameter is loaded into rX and a value of zero is loaded into rY. The integer parameter specifies the number of times the transaction repeatedly aborted.

int __builtin_tx_nesting_depth (*void*)   [Built-in Function]
> Generates the etnd machine instruction. The current nesting depth is returned as integer value. For a nesting depth of 0 the code is not executed as part of an transaction.

void __builtin_non_tx_store (*uint64_t **, *uint64_t*)   [Built-in Function]
> Generates the ntstg machine instruction. The second argument is written to the first arguments location. The store operation will not be rolled-back in case of an transaction abort.

6.60.26 SH Built-in Functions

The following built-in functions are supported on the SH1, SH2, SH3 and SH4 families of processors:

void __builtin_set_thread_pointer (*void *ptr*)   [Built-in Function]
> Sets the 'GBR' register to the specified value *ptr*. This is usually used by system code that manages threads and execution contexts. The compiler normally does not generate code that modifies the contents of 'GBR' and thus the value is preserved across function calls. Changing the 'GBR' value in user code must be done with caution, since the compiler might use 'GBR' in order to access thread local variables.

void * __builtin_thread_pointer (*void*)   [Built-in Function]
    Returns the value that is currently set in the 'GBR' register. Memory loads and stores
    that use the thread pointer as a base address are turned into 'GBR' based displacement
    loads and stores, if possible. For example:

```
struct my_tcb
{
   int a, b, c, d, e;
};

int get_tcb_value (void)
{
  // Generate 'mov.l @(8,gbr),r0' instruction
  return ((my_tcb*)__builtin_thread_pointer ())->c;
}
```

unsigned int __builtin_sh_get_fpscr (*void*)   [Built-in Function]
    Returns the value that is currently set in the 'FPSCR' register.

void __builtin_sh_set_fpscr (*unsigned int* val)   [Built-in Function]
    Sets the 'FPSCR' register to the specified value *val*, while preserving the current values
    of the FR, SZ and PR bits.

6.60.27 SPARC VIS Built-in Functions

GCC supports SIMD operations on the SPARC using both the generic vector extensions
(see Section 6.50 [Vector Extensions], page 552) as well as built-in functions for the SPARC
Visual Instruction Set (VIS). When you use the '-mvis' switch, the VIS extension is exposed
as the following built-in functions:

```
typedef int v1si __attribute__ ((vector_size (4)));
typedef int v2si __attribute__ ((vector_size (8)));
typedef short v4hi __attribute__ ((vector_size (8)));
typedef short v2hi __attribute__ ((vector_size (4)));
typedef unsigned char v8qi __attribute__ ((vector_size (8)));
typedef unsigned char v4qi __attribute__ ((vector_size (4)));

void __builtin_vis_write_gsr (int64_t);
int64_t __builtin_vis_read_gsr (void);

void * __builtin_vis_alignaddr (void *, long);
void * __builtin_vis_alignaddrl (void *, long);
int64_t __builtin_vis_faligndatadi (int64_t, int64_t);
v2si __builtin_vis_faligndatav2si (v2si, v2si);
v4hi __builtin_vis_faligndatav4hi (v4si, v4si);
v8qi __builtin_vis_faligndatav8qi (v8qi, v8qi);

v4hi __builtin_vis_fexpand (v4qi);

v4hi __builtin_vis_fmul8x16 (v4qi, v4hi);
v4hi __builtin_vis_fmul8x16au (v4qi, v2hi);
v4hi __builtin_vis_fmul8x16al (v4qi, v2hi);
v4hi __builtin_vis_fmul8sux16 (v8qi, v4hi);
v4hi __builtin_vis_fmul8ulx16 (v8qi, v4hi);
v2si __builtin_vis_fmuld8sux16 (v4qi, v2hi);
v2si __builtin_vis_fmuld8ulx16 (v4qi, v2hi);
```

```
v4qi __builtin_vis_fpack16 (v4hi);
v8qi __builtin_vis_fpack32 (v2si, v8qi);
v2hi __builtin_vis_fpackfix (v2si);
v8qi __builtin_vis_fpmerge (v4qi, v4qi);

int64_t __builtin_vis_pdist (v8qi, v8qi, int64_t);

long __builtin_vis_edge8 (void *, void *);
long __builtin_vis_edge8l (void *, void *);
long __builtin_vis_edge16 (void *, void *);
long __builtin_vis_edge16l (void *, void *);
long __builtin_vis_edge32 (void *, void *);
long __builtin_vis_edge32l (void *, void *);

long __builtin_vis_fcmple16 (v4hi, v4hi);
long __builtin_vis_fcmple32 (v2si, v2si);
long __builtin_vis_fcmpne16 (v4hi, v4hi);
long __builtin_vis_fcmpne32 (v2si, v2si);
long __builtin_vis_fcmpgt16 (v4hi, v4hi);
long __builtin_vis_fcmpgt32 (v2si, v2si);
long __builtin_vis_fcmpeq16 (v4hi, v4hi);
long __builtin_vis_fcmpeq32 (v2si, v2si);

v4hi __builtin_vis_fpadd16 (v4hi, v4hi);
v2hi __builtin_vis_fpadd16s (v2hi, v2hi);
v2si __builtin_vis_fpadd32 (v2si, v2si);
v1si __builtin_vis_fpadd32s (v1si, v1si);
v4hi __builtin_vis_fpsub16 (v4hi, v4hi);
v2hi __builtin_vis_fpsub16s (v2hi, v2hi);
v2si __builtin_vis_fpsub32 (v2si, v2si);
v1si __builtin_vis_fpsub32s (v1si, v1si);

long __builtin_vis_array8 (long, long);
long __builtin_vis_array16 (long, long);
long __builtin_vis_array32 (long, long);
```

When you use the '-mvis2' switch, the VIS version 2.0 built-in functions also become available:

```
long __builtin_vis_bmask (long, long);
int64_t __builtin_vis_bshuffledi (int64_t, int64_t);
v2si __builtin_vis_bshufflev2si (v2si, v2si);
v4hi __builtin_vis_bshufflev2si (v4hi, v4hi);
v8qi __builtin_vis_bshufflev2si (v8qi, v8qi);

long __builtin_vis_edge8n (void *, void *);
long __builtin_vis_edge8ln (void *, void *);
long __builtin_vis_edge16n (void *, void *);
long __builtin_vis_edge16ln (void *, void *);
long __builtin_vis_edge32n (void *, void *);
long __builtin_vis_edge32ln (void *, void *);
```

When you use the '-mvis3' switch, the VIS version 3.0 built-in functions also become available:

```
void __builtin_vis_cmask8 (long);
void __builtin_vis_cmask16 (long);
void __builtin_vis_cmask32 (long);

v4hi __builtin_vis_fchksm16 (v4hi, v4hi);
```

```
v4hi __builtin_vis_fsll16 (v4hi, v4hi);
v4hi __builtin_vis_fslas16 (v4hi, v4hi);
v4hi __builtin_vis_fsrl16 (v4hi, v4hi);
v4hi __builtin_vis_fsra16 (v4hi, v4hi);
v2si __builtin_vis_fsll16 (v2si, v2si);
v2si __builtin_vis_fslas16 (v2si, v2si);
v2si __builtin_vis_fsrl16 (v2si, v2si);
v2si __builtin_vis_fsra16 (v2si, v2si);

long __builtin_vis_pdistn (v8qi, v8qi);

v4hi __builtin_vis_fmean16 (v4hi, v4hi);

int64_t __builtin_vis_fpadd64 (int64_t, int64_t);
int64_t __builtin_vis_fpsub64 (int64_t, int64_t);

v4hi __builtin_vis_fpadds16 (v4hi, v4hi);
v2hi __builtin_vis_fpadds16s (v2hi, v2hi);
v4hi __builtin_vis_fpsubs16 (v4hi, v4hi);
v2hi __builtin_vis_fpsubs16s (v2hi, v2hi);
v2si __builtin_vis_fpadds32 (v2si, v2si);
v1si __builtin_vis_fpadds32s (v1si, v1si);
v2si __builtin_vis_fpsubs32 (v2si, v2si);
v1si __builtin_vis_fpsubs32s (v1si, v1si);

long __builtin_vis_fucmple8 (v8qi, v8qi);
long __builtin_vis_fucmpne8 (v8qi, v8qi);
long __builtin_vis_fucmpgt8 (v8qi, v8qi);
long __builtin_vis_fucmpeq8 (v8qi, v8qi);

float __builtin_vis_fhadds (float, float);
double __builtin_vis_fhaddd (double, double);
float __builtin_vis_fhsubs (float, float);
double __builtin_vis_fhsubd (double, double);
float __builtin_vis_fnhadds (float, float);
double __builtin_vis_fnhaddd (double, double);

int64_t __builtin_vis_umulxhi (int64_t, int64_t);
int64_t __builtin_vis_xmulx (int64_t, int64_t);
int64_t __builtin_vis_xmulxhi (int64_t, int64_t);
```

When you use the '-mvis4' switch, the VIS version 4.0 built-in functions also become available:

```
v8qi __builtin_vis_fpadd8 (v8qi, v8qi);
v8qi __builtin_vis_fpadds8 (v8qi, v8qi);
v8qi __builtin_vis_fpaddus8 (v8qi, v8qi);
v4hi __builtin_vis_fpaddus16 (v4hi, v4hi);

v8qi __builtin_vis_fpsub8 (v8qi, v8qi);
v8qi __builtin_vis_fpsubs8 (v8qi, v8qi);
v8qi __builtin_vis_fpsubus8 (v8qi, v8qi);
v4hi __builtin_vis_fpsubus16 (v4hi, v4hi);

long __builtin_vis_fpcmple8 (v8qi, v8qi);
long __builtin_vis_fpcmpgt8 (v8qi, v8qi);
long __builtin_vis_fpcmpule16 (v4hi, v4hi);
long __builtin_vis_fpcmpugt16 (v4hi, v4hi);
```

```
long __builtin_vis_fpcmpule32 (v2si, v2si);
long __builtin_vis_fpcmpugt32 (v2si, v2si);

v8qi __builtin_vis_fpmax8 (v8qi, v8qi);
v4hi __builtin_vis_fpmax16 (v4hi, v4hi);
v2si __builtin_vis_fpmax32 (v2si, v2si);

v8qi __builtin_vis_fpmaxu8 (v8qi, v8qi);
v4hi __builtin_vis_fpmaxu16 (v4hi, v4hi);
v2si __builtin_vis_fpmaxu32 (v2si, v2si);


v8qi __builtin_vis_fpmin8 (v8qi, v8qi);
v4hi __builtin_vis_fpmin16 (v4hi, v4hi);
v2si __builtin_vis_fpmin32 (v2si, v2si);

v8qi __builtin_vis_fpminu8 (v8qi, v8qi);
v4hi __builtin_vis_fpminu16 (v4hi, v4hi);
v2si __builtin_vis_fpminu32 (v2si, v2si);
```

6.60.28 SPU Built-in Functions

GCC provides extensions for the SPU processor as described in the Sony/Toshiba/IBM SPU Language Extensions Specification. GCC's implementation differs in several ways.

- The optional extension of specifying vector constants in parentheses is not supported.

- A vector initializer requires no cast if the vector constant is of the same type as the variable it is initializing.

- If `signed` or `unsigned` is omitted, the signedness of the vector type is the default signedness of the base type. The default varies depending on the operating system, so a portable program should always specify the signedness.

- By default, the keyword `__vector` is added. The macro `vector` is defined in `<spu_intrinsics.h>` and can be undefined.

- GCC allows using a `typedef` name as the type specifier for a vector type.

- For C, overloaded functions are implemented with macros so the following does not work:

  ```
  spu_add ((vector signed int){1, 2, 3, 4}, foo);
  ```

  Since `spu_add` is a macro, the vector constant in the example is treated as four separate arguments. Wrap the entire argument in parentheses for this to work.

- The extended version of `__builtin_expect` is not supported.

Note: Only the interface described in the aforementioned specification is supported. Internally, GCC uses built-in functions to implement the required functionality, but these are not supported and are subject to change without notice.

6.60.29 TI C6X Built-in Functions

GCC provides intrinsics to access certain instructions of the TI C6X processors. These intrinsics, listed below, are available after inclusion of the `c6x_intrinsics.h` header file. They map directly to C6X instructions.

```
int _sadd (int, int)
```

```
int _ssub (int, int)
int _sadd2 (int, int)
int _ssub2 (int, int)
long long _mpy2 (int, int)
long long _smpy2 (int, int)
int _add4 (int, int)
int _sub4 (int, int)
int _saddu4 (int, int)

int _smpy (int, int)
int _smpyh (int, int)
int _smpyhl (int, int)
int _smpylh (int, int)

int _sshl (int, int)
int _subc (int, int)

int _avg2 (int, int)
int _avgu4 (int, int)

int _clrr (int, int)
int _extr (int, int)
int _extru (int, int)
int _abs (int)
int _abs2 (int)
```

6.60.30 TILE-Gx Built-in Functions

GCC provides intrinsics to access every instruction of the TILE-Gx processor. The intrinsics are of the form:

```
unsigned long long __insn_op (...)
```

Where op is the name of the instruction. Refer to the ISA manual for the complete list of instructions.

GCC also provides intrinsics to directly access the network registers. The intrinsics are:

```
unsigned long long __tile_idn0_receive (void)
unsigned long long __tile_idn1_receive (void)
unsigned long long __tile_udn0_receive (void)
unsigned long long __tile_udn1_receive (void)
unsigned long long __tile_udn2_receive (void)
unsigned long long __tile_udn3_receive (void)
void __tile_idn_send (unsigned long long)
void __tile_udn_send (unsigned long long)
```

The intrinsic `void __tile_network_barrier (void)` is used to guarantee that no network operations before it are reordered with those after it.

6.60.31 TILEPro Built-in Functions

GCC provides intrinsics to access every instruction of the TILEPro processor. The intrinsics are of the form:

```
unsigned __insn_op (...)
```

where *op* is the name of the instruction. Refer to the ISA manual for the complete list of instructions.

GCC also provides intrinsics to directly access the network registers. The intrinsics are:

```
unsigned __tile_idn0_receive (void)
unsigned __tile_idn1_receive (void)
unsigned __tile_sn_receive (void)
unsigned __tile_udn0_receive (void)
unsigned __tile_udn1_receive (void)
unsigned __tile_udn2_receive (void)
unsigned __tile_udn3_receive (void)
void __tile_idn_send (unsigned)
void __tile_sn_send (unsigned)
void __tile_udn_send (unsigned)
```

The intrinsic `void __tile_network_barrier (void)` is used to guarantee that no network operations before it are reordered with those after it.

6.60.32 x86 Built-in Functions

These built-in functions are available for the x86-32 and x86-64 family of computers, depending on the command-line switches used.

If you specify command-line switches such as '`-msse`', the compiler could use the extended instruction sets even if the built-ins are not used explicitly in the program. For this reason, applications that perform run-time CPU detection must compile separate files for each supported architecture, using the appropriate flags. In particular, the file containing the CPU detection code should be compiled without these options.

The following machine modes are available for use with MMX built-in functions (see Section 6.50 [Vector Extensions], page 552): `V2SI` for a vector of two 32-bit integers, `V4HI` for a vector of four 16-bit integers, and `V8QI` for a vector of eight 8-bit integers. Some of the built-in functions operate on MMX registers as a whole 64-bit entity, these use `V1DI` as their mode.

If 3DNow! extensions are enabled, `V2SF` is used as a mode for a vector of two 32-bit floating-point values.

If SSE extensions are enabled, `V4SF` is used for a vector of four 32-bit floating-point values. Some instructions use a vector of four 32-bit integers, these use `V4SI`. Finally, some instructions operate on an entire vector register, interpreting it as a 128-bit integer, these use mode `TI`.

The x86-32 and x86-64 family of processors use additional built-in functions for efficient use of `TF` (`__float128`) 128-bit floating point and `TC` 128-bit complex floating-point values.

The following floating-point built-in functions are always available. All of them implement the function that is part of the name.

```
__float128 __builtin_fabsq (__float128)
__float128 __builtin_copysignq (__float128, __float128)
```

The following built-in functions are always available.

`__float128 __builtin_infq (void)`
>   Similar to `__builtin_inf`, except the return type is `__float128`.

`__float128 __builtin_huge_valq (void)`
>   Similar to `__builtin_huge_val`, except the return type is `__float128`.

`__float128 __builtin_nanq (void)`
>   Similar to `__builtin_nan`, except the return type is `__float128`.

`__float128 __builtin_nansq (void)`
>   Similar to `__builtin_nans`, except the return type is `__float128`.

The following built-in function is always available.

`void __builtin_ia32_pause (void)`
>   Generates the **pause** machine instruction with a compiler memory barrier.

The following built-in functions are always available and can be used to check the target platform type.

`void __builtin_cpu_init` (*void*)   [Built-in Function]
>   This function runs the CPU detection code to check the type of CPU and the features supported. This built-in function needs to be invoked along with the built-in functions to check CPU type and features, `__builtin_cpu_is` and `__builtin_cpu_supports`, only when used in a function that is executed before any constructors are called. The CPU detection code is automatically executed in a very high priority constructor.
>
>   For example, this function has to be used in **ifunc** resolvers that check for CPU type using the built-in functions `__builtin_cpu_is` and `__builtin_cpu_supports`, or in constructors on targets that don't support constructor priority.

```
static void (*resolve_memcpy (void)) (void)
{
  // ifunc resolvers fire before constructors, explicitly call the init
  // function.
  __builtin_cpu_init ();
  if (__builtin_cpu_supports ("ssse3"))
    return ssse3_memcpy; // super fast memcpy with ssse3 instructions.
  else
    return default_memcpy;
}

void *memcpy (void *, const void *, size_t)
     __attribute__ ((ifunc ("resolve_memcpy")));
```

`int __builtin_cpu_is` (*const char *cpuname*)   [Built-in Function]
>   This function returns a positive integer if the run-time CPU is of type *cpuname* and returns 0 otherwise. The following CPU names can be detected:

‘intel’   Intel CPU.

‘atom’   Intel Atom CPU.

‘core2’   Intel Core 2 CPU.

‘corei7’   Intel Core i7 CPU.

'nehalem'   Intel Core i7 Nehalem CPU.

'westmere'
            Intel Core i7 Westmere CPU.

'sandybridge'
            Intel Core i7 Sandy Bridge CPU.

'amd'   AMD CPU.

'amdfam10h'
            AMD Family 10h CPU.

'barcelona'
            AMD Family 10h Barcelona CPU.

'shanghai'
            AMD Family 10h Shanghai CPU.

'istanbul'
            AMD Family 10h Istanbul CPU.

'btver1'   AMD Family 14h CPU.

'amdfam15h'
            AMD Family 15h CPU.

'bdver1'   AMD Family 15h Bulldozer version 1.

'bdver2'   AMD Family 15h Bulldozer version 2.

'bdver3'   AMD Family 15h Bulldozer version 3.

'bdver4'   AMD Family 15h Bulldozer version 4.

'btver2'   AMD Family 16h CPU.

'znver1'   AMD Family 17h CPU.

Here is an example:

```
if (__builtin_cpu_is ("corei7"))
  {
     do_corei7 (); // Core i7 specific implementation.
  }
else
  {
     do_generic (); // Generic implementation.
  }
```

int __builtin_cpu_supports (*const char *feature*)   [Built-in Function]
     This function returns a positive integer if the run-time CPU supports *feature* and
     returns 0 otherwise. The following features can be detected:

'cmov'   CMOV instruction.

'mmx'   MMX instructions.

'popcnt'   POPCNT instruction.

'sse'   SSE instructions.

'sse2'   SSE2 instructions.

'sse3'   SSE3 instructions.

'ssse3'   SSSE3 instructions.

'sse4.1'   SSE4.1 instructions.

'sse4.2'   SSE4.2 instructions.

'avx'   AVX instructions.

'avx2'   AVX2 instructions.

'avx512f'   AVX512F instructions.

Here is an example:

```
if (__builtin_cpu_supports ("popcnt"))
  {
      asm("popcnt %1,%0" : "=r"(count) : "rm"(n) : "cc");
  }
else
  {
      count = generic_countbits (n); //generic implementation.
  }
```

The following built-in functions are made available by '-mmmx'. All of them generate the machine instruction that is part of the name.

```
v8qi __builtin_ia32_paddb (v8qi, v8qi)
v4hi __builtin_ia32_paddw (v4hi, v4hi)
v2si __builtin_ia32_paddd (v2si, v2si)
v8qi __builtin_ia32_psubb (v8qi, v8qi)
v4hi __builtin_ia32_psubw (v4hi, v4hi)
v2si __builtin_ia32_psubd (v2si, v2si)
v8qi __builtin_ia32_paddsb (v8qi, v8qi)
v4hi __builtin_ia32_paddsw (v4hi, v4hi)
v8qi __builtin_ia32_psubsb (v8qi, v8qi)
v4hi __builtin_ia32_psubsw (v4hi, v4hi)
v8qi __builtin_ia32_paddusb (v8qi, v8qi)
v4hi __builtin_ia32_paddusw (v4hi, v4hi)
v8qi __builtin_ia32_psubusb (v8qi, v8qi)
v4hi __builtin_ia32_psubusw (v4hi, v4hi)
v4hi __builtin_ia32_pmullw (v4hi, v4hi)
v4hi __builtin_ia32_pmulhw (v4hi, v4hi)
di __builtin_ia32_pand (di, di)
di __builtin_ia32_pandn (di,di)
di __builtin_ia32_por (di, di)
di __builtin_ia32_pxor (di, di)
v8qi __builtin_ia32_pcmpeqb (v8qi, v8qi)
v4hi __builtin_ia32_pcmpeqw (v4hi, v4hi)
v2si __builtin_ia32_pcmpeqd (v2si, v2si)
v8qi __builtin_ia32_pcmpgtb (v8qi, v8qi)
v4hi __builtin_ia32_pcmpgtw (v4hi, v4hi)
v2si __builtin_ia32_pcmpgtd (v2si, v2si)
v8qi __builtin_ia32_punpckhbw (v8qi, v8qi)
v4hi __builtin_ia32_punpckhwd (v4hi, v4hi)
v2si __builtin_ia32_punpckhdq (v2si, v2si)
v8qi __builtin_ia32_punpcklbw (v8qi, v8qi)
v4hi __builtin_ia32_punpcklwd (v4hi, v4hi)
```

```
v2si __builtin_ia32_punpckldq (v2si, v2si)
v8qi __builtin_ia32_packsswb (v4hi, v4hi)
v4hi __builtin_ia32_packssdw (v2si, v2si)
v8qi __builtin_ia32_packuswb (v4hi, v4hi)

v4hi __builtin_ia32_psllw (v4hi, v4hi)
v2si __builtin_ia32_pslld (v2si, v2si)
v1di __builtin_ia32_psllq (v1di, v1di)
v4hi __builtin_ia32_psrlw (v4hi, v4hi)
v2si __builtin_ia32_psrld (v2si, v2si)
v1di __builtin_ia32_psrlq (v1di, v1di)
v4hi __builtin_ia32_psraw (v4hi, v4hi)
v2si __builtin_ia32_psrad (v2si, v2si)
v4hi __builtin_ia32_psllwi (v4hi, int)
v2si __builtin_ia32_pslldi (v2si, int)
v1di __builtin_ia32_psllqi (v1di, int)
v4hi __builtin_ia32_psrlwi (v4hi, int)
v2si __builtin_ia32_psrldi (v2si, int)
v1di __builtin_ia32_psrlqi (v1di, int)
v4hi __builtin_ia32_psrawi (v4hi, int)
v2si __builtin_ia32_psradi (v2si, int)
```

The following built-in functions are made available either with '-msse', or with a combination of '-m3dnow' and '-march=athlon'. All of them generate the machine instruction that is part of the name.

```
v4hi __builtin_ia32_pmulhuw (v4hi, v4hi)
v8qi __builtin_ia32_pavgb (v8qi, v8qi)
v4hi __builtin_ia32_pavgw (v4hi, v4hi)
v1di __builtin_ia32_psadbw (v8qi, v8qi)
v8qi __builtin_ia32_pmaxub (v8qi, v8qi)
v4hi __builtin_ia32_pmaxsw (v4hi, v4hi)
v8qi __builtin_ia32_pminub (v8qi, v8qi)
v4hi __builtin_ia32_pminsw (v4hi, v4hi)
int __builtin_ia32_pmovmskb (v8qi)
void __builtin_ia32_maskmovq (v8qi, v8qi, char *)
void __builtin_ia32_movntq (di *, di)
void __builtin_ia32_sfence (void)
```

The following built-in functions are available when '-msse' is used. All of them generate the machine instruction that is part of the name.

```
int __builtin_ia32_comieq (v4sf, v4sf)
int __builtin_ia32_comineq (v4sf, v4sf)
int __builtin_ia32_comilt (v4sf, v4sf)
int __builtin_ia32_comile (v4sf, v4sf)
int __builtin_ia32_comigt (v4sf, v4sf)
int __builtin_ia32_comige (v4sf, v4sf)
int __builtin_ia32_ucomieq (v4sf, v4sf)
int __builtin_ia32_ucomineq (v4sf, v4sf)
int __builtin_ia32_ucomilt (v4sf, v4sf)
int __builtin_ia32_ucomile (v4sf, v4sf)
int __builtin_ia32_ucomigt (v4sf, v4sf)
int __builtin_ia32_ucomige (v4sf, v4sf)
v4sf __builtin_ia32_addps (v4sf, v4sf)
v4sf __builtin_ia32_subps (v4sf, v4sf)
v4sf __builtin_ia32_mulps (v4sf, v4sf)
v4sf __builtin_ia32_divps (v4sf, v4sf)
v4sf __builtin_ia32_addss (v4sf, v4sf)
```

```
v4sf __builtin_ia32_subss (v4sf, v4sf)
v4sf __builtin_ia32_mulss (v4sf, v4sf)
v4sf __builtin_ia32_divss (v4sf, v4sf)
v4sf __builtin_ia32_cmpeqps (v4sf, v4sf)
v4sf __builtin_ia32_cmpltps (v4sf, v4sf)
v4sf __builtin_ia32_cmpleps (v4sf, v4sf)
v4sf __builtin_ia32_cmpgtps (v4sf, v4sf)
v4sf __builtin_ia32_cmpgeps (v4sf, v4sf)
v4sf __builtin_ia32_cmpunordps (v4sf, v4sf)
v4sf __builtin_ia32_cmpneqps (v4sf, v4sf)
v4sf __builtin_ia32_cmpnltps (v4sf, v4sf)
v4sf __builtin_ia32_cmpnleps (v4sf, v4sf)
v4sf __builtin_ia32_cmpngtps (v4sf, v4sf)
v4sf __builtin_ia32_cmpngeps (v4sf, v4sf)
v4sf __builtin_ia32_cmpordps (v4sf, v4sf)
v4sf __builtin_ia32_cmpeqss (v4sf, v4sf)
v4sf __builtin_ia32_cmpltss (v4sf, v4sf)
v4sf __builtin_ia32_cmpless (v4sf, v4sf)
v4sf __builtin_ia32_cmpunordss (v4sf, v4sf)
v4sf __builtin_ia32_cmpneqss (v4sf, v4sf)
v4sf __builtin_ia32_cmpnltss (v4sf, v4sf)
v4sf __builtin_ia32_cmpnless (v4sf, v4sf)
v4sf __builtin_ia32_cmpordss (v4sf, v4sf)
v4sf __builtin_ia32_maxps (v4sf, v4sf)
v4sf __builtin_ia32_maxss (v4sf, v4sf)
v4sf __builtin_ia32_minps (v4sf, v4sf)
v4sf __builtin_ia32_minss (v4sf, v4sf)
v4sf __builtin_ia32_andps (v4sf, v4sf)
v4sf __builtin_ia32_andnps (v4sf, v4sf)
v4sf __builtin_ia32_orps (v4sf, v4sf)
v4sf __builtin_ia32_xorps (v4sf, v4sf)
v4sf __builtin_ia32_movss (v4sf, v4sf)
v4sf __builtin_ia32_movhlps (v4sf, v4sf)
v4sf __builtin_ia32_movlhps (v4sf, v4sf)
v4sf __builtin_ia32_unpckhps (v4sf, v4sf)
v4sf __builtin_ia32_unpcklps (v4sf, v4sf)
v4sf __builtin_ia32_cvtpi2ps (v4sf, v2si)
v4sf __builtin_ia32_cvtsi2ss (v4sf, int)
v2si __builtin_ia32_cvtps2pi (v4sf)
int __builtin_ia32_cvtss2si (v4sf)
v2si __builtin_ia32_cvttps2pi (v4sf)
int __builtin_ia32_cvttss2si (v4sf)
v4sf __builtin_ia32_rcpps (v4sf)
v4sf __builtin_ia32_rsqrtps (v4sf)
v4sf __builtin_ia32_sqrtps (v4sf)
v4sf __builtin_ia32_rcpss (v4sf)
v4sf __builtin_ia32_rsqrtss (v4sf)
v4sf __builtin_ia32_sqrtss (v4sf)
v4sf __builtin_ia32_shufps (v4sf, v4sf, int)
void __builtin_ia32_movntps (float *, v4sf)
int __builtin_ia32_movmskps (v4sf)
```

The following built-in functions are available when '-msse' is used.

`v4sf __builtin_ia32_loadups (float *)`

> Generates the movups machine instruction as a load from memory.

`void __builtin_ia32_storeups (float *, v4sf)`

> Generates the movups machine instruction as a store to memory.

`v4sf __builtin_ia32_loadss (float *)`
> Generates the `movss` machine instruction as a load from memory.

`v4sf __builtin_ia32_loadhps (v4sf, const v2sf *)`
> Generates the `movhps` machine instruction as a load from memory.

`v4sf __builtin_ia32_loadlps (v4sf, const v2sf *)`
> Generates the `movlps` machine instruction as a load from memory

`void __builtin_ia32_storehps (v2sf *, v4sf)`
> Generates the `movhps` machine instruction as a store to memory.

`void __builtin_ia32_storelps (v2sf *, v4sf)`
> Generates the `movlps` machine instruction as a store to memory.

The following built-in functions are available when '`-msse2`' is used. All of them generate the machine instruction that is part of the name.

```
int __builtin_ia32_comisdeq (v2df, v2df)
int __builtin_ia32_comisdlt (v2df, v2df)
int __builtin_ia32_comisdle (v2df, v2df)
int __builtin_ia32_comisdgt (v2df, v2df)
int __builtin_ia32_comisdge (v2df, v2df)
int __builtin_ia32_comisdneq (v2df, v2df)
int __builtin_ia32_ucomisdeq (v2df, v2df)
int __builtin_ia32_ucomisdlt (v2df, v2df)
int __builtin_ia32_ucomisdle (v2df, v2df)
int __builtin_ia32_ucomisdgt (v2df, v2df)
int __builtin_ia32_ucomisdge (v2df, v2df)
int __builtin_ia32_ucomisdneq (v2df, v2df)
v2df __builtin_ia32_cmpeqpd (v2df, v2df)
v2df __builtin_ia32_cmpltpd (v2df, v2df)
v2df __builtin_ia32_cmplepd (v2df, v2df)
v2df __builtin_ia32_cmpgtpd (v2df, v2df)
v2df __builtin_ia32_cmpgepd (v2df, v2df)
v2df __builtin_ia32_cmpunordpd (v2df, v2df)
v2df __builtin_ia32_cmpneqpd (v2df, v2df)
v2df __builtin_ia32_cmpnltpd (v2df, v2df)
v2df __builtin_ia32_cmpnlepd (v2df, v2df)
v2df __builtin_ia32_cmpngtpd (v2df, v2df)
v2df __builtin_ia32_cmpngepd (v2df, v2df)
v2df __builtin_ia32_cmpordpd (v2df, v2df)
v2df __builtin_ia32_cmpeqsd (v2df, v2df)
v2df __builtin_ia32_cmpltsd (v2df, v2df)
v2df __builtin_ia32_cmplesd (v2df, v2df)
v2df __builtin_ia32_cmpunordsd (v2df, v2df)
v2df __builtin_ia32_cmpneqsd (v2df, v2df)
v2df __builtin_ia32_cmpnltsd (v2df, v2df)
v2df __builtin_ia32_cmpnlesd (v2df, v2df)
v2df __builtin_ia32_cmpordsd (v2df, v2df)
v2di __builtin_ia32_paddq (v2di, v2di)
v2di __builtin_ia32_psubq (v2di, v2di)
v2df __builtin_ia32_addpd (v2df, v2df)
v2df __builtin_ia32_subpd (v2df, v2df)
v2df __builtin_ia32_mulpd (v2df, v2df)
v2df __builtin_ia32_divpd (v2df, v2df)
v2df __builtin_ia32_addsd (v2df, v2df)
v2df __builtin_ia32_subsd (v2df, v2df)
v2df __builtin_ia32_mulsd (v2df, v2df)
```

```
v2df __builtin_ia32_divsd (v2df, v2df)
v2df __builtin_ia32_minpd (v2df, v2df)
v2df __builtin_ia32_maxpd (v2df, v2df)
v2df __builtin_ia32_minsd (v2df, v2df)
v2df __builtin_ia32_maxsd (v2df, v2df)
v2df __builtin_ia32_andpd (v2df, v2df)
v2df __builtin_ia32_andnpd (v2df, v2df)
v2df __builtin_ia32_orpd (v2df, v2df)
v2df __builtin_ia32_xorpd (v2df, v2df)
v2df __builtin_ia32_movsd (v2df, v2df)
v2df __builtin_ia32_unpckhpd (v2df, v2df)
v2df __builtin_ia32_unpcklpd (v2df, v2df)
v16qi __builtin_ia32_paddb128 (v16qi, v16qi)
v8hi __builtin_ia32_paddw128 (v8hi, v8hi)
v4si __builtin_ia32_paddd128 (v4si, v4si)
v2di __builtin_ia32_paddq128 (v2di, v2di)
v16qi __builtin_ia32_psubb128 (v16qi, v16qi)
v8hi __builtin_ia32_psubw128 (v8hi, v8hi)
v4si __builtin_ia32_psubd128 (v4si, v4si)
v2di __builtin_ia32_psubq128 (v2di, v2di)
v8hi __builtin_ia32_pmullw128 (v8hi, v8hi)
v8hi __builtin_ia32_pmulhw128 (v8hi, v8hi)
v2di __builtin_ia32_pand128 (v2di, v2di)
v2di __builtin_ia32_pandn128 (v2di, v2di)
v2di __builtin_ia32_por128 (v2di, v2di)
v2di __builtin_ia32_pxor128 (v2di, v2di)
v16qi __builtin_ia32_pavgb128 (v16qi, v16qi)
v8hi __builtin_ia32_pavgw128 (v8hi, v8hi)
v16qi __builtin_ia32_pcmpeqb128 (v16qi, v16qi)
v8hi __builtin_ia32_pcmpeqw128 (v8hi, v8hi)
v4si __builtin_ia32_pcmpeqd128 (v4si, v4si)
v16qi __builtin_ia32_pcmpgtb128 (v16qi, v16qi)
v8hi __builtin_ia32_pcmpgtw128 (v8hi, v8hi)
v4si __builtin_ia32_pcmpgtd128 (v4si, v4si)
v16qi __builtin_ia32_pmaxub128 (v16qi, v16qi)
v8hi __builtin_ia32_pmaxsw128 (v8hi, v8hi)
v16qi __builtin_ia32_pminub128 (v16qi, v16qi)
v8hi __builtin_ia32_pminsw128 (v8hi, v8hi)
v16qi __builtin_ia32_punpckhbw128 (v16qi, v16qi)
v8hi __builtin_ia32_punpckhwd128 (v8hi, v8hi)
v4si __builtin_ia32_punpckhdq128 (v4si, v4si)
v2di __builtin_ia32_punpckhqdq128 (v2di, v2di)
v16qi __builtin_ia32_punpcklbw128 (v16qi, v16qi)
v8hi __builtin_ia32_punpcklwd128 (v8hi, v8hi)
v4si __builtin_ia32_punpckldq128 (v4si, v4si)
v2di __builtin_ia32_punpcklqdq128 (v2di, v2di)
v16qi __builtin_ia32_packsswb128 (v8hi, v8hi)
v8hi __builtin_ia32_packssdw128 (v4si, v4si)
v16qi __builtin_ia32_packuswb128 (v8hi, v8hi)
v8hi __builtin_ia32_pmulhuw128 (v8hi, v8hi)
void __builtin_ia32_maskmovdqu (v16qi, v16qi)
v2df __builtin_ia32_loadupd (double *)
void __builtin_ia32_storeupd (double *, v2df)
v2df __builtin_ia32_loadhpd (v2df, double const *)
v2df __builtin_ia32_loadlpd (v2df, double const *)
int __builtin_ia32_movmskpd (v2df)
int __builtin_ia32_pmovmskb128 (v16qi)
void __builtin_ia32_movnti (int *, int)
```

```
void __builtin_ia32_movnti64 (long long int *, long long int)
void __builtin_ia32_movntpd (double *, v2df)
void __builtin_ia32_movntdq (v2df *, v2df)
v4si __builtin_ia32_pshufd (v4si, int)
v8hi __builtin_ia32_pshuflw (v8hi, int)
v8hi __builtin_ia32_pshufhw (v8hi, int)
v2di __builtin_ia32_psadbw128 (v16qi, v16qi)
v2df __builtin_ia32_sqrtpd (v2df)
v2df __builtin_ia32_sqrtsd (v2df)
v2df __builtin_ia32_shufpd (v2df, v2df, int)
v2df __builtin_ia32_cvtdq2pd (v4si)
v4sf __builtin_ia32_cvtdq2ps (v4si)
v4si __builtin_ia32_cvtpd2dq (v2df)
v2si __builtin_ia32_cvtpd2pi (v2df)
v4sf __builtin_ia32_cvtpd2ps (v2df)
v4si __builtin_ia32_cvttpd2dq (v2df)
v2si __builtin_ia32_cvttpd2pi (v2df)
v2df __builtin_ia32_cvtpi2pd (v2si)
int __builtin_ia32_cvtsd2si (v2df)
int __builtin_ia32_cvttsd2si (v2df)
long long __builtin_ia32_cvtsd2si64 (v2df)
long long __builtin_ia32_cvttsd2si64 (v2df)
v4si __builtin_ia32_cvtps2dq (v4sf)
v2df __builtin_ia32_cvtps2pd (v4sf)
v4si __builtin_ia32_cvttps2dq (v4sf)
v2df __builtin_ia32_cvtsi2sd (v2df, int)
v2df __builtin_ia32_cvtsi642sd (v2df, long long)
v4sf __builtin_ia32_cvtsd2ss (v4sf, v2df)
v2df __builtin_ia32_cvtss2sd (v2df, v4sf)
void __builtin_ia32_clflush (const void *)
void __builtin_ia32_lfence (void)
void __builtin_ia32_mfence (void)
v16qi __builtin_ia32_loaddqu (const char *)
void __builtin_ia32_storedqu (char *, v16qi)
v1di __builtin_ia32_pmuludq (v2si, v2si)
v2di __builtin_ia32_pmuludq128 (v4si, v4si)
v8hi __builtin_ia32_psllw128 (v8hi, v8hi)
v4si __builtin_ia32_pslld128 (v4si, v4si)
v2di __builtin_ia32_psllq128 (v2di, v2di)
v8hi __builtin_ia32_psrlw128 (v8hi, v8hi)
v4si __builtin_ia32_psrld128 (v4si, v4si)
v2di __builtin_ia32_psrlq128 (v2di, v2di)
v8hi __builtin_ia32_psraw128 (v8hi, v8hi)
v4si __builtin_ia32_psrad128 (v4si, v4si)
v2di __builtin_ia32_pslldqi128 (v2di, int)
v8hi __builtin_ia32_psllwi128 (v8hi, int)
v4si __builtin_ia32_pslldi128 (v4si, int)
v2di __builtin_ia32_psllqi128 (v2di, int)
v2di __builtin_ia32_psrldqi128 (v2di, int)
v8hi __builtin_ia32_psrlwi128 (v8hi, int)
v4si __builtin_ia32_psrldi128 (v4si, int)
v2di __builtin_ia32_psrlqi128 (v2di, int)
v8hi __builtin_ia32_psrawi128 (v8hi, int)
v4si __builtin_ia32_psradi128 (v4si, int)
v4si __builtin_ia32_pmaddwd128 (v8hi, v8hi)
v2di __builtin_ia32_movq128 (v2di)
```

The following built-in functions are available when '-msse3' is used. All of them generate the machine instruction that is part of the name.

```
v2df __builtin_ia32_addsubpd (v2df, v2df)
v4sf __builtin_ia32_addsubps (v4sf, v4sf)
v2df __builtin_ia32_haddpd (v2df, v2df)
v4sf __builtin_ia32_haddps (v4sf, v4sf)
v2df __builtin_ia32_hsubpd (v2df, v2df)
v4sf __builtin_ia32_hsubps (v4sf, v4sf)
v16qi __builtin_ia32_lddqu (char const *)
void __builtin_ia32_monitor (void *, unsigned int, unsigned int)
v4sf __builtin_ia32_movshdup (v4sf)
v4sf __builtin_ia32_movsldup (v4sf)
void __builtin_ia32_mwait (unsigned int, unsigned int)
```

The following built-in functions are available when '-mssse3' is used. All of them generate the machine instruction that is part of the name.

```
v2si __builtin_ia32_phaddd (v2si, v2si)
v4hi __builtin_ia32_phaddw (v4hi, v4hi)
v4hi __builtin_ia32_phaddsw (v4hi, v4hi)
v2si __builtin_ia32_phsubd (v2si, v2si)
v4hi __builtin_ia32_phsubw (v4hi, v4hi)
v4hi __builtin_ia32_phsubsw (v4hi, v4hi)
v4hi __builtin_ia32_pmaddubsw (v8qi, v8qi)
v4hi __builtin_ia32_pmulhrsw (v4hi, v4hi)
v8qi __builtin_ia32_pshufb (v8qi, v8qi)
v8qi __builtin_ia32_psignb (v8qi, v8qi)
v2si __builtin_ia32_psignd (v2si, v2si)
v4hi __builtin_ia32_psignw (v4hi, v4hi)
v1di __builtin_ia32_palignr (v1di, v1di, int)
v8qi __builtin_ia32_pabsb (v8qi)
v2si __builtin_ia32_pabsd (v2si)
v4hi __builtin_ia32_pabsw (v4hi)
```

The following built-in functions are available when '-mssse3' is used. All of them generate the machine instruction that is part of the name.

```
v4si __builtin_ia32_phaddd128 (v4si, v4si)
v8hi __builtin_ia32_phaddw128 (v8hi, v8hi)
v8hi __builtin_ia32_phaddsw128 (v8hi, v8hi)
v4si __builtin_ia32_phsubd128 (v4si, v4si)
v8hi __builtin_ia32_phsubw128 (v8hi, v8hi)
v8hi __builtin_ia32_phsubsw128 (v8hi, v8hi)
v8hi __builtin_ia32_pmaddubsw128 (v16qi, v16qi)
v8hi __builtin_ia32_pmulhrsw128 (v8hi, v8hi)
v16qi __builtin_ia32_pshufb128 (v16qi, v16qi)
v16qi __builtin_ia32_psignb128 (v16qi, v16qi)
v4si __builtin_ia32_psignd128 (v4si, v4si)
v8hi __builtin_ia32_psignw128 (v8hi, v8hi)
v2di __builtin_ia32_palignr128 (v2di, v2di, int)
v16qi __builtin_ia32_pabsb128 (v16qi)
v4si __builtin_ia32_pabsd128 (v4si)
v8hi __builtin_ia32_pabsw128 (v8hi)
```

The following built-in functions are available when '-msse4.1' is used. All of them generate the machine instruction that is part of the name.

```
v2df __builtin_ia32_blendpd (v2df, v2df, const int)
v4sf __builtin_ia32_blendps (v4sf, v4sf, const int)
v2df __builtin_ia32_blendvpd (v2df, v2df, v2df)
v4sf __builtin_ia32_blendvps (v4sf, v4sf, v4sf)
v2df __builtin_ia32_dppd (v2df, v2df, const int)
v4sf __builtin_ia32_dpps (v4sf, v4sf, const int)
```

```
v4sf __builtin_ia32_insertps128 (v4sf, v4sf, const int)
v2di __builtin_ia32_movntdqa (v2di *);
v16qi __builtin_ia32_mpsadbw128 (v16qi, v16qi, const int)
v8hi __builtin_ia32_packusdw128 (v4si, v4si)
v16qi __builtin_ia32_pblendvb128 (v16qi, v16qi, v16qi)
v8hi __builtin_ia32_pblendw128 (v8hi, v8hi, const int)
v2di __builtin_ia32_pcmpeqq (v2di, v2di)
v8hi __builtin_ia32_phminposuw128 (v8hi)
v16qi __builtin_ia32_pmaxsb128 (v16qi, v16qi)
v4si __builtin_ia32_pmaxsd128 (v4si, v4si)
v4si __builtin_ia32_pmaxud128 (v4si, v4si)
v8hi __builtin_ia32_pmaxuw128 (v8hi, v8hi)
v16qi __builtin_ia32_pminsb128 (v16qi, v16qi)
v4si __builtin_ia32_pminsd128 (v4si, v4si)
v4si __builtin_ia32_pminud128 (v4si, v4si)
v8hi __builtin_ia32_pminuw128 (v8hi, v8hi)
v4si __builtin_ia32_pmovsxbd128 (v16qi)
v2di __builtin_ia32_pmovsxbq128 (v16qi)
v8hi __builtin_ia32_pmovsxbw128 (v16qi)
v2di __builtin_ia32_pmovsxdq128 (v4si)
v4si __builtin_ia32_pmovsxwd128 (v8hi)
v2di __builtin_ia32_pmovsxwq128 (v8hi)
v4si __builtin_ia32_pmovzxbd128 (v16qi)
v2di __builtin_ia32_pmovzxbq128 (v16qi)
v8hi __builtin_ia32_pmovzxbw128 (v16qi)
v2di __builtin_ia32_pmovzxdq128 (v4si)
v4si __builtin_ia32_pmovzxwd128 (v8hi)
v2di __builtin_ia32_pmovzxwq128 (v8hi)
v2di __builtin_ia32_pmuldq128 (v4si, v4si)
v4si __builtin_ia32_pmulld128 (v4si, v4si)
int __builtin_ia32_ptestc128 (v2di, v2di)
int __builtin_ia32_ptestnzc128 (v2di, v2di)
int __builtin_ia32_ptestz128 (v2di, v2di)
v2df __builtin_ia32_roundpd (v2df, const int)
v4sf __builtin_ia32_roundps (v4sf, const int)
v2df __builtin_ia32_roundsd (v2df, v2df, const int)
v4sf __builtin_ia32_roundss (v4sf, v4sf, const int)
```

The following built-in functions are available when '-msse4.1' is used.

`v4sf __builtin_ia32_vec_set_v4sf (v4sf, float, const int)`
   Generates the **insertps** machine instruction.

`int __builtin_ia32_vec_ext_v16qi (v16qi, const int)`
   Generates the **pextrb** machine instruction.

`v16qi __builtin_ia32_vec_set_v16qi (v16qi, int, const int)`
   Generates the **pinsrb** machine instruction.

`v4si __builtin_ia32_vec_set_v4si (v4si, int, const int)`
   Generates the **pinsrd** machine instruction.

`v2di __builtin_ia32_vec_set_v2di (v2di, long long, const int)`
   Generates the **pinsrq** machine instruction in 64bit mode.

The following built-in functions are changed to generate new SSE4.1 instructions when '-msse4.1' is used.

`float __builtin_ia32_vec_ext_v4sf (v4sf, const int)`
   Generates the **extractps** machine instruction.

```
int __builtin_ia32_vec_ext_v4si (v4si, const int)
```
>   Generates the `pextrd` machine instruction.

```
long long __builtin_ia32_vec_ext_v2di (v2di, const int)
```
>   Generates the `pextrq` machine instruction in 64bit mode.

The following built-in functions are available when '-msse4.2' is used. All of them generate the machine instruction that is part of the name.

```
v16qi __builtin_ia32_pcmpestrm128 (v16qi, int, v16qi, int, const int)
int __builtin_ia32_pcmpestri128 (v16qi, int, v16qi, int, const int)
int __builtin_ia32_pcmpestria128 (v16qi, int, v16qi, int, const int)
int __builtin_ia32_pcmpestric128 (v16qi, int, v16qi, int, const int)
int __builtin_ia32_pcmpestrio128 (v16qi, int, v16qi, int, const int)
int __builtin_ia32_pcmpestris128 (v16qi, int, v16qi, int, const int)
int __builtin_ia32_pcmpestriz128 (v16qi, int, v16qi, int, const int)
v16qi __builtin_ia32_pcmpistrm128 (v16qi, v16qi, const int)
int __builtin_ia32_pcmpistri128 (v16qi, v16qi, const int)
int __builtin_ia32_pcmpistria128 (v16qi, v16qi, const int)
int __builtin_ia32_pcmpistric128 (v16qi, v16qi, const int)
int __builtin_ia32_pcmpistrio128 (v16qi, v16qi, const int)
int __builtin_ia32_pcmpistris128 (v16qi, v16qi, const int)
int __builtin_ia32_pcmpistriz128 (v16qi, v16qi, const int)
v2di __builtin_ia32_pcmpgtq (v2di, v2di)
```

The following built-in functions are available when '-msse4.2' is used.

```
unsigned int __builtin_ia32_crc32qi (unsigned int, unsigned char)
```
>   Generates the `crc32b` machine instruction.

```
unsigned int __builtin_ia32_crc32hi (unsigned int, unsigned short)
```
>   Generates the `crc32w` machine instruction.

```
unsigned int __builtin_ia32_crc32si (unsigned int, unsigned int)
```
>   Generates the `crc32l` machine instruction.

```
unsigned long long __builtin_ia32_crc32di (unsigned long long, unsigned long long)
```
>   Generates the `crc32q` machine instruction.

The following built-in functions are changed to generate new SSE4.2 instructions when '-msse4.2' is used.

```
int __builtin_popcount (unsigned int)
```
>   Generates the `popcntl` machine instruction.

```
int __builtin_popcountl (unsigned long)
```
>   Generates the `popcntl` or `popcntq` machine instruction, depending on the size of `unsigned long`.

```
int __builtin_popcountll (unsigned long long)
```
>   Generates the `popcntq` machine instruction.

The following built-in functions are available when '-mavx' is used. All of them generate the machine instruction that is part of the name.

```
v4df __builtin_ia32_addpd256 (v4df,v4df)
v8sf __builtin_ia32_addps256 (v8sf,v8sf)
v4df __builtin_ia32_addsubpd256 (v4df,v4df)
```

```
v8sf __builtin_ia32_addsubps256 (v8sf,v8sf)
v4df __builtin_ia32_andnpd256 (v4df,v4df)
v8sf __builtin_ia32_andnps256 (v8sf,v8sf)
v4df __builtin_ia32_andpd256 (v4df,v4df)
v8sf __builtin_ia32_andps256 (v8sf,v8sf)
v4df __builtin_ia32_blendpd256 (v4df,v4df,int)
v8sf __builtin_ia32_blendps256 (v8sf,v8sf,int)
v4df __builtin_ia32_blendvpd256 (v4df,v4df,v4df)
v8sf __builtin_ia32_blendvps256 (v8sf,v8sf,v8sf)
v2df __builtin_ia32_cmppd (v2df,v2df,int)
v4df __builtin_ia32_cmppd256 (v4df,v4df,int)
v4sf __builtin_ia32_cmpps (v4sf,v4sf,int)
v8sf __builtin_ia32_cmpps256 (v8sf,v8sf,int)
v2df __builtin_ia32_cmpsd (v2df,v2df,int)
v4sf __builtin_ia32_cmpss (v4sf,v4sf,int)
v4df __builtin_ia32_cvtdq2pd256 (v4si)
v8sf __builtin_ia32_cvtdq2ps256 (v8si)
v4si __builtin_ia32_cvtpd2dq256 (v4df)
v4sf __builtin_ia32_cvtpd2ps256 (v4df)
v8si __builtin_ia32_cvtps2dq256 (v8sf)
v4df __builtin_ia32_cvtps2pd256 (v4sf)
v4si __builtin_ia32_cvttpd2dq256 (v4df)
v8si __builtin_ia32_cvttps2dq256 (v8sf)
v4df __builtin_ia32_divpd256 (v4df,v4df)
v8sf __builtin_ia32_divps256 (v8sf,v8sf)
v8sf __builtin_ia32_dpps256 (v8sf,v8sf,int)
v4df __builtin_ia32_haddpd256 (v4df,v4df)
v8sf __builtin_ia32_haddps256 (v8sf,v8sf)
v4df __builtin_ia32_hsubpd256 (v4df,v4df)
v8sf __builtin_ia32_hsubps256 (v8sf,v8sf)
v32qi __builtin_ia32_lddqu256 (pcchar)
v32qi __builtin_ia32_loaddqu256 (pcchar)
v4df __builtin_ia32_loadupd256 (pcdouble)
v8sf __builtin_ia32_loadups256 (pcfloat)
v2df __builtin_ia32_maskloadpd (pcv2df,v2df)
v4df __builtin_ia32_maskloadpd256 (pcv4df,v4df)
v4sf __builtin_ia32_maskloadps (pcv4sf,v4sf)
v8sf __builtin_ia32_maskloadps256 (pcv8sf,v8sf)
void __builtin_ia32_maskstorepd (pv2df,v2df,v2df)
void __builtin_ia32_maskstorepd256 (pv4df,v4df,v4df)
void __builtin_ia32_maskstoreps (pv4sf,v4sf,v4sf)
void __builtin_ia32_maskstoreps256 (pv8sf,v8sf,v8sf)
v4df __builtin_ia32_maxpd256 (v4df,v4df)
v8sf __builtin_ia32_maxps256 (v8sf,v8sf)
v4df __builtin_ia32_minpd256 (v4df,v4df)
v8sf __builtin_ia32_minps256 (v8sf,v8sf)
v4df __builtin_ia32_movddup256 (v4df)
int __builtin_ia32_movmskpd256 (v4df)
int __builtin_ia32_movmskps256 (v8sf)
v8sf __builtin_ia32_movshdup256 (v8sf)
v8sf __builtin_ia32_movsldup256 (v8sf)
v4df __builtin_ia32_mulpd256 (v4df,v4df)
v8sf __builtin_ia32_mulps256 (v8sf,v8sf)
v4df __builtin_ia32_orpd256 (v4df,v4df)
v8sf __builtin_ia32_orps256 (v8sf,v8sf)
v2df __builtin_ia32_pd_pd256 (v4df)
v4df __builtin_ia32_pd256_pd (v2df)
v4sf __builtin_ia32_ps_ps256 (v8sf)
```

```
v8sf __builtin_ia32_ps256_ps (v4sf)
int __builtin_ia32_ptestc256 (v4di,v4di,ptest)
int __builtin_ia32_ptestnzc256 (v4di,v4di,ptest)
int __builtin_ia32_ptestz256 (v4di,v4di,ptest)
v8sf __builtin_ia32_rcpps256 (v8sf)
v4df __builtin_ia32_roundpd256 (v4df,int)
v8sf __builtin_ia32_roundps256 (v8sf,int)
v8sf __builtin_ia32_rsqrtps_nr256 (v8sf)
v8sf __builtin_ia32_rsqrtps256 (v8sf)
v4df __builtin_ia32_shufpd256 (v4df,v4df,int)
v8sf __builtin_ia32_shufps256 (v8sf,v8sf,int)
v4si __builtin_ia32_si_si256 (v8si)
v8si __builtin_ia32_si256_si (v4si)
v4df __builtin_ia32_sqrtpd256 (v4df)
v8sf __builtin_ia32_sqrtps_nr256 (v8sf)
v8sf __builtin_ia32_sqrtps256 (v8sf)
void __builtin_ia32_storedqu256 (pchar,v32qi)
void __builtin_ia32_storeupd256 (pdouble,v4df)
void __builtin_ia32_storeups256 (pfloat,v8sf)
v4df __builtin_ia32_subpd256 (v4df,v4df)
v8sf __builtin_ia32_subps256 (v8sf,v8sf)
v4df __builtin_ia32_unpckhpd256 (v4df,v4df)
v8sf __builtin_ia32_unpckhps256 (v8sf,v8sf)
v4df __builtin_ia32_unpcklpd256 (v4df,v4df)
v8sf __builtin_ia32_unpcklps256 (v8sf,v8sf)
v4df __builtin_ia32_vbroadcastf128_pd256 (pcv2df)
v8sf __builtin_ia32_vbroadcastf128_ps256 (pcv4sf)
v4df __builtin_ia32_vbroadcastsd256 (pcdouble)
v4sf __builtin_ia32_vbroadcastss (pcfloat)
v8sf __builtin_ia32_vbroadcastss256 (pcfloat)
v2df __builtin_ia32_vextractf128_pd256 (v4df,int)
v4sf __builtin_ia32_vextractf128_ps256 (v8sf,int)
v4si __builtin_ia32_vextractf128_si256 (v8si,int)
v4df __builtin_ia32_vinsertf128_pd256 (v4df,v2df,int)
v8sf __builtin_ia32_vinsertf128_ps256 (v8sf,v4sf,int)
v8si __builtin_ia32_vinsertf128_si256 (v8si,v4si,int)
v4df __builtin_ia32_vperm2f128_pd256 (v4df,v4df,int)
v8sf __builtin_ia32_vperm2f128_ps256 (v8sf,v8sf,int)
v8si __builtin_ia32_vperm2f128_si256 (v8si,v8si,int)
v2df __builtin_ia32_vpermil2pd (v2df,v2df,v2di,int)
v4df __builtin_ia32_vpermil2pd256 (v4df,v4df,v4di,int)
v4sf __builtin_ia32_vpermil2ps (v4sf,v4sf,v4si,int)
v8sf __builtin_ia32_vpermil2ps256 (v8sf,v8sf,v8si,int)
v2df __builtin_ia32_vpermilpd (v2df,int)
v4df __builtin_ia32_vpermilpd256 (v4df,int)
v4sf __builtin_ia32_vpermilps (v4sf,int)
v8sf __builtin_ia32_vpermilps256 (v8sf,int)
v2df __builtin_ia32_vpermilvarpd (v2df,v2di)
v4df __builtin_ia32_vpermilvarpd256 (v4df,v4di)
v4sf __builtin_ia32_vpermilvarps (v4sf,v4si)
v8sf __builtin_ia32_vpermilvarps256 (v8sf,v8si)
int __builtin_ia32_vtestcpd (v2df,v2df,ptest)
int __builtin_ia32_vtestcpd256 (v4df,v4df,ptest)
int __builtin_ia32_vtestcps (v4sf,v4sf,ptest)
int __builtin_ia32_vtestcps256 (v8sf,v8sf,ptest)
int __builtin_ia32_vtestnzcpd (v2df,v2df,ptest)
int __builtin_ia32_vtestnzcpd256 (v4df,v4df,ptest)
int __builtin_ia32_vtestnzcps (v4sf,v4sf,ptest)
```

```
int __builtin_ia32_vtestnzcps256 (v8sf,v8sf,ptest)
int __builtin_ia32_vtestzpd (v2df,v2df,ptest)
int __builtin_ia32_vtestzpd256 (v4df,v4df,ptest)
int __builtin_ia32_vtestzps (v4sf,v4sf,ptest)
int __builtin_ia32_vtestzps256 (v8sf,v8sf,ptest)
void __builtin_ia32_vzeroall (void)
void __builtin_ia32_vzeroupper (void)
v4df __builtin_ia32_xorpd256 (v4df,v4df)
v8sf __builtin_ia32_xorps256 (v8sf,v8sf)
```

The following built-in functions are available when '-mavx2' is used. All of them generate the machine instruction that is part of the name.

```
v32qi __builtin_ia32_mpsadbw256 (v32qi,v32qi,int)
v32qi __builtin_ia32_pabsb256 (v32qi)
v16hi __builtin_ia32_pabsw256 (v16hi)
v8si __builtin_ia32_pabsd256 (v8si)
v16hi __builtin_ia32_packssdw256 (v8si,v8si)
v32qi __builtin_ia32_packsswb256 (v16hi,v16hi)
v16hi __builtin_ia32_packusdw256 (v8si,v8si)
v32qi __builtin_ia32_packuswb256 (v16hi,v16hi)
v32qi __builtin_ia32_paddb256 (v32qi,v32qi)
v16hi __builtin_ia32_paddw256 (v16hi,v16hi)
v8si __builtin_ia32_paddd256 (v8si,v8si)
v4di __builtin_ia32_paddq256 (v4di,v4di)
v32qi __builtin_ia32_paddsb256 (v32qi,v32qi)
v16hi __builtin_ia32_paddsw256 (v16hi,v16hi)
v32qi __builtin_ia32_paddusb256 (v32qi,v32qi)
v16hi __builtin_ia32_paddusw256 (v16hi,v16hi)
v4di __builtin_ia32_palignr256 (v4di,v4di,int)
v4di __builtin_ia32_andsi256 (v4di,v4di)
v4di __builtin_ia32_andnotsi256 (v4di,v4di)
v32qi __builtin_ia32_pavgb256 (v32qi,v32qi)
v16hi __builtin_ia32_pavgw256 (v16hi,v16hi)
v32qi __builtin_ia32_pblendvb256 (v32qi,v32qi,v32qi)
v16hi __builtin_ia32_pblendw256 (v16hi,v16hi,int)
v32qi __builtin_ia32_pcmpeqb256 (v32qi,v32qi)
v16hi __builtin_ia32_pcmpeqw256 (v16hi,v16hi)
v8si __builtin_ia32_pcmpeqd256 (c8si,v8si)
v4di __builtin_ia32_pcmpeqq256 (v4di,v4di)
v32qi __builtin_ia32_pcmpgtb256 (v32qi,v32qi)
v16hi __builtin_ia32_pcmpgtw256 (16hi,v16hi)
v8si __builtin_ia32_pcmpgtd256 (v8si,v8si)
v4di __builtin_ia32_pcmpgtq256 (v4di,v4di)
v16hi __builtin_ia32_phaddw256 (v16hi,v16hi)
v8si __builtin_ia32_phaddd256 (v8si,v8si)
v16hi __builtin_ia32_phaddsw256 (v16hi,v16hi)
v16hi __builtin_ia32_phsubw256 (v16hi,v16hi)
v8si __builtin_ia32_phsubd256 (v8si,v8si)
v16hi __builtin_ia32_phsubsw256 (v16hi,v16hi)
v32qi __builtin_ia32_pmaddubsw256 (v32qi,v32qi)
v16hi __builtin_ia32_pmaddwd256 (v16hi,v16hi)
v32qi __builtin_ia32_pmaxsb256 (v32qi,v32qi)
v16hi __builtin_ia32_pmaxsw256 (v16hi,v16hi)
v8si __builtin_ia32_pmaxsd256 (v8si,v8si)
v32qi __builtin_ia32_pmaxub256 (v32qi,v32qi)
v16hi __builtin_ia32_pmaxuw256 (v16hi,v16hi)
v8si __builtin_ia32_pmaxud256 (v8si,v8si)
v32qi __builtin_ia32_pminsb256 (v32qi,v32qi)
```

```
v16hi __builtin_ia32_pminsw256 (v16hi,v16hi)
v8si __builtin_ia32_pminsd256 (v8si,v8si)
v32qi __builtin_ia32_pminub256 (v32qi,v32qi)
v16hi __builtin_ia32_pminuw256 (v16hi,v16hi)
v8si __builtin_ia32_pminud256 (v8si,v8si)
int __builtin_ia32_pmovmskb256 (v32qi)
v16hi __builtin_ia32_pmovsxbw256 (v16qi)
v8si __builtin_ia32_pmovsxbd256 (v16qi)
v4di __builtin_ia32_pmovsxbq256 (v16qi)
v8si __builtin_ia32_pmovsxwd256 (v8hi)
v4di __builtin_ia32_pmovsxwq256 (v8hi)
v4di __builtin_ia32_pmovsxdq256 (v4si)
v16hi __builtin_ia32_pmovzxbw256 (v16qi)
v8si __builtin_ia32_pmovzxbd256 (v16qi)
v4di __builtin_ia32_pmovzxbq256 (v16qi)
v8si __builtin_ia32_pmovzxwd256 (v8hi)
v4di __builtin_ia32_pmovzxwq256 (v8hi)
v4di __builtin_ia32_pmovzxdq256 (v4si)
v4di __builtin_ia32_pmuldq256 (v8si,v8si)
v16hi __builtin_ia32_pmulhrsw256 (v16hi, v16hi)
v16hi __builtin_ia32_pmulhuw256 (v16hi,v16hi)
v16hi __builtin_ia32_pmulhw256 (v16hi,v16hi)
v16hi __builtin_ia32_pmullw256 (v16hi,v16hi)
v8si __builtin_ia32_pmulld256 (v8si,v8si)
v4di __builtin_ia32_pmuludq256 (v8si,v8si)
v4di __builtin_ia32_por256 (v4di,v4di)
v16hi __builtin_ia32_psadbw256 (v32qi,v32qi)
v32qi __builtin_ia32_pshufb256 (v32qi,v32qi)
v8si __builtin_ia32_pshufd256 (v8si,int)
v16hi __builtin_ia32_pshufhw256 (v16hi,int)
v16hi __builtin_ia32_pshuflw256 (v16hi,int)
v32qi __builtin_ia32_psignb256 (v32qi,v32qi)
v16hi __builtin_ia32_psignw256 (v16hi,v16hi)
v8si __builtin_ia32_psignd256 (v8si,v8si)
v4di __builtin_ia32_pslldqi256 (v4di,int)
v16hi __builtin_ia32_psllwi256 (16hi,int)
v16hi __builtin_ia32_psllw256(v16hi,v8hi)
v8si __builtin_ia32_pslldi256 (v8si,int)
v8si __builtin_ia32_pslld256(v8si,v4si)
v4di __builtin_ia32_psllqi256 (v4di,int)
v4di __builtin_ia32_psllq256(v4di,v2di)
v16hi __builtin_ia32_psrawi256 (v16hi,int)
v16hi __builtin_ia32_psraw256 (v16hi,v8hi)
v8si __builtin_ia32_psradi256 (v8si,int)
v8si __builtin_ia32_psrad256 (v8si,v4si)
v4di __builtin_ia32_psrldqi256 (v4di, int)
v16hi __builtin_ia32_psrlwi256 (v16hi,int)
v16hi __builtin_ia32_psrlw256 (v16hi,v8hi)
v8si __builtin_ia32_psrldi256 (v8si,int)
v8si __builtin_ia32_psrld256 (v8si,v4si)
v4di __builtin_ia32_psrlqi256 (v4di,int)
v4di __builtin_ia32_psrlq256(v4di,v2di)
v32qi __builtin_ia32_psubb256 (v32qi,v32qi)
v32hi __builtin_ia32_psubw256 (v16hi,v16hi)
v8si __builtin_ia32_psubd256 (v8si,v8si)
v4di __builtin_ia32_psubq256 (v4di,v4di)
v32qi __builtin_ia32_psubsb256 (v32qi,v32qi)
v16hi __builtin_ia32_psubsw256 (v16hi,v16hi)
```

```
v32qi __builtin_ia32_psubusb256 (v32qi,v32qi)
v16hi __builtin_ia32_psubusw256 (v16hi,v16hi)
v32qi __builtin_ia32_punpckhbw256 (v32qi,v32qi)
v16hi __builtin_ia32_punpckhwd256 (v16hi,v16hi)
v8si __builtin_ia32_punpckhdq256 (v8si,v8si)
v4di __builtin_ia32_punpckhqdq256 (v4di,v4di)
v32qi __builtin_ia32_punpcklbw256 (v32qi,v32qi)
v16hi __builtin_ia32_punpcklwd256 (v16hi,v16hi)
v8si __builtin_ia32_punpckldq256 (v8si,v8si)
v4di __builtin_ia32_punpcklqdq256 (v4di,v4di)
v4di __builtin_ia32_pxor256 (v4di,v4di)
v4di __builtin_ia32_movntdqa256 (pv4di)
v4sf __builtin_ia32_vbroadcastss_ps (v4sf)
v8sf __builtin_ia32_vbroadcastss_ps256 (v4sf)
v4df __builtin_ia32_vbroadcastsd_pd256 (v2df)
v4di __builtin_ia32_vbroadcastsi256 (v2di)
v4si __builtin_ia32_pblendd128 (v4si,v4si)
v8si __builtin_ia32_pblendd256 (v8si,v8si)
v32qi __builtin_ia32_pbroadcastb256 (v16qi)
v16hi __builtin_ia32_pbroadcastw256 (v8hi)
v8si __builtin_ia32_pbroadcastd256 (v4si)
v4di __builtin_ia32_pbroadcastq256 (v2di)
v16qi __builtin_ia32_pbroadcastb128 (v16qi)
v8hi __builtin_ia32_pbroadcastw128 (v8hi)
v4si __builtin_ia32_pbroadcastd128 (v4si)
v2di __builtin_ia32_pbroadcastq128 (v2di)
v8si __builtin_ia32_permvarsi256 (v8si,v8si)
v4df __builtin_ia32_permdf256 (v4df,int)
v8sf __builtin_ia32_permvarsf256 (v8sf,v8sf)
v4di __builtin_ia32_permdi256 (v4di,int)
v4di __builtin_ia32_permti256 (v4di,v4di,int)
v4di __builtin_ia32_extract128i256 (v4di,int)
v4di __builtin_ia32_insert128i256 (v4di,v2di,int)
v8si __builtin_ia32_maskloadd256 (pcv8si,v8si)
v4di __builtin_ia32_maskloadq256 (pcv4di,v4di)
v4si __builtin_ia32_maskloadd (pcv4si,v4si)
v2di __builtin_ia32_maskloadq (pcv2di,v2di)
void __builtin_ia32_maskstored256 (pv8si,v8si,v8si)
void __builtin_ia32_maskstoreq256 (pv4di,v4di,v4di)
void __builtin_ia32_maskstored (pv4si,v4si,v4si)
void __builtin_ia32_maskstoreq (pv2di,v2di,v2di)
v8si __builtin_ia32_psllv8si (v8si,v8si)
v4si __builtin_ia32_psllv4si (v4si,v4si)
v4di __builtin_ia32_psllv4di (v4di,v4di)
v2di __builtin_ia32_psllv2di (v2di,v2di)
v8si __builtin_ia32_psrav8si (v8si,v8si)
v4si __builtin_ia32_psrav4si (v4si,v4si)
v8si __builtin_ia32_psrlv8si (v8si,v8si)
v4si __builtin_ia32_psrlv4si (v4si,v4si)
v4di __builtin_ia32_psrlv4di (v4di,v4di)
v2di __builtin_ia32_psrlv2di (v2di,v2di)
v2df __builtin_ia32_gathersiv2df (v2df, pcdouble,v4si,v2df,int)
v4df __builtin_ia32_gathersiv4df (v4df, pcdouble,v4si,v4df,int)
v2df __builtin_ia32_gatherdiv2df (v2df, pcdouble,v2di,v2df,int)
v4df __builtin_ia32_gatherdiv4df (v4df, pcdouble,v4di,v4df,int)
v4sf __builtin_ia32_gathersiv4sf (v4sf, pcfloat,v4si,v4sf,int)
v8sf __builtin_ia32_gathersiv8sf (v8sf, pcfloat,v8si,v8sf,int)
v4sf __builtin_ia32_gatherdiv4sf (v4sf, pcfloat,v2di,v4sf,int)
```

```
v4sf __builtin_ia32_gatherdiv4sf256 (v4sf, pcfloat,v4di,v4sf,int)
v2di __builtin_ia32_gathersiv2di (v2di, pcint64,v4si,v2di,int)
v4di __builtin_ia32_gathersiv4di (v4di, pcint64,v4si,v4di,int)
v2di __builtin_ia32_gatherdiv2di (v2di, pcint64,v2di,v2di,int)
v4di __builtin_ia32_gatherdiv4di (v4di, pcint64,v4di,v4di,int)
v4si __builtin_ia32_gathersiv4si (v4si, pcint,v4si,v4si,int)
v8si __builtin_ia32_gathersiv8si (v8si, pcint,v8si,v8si,int)
v4si __builtin_ia32_gatherdiv4si (v4si, pcint,v2di,v4si,int)
v4si __builtin_ia32_gatherdiv4si256 (v4si, pcint,v4di,v4si,int)
```

The following built-in functions are available when '-maes' is used. All of them generate the machine instruction that is part of the name.

```
v2di __builtin_ia32_aesenc128 (v2di, v2di)
v2di __builtin_ia32_aesenclast128 (v2di, v2di)
v2di __builtin_ia32_aesdec128 (v2di, v2di)
v2di __builtin_ia32_aesdeclast128 (v2di, v2di)
v2di __builtin_ia32_aeskeygenassist128 (v2di, const int)
v2di __builtin_ia32_aesimc128 (v2di)
```

The following built-in function is available when '-mpclmul' is used.

`v2di __builtin_ia32_pclmulqdq128 (v2di, v2di, const int)`
> Generates the `pclmulqdq` machine instruction.

The following built-in function is available when '-mfsgsbase' is used. All of them generate the machine instruction that is part of the name.

```
unsigned int __builtin_ia32_rdfsbase32 (void)
unsigned long long __builtin_ia32_rdfsbase64 (void)
unsigned int __builtin_ia32_rdgsbase32 (void)
unsigned long long __builtin_ia32_rdgsbase64 (void)
void _writefsbase_u32 (unsigned int)
void _writefsbase_u64 (unsigned long long)
void _writegsbase_u32 (unsigned int)
void _writegsbase_u64 (unsigned long long)
```

The following built-in function is available when '-mrdrnd' is used. All of them generate the machine instruction that is part of the name.

```
unsigned int __builtin_ia32_rdrand16_step (unsigned short *)
unsigned int __builtin_ia32_rdrand32_step (unsigned int *)
unsigned int __builtin_ia32_rdrand64_step (unsigned long long *)
```

The following built-in functions are available when '-msse4a' is used. All of them generate the machine instruction that is part of the name.

```
void __builtin_ia32_movntsd (double *, v2df)
void __builtin_ia32_movntss (float *, v4sf)
v2di __builtin_ia32_extrq  (v2di, v16qi)
v2di __builtin_ia32_extrqi (v2di, const unsigned int, const unsigned int)
v2di __builtin_ia32_insertq (v2di, v2di)
v2di __builtin_ia32_insertqi (v2di, v2di, const unsigned int, const unsigned int)
```

The following built-in functions are available when '-mxop' is used.

```
v2df __builtin_ia32_vfrczpd (v2df)
v4sf __builtin_ia32_vfrczps (v4sf)
v2df __builtin_ia32_vfrczsd (v2df)
v4sf __builtin_ia32_vfrczss (v4sf)
v4df __builtin_ia32_vfrczpd256 (v4df)
v8sf __builtin_ia32_vfrczps256 (v8sf)
v2di __builtin_ia32_vpcmov (v2di, v2di, v2di)
v2di __builtin_ia32_vpcmov_v2di (v2di, v2di, v2di)
```

```
v4si __builtin_ia32_vpcmov_v4si (v4si, v4si, v4si)
v8hi __builtin_ia32_vpcmov_v8hi (v8hi, v8hi, v8hi)
v16qi __builtin_ia32_vpcmov_v16qi (v16qi, v16qi, v16qi)
v2df __builtin_ia32_vpcmov_v2df (v2df, v2df, v2df)
v4sf __builtin_ia32_vpcmov_v4sf (v4sf, v4sf, v4sf)
v4di __builtin_ia32_vpcmov_v4di256 (v4di, v4di, v4di)
v8si __builtin_ia32_vpcmov_v8si256 (v8si, v8si, v8si)
v16hi __builtin_ia32_vpcmov_v16hi256 (v16hi, v16hi, v16hi)
v32qi __builtin_ia32_vpcmov_v32qi256 (v32qi, v32qi, v32qi)
v4df __builtin_ia32_vpcmov_v4df256 (v4df, v4df, v4df)
v8sf __builtin_ia32_vpcmov_v8sf256 (v8sf, v8sf, v8sf)
v16qi __builtin_ia32_vpcomeqb (v16qi, v16qi)
v8hi __builtin_ia32_vpcomeqw (v8hi, v8hi)
v4si __builtin_ia32_vpcomeqd (v4si, v4si)
v2di __builtin_ia32_vpcomeqq (v2di, v2di)
v16qi __builtin_ia32_vpcomequb (v16qi, v16qi)
v4si __builtin_ia32_vpcomequd (v4si, v4si)
v2di __builtin_ia32_vpcomequq (v2di, v2di)
v8hi __builtin_ia32_vpcomequw (v8hi, v8hi)
v8hi __builtin_ia32_vpcomeqw (v8hi, v8hi)
v16qi __builtin_ia32_vpcomfalseb (v16qi, v16qi)
v4si __builtin_ia32_vpcomfalsed (v4si, v4si)
v2di __builtin_ia32_vpcomfalseq (v2di, v2di)
v16qi __builtin_ia32_vpcomfalseub (v16qi, v16qi)
v4si __builtin_ia32_vpcomfalseud (v4si, v4si)
v2di __builtin_ia32_vpcomfalseuq (v2di, v2di)
v8hi __builtin_ia32_vpcomfalseuw (v8hi, v8hi)
v8hi __builtin_ia32_vpcomfalsew (v8hi, v8hi)
v16qi __builtin_ia32_vpcomgeb (v16qi, v16qi)
v4si __builtin_ia32_vpcomged (v4si, v4si)
v2di __builtin_ia32_vpcomgeq (v2di, v2di)
v16qi __builtin_ia32_vpcomgeub (v16qi, v16qi)
v4si __builtin_ia32_vpcomgeud (v4si, v4si)
v2di __builtin_ia32_vpcomgeuq (v2di, v2di)
v8hi __builtin_ia32_vpcomgeuw (v8hi, v8hi)
v8hi __builtin_ia32_vpcomgew (v8hi, v8hi)
v16qi __builtin_ia32_vpcomgtb (v16qi, v16qi)
v4si __builtin_ia32_vpcomgtd (v4si, v4si)
v2di __builtin_ia32_vpcomgtq (v2di, v2di)
v16qi __builtin_ia32_vpcomgtub (v16qi, v16qi)
v4si __builtin_ia32_vpcomgtud (v4si, v4si)
v2di __builtin_ia32_vpcomgtuq (v2di, v2di)
v8hi __builtin_ia32_vpcomgtuw (v8hi, v8hi)
v8hi __builtin_ia32_vpcomgtw (v8hi, v8hi)
v16qi __builtin_ia32_vpcomleb (v16qi, v16qi)
v4si __builtin_ia32_vpcomled (v4si, v4si)
v2di __builtin_ia32_vpcomleq (v2di, v2di)
v16qi __builtin_ia32_vpcomleub (v16qi, v16qi)
v4si __builtin_ia32_vpcomleud (v4si, v4si)
v2di __builtin_ia32_vpcomleuq (v2di, v2di)
v8hi __builtin_ia32_vpcomleuw (v8hi, v8hi)
v8hi __builtin_ia32_vpcomlew (v8hi, v8hi)
v16qi __builtin_ia32_vpcomltb (v16qi, v16qi)
v4si __builtin_ia32_vpcomltd (v4si, v4si)
v2di __builtin_ia32_vpcomltq (v2di, v2di)
v16qi __builtin_ia32_vpcomltub (v16qi, v16qi)
v4si __builtin_ia32_vpcomltud (v4si, v4si)
v2di __builtin_ia32_vpcomltuq (v2di, v2di)
```

```
v8hi __builtin_ia32_vpcomltuw (v8hi, v8hi)
v8hi __builtin_ia32_vpcomltw (v8hi, v8hi)
v16qi __builtin_ia32_vpcomneb (v16qi, v16qi)
v4si __builtin_ia32_vpcomned (v4si, v4si)
v2di __builtin_ia32_vpcomneq (v2di, v2di)
v16qi __builtin_ia32_vpcomneub (v16qi, v16qi)
v4si __builtin_ia32_vpcomneud (v4si, v4si)
v2di __builtin_ia32_vpcomneuq (v2di, v2di)
v8hi __builtin_ia32_vpcomneuw (v8hi, v8hi)
v8hi __builtin_ia32_vpcomnew (v8hi, v8hi)
v16qi __builtin_ia32_vpcomtrueb (v16qi, v16qi)
v4si __builtin_ia32_vpcomtrued (v4si, v4si)
v2di __builtin_ia32_vpcomtrueq (v2di, v2di)
v16qi __builtin_ia32_vpcomtrueub (v16qi, v16qi)
v4si __builtin_ia32_vpcomtrueud (v4si, v4si)
v2di __builtin_ia32_vpcomtrueuq (v2di, v2di)
v8hi __builtin_ia32_vpcomtrueuw (v8hi, v8hi)
v8hi __builtin_ia32_vpcomtruew (v8hi, v8hi)
v4si __builtin_ia32_vphaddbd (v16qi)
v2di __builtin_ia32_vphaddbq (v16qi)
v8hi __builtin_ia32_vphaddbw (v16qi)
v2di __builtin_ia32_vphadddq (v4si)
v4si __builtin_ia32_vphaddubd (v16qi)
v2di __builtin_ia32_vphaddubq (v16qi)
v8hi __builtin_ia32_vphaddubw (v16qi)
v2di __builtin_ia32_vphaddudq (v4si)
v4si __builtin_ia32_vphadduwd (v8hi)
v2di __builtin_ia32_vphadduwq (v8hi)
v4si __builtin_ia32_vphaddwd (v8hi)
v2di __builtin_ia32_vphaddwq (v8hi)
v8hi __builtin_ia32_vphsubbw (v16qi)
v2di __builtin_ia32_vphsubdq (v4si)
v4si __builtin_ia32_vphsubwd (v8hi)
v4si __builtin_ia32_vpmacsdd (v4si, v4si, v4si)
v2di __builtin_ia32_vpmacsdqh (v4si, v4si, v2di)
v2di __builtin_ia32_vpmacsdql (v4si, v4si, v2di)
v4si __builtin_ia32_vpmacssdd (v4si, v4si, v4si)
v2di __builtin_ia32_vpmacssdqh (v4si, v4si, v2di)
v2di __builtin_ia32_vpmacssdql (v4si, v4si, v2di)
v4si __builtin_ia32_vpmacsswd (v8hi, v8hi, v4si)
v8hi __builtin_ia32_vpmacssww (v8hi, v8hi, v8hi)
v4si __builtin_ia32_vpmacswd (v8hi, v8hi, v4si)
v8hi __builtin_ia32_vpmacsww (v8hi, v8hi, v8hi)
v4si __builtin_ia32_vpmadcsswd (v8hi, v8hi, v4si)
v4si __builtin_ia32_vpmadcswd (v8hi, v8hi, v4si)
v16qi __builtin_ia32_vpperm (v16qi, v16qi, v16qi)
v16qi __builtin_ia32_vprotb (v16qi, v16qi)
v4si __builtin_ia32_vprotd (v4si, v4si)
v2di __builtin_ia32_vprotq (v2di, v2di)
v8hi __builtin_ia32_vprotw (v8hi, v8hi)
v16qi __builtin_ia32_vpshab (v16qi, v16qi)
v4si __builtin_ia32_vpshad (v4si, v4si)
v2di __builtin_ia32_vpshaq (v2di, v2di)
v8hi __builtin_ia32_vpshaw (v8hi, v8hi)
v16qi __builtin_ia32_vpshlb (v16qi, v16qi)
v4si __builtin_ia32_vpshld (v4si, v4si)
v2di __builtin_ia32_vpshlq (v2di, v2di)
v8hi __builtin_ia32_vpshlw (v8hi, v8hi)
```

The following built-in functions are available when '-mfma4' is used. All of them generate the machine instruction that is part of the name.

```
v2df __builtin_ia32_vfmaddpd (v2df, v2df, v2df)
v4sf __builtin_ia32_vfmaddps (v4sf, v4sf, v4sf)
v2df __builtin_ia32_vfmaddsd (v2df, v2df, v2df)
v4sf __builtin_ia32_vfmaddss (v4sf, v4sf, v4sf)
v2df __builtin_ia32_vfmsubpd (v2df, v2df, v2df)
v4sf __builtin_ia32_vfmsubps (v4sf, v4sf, v4sf)
v2df __builtin_ia32_vfmsubsd (v2df, v2df, v2df)
v4sf __builtin_ia32_vfmsubss (v4sf, v4sf, v4sf)
v2df __builtin_ia32_vfnmaddpd (v2df, v2df, v2df)
v4sf __builtin_ia32_vfnmaddps (v4sf, v4sf, v4sf)
v2df __builtin_ia32_vfnmaddsd (v2df, v2df, v2df)
v4sf __builtin_ia32_vfnmaddss (v4sf, v4sf, v4sf)
v2df __builtin_ia32_vfnmsubpd (v2df, v2df, v2df)
v4sf __builtin_ia32_vfnmsubps (v4sf, v4sf, v4sf)
v2df __builtin_ia32_vfnmsubsd (v2df, v2df, v2df)
v4sf __builtin_ia32_vfnmsubss (v4sf, v4sf, v4sf)
v2df __builtin_ia32_vfmaddsubpd  (v2df, v2df, v2df)
v4sf __builtin_ia32_vfmaddsubps  (v4sf, v4sf, v4sf)
v2df __builtin_ia32_vfmsubaddpd  (v2df, v2df, v2df)
v4sf __builtin_ia32_vfmsubaddps  (v4sf, v4sf, v4sf)
v4df __builtin_ia32_vfmaddpd256 (v4df, v4df, v4df)
v8sf __builtin_ia32_vfmaddps256 (v8sf, v8sf, v8sf)
v4df __builtin_ia32_vfmsubpd256 (v4df, v4df, v4df)
v8sf __builtin_ia32_vfmsubps256 (v8sf, v8sf, v8sf)
v4df __builtin_ia32_vfnmaddpd256 (v4df, v4df, v4df)
v8sf __builtin_ia32_vfnmaddps256 (v8sf, v8sf, v8sf)
v4df __builtin_ia32_vfnmsubpd256 (v4df, v4df, v4df)
v8sf __builtin_ia32_vfnmsubps256 (v8sf, v8sf, v8sf)
v4df __builtin_ia32_vfmaddsubpd256 (v4df, v4df, v4df)
v8sf __builtin_ia32_vfmaddsubps256 (v8sf, v8sf, v8sf)
v4df __builtin_ia32_vfmsubaddpd256 (v4df, v4df, v4df)
v8sf __builtin_ia32_vfmsubaddps256 (v8sf, v8sf, v8sf)
```

The following built-in functions are available when '-mlwp' is used.

```
void __builtin_ia32_llwpcb16 (void *);
void __builtin_ia32_llwpcb32 (void *);
void __builtin_ia32_llwpcb64 (void *);
void * __builtin_ia32_llwpcb16 (void);
void * __builtin_ia32_llwpcb32 (void);
void * __builtin_ia32_llwpcb64 (void);
void __builtin_ia32_lwpval16 (unsigned short, unsigned int, unsigned short)
void __builtin_ia32_lwpval32 (unsigned int, unsigned int, unsigned int)
void __builtin_ia32_lwpval64 (unsigned __int64, unsigned int, unsigned int)
unsigned char __builtin_ia32_lwpins16 (unsigned short, unsigned int, unsigned short)
unsigned char __builtin_ia32_lwpins32 (unsigned int, unsigned int, unsigned int)
unsigned char __builtin_ia32_lwpins64 (unsigned __int64, unsigned int, unsigned int)
```

The following built-in functions are available when '-mbmi' is used. All of them generate the machine instruction that is part of the name.

```
unsigned int __builtin_ia32_bextr_u32(unsigned int, unsigned int);
unsigned long long __builtin_ia32_bextr_u64 (unsigned long long, unsigned long long);
```

The following built-in functions are available when '-mbmi2' is used. All of them generate the machine instruction that is part of the name.

```
unsigned int _bzhi_u32 (unsigned int, unsigned int)
```

```
unsigned int _pdep_u32 (unsigned int, unsigned int)
unsigned int _pext_u32 (unsigned int, unsigned int)
unsigned long long _bzhi_u64 (unsigned long long, unsigned long long)
unsigned long long _pdep_u64 (unsigned long long, unsigned long long)
unsigned long long _pext_u64 (unsigned long long, unsigned long long)
```

The following built-in functions are available when '-mlzcnt' is used. All of them generate the machine instruction that is part of the name.

```
unsigned short __builtin_ia32_lzcnt_16(unsigned short);
unsigned int __builtin_ia32_lzcnt_u32(unsigned int);
unsigned long long __builtin_ia32_lzcnt_u64 (unsigned long long);
```

The following built-in functions are available when '-mfxsr' is used. All of them generate the machine instruction that is part of the name.

```
void __builtin_ia32_fxsave (void *)
void __builtin_ia32_fxrstor (void *)
void __builtin_ia32_fxsave64 (void *)
void __builtin_ia32_fxrstor64 (void *)
```

The following built-in functions are available when '-mxsave' is used. All of them generate the machine instruction that is part of the name.

```
void __builtin_ia32_xsave (void *, long long)
void __builtin_ia32_xrstor (void *, long long)
void __builtin_ia32_xsave64 (void *, long long)
void __builtin_ia32_xrstor64 (void *, long long)
```

The following built-in functions are available when '-mxsaveopt' is used. All of them generate the machine instruction that is part of the name.

```
void __builtin_ia32_xsaveopt (void *, long long)
void __builtin_ia32_xsaveopt64 (void *, long long)
```

The following built-in functions are available when '-mtbm' is used. Both of them generate the immediate form of the bextr machine instruction.

```
unsigned int __builtin_ia32_bextri_u32 (unsigned int, const unsigned int);
unsigned long long __builtin_ia32_bextri_u64 (unsigned long long, const unsigned long long);
```

The following built-in functions are available when '-m3dnow' is used. All of them generate the machine instruction that is part of the name.

```
void __builtin_ia32_femms (void)
v8qi __builtin_ia32_pavgusb (v8qi, v8qi)
v2si __builtin_ia32_pf2id (v2sf)
v2sf __builtin_ia32_pfacc (v2sf, v2sf)
v2sf __builtin_ia32_pfadd (v2sf, v2sf)
v2si __builtin_ia32_pfcmpeq (v2sf, v2sf)
v2si __builtin_ia32_pfcmpge (v2sf, v2sf)
v2si __builtin_ia32_pfcmpgt (v2sf, v2sf)
v2sf __builtin_ia32_pfmax (v2sf, v2sf)
v2sf __builtin_ia32_pfmin (v2sf, v2sf)
v2sf __builtin_ia32_pfmul (v2sf, v2sf)
v2sf __builtin_ia32_pfrcp (v2sf)
v2sf __builtin_ia32_pfrcpit1 (v2sf, v2sf)
v2sf __builtin_ia32_pfrcpit2 (v2sf, v2sf)
v2sf __builtin_ia32_pfrsqrt (v2sf)
v2sf __builtin_ia32_pfsub (v2sf, v2sf)
v2sf __builtin_ia32_pfsubr (v2sf, v2sf)
v2sf __builtin_ia32_pi2fd (v2si)
v4hi __builtin_ia32_pmulhrw (v4hi, v4hi)
```

The following built-in functions are available when both '-m3dnow' and '-march=athlon' are used. All of them generate the machine instruction that is part of the name.

```
v2si __builtin_ia32_pf2iw (v2sf)
v2sf __builtin_ia32_pfnacc (v2sf, v2sf)
v2sf __builtin_ia32_pfpnacc (v2sf, v2sf)
v2sf __builtin_ia32_pi2fw (v2si)
v2sf __builtin_ia32_pswapdsf (v2sf)
v2si __builtin_ia32_pswapdsi (v2si)
```

The following built-in functions are available when '-mrtm' is used They are used for restricted transactional memory. These are the internal low level functions. Normally the functions in Section 6.60.33 [x86 transactional memory intrinsics], page 713 should be used instead.

```
int __builtin_ia32_xbegin ()
void __builtin_ia32_xend ()
void __builtin_ia32_xabort (status)
int __builtin_ia32_xtest ()
```

The following built-in functions are available when '-mmwaitx' is used. All of them generate the machine instruction that is part of the name.

```
void __builtin_ia32_monitorx (void *, unsigned int, unsigned int)
void __builtin_ia32_mwaitx (unsigned int, unsigned int, unsigned int)
```

The following built-in functions are available when '-mclzero' is used. All of them generate the machine instruction that is part of the name.

```
void __builtin_i32_clzero (void *)
```

The following built-in functions are available when '-mpku' is used. They generate reads and writes to PKRU.

```
void __builtin_ia32_wrpkru (unsigned int)
unsigned int __builtin_ia32_rdpkru ()
```

6.60.33 x86 Transactional Memory Intrinsics

These hardware transactional memory intrinsics for x86 allow you to use memory transactions with RTM (Restricted Transactional Memory). This support is enabled with the '-mrtm' option. For using HLE (Hardware Lock Elision) see Section 6.55 [x86 specific memory model extensions for transactional memory], page 563 instead.

A memory transaction commits all changes to memory in an atomic way, as visible to other threads. If the transaction fails it is rolled back and all side effects discarded.

Generally there is no guarantee that a memory transaction ever succeeds and suitable fallback code always needs to be supplied.

unsigned _xbegin ()   [RTM Function]

Start a RTM (Restricted Transactional Memory) transaction. Returns _XBEGIN_ STARTED when the transaction started successfully (note this is not 0, so the constant has to be explicitly tested).

If the transaction aborts, all side-effects are undone and an abort code encoded as a bit mask is returned. The following macros are defined:

_XABORT_EXPLICIT

Transaction was explicitly aborted with _xabort. The parameter passed to _xabort is available with _XABORT_CODE(status).

_XABORT_RETRY

>   Transaction retry is possible.

_XABORT_CONFLICT

>   Transaction abort due to a memory conflict with another thread.

_XABORT_CAPACITY

>   Transaction abort due to the transaction using too much memory.

_XABORT_DEBUG

>   Transaction abort due to a debug trap.

_XABORT_NESTED

>   Transaction abort in an inner nested transaction.

There is no guarantee any transaction ever succeeds, so there always needs to be a valid fallback path.

void _xend ()   [RTM Function]

>   Commit the current transaction. When no transaction is active this faults. All memory side-effects of the transaction become visible to other threads in an atomic manner.

int _xtest ()   [RTM Function]

>   Return a nonzero value if a transaction is currently active, otherwise 0.

void _xabort (*status*)   [RTM Function]

>   Abort the current transaction. When no transaction is active this is a no-op. The *status* is an 8-bit constant; its value is encoded in the return value from **_xbegin**.

Here is an example showing handling for **_XABORT_RETRY** and a fallback path for other failures:

```
#include <immintrin.h>

int n_tries, max_tries;
unsigned status = _XABORT_EXPLICIT;
...

for (n_tries = 0; n_tries < max_tries; n_tries++)
  {
    status = _xbegin ();
    if (status == _XBEGIN_STARTED || !(status & _XABORT_RETRY))
      break;
  }
if (status == _XBEGIN_STARTED)
  {
    ... transaction code...
    _xend ();
  }
else
  {
    ... non-transactional fallback path...
  }
```

Note that, in most cases, the transactional and non-transactional code must synchronize together to ensure consistency.

6.61 Format Checks Specific to Particular Target Machines

For some target machines, GCC supports additional options to the format attribute (see Section 6.31 [Declaring Attributes of Functions], page 427).

6.61.1 Solaris Format Checks

Solaris targets support the `cmn_err` (or `__cmn_err__`) format check. `cmn_err` accepts a subset of the standard `printf` conversions, and the two-argument `%b` conversion for displaying bit-fields. See the Solaris man page for `cmn_err` for more information.

6.61.2 Darwin Format Checks

Darwin targets support the `CFString` (or `__CFString__`) in the format attribute context. Declarations made with such attribution are parsed for correct syntax and format argument types. However, parsing of the format string itself is currently undefined and is not carried out by this version of the compiler.

Additionally, `CFStringRefs` (defined by the `CoreFoundation` headers) may also be used as format arguments. Note that the relevant headers are only likely to be available on Darwin (OSX) installations. On such installations, the XCode and system documentation provide descriptions of `CFString`, `CFStringRefs` and associated functions.

6.62 Pragmas Accepted by GCC

GCC supports several types of pragmas, primarily in order to compile code originally written for other compilers. Note that in general we do not recommend the use of pragmas; See Section 6.31 [Function Attributes], page 427, for further explanation.

6.62.1 AArch64 Pragmas

The pragmas defined by the AArch64 target correspond to the AArch64 target function attributes. They can be specified as below:

```
#pragma GCC target("string")
```

where *string* can be any string accepted as an AArch64 target attribute. See Section 6.31.2 [AArch64 Function Attributes], page 443, for more details on the permissible values of `string`.

6.62.2 ARM Pragmas

The ARM target defines pragmas for controlling the default addition of `long_call` and `short_call` attributes to functions. See Section 6.31 [Function Attributes], page 427, for information about the effects of these attributes.

`long_calls`
> Set all subsequent functions to have the `long_call` attribute.

`no_long_calls`
> Set all subsequent functions to have the `short_call` attribute.

`long_calls_off`
> Do not affect the `long_call` or `short_call` attributes of subsequent functions.

6.62.3 M32C Pragmas

GCC memregs *number*

> Overrides the command-line option -memregs= for the current file. Use with care! This pragma must be before any function in the file, and mixing different memregs values in different objects may make them incompatible. This pragma is useful when a performance-critical function uses a memreg for temporary values, as it may allow you to reduce the number of memregs used.

ADDRESS *name address*

> For any declared symbols matching *name*, this does three things to that symbol: it forces the symbol to be located at the given address (a number), it forces the symbol to be volatile, and it changes the symbol's scope to be static. This pragma exists for compatibility with other compilers, but note that the common 1234H numeric syntax is not supported (use 0x1234 instead). Example:
>
> ```
> #pragma ADDRESS port3 0x103
> char port3;
> ```

6.62.4 MeP Pragmas

custom io_volatile (on|off)

> Overrides the command-line option -mio-volatile for the current file. Note that for compatibility with future GCC releases, this option should only be used once before any io variables in each file.

GCC coprocessor available *registers*

> Specifies which coprocessor registers are available to the register allocator. *registers* may be a single register, register range separated by ellipses, or comma-separated list of those. Example:
>
> ```
> #pragma GCC coprocessor available $c0...$c10, $c28
> ```

GCC coprocessor call_saved *registers*

> Specifies which coprocessor registers are to be saved and restored by any function using them. *registers* may be a single register, register range separated by ellipses, or comma-separated list of those. Example:
>
> ```
> #pragma GCC coprocessor call_saved $c4...$c6, $c31
> ```

GCC coprocessor subclass '(A|B|C|D)' = *registers*

> Creates and defines a register class. These register classes can be used by inline asm constructs. *registers* may be a single register, register range separated by ellipses, or comma-separated list of those. Example:
>
> ```
> #pragma GCC coprocessor subclass 'B' = $c2, $c4, $c6
>
> asm ("cpfoo %0" : "=B" (x));
> ```

GCC disinterrupt *name , name ...*

> For the named functions, the compiler adds code to disable interrupts for the duration of those functions. If any functions so named are not encountered in the source, a warning is emitted that the pragma is not used. Examples:
>
> ```
> #pragma disinterrupt foo
> #pragma disinterrupt bar, grill
> int foo () { ... }
> ```

GCC call *name* , *name* ...

> For the named functions, the compiler always uses a register-indirect call model when calling the named functions. Examples:
>
> ```
> extern int foo ();
> #pragma call foo
> ```

6.62.5 RS/6000 and PowerPC Pragmas

The RS/6000 and PowerPC targets define one pragma for controlling whether or not the **longcall** attribute is added to function declarations by default. This pragma overrides the '-mlongcall' option, but not the **longcall** and **shortcall** attributes. See Section 3.18.38 [RS/6000 and PowerPC Options], page 311, for more information about when long calls are and are not necessary.

longcall (1)

> Apply the **longcall** attribute to all subsequent function declarations.

longcall (0)

> Do not apply the **longcall** attribute to subsequent function declarations.

6.62.6 S/390 Pragmas

The pragmas defined by the S/390 target correspond to the S/390 target function attributes and some the additional options:

'zvector'

'no-zvector'

Note that options of the pragma, unlike options of the target attribute, do change the value of preprocessor macros like __VEC__. They can be specified as below:

```
#pragma GCC target("string[,string]...")
#pragma GCC target("string"[,"string"]...)
```

6.62.7 Darwin Pragmas

The following pragmas are available for all architectures running the Darwin operating system. These are useful for compatibility with other Mac OS compilers.

mark *tokens*...

> This pragma is accepted, but has no effect.

options align=*alignment*

> This pragma sets the alignment of fields in structures. The values of *alignment* may be **mac68k**, to emulate m68k alignment, or **power**, to emulate PowerPC alignment. Uses of this pragma nest properly; to restore the previous setting, use **reset** for the *alignment*.

segment *tokens*...

> This pragma is accepted, but has no effect.

unused (*var* [, *var*]...)

> This pragma declares variables to be possibly unused. GCC does not produce warnings for the listed variables. The effect is similar to that of the **unused** attribute, except that this pragma may appear anywhere within the variables' scopes.

6.62.8 Solaris Pragmas

The Solaris target supports `#pragma redefine_extname` (see Section 6.62.9 [Symbol-Renaming Pragmas], page 718). It also supports additional `#pragma` directives for compatibility with the system compiler.

`align alignment (variable [, variable]...)`
> Increase the minimum alignment of each *variable* to *alignment*. This is the same as GCC's `aligned` attribute see Section 6.32 [Variable Attributes], page 471). Macro expansion occurs on the arguments to this pragma when compiling C and Objective-C. It does not currently occur when compiling C++, but this is a bug which may be fixed in a future release.

`fini (function [, function]...)`
> This pragma causes each listed *function* to be called after main, or during shared module unloading, by adding a call to the `.fini` section.

`init (function [, function]...)`
> This pragma causes each listed *function* to be called during initialization (before `main`) or during shared module loading, by adding a call to the `.init` section.

6.62.9 Symbol-Renaming Pragmas

GCC supports a `#pragma` directive that changes the name used in assembly for a given declaration. While this pragma is supported on all platforms, it is intended primarily to provide compatibility with the Solaris system headers. This effect can also be achieved using the asm labels extension (see Section 6.45.4 [Asm Labels], page 546).

`redefine_extname oldname newname`
> This pragma gives the C function *oldname* the assembly symbol *newname*. The preprocessor macro `__PRAGMA_REDEFINE_EXTNAME` is defined if this pragma is available (currently on all platforms).

This pragma and the asm labels extension interact in a complicated manner. Here are some corner cases you may want to be aware of:

1. This pragma silently applies only to declarations with external linkage. Asm labels do not have this restriction.

2. In C++, this pragma silently applies only to declarations with "C" linkage. Again, asm labels do not have this restriction.

3. If either of the ways of changing the assembly name of a declaration are applied to a declaration whose assembly name has already been determined (either by a previous use of one of these features, or because the compiler needed the assembly name in order to generate code), and the new name is different, a warning issues and the name does not change.

4. The *oldname* used by `#pragma redefine_extname` is always the C-language name.

6.62.10 Structure-Layout Pragmas

For compatibility with Microsoft Windows compilers, GCC supports a set of `#pragma` directives that change the maximum alignment of members of structures (other than zero-width bit-fields), unions, and classes subsequently defined. The n value below always is required to be a small power of two and specifies the new alignment in bytes.

1. `#pragma pack(n)` simply sets the new alignment.

2. `#pragma pack()` sets the alignment to the one that was in effect when compilation started (see also command-line option '`-fpack-struct[=n]`' see Section 3.16 [Code Gen Options], page 190).

3. `#pragma pack(push[,n])` pushes the current alignment setting on an internal stack and then optionally sets the new alignment.

4. `#pragma pack(pop)` restores the alignment setting to the one saved at the top of the internal stack (and removes that stack entry). Note that `#pragma pack([n])` does not influence this internal stack; thus it is possible to have `#pragma pack(push)` followed by multiple `#pragma pack(n)` instances and finalized by a single `#pragma pack(pop)`.

Some targets, e.g. x86 and PowerPC, support the `#pragma ms_struct` directive which lays out structures and unions subsequently defined as the documented `__attribute__ ((ms_struct))`.

1. `#pragma ms_struct on` turns on the Microsoft layout.

2. `#pragma ms_struct off` turns off the Microsoft layout.

3. `#pragma ms_struct reset` goes back to the default layout.

Most targets also support the `#pragma scalar_storage_order` directive which lays out structures and unions subsequently defined as the documented `__attribute__ ((scalar_storage_order))`.

1. `#pragma scalar_storage_order big-endian` sets the storage order of the scalar fields to big-endian.

2. `#pragma scalar_storage_order little-endian` sets the storage order of the scalar fields to little-endian.

3. `#pragma scalar_storage_order default` goes back to the endianness that was in effect when compilation started (see also command-line option '`-fsso-struct=endianness`' see Section 3.4 [C Dialect Options], page 33).

6.62.11 Weak Pragmas

For compatibility with SVR4, GCC supports a set of `#pragma` directives for declaring symbols to be weak, and defining weak aliases.

`#pragma weak symbol`

> This pragma declares *symbol* to be weak, as if the declaration had the attribute of the same name. The pragma may appear before or after the declaration of *symbol*. It is not an error for *symbol* to never be defined at all.

`#pragma weak symbol1 = symbol2`

> This pragma declares *symbol1* to be a weak alias of *symbol2*. It is an error if *symbol2* is not defined in the current translation unit.

6.62.12 Diagnostic Pragmas

GCC allows the user to selectively enable or disable certain types of diagnostics, and change the kind of the diagnostic. For example, a project's policy might require that all sources compile with '`-Werror`' but certain files might have exceptions allowing specific types of warnings. Or, a project might selectively enable diagnostics and treat them as errors depending on which preprocessor macros are defined.

`#pragma GCC diagnostic` *kind option*

> Modifies the disposition of a diagnostic. Note that not all diagnostics are modifiable; at the moment only warnings (normally controlled by '-W...') can be controlled, and not all of them. Use '-fdiagnostics-show-option' to determine which diagnostics are controllable and which option controls them.
>
> *kind* is 'error' to treat this diagnostic as an error, 'warning' to treat it like a warning (even if '-Werror' is in effect), or 'ignored' if the diagnostic is to be ignored. *option* is a double quoted string that matches the command-line option.
>
> ```
> #pragma GCC diagnostic warning "-Wformat"
> #pragma GCC diagnostic error "-Wformat"
> #pragma GCC diagnostic ignored "-Wformat"
> ```
>
> Note that these pragmas override any command-line options. GCC keeps track of the location of each pragma, and issues diagnostics according to the state as of that point in the source file. Thus, pragmas occurring after a line do not affect diagnostics caused by that line.

`#pragma GCC diagnostic push`
`#pragma GCC diagnostic pop`

> Causes GCC to remember the state of the diagnostics as of each `push`, and restore to that point at each `pop`. If a `pop` has no matching `push`, the command-line options are restored.
>
> ```
> #pragma GCC diagnostic error "-Wuninitialized"
>   foo(a);                          /* error is given for this one */
> #pragma GCC diagnostic push
> #pragma GCC diagnostic ignored "-Wuninitialized"
>   foo(b);                          /* no diagnostic for this one */
> #pragma GCC diagnostic pop
>   foo(c);                          /* error is given for this one */
> #pragma GCC diagnostic pop
>   foo(d);                          /* depends on command-line options */
> ```

GCC also offers a simple mechanism for printing messages during compilation.

`#pragma message` *string*

> Prints *string* as a compiler message on compilation. The message is informational only, and is neither a compilation warning nor an error.
>
> ```
> #pragma message "Compiling " __FILE__ "..."
> ```
>
> *string* may be parenthesized, and is printed with location information. For example,
>
> ```
> #define DO_PRAGMA(x) _Pragma (#x)
> #define TODO(x) DO_PRAGMA(message ("TODO - " #x))
>
> TODO(Remember to fix this)
> ```
>
> prints   '/tmp/file.c:4: note: #pragma message: TODO - Remember to fix this'.

6.62.13 Visibility Pragmas

`#pragma GCC visibility push(visibility)`
`#pragma GCC visibility pop`

> This pragma allows the user to set the visibility for multiple declarations without having to give each a visibility attribute (see Section 6.31 [Function Attributes], page 427).
>
> In C++, '`#pragma GCC visibility`' affects only namespace-scope declarations. Class members and template specializations are not affected; if you want to override the visibility for a particular member or instantiation, you must use an attribute.

6.62.14 Push/Pop Macro Pragmas

For compatibility with Microsoft Windows compilers, GCC supports '`#pragma push_macro("macro_name")`' and '`#pragma pop_macro("macro_name")`'.

`#pragma push_macro("macro_name")`

> This pragma saves the value of the macro named as macro_name to the top of the stack for this macro.

`#pragma pop_macro("macro_name")`

> This pragma sets the value of the macro named as macro_name to the value on top of the stack for this macro. If the stack for macro_name is empty, the value of the macro remains unchanged.

For example:

```
#define X  1
#pragma push_macro("X")
#undef X
#define X -1
#pragma pop_macro("X")
int x [X];
```

In this example, the definition of X as 1 is saved by `#pragma push_macro` and restored by `#pragma pop_macro`.

6.62.15 Function Specific Option Pragmas

`#pragma GCC target ("string"...)`

> This pragma allows you to set target specific options for functions defined later in the source file. One or more strings can be specified. Each function that is defined after this point is as if `attribute((target("STRING")))` was specified for that function. The parenthesis around the options is optional. See Section 6.31 [Function Attributes], page 427, for more information about the **target** attribute and the attribute syntax.
>
> The `#pragma GCC target` pragma is presently implemented for x86, PowerPC, and Nios II targets only.

`#pragma GCC optimize ("string"...)`

> This pragma allows you to set global optimization options for functions defined later in the source file. One or more strings can be specified. Each function

that is defined after this point is as if `attribute((optimize("STRING")))` was specified for that function. The parenthesis around the options is optional. See Section 6.31 [Function Attributes], page 427, for more information about the `optimize` attribute and the attribute syntax.

`#pragma GCC push_options`
`#pragma GCC pop_options`

These pragmas maintain a stack of the current target and optimization options. It is intended for include files where you temporarily want to switch to using a different '`#pragma GCC target`' or '`#pragma GCC optimize`' and then to pop back to the previous options.

`#pragma GCC reset_options`

This pragma clears the current `#pragma GCC target` and `#pragma GCC optimize` to use the default switches as specified on the command line.

6.62.16 Loop-Specific Pragmas

`#pragma GCC ivdep`

With this pragma, the programmer asserts that there are no loop-carried dependencies which would prevent consecutive iterations of the following loop from executing concurrently with SIMD (single instruction multiple data) instructions.

For example, the compiler can only unconditionally vectorize the following loop with the pragma:

```
void foo (int n, int *a, int *b, int *c)
{
  int i, j;
#pragma GCC ivdep
  for (i = 0; i < n; ++i)
    a[i] = b[i] + c[i];
}
```

In this example, using the `restrict` qualifier had the same effect. In the following example, that would not be possible. Assume $k < -m$ or $k >= m$. Only with the pragma, the compiler knows that it can unconditionally vectorize the following loop:

```
void ignore_vec_dep (int *a, int k, int c, int m)
{
#pragma GCC ivdep
  for (int i = 0; i < m; i++)
    a[i] = a[i + k] * c;
}
```

6.63 Unnamed Structure and Union Fields

As permitted by ISO C11 and for compatibility with other compilers, GCC allows you to define a structure or union that contains, as fields, structures and unions without names. For example:

```
struct {
  int a;
  union {
    int b;
    float c;
```

```
  };
  int d;
} foo;
```

In this example, you are able to access members of the unnamed union with code like 'foo.b'. Note that only unnamed structs and unions are allowed, you may not have, for example, an unnamed int.

You must never create such structures that cause ambiguous field definitions. For example, in this structure:

```
struct {
  int a;
  struct {
    int a;
  };
} foo;
```

it is ambiguous which a is being referred to with 'foo.a'. The compiler gives errors for such constructs.

Unless '-fms-extensions' is used, the unnamed field must be a structure or union definition without a tag (for example, 'struct { int a; };'). If '-fms-extensions' is used, the field may also be a definition with a tag such as 'struct foo { int a; };', a reference to a previously defined structure or union such as 'struct foo;', or a reference to a typedef name for a previously defined structure or union type.

The option '-fplan9-extensions' enables '-fms-extensions' as well as two other extensions. First, a pointer to a structure is automatically converted to a pointer to an anonymous field for assignments and function calls. For example:

```
struct s1 { int a; };
struct s2 { struct s1; };
extern void f1 (struct s1 *);
void f2 (struct s2 *p) { f1 (p); }
```

In the call to f1 inside f2, the pointer p is converted into a pointer to the anonymous field.

Second, when the type of an anonymous field is a typedef for a struct or union, code may refer to the field using the name of the typedef.

```
typedef struct { int a; } s1;
struct s2 { s1; };
s1 f1 (struct s2 *p) { return p->s1; }
```

These usages are only permitted when they are not ambiguous.

6.64 Thread-Local Storage

Thread-local storage (TLS) is a mechanism by which variables are allocated such that there is one instance of the variable per extant thread. The runtime model GCC uses to implement this originates in the IA-64 processor-specific ABI, but has since been migrated to other processors as well. It requires significant support from the linker (ld), dynamic linker (ld.so), and system libraries ('libc.so' and 'libpthread.so'), so it is not available everywhere.

At the user level, the extension is visible with a new storage class keyword: __thread. For example:

```
__thread int i;
extern __thread struct state s;
```

```
static __thread char *p;
```

The `__thread` specifier may be used alone, with the `extern` or `static` specifiers, but with no other storage class specifier. When used with `extern` or `static`, `__thread` must appear immediately after the other storage class specifier.

The `__thread` specifier may be applied to any global, file-scoped static, function-scoped static, or static data member of a class. It may not be applied to block-scoped automatic or non-static data member.

When the address-of operator is applied to a thread-local variable, it is evaluated at run time and returns the address of the current thread's instance of that variable. An address so obtained may be used by any thread. When a thread terminates, any pointers to thread-local variables in that thread become invalid.

No static initialization may refer to the address of a thread-local variable.

In C++, if an initializer is present for a thread-local variable, it must be a *constant-expression*, as defined in 5.19.2 of the ANSI/ISO C++ standard.

See ELF Handling For Thread-Local Storage for a detailed explanation of the four thread-local storage addressing models, and how the runtime is expected to function.

6.64.1 ISO/IEC 9899:1999 Edits for Thread-Local Storage

The following are a set of changes to ISO/IEC 9899:1999 (aka C99) that document the exact semantics of the language extension.

- *5.1.2 Execution environments*

  Add new text after paragraph 1

  > Within either execution environment, a *thread* is a flow of control within a program. It is implementation defined whether or not there may be more than one thread associated with a program. It is implementation defined how threads beyond the first are created, the name and type of the function called at thread startup, and how threads may be terminated. However, objects with thread storage duration shall be initialized before thread startup.

- *6.2.4 Storage durations of objects*

  Add new text before paragraph 3

  > An object whose identifier is declared with the storage-class specifier `__thread` has *thread storage duration*. Its lifetime is the entire execution of the thread, and its stored value is initialized only once, prior to thread startup.

- *6.4.1 Keywords*

  Add `__thread`.

- *6.7.1 Storage-class specifiers*

  Add `__thread` to the list of storage class specifiers in paragraph 1.

  Change paragraph 2 to

  > With the exception of `__thread`, at most one storage-class specifier may be given [...]. The `__thread` specifier may be used alone, or immediately following `extern` or `static`.

Add new text after paragraph 6

> The declaration of an identifier for a variable that has block scope that specifies `__thread` shall also specify either `extern` or `static`.

> The `__thread` specifier shall be used only with variables.

6.64.2 ISO/IEC 14882:1998 Edits for Thread-Local Storage

The following are a set of changes to ISO/IEC 14882:1998 (aka C++98) that document the exact semantics of the language extension.

- **[intro.execution]**

  New text after paragraph 4

  > A *thread* is a flow of control within the abstract machine. It is implementation defined whether or not there may be more than one thread.

  New text after paragraph 7

  > It is unspecified whether additional action must be taken to ensure when and whether side effects are visible to other threads.

- **[lex.key]**

  Add `__thread`.

- **[basic.start.main]**

  Add after paragraph 5

  > The thread that begins execution at the `main` function is called the *main thread*. It is implementation defined how functions beginning threads other than the main thread are designated or typed. A function so designated, as well as the `main` function, is called a *thread startup function*. It is implementation defined what happens if a thread startup function returns. It is implementation defined what happens to other threads when any thread calls `exit`.

- **[basic.start.init]**

  Add after paragraph 4

  > The storage for an object of thread storage duration shall be statically initialized before the first statement of the thread startup function. An object of thread storage duration shall not require dynamic initialization.

- **[basic.start.term]**

  Add after paragraph 3

  > The type of an object with thread storage duration shall not have a non-trivial destructor, nor shall it be an array type whose elements (directly or indirectly) have non-trivial destructors.

- **[basic.stc]**

  Add "thread storage duration" to the list in paragraph 1.

  Change paragraph 2

  > Thread, static, and automatic storage durations are associated with objects introduced by declarations [. . .].

  Add `__thread` to the list of specifiers in paragraph 3.

- [**basic.stc.thread**]

  New section before [**basic.stc.static**]

  > The keyword `__thread` applied to a non-local object gives the object thread storage duration.
  >
  > A local variable or class data member declared both `static` and `__thread` gives the variable or member thread storage duration.

- [**basic.stc.static**]

  Change paragraph 1

  > All objects that have neither thread storage duration, dynamic storage duration nor are local [...].

- [**dcl.stc**]

  Add `__thread` to the list in paragraph 1.

  Change paragraph 1

  > With the exception of `__thread`, at most one *storage-class-specifier* shall appear in a given *decl-specifier-seq*. The `__thread` specifier may be used alone, or immediately following the `extern` or `static` specifiers. [...]

  Add after paragraph 5

  > The `__thread` specifier can be applied only to the names of objects and to anonymous unions.

- [**class.mem**]

  Add after paragraph 6

  > Non-`static` members shall not be `__thread`.

6.65 Binary Constants using the '0b' Prefix

Integer constants can be written as binary constants, consisting of a sequence of '0' and '1' digits, prefixed by '0b' or '0B'. This is particularly useful in environments that operate a lot on the bit level (like microcontrollers).

The following statements are identical:

```
i =        42;
i =      0x2a;
i =       052;
i = 0b101010;
```

The type of these constants follows the same rules as for octal or hexadecimal integer constants, so suffixes like 'L' or 'UL' can be applied.

7 Extensions to the C++ Language

The GNU compiler provides these extensions to the C++ language (and you can also use most of the C language extensions in your C++ programs). If you want to write code that checks whether these features are available, you can test for the GNU compiler the same way as for C programs: check for a predefined macro `__GNUC__`. You can also use `__GNUG__` to test specifically for GNU C++ (see Section "Predefined Macros" in *The GNU C Preprocessor*).

7.1 When is a Volatile C++ Object Accessed?

The C++ standard differs from the C standard in its treatment of volatile objects. It fails to specify what constitutes a volatile access, except to say that C++ should behave in a similar manner to C with respect to volatiles, where possible. However, the different lvalueness of expressions between C and C++ complicate the behavior. G++ behaves the same as GCC for volatile access, See Chapter 6 [Volatiles], page 403, for a description of GCC's behavior.

The C and C++ language specifications differ when an object is accessed in a void context:

```
volatile int *src = somevalue;
*src;
```

The C++ standard specifies that such expressions do not undergo lvalue to rvalue conversion, and that the type of the dereferenced object may be incomplete. The C++ standard does not specify explicitly that it is lvalue to rvalue conversion that is responsible for causing an access. There is reason to believe that it is, because otherwise certain simple expressions become undefined. However, because it would surprise most programmers, G++ treats dereferencing a pointer to volatile object of complete type as GCC would do for an equivalent type in C. When the object has incomplete type, G++ issues a warning; if you wish to force an error, you must force a conversion to rvalue with, for instance, a static cast.

When using a reference to volatile, G++ does not treat equivalent expressions as accesses to volatiles, but instead issues a warning that no volatile is accessed. The rationale for this is that otherwise it becomes difficult to determine where volatile access occur, and not possible to ignore the return value from functions returning volatile references. Again, if you wish to force a read, cast the reference to an rvalue.

G++ implements the same behavior as GCC does when assigning to a volatile object— there is no reread of the assigned-to object, the assigned rvalue is reused. Note that in C++ assignment expressions are lvalues, and if used as an lvalue, the volatile object is referred to. For instance, *vref* refers to *vobj*, as expected, in the following example:

```
volatile int vobj;
volatile int &vref = vobj = something;
```

7.2 Restricting Pointer Aliasing

As with the C front end, G++ understands the C99 feature of restricted pointers, specified with the `__restrict__`, or `__restrict` type qualifier. Because you cannot compile C++ by specifying the '`-std=c99`' language flag, `restrict` is not a keyword in C++.

In addition to allowing restricted pointers, you can specify restricted references, which indicate that the reference is not aliased in the local context.

```
void fn (int *__restrict__ rptr, int &__restrict__ rref)
{
  /* ... */
}
```

In the body of **fn**, *rptr* points to an unaliased integer and *rref* refers to a (different) unaliased integer.

You may also specify whether a member function's *this* pointer is unaliased by using **__restrict__** as a member function qualifier.

```
void T::fn () __restrict__
{
  /* ... */
}
```

Within the body of T::**fn**, *this* has the effective definition T *__restrict__ const this. Notice that the interpretation of a **__restrict__** member function qualifier is different to that of **const** or **volatile** qualifier, in that it is applied to the pointer rather than the object. This is consistent with other compilers that implement restricted pointers.

As with all outermost parameter qualifiers, **__restrict__** is ignored in function definition matching. This means you only need to specify **__restrict__** in a function definition, rather than in a function prototype as well.

7.3 Vague Linkage

There are several constructs in C++ that require space in the object file but are not clearly tied to a single translation unit. We say that these constructs have "vague linkage". Typically such constructs are emitted wherever they are needed, though sometimes we can be more clever.

Inline Functions

Inline functions are typically defined in a header file which can be included in many different compilations. Hopefully they can usually be inlined, but sometimes an out-of-line copy is necessary, if the address of the function is taken or if inlining fails. In general, we emit an out-of-line copy in all translation units where one is needed. As an exception, we only emit inline virtual functions with the vtable, since it always requires a copy.

Local static variables and string constants used in an inline function are also considered to have vague linkage, since they must be shared between all inlined and out-of-line instances of the function.

VTables   C++ virtual functions are implemented in most compilers using a lookup table, known as a vtable. The vtable contains pointers to the virtual functions provided by a class, and each object of the class contains a pointer to its vtable (or vtables, in some multiple-inheritance situations). If the class declares any non-inline, non-pure virtual functions, the first one is chosen as the "key method" for the class, and the vtable is only emitted in the translation unit where the key method is defined.

Note: If the chosen key method is later defined as inline, the vtable is still emitted in every translation unit that defines it. Make sure that any inline virtuals are declared inline in the class body, even if they are not defined there.

`type_info` objects

>C++ requires information about types to be written out in order to implement 'dynamic_cast', 'typeid' and exception handling. For polymorphic classes (classes with virtual functions), the 'type_info' object is written out along with the vtable so that 'dynamic_cast' can determine the dynamic type of a class object at run time. For all other types, we write out the 'type_info' object when it is used: when applying 'typeid' to an expression, throwing an object, or referring to a type in a catch clause or exception specification.

Template Instantiations

>Most everything in this section also applies to template instantiations, but there are other options as well. See Section 7.5 [Where's the Template?], page 730.

When used with GNU ld version 2.8 or later on an ELF system such as GNU/Linux or Solaris 2, or on Microsoft Windows, duplicate copies of these constructs will be discarded at link time. This is known as COMDAT support.

On targets that don't support COMDAT, but do support weak symbols, GCC uses them. This way one copy overrides all the others, but the unused copies still take up space in the executable.

For targets that do not support either COMDAT or weak symbols, most entities with vague linkage are emitted as local symbols to avoid duplicate definition errors from the linker. This does not happen for local statics in inlines, however, as having multiple copies almost certainly breaks things.

See Section 7.4 [Declarations and Definitions in One Header], page 729, for another way to control placement of these constructs.

7.4 C++ Interface and Implementation Pragmas

`#pragma interface` and `#pragma implementation` provide the user with a way of explicitly directing the compiler to emit entities with vague linkage (and debugging information) in a particular translation unit.

Note: These `#pragma`s have been superceded as of GCC 2.7.2 by COMDAT support and the "key method" heuristic mentioned in Section 7.3 [Vague Linkage], page 728. Using them can actually cause your program to grow due to unnecessary out-of-line copies of inline functions.

`#pragma interface`
`#pragma interface "subdir/objects.h"`

>Use this directive in *header files* that define object classes, to save space in most of the object files that use those classes. Normally, local copies of certain information (backup copies of inline member functions, debugging information, and the internal tables that implement virtual functions) must be kept in each object file that includes class definitions. You can use this pragma to avoid such duplication. When a header file containing '#pragma interface' is included in a compilation, this auxiliary information is not generated (unless the main input source file itself uses '#pragma implementation'). Instead, the object files contain references to be resolved at link time.

The second form of this directive is useful for the case where you have multiple headers with the same name in different directories. If you use this form, you must specify the same string to '#pragma implementation'.

#pragma implementation
#pragma implementation "objects.h"

Use this pragma in a *main input file*, when you want full output from included header files to be generated (and made globally visible). The included header file, in turn, should use '#pragma interface'. Backup copies of inline member functions, debugging information, and the internal tables used to implement virtual functions are all generated in implementation files.

If you use '#pragma implementation' with no argument, it applies to an include file with the same basename[1] as your source file. For example, in 'allclass.cc', giving just '#pragma implementation' by itself is equivalent to '#pragma implementation "allclass.h"'.

Use the string argument if you want a single implementation file to include code from multiple header files. (You must also use '#include' to include the header file; '#pragma implementation' only specifies how to use the file—it doesn't actually include it.)

There is no way to split up the contents of a single header file into multiple implementation files.

'#pragma implementation' and '#pragma interface' also have an effect on function inlining.

If you define a class in a header file marked with '#pragma interface', the effect on an inline function defined in that class is similar to an explicit extern declaration—the compiler emits no code at all to define an independent version of the function. Its definition is used only for inlining with its callers.

Conversely, when you include the same header file in a main source file that declares it as '#pragma implementation', the compiler emits code for the function itself; this defines a version of the function that can be found via pointers (or by callers compiled without inlining). If all calls to the function can be inlined, you can avoid emitting the function by compiling with '-fno-implement-inlines'. If any calls are not inlined, you will get linker errors.

7.5 Where's the Template?

C++ templates were the first language feature to require more intelligence from the environment than was traditionally found on a UNIX system. Somehow the compiler and linker have to make sure that each template instance occurs exactly once in the executable if it is needed, and not at all otherwise. There are two basic approaches to this problem, which are referred to as the Borland model and the Cfront model.

Borland model

Borland C++ solved the template instantiation problem by adding the code equivalent of common blocks to their linker; the compiler emits template in-

---

[1] A file's *basename* is the name stripped of all leading path information and of trailing suffixes, such as '.h' or '.C' or '.cc'.

stances in each translation unit that uses them, and the linker collapses them together. The advantage of this model is that the linker only has to consider the object files themselves; there is no external complexity to worry about. The disadvantage is that compilation time is increased because the template code is being compiled repeatedly. Code written for this model tends to include definitions of all templates in the header file, since they must be seen to be instantiated.

Cfront model

The AT&T C++ translator, Cfront, solved the template instantiation problem by creating the notion of a template repository, an automatically maintained place where template instances are stored. A more modern version of the repository works as follows: As individual object files are built, the compiler places any template definitions and instantiations encountered in the repository. At link time, the link wrapper adds in the objects in the repository and compiles any needed instances that were not previously emitted. The advantages of this model are more optimal compilation speed and the ability to use the system linker; to implement the Borland model a compiler vendor also needs to replace the linker. The disadvantages are vastly increased complexity, and thus potential for error; for some code this can be just as transparent, but in practice it can been very difficult to build multiple programs in one directory and one program in multiple directories. Code written for this model tends to separate definitions of non-inline member templates into a separate file, which should be compiled separately.

G++ implements the Borland model on targets where the linker supports it, including ELF targets (such as GNU/Linux), Mac OS X and Microsoft Windows. Otherwise G++ implements neither automatic model.

You have the following options for dealing with template instantiations:

1. Do nothing. Code written for the Borland model works fine, but each translation unit contains instances of each of the templates it uses. The duplicate instances will be discarded by the linker, but in a large program, this can lead to an unacceptable amount of code duplication in object files or shared libraries.

   Duplicate instances of a template can be avoided by defining an explicit instantiation in one object file, and preventing the compiler from doing implicit instantiations in any other object files by using an explicit instantiation declaration, using the **extern template** syntax:

   ```
   extern template int max (int, int);
   ```

   This syntax is defined in the C++ 2011 standard, but has been supported by G++ and other compilers since well before 2011.

   Explicit instantiations can be used for the largest or most frequently duplicated instances, without having to know exactly which other instances are used in the rest of the program. You can scatter the explicit instantiations throughout your program, perhaps putting them in the translation units where the instances are used or the translation units that define the templates themselves; you can put all of the explicit instantiations you need into one big file; or you can create small files like

   ```
   #include "Foo.h"
   ```

```
#include "Foo.cc"

template class Foo<int>;
template ostream& operator <<
                  (ostream&, const Foo<int>&);
```

for each of the instances you need, and create a template instantiation library from
those.

This is the simplest option, but also offers flexibility and fine-grained control when
necessary. It is also the most portable alternative and programs using this approach
will work with most modern compilers.

2. Compile your template-using code with '-frepo'. The compiler generates files with
   the extension '.rpo' listing all of the template instantiations used in the corresponding
   object files that could be instantiated there; the link wrapper, 'collect2', then updates
   the '.rpo' files to tell the compiler where to place those instantiations and rebuild any
   affected object files. The link-time overhead is negligible after the first pass, as the
   compiler continues to place the instantiations in the same files.

   This can be a suitable option for application code written for the Borland model, as it
   usually just works. Code written for the Cfront model needs to be modified so that the
   template definitions are available at one or more points of instantiation; usually this is
   as simple as adding #include <tmethods.cc> to the end of each template header.

   For library code, if you want the library to provide all of the template instantiations
   it needs, just try to link all of its object files together; the link will fail, but cause
   the instantiations to be generated as a side effect. Be warned, however, that this may
   cause conflicts if multiple libraries try to provide the same instantiations. For greater
   control, use explicit instantiation as described in the next option.

3. Compile your code with '-fno-implicit-templates' to disable the implicit generation
   of template instances, and explicitly instantiate all the ones you use. This approach
   requires more knowledge of exactly which instances you need than do the others, but it's
   less mysterious and allows greater control if you want to ensure that only the intended
   instances are used.

   If you are using Cfront-model code, you can probably get away with not using
   '-fno-implicit-templates' when compiling files that don't '#include' the member
   template definitions.

   If you use one big file to do the instantiations, you may want to compile it without
   '-fno-implicit-templates' so you get all of the instances required by your explicit
   instantiations (but not by any other files) without having to specify them as well.

   In addition to forward declaration of explicit instantiations (with **extern**), G++ has
   extended the template instantiation syntax to support instantiation of the compiler
   support data for a template class (i.e. the vtable) without instantiating any of its
   members (with **inline**), and instantiation of only the static data members of a template
   class, without the support data or member functions (with **static**):

```
inline template class Foo<int>;
static template class Foo<int>;
```

7.6 Extracting the Function Pointer from a Bound Pointer to Member Function

In C++, pointer to member functions (PMFs) are implemented using a wide pointer of sorts to handle all the possible call mechanisms; the PMF needs to store information about how to adjust the 'this' pointer, and if the function pointed to is virtual, where to find the vtable, and where in the vtable to look for the member function. If you are using PMFs in an inner loop, you should really reconsider that decision. If that is not an option, you can extract the pointer to the function that would be called for a given object/PMF pair and call it directly inside the inner loop, to save a bit of time.

Note that you still pay the penalty for the call through a function pointer; on most modern architectures, such a call defeats the branch prediction features of the CPU. This is also true of normal virtual function calls.

The syntax for this extension is

```
extern A a;
extern int (A::*fp)();
typedef int (*fptr)(A *);

fptr p = (fptr)(a.*fp);
```

For PMF constants (i.e. expressions of the form '&Klasse::Member'), no object is needed to obtain the address of the function. They can be converted to function pointers directly:

```
fptr p1 = (fptr)(&A::foo);
```

You must specify '-Wno-pmf-conversions' to use this extension.

7.7 C++-Specific Variable, Function, and Type Attributes

Some attributes only make sense for C++ programs.

abi_tag ("*tag*", ...)

The abi_tag attribute can be applied to a function, variable, or class declaration. It modifies the mangled name of the entity to incorporate the tag name, in order to distinguish the function or class from an earlier version with a different ABI; perhaps the class has changed size, or the function has a different return type that is not encoded in the mangled name.

The attribute can also be applied to an inline namespace, but does not affect the mangled name of the namespace; in this case it is only used for '-Wabi-tag' warnings and automatic tagging of functions and variables. Tagging inline namespaces is generally preferable to tagging individual declarations, but the latter is sometimes necessary, such as when only certain members of a class need to be tagged.

The argument can be a list of strings of arbitrary length. The strings are sorted on output, so the order of the list is unimportant.

A redeclaration of an entity must not add new ABI tags, since doing so would change the mangled name.

The ABI tags apply to a name, so all instantiations and specializations of a template have the same tags. The attribute will be ignored if applied to an explicit specialization or instantiation.

The '-Wabi-tag' flag enables a warning about a class which does not have all the ABI tags used by its subobjects and virtual functions; for users with code that needs to coexist with an earlier ABI, using this option can help to find all affected types that need to be tagged.

When a type involving an ABI tag is used as the type of a variable or return type of a function where that tag is not already present in the signature of the function, the tag is automatically applied to the variable or function. '-Wabi-tag' also warns about this situation; this warning can be avoided by explicitly tagging the variable or function or moving it into a tagged inline namespace.

init_priority (*priority*)

In Standard C++, objects defined at namespace scope are guaranteed to be initialized in an order in strict accordance with that of their definitions *in a given translation unit*. No guarantee is made for initializations across translation units. However, GNU C++ allows users to control the order of initialization of objects defined at namespace scope with the init_priority attribute by specifying a relative *priority*, a constant integral expression currently bounded between 101 and 65535 inclusive. Lower numbers indicate a higher priority.

In the following example, A would normally be created before B, but the init_priority attribute reverses that order:

```
Some_Class  A  __attribute__ ((init_priority (2000)));
Some_Class  B  __attribute__ ((init_priority (543)));
```

Note that the particular values of *priority* do not matter; only their relative ordering.

warn_unused

For C++ types with non-trivial constructors and/or destructors it is impossible for the compiler to determine whether a variable of this type is truly unused if it is not referenced. This type attribute informs the compiler that variables of this type should be warned about if they appear to be unused, just like variables of fundamental types.

This attribute is appropriate for types which just represent a value, such as std::string; it is not appropriate for types which control a resource, such as std::lock_guard.

This attribute is also accepted in C, but it is unnecessary because C does not have constructors or destructors.

See also Section 7.9 [Namespace Association], page 735.

7.8 Function Multiversioning

With the GNU C++ front end, for x86 targets, you may specify multiple versions of a function, where each function is specialized for a specific target feature. At runtime, the appropriate version of the function is automatically executed depending on the characteristics of the execution platform. Here is an example.

```
__attribute__ ((target ("default")))
int foo ()
{
  // The default version of foo.
  return 0;
```

```
}

__attribute__ ((target ("sse4.2")))
int foo ()
{
  // foo version for SSE4.2
  return 1;
}


__attribute__ ((target ("arch=atom")))
int foo ()
{
  // foo version for the Intel ATOM processor
  return 2;
}


__attribute__ ((target ("arch=amdfam10")))
int foo ()
{
  // foo version for the AMD Family 0x10 processors.
  return 3;
}

int main ()
{
  int (*p)() = &foo;
  assert ((*p) () == foo ());
  return 0;
}
```

In the above example, four versions of function foo are created. The first version of foo
with the target attribute "default" is the default version. This version gets executed when
no other target specific version qualifies for execution on a particular platform. A new
version of foo is created by using the same function signature but with a different target
string. Function foo is called or a pointer to it is taken just like a regular function. GCC
takes care of doing the dispatching to call the right version at runtime. Refer to the GCC
wiki on Function Multiversioning for more details.

7.9 Namespace Association

Caution: The semantics of this extension are equivalent to C++ 2011 inline namespaces.
Users should use inline namespaces instead as this extension will be removed in future
versions of G++.

A using-directive with `__attribute ((strong))` is stronger than a normal using-directive
in two ways:

- Templates from the used namespace can be specialized and explicitly instantiated as
  though they were members of the using namespace.

- The using namespace is considered an associated namespace of all templates in the
  used namespace for purposes of argument-dependent name lookup.

The used namespace must be nested within the using namespace so that normal unqual-
ified lookup works properly.

This is useful for composing a namespace transparently from implementation namespaces.
For example:

```
namespace std {
  namespace debug {
    template <class T> struct A { };
  }
  using namespace debug __attribute ((__strong__));
  template <> struct A<int> { };    // OK to specialize

  template <class T> void f (A<T>);
}

int main()
{
  f (std::A<float>());                   // lookup finds std::f
  f (std::A<int>());
}
```

7.10 Type Traits

The C++ front end implements syntactic extensions that allow compile-time determination of various characteristics of a type (or of a pair of types).

__has_nothrow_assign (type)

> If type is const qualified or is a reference type then the trait is false. Otherwise if __has_trivial_assign (type) is true then the trait is true, else if type is a cv class or union type with copy assignment operators that are known not to throw an exception then the trait is true, else it is false. Requires: type shall be a complete type, (possibly cv-qualified) void, or an array of unknown bound.

__has_nothrow_copy (type)

> If __has_trivial_copy (type) is true then the trait is true, else if type is a cv class or union type with copy constructors that are known not to throw an exception then the trait is true, else it is false. Requires: type shall be a complete type, (possibly cv-qualified) void, or an array of unknown bound.

__has_nothrow_constructor (type)

> If __has_trivial_constructor (type) is true then the trait is true, else if type is a cv class or union type (or array thereof) with a default constructor that is known not to throw an exception then the trait is true, else it is false. Requires: type shall be a complete type, (possibly cv-qualified) void, or an array of unknown bound.

__has_trivial_assign (type)

> If type is const qualified or is a reference type then the trait is false. Otherwise if __is_pod (type) is true then the trait is true, else if type is a cv class or union type with a trivial copy assignment ([class.copy]) then the trait is true, else it is false. Requires: type shall be a complete type, (possibly cv-qualified) void, or an array of unknown bound.

__has_trivial_copy (type)

> If __is_pod (type) is true or type is a reference type then the trait is true, else if type is a cv class or union type with a trivial copy constructor ([class.copy])

then the trait is true, else it is false. Requires: **type** shall be a complete type, (possibly cv-qualified) **void**, or an array of unknown bound.

__has_trivial_constructor (type)

If **__is_pod (type)** is true then the trait is true, else if **type** is a cv class or union type (or array thereof) with a trivial default constructor ([class.ctor]) then the trait is true, else it is false. Requires: **type** shall be a complete type, (possibly cv-qualified) **void**, or an array of unknown bound.

__has_trivial_destructor (type)

If **__is_pod (type)** is true or **type** is a reference type then the trait is true, else if **type** is a cv class or union type (or array thereof) with a trivial destructor ([class.dtor]) then the trait is true, else it is false. Requires: **type** shall be a complete type, (possibly cv-qualified) **void**, or an array of unknown bound.

__has_virtual_destructor (type)

If **type** is a class type with a virtual destructor ([class.dtor]) then the trait is true, else it is false. Requires: **type** shall be a complete type, (possibly cv-qualified) **void**, or an array of unknown bound.

__is_abstract (type)

If **type** is an abstract class ([class.abstract]) then the trait is true, else it is false. Requires: **type** shall be a complete type, (possibly cv-qualified) **void**, or an array of unknown bound.

__is_base_of (base_type, derived_type)

If **base_type** is a base class of **derived_type** ([class.derived]) then the trait is true, otherwise it is false. Top-level cv qualifications of **base_type** and **derived_type** are ignored. For the purposes of this trait, a class type is considered is own base. Requires: if **__is_class (base_type)** and **__is_class (derived_type)** are true and **base_type** and **derived_type** are not the same type (disregarding cv-qualifiers), **derived_type** shall be a complete type. A diagnostic is produced if this requirement is not met.

__is_class (type)

If **type** is a cv class type, and not a union type ([basic.compound]) the trait is true, else it is false.

__is_empty (type)

If **__is_class (type)** is false then the trait is false. Otherwise **type** is considered empty if and only if: **type** has no non-static data members, or all non-static data members, if any, are bit-fields of length 0, and **type** has no virtual members, and **type** has no virtual base classes, and **type** has no base classes **base_type** for which **__is_empty (base_type)** is false. Requires: **type** shall be a complete type, (possibly cv-qualified) **void**, or an array of unknown bound.

__is_enum (type)

If **type** is a cv enumeration type ([basic.compound]) the trait is true, else it is false.

`__is_literal_type (type)`

        If `type` is a literal type ([basic.types]) the trait is true, else it is false. Requires: `type` shall be a complete type, (possibly cv-qualified) `void`, or an array of unknown bound.

`__is_pod (type)`

        If `type` is a cv POD type ([basic.types]) then the trait is true, else it is false. Requires: `type` shall be a complete type, (possibly cv-qualified) `void`, or an array of unknown bound.

`__is_polymorphic (type)`

        If `type` is a polymorphic class ([class.virtual]) then the trait is true, else it is false. Requires: `type` shall be a complete type, (possibly cv-qualified) `void`, or an array of unknown bound.

`__is_standard_layout (type)`

        If `type` is a standard-layout type ([basic.types]) the trait is true, else it is false. Requires: `type` shall be a complete type, (possibly cv-qualified) `void`, or an array of unknown bound.

`__is_trivial (type)`

        If `type` is a trivial type ([basic.types]) the trait is true, else it is false. Requires: `type` shall be a complete type, (possibly cv-qualified) `void`, or an array of unknown bound.

`__is_union (type)`

        If `type` is a cv union type ([basic.compound]) the trait is true, else it is false.

`__underlying_type (type)`

        The underlying type of `type`. Requires: `type` shall be an enumeration type ([dcl.enum]).

7.11 C++ Concepts

C++ concepts provide much-improved support for generic programming. In particular, they allow the specification of constraints on template arguments. The constraints are used to extend the usual overloading and partial specialization capabilities of the language, allowing generic data structures and algorithms to be "refined" based on their properties rather than their type names.

The following keywords are reserved for concepts.

`assumes`   States an expression as an assumption, and if possible, verifies that the assumption is valid. For example, `assume(n > 0)`.

`axiom`   Introduces an axiom definition. Axioms introduce requirements on values.

`forall`   Introduces a universally quantified object in an axiom. For example, `forall (int n) n + 0 == n)`.

`concept`   Introduces a concept definition. Concepts are sets of syntactic and semantic requirements on types and their values.

`requires`   Introduces constraints on template arguments or requirements for a member function of a class template.

The front end also exposes a number of internal mechanism that can be used to simplify the writing of type traits. Note that some of these traits are likely to be removed in the future.

`__is_same (type1, type2)`
> A binary type trait: true whenever the type arguments are the same.

7.12 Deprecated Features

In the past, the GNU C++ compiler was extended to experiment with new features, at a time when the C++ language was still evolving. Now that the C++ standard is complete, some of those features are superseded by superior alternatives. Using the old features might cause a warning in some cases that the feature will be dropped in the future. In other cases, the feature might be gone already.

While the list below is not exhaustive, it documents some of the options that are now deprecated:

`-fexternal-templates`
`-falt-external-templates`
> These are two of the many ways for G++ to implement template instantiation. See Section 7.5 [Template Instantiation], page 730. The C++ standard clearly defines how template definitions have to be organized across implementation units. G++ has an implicit instantiation mechanism that should work just fine for standard-conforming code.

`-fstrict-prototype`
`-fno-strict-prototype`
> Previously it was possible to use an empty prototype parameter list to indicate an unspecified number of parameters (like C), rather than no parameters, as C++ demands. This feature has been removed, except where it is required for backwards compatibility. See Section 7.13 [Backwards Compatibility], page 740.

G++ allows a virtual function returning 'void *' to be overridden by one returning a different pointer type. This extension to the covariant return type rules is now deprecated and will be removed from a future version.

The G++ minimum and maximum operators ('<?' and '>?') and their compound forms ('<?=') and '>?=') have been deprecated and are now removed from G++. Code using these operators should be modified to use std::min and std::max instead.

The named return value extension has been deprecated, and is now removed from G++.

The use of initializer lists with new expressions has been deprecated, and is now removed from G++.

Floating and complex non-type template parameters have been deprecated, and are now removed from G++.

The implicit typename extension has been deprecated and is now removed from G++.

The use of default arguments in function pointers, function typedefs and other places where they are not permitted by the standard is deprecated and will be removed from a future version of G++.

G++ allows floating-point literals to appear in integral constant expressions, e.g. ' `enum E { e = int(2.2 * 3.7) }` ' This extension is deprecated and will be removed from a future version.

G++ allows static data members of const floating-point type to be declared with an initializer in a class definition. The standard only allows initializers for static members of const integral types and const enumeration types so this extension has been deprecated and will be removed from a future version.

7.13 Backwards Compatibility

Now that there is a definitive ISO standard C++, G++ has a specification to adhere to. The C++ language evolved over time, and features that used to be acceptable in previous drafts of the standard, such as the ARM [Annotated C++ Reference Manual], are no longer accepted. In order to allow compilation of C++ written to such drafts, G++ contains some backwards compatibilities. *All such backwards compatibility features are liable to disappear in future versions of G++.* They should be considered deprecated. See Section 7.12 [Deprecated Features], page 739.

For scope   If a variable is declared at for scope, it used to remain in scope until the end of the scope that contained the for statement (rather than just within the for scope). G++ retains this, but issues a warning, if such a variable is accessed outside the for scope.

Implicit C language
              Old C system header files did not contain an **extern "C"** {...} scope to set the language. On such systems, all header files are implicitly scoped inside a C language scope. Also, an empty prototype () is treated as an unspecified number of arguments, rather than no arguments, as C++ demands.

8 GNU Objective-C Features

This document is meant to describe some of the GNU Objective-C features. It is not intended to teach you Objective-C. There are several resources on the Internet that present the language.

8.1 GNU Objective-C Runtime API

This section is specific for the GNU Objective-C runtime. If you are using a different runtime, you can skip it.

The GNU Objective-C runtime provides an API that allows you to interact with the Objective-C runtime system, querying the live runtime structures and even manipulating them. This allows you for example to inspect and navigate classes, methods and protocols; to define new classes or new methods, and even to modify existing classes or protocols.

If you are using a "Foundation" library such as GNUstep-Base, this library will provide you with a rich set of functionality to do most of the inspection tasks, and you probably will only need direct access to the GNU Objective-C runtime API to define new classes or methods.

8.1.1 Modern GNU Objective-C Runtime API

The GNU Objective-C runtime provides an API which is similar to the one provided by the "Objective-C 2.0" Apple/NeXT Objective-C runtime. The API is documented in the public header files of the GNU Objective-C runtime:

- 'objc/objc.h': this is the basic Objective-C header file, defining the basic Objective-C types such as id, Class and BOOL. You have to include this header to do almost anything with Objective-C.

- 'objc/runtime.h': this header declares most of the public runtime API functions allowing you to inspect and manipulate the Objective-C runtime data structures. These functions are fairly standardized across Objective-C runtimes and are almost identical to the Apple/NeXT Objective-C runtime ones. It does not declare functions in some specialized areas (constructing and forwarding message invocations, threading) which are in the other headers below. You have to include 'objc/objc.h' and 'objc/runtime.h' to use any of the functions, such as class_getName(), declared in 'objc/runtime.h'.

- 'objc/message.h': this header declares public functions used to construct, deconstruct and forward message invocations. Because messaging is done in quite a different way on different runtimes, functions in this header are specific to the GNU Objective-C runtime implementation.

- 'objc/objc-exception.h': this header declares some public functions related to Objective-C exceptions. For example functions in this header allow you to throw an Objective-C exception from plain C/C++ code.

- 'objc/objc-sync.h': this header declares some public functions related to the Objective-C @synchronized() syntax, allowing you to emulate an Objective-C @synchronized() block in plain C/C++ code.

- 'objc/thr.h': this header declares a public runtime API threading layer that is only provided by the GNU Objective-C runtime. It declares functions such as objc_mutex_lock(), which provide a platform-independent set of threading functions.

The header files contain detailed documentation for each function in the GNU Objective-C runtime API.

8.1.2 Traditional GNU Objective-C Runtime API

The GNU Objective-C runtime used to provide a different API, which we call the "traditional" GNU Objective-C runtime API. Functions belonging to this API are easy to recognize because they use a different naming convention, such as class_get_super_class() (traditional API) instead of class_getSuperclass() (modern API). Software using this API includes the file 'objc/objc-api.h' where it is declared.

Starting with GCC 4.7.0, the traditional GNU runtime API is no longer available.

8.2 +load: Executing Code before main

This section is specific for the GNU Objective-C runtime. If you are using a different runtime, you can skip it.

The GNU Objective-C runtime provides a way that allows you to execute code before the execution of the program enters the main function. The code is executed on a per-class and a per-category basis, through a special class method +load.

This facility is very useful if you want to initialize global variables which can be accessed by the program directly, without sending a message to the class first. The usual way to initialize global variables, in the +initialize method, might not be useful because +initialize is only called when the first message is sent to a class object, which in some cases could be too late.

Suppose for example you have a FileStream class that declares Stdin, Stdout and Stderr as global variables, like below:

```
FileStream *Stdin = nil;
FileStream *Stdout = nil;
FileStream *Stderr = nil;

@implementation FileStream

+ (void)initialize
{
    Stdin = [[FileStream new] initWithFd:0];
    Stdout = [[FileStream new] initWithFd:1];
    Stderr = [[FileStream new] initWithFd:2];
}

/* Other methods here */
@end
```

In this example, the initialization of Stdin, Stdout and Stderr in +initialize occurs too late. The programmer can send a message to one of these objects before the variables are actually initialized, thus sending messages to the nil object. The +initialize method which actually initializes the global variables is not invoked until the first message is sent to the class object. The solution would require these variables to be initialized just before entering `main`.

The correct solution of the above problem is to use the `+load` method instead of `+initialize`:

```
@implementation FileStream

+ (void)load
{
    Stdin = [[FileStream new] initWithFd:0];
    Stdout = [[FileStream new] initWithFd:1];
    Stderr = [[FileStream new] initWithFd:2];
}

/* Other methods here */
@end
```

The `+load` is a method that is not overridden by categories. If a class and a category of it both implement `+load`, both methods are invoked. This allows some additional initializations to be performed in a category.

This mechanism is not intended to be a replacement for `+initialize`. You should be aware of its limitations when you decide to use it instead of `+initialize`.

8.2.1 What You Can and Cannot Do in `+load`

`+load` is to be used only as a last resort. Because it is executed very early, most of the Objective-C runtime machinery will not be ready when `+load` is executed; hence `+load` works best for executing C code that is independent on the Objective-C runtime.

The `+load` implementation in the GNU runtime guarantees you the following things:

- you can write whatever C code you like;
- you can allocate and send messages to objects whose class is implemented in the same file;
- the `+load` implementation of all super classes of a class are executed before the `+load` of that class is executed;
- the `+load` implementation of a class is executed before the `+load` implementation of any category.

In particular, the following things, even if they can work in a particular case, are not guaranteed:

- allocation of or sending messages to arbitrary objects;
- allocation of or sending messages to objects whose classes have a category implemented in the same file;
- sending messages to Objective-C constant strings (`@"this is a constant string"`);

You should make no assumptions about receiving `+load` in sibling classes when you write `+load` of a class. The order in which sibling classes receive `+load` is not guaranteed.

The order in which `+load` and `+initialize` are called could be problematic if this matters. If you don't allocate objects inside `+load`, it is guaranteed that `+load` is called before `+initialize`. If you create an object inside `+load` the `+initialize` method of object's class is invoked even if +load was not invoked. Note if you explicitly call +load on a class, +initialize will be called first. To avoid possible problems try to implement only one of these methods.

The +load method is also invoked when a bundle is dynamically loaded into your running program. This happens automatically without any intervening operation from you. When you write bundles and you need to write +load you can safely create and send messages to objects whose classes already exist in the running program. The same restrictions as above apply to classes defined in bundle.

8.3 Type Encoding

This is an advanced section. Type encodings are used extensively by the compiler and by the runtime, but you generally do not need to know about them to use Objective-C.

The Objective-C compiler generates type encodings for all the types. These type encodings are used at runtime to find out information about selectors and methods and about objects and classes.

The types are encoded in the following way:

_Bool	B
char	c
unsigned char	C
short	s
unsigned short	S
int	i
unsigned int	I
long	l
unsigned long	L
long long	q
unsigned long long	Q
float	f
double	d
long double	D
void	v
id	@
Class	#
SEL	:
char*	*
enum	an enum is encoded exactly as the integer type that the compiler uses for it, which depends on the enumeration values. Often the compiler users unsigned int, which is then encoded as I.
unknown type	?
Complex types	j followed by the inner type. For example _Complex double is encoded as "jd".
bit-fields	b followed by the starting position of the bit-field, the type of the bit-field and the size of the bit-field (the bit-fields encoding was changed from the NeXT's compiler encoding, see below)

The encoding of bit-fields has changed to allow bit-fields to be properly handled by the runtime functions that compute sizes and alignments of types that contain bit-fields. The previous encoding contained only the size of the bit-field. Using only this information it is not possible to reliably compute the size occupied by the bit-field. This is very important in the presence of the Boehm's garbage collector because the objects are allocated using the typed memory facility available in this collector. The typed memory allocation requires information about where the pointers are located inside the object.

The position in the bit-field is the position, counting in bits, of the bit closest to the beginning of the structure.

The non-atomic types are encoded as follows:

pointers	'^' followed by the pointed type.
arrays	'[' followed by the number of elements in the array followed by the type of the elements followed by ']'
structures	'{' followed by the name of the structure (or '?' if the structure is unnamed), the '=' sign, the type of the members and by '}'
unions	'(' followed by the name of the structure (or '?' if the union is unnamed), the '=' sign, the type of the members followed by ')'
vectors	'![' followed by the vector_size (the number of bytes composing the vector) followed by a comma, followed by the alignment (in bytes) of the vector, followed by the type of the elements followed by ']'

Here are some types and their encodings, as they are generated by the compiler on an i386 machine:

```
Objective-C type          Compiler encoding
    int a[10];            [10i]

    struct {              {?=i[3f]b128i3b131i2c}
      int i;
      float f[3];
      int a:3;
      int b:2;
      char c;
    }

    int a __attribute__ !(16,16i (vector_size) (the alignment would depend on the machine)
```

In addition to the types the compiler also encodes the type specifiers. The table below describes the encoding of the current Objective-C type specifiers:

Specifier	Encoding
const	r
in	n
inout	N
out	o
bycopy	O

```
byref                      R
oneway                     V
```

The type specifiers are encoded just before the type. Unlike types however, the type specifiers are only encoded when they appear in method argument types.

Note how `const` interacts with pointers:

Objective-C type	Compiler encoding
const int	ri
const int*	^ri
int *const	r^i

`const int*` is a pointer to a `const int`, and so is encoded as `^ri`. `int* const`, instead, is a `const` pointer to an `int`, and so is encoded as `r^i`.

Finally, there is a complication when encoding `const char *` versus `char * const`. Because `char *` is encoded as `*` and not as `^c`, there is no way to express the fact that `r` applies to the pointer or to the pointee.

Hence, it is assumed as a convention that `r*` means `const char *` (since it is what is most often meant), and there is no way to encode `char *const`. `char *const` would simply be encoded as `*`, and the `const` is lost.

8.3.1 Legacy Type Encoding

Unfortunately, historically GCC used to have a number of bugs in its encoding code. The NeXT runtime expects GCC to emit type encodings in this historical format (compatible with GCC-3.3), so when using the NeXT runtime, GCC will introduce on purpose a number of incorrect encodings:

- the read-only qualifier of the pointee gets emitted before the '^'. The read-only qualifier of the pointer itself gets ignored, unless it is a typedef. Also, the 'r' is only emitted for the outermost type.
- 32-bit longs are encoded as 'l' or 'L', but not always. For typedefs, the compiler uses 'i' or 'I' instead if encoding a struct field or a pointer.
- enums are always encoded as 'i' (int) even if they are actually unsigned or long.

In addition to that, the NeXT runtime uses a different encoding for bitfields. It encodes them as `b` followed by the size, without a bit offset or the underlying field type.

8.3.2 @encode

GNU Objective-C supports the `@encode` syntax that allows you to create a type encoding from a C/Objective-C type. For example, `@encode(int)` is compiled by the compiler into `"i"`.

`@encode` does not support type qualifiers other than `const`. For example, `@encode(const char*)` is valid and is compiled into `"r*"`, while `@encode(bycopy char *)` is invalid and will cause a compilation error.

8.3.3 Method Signatures

This section documents the encoding of method types, which is rarely needed to use Objective-C. You should skip it at a first reading; the runtime provides functions that will work on methods and can walk through the list of parameters and interpret them for you. These functions are part of the public "API" and are the preferred way to interact with method signatures from user code.

But if you need to debug a problem with method signatures and need to know how they are implemented (i.e., the "ABI"), read on.

Methods have their "signature" encoded and made available to the runtime. The "signature" encodes all the information required to dynamically build invocations of the method at runtime: return type and arguments.

The "signature" is a null-terminated string, composed of the following:

- The return type, including type qualifiers. For example, a method returning `int` would have `i` here.

- The total size (in bytes) required to pass all the parameters. This includes the two hidden parameters (the object `self` and the method selector `_cmd`).

- Each argument, with the type encoding, followed by the offset (in bytes) of the argument in the list of parameters.

For example, a method with no arguments and returning `int` would have the signature `i8@0:4` if the size of a pointer is 4. The signature is interpreted as follows: the `i` is the return type (an `int`), the `8` is the total size of the parameters in bytes (two pointers each of size 4), the `@0` is the first parameter (an object at byte offset 0) and `:4` is the second parameter (a `SEL` at byte offset 4).

You can easily find more examples by running the "strings" program on an Objective-C object file compiled by GCC. You'll see a lot of strings that look very much like `i8@0:4`. They are signatures of Objective-C methods.

8.4 Garbage Collection

This section is specific for the GNU Objective-C runtime. If you are using a different runtime, you can skip it.

Support for garbage collection with the GNU runtime has been added by using a powerful conservative garbage collector, known as the Boehm-Demers-Weiser conservative garbage collector.

To enable the support for it you have to configure the compiler using an additional argument, '`--enable-objc-gc`'. This will build the boehm-gc library, and build an additional runtime library which has several enhancements to support the garbage collector. The new library has a new name, '`libobjc_gc.a`' to not conflict with the non-garbage-collected library.

When the garbage collector is used, the objects are allocated using the so-called typed memory allocation mechanism available in the Boehm-Demers-Weiser collector. This mode requires precise information on where pointers are located inside objects. This information is computed once per class, immediately after the class has been initialized.

There is a new runtime function `class_ivar_set_gcinvisible()` which can be used to declare a so-called *weak pointer* reference. Such a pointer is basically hidden for the garbage collector; this can be useful in certain situations, especially when you want to keep track of the allocated objects, yet allow them to be collected. This kind of pointers can only be members of objects, you cannot declare a global pointer as a weak reference. Every type which is a pointer type can be declared a weak pointer, including `id`, `Class` and `SEL`.

Here is an example of how to use this feature. Suppose you want to implement a class whose instances hold a weak pointer reference; the following class does this:

```
@interface WeakPointer : Object
{
    const void* weakPointer;
}

- initWithPointer:(const void*)p;
- (const void*)weakPointer;
@end


@implementation WeakPointer

+ (void)initialize
{
  if (self == objc_lookUpClass ("WeakPointer"))
    class_ivar_set_gcinvisible (self, "weakPointer", YES);
}

- initWithPointer:(const void*)p
{
  weakPointer = p;
  return self;
}

- (const void*)weakPointer
{
  return weakPointer;
}

@end
```

Weak pointers are supported through a new type character specifier represented by the '!' character. The `class_ivar_set_gcinvisible()` function adds or removes this specifier to the string type description of the instance variable named as argument.

8.5 Constant String Objects

GNU Objective-C provides constant string objects that are generated directly by the compiler. You declare a constant string object by prefixing a C constant string with the character '@':

```
id myString = @"this is a constant string object";
```

The constant string objects are by default instances of the `NXConstantString` class which is provided by the GNU Objective-C runtime. To get the definition of this class you must include the 'objc/NXConstStr.h' header file.

User defined libraries may want to implement their own constant string class. To be able to support them, the GNU Objective-C compiler provides a new command line options '-fconstant-string-class=*class-name*'. The provided class should adhere to a strict structure, the same as NXConstantString's structure:

```
@interface MyConstantStringClass
{
  Class isa;
  char *c_string;
  unsigned int len;
}
@end
```

NXConstantString inherits from Object; user class libraries may choose to inherit the customized constant string class from a different class than Object. There is no requirement in the methods the constant string class has to implement, but the final ivar layout of the class must be the compatible with the given structure.

When the compiler creates the statically allocated constant string object, the c_string field will be filled by the compiler with the string; the length field will be filled by the compiler with the string length; the isa pointer will be filled with NULL by the compiler, and it will later be fixed up automatically at runtime by the GNU Objective-C runtime library to point to the class which was set by the '-fconstant-string-class' option when the object file is loaded (if you wonder how it works behind the scenes, the name of the class to use, and the list of static objects to fixup, are stored by the compiler in the object file in a place where the GNU runtime library will find them at runtime).

As a result, when a file is compiled with the '-fconstant-string-class' option, all the constant string objects will be instances of the class specified as argument to this option. It is possible to have multiple compilation units referring to different constant string classes, neither the compiler nor the linker impose any restrictions in doing this.

8.6 compatibility_alias

The keyword @compatibility_alias allows you to define a class name as equivalent to another class name. For example:

```
@compatibility_alias WOApplication GSWApplication;
```

tells the compiler that each time it encounters WOApplication as a class name, it should replace it with GSWApplication (that is, WOApplication is just an alias for GSWApplication).

There are some constraints on how this can be used—

- WOApplication (the alias) must not be an existing class;
- GSWApplication (the real class) must be an existing class.

8.7 Exceptions

GNU Objective-C provides exception support built into the language, as in the following example:

```
@try {
  ...
```

```
        @throw expr;
    ...
}
@catch (AnObjCClass *exc) {
    ...
        @throw expr;
    ...
        @throw;
    ...
}
@catch (AnotherClass *exc) {
    ...
}
@catch (id allOthers) {
    ...
}
@finally {
    ...
        @throw expr;
    ...
}
```

The `@throw` statement may appear anywhere in an Objective-C or Objective-C++ program; when used inside of a `@catch` block, the `@throw` may appear without an argument (as shown above), in which case the object caught by the `@catch` will be rethrown.

Note that only (pointers to) Objective-C objects may be thrown and caught using this scheme. When an object is thrown, it will be caught by the nearest `@catch` clause capable of handling objects of that type, analogously to how `catch` blocks work in C++ and Java. A `@catch(id ...)` clause (as shown above) may also be provided to catch any and all Objective-C exceptions not caught by previous `@catch` clauses (if any).

The `@finally` clause, if present, will be executed upon exit from the immediately preceding `@try ... @catch` section. This will happen regardless of whether any exceptions are thrown, caught or rethrown inside the `@try ... @catch` section, analogously to the behavior of the `finally` clause in Java.

There are several caveats to using the new exception mechanism:

- The '`-fobjc-exceptions`' command line option must be used when compiling Objective-C files that use exceptions.

- With the GNU runtime, exceptions are always implemented as "native" exceptions and it is recommended that the '`-fexceptions`' and '`-shared-libgcc`' options are used when linking.

- With the NeXT runtime, although currently designed to be binary compatible with `NS_HANDLER`-style idioms provided by the `NSException` class, the new exceptions can only be used on Mac OS X 10.3 (Panther) and later systems, due to additional functionality needed in the NeXT Objective-C runtime.

- As mentioned above, the new exceptions do not support handling types other than Objective-C objects. Furthermore, when used from Objective-C++, the Objective-C exception model does not interoperate with C++ exceptions at this time. This means you cannot `@throw` an exception from Objective-C and `catch` it in C++, or vice versa (i.e., `throw ... @catch`).

8.8 Synchronization

GNU Objective-C provides support for synchronized blocks:

```
@synchronized (ObjCClass *guard) {
  ...
}
```

Upon entering the @synchronized block, a thread of execution shall first check whether a lock has been placed on the corresponding guard object by another thread. If it has, the current thread shall wait until the other thread relinquishes its lock. Once guard becomes available, the current thread will place its own lock on it, execute the code contained in the @synchronized block, and finally relinquish the lock (thereby making guard available to other threads).

Unlike Java, Objective-C does not allow for entire methods to be marked @synchronized. Note that throwing exceptions out of @synchronized blocks is allowed, and will cause the guarding object to be unlocked properly.

Because of the interactions between synchronization and exception handling, you can only use @synchronized when compiling with exceptions enabled, that is with the command line option '-fobjc-exceptions'.

8.9 Fast Enumeration

8.9.1 Using Fast Enumeration

GNU Objective-C provides support for the fast enumeration syntax:

```
id array = ...;
id object;

for (object in array)
{
  /* Do something with 'object' */
}
```

array needs to be an Objective-C object (usually a collection object, for example an array, a dictionary or a set) which implements the "Fast Enumeration Protocol" (see below). If you are using a Foundation library such as GNUstep Base or Apple Cocoa Foundation, all collection objects in the library implement this protocol and can be used in this way.

The code above would iterate over all objects in array. For each of them, it assigns it to object, then executes the Do something with 'object' statements.

Here is a fully worked-out example using a Foundation library (which provides the implementation of NSArray, NSString and NSLog):

```
NSArray *array = [NSArray arrayWithObjects: @"1", @"2", @"3", nil];
NSString *object;

for (object in array)
  NSLog (@"Iterating over %@", object);
```

8.9.2 C99-Like Fast Enumeration Syntax

A c99-like declaration syntax is also allowed:

```
id array = ...;
```

```
     for (id object in array)
     {
       /* Do something with 'object' */
     }
```
this is completely equivalent to:
```
     id array = ...;

     {
       id object;
       for (object in array)
       {
         /* Do something with 'object' */
       }
     }
```
but can save some typing.

Note that the option '-std=c99' is not required to allow this syntax in Objective-C.

8.9.3 Fast Enumeration Details

Here is a more technical description with the gory details. Consider the code
```
     for (object expression in collection expression)
     {
       statements
     }
```
here is what happens when you run it:

- *collection expression* is evaluated exactly once and the result is used as the collection object to iterate over. This means it is safe to write code such as `for (object in [NSDictionary keyEnumerator])` ....

- the iteration is implemented by the compiler by repeatedly getting batches of objects from the collection object using the fast enumeration protocol (see below), then iterating over all objects in the batch. This is faster than a normal enumeration where objects are retrieved one by one (hence the name "fast enumeration").

- if there are no objects in the collection, then *object expression* is set to `nil` and the loop immediately terminates.

- if there are objects in the collection, then for each object in the collection (in the order they are returned) *object expression* is set to the object, then *statements* are executed.

- *statements* can contain `break` and `continue` commands, which will abort the iteration or skip to the next loop iteration as expected.

- when the iteration ends because there are no more objects to iterate over, *object expression* is set to `nil`. This allows you to determine whether the iteration finished because a `break` command was used (in which case *object expression* will remain set to the last object that was iterated over) or because it iterated over all the objects (in which case *object expression* will be set to `nil`).

- *statements* must not make any changes to the collection object; if they do, it is a hard error and the fast enumeration terminates by invoking `objc_enumerationMutation`, a runtime function that normally aborts the program but which can be customized by Foundation libraries via `objc_set_mutation_handler` to do something different, such as raising an exception.

8.9.4 Fast Enumeration Protocol

If you want your own collection object to be usable with fast enumeration, you need to have it implement the method

```
- (unsigned long) countByEnumeratingWithState: (NSFastEnumerationState *)state
                                      objects: (id *)objects
                                        count: (unsigned long)len;
```

where NSFastEnumerationState must be defined in your code as follows:

```
typedef struct
{
  unsigned long state;
  id            *itemsPtr;
  unsigned long *mutationsPtr;
  unsigned long extra[5];
} NSFastEnumerationState;
```

If no NSFastEnumerationState is defined in your code, the compiler will automatically replace NSFastEnumerationState * with struct __objcFastEnumerationState *, where that type is silently defined by the compiler in an identical way. This can be confusing and we recommend that you define NSFastEnumerationState (as shown above) instead.

The method is called repeatedly during a fast enumeration to retrieve batches of objects. Each invocation of the method should retrieve the next batch of objects.

The return value of the method is the number of objects in the current batch; this should not exceed len, which is the maximum size of a batch as requested by the caller. The batch itself is returned in the itemsPtr field of the NSFastEnumerationState struct.

To help with returning the objects, the objects array is a C array preallocated by the caller (on the stack) of size len. In many cases you can put the objects you want to return in that objects array, then do itemsPtr = objects. But you don't have to; if your collection already has the objects to return in some form of C array, it could return them from there instead.

The state and extra fields of the NSFastEnumerationState structure allows your collection object to keep track of the state of the enumeration. In a simple array implementation, state may keep track of the index of the last object that was returned, and extra may be unused.

The mutationsPtr field of the NSFastEnumerationState is used to keep track of mutations. It should point to a number; before working on each object, the fast enumeration loop will check that this number has not changed. If it has, a mutation has happened and the fast enumeration will abort. So, mutationsPtr could be set to point to some sort of version number of your collection, which is increased by one every time there is a change (for example when an object is added or removed). Or, if you are content with less strict mutation checks, it could point to the number of objects in your collection or some other value that can be checked to perform an approximate check that the collection has not been mutated.

Finally, note how we declared the len argument and the return value to be of type unsigned long. They could also be declared to be of type unsigned int and everything would still work.

8.10 Messaging with the GNU Objective-C Runtime

This section is specific for the GNU Objective-C runtime. If you are using a different runtime, you can skip it.

The implementation of messaging in the GNU Objective-C runtime is designed to be portable, and so is based on standard C.

Sending a message in the GNU Objective-C runtime is composed of two separate steps. First, there is a call to the lookup function, `objc_msg_lookup ()` (or, in the case of messages to super, `objc_msg_lookup_super ()`). This runtime function takes as argument the receiver and the selector of the method to be called; it returns the IMP, that is a pointer to the function implementing the method. The second step of method invocation consists of casting this pointer function to the appropriate function pointer type, and calling the function pointed to it with the right arguments.

For example, when the compiler encounters a method invocation such as `[object init]`, it compiles it into a call to `objc_msg_lookup (object, @selector(init))` followed by a cast of the returned value to the appropriate function pointer type, and then it calls it.

8.10.1 Dynamically Registering Methods

If `objc_msg_lookup()` does not find a suitable method implementation, because the receiver does not implement the required method, it tries to see if the class can dynamically register the method.

To do so, the runtime checks if the class of the receiver implements the method

```
+ (BOOL) resolveInstanceMethod: (SEL)selector;
```

in the case of an instance method, or

```
+ (BOOL) resolveClassMethod: (SEL)selector;
```

in the case of a class method. If the class implements it, the runtime invokes it, passing as argument the selector of the original method, and if it returns YES, the runtime tries the lookup again, which could now succeed if a matching method was added dynamically by `+resolveInstanceMethod:` or `+resolveClassMethod:`.

This allows classes to dynamically register methods (by adding them to the class using `class_addMethod`) when they are first called. To do so, a class should implement `+resolveInstanceMethod:` (or, depending on the case, `+resolveClassMethod:`) and have it recognize the selectors of methods that can be registered dynamically at runtime, register them, and return YES. It should return NO for methods that it does not dynamically registered at runtime.

If `+resolveInstanceMethod:` (or `+resolveClassMethod:`) is not implemented or returns NO, the runtime then tries the forwarding hook.

Support for `+resolveInstanceMethod:` and `resolveClassMethod:` was added to the GNU Objective-C runtime in GCC version 4.6.

8.10.2 Forwarding Hook

The GNU Objective-C runtime provides a hook, called `__objc_msg_forward2`, which is called by `objc_msg_lookup()` when it can't find a method implementation in the runtime tables and after calling `+resolveInstanceMethod:` and `+resolveClassMethod:` has been attempted and did not succeed in dynamically registering the method.

To configure the hook, you set the global variable `__objc_msg_forward2` to a function with the same argument and return types of `objc_msg_lookup()`. When `objc_msg_lookup()` can not find a method implementation, it invokes the hook function you provided to get a method implementation to return. So, in practice `__objc_msg_forward2` allows you to extend `objc_msg_lookup()` by adding some custom code that is called to do a further lookup when no standard method implementation can be found using the normal lookup.

This hook is generally reserved for "Foundation" libraries such as GNUstep Base, which use it to implement their high-level method forwarding API, typically based around the `forwardInvocation:` method. So, unless you are implementing your own "Foundation" library, you should not set this hook.

In a typical forwarding implementation, the `__objc_msg_forward2` hook function determines the argument and return type of the method that is being looked up, and then creates a function that takes these arguments and has that return type, and returns it to the caller. Creating this function is non-trivial and is typically performed using a dedicated library such as `libffi`.

The forwarding method implementation thus created is returned by `objc_msg_lookup()` and is executed as if it was a normal method implementation. When the forwarding method implementation is called, it is usually expected to pack all arguments into some sort of object (typically, an `NSInvocation` in a "Foundation" library), and hand it over to the programmer (`forwardInvocation:`) who is then allowed to manipulate the method invocation using a high-level API provided by the "Foundation" library. For example, the programmer may want to examine the method invocation arguments and name and potentially change them before forwarding the method invocation to one or more local objects (`performInvocation:`) or even to remote objects (by using Distributed Objects or some other mechanism). When all this completes, the return value is passed back and must be returned correctly to the original caller.

Note that the GNU Objective-C runtime currently provides no support for method forwarding or method invocations other than the `__objc_msg_forward2` hook.

If the forwarding hook does not exist or returns `NULL`, the runtime currently attempts forwarding using an older, deprecated API, and if that fails, it aborts the program. In future versions of the GNU Objective-C runtime, the runtime will immediately abort.

9 Binary Compatibility

Binary compatibility encompasses several related concepts:

application binary interface (ABI)
> The set of runtime conventions followed by all of the tools that deal with binary representations of a program, including compilers, assemblers, linkers, and language runtime support. Some ABIs are formal with a written specification, possibly designed by multiple interested parties. Others are simply the way things are actually done by a particular set of tools.

ABI conformance
> A compiler conforms to an ABI if it generates code that follows all of the specifications enumerated by that ABI. A library conforms to an ABI if it is implemented according to that ABI. An application conforms to an ABI if it is built using tools that conform to that ABI and does not contain source code that specifically changes behavior specified by the ABI.

calling conventions
> Calling conventions are a subset of an ABI that specify of how arguments are passed and function results are returned.

interoperability
> Different sets of tools are interoperable if they generate files that can be used in the same program. The set of tools includes compilers, assemblers, linkers, libraries, header files, startup files, and debuggers. Binaries produced by different sets of tools are not interoperable unless they implement the same ABI. This applies to different versions of the same tools as well as tools from different vendors.

intercallability
> Whether a function in a binary built by one set of tools can call a function in a binary built by a different set of tools is a subset of interoperability.

implementation-defined features
> Language standards include lists of implementation-defined features whose behavior can vary from one implementation to another. Some of these features are normally covered by a platform's ABI and others are not. The features that are not covered by an ABI generally affect how a program behaves, but not intercallability.

compatibility
> Conformance to the same ABI and the same behavior of implementation-defined features are both relevant for compatibility.

The application binary interface implemented by a C or C++ compiler affects code generation and runtime support for:

- size and alignment of data types
- layout of structured types
- calling conventions

- register usage conventions
- interfaces for runtime arithmetic support
- object file formats

In addition, the application binary interface implemented by a C++ compiler affects code generation and runtime support for:

- name mangling
- exception handling
- invoking constructors and destructors
- layout, alignment, and padding of classes
- layout and alignment of virtual tables

Some GCC compilation options cause the compiler to generate code that does not conform to the platform's default ABI. Other options cause different program behavior for implementation-defined features that are not covered by an ABI. These options are provided for consistency with other compilers that do not follow the platform's default ABI or the usual behavior of implementation-defined features for the platform. Be very careful about using such options.

Most platforms have a well-defined ABI that covers C code, but ABIs that cover C++ functionality are not yet common.

Starting with GCC 3.2, GCC binary conventions for C++ are based on a written, vendor-neutral C++ ABI that was designed to be specific to 64-bit Itanium but also includes generic specifications that apply to any platform. This C++ ABI is also implemented by other compiler vendors on some platforms, notably GNU/Linux and BSD systems. We have tried hard to provide a stable ABI that will be compatible with future GCC releases, but it is possible that we will encounter problems that make this difficult. Such problems could include different interpretations of the C++ ABI by different vendors, bugs in the ABI, or bugs in the implementation of the ABI in different compilers. GCC's '-Wabi' switch warns when G++ generates code that is probably not compatible with the C++ ABI.

The C++ library used with a C++ compiler includes the Standard C++ Library, with functionality defined in the C++ Standard, plus language runtime support. The runtime support is included in a C++ ABI, but there is no formal ABI for the Standard C++ Library. Two implementations of that library are interoperable if one follows the de-facto ABI of the other and if they are both built with the same compiler, or with compilers that conform to the same ABI for C++ compiler and runtime support.

When G++ and another C++ compiler conform to the same C++ ABI, but the implementations of the Standard C++ Library that they normally use do not follow the same ABI for the Standard C++ Library, object files built with those compilers can be used in the same program only if they use the same C++ library. This requires specifying the location of the C++ library header files when invoking the compiler whose usual library is not being used. The location of GCC's C++ header files depends on how the GCC build was configured, but can be seen by using the G++ '-v' option. With default configuration options for G++ 3.3 the compile line for a different C++ compiler needs to include

```
-Igcc_install_directory/include/c++/3.3
```

Similarly, compiling code with G++ that must use a C++ library other than the GNU C++ library requires specifying the location of the header files for that other library.

The most straightforward way to link a program to use a particular C++ library is to use a C++ driver that specifies that C++ library by default. The g++ driver, for example, tells the linker where to find GCC's C++ library ('libstdc++') plus the other libraries and startup files it needs, in the proper order.

If a program must use a different C++ library and it's not possible to do the final link using a C++ driver that uses that library by default, it is necessary to tell g++ the location and name of that library. It might also be necessary to specify different startup files and other runtime support libraries, and to suppress the use of GCC's support libraries with one or more of the options '-nostdlib', '-nostartfiles', and '-nodefaultlibs'.

10 gcov—a Test Coverage Program

gcov is a tool you can use in conjunction with GCC to test code coverage in your programs.

10.1 Introduction to gcov

gcov is a test coverage program. Use it in concert with GCC to analyze your programs to help create more efficient, faster running code and to discover untested parts of your program. You can use gcov as a profiling tool to help discover where your optimization efforts will best affect your code. You can also use gcov along with the other profiling tool, gprof, to assess which parts of your code use the greatest amount of computing time.

Profiling tools help you analyze your code's performance. Using a profiler such as gcov or gprof, you can find out some basic performance statistics, such as:

- how often each line of code executes
- what lines of code are actually executed
- how much computing time each section of code uses

Once you know these things about how your code works when compiled, you can look at each module to see which modules should be optimized. gcov helps you determine where to work on optimization.

Software developers also use coverage testing in concert with testsuites, to make sure software is actually good enough for a release. Testsuites can verify that a program works as expected; a coverage program tests to see how much of the program is exercised by the testsuite. Developers can then determine what kinds of test cases need to be added to the testsuites to create both better testing and a better final product.

You should compile your code without optimization if you plan to use gcov because the optimization, by combining some lines of code into one function, may not give you as much information as you need to look for 'hot spots' where the code is using a great deal of computer time. Likewise, because gcov accumulates statistics by line (at the lowest resolution), it works best with a programming style that places only one statement on each line. If you use complicated macros that expand to loops or to other control structures, the statistics are less helpful—they only report on the line where the macro call appears. If your complex macros behave like functions, you can replace them with inline functions to solve this problem.

gcov creates a logfile called 'sourcefile.gcov' which indicates how many times each line of a source file 'sourcefile.c' has executed. You can use these logfiles along with gprof to aid in fine-tuning the performance of your programs. gprof gives timing information you can use along with the information you get from gcov.

gcov works only on code compiled with GCC. It is not compatible with any other profiling or test coverage mechanism.

10.2 Invoking gcov

```
gcov [options] files
```

gcov accepts the following options:

`-h`
`--help`   Display help about using `gcov` (on the standard output), and exit without doing
            any further processing.

`-v`
`--version`
            Display the `gcov` version number (on the standard output), and exit without
            doing any further processing.

`-a`
`--all-blocks`
            Write individual execution counts for every basic block. Normally gcov outputs
            execution counts only for the main blocks of a line. With this option you can
            determine if blocks within a single line are not being executed.

`-b`
`--branch-probabilities`
            Write branch frequencies to the output file, and write branch summary info to
            the standard output. This option allows you to see how often each branch in
            your program was taken. Unconditional branches will not be shown, unless the
            '-u' option is given.

`-c`
`--branch-counts`
            Write branch frequencies as the number of branches taken, rather than the
            percentage of branches taken.

`-n`
`--no-output`
            Do not create the `gcov` output file.

`-l`
`--long-file-names`
            Create long file names for included source files. For example, if the header
            file 'x.h' contains code, and was included in the file 'a.c', then running `gcov`
            on the file 'a.c' will produce an output file called 'a.c##x.h.gcov' instead of
            'x.h.gcov'. This can be useful if 'x.h' is included in multiple source files and
            you want to see the individual contributions. If you use the '-p' option, both
            the including and included file names will be complete path names.

`-p`
`--preserve-paths`
            Preserve complete path information in the names of generated '.gcov' files.
            Without this option, just the filename component is used. With this option, all
            directories are used, with '/' characters translated to '#' characters, '.' directory
            components removed and unremoveable '..' components renamed to '^'. This
            is useful if sourcefiles are in several different directories.

`-r`
`--relative-only`

> Only output information about source files with a relative pathname (after source prefix elision). Absolute paths are usually system header files and coverage of any inline functions therein is normally uninteresting.

`-f`
`--function-summaries`

> Output summaries for each function in addition to the file level summary.

`-o` *directory|file*
`--object-directory` *directory*
`--object-file` *file*

> Specify either the directory containing the gcov data files, or the object path name. The '`.gcno`', and '`.gcda`' data files are searched for using this option. If a directory is specified, the data files are in that directory and named after the input file name, without its extension. If a file is specified here, the data files are named after that file, without its extension.

`-s` *directory*
`--source-prefix` *directory*

> A prefix for source file names to remove when generating the output coverage files. This option is useful when building in a separate directory, and the path-name to the source directory is not wanted when determining the output file names. Note that this prefix detection is applied before determining whether the source file is absolute.

`-u`
`--unconditional-branches`

> When branch probabilities are given, include those of unconditional branches. Unconditional branches are normally not interesting.

`-d`
`--display-progress`

> Display the progress on the standard output.

`-i`
`--intermediate-format`

> Output gcov file in an easy-to-parse intermediate text format that can be used by `lcov` or other tools. The output is a single '`.gcov`' file per '`.gcda`' file. No source code is required.
>
> The format of the intermediate '`.gcov`' file is plain text with one entry per line
>
> ```
> file:source_file_name
> function:line_number,execution_count,function_name
> lcount:line number,execution_count
> branch:line_number,branch_coverage_type
>
> Where the branch_coverage_type is
>    notexec (Branch not executed)
>    taken (Branch executed and taken)
>    nottaken (Branch executed, but not taken)
> ```

There can be multiple *file* entries in an intermediate gcov
file. All entries following a *file* pertain to that source file
until the next *file* entry.

Here is a sample when '-i' is used in conjunction with '-b' option:

```
file:array.cc
function:11,1,_Z3sumRKSt6vectorIPiSaIS0_EE
function:22,1,main
lcount:11,1
lcount:12,1
lcount:14,1
branch:14,taken
lcount:26,1
branch:28,nottaken
```

-m

--demangled-names

> Display demangled function names in output. The default is to show mangled function names.

-x

--hash-filenames

> By default, gcov uses the full pathname of the source files to to create an output filename. This can lead to long filenames that can overflow filesystem limits. This option creates names of the form '*source-file*##*md5*.gcov', where the *source-file* component is the final filename part and the *md5* component is calculated from the full mangled name that would have been used otherwise.

gcov should be run with the current directory the same as that when you invoked the compiler. Otherwise it will not be able to locate the source files. gcov produces files called '*mangledname*.gcov' in the current directory. These contain the coverage information of the source file they correspond to. One '.gcov' file is produced for each source (or header) file containing code, which was compiled to produce the data files. The *mangledname* part of the output file name is usually simply the source file name, but can be something more complicated if the '-l' or '-p' options are given. Refer to those options for details.

If you invoke gcov with multiple input files, the contributions from each input file are summed. Typically you would invoke it with the same list of files as the final link of your executable.

The '.gcov' files contain the ':' separated fields along with program source code. The format is

```
execution_count:line_number:source line text
```

Additional block information may succeed each line, when requested by command line option. The *execution_count* is '-' for lines containing no code. Unexecuted lines are marked '#####' or '=====', depending on whether they are reachable by non-exceptional paths or only exceptional paths such as C++ exception handlers, respectively.

Some lines of information at the start have *line_number* of zero. These preamble lines are of the form

```
-:0:tag:value
```

The ordering and number of these preamble lines will be augmented as gcov development progresses — do not rely on them remaining unchanged. Use *tag* to locate a particular preamble line.

The additional block information is of the form

```
tag information
```

The *information* is human readable, but designed to be simple enough for machine parsing too.

When printing percentages, 0% and 100% are only printed when the values are *exactly* 0% and 100% respectively. Other values which would conventionally be rounded to 0% or 100% are instead printed as the nearest non-boundary value.

When using gcov, you must first compile your program with two special GCC options: '-fprofile-arcs -ftest-coverage'. This tells the compiler to generate additional information needed by gcov (basically a flow graph of the program) and also includes additional code in the object files for generating the extra profiling information needed by gcov. These additional files are placed in the directory where the object file is located.

Running the program will cause profile output to be generated. For each source file compiled with '-fprofile-arcs', an accompanying '.gcda' file will be placed in the object file directory.

Running gcov with your program's source file names as arguments will now produce a listing of the code along with frequency of execution for each line. For example, if your program is called 'tmp.c', this is what you see when you use the basic gcov facility:

```
$ gcc -fprofile-arcs -ftest-coverage tmp.c
$ a.out
$ gcov tmp.c
File 'tmp.c'
Lines executed:90.00% of 10
Creating 'tmp.c.gcov'
```

The file 'tmp.c.gcov' contains output from gcov. Here is a sample:

```
        -:    0:Source:tmp.c
        -:    0:Graph:tmp.gcno
        -:    0:Data:tmp.gcda
        -:    0:Runs:1
        -:    0:Programs:1
        -:    1:#include <stdio.h>
        -:    2:
        -:    3:int main (void)
        1:    4:{
        1:    5:  int i, total;
        -:    6:
        1:    7:  total = 0;
        -:    8:
       11:    9:  for (i = 0; i < 10; i++)
       10:   10:    total += i;
        -:   11:
        1:   12:  if (total != 45)
    #####:   13:    printf ("Failure\n");
        -:   14:  else
        1:   15:    printf ("Success\n");
        1:   16:  return 0;
        -:   17:}
```

When you use the '-a' option, you will get individual block counts, and the output looks like this:

```
        -:    0:Source:tmp.c
        -:    0:Graph:tmp.gcno
```

```
       -:    0:Data:tmp.gcda
       -:    0:Runs:1
       -:    0:Programs:1
       -:    1:#include <stdio.h>
       -:    2:
       -:    3:int main (void)
       1:    4:{
       1:    4-block  0
       1:    5:  int i, total;
       -:    6:
       1:    7:  total = 0;
       -:    8:
      11:    9:  for (i = 0; i < 10; i++)
      11:    9-block  0
      10:   10:    total += i;
      10:   10-block  0
       -:   11:
       1:   12:  if (total != 45)
       1:   12-block  0
   #####:   13:    printf ("Failure\n");
  $$$$$:   13-block  0
       -:   14:  else
       1:   15:    printf ("Success\n");
       1:   15-block  0
       1:   16:  return 0;
       1:   16-block  0
       -:   17:}
```

In this mode, each basic block is only shown on one line – the last line of the block. A multi-line block will only contribute to the execution count of that last line, and other lines will not be shown to contain code, unless previous blocks end on those lines. The total execution count of a line is shown and subsequent lines show the execution counts for individual blocks that end on that line. After each block, the branch and call counts of the block will be shown, if the '-b' option is given.

Because of the way GCC instruments calls, a call count can be shown after a line with no individual blocks. As you can see, line 13 contains a basic block that was not executed.

When you use the '-b' option, your output looks like this:

```
$ gcov -b tmp.c
File 'tmp.c'
Lines executed:90.00% of 10
Branches executed:80.00% of 5
Taken at least once:80.00% of 5
Calls executed:50.00% of 2
Creating 'tmp.c.gcov'
```

Here is a sample of a resulting 'tmp.c.gcov' file:

```
       -:    0:Source:tmp.c
       -:    0:Graph:tmp.gcno
       -:    0:Data:tmp.gcda
       -:    0:Runs:1
       -:    0:Programs:1
       -:    1:#include <stdio.h>
       -:    2:
       -:    3:int main (void)
function main called 1 returned 1 blocks executed 75%
       1:    4:{
```

```
        1:    5:    int i, total;
       -:    6:
        1:    7:    total = 0;
       -:    8:
       11:    9:    for (i = 0; i < 10; i++)
branch  0 taken 91% (fallthrough)
branch  1 taken 9%
       10:   10:       total += i;
       -:   11:
        1:   12:    if (total != 45)
branch  0 taken 0% (fallthrough)
branch  1 taken 100%
    #####:   13:       printf ("Failure\n");
call    0 never executed
       -:   14:    else
        1:   15:       printf ("Success\n");
call    0 called 1 returned 100%
        1:   16:    return 0;
       -:   17:}
```

For each function, a line is printed showing how many times the function is called, how many times it returns and what percentage of the function's blocks were executed.

For each basic block, a line is printed after the last line of the basic block describing the branch or call that ends the basic block. There can be multiple branches and calls listed for a single source line if there are multiple basic blocks that end on that line. In this case, the branches and calls are each given a number. There is no simple way to map these branches and calls back to source constructs. In general, though, the lowest numbered branch or call will correspond to the leftmost construct on the source line.

For a branch, if it was executed at least once, then a percentage indicating the number of times the branch was taken divided by the number of times the branch was executed will be printed. Otherwise, the message "never executed" is printed.

For a call, if it was executed at least once, then a percentage indicating the number of times the call returned divided by the number of times the call was executed will be printed. This will usually be 100%, but may be less for functions that call **exit** or **longjmp**, and thus may not return every time they are called.

The execution counts are cumulative. If the example program were executed again without removing the '.gcda' file, the count for the number of times each line in the source was executed would be added to the results of the previous run(s). This is potentially useful in several ways. For example, it could be used to accumulate data over a number of program runs as part of a test verification suite, or to provide more accurate long-term information over a large number of program runs.

The data in the '.gcda' files is saved immediately before the program exits. For each source file compiled with '-fprofile-arcs', the profiling code first attempts to read in an existing '.gcda' file; if the file doesn't match the executable (differing number of basic block counts) it will ignore the contents of the file. It then adds in the new execution counts and finally writes the data to the file.

10.3 Using gcov with GCC Optimization

If you plan to use gcov to help optimize your code, you must first compile your program with two special GCC options: '-fprofile-arcs -ftest-coverage'. Aside from that, you can use any other GCC options; but if you want to prove that every single line in your program was executed, you should not compile with optimization at the same time. On some machines the optimizer can eliminate some simple code lines by combining them with other lines. For example, code like this:

```
if (a != b)
  c = 1;
else
  c = 0;
```

can be compiled into one instruction on some machines. In this case, there is no way for gcov to calculate separate execution counts for each line because there isn't separate code for each line. Hence the gcov output looks like this if you compiled the program with optimization:

```
100:    12:if (a != b)
100:    13:  c = 1;
100:    14:else
100:    15:  c = 0;
```

The output shows that this block of code, combined by optimization, executed 100 times. In one sense this result is correct, because there was only one instruction representing all four of these lines. However, the output does not indicate how many times the result was 0 and how many times the result was 1.

Inlineable functions can create unexpected line counts. Line counts are shown for the source code of the inlineable function, but what is shown depends on where the function is inlined, or if it is not inlined at all.

If the function is not inlined, the compiler must emit an out of line copy of the function, in any object file that needs it. If 'fileA.o' and 'fileB.o' both contain out of line bodies of a particular inlineable function, they will also both contain coverage counts for that function. When 'fileA.o' and 'fileB.o' are linked together, the linker will, on many systems, select one of those out of line bodies for all calls to that function, and remove or ignore the other. Unfortunately, it will not remove the coverage counters for the unused function body. Hence when instrumented, all but one use of that function will show zero counts.

If the function is inlined in several places, the block structure in each location might not be the same. For instance, a condition might now be calculable at compile time in some instances. Because the coverage of all the uses of the inline function will be shown for the same source lines, the line counts themselves might seem inconsistent.

Long-running applications can use the __gcov_reset and __gcov_dump facilities to restrict profile collection to the program region of interest. Calling __gcov_reset(void) will clear all profile counters to zero, and calling __gcov_dump(void) will cause the profile information collected at that point to be dumped to '.gcda' output files. Instrumented applications use a static destructor with priority 99 to invoke the __gcov_dump function. Thus __gcov_dump is executed after all user defined static destructors, as well as handlers registered with atexit.

10.4 Brief Description of gcov Data Files

gcov uses two files for profiling. The names of these files are derived from the original *object* file by substituting the file suffix with either '.gcno', or '.gcda'. The files contain coverage and profile data stored in a platform-independent format. The '.gcno' files are placed in the same directory as the object file. By default, the '.gcda' files are also stored in the same directory as the object file, but the GCC '-fprofile-dir' option may be used to store the '.gcda' files in a separate directory.

The '.gcno' notes file is generated when the source file is compiled with the GCC '-ftest-coverage' option. It contains information to reconstruct the basic block graphs and assign source line numbers to blocks.

The '.gcda' count data file is generated when a program containing object files built with the GCC '-fprofile-arcs' option is executed. A separate '.gcda' file is created for each object file compiled with this option. It contains arc transition counts, value profile counts, and some summary information.

The full details of the file format is specified in 'gcov-io.h', and functions provided in that header file should be used to access the coverage files.

10.5 Data File Relocation to Support Cross-Profiling

Running the program will cause profile output to be generated. For each source file compiled with '-fprofile-arcs', an accompanying '.gcda' file will be placed in the object file directory. That implicitly requires running the program on the same system as it was built or having the same absolute directory structure on the target system. The program will try to create the needed directory structure, if it is not already present.

To support cross-profiling, a program compiled with '-fprofile-arcs' can relocate the data files based on two environment variables:

- GCOV_PREFIX contains the prefix to add to the absolute paths in the object file. Prefix can be absolute, or relative. The default is no prefix.

- GCOV_PREFIX_STRIP indicates the how many initial directory names to strip off the hardwired absolute paths. Default value is 0.

  Note: If GCOV_PREFIX_STRIP is set without GCOV_PREFIX is undefined, then a relative path is made out of the hardwired absolute paths.

For example, if the object file '/user/build/foo.o' was built with '-fprofile-arcs', the final executable will try to create the data file '/user/build/foo.gcda' when running on the target system. This will fail if the corresponding directory does not exist and it is unable to create it. This can be overcome by, for example, setting the environment as 'GCOV_PREFIX=/target/run' and 'GCOV_PREFIX_STRIP=1'. Such a setting will name the data file '/target/run/build/foo.gcda'.

You must move the data files to the expected directory tree in order to use them for profile directed optimizations ('--use-profile'), or to use the `gcov` tool.

11 gcov-tool—an Offline Gcda Profile Processing Tool

`gcov-tool` is a tool you can use in conjunction with GCC to manipulate or process gcda profile files offline.

11.1 Introduction to `gcov-tool`

`gcov-tool` is an offline tool to process gcc's gcda profile files.

Current gcov-tool supports the following functionalities:

- merge two sets of profiles with weights.
- read one set of profile and rewrite profile contents. One can scale or normalize the count values.

Examples of the use cases for this tool are:

- Collect the profiles for different set of inputs, and use this tool to merge them. One can specify the weight to factor in the relative importance of each input.
- Rewrite the profile after removing a subset of the gcda files, while maintaining the consistency of the summary and the histogram.
- It can also be used to debug or libgcov code as the tools shares the majority code as the runtime library.

Note that for the merging operation, this profile generated offline may contain slight different values from the online merged profile. Here are a list of typical differences:

- histogram difference: This offline tool recomputes the histogram after merging the counters. The resulting histogram, therefore, is precise. The online merging does not have this capability – the histogram is merged from two histograms and the result is an approximation.
- summary checksum difference: Summary checksum uses a CRC32 operation. The value depends on the link list order of gcov-info objects. This order is different in gcov-tool from that in the online merge. It's expected to have different summary checksums. It does not really matter as the compiler does not use this checksum anywhere.
- value profile counter values difference: Some counter values for value profile are runtime dependent, like heap addresses. It's normal to see some difference in these kind of counters.

11.2 Invoking `gcov-tool`

```
gcov-tool [global-options] SUB_COMMAND [sub_command-options] profile_dir
```

`gcov-tool` accepts the following options:

`-h`
`--help`   Display help about using `gcov-tool` (on the standard output), and exit without doing any further processing.

`-v`
`--version`
Display the `gcov-tool` version number (on the standard output), and exit without doing any further processing.

merge   Merge two profile directories.

               `-v`
               `--verbose`
                       Set the verbose mode.

               `-o directory`
               `--output directory`
                       Set the output profile directory. Default output directory name is
                       merged_profile.

               `-w w1,w2`
               `--weight w1,w2`
                       Set the merge weights of the directory1 and directory2, respectively.
                       The default weights are 1 for both.

rewrite   Read the specified profile directory and rewrite to a new directory.

               `-v`
               `--verbose`
                       Set the verbose mode.

               `-o directory`
               `--output directory`
                       Set the output profile directory.   Default output name is
                       rewrite_profile.

               `-s float_or_simple-frac_value`
               `--scale float_or_simple-frac_value`
                       Scale the profile counters. The specified value can be in floating
                       point value, or simple fraction value form, such 1, 2, 2/3, and 5/3.

               `-n long_long_value`
               `--normalize <long_long_value>`
                       Normalize the profile. The specified value is the max counter value
                       in the new profile.

overlap   Compute the overlap score between the two specified profile directories. The
               overlap score is computed based on the arc profiles. It is defined as the sum
               of min ($p1\_counter[i]$ / $p1\_sum\_all$, $p2\_counter[i]$ / $p2\_sum\_all$), for all arc
               counter i, where $p1\_counter[i]$ and $p2\_counter[i]$ are two matched counters and
               $p1\_sum\_all$ and $p2\_sum\_all$ are the sum of counter values in profile 1 and profile
               2, respectively.

               `-v`
               `--verbose`
                       Set the verbose mode.

               `-h`
               `--hotonly`
                       Only print info for hot objects/functions.

               `-f`
               `--function`
                       Print function level overlap score.

`-F`
`--fullname`
> Print full gcda filename.

`-o`
`--object`   Print object level overlap score.

`-t` *float*
`--hot_threshold <float>`
> Set the threshold for hot counter value.

12 Known Causes of Trouble with GCC

This section describes known problems that affect users of GCC. Most of these are not GCC bugs per se—if they were, we would fix them. But the result for a user may be like the result of a bug.

Some of these problems are due to bugs in other software, some are missing features that are too much work to add, and some are places where people's opinions differ as to what is best.

12.1 Actual Bugs We Haven't Fixed Yet

- The `fixincludes` script interacts badly with automounters; if the directory of system header files is automounted, it tends to be unmounted while `fixincludes` is running. This would seem to be a bug in the automounter. We don't know any good way to work around it.

12.2 Interoperation

This section lists various difficulties encountered in using GCC together with other compilers or with the assemblers, linkers, libraries and debuggers on certain systems.

- On many platforms, GCC supports a different ABI for C++ than do other compilers, so the object files compiled by GCC cannot be used with object files generated by another C++ compiler.

  An area where the difference is most apparent is name mangling. The use of different name mangling is intentional, to protect you from more subtle problems. Compilers differ as to many internal details of C++ implementation, including: how class instances are laid out, how multiple inheritance is implemented, and how virtual function calls are handled. If the name encoding were made the same, your programs would link against libraries provided from other compilers—but the programs would then crash when run. Incompatible libraries are then detected at link time, rather than at run time.

- On some BSD systems, including some versions of Ultrix, use of profiling causes static variable destructors (currently used only in C++) not to be run.

- On a SPARC, GCC aligns all values of type `double` on an 8-byte boundary, and it expects every `double` to be so aligned. The Sun compiler usually gives `double` values 8-byte alignment, with one exception: function arguments of type `double` may not be aligned.

  As a result, if a function compiled with Sun CC takes the address of an argument of type `double` and passes this pointer of type `double *` to a function compiled with GCC, dereferencing the pointer may cause a fatal signal.

  One way to solve this problem is to compile your entire program with GCC. Another solution is to modify the function that is compiled with Sun CC to copy the argument into a local variable; local variables are always properly aligned. A third solution is to modify the function that uses the pointer to dereference it via the following function `access_double` instead of directly with '`*`':

```
inline double
access_double (double *unaligned_ptr)
{
  union d2i { double d; int i[2]; };

  union d2i *p = (union d2i *) unaligned_ptr;
  union d2i u;

  u.i[0] = p->i[0];
  u.i[1] = p->i[1];

  return u.d;
}
```

Storing into the pointer can be done likewise with the same union.

- On Solaris, the `malloc` function in the 'libmalloc.a' library may allocate memory that is only 4 byte aligned. Since GCC on the SPARC assumes that doubles are 8 byte aligned, this may result in a fatal signal if doubles are stored in memory allocated by the 'libmalloc.a' library.

  The solution is to not use the 'libmalloc.a' library. Use instead `malloc` and related functions from 'libc.a'; they do not have this problem.

- On the HP PA machine, ADB sometimes fails to work on functions compiled with GCC. Specifically, it fails to work on functions that use `alloca` or variable-size arrays. This is because GCC doesn't generate HP-UX unwind descriptors for such functions. It may even be impossible to generate them.

- Debugging ('-g') is not supported on the HP PA machine, unless you use the preliminary GNU tools.

- Taking the address of a label may generate errors from the HP-UX PA assembler. GAS for the PA does not have this problem.

- Using floating point parameters for indirect calls to static functions will not work when using the HP assembler. There simply is no way for GCC to specify what registers hold arguments for static functions when using the HP assembler. GAS for the PA does not have this problem.

- In extremely rare cases involving some very large functions you may receive errors from the HP linker complaining about an out of bounds unconditional branch offset. This used to occur more often in previous versions of GCC, but is now exceptionally rare. If you should run into it, you can work around by making your function smaller.

- GCC compiled code sometimes emits warnings from the HP-UX assembler of the form:
  ```
  (warning) Use of GR3 when
     frame >= 8192 may cause conflict.
  ```
  These warnings are harmless and can be safely ignored.

- In extremely rare cases involving some very large functions you may receive errors from the AIX Assembler complaining about a displacement that is too large. If you should run into it, you can work around by making your function smaller.

- The 'libstdc++.a' library in GCC relies on the SVR4 dynamic linker semantics which merges global symbols between libraries and applications, especially necessary for C++ streams functionality. This is not the default behavior of AIX shared libraries and dynamic linking. 'libstdc++.a' is built on AIX with "runtime-linking" enabled so that symbol merging can occur. To utilize this feature, the application linked with 'libstdc++.a' must include the '-Wl,-brtl' flag on the link line. G++ cannot impose this because this option may interfere with the semantics of the user program and users may not always use 'g++' to link his or her application. Applications are not required to use the '-Wl,-brtl' flag on the link line—the rest of the 'libstdc++.a' library which is not dependent on the symbol merging semantics will continue to function correctly.

- An application can interpose its own definition of functions for functions invoked by 'libstdc++.a' with "runtime-linking" enabled on AIX. To accomplish this the application must be linked with "runtime-linking" option and the functions explicitly must be exported by the application ('-Wl,-brtl,-bE:exportfile').

- AIX on the RS/6000 provides support (NLS) for environments outside of the United States. Compilers and assemblers use NLS to support locale-specific representations of various objects including floating-point numbers ('.' vs ',' for separating decimal fractions). There have been problems reported where the library linked with GCC does not produce the same floating-point formats that the assembler accepts. If you have this problem, set the LANG environment variable to 'C' or 'En_US'.

- Even if you specify '-fdollars-in-identifiers', you cannot successfully use '$' in identifiers on the RS/6000 due to a restriction in the IBM assembler. GAS supports these identifiers.

12.3 Incompatibilities of GCC

There are several noteworthy incompatibilities between GNU C and K&R (non-ISO) versions of C.

- GCC normally makes string constants read-only. If several identical-looking string constants are used, GCC stores only one copy of the string.

  One consequence is that you cannot call mktemp with a string constant argument. The function mktemp always alters the string its argument points to.

  Another consequence is that sscanf does not work on some very old systems when passed a string constant as its format control string or input. This is because sscanf incorrectly tries to write into the string constant. Likewise fscanf and scanf.

  The solution to these problems is to change the program to use char-array variables with initialization strings for these purposes instead of string constants.

- -2147483648 is positive.

  This is because 2147483648 cannot fit in the type int, so (following the ISO C rules) its data type is unsigned long int. Negating this value yields 2147483648 again.

- GCC does not substitute macro arguments when they appear inside of string constants. For example, the following macro in GCC

      #define foo(a) "a"

  will produce output "a" regardless of what the argument a is.

- When you use setjmp and longjmp, the only automatic variables guaranteed to remain valid are those declared volatile. This is a consequence of automatic register allocation. Consider this function:

      jmp_buf j;

```
foo ()
{
  int a, b;

  a = fun1 ();
  if (setjmp (j))
    return a;

  a = fun2 ();
  /* longjmp (j) may occur in fun3. */
  return a + fun3 ();
}
```

Here a may or may not be restored to its first value when the longjmp occurs. If a is allocated in a register, then its first value is restored; otherwise, it keeps the last value stored in it.

If you use the '-W' option with the '-O' option, you will get a warning when GCC thinks such a problem might be possible.

- Programs that use preprocessing directives in the middle of macro arguments do not work with GCC. For example, a program like this will not work:

```
foobar (
#define luser
        hack)
```

ISO C does not permit such a construct.

- K&R compilers allow comments to cross over an inclusion boundary (i.e. started in an include file and ended in the including file).

- Declarations of external variables and functions within a block apply only to the block containing the declaration. In other words, they have the same scope as any other declaration in the same place.

In some other C compilers, an **extern** declaration affects all the rest of the file even if it happens within a block.

- In traditional C, you can combine long, etc., with a typedef name, as shown here:

```
typedef int foo;
typedef long foo bar;
```

In ISO C, this is not allowed: long and other type modifiers require an explicit int.

- PCC allows typedef names to be used as function parameters.

- Traditional C allows the following erroneous pair of declarations to appear together in a given scope:

```
typedef int foo;
typedef foo foo;
```

- GCC treats all characters of identifiers as significant. According to K&R-1 (2.2), "No more than the first eight characters are significant, although more may be used.". Also according to K&R-1 (2.2), "An identifier is a sequence of letters and digits; the first character must be a letter. The underscore _ counts as a letter.", but GCC also allows dollar signs in identifiers.

- PCC allows whitespace in the middle of compound assignment operators such as '+='. GCC, following the ISO standard, does not allow this.

- GCC complains about unterminated character constants inside of preprocessing conditionals that fail. Some programs have English comments enclosed in conditionals that are guaranteed to fail; if these comments contain apostrophes, GCC will probably report an error. For example, this code would produce an error:

  ```
  #if 0
  You can't expect this to work.
  #endif
  ```

  The best solution to such a problem is to put the text into an actual C comment delimited by '/*...*/'.

- Many user programs contain the declaration 'long time ();'. In the past, the system header files on many systems did not actually declare time, so it did not matter what type your program declared it to return. But in systems with ISO C headers, time is declared to return time_t, and if that is not the same as long, then 'long time ();' is erroneous.

  The solution is to change your program to use appropriate system headers (<time.h> on systems with ISO C headers) and not to declare time if the system header files declare it, or failing that to use time_t as the return type of time.

- When compiling functions that return float, PCC converts it to a double. GCC actually returns a float. If you are concerned with PCC compatibility, you should declare your functions to return double; you might as well say what you mean.

- When compiling functions that return structures or unions, GCC output code normally uses a method different from that used on most versions of Unix. As a result, code compiled with GCC cannot call a structure-returning function compiled with PCC, and vice versa.

  The method used by GCC is as follows: a structure or union which is 1, 2, 4 or 8 bytes long is returned like a scalar. A structure or union with any other size is stored into an address supplied by the caller (usually in a special, fixed register, but on some machines it is passed on the stack). The target hook TARGET_STRUCT_VALUE_RTX tells GCC where to pass this address.

  By contrast, PCC on most target machines returns structures and unions of any size by copying the data into an area of static storage, and then returning the address of that storage as if it were a pointer value. The caller must copy the data from that memory area to the place where the value is wanted. GCC does not use this method because it is slower and nonreentrant.

  On some newer machines, PCC uses a reentrant convention for all structure and union returning. GCC on most of these machines uses a compatible convention when returning structures and unions in memory, but still returns small structures and unions in registers.

  You can tell GCC to use a compatible convention for all structure and union returning with the option '-fpcc-struct-return'.

- GCC complains about program fragments such as '0x74ae-0x4000' which appear to be two hexadecimal constants separated by the minus operator. Actually, this string is a single *preprocessing token*. Each such token must correspond to one token in C. Since this does not, GCC prints an error message. Although it may appear obvious that what is meant is an operator and two values, the ISO C standard specifically requires that this be treated as erroneous.

A *preprocessing token* is a *preprocessing number* if it begins with a digit and is followed by letters, underscores, digits, periods and 'e+', 'e-', 'E+', 'E-', 'p+', 'p-', 'P+', or 'P-' character sequences. (In strict C90 mode, the sequences 'p+', 'p-', 'P+' and 'P-' cannot appear in preprocessing numbers.)

To make the above program fragment valid, place whitespace in front of the minus sign. This whitespace will end the preprocessing number.

12.4 Fixed Header Files

GCC needs to install corrected versions of some system header files. This is because most target systems have some header files that won't work with GCC unless they are changed. Some have bugs, some are incompatible with ISO C, and some depend on special features of other compilers.

Installing GCC automatically creates and installs the fixed header files, by running a program called `fixincludes`. Normally, you don't need to pay attention to this. But there are cases where it doesn't do the right thing automatically.

- If you update the system's header files, such as by installing a new system version, the fixed header files of GCC are not automatically updated. They can be updated using the `mkheaders` script installed in '`libexecdir/gcc/target/version/install-tools/`'.

- On some systems, header file directories contain machine-specific symbolic links in certain places. This makes it possible to share most of the header files among hosts running the same version of the system on different machine models.

  The programs that fix the header files do not understand this special way of using symbolic links; therefore, the directory of fixed header files is good only for the machine model used to build it.

  It is possible to make separate sets of fixed header files for the different machine models, and arrange a structure of symbolic links so as to use the proper set, but you'll have to do this by hand.

12.5 Standard Libraries

GCC by itself attempts to be a conforming freestanding implementation. See Chapter 2 [Language Standards Supported by GCC], page 5, for details of what this means. Beyond the library facilities required of such an implementation, the rest of the C library is supplied by the vendor of the operating system. If that C library doesn't conform to the C standards, then your programs might get warnings (especially when using '-Wall') that you don't expect.

For example, the `sprintf` function on SunOS 4.1.3 returns `char *` while the C standard says that `sprintf` returns an `int`. The `fixincludes` program could make the prototype for this function match the Standard, but that would be wrong, since the function will still return `char *`.

If you need a Standard compliant library, then you need to find one, as GCC does not provide one. The GNU C library (called `glibc`) provides ISO C, POSIX, BSD, SystemV and

X/Open compatibility for GNU/Linux and HURD-based GNU systems; no recent version of it supports other systems, though some very old versions did. Version 2.2 of the GNU C library includes nearly complete C99 support. You could also ask your operating system vendor if newer libraries are available.

12.6 Disappointments and Misunderstandings

These problems are perhaps regrettable, but we don't know any practical way around them.

- Certain local variables aren't recognized by debuggers when you compile with optimization.

  This occurs because sometimes GCC optimizes the variable out of existence. There is no way to tell the debugger how to compute the value such a variable "would have had", and it is not clear that would be desirable anyway. So GCC simply does not mention the eliminated variable when it writes debugging information.

  You have to expect a certain amount of disagreement between the executable and your source code, when you use optimization.

- Users often think it is a bug when GCC reports an error for code like this:

    ```
    int foo (struct mumble *);

    struct mumble { ... };

    int foo (struct mumble *x)
    { ... }
    ```

  This code really is erroneous, because the scope of struct mumble in the prototype is limited to the argument list containing it. It does not refer to the struct mumble defined with file scope immediately below—they are two unrelated types with similar names in different scopes.

  But in the definition of foo, the file-scope type is used because that is available to be inherited. Thus, the definition and the prototype do not match, and you get an error.

  This behavior may seem silly, but it's what the ISO standard specifies. It is easy enough for you to make your code work by moving the definition of struct mumble above the prototype. It's not worth being incompatible with ISO C just to avoid an error for the example shown above.

- Accesses to bit-fields even in volatile objects works by accessing larger objects, such as a byte or a word. You cannot rely on what size of object is accessed in order to read or write the bit-field; it may even vary for a given bit-field according to the precise usage.

  If you care about controlling the amount of memory that is accessed, use volatile but do not use bit-fields.

- GCC comes with shell scripts to fix certain known problems in system header files. They install corrected copies of various header files in a special directory where only GCC will normally look for them. The scripts adapt to various systems by searching all the system header files for the problem cases that we know about.

  If new system header files are installed, nothing automatically arranges to update the corrected header files. They can be updated using the mkheaders script installed in 'libexecdir/gcc/target/version/install-tools/'.

- On 68000 and x86 systems, for instance, you can get paradoxical results if you test the precise values of floating point numbers. For example, you can find that a floating point value which is not a NaN is not equal to itself. This results from the fact that the floating point registers hold a few more bits of precision than fit in a `double` in memory. Compiled code moves values between memory and floating point registers at its convenience, and moving them into memory truncates them.

  You can partially avoid this problem by using the '`-ffloat-store`' option (see Section 3.10 [Optimize Options], page 102).

- On AIX and other platforms without weak symbol support, templates need to be instantiated explicitly and symbols for static members of templates will not be generated.

- On AIX, GCC scans object files and library archives for static constructors and destructors when linking an application before the linker prunes unreferenced symbols. This is necessary to prevent the AIX linker from mistakenly assuming that static constructor or destructor are unused and removing them before the scanning can occur. All static constructors and destructors found will be referenced even though the modules in which they occur may not be used by the program. This may lead to both increased executable size and unexpected symbol references.

12.7 Common Misunderstandings with GNU C++

C++ is a complex language and an evolving one, and its standard definition (the ISO C++ standard) was only recently completed. As a result, your C++ compiler may occasionally surprise you, even when its behavior is correct. This section discusses some areas that frequently give rise to questions of this sort.

12.7.1 Declare *and* Define Static Members

When a class has static data members, it is not enough to *declare* the static member; you must also *define* it. For example:

```
class Foo
{
  ...
  void method();
  static int bar;
};
```

This declaration only establishes that the class `Foo` has an `int` named `Foo::bar`, and a member function named `Foo::method`. But you still need to define *both* method and `bar` elsewhere. According to the ISO standard, you must supply an initializer in one (and only one) source file, such as:

```
int Foo::bar = 0;
```

Other C++ compilers may not correctly implement the standard behavior. As a result, when you switch to g++ from one of these compilers, you may discover that a program that appeared to work correctly in fact does not conform to the standard: g++ reports as undefined symbols any static data members that lack definitions.

12.7.2 Name Lookup, Templates, and Accessing Members of Base Classes

The C++ standard prescribes that all names that are not dependent on template parameters are bound to their present definitions when parsing a template function or class.[1] Only names that are dependent are looked up at the point of instantiation. For example, consider

```
void foo(double);

struct A {
  template <typename T>
  void f () {
    foo (1);        // 1
    int i = N;      // 2
    T t;
    t.bar();        // 3
    foo (t);        // 4
  }

  static const int N;
};
```

Here, the names `foo` and `N` appear in a context that does not depend on the type of `T`. The compiler will thus require that they are defined in the context of use in the template, not only before the point of instantiation, and will here use `::foo(double)` and `A::N`, respectively. In particular, it will convert the integer value to a `double` when passing it to `::foo(double)`.

Conversely, `bar` and the call to `foo` in the fourth marked line are used in contexts that do depend on the type of `T`, so they are only looked up at the point of instantiation, and you can provide declarations for them after declaring the template, but before instantiating it. In particular, if you instantiate `A::f<int>`, the last line will call an overloaded `::foo(int)` if one was provided, even if after the declaration of `struct A`.

This distinction between lookup of dependent and non-dependent names is called two-stage (or dependent) name lookup. G++ implements it since version 3.4.

Two-stage name lookup sometimes leads to situations with behavior different from non-template codes. The most common is probably this:

```
template <typename T> struct Base {
  int i;
};

template <typename T> struct Derived : public Base<T> {
  int get_i() { return i; }
};
```

In `get_i()`, `i` is not used in a dependent context, so the compiler will look for a name declared at the enclosing namespace scope (which is the global scope here). It will not look into the base class, since that is dependent and you may declare specializations of `Base` even after declaring `Derived`, so the compiler can't really know what `i` would refer to. If there is no global variable `i`, then you will get an error message.

In order to make it clear that you want the member of the base class, you need to defer lookup until instantiation time, at which the base class is known. For this, you need to

---

[1] The C++ standard just uses the term "dependent" for names that depend on the type or value of template parameters. This shorter term will also be used in the rest of this section.

access i in a dependent context, by either using this->i (remember that this is of type Derived<T>*, so is obviously dependent), or using Base<T>::i. Alternatively, Base<T>::i might be brought into scope by a using-declaration.

Another, similar example involves calling member functions of a base class:

```
template <typename T> struct Base {
    int f();
};


template <typename T> struct Derived : Base<T> {
    int g() { return f(); };
};
```

Again, the call to f() is not dependent on template arguments (there are no arguments that depend on the type T, and it is also not otherwise specified that the call should be in a dependent context). Thus a global declaration of such a function must be available, since the one in the base class is not visible until instantiation time. The compiler will consequently produce the following error message:

```
x.cc: In member function 'int Derived<T>::g()':
x.cc:6: error: there are no arguments to 'f' that depend on a template
    parameter, so a declaration of 'f' must be available
x.cc:6: error: (if you use '-fpermissive', G++ will accept your code, but
    allowing the use of an undeclared name is deprecated)
```

To make the code valid either use this->f(), or Base<T>::f(). Using the '-fpermissive' flag will also let the compiler accept the code, by marking all function calls for which no declaration is visible at the time of definition of the template for later lookup at instantiation time, as if it were a dependent call. We do not recommend using '-fpermissive' to work around invalid code, and it will also only catch cases where functions in base classes are called, not where variables in base classes are used (as in the example above).

Note that some compilers (including G++ versions prior to 3.4) get these examples wrong and accept above code without an error. Those compilers do not implement two-stage name lookup correctly.

12.7.3 Temporaries May Vanish Before You Expect

It is dangerous to use pointers or references to *portions* of a temporary object. The compiler may very well delete the object before you expect it to, leaving a pointer to garbage. The most common place where this problem crops up is in classes like string classes, especially ones that define a conversion function to type char * or const char *—which is one reason why the standard string class requires you to call the c_str member function. However, any class that returns a pointer to some internal structure is potentially subject to this problem.

For example, a program may use a function strfunc that returns string objects, and another function charfunc that operates on pointers to char:

```
string strfunc ();
void charfunc (const char *);

void
f ()
{
  const char *p = strfunc().c_str();
```

```
    ...
    charfunc (p);
    ...
    charfunc (p);
}
```

In this situation, it may seem reasonable to save a pointer to the C string returned by the c_str member function and use that rather than call c_str repeatedly. However, the temporary string created by the call to strfunc is destroyed after p is initialized, at which point p is left pointing to freed memory.

Code like this may run successfully under some other compilers, particularly obsolete cfront-based compilers that delete temporaries along with normal local variables. However, the GNU C++ behavior is standard-conforming, so if your program depends on late destruction of temporaries it is not portable.

The safe way to write such code is to give the temporary a name, which forces it to remain until the end of the scope of the name. For example:

```
const string& tmp = strfunc ();
charfunc (tmp.c_str ());
```

12.7.4 Implicit Copy-Assignment for Virtual Bases

When a base class is virtual, only one subobject of the base class belongs to each full object. Also, the constructors and destructors are invoked only once, and called from the most-derived class. However, such objects behave unspecified when being assigned. For example:

```
struct Base{
  char *name;
  Base(char *n) : name(strdup(n)){}
  Base& operator= (const Base& other){
   free (name);
   name = strdup (other.name);
  }
};

struct A:virtual Base{
  int val;
  A():Base("A"){}
};

struct B:virtual Base{
  int bval;
  B():Base("B"){}
};

struct Derived:public A, public B{
  Derived():Base("Derived"){}
};

void func(Derived &d1, Derived &d2)
{
   d1 = d2;
}
```

The C++ standard specifies that 'Base::Base' is only called once when constructing or copy-constructing a Derived object. It is unspecified whether 'Base::operator=' is called more than once when the implicit copy-assignment for Derived objects is invoked (as it is inside 'func' in the example).

G++ implements the "intuitive" algorithm for copy-assignment: assign all direct bases, then assign all members. In that algorithm, the virtual base subobject can be encountered more than once. In the example, copying proceeds in the following order: 'val', 'name' (via strdup), 'bval', and 'name' again.

If application code relies on copy-assignment, a user-defined copy-assignment operator removes any uncertainties. With such an operator, the application can define whether and how the virtual base subobject is assigned.

12.8 Certain Changes We Don't Want to Make

This section lists changes that people frequently request, but which we do not make because we think GCC is better without them.

- Checking the number and type of arguments to a function which has an old-fashioned definition and no prototype.

  Such a feature would work only occasionally—only for calls that appear in the same file as the called function, following the definition. The only way to check all calls reliably is to add a prototype for the function. But adding a prototype eliminates the motivation for this feature. So the feature is not worthwhile.

- Warning about using an expression whose type is signed as a shift count.

  Shift count operands are probably signed more often than unsigned. Warning about this would cause far more annoyance than good.

- Warning about assigning a signed value to an unsigned variable.

  Such assignments must be very common; warning about them would cause more annoyance than good.

- Warning when a non-void function value is ignored.

  C contains many standard functions that return a value that most programs choose to ignore. One obvious example is printf. Warning about this practice only leads the defensive programmer to clutter programs with dozens of casts to void. Such casts are required so frequently that they become visual noise. Writing those casts becomes so automatic that they no longer convey useful information about the intentions of the programmer. For functions where the return value should never be ignored, use the warn_unused_result function attribute (see Section 6.31 [Function Attributes], page 427).

- Making '-fshort-enums' the default.

  This would cause storage layout to be incompatible with most other C compilers. And it doesn't seem very important, given that you can get the same result in other ways. The case where it matters most is when the enumeration-valued object is inside a structure, and in that case you can specify a field width explicitly.

- Making bit-fields unsigned by default on particular machines where "the ABI standard" says to do so.

  The ISO C standard leaves it up to the implementation whether a bit-field declared plain int is signed or not. This in effect creates two alternative dialects of C.

The GNU C compiler supports both dialects; you can specify the signed dialect with '-fsigned-bitfields' and the unsigned dialect with '-funsigned-bitfields'. However, this leaves open the question of which dialect to use by default.

Currently, the preferred dialect makes plain bit-fields signed, because this is simplest. Since int is the same as signed int in every other context, it is cleanest for them to be the same in bit-fields as well.

Some computer manufacturers have published Application Binary Interface standards which specify that plain bit-fields should be unsigned. It is a mistake, however, to say anything about this issue in an ABI. This is because the handling of plain bit-fields distinguishes two dialects of C. Both dialects are meaningful on every type of machine. Whether a particular object file was compiled using signed bit-fields or unsigned is of no concern to other object files, even if they access the same bit-fields in the same data structures.

A given program is written in one or the other of these two dialects. The program stands a chance to work on most any machine if it is compiled with the proper dialect. It is unlikely to work at all if compiled with the wrong dialect.

Many users appreciate the GNU C compiler because it provides an environment that is uniform across machines. These users would be inconvenienced if the compiler treated plain bit-fields differently on certain machines.

Occasionally users write programs intended only for a particular machine type. On these occasions, the users would benefit if the GNU C compiler were to support by default the same dialect as the other compilers on that machine. But such applications are rare. And users writing a program to run on more than one type of machine cannot possibly benefit from this kind of compatibility.

This is why GCC does and will treat plain bit-fields in the same fashion on all types of machines (by default).

There are some arguments for making bit-fields unsigned by default on all machines. If, for example, this becomes a universal de facto standard, it would make sense for GCC to go along with it. This is something to be considered in the future.

(Of course, users strongly concerned about portability should indicate explicitly in each bit-field whether it is signed or not. In this way, they write programs which have the same meaning in both C dialects.)

- Undefining __STDC__ when '-ansi' is not used.

  Currently, GCC defines __STDC__ unconditionally. This provides good results in practice.

  Programmers normally use conditionals on __STDC__ to ask whether it is safe to use certain features of ISO C, such as function prototypes or ISO token concatenation. Since plain gcc supports all the features of ISO C, the correct answer to these questions is "yes".

  Some users try to use __STDC__ to check for the availability of certain library facilities. This is actually incorrect usage in an ISO C program, because the ISO C standard says that a conforming freestanding implementation should define __STDC__ even though it does not have the library facilities. 'gcc -ansi -pedantic' is a conforming freestanding implementation, and it is therefore required to define __STDC__, even though it does not come with an ISO C library.

Sometimes people say that defining `__STDC__` in a compiler that does not completely conform to the ISO C standard somehow violates the standard. This is illogical. The standard is a standard for compilers that claim to support ISO C, such as 'gcc -ansi'—not for other compilers such as plain gcc. Whatever the ISO C standard says is relevant to the design of plain gcc without '-ansi' only for pragmatic reasons, not as a requirement.

GCC normally defines `__STDC__` to be 1, and in addition defines `__STRICT_ANSI__` if you specify the '-ansi' option, or a '-std' option for strict conformance to some version of ISO C. On some hosts, system include files use a different convention, where `__STDC__` is normally 0, but is 1 if the user specifies strict conformance to the C Standard. GCC follows the host convention when processing system include files, but when processing user files it follows the usual GNU C convention.

- Undefining `__STDC__` in C++.

  Programs written to compile with C++-to-C translators get the value of `__STDC__` that goes with the C compiler that is subsequently used. These programs must test `__STDC__` to determine what kind of C preprocessor that compiler uses: whether they should concatenate tokens in the ISO C fashion or in the traditional fashion.

  These programs work properly with GNU C++ if `__STDC__` is defined. They would not work otherwise.

  In addition, many header files are written to provide prototypes in ISO C but not in traditional C. Many of these header files can work without change in C++ provided `__STDC__` is defined. If `__STDC__` is not defined, they will all fail, and will all need to be changed to test explicitly for C++ as well.

- Deleting "empty" loops.

  Historically, GCC has not deleted "empty" loops under the assumption that the most likely reason you would put one in a program is to have a delay, so deleting them will not make real programs run any faster.

  However, the rationale here is that optimization of a nonempty loop cannot produce an empty one. This held for carefully written C compiled with less powerful optimizers but is not always the case for carefully written C++ or with more powerful optimizers. Thus GCC will remove operations from loops whenever it can determine those operations are not externally visible (apart from the time taken to execute them, of course). In case the loop can be proved to be finite, GCC will also remove the loop itself.

  Be aware of this when performing timing tests, for instance the following loop can be completely removed, provided `some_expression` can provably not change any global state.

  ```
  {
      int sum = 0;
      int ix;

      for (ix = 0; ix != 10000; ix++)
          sum += some_expression;
  }
  ```

  Even though `sum` is accumulated in the loop, no use is made of that summation, so the accumulation can be removed.

- Making side effects happen in the same order as in some other compiler.

It is never safe to depend on the order of evaluation of side effects. For example, a function call like this may very well behave differently from one compiler to another:

```
void func (int, int);

int i = 2;
func (i++, i++);
```

There is no guarantee (in either the C or the C++ standard language definitions) that the increments will be evaluated in any particular order. Either increment might happen first. func might get the arguments '2, 3', or it might get '3, 2', or even '2, 2'.

- Making certain warnings into errors by default.

  Some ISO C testsuites report failure when the compiler does not produce an error message for a certain program.

  ISO C requires a "diagnostic" message for certain kinds of invalid programs, but a warning is defined by GCC to count as a diagnostic. If GCC produces a warning but not an error, that is correct ISO C support. If testsuites call this "failure", they should be run with the GCC option '-pedantic-errors', which will turn these warnings into errors.

12.9 Warning Messages and Error Messages

The GNU compiler can produce two kinds of diagnostics: errors and warnings. Each kind has a different purpose:

Errors report problems that make it impossible to compile your program. GCC reports errors with the source file name and line number where the problem is apparent.

Warnings report other unusual conditions in your code that *may* indicate a problem, although compilation can (and does) proceed. Warning messages also report the source file name and line number, but include the text 'warning:' to distinguish them from error messages.

Warnings may indicate danger points where you should check to make sure that your program really does what you intend; or the use of obsolete features; or the use of nonstandard features of GNU C or C++. Many warnings are issued only if you ask for them, with one of the '-W' options (for instance, '-Wall' requests a variety of useful warnings).

GCC always tries to compile your program if possible; it never gratuitously rejects a program whose meaning is clear merely because (for instance) it fails to conform to a standard. In some cases, however, the C and C++ standards specify that certain extensions are forbidden, and a diagnostic *must* be issued by a conforming compiler. The '-pedantic' option tells GCC to issue warnings in such cases; '-pedantic-errors' says to make them errors instead. This does not mean that *all* non-ISO constructs get warnings or errors.

See Section 3.8 [Options to Request or Suppress Warnings], page 59, for more detail on these and related command-line options.

13 Reporting Bugs

Your bug reports play an essential role in making GCC reliable.

When you encounter a problem, the first thing to do is to see if it is already known. See Chapter 12 [Trouble], page 775. If it isn't known, then you should report the problem.

13.1 Have You Found a Bug?

If you are not sure whether you have found a bug, here are some guidelines:

- If the compiler gets a fatal signal, for any input whatever, that is a compiler bug. Reliable compilers never crash.

- If the compiler produces invalid assembly code, for any input whatever (except an `asm` statement), that is a compiler bug, unless the compiler reports errors (not just warnings) which would ordinarily prevent the assembler from being run.

- If the compiler produces valid assembly code that does not correctly execute the input source code, that is a compiler bug.

  However, you must double-check to make sure, because you may have a program whose behavior is undefined, which happened by chance to give the desired results with another C or C++ compiler.

  For example, in many nonoptimizing compilers, you can write 'x;' at the end of a function instead of 'return x;', with the same results. But the value of the function is undefined if `return` is omitted; it is not a bug when GCC produces different results.

  Problems often result from expressions with two increment operators, as in f (*p++, *p++). Your previous compiler might have interpreted that expression the way you intended; GCC might interpret it another way. Neither compiler is wrong. The bug is in your code.

  After you have localized the error to a single source line, it should be easy to check for these things. If your program is correct and well defined, you have found a compiler bug.

- If the compiler produces an error message for valid input, that is a compiler bug.

- If the compiler does not produce an error message for invalid input, that is a compiler bug. However, you should note that your idea of "invalid input" might be someone else's idea of "an extension" or "support for traditional practice".

- If you are an experienced user of one of the languages GCC supports, your suggestions for improvement of GCC are welcome in any case.

13.2 How and Where to Report Bugs

Bugs should be reported to the bug database at `http://gcc.gnu.org/bugs/`.

14 How To Get Help with GCC

If you need help installing, using or changing GCC, there are two ways to find it:

- Send a message to a suitable network mailing list. First try `gcc-help@gcc.gnu.org` (for help installing or using GCC), and if that brings no response, try `gcc@gcc.gnu.org`. For help changing GCC, ask `gcc@gcc.gnu.org`. If you think you have found a bug in GCC, please report it following the instructions at see Section 13.2 [Bug Reporting], page 791.

- Look in the service directory for someone who might help you for a fee. The service directory is found at `http://www.fsf.org/resources/service`.

For further information, see `http://gcc.gnu.org/faq.html#support`.

15 Contributing to GCC Development

If you would like to help pretest GCC releases to assure they work well, current development sources are available by SVN (see `http://gcc.gnu.org/svn.html`). Source and binary snapshots are also available for FTP; see `http://gcc.gnu.org/snapshots.html`.

If you would like to work on improvements to GCC, please read the advice at these URLs:

```
http://gcc.gnu.org/contribute.html
http://gcc.gnu.org/contributewhy.html
```

for information on how to make useful contributions and avoid duplication of effort. Suggested projects are listed at `http://gcc.gnu.org/projects/`.

Funding Free Software

If you want to have more free software a few years from now, it makes sense for you to help encourage people to contribute funds for its development. The most effective approach known is to encourage commercial redistributors to donate.

Users of free software systems can boost the pace of development by encouraging for-a-fee distributors to donate part of their selling price to free software developers—the Free Software Foundation, and others.

The way to convince distributors to do this is to demand it and expect it from them. So when you compare distributors, judge them partly by how much they give to free software development. Show distributors they must compete to be the one who gives the most.

To make this approach work, you must insist on numbers that you can compare, such as, "We will donate ten dollars to the Frobnitz project for each disk sold." Don't be satisfied with a vague promise, such as "A portion of the profits are donated," since it doesn't give a basis for comparison.

Even a precise fraction "of the profits from this disk" is not very meaningful, since creative accounting and unrelated business decisions can greatly alter what fraction of the sales price counts as profit. If the price you pay is $50, ten percent of the profit is probably less than a dollar; it might be a few cents, or nothing at all.

Some redistributors do development work themselves. This is useful too; but to keep everyone honest, you need to inquire how much they do, and what kind. Some kinds of development make much more long-term difference than others. For example, maintaining a separate version of a program contributes very little; maintaining the standard version of a program for the whole community contributes much. Easy new ports contribute little, since someone else would surely do them; difficult ports such as adding a new CPU to the GNU Compiler Collection contribute more; major new features or packages contribute the most.

By establishing the idea that supporting further development is "the proper thing to do" when distributing free software for a fee, we can assure a steady flow of resources into making more free software.

The GNU Project and GNU/Linux

The GNU Project was launched in 1984 to develop a complete Unix-like operating system which is free software: the GNU system. (GNU is a recursive acronym for "GNU's Not Unix"; it is pronounced "guh-NEW".) Variants of the GNU operating system, which use the kernel Linux, are now widely used; though these systems are often referred to as "Linux", they are more accurately called GNU/Linux systems.

For more information, see:

```
http://www.gnu.org/
http://www.gnu.org/gnu/linux-and-gnu.html
```

GNU General Public License

Version 3, 29 June 2007

Copyright © 2007 Free Software Foundation, Inc. http://fsf.org/

Preamble

The GNU General Public License is a free, copyleft license for software and other kinds of works.

The licenses for most software and other practical works are designed to take away your freedom to share and change the works. By contrast, the GNU General Public License is intended to guarantee your freedom to share and change all versions of a program–to make sure it remains free software for all its users. We, the Free Software Foundation, use the GNU General Public License for most of our software; it applies also to any other work released this way by its authors. You can apply it to your programs, too.

When we speak of free software, we are referring to freedom, not price. Our General Public Licenses are designed to make sure that you have the freedom to distribute copies of free software (and charge for them if you wish), that you receive source code or can get it if you want it, that you can change the software or use pieces of it in new free programs, and that you know you can do these things.

To protect your rights, we need to prevent others from denying you these rights or asking you to surrender the rights. Therefore, you have certain responsibilities if you distribute copies of the software, or if you modify it: responsibilities to respect the freedom of others.

For example, if you distribute copies of such a program, whether gratis or for a fee, you must pass on to the recipients the same freedoms that you received. You must make sure that they, too, receive or can get the source code. And you must show them these terms so they know their rights.

Developers that use the GNU GPL protect your rights with two steps: (1) assert copyright on the software, and (2) offer you this License giving you legal permission to copy, distribute and/or modify it.

For the developers' and authors' protection, the GPL clearly explains that there is no warranty for this free software. For both users' and authors' sake, the GPL requires that modified versions be marked as changed, so that their problems will not be attributed erroneously to authors of previous versions.

Some devices are designed to deny users access to install or run modified versions of the software inside them, although the manufacturer can do so. This is fundamentally incompatible with the aim of protecting users' freedom to change the software. The systematic pattern of such abuse occurs in the area of products for individuals to use, which is precisely where it is most unacceptable. Therefore, we have designed this version of the GPL to prohibit the practice for those products. If such problems arise substantially in other domains, we stand ready to extend this provision to those domains in future versions of the GPL, as needed to protect the freedom of users.

Finally, every program is threatened constantly by software patents. States should not allow patents to restrict development and use of software on general-purpose computers, but in those that do, we wish to avoid the special danger that patents applied to a free program could make it effectively proprietary. To prevent this, the GPL assures that patents cannot be used to render the program non-free.

The precise terms and conditions for copying, distribution and modification follow.

TERMS AND CONDITIONS

0. Definitions.

   "This License" refers to version 3 of the GNU General Public License.

   "Copyright" also means copyright-like laws that apply to other kinds of works, such as semiconductor masks.

   "The Program" refers to any copyrightable work licensed under this License. Each licensee is addressed as "you". "Licensees" and "recipients" may be individuals or organizations.

   To "modify" a work means to copy from or adapt all or part of the work in a fashion requiring copyright permission, other than the making of an exact copy. The resulting work is called a "modified version" of the earlier work or a work "based on" the earlier work.

   A "covered work" means either the unmodified Program or a work based on the Program.

   To "propagate" a work means to do anything with it that, without permission, would make you directly or secondarily liable for infringement under applicable copyright law, except executing it on a computer or modifying a private copy. Propagation includes copying, distribution (with or without modification), making available to the public, and in some countries other activities as well.

   To "convey" a work means any kind of propagation that enables other parties to make or receive copies. Mere interaction with a user through a computer network, with no transfer of a copy, is not conveying.

   An interactive user interface displays "Appropriate Legal Notices" to the extent that it includes a convenient and prominently visible feature that (1) displays an appropriate copyright notice, and (2) tells the user that there is no warranty for the work (except to the extent that warranties are provided), that licensees may convey the work under this License, and how to view a copy of this License. If the interface presents a list of user commands or options, such as a menu, a prominent item in the list meets this criterion.

1. Source Code.

   The "source code" for a work means the preferred form of the work for making modifications to it. "Object code" means any non-source form of a work.

   A "Standard Interface" means an interface that either is an official standard defined by a recognized standards body, or, in the case of interfaces specified for a particular programming language, one that is widely used among developers working in that language.

The "System Libraries" of an executable work include anything, other than the work as a whole, that (a) is included in the normal form of packaging a Major Component, but which is not part of that Major Component, and (b) serves only to enable use of the work with that Major Component, or to implement a Standard Interface for which an implementation is available to the public in source code form. A "Major Component", in this context, means a major essential component (kernel, window system, and so on) of the specific operating system (if any) on which the executable work runs, or a compiler used to produce the work, or an object code interpreter used to run it.

The "Corresponding Source" for a work in object code form means all the source code needed to generate, install, and (for an executable work) run the object code and to modify the work, including scripts to control those activities. However, it does not include the work's System Libraries, or general-purpose tools or generally available free programs which are used unmodified in performing those activities but which are not part of the work. For example, Corresponding Source includes interface definition files associated with source files for the work, and the source code for shared libraries and dynamically linked subprograms that the work is specifically designed to require, such as by intimate data communication or control flow between those subprograms and other parts of the work.

The Corresponding Source need not include anything that users can regenerate automatically from other parts of the Corresponding Source.

The Corresponding Source for a work in source code form is that same work.

2. Basic Permissions.

All rights granted under this License are granted for the term of copyright on the Program, and are irrevocable provided the stated conditions are met. This License explicitly affirms your unlimited permission to run the unmodified Program. The output from running a covered work is covered by this License only if the output, given its content, constitutes a covered work. This License acknowledges your rights of fair use or other equivalent, as provided by copyright law.

You may make, run and propagate covered works that you do not convey, without conditions so long as your license otherwise remains in force. You may convey covered works to others for the sole purpose of having them make modifications exclusively for you, or provide you with facilities for running those works, provided that you comply with the terms of this License in conveying all material for which you do not control copyright. Those thus making or running the covered works for you must do so exclusively on your behalf, under your direction and control, on terms that prohibit them from making any copies of your copyrighted material outside their relationship with you.

Conveying under any other circumstances is permitted solely under the conditions stated below. Sublicensing is not allowed; section 10 makes it unnecessary.

3. Protecting Users' Legal Rights From Anti-Circumvention Law.

No covered work shall be deemed part of an effective technological measure under any applicable law fulfilling obligations under article 11 of the WIPO copyright treaty adopted on 20 December 1996, or similar laws prohibiting or restricting circumvention of such measures.

When you convey a covered work, you waive any legal power to forbid circumvention of technological measures to the extent such circumvention is effected by exercising rights under this License with respect to the covered work, and you disclaim any intention to limit operation or modification of the work as a means of enforcing, against the work's users, your or third parties' legal rights to forbid circumvention of technological measures.

4. Conveying Verbatim Copies.

   You may convey verbatim copies of the Program's source code as you receive it, in any medium, provided that you conspicuously and appropriately publish on each copy an appropriate copyright notice; keep intact all notices stating that this License and any non-permissive terms added in accord with section 7 apply to the code; keep intact all notices of the absence of any warranty; and give all recipients a copy of this License along with the Program.

   You may charge any price or no price for each copy that you convey, and you may offer support or warranty protection for a fee.

5. Conveying Modified Source Versions.

   You may convey a work based on the Program, or the modifications to produce it from the Program, in the form of source code under the terms of section 4, provided that you also meet all of these conditions:

   a. The work must carry prominent notices stating that you modified it, and giving a relevant date.

   b. The work must carry prominent notices stating that it is released under this License and any conditions added under section 7. This requirement modifies the requirement in section 4 to "keep intact all notices".

   c. You must license the entire work, as a whole, under this License to anyone who comes into possession of a copy. This License will therefore apply, along with any applicable section 7 additional terms, to the whole of the work, and all its parts, regardless of how they are packaged. This License gives no permission to license the work in any other way, but it does not invalidate such permission if you have separately received it.

   d. If the work has interactive user interfaces, each must display Appropriate Legal Notices; however, if the Program has interactive interfaces that do not display Appropriate Legal Notices, your work need not make them do so.

   A compilation of a covered work with other separate and independent works, which are not by their nature extensions of the covered work, and which are not combined with it such as to form a larger program, in or on a volume of a storage or distribution medium, is called an "aggregate" if the compilation and its resulting copyright are not used to limit the access or legal rights of the compilation's users beyond what the individual works permit. Inclusion of a covered work in an aggregate does not cause this License to apply to the other parts of the aggregate.

6. Conveying Non-Source Forms.

   You may convey a covered work in object code form under the terms of sections 4 and 5, provided that you also convey the machine-readable Corresponding Source under the terms of this License, in one of these ways:

a. Convey the object code in, or embodied in, a physical product (including a physical distribution medium), accompanied by the Corresponding Source fixed on a durable physical medium customarily used for software interchange.

b. Convey the object code in, or embodied in, a physical product (including a physical distribution medium), accompanied by a written offer, valid for at least three years and valid for as long as you offer spare parts or customer support for that product model, to give anyone who possesses the object code either (1) a copy of the Corresponding Source for all the software in the product that is covered by this License, on a durable physical medium customarily used for software interchange, for a price no more than your reasonable cost of physically performing this conveying of source, or (2) access to copy the Corresponding Source from a network server at no charge.

c. Convey individual copies of the object code with a copy of the written offer to provide the Corresponding Source. This alternative is allowed only occasionally and noncommercially, and only if you received the object code with such an offer, in accord with subsection 6b.

d. Convey the object code by offering access from a designated place (gratis or for a charge), and offer equivalent access to the Corresponding Source in the same way through the same place at no further charge. You need not require recipients to copy the Corresponding Source along with the object code. If the place to copy the object code is a network server, the Corresponding Source may be on a different server (operated by you or a third party) that supports equivalent copying facilities, provided you maintain clear directions next to the object code saying where to find the Corresponding Source. Regardless of what server hosts the Corresponding Source, you remain obligated to ensure that it is available for as long as needed to satisfy these requirements.

e. Convey the object code using peer-to-peer transmission, provided you inform other peers where the object code and Corresponding Source of the work are being offered to the general public at no charge under subsection 6d.

A separable portion of the object code, whose source code is excluded from the Corresponding Source as a System Library, need not be included in conveying the object code work.

A "User Product" is either (1) a "consumer product", which means any tangible personal property which is normally used for personal, family, or household purposes, or (2) anything designed or sold for incorporation into a dwelling. In determining whether a product is a consumer product, doubtful cases shall be resolved in favor of coverage. For a particular product received by a particular user, "normally used" refers to a typical or common use of that class of product, regardless of the status of the particular user or of the way in which the particular user actually uses, or expects or is expected to use, the product. A product is a consumer product regardless of whether the product has substantial commercial, industrial or non-consumer uses, unless such uses represent the only significant mode of use of the product.

"Installation Information" for a User Product means any methods, procedures, authorization keys, or other information required to install and execute modified versions of a covered work in that User Product from a modified version of its Corresponding Source.

The information must suffice to ensure that the continued functioning of the modified object code is in no case prevented or interfered with solely because modification has been made.

If you convey an object code work under this section in, or with, or specifically for use in, a User Product, and the conveying occurs as part of a transaction in which the right of possession and use of the User Product is transferred to the recipient in perpetuity or for a fixed term (regardless of how the transaction is characterized), the Corresponding Source conveyed under this section must be accompanied by the Installation Information. But this requirement does not apply if neither you nor any third party retains the ability to install modified object code on the User Product (for example, the work has been installed in ROM).

The requirement to provide Installation Information does not include a requirement to continue to provide support service, warranty, or updates for a work that has been modified or installed by the recipient, or for the User Product in which it has been modified or installed. Access to a network may be denied when the modification itself materially and adversely affects the operation of the network or violates the rules and protocols for communication across the network.

Corresponding Source conveyed, and Installation Information provided, in accord with this section must be in a format that is publicly documented (and with an implementation available to the public in source code form), and must require no special password or key for unpacking, reading or copying.

7. Additional Terms.

"Additional permissions" are terms that supplement the terms of this License by making exceptions from one or more of its conditions. Additional permissions that are applicable to the entire Program shall be treated as though they were included in this License, to the extent that they are valid under applicable law. If additional permissions apply only to part of the Program, that part may be used separately under those permissions, but the entire Program remains governed by this License without regard to the additional permissions.

When you convey a copy of a covered work, you may at your option remove any additional permissions from that copy, or from any part of it. (Additional permissions may be written to require their own removal in certain cases when you modify the work.) You may place additional permissions on material, added by you to a covered work, for which you have or can give appropriate copyright permission.

Notwithstanding any other provision of this License, for material you add to a covered work, you may (if authorized by the copyright holders of that material) supplement the terms of this License with terms:

a. Disclaiming warranty or limiting liability differently from the terms of sections 15 and 16 of this License; or

b. Requiring preservation of specified reasonable legal notices or author attributions in that material or in the Appropriate Legal Notices displayed by works containing it; or

c. Prohibiting misrepresentation of the origin of that material, or requiring that modified versions of such material be marked in reasonable ways as different from the original version; or

d. Limiting the use for publicity purposes of names of licensors or authors of the material; or

e. Declining to grant rights under trademark law for use of some trade names, trademarks, or service marks; or

f. Requiring indemnification of licensors and authors of that material by anyone who conveys the material (or modified versions of it) with contractual assumptions of liability to the recipient, for any liability that these contractual assumptions directly impose on those licensors and authors.

All other non-permissive additional terms are considered "further restrictions" within the meaning of section 10. If the Program as you received it, or any part of it, contains a notice stating that it is governed by this License along with a term that is a further restriction, you may remove that term. If a license document contains a further restriction but permits relicensing or conveying under this License, you may add to a covered work material governed by the terms of that license document, provided that the further restriction does not survive such relicensing or conveying.

If you add terms to a covered work in accord with this section, you must place, in the relevant source files, a statement of the additional terms that apply to those files, or a notice indicating where to find the applicable terms.

Additional terms, permissive or non-permissive, may be stated in the form of a separately written license, or stated as exceptions; the above requirements apply either way.

8. Termination.

You may not propagate or modify a covered work except as expressly provided under this License. Any attempt otherwise to propagate or modify it is void, and will automatically terminate your rights under this License (including any patent licenses granted under the third paragraph of section 11).

However, if you cease all violation of this License, then your license from a particular copyright holder is reinstated (a) provisionally, unless and until the copyright holder explicitly and finally terminates your license, and (b) permanently, if the copyright holder fails to notify you of the violation by some reasonable means prior to 60 days after the cessation.

Moreover, your license from a particular copyright holder is reinstated permanently if the copyright holder notifies you of the violation by some reasonable means, this is the first time you have received notice of violation of this License (for any work) from that copyright holder, and you cure the violation prior to 30 days after your receipt of the notice.

Termination of your rights under this section does not terminate the licenses of parties who have received copies or rights from you under this License. If your rights have been terminated and not permanently reinstated, you do not qualify to receive new licenses for the same material under section 10.

9. Acceptance Not Required for Having Copies.

You are not required to accept this License in order to receive or run a copy of the Program. Ancillary propagation of a covered work occurring solely as a consequence of using peer-to-peer transmission to receive a copy likewise does not require acceptance.

However, nothing other than this License grants you permission to propagate or modify any covered work. These actions infringe copyright if you do not accept this License. Therefore, by modifying or propagating a covered work, you indicate your acceptance of this License to do so.

10. Automatic Licensing of Downstream Recipients.

Each time you convey a covered work, the recipient automatically receives a license from the original licensors, to run, modify and propagate that work, subject to this License. You are not responsible for enforcing compliance by third parties with this License.

An "entity transaction" is a transaction transferring control of an organization, or substantially all assets of one, or subdividing an organization, or merging organizations. If propagation of a covered work results from an entity transaction, each party to that transaction who receives a copy of the work also receives whatever licenses to the work the party's predecessor in interest had or could give under the previous paragraph, plus a right to possession of the Corresponding Source of the work from the predecessor in interest, if the predecessor has it or can get it with reasonable efforts.

You may not impose any further restrictions on the exercise of the rights granted or affirmed under this License. For example, you may not impose a license fee, royalty, or other charge for exercise of rights granted under this License, and you may not initiate litigation (including a cross-claim or counterclaim in a lawsuit) alleging that any patent claim is infringed by making, using, selling, offering for sale, or importing the Program or any portion of it.

11. Patents.

A "contributor" is a copyright holder who authorizes use under this License of the Program or a work on which the Program is based. The work thus licensed is called the contributor's "contributor version".

A contributor's "essential patent claims" are all patent claims owned or controlled by the contributor, whether already acquired or hereafter acquired, that would be infringed by some manner, permitted by this License, of making, using, or selling its contributor version, but do not include claims that would be infringed only as a consequence of further modification of the contributor version. For purposes of this definition, "control" includes the right to grant patent sublicenses in a manner consistent with the requirements of this License.

Each contributor grants you a non-exclusive, worldwide, royalty-free patent license under the contributor's essential patent claims, to make, use, sell, offer for sale, import and otherwise run, modify and propagate the contents of its contributor version.

In the following three paragraphs, a "patent license" is any express agreement or commitment, however denominated, not to enforce a patent (such as an express permission to practice a patent or covenant not to sue for patent infringement). To "grant" such a patent license to a party means to make such an agreement or commitment not to enforce a patent against the party.

If you convey a covered work, knowingly relying on a patent license, and the Corresponding Source of the work is not available for anyone to copy, free of charge and under the terms of this License, through a publicly available network server or other readily accessible means, then you must either (1) cause the Corresponding Source to be so available, or (2) arrange to deprive yourself of the benefit of the patent license for this particular work, or (3) arrange, in a manner consistent with the requirements of this License, to extend the patent license to downstream recipients. "Knowingly relying" means you have actual knowledge that, but for the patent license, your conveying the covered work in a country, or your recipient's use of the covered work in a country, would infringe one or more identifiable patents in that country that you have reason to believe are valid.

If, pursuant to or in connection with a single transaction or arrangement, you convey, or propagate by procuring conveyance of, a covered work, and grant a patent license to some of the parties receiving the covered work authorizing them to use, propagate, modify or convey a specific copy of the covered work, then the patent license you grant is automatically extended to all recipients of the covered work and works based on it.

A patent license is "discriminatory" if it does not include within the scope of its coverage, prohibits the exercise of, or is conditioned on the non-exercise of one or more of the rights that are specifically granted under this License. You may not convey a covered work if you are a party to an arrangement with a third party that is in the business of distributing software, under which you make payment to the third party based on the extent of your activity of conveying the work, and under which the third party grants, to any of the parties who would receive the covered work from you, a discriminatory patent license (a) in connection with copies of the covered work conveyed by you (or copies made from those copies), or (b) primarily for and in connection with specific products or compilations that contain the covered work, unless you entered into that arrangement, or that patent license was granted, prior to 28 March 2007.

Nothing in this License shall be construed as excluding or limiting any implied license or other defenses to infringement that may otherwise be available to you under applicable patent law.

12. No Surrender of Others' Freedom.

If conditions are imposed on you (whether by court order, agreement or otherwise) that contradict the conditions of this License, they do not excuse you from the conditions of this License. If you cannot convey a covered work so as to satisfy simultaneously your obligations under this License and any other pertinent obligations, then as a consequence you may not convey it at all. For example, if you agree to terms that obligate you to collect a royalty for further conveying from those to whom you convey the Program, the only way you could satisfy both those terms and this License would be to refrain entirely from conveying the Program.

13. Use with the GNU Affero General Public License.

Notwithstanding any other provision of this License, you have permission to link or combine any covered work with a work licensed under version 3 of the GNU Affero General Public License into a single combined work, and to convey the resulting work. The terms of this License will continue to apply to the part which is the covered work, but the special requirements of the GNU Affero General Public License, section 13, concerning interaction through a network will apply to the combination as such.

14. Revised Versions of this License.

The Free Software Foundation may publish revised and/or new versions of the GNU General Public License from time to time. Such new versions will be similar in spirit to the present version, but may differ in detail to address new problems or concerns.

Each version is given a distinguishing version number. If the Program specifies that a certain numbered version of the GNU General Public License "or any later version" applies to it, you have the option of following the terms and conditions either of that numbered version or of any later version published by the Free Software Foundation. If the Program does not specify a version number of the GNU General Public License, you may choose any version ever published by the Free Software Foundation.

If the Program specifies that a proxy can decide which future versions of the GNU General Public License can be used, that proxy's public statement of acceptance of a version permanently authorizes you to choose that version for the Program.

Later license versions may give you additional or different permissions. However, no additional obligations are imposed on any author or copyright holder as a result of your choosing to follow a later version.

15. Disclaimer of Warranty.

THERE IS NO WARRANTY FOR THE PROGRAM, TO THE EXTENT PER-MITTED BY APPLICABLE LAW. EXCEPT WHEN OTHERWISE STATED IN WRITING THE COPYRIGHT HOLDERS AND/OR OTHER PARTIES PROVIDE THE PROGRAM "AS IS" WITHOUT WARRANTY OF ANY KIND, EITHER EX-PRESSED OR IMPLIED, INCLUDING, BUT NOT LIMITED TO, THE IMPLIED WARRANTIES OF MERCHANTABILITY AND FITNESS FOR A PARTICULAR PURPOSE. THE ENTIRE RISK AS TO THE QUALITY AND PERFORMANCE OF THE PROGRAM IS WITH YOU. SHOULD THE PROGRAM PROVE DEFEC-TIVE, YOU ASSUME THE COST OF ALL NECESSARY SERVICING, REPAIR OR CORRECTION.

16. Limitation of Liability.

IN NO EVENT UNLESS REQUIRED BY APPLICABLE LAW OR AGREED TO IN WRITING WILL ANY COPYRIGHT HOLDER, OR ANY OTHER PARTY WHO MODIFIES AND/OR CONVEYS THE PROGRAM AS PERMITTED ABOVE, BE LIABLE TO YOU FOR DAMAGES, INCLUDING ANY GENERAL, SPECIAL, IN-CIDENTAL OR CONSEQUENTIAL DAMAGES ARISING OUT OF THE USE OR INABILITY TO USE THE PROGRAM (INCLUDING BUT NOT LIMITED TO LOSS OF DATA OR DATA BEING RENDERED INACCURATE OR LOSSES SUS-TAINED BY YOU OR THIRD PARTIES OR A FAILURE OF THE PROGRAM TO OPERATE WITH ANY OTHER PROGRAMS), EVEN IF SUCH HOLDER OR OTHER PARTY HAS BEEN ADVISED OF THE POSSIBILITY OF SUCH DAM-AGES.

17. Interpretation of Sections 15 and 16.

If the disclaimer of warranty and limitation of liability provided above cannot be given local legal effect according to their terms, reviewing courts shall apply local law that most closely approximates an absolute waiver of all civil liability in connection with the Program, unless a warranty or assumption of liability accompanies a copy of the Program in return for a fee.

END OF TERMS AND CONDITIONS

How to Apply These Terms to Your New Programs

If you develop a new program, and you want it to be of the greatest possible use to the public, the best way to achieve this is to make it free software which everyone can redistribute and change under these terms.

To do so, attach the following notices to the program. It is safest to attach them to the start of each source file to most effectively state the exclusion of warranty; and each file should have at least the "copyright" line and a pointer to where the full notice is found.

```
one line to give the program's name and a brief idea of what it does.
Copyright (C) year name of author

This program is free software: you can redistribute it and/or modify
it under the terms of the GNU General Public License as published by
the Free Software Foundation, either version 3 of the License, or (at
your option) any later version.

This program is distributed in the hope that it will be useful, but
WITHOUT ANY WARRANTY; without even the implied warranty of
MERCHANTABILITY or FITNESS FOR A PARTICULAR PURPOSE.  See the GNU
General Public License for more details.

You should have received a copy of the GNU General Public License
along with this program.  If not, see http://www.gnu.org/licenses/.
```

Also add information on how to contact you by electronic and paper mail.

If the program does terminal interaction, make it output a short notice like this when it starts in an interactive mode:

```
program Copyright (C) year name of author
This program comes with ABSOLUTELY NO WARRANTY; for details type 'show w'.
This is free software, and you are welcome to redistribute it
under certain conditions; type 'show c' for details.
```

The hypothetical commands 'show w' and 'show c' should show the appropriate parts of the General Public License. Of course, your program's commands might be different; for a GUI interface, you would use an "about box".

You should also get your employer (if you work as a programmer) or school, if any, to sign a "copyright disclaimer" for the program, if necessary. For more information on this, and how to apply and follow the GNU GPL, see http://www.gnu.org/licenses/.

The GNU General Public License does not permit incorporating your program into proprietary programs. If your program is a subroutine library, you may consider it more useful to permit linking proprietary applications with the library. If this is what you want to do, use the GNU Lesser General Public License instead of this License. But first, please read http://www.gnu.org/philosophy/why-not-lgpl.html.

GNU Free Documentation License

Version 1.3, 3 November 2008

Copyright © 2000, 2001, 2002, 2007, 2008 Free Software Foundation, Inc.
`http://fsf.org/`

Everyone is permitted to copy and distribute verbatim copies
of this license document, but changing it is not allowed.

0. PREAMBLE

The purpose of this License is to make a manual, textbook, or other functional and useful document *free* in the sense of freedom: to assure everyone the effective freedom to copy and redistribute it, with or without modifying it, either commercially or non-commercially. Secondarily, this License preserves for the author and publisher a way to get credit for their work, while not being considered responsible for modifications made by others.

This License is a kind of "copyleft", which means that derivative works of the document must themselves be free in the same sense. It complements the GNU General Public License, which is a copyleft license designed for free software.

We have designed this License in order to use it for manuals for free software, because free software needs free documentation: a free program should come with manuals providing the same freedoms that the software does. But this License is not limited to software manuals; it can be used for any textual work, regardless of subject matter or whether it is published as a printed book. We recommend this License principally for works whose purpose is instruction or reference.

1. APPLICABILITY AND DEFINITIONS

This License applies to any manual or other work, in any medium, that contains a notice placed by the copyright holder saying it can be distributed under the terms of this License. Such a notice grants a world-wide, royalty-free license, unlimited in duration, to use that work under the conditions stated herein. The "Document", below, refers to any such manual or work. Any member of the public is a licensee, and is addressed as "you". You accept the license if you copy, modify or distribute the work in a way requiring permission under copyright law.

A "Modified Version" of the Document means any work containing the Document or a portion of it, either copied verbatim, or with modifications and/or translated into another language.

A "Secondary Section" is a named appendix or a front-matter section of the Document that deals exclusively with the relationship of the publishers or authors of the Document to the Document's overall subject (or to related matters) and contains nothing that could fall directly within that overall subject. (Thus, if the Document is in part a textbook of mathematics, a Secondary Section may not explain any mathematics.) The relationship could be a matter of historical connection with the subject or with related matters, or of legal, commercial, philosophical, ethical or political position regarding them.

The "Invariant Sections" are certain Secondary Sections whose titles are designated, as being those of Invariant Sections, in the notice that says that the Document is released under this License. If a section does not fit the above definition of Secondary then it is not allowed to be designated as Invariant. The Document may contain zero Invariant Sections. If the Document does not identify any Invariant Sections then there are none.

The "Cover Texts" are certain short passages of text that are listed, as Front-Cover Texts or Back-Cover Texts, in the notice that says that the Document is released under this License. A Front-Cover Text may be at most 5 words, and a Back-Cover Text may be at most 25 words.

A "Transparent" copy of the Document means a machine-readable copy, represented in a format whose specification is available to the general public, that is suitable for revising the document straightforwardly with generic text editors or (for images composed of pixels) generic paint programs or (for drawings) some widely available drawing editor, and that is suitable for input to text formatters or for automatic translation to a variety of formats suitable for input to text formatters. A copy made in an otherwise Transparent file format whose markup, or absence of markup, has been arranged to thwart or discourage subsequent modification by readers is not Transparent. An image format is not Transparent if used for any substantial amount of text. A copy that is not "Transparent" is called "Opaque".

Examples of suitable formats for Transparent copies include plain ASCII without markup, Texinfo input format, LaTeX input format, SGML or XML using a publicly available DTD, and standard-conforming simple HTML, PostScript or PDF designed for human modification. Examples of transparent image formats include PNG, XCF and JPG. Opaque formats include proprietary formats that can be read and edited only by proprietary word processors, SGML or XML for which the DTD and/or processing tools are not generally available, and the machine-generated HTML, PostScript or PDF produced by some word processors for output purposes only.

The "Title Page" means, for a printed book, the title page itself, plus such following pages as are needed to hold, legibly, the material this License requires to appear in the title page. For works in formats which do not have any title page as such, "Title Page" means the text near the most prominent appearance of the work's title, preceding the beginning of the body of the text.

The "publisher" means any person or entity that distributes copies of the Document to the public.

A section "Entitled XYZ" means a named subunit of the Document whose title either is precisely XYZ or contains XYZ in parentheses following text that translates XYZ in another language. (Here XYZ stands for a specific section name mentioned below, such as "Acknowledgements", "Dedications", "Endorsements", or "History".) To "Preserve the Title" of such a section when you modify the Document means that it remains a section "Entitled XYZ" according to this definition.

The Document may include Warranty Disclaimers next to the notice which states that this License applies to the Document. These Warranty Disclaimers are considered to be included by reference in this License, but only as regards disclaiming warranties: any other implication that these Warranty Disclaimers may have is void and has no effect on the meaning of this License.

2. VERBATIM COPYING

You may copy and distribute the Document in any medium, either commercially or noncommercially, provided that this License, the copyright notices, and the license notice saying this License applies to the Document are reproduced in all copies, and that you add no other conditions whatsoever to those of this License. You may not use technical measures to obstruct or control the reading or further copying of the copies you make or distribute. However, you may accept compensation in exchange for copies. If you distribute a large enough number of copies you must also follow the conditions in section 3.

You may also lend copies, under the same conditions stated above, and you may publicly display copies.

3. COPYING IN QUANTITY

If you publish printed copies (or copies in media that commonly have printed covers) of the Document, numbering more than 100, and the Document's license notice requires Cover Texts, you must enclose the copies in covers that carry, clearly and legibly, all these Cover Texts: Front-Cover Texts on the front cover, and Back-Cover Texts on the back cover. Both covers must also clearly and legibly identify you as the publisher of these copies. The front cover must present the full title with all words of the title equally prominent and visible. You may add other material on the covers in addition. Copying with changes limited to the covers, as long as they preserve the title of the Document and satisfy these conditions, can be treated as verbatim copying in other respects.

If the required texts for either cover are too voluminous to fit legibly, you should put the first ones listed (as many as fit reasonably) on the actual cover, and continue the rest onto adjacent pages.

If you publish or distribute Opaque copies of the Document numbering more than 100, you must either include a machine-readable Transparent copy along with each Opaque copy, or state in or with each Opaque copy a computer-network location from which the general network-using public has access to download using public-standard network protocols a complete Transparent copy of the Document, free of added material. If you use the latter option, you must take reasonably prudent steps, when you begin distribution of Opaque copies in quantity, to ensure that this Transparent copy will remain thus accessible at the stated location until at least one year after the last time you distribute an Opaque copy (directly or through your agents or retailers) of that edition to the public.

It is requested, but not required, that you contact the authors of the Document well before redistributing any large number of copies, to give them a chance to provide you with an updated version of the Document.

4. MODIFICATIONS

You may copy and distribute a Modified Version of the Document under the conditions of sections 2 and 3 above, provided that you release the Modified Version under precisely this License, with the Modified Version filling the role of the Document, thus licensing distribution and modification of the Modified Version to whoever possesses a copy of it. In addition, you must do these things in the Modified Version:

A. Use in the Title Page (and on the covers, if any) a title distinct from that of the Document, and from those of previous versions (which should, if there were any, be listed in the History section of the Document). You may use the same title as a previous version if the original publisher of that version gives permission.

B. List on the Title Page, as authors, one or more persons or entities responsible for authorship of the modifications in the Modified Version, together with at least five of the principal authors of the Document (all of its principal authors, if it has fewer than five), unless they release you from this requirement.

C. State on the Title page the name of the publisher of the Modified Version, as the publisher.

D. Preserve all the copyright notices of the Document.

E. Add an appropriate copyright notice for your modifications adjacent to the other copyright notices.

F. Include, immediately after the copyright notices, a license notice giving the public permission to use the Modified Version under the terms of this License, in the form shown in the Addendum below.

G. Preserve in that license notice the full lists of Invariant Sections and required Cover Texts given in the Document's license notice.

H. Include an unaltered copy of this License.

I. Preserve the section Entitled "History", Preserve its Title, and add to it an item stating at least the title, year, new authors, and publisher of the Modified Version as given on the Title Page. If there is no section Entitled "History" in the Document, create one stating the title, year, authors, and publisher of the Document as given on its Title Page, then add an item describing the Modified Version as stated in the previous sentence.

J. Preserve the network location, if any, given in the Document for public access to a Transparent copy of the Document, and likewise the network locations given in the Document for previous versions it was based on. These may be placed in the "History" section. You may omit a network location for a work that was published at least four years before the Document itself, or if the original publisher of the version it refers to gives permission.

K. For any section Entitled "Acknowledgements" or "Dedications", Preserve the Title of the section, and preserve in the section all the substance and tone of each of the contributor acknowledgements and/or dedications given therein.

L. Preserve all the Invariant Sections of the Document, unaltered in their text and in their titles. Section numbers or the equivalent are not considered part of the section titles.

M. Delete any section Entitled "Endorsements". Such a section may not be included in the Modified Version.

N. Do not retitle any existing section to be Entitled "Endorsements" or to conflict in title with any Invariant Section.

O. Preserve any Warranty Disclaimers.

If the Modified Version includes new front-matter sections or appendices that qualify as Secondary Sections and contain no material copied from the Document, you may at your option designate some or all of these sections as invariant. To do this, add their titles to the list of Invariant Sections in the Modified Version's license notice. These titles must be distinct from any other section titles.

You may add a section Entitled "Endorsements", provided it contains nothing but endorsements of your Modified Version by various parties—for example, statements of peer review or that the text has been approved by an organization as the authoritative definition of a standard.

You may add a passage of up to five words as a Front-Cover Text, and a passage of up to 25 words as a Back-Cover Text, to the end of the list of Cover Texts in the Modified Version. Only one passage of Front-Cover Text and one of Back-Cover Text may be added by (or through arrangements made by) any one entity. If the Document already includes a cover text for the same cover, previously added by you or by arrangement made by the same entity you are acting on behalf of, you may not add another; but you may replace the old one, on explicit permission from the previous publisher that added the old one.

The author(s) and publisher(s) of the Document do not by this License give permission to use their names for publicity for or to assert or imply endorsement of any Modified Version.

5. COMBINING DOCUMENTS

You may combine the Document with other documents released under this License, under the terms defined in section 4 above for modified versions, provided that you include in the combination all of the Invariant Sections of all of the original documents, unmodified, and list them all as Invariant Sections of your combined work in its license notice, and that you preserve all their Warranty Disclaimers.

The combined work need only contain one copy of this License, and multiple identical Invariant Sections may be replaced with a single copy. If there are multiple Invariant Sections with the same name but different contents, make the title of each such section unique by adding at the end of it, in parentheses, the name of the original author or publisher of that section if known, or else a unique number. Make the same adjustment to the section titles in the list of Invariant Sections in the license notice of the combined work.

In the combination, you must combine any sections Entitled "History" in the various original documents, forming one section Entitled "History"; likewise combine any sections Entitled "Acknowledgements", and any sections Entitled "Dedications". You must delete all sections Entitled "Endorsements."

6. COLLECTIONS OF DOCUMENTS

You may make a collection consisting of the Document and other documents released under this License, and replace the individual copies of this License in the various documents with a single copy that is included in the collection, provided that you follow the rules of this License for verbatim copying of each of the documents in all other respects.

You may extract a single document from such a collection, and distribute it individually under this License, provided you insert a copy of this License into the extracted document, and follow this License in all other respects regarding verbatim copying of that document.

7. AGGREGATION WITH INDEPENDENT WORKS

A compilation of the Document or its derivatives with other separate and independent documents or works, in or on a volume of a storage or distribution medium, is called an "aggregate" if the copyright resulting from the compilation is not used to limit the legal rights of the compilation's users beyond what the individual works permit. When the Document is included in an aggregate, this License does not apply to the other works in the aggregate which are not themselves derivative works of the Document.

If the Cover Text requirement of section 3 is applicable to these copies of the Document, then if the Document is less than one half of the entire aggregate, the Document's Cover Texts may be placed on covers that bracket the Document within the aggregate, or the electronic equivalent of covers if the Document is in electronic form. Otherwise they must appear on printed covers that bracket the whole aggregate.

8. TRANSLATION

Translation is considered a kind of modification, so you may distribute translations of the Document under the terms of section 4. Replacing Invariant Sections with translations requires special permission from their copyright holders, but you may include translations of some or all Invariant Sections in addition to the original versions of these Invariant Sections. You may include a translation of this License, and all the license notices in the Document, and any Warranty Disclaimers, provided that you also include the original English version of this License and the original versions of those notices and disclaimers. In case of a disagreement between the translation and the original version of this License or a notice or disclaimer, the original version will prevail.

If a section in the Document is Entitled "Acknowledgements", "Dedications", or "History", the requirement (section 4) to Preserve its Title (section 1) will typically require changing the actual title.

9. TERMINATION

You may not copy, modify, sublicense, or distribute the Document except as expressly provided under this License. Any attempt otherwise to copy, modify, sublicense, or distribute it is void, and will automatically terminate your rights under this License.

However, if you cease all violation of this License, then your license from a particular copyright holder is reinstated (a) provisionally, unless and until the copyright holder explicitly and finally terminates your license, and (b) permanently, if the copyright holder fails to notify you of the violation by some reasonable means prior to 60 days after the cessation.

Moreover, your license from a particular copyright holder is reinstated permanently if the copyright holder notifies you of the violation by some reasonable means, this is the first time you have received notice of violation of this License (for any work) from that copyright holder, and you cure the violation prior to 30 days after your receipt of the notice.

Termination of your rights under this section does not terminate the licenses of parties who have received copies or rights from you under this License. If your rights have been terminated and not permanently reinstated, receipt of a copy of some or all of the same material does not give you any rights to use it.

10. FUTURE REVISIONS OF THIS LICENSE

The Free Software Foundation may publish new, revised versions of the GNU Free Documentation License from time to time. Such new versions will be similar in spirit to the present version, but may differ in detail to address new problems or concerns. See http://www.gnu.org/copyleft/.

Each version of the License is given a distinguishing version number. If the Document specifies that a particular numbered version of this License "or any later version" applies to it, you have the option of following the terms and conditions either of that specified version or of any later version that has been published (not as a draft) by the Free Software Foundation. If the Document does not specify a version number of this License, you may choose any version ever published (not as a draft) by the Free Software Foundation. If the Document specifies that a proxy can decide which future versions of this License can be used, that proxy's public statement of acceptance of a version permanently authorizes you to choose that version for the Document.

11. RELICENSING

"Massive Multiauthor Collaboration Site" (or "MMC Site") means any World Wide Web server that publishes copyrightable works and also provides prominent facilities for anybody to edit those works. A public wiki that anybody can edit is an example of such a server. A "Massive Multiauthor Collaboration" (or "MMC") contained in the site means any set of copyrightable works thus published on the MMC site.

"CC-BY-SA" means the Creative Commons Attribution-Share Alike 3.0 license published by Creative Commons Corporation, a not-for-profit corporation with a principal place of business in San Francisco, California, as well as future copyleft versions of that license published by that same organization.

"Incorporate" means to publish or republish a Document, in whole or in part, as part of another Document.

An MMC is "eligible for relicensing" if it is licensed under this License, and if all works that were first published under this License somewhere other than this MMC, and subsequently incorporated in whole or in part into the MMC, (1) had no cover texts or invariant sections, and (2) were thus incorporated prior to November 1, 2008.

The operator of an MMC Site may republish an MMC contained in the site under CC-BY-SA on the same site at any time before August 1, 2009, provided the MMC is eligible for relicensing.

ADDENDUM: How to use this License for your documents

To use this License in a document you have written, include a copy of the License in the document and put the following copyright and license notices just after the title page:

```
Copyright (C)  year  your name.
Permission is granted to copy, distribute and/or modify this document
under the terms of the GNU Free Documentation License, Version 1.3
or any later version published by the Free Software Foundation;
with no Invariant Sections, no Front-Cover Texts, and no Back-Cover
Texts.  A copy of the license is included in the section entitled ''GNU
Free Documentation License''.
```

If you have Invariant Sections, Front-Cover Texts and Back-Cover Texts, replace the "with...Texts." line with this:

```
with the Invariant Sections being list their titles, with
the Front-Cover Texts being list, and with the Back-Cover Texts
being list.
```

If you have Invariant Sections without Cover Texts, or some other combination of the three, merge those two alternatives to suit the situation.

If your document contains nontrivial examples of program code, we recommend releasing these examples in parallel under your choice of free software license, such as the GNU General Public License, to permit their use in free software.

Contributors to GCC

The GCC project would like to thank its many contributors. Without them the project would not have been nearly as successful as it has been. Any omissions in this list are accidental. Feel free to contact law@redhat.com or gerald@pfeifer.com if you have been left out or some of your contributions are not listed. Please keep this list in alphabetical order.

- Analog Devices helped implement the support for complex data types and iterators.
- John David Anglin for threading-related fixes and improvements to libstdc++-v3, and the HP-UX port.
- James van Artsdalen wrote the code that makes efficient use of the Intel 80387 register stack.
- Abramo and Roberto Bagnara for the SysV68 Motorola 3300 Delta Series port.
- Alasdair Baird for various bug fixes.
- Giovanni Bajo for analyzing lots of complicated C++ problem reports.
- Peter Barada for his work to improve code generation for new ColdFire cores.
- Gerald Baumgartner added the signature extension to the C++ front end.
- Godmar Back for his Java improvements and encouragement.
- Scott Bambrough for help porting the Java compiler.
- Wolfgang Bangerth for processing tons of bug reports.
- Jon Beniston for his Microsoft Windows port of Java and port to Lattice Mico32.
- Daniel Berlin for better DWARF 2 support, faster/better optimizations, improved alias analysis, plus migrating GCC to Bugzilla.
- Geoff Berry for his Java object serialization work and various patches.
- David Binderman tests weekly snapshots of GCC trunk against Fedora Rawhide for several architectures.
- Laurynas Biveinis for memory management work and DJGPP port fixes.
- Uros Bizjak for the implementation of x87 math built-in functions and for various middle end and i386 back end improvements and bug fixes.
- Eric Blake for helping to make GCJ and libgcj conform to the specifications.
- Janne Blomqvist for contributions to GNU Fortran.
- Segher Boessenkool for various fixes.
- Hans-J. Boehm for his garbage collector, IA-64 libffi port, and other Java work.
- Neil Booth for work on cpplib, lang hooks, debug hooks and other miscellaneous cleanups.
- Steven Bosscher for integrating the GNU Fortran front end into GCC and for contributing to the tree-ssa branch.
- Eric Botcazou for fixing middle- and backend bugs left and right.
- Per Bothner for his direction via the steering committee and various improvements to the infrastructure for supporting new languages. Chill front end implementation. Initial implementations of cpplib, fix-header, config.guess, libio, and past C++ library (libg++) maintainer. Dreaming up, designing and implementing much of GCJ.

- Devon Bowen helped port GCC to the Tahoe.
- Don Bowman for mips-vxworks contributions.
- James Bowman for the FT32 port.
- Dave Brolley for work on cpplib and Chill.
- Paul Brook for work on the ARM architecture and maintaining GNU Fortran.
- Robert Brown implemented the support for Encore 32000 systems.
- Christian Bruel for improvements to local store elimination.
- Herman A.J. ten Brugge for various fixes.
- Joerg Brunsmann for Java compiler hacking and help with the GCJ FAQ.
- Joe Buck for his direction via the steering committee from its creation to 2013.
- Craig Burley for leadership of the G77 Fortran effort.
- Tobias Burnus for contributions to GNU Fortran.
- Stephan Buys for contributing Doxygen notes for libstdc++.
- Paolo Carlini for libstdc++ work: lots of efficiency improvements to the C++ strings, streambufs and formatted I/O, hard detective work on the frustrating localization issues, and keeping up with the problem reports.
- John Carr for his alias work, SPARC hacking, infrastructure improvements, previous contributions to the steering committee, loop optimizations, etc.
- Stephane Carrez for 68HC11 and 68HC12 ports.
- Steve Chamberlain for support for the Renesas SH and H8 processors and the PicoJava processor, and for GCJ config fixes.
- Glenn Chambers for help with the GCJ FAQ.
- John-Marc Chandonia for various libgcj patches.
- Denis Chertykov for contributing and maintaining the AVR port, the first GCC port for an 8-bit architecture.
- Scott Christley for his Objective-C contributions.
- Eric Christopher for his Java porting help and clean-ups.
- Branko Cibej for more warning contributions.
- The GNU Classpath project for all of their merged runtime code.
- Nick Clifton for arm, mcore, fr30, v850, m32r, msp430 rx work, '`--help`', and other random hacking.
- Michael Cook for libstdc++ cleanup patches to reduce warnings.
- R. Kelley Cook for making GCC buildable from a read-only directory as well as other miscellaneous build process and documentation clean-ups.
- Ralf Corsepius for SH testing and minor bug fixing.
- François-Xavier Coudert for contributions to GNU Fortran.
- Stan Cox for care and feeding of the x86 port and lots of behind the scenes hacking.
- Alex Crain provided changes for the 3b1.
- Ian Dall for major improvements to the NS32k port.
- Paul Dale for his work to add uClinux platform support to the m68k backend.

- Dario Dariol contributed the four varieties of sample programs that print a copy of their source.

- Russell Davidson for fstream and stringstream fixes in libstdc++.

- Bud Davis for work on the G77 and GNU Fortran compilers.

- Mo DeJong for GCJ and libgcj bug fixes.

- Jerry DeLisle for contributions to GNU Fortran.

- DJ Delorie for the DJGPP port, build and libiberty maintenance, various bug fixes, and the M32C, MeP, MSP430, and RL78 ports.

- Arnaud Desitter for helping to debug GNU Fortran.

- Gabriel Dos Reis for contributions to G++, contributions and maintenance of GCC diagnostics infrastructure, libstdc++-v3, including `valarray<>`, `complex<>`, maintaining the numerics library (including that pesky `<limits>` :-) and keeping up-to-date anything to do with numbers.

- Ulrich Drepper for his work on glibc, testing of GCC using glibc, ISO C99 support, CFG dumping support, etc., plus support of the C++ runtime libraries including for all kinds of C interface issues, contributing and maintaining `complex<>`, sanity checking and disbursement, configuration architecture, libio maintenance, and early math work.

- François Dumont for his work on libstdc++-v3, especially maintaining and improving `debug-mode` and associative and unordered containers.

- Zdenek Dvorak for a new loop unroller and various fixes.

- Michael Eager for his work on the Xilinx MicroBlaze port.

- Richard Earnshaw for his ongoing work with the ARM.

- David Edelsohn for his direction via the steering committee, ongoing work with the RS6000/PowerPC port, help cleaning up Haifa loop changes, doing the entire AIX port of libstdc++ with his bare hands, and for ensuring GCC properly keeps working on AIX.

- Kevin Ediger for the floating point formatting of num_put::do_put in libstdc++.

- Phil Edwards for libstdc++ work including configuration hackery, documentation maintainer, chief breaker of the web pages, the occasional iostream bug fix, and work on shared library symbol versioning.

- Paul Eggert for random hacking all over GCC.

- Mark Elbrecht for various DJGPP improvements, and for libstdc++ configuration support for locales and fstream-related fixes.

- Vadim Egorov for libstdc++ fixes in strings, streambufs, and iostreams.

- Christian Ehrhardt for dealing with bug reports.

- Ben Elliston for his work to move the Objective-C runtime into its own subdirectory and for his work on autoconf.

- Revital Eres for work on the PowerPC 750CL port.

- Marc Espie for OpenBSD support.

- Doug Evans for much of the global optimization framework, arc, m32r, and SPARC work.

- Christopher Faylor for his work on the Cygwin port and for caring and feeding the gcc.gnu.org box and saving its users tons of spam.
- Fred Fish for BeOS support and Ada fixes.
- Ivan Fontes Garcia for the Portuguese translation of the GCJ FAQ.
- Peter Gerwinski for various bug fixes and the Pascal front end.
- Kaveh R. Ghazi for his direction via the steering committee, amazing work to make '-W -Wall -W* -Werror' useful, and testing GCC on a plethora of platforms. Kaveh extends his gratitude to the CAIP Center at Rutgers University for providing him with computing resources to work on Free Software from the late 1980s to 2010.
- John Gilmore for a donation to the FSF earmarked improving GNU Java.
- Judy Goldberg for c++ contributions.
- Torbjorn Granlund for various fixes and the c-torture testsuite, multiply- and divide-by-constant optimization, improved long long support, improved leaf function register allocation, and his direction via the steering committee.
- Jonny Grant for improvements to collect2's '--help' documentation.
- Anthony Green for his '-Os' contributions, the moxie port, and Java front end work.
- Stu Grossman for gdb hacking, allowing GCJ developers to debug Java code.
- Michael K. Gschwind contributed the port to the PDP-11.
- Richard Biener for his ongoing middle-end contributions and bug fixes and for release management.
- Ron Guilmette implemented the protoize and unprotoize tools, the support for DWARF 1 symbolic debugging information, and much of the support for System V Release 4. He has also worked heavily on the Intel 386 and 860 support.
- Sumanth Gundapaneni for contributing the CR16 port.
- Mostafa Hagog for Swing Modulo Scheduling (SMS) and post reload GCSE.
- Bruno Haible for improvements in the runtime overhead for EH, new warnings and assorted bug fixes.
- Andrew Haley for his amazing Java compiler and library efforts.
- Chris Hanson assisted in making GCC work on HP-UX for the 9000 series 300.
- Michael Hayes for various thankless work he's done trying to get the c30/c40 ports functional. Lots of loop and unroll improvements and fixes.
- Dara Hazeghi for wading through myriads of target-specific bug reports.
- Kate Hedstrom for staking the G77 folks with an initial testsuite.
- Richard Henderson for his ongoing SPARC, alpha, ia32, and ia64 work, loop opts, and generally fixing lots of old problems we've ignored for years, flow rewrite and lots of further stuff, including reviewing tons of patches.
- Aldy Hernandez for working on the PowerPC port, SIMD support, and various fixes.
- Nobuyuki Hikichi of Software Research Associates, Tokyo, contributed the support for the Sony NEWS machine.
- Kazu Hirata for caring and feeding the Renesas H8/300 port and various fixes.
- Katherine Holcomb for work on GNU Fortran.

- Manfred Hollstein for his ongoing work to keep the m88k alive, lots of testing and bug fixing, particularly of GCC configury code.

- Steve Holmgren for MachTen patches.

- Mat Hostetter for work on the TILE-Gx and TILEPro ports.

- Jan Hubicka for his x86 port improvements.

- Falk Hueffner for working on C and optimization bug reports.

- Bernardo Innocenti for his m68k work, including merging of ColdFire improvements and uClinux support.

- Christian Iseli for various bug fixes.

- Kamil Iskra for general m68k hacking.

- Lee Iverson for random fixes and MIPS testing.

- Balaji V. Iyer for Cilk+ development and merging.

- Andreas Jaeger for testing and benchmarking of GCC and various bug fixes.

- Martin Jambor for his work on inter-procedural optimizations, the switch conversion pass, and scalar replacement of aggregates.

- Jakub Jelinek for his SPARC work and sibling call optimizations as well as lots of bug fixes and test cases, and for improving the Java build system.

- Janis Johnson for ia64 testing and fixes, her quality improvement sidetracks, and web page maintenance.

- Kean Johnston for SCO OpenServer support and various fixes.

- Tim Josling for the sample language treelang based originally on Richard Kenner's "toy" language.

- Nicolai Josuttis for additional libstdc++ documentation.

- Klaus Kaempf for his ongoing work to make alpha-vms a viable target.

- Steven G. Kargl for work on GNU Fortran.

- David Kashtan of SRI adapted GCC to VMS.

- Ryszard Kabatek for many, many libstdc++ bug fixes and optimizations of strings, especially member functions, and for auto_ptr fixes.

- Geoffrey Keating for his ongoing work to make the PPC work for GNU/Linux and his automatic regression tester.

- Brendan Kehoe for his ongoing work with G++ and for a lot of early work in just about every part of libstdc++.

- Oliver M. Kellogg of Deutsche Aerospace contributed the port to the MIL-STD-1750A.

- Richard Kenner of the New York University Ultracomputer Research Laboratory wrote the machine descriptions for the AMD 29000, the DEC Alpha, the IBM RT PC, and the IBM RS/6000 as well as the support for instruction attributes. He also made changes to better support RISC processors including changes to common subexpression elimination, strength reduction, function calling sequence handling, and condition code support, in addition to generalizing the code for frame pointer elimination and delay slot scheduling. Richard Kenner was also the head maintainer of GCC for several years.

- Mumit Khan for various contributions to the Cygwin and Mingw32 ports and maintaining binary releases for Microsoft Windows hosts, and for massive libstdc++ porting work to Cygwin/Mingw32.

- Robin Kirkham for cpu32 support.

- Mark Klein for PA improvements.

- Thomas Koenig for various bug fixes.

- Bruce Korb for the new and improved fixincludes code.

- Benjamin Kosnik for his G++ work and for leading the libstdc++-v3 effort.

- Maxim Kuvyrkov for contributions to the instruction scheduler, the Android and m68k/Coldfire ports, and optimizations.

- Charles LaBrec contributed the support for the Integrated Solutions 68020 system.

- Asher Langton and Mike Kumbera for contributing Cray pointer support to GNU Fortran, and for other GNU Fortran improvements.

- Jeff Law for his direction via the steering committee, coordinating the entire egcs project and GCC 2.95, rolling out snapshots and releases, handling merges from GCC2, reviewing tons of patches that might have fallen through the cracks else, and random but extensive hacking.

- Walter Lee for work on the TILE-Gx and TILEPro ports.

- Marc Lehmann for his direction via the steering committee and helping with analysis and improvements of x86 performance.

- Victor Leikehman for work on GNU Fortran.

- Ted Lemon wrote parts of the RTL reader and printer.

- Kriang Lerdsuwanakij for C++ improvements including template as template parameter support, and many C++ fixes.

- Warren Levy for tremendous work on libgcj (Java Runtime Library) and random work on the Java front end.

- Alain Lichnewsky ported GCC to the MIPS CPU.

- Oskar Liljeblad for hacking on AWT and his many Java bug reports and patches.

- Robert Lipe for OpenServer support, new testsuites, testing, etc.

- Chen Liqin for various S+core related fixes/improvement, and for maintaining the S+core port.

- Weiwen Liu for testing and various bug fixes.

- Manuel López-Ibáñez for improving '-Wconversion' and many other diagnostics fixes and improvements.

- Dave Love for his ongoing work with the Fortran front end and runtime libraries.

- Martin von Löwis for internal consistency checking infrastructure, various C++ improvements including namespace support, and tons of assistance with libstdc++/compiler merges.

- H.J. Lu for his previous contributions to the steering committee, many x86 bug reports, prototype patches, and keeping the GNU/Linux ports working.

- Greg McGary for random fixes and (someday) bounded pointers.

- Andrew MacLeod for his ongoing work in building a real EH system, various code generation improvements, work on the global optimizer, etc.

- Vladimir Makarov for hacking some ugly i960 problems, PowerPC hacking improvements to compile-time performance, overall knowledge and direction in the area of instruction scheduling, and design and implementation of the automaton based instruction scheduler.

- Bob Manson for his behind the scenes work on dejagnu.

- John Marino for contributing the DragonFly BSD port.

- Philip Martin for lots of libstdc++ string and vector iterator fixes and improvements, and string clean up and testsuites.

- Michael Matz for his work on dominance tree discovery, the x86-64 port, link-time optimization framework and general optimization improvements.

- All of the Mauve project contributors, for Java test code.

- Bryce McKinlay for numerous GCJ and libgcj fixes and improvements.

- Adam Megacz for his work on the Microsoft Windows port of GCJ.

- Michael Meissner for LRS framework, ia32, m32r, v850, m88k, MIPS, powerpc, haifa, ECOFF debug support, and other assorted hacking.

- Jason Merrill for his direction via the steering committee and leading the G++ effort.

- Martin Michlmayr for testing GCC on several architectures using the entire Debian archive.

- David Miller for his direction via the steering committee, lots of SPARC work, improvements in jump.c and interfacing with the Linux kernel developers.

- Gary Miller ported GCC to Charles River Data Systems machines.

- Alfred Minarik for libstdc++ string and ios bug fixes, and turning the entire libstdc++ testsuite namespace-compatible.

- Mark Mitchell for his direction via the steering committee, mountains of C++ work, load/store hoisting out of loops, alias analysis improvements, ISO C `restrict` support, and serving as release manager from 2000 to 2011.

- Alan Modra for various GNU/Linux bits and testing.

- Toon Moene for his direction via the steering committee, Fortran maintenance, and his ongoing work to make us make Fortran run fast.

- Jason Molenda for major help in the care and feeding of all the services on the gcc.gnu.org (formerly egcs.cygnus.com) machine—mail, web services, ftp services, etc etc. Doing all this work on scrap paper and the backs of envelopes would have been... difficult.

- Catherine Moore for fixing various ugly problems we have sent her way, including the haifa bug which was killing the Alpha & PowerPC Linux kernels.

- Mike Moreton for his various Java patches.

- David Mosberger-Tang for various Alpha improvements, and for the initial IA-64 port.

- Stephen Moshier contributed the floating point emulator that assists in cross-compilation and permits support for floating point numbers wider than 64 bits and for ISO C99 support.

- Bill Moyer for his behind the scenes work on various issues.
- Philippe De Muyter for his work on the m68k port.
- Joseph S. Myers for his work on the PDP-11 port, format checking and ISO C99 support, and continuous emphasis on (and contributions to) documentation.
- Nathan Myers for his work on libstdc++-v3: architecture and authorship through the first three snapshots, including implementation of locale infrastructure, string, shadow C headers, and the initial project documentation (DESIGN, CHECKLIST, and so forth). Later, more work on MT-safe string and shadow headers.
- Felix Natter for documentation on porting libstdc++.
- Nathanael Nerode for cleaning up the configuration/build process.
- NeXT, Inc. donated the front end that supports the Objective-C language.
- Hans-Peter Nilsson for the CRIS and MMIX ports, improvements to the search engine setup, various documentation fixes and other small fixes.
- Geoff Noer for his work on getting cygwin native builds working.
- Diego Novillo for his work on Tree SSA, OpenMP, SPEC performance tracking web pages, GIMPLE tuples, and assorted fixes.
- David O'Brien for the FreeBSD/alpha, FreeBSD/AMD x86-64, FreeBSD/ARM, FreeBSD/PowerPC, and FreeBSD/SPARC64 ports and related infrastructure improvements.
- Alexandre Oliva for various build infrastructure improvements, scripts and amazing testing work, including keeping libtool issues sane and happy.
- Stefan Olsson for work on mt_alloc.
- Melissa O'Neill for various NeXT fixes.
- Rainer Orth for random MIPS work, including improvements to GCC's o32 ABI support, improvements to dejagnu's MIPS support, Java configuration clean-ups and porting work, and maintaining the IRIX, Solaris 2, and Tru64 UNIX ports.
- Hartmut Penner for work on the s390 port.
- Paul Petersen wrote the machine description for the Alliant FX/8.
- Alexandre Petit-Bianco for implementing much of the Java compiler and continued Java maintainership.
- Matthias Pfaller for major improvements to the NS32k port.
- Gerald Pfeifer for his direction via the steering committee, pointing out lots of problems we need to solve, maintenance of the web pages, and taking care of documentation maintenance in general.
- Andrew Pinski for processing bug reports by the dozen.
- Ovidiu Predescu for his work on the Objective-C front end and runtime libraries.
- Jerry Quinn for major performance improvements in C++ formatted I/O.
- Ken Raeburn for various improvements to checker, MIPS ports and various cleanups in the compiler.
- Rolf W. Rasmussen for hacking on AWT.
- David Reese of Sun Microsystems contributed to the Solaris on PowerPC port.

- Volker Reichelt for keeping up with the problem reports.

- Joern Rennecke for maintaining the sh port, loop, regmove & reload hacking and developing and maintaining the Epiphany port.

- Loren J. Rittle for improvements to libstdc++-v3 including the FreeBSD port, threading fixes, thread-related configury changes, critical threading documentation, and solutions to really tricky I/O problems, as well as keeping GCC properly working on FreeBSD and continuous testing.

- Craig Rodrigues for processing tons of bug reports.

- Ola Rönnerup for work on mt_alloc.

- Gavin Romig-Koch for lots of behind the scenes MIPS work.

- David Ronis inspired and encouraged Craig to rewrite the G77 documentation in texinfo format by contributing a first pass at a translation of the old 'g77-0.5.16/f/DOC' file.

- Ken Rose for fixes to GCC's delay slot filling code.

- Ira Rosen for her contributions to the auto-vectorizer.

- Paul Rubin wrote most of the preprocessor.

- Pétur Runólfsson for major performance improvements in C++ formatted I/O and large file support in C++ filebuf.

- Chip Salzenberg for libstdc++ patches and improvements to locales, traits, Makefiles, libio, libtool hackery, and "long long" support.

- Juha Sarlin for improvements to the H8 code generator.

- Greg Satz assisted in making GCC work on HP-UX for the 9000 series 300.

- Roger Sayle for improvements to constant folding and GCC's RTL optimizers as well as for fixing numerous bugs.

- Bradley Schatz for his work on the GCJ FAQ.

- Peter Schauer wrote the code to allow debugging to work on the Alpha.

- William Schelter did most of the work on the Intel 80386 support.

- Tobias Schlüter for work on GNU Fortran.

- Bernd Schmidt for various code generation improvements and major work in the reload pass, serving as release manager for GCC 2.95.3, and work on the Blackfin and C6X ports.

- Peter Schmid for constant testing of libstdc++—especially application testing, going above and beyond what was requested for the release criteria—and libstdc++ header file tweaks.

- Jason Schroeder for jcf-dump patches.

- Andreas Schwab for his work on the m68k port.

- Lars Segerlund for work on GNU Fortran.

- Dodji Seketeli for numerous C++ bug fixes and debug info improvements.

- Tim Shen for major work on <regex>.

- Joel Sherrill for his direction via the steering committee, RTEMS contributions and RTEMS testing.

- Nathan Sidwell for many C++ fixes/improvements.

- Jeffrey Siegal for helping RMS with the original design of GCC, some code which handles the parse tree and RTL data structures, constant folding and help with the original VAX & m68k ports.
- Kenny Simpson for prompting libstdc++ fixes due to defect reports from the LWG (thereby keeping GCC in line with updates from the ISO).
- Franz Sirl for his ongoing work with making the PPC port stable for GNU/Linux.
- Andrey Slepuhin for assorted AIX hacking.
- Trevor Smigiel for contributing the SPU port.
- Christopher Smith did the port for Convex machines.
- Danny Smith for his major efforts on the Mingw (and Cygwin) ports. Retired from GCC maintainership August 2010, having mentored two new maintainers into the role.
- Randy Smith finished the Sun FPA support.
- Ed Smith-Rowland for his continuous work on libstdc++-v3, special functions, <random>, and various improvements to C++11 features.
- Scott Snyder for queue, iterator, istream, and string fixes and libstdc++ testsuite entries. Also for providing the patch to G77 to add rudimentary support for INTEGER*1, INTEGER*2, and LOGICAL*1.
- Zdenek Sojka for running automated regression testing of GCC and reporting numerous bugs.
- Jayant Sonar for contributing the CR16 port.
- Brad Spencer for contributions to the GLIBCPP_FORCE_NEW technique.
- Richard Stallman, for writing the original GCC and launching the GNU project.
- Jan Stein of the Chalmers Computer Society provided support for Genix, as well as part of the 32000 machine description.
- Nigel Stephens for various mips16 related fixes/improvements.
- Jonathan Stone wrote the machine description for the Pyramid computer.
- Graham Stott for various infrastructure improvements.
- John Stracke for his Java HTTP protocol fixes.
- Mike Stump for his Elxsi port, G++ contributions over the years and more recently his vxworks contributions
- Jeff Sturm for Java porting help, bug fixes, and encouragement.
- Shigeya Suzuki for this fixes for the bsdi platforms.
- Ian Lance Taylor for the Go frontend, the initial mips16 and mips64 support, general configury hacking, fixincludes, etc.
- Holger Teutsch provided the support for the Clipper CPU.
- Gary Thomas for his ongoing work to make the PPC work for GNU/Linux.
- Paul Thomas for contributions to GNU Fortran.
- Philipp Thomas for random bug fixes throughout the compiler
- Jason Thorpe for thread support in libstdc++ on NetBSD.
- Kresten Krab Thorup wrote the run time support for the Objective-C language and the fantastic Java bytecode interpreter.

- Michael Tiemann for random bug fixes, the first instruction scheduler, initial C++ support, function integration, NS32k, SPARC and M88k machine description work, delay slot scheduling.

- Andreas Tobler for his work porting libgcj to Darwin.

- Teemu Torma for thread safe exception handling support.

- Leonard Tower wrote parts of the parser, RTL generator, and RTL definitions, and of the VAX machine description.

- Daniel Towner and Hariharan Sandanagobalane contributed and maintain the picoChip port.

- Tom Tromey for internationalization support and for his many Java contributions and libgcj maintainership.

- Lassi Tuura for improvements to config.guess to determine HP processor types.

- Petter Urkedal for libstdc++ CXXFLAGS, math, and algorithms fixes.

- Andy Vaught for the design and initial implementation of the GNU Fortran front end.

- Brent Verner for work with the libstdc++ cshadow files and their associated configure steps.

- Todd Vierling for contributions for NetBSD ports.

- Jonathan Wakely for contributing libstdc++ Doxygen notes and XHTML guidance.

- Dean Wakerley for converting the install documentation from HTML to texinfo in time for GCC 3.0.

- Krister Walfridsson for random bug fixes.

- Feng Wang for contributions to GNU Fortran.

- Stephen M. Webb for time and effort on making libstdc++ shadow files work with the tricky Solaris 8+ headers, and for pushing the build-time header tree. Also, for starting and driving the `<regex>` effort.

- John Wehle for various improvements for the x86 code generator, related infrastructure improvements to help x86 code generation, value range propagation and other work, WE32k port.

- Ulrich Weigand for work on the s390 port.

- Janus Weil for contributions to GNU Fortran.

- Zack Weinberg for major work on cpplib and various other bug fixes.

- Matt Welsh for help with Linux Threads support in GCJ.

- Urban Widmark for help fixing java.io.

- Mark Wielaard for new Java library code and his work integrating with Classpath.

- Dale Wiles helped port GCC to the Tahoe.

- Bob Wilson from Tensilica, Inc. for the Xtensa port.

- Jim Wilson for his direction via the steering committee, tackling hard problems in various places that nobody else wanted to work on, strength reduction and other loop optimizations.

- Paul Woegerer and Tal Agmon for the CRX port.

- Carlo Wood for various fixes.

- Tom Wood for work on the m88k port.
- Chung-Ju Wu for his work on the Andes NDS32 port.
- Canqun Yang for work on GNU Fortran.
- Masanobu Yuhara of Fujitsu Laboratories implemented the machine description for the Tron architecture (specifically, the Gmicro).
- Kevin Zachmann helped port GCC to the Tahoe.
- Ayal Zaks for Swing Modulo Scheduling (SMS).
- Xiaoqiang Zhang for work on GNU Fortran.
- Gilles Zunino for help porting Java to Irix.

The following people are recognized for their contributions to GNAT, the Ada front end of GCC:

- Bernard Banner
- Romain Berrendonner
- Geert Bosch
- Emmanuel Briot
- Joel Brobecker
- Ben Brosgol
- Vincent Celier
- Arnaud Charlet
- Chien Chieng
- Cyrille Comar
- Cyrille Crozes
- Robert Dewar
- Gary Dismukes
- Robert Duff
- Ed Falis
- Ramon Fernandez
- Sam Figueroa
- Vasiliy Fofanov
- Michael Friess
- Franco Gasperoni
- Ted Giering
- Matthew Gingell
- Laurent Guerby
- Jerome Guitton
- Olivier Hainque
- Jerome Hugues
- Hristian Kirtchev
- Jerome Lambourg

- Bruno Leclerc
- Albert Lee
- Sean McNeil
- Javier Miranda
- Laurent Nana
- Pascal Obry
- Dong-Ik Oh
- Laurent Pautet
- Brett Porter
- Thomas Quinot
- Nicolas Roche
- Pat Rogers
- Jose Ruiz
- Douglas Rupp
- Sergey Rybin
- Gail Schenker
- Ed Schonberg
- Nicolas Setton
- Samuel Tardieu

The following people are recognized for their contributions of new features, bug reports, testing and integration of classpath/libgcj for GCC version 4.1:

- Lillian Angel for `JTree` implementation and lots Free Swing additions and bug fixes.
- Wolfgang Baer for `GapContent` bug fixes.
- Anthony Balkissoon for `JList`, Free Swing 1.5 updates and mouse event fixes, lots of Free Swing work including `JTable` editing.
- Stuart Ballard for RMI constant fixes.
- Goffredo Baroncelli for `HTTPURLConnection` fixes.
- Gary Benson for `MessageFormat` fixes.
- Daniel Bonniot for `Serialization` fixes.
- Chris Burdess for lots of gnu.xml and http protocol fixes, `StAX` and `DOM` `xml:id` support.
- Ka-Hing Cheung for `TreePath` and `TreeSelection` fixes.
- Archie Cobbs for build fixes, VM interface updates, `URLClassLoader` updates.
- Kelley Cook for build fixes.
- Martin Cordova for Suggestions for better `SocketTimeoutException`.
- David Daney for `BitSet` bug fixes, `HttpURLConnection` rewrite and improvements.
- Thomas Fitzsimmons for lots of upgrades to the gtk+ AWT and Cairo 2D support. Lots of imageio framework additions, lots of AWT and Free Swing bug fixes.
- Jeroen Frijters for `ClassLoader` and nio cleanups, serialization fixes, better `Proxy` support, bug fixes and IKVM integration.

- Santiago Gala for `AccessControlContext` fixes.
- Nicolas Geoffray for `VMClassLoader` and `AccessController` improvements.
- David Gilbert for `basic` and `metal` icon and plaf support and lots of documenting, Lots of Free Swing and metal theme additions. `MetalIconFactory` implementation.
- Anthony Green for `MIDI` framework, `ALSA` and `DSSI` providers.
- Andrew Haley for `Serialization` and `URLClassLoader` fixes, gcj build speedups.
- Kim Ho for `JFileChooser` implementation.
- Andrew John Hughes for `Locale` and net fixes, URI RFC2986 updates, `Serialization` fixes, `Properties` XML support and generic branch work, VMIntegration guide update.
- Bastiaan Huisman for `TimeZone` bug fixing.
- Andreas Jaeger for mprec updates.
- Paul Jenner for better '`-Werror`' support.
- Ito Kazumitsu for `NetworkInterface` implementation and updates.
- Roman Kennke for `BoxLayout`, `GrayFilter` and `SplitPane`, plus bug fixes all over. Lots of Free Swing work including styled text.
- Simon Kitching for `String` cleanups and optimization suggestions.
- Michael Koch for configuration fixes, `Locale` updates, bug and build fixes.
- Guilhem Lavaux for configuration, thread and channel fixes and Kaffe integration. JCL native `Pointer` updates. Logger bug fixes.
- David Lichteblau for JCL support library global/local reference cleanups.
- Aaron Luchko for JDWP updates and documentation fixes.
- Ziga Mahkovec for `Graphics2D` upgraded to Cairo 0.5 and new regex features.
- Sven de Marothy for BMP imageio support, CSS and `TextLayout` fixes. `GtkImage` rewrite, 2D, awt, free swing and date/time fixes and implementing the Qt4 peers.
- Casey Marshall for crypto algorithm fixes, `FileChannel` lock, `SystemLogger` and `FileHandler` rotate implementations, NIO `FileChannel.map` support, security and policy updates.
- Bryce McKinlay for RMI work.
- Audrius Meskauskas for lots of Free Corba, RMI and HTML work plus testing and documenting.
- Kalle Olavi Niemitalo for build fixes.
- Rainer Orth for build fixes.
- Andrew Overholt for `File` locking fixes.
- Ingo Proetel for `Image`, `Logger` and `URLClassLoader` updates.
- Olga Rodimina for `MenuSelectionManager` implementation.
- Jan Roehrich for `BasicTreeUI` and `JTree` fixes.
- Julian Scheid for documentation updates and gjdoc support.
- Christian Schlichtherle for zip fixes and cleanups.
- Robert Schuster for documentation updates and beans fixes, `TreeNode` enumerations and `ActionCommand` and various fixes, XML and URL, AWT and Free Swing bug fixes.

- Keith Seitz for lots of JDWP work.
- Christian Thalinger for 64-bit cleanups, Configuration and VM interface fixes and `CACAO` integration, `fdlibm` updates.
- Gael Thomas for `VMClassLoader` boot packages support suggestions.
- Andreas Tobler for Darwin and Solaris testing and fixing, `Qt4` support for Darwin/OS X, `Graphics2D` support, `gtk+` updates.
- Dalibor Topic for better `DEBUG` support, build cleanups and Kaffe integration. `Qt4` build infrastructure, `SHA1PRNG` and `GdkPixbugDecoder` updates.
- Tom Tromey for Eclipse integration, generics work, lots of bug fixes and gcj integration including coordinating The Big Merge.
- Mark Wielaard for bug fixes, packaging and release management, `Clipboard` implementation, system call interrupts and network timeouts and `GdkPixpufDecoder` fixes.

In addition to the above, all of which also contributed time and energy in testing GCC, we would like to thank the following for their contributions to testing:

- Michael Abd-El-Malek
- Thomas Arend
- Bonzo Armstrong
- Steven Ashe
- Chris Baldwin
- David Billinghurst
- Jim Blandy
- Stephane Bortzmeyer
- Horst von Brand
- Frank Braun
- Rodney Brown
- Sidney Cadot
- Bradford Castalia
- Robert Clark
- Jonathan Corbet
- Ralph Doncaster
- Richard Emberson
- Levente Farkas
- Graham Fawcett
- Mark Fernyhough
- Robert A. French
- Jörgen Freyh
- Mark K. Gardner
- Charles-Antoine Gauthier
- Yung Shing Gene

- David Gilbert
- Simon Gornall
- Fred Gray
- John Griffin
- Patrik Hagglund
- Phil Hargett
- Amancio Hasty
- Takafumi Hayashi
- Bryan W. Headley
- Kevin B. Hendricks
- Joep Jansen
- Christian Joensson
- Michel Kern
- David Kidd
- Tobias Kuipers
- Anand Krishnaswamy
- A. O. V. Le Blanc
- llewelly
- Damon Love
- Brad Lucier
- Matthias Klose
- Martin Knoblauch
- Rick Lutowski
- Jesse Macnish
- Stefan Morrell
- Anon A. Mous
- Matthias Mueller
- Pekka Nikander
- Rick Niles
- Jon Olson
- Magnus Persson
- Chris Pollard
- Richard Polton
- Derk Reefman
- David Rees
- Paul Reilly
- Tom Reilly
- Torsten Rueger
- Danny Sadinoff

- Marc Schifer
- Erik Schnetter
- Wayne K. Schroll
- David Schuler
- Vin Shelton
- Tim Souder
- Adam Sulmicki
- Bill Thorson
- George Talbot
- Pedro A. M. Vazquez
- Gregory Warnes
- Ian Watson
- David E. Young
- And many others

And finally we'd like to thank everyone who uses the compiler, provides feedback and generally reminds us why we're doing this work in the first place.

Option Index

GCC's command line options are indexed here without any initial '-' or '--'. Where an option has both positive and negative forms (such as '*-foption*' and '*-fno-option*'), relevant entries in the manual are indexed under the most appropriate form; it may sometimes be useful to look up both forms.

N

O

P

X

Y

Z

Keyword Index